Adelaide Darby
of Coalbrookdale

Her Private Journal
From 1833 to 1861

Transcribed by
Rachel Labouchere
and Edited by
Emyr Thomas, CBE, LL.B, DL

SESSIONS BOOK TRUST
in association with
IRONBRIDGE GORGE MUSEUM TRUST

Publishers Note

THE FOLLOWING WORDS appeared in Rachel Labouchere's *Times* obituary of April 1996, after reference to her first two books *Abiah Darby* and *Deborah Darby*: "A political diary of Adelaide Whitmore is currently at the press..."

In fact at the time of Rachel's death she had made extensive marginal notes upon a rough typing of Adelaide's substantial journal, and she had also drafted a helpful Foreword, of which an edited version is printed here on pages vii-xi. Otherwise, the work was considerably incomplete and was not in a state to justify its description as being "currently at the press".

Three years later, in 1999 the Sessions Book Trust, in association with the Ironbridge Gorge Museum Trust published *Coalbrookdale and the Darby Family: the story of the world's first industrial dynasty*. Its author, our good friend Emyr Thomas, was persuaded next to undertake the formidable task of editing Rachel's transcript. "Tommy" Thomas was the secretary and solicitor of Dawley Development Corporation from 1964 to 1969 and general manager of Telford Development Corporation from 1969 to 1980. As solicitor to the Dawley Development Corporation he had brought the Ironbridge Gorge Museum into existence in 1968 and he remained its founding honorary secretary for the next 21 years.

With his extensive knowledge of the Darby family and his familiarity with the people and places in the Coalbrookdale area, he has been able to "bring to life" the sometimes obscure and elusive references in Adelaide's private journal, by means of "comment" and "notes" for each of her journal years. The publishers express deep appreciation of his achievement, which as he writes on page 501 is in testimony to "a lovely English lady", Rachel Labouchere, as well as to her forebear who Rachel once described as the "naughty fascinating Adelaide".

The publishers regret that the substantial size of this single volume has precluded the inclusion of what would have been a lengthy index. It is hoped to deposit one in the library of the Ironbridge Gorge Museum Trust at Coalbrookdale.

WILLIAM K. SESSIONS

ISBN 1 85072 316 8

Printed in 10 on 11 point Plantin Typeface
by William Sessions Limited
The Ebor Press
York, England

Contents

Illustrations

Family Trees

Maps

Foreword

by Rachel Labouchere

ADELAIDE ANNA DARBY was born on 10th August 1817, the younger daughter of Francis Darby of Coalbrookdale and Hannah Grant of Leighton Buzzard. Francis was the eldest living son of Abraham Darby III, builder of the famous Iron Bridge over the River Severn and Rebecca Smith of Doncaster. He was born at The Haye in 1783, a house to which his parents had moved three years before, in part to accommodate their growing family, but also to be able to receive the increasing number of visitors to view the new and unique construction in iron.

The Haye was on the hill above Coalport and was an ancient dwelling originally in the ecclesiastical possession of the Abbey of Wenlock, a few miles distant, there being evidence of this connection in the upper part of the building, although most of the house was of more recent date. There were pleasant panelled rooms and the hall had a stone floor. One of these rooms to the west was to be Abraham's study containing his library of books and from the windows he could see, as he sat at his desk, the slender bow of his famous iron bridge. The entrance was on the north side beneath large chimneys of elaborate design and was reached along a country road from Madeley. On the left of the entrance and close to the house were walled kitchen gardens and orchard, newly planted by Abraham with different vegetables and fruit trees.

Abraham had been preparing for this move for some time and had had constructed barns to the west of the house, and acquired more land to add to his fine original holding. These barns were constructed of bricks, tiles and iron fittings supplied by the Company - they were large and useful agricultural buildings, remaining in the original form until quite recently, an historical witness to the farming procedures of that period. Being close to the house the Darby children were brought into close daily proximity with the animals - the horses bred for work on the farm and in the Company's ironworks and railroads; the cattle, sheep, pigs and poultry. Sparrows twittered in the roof and in summer swallows and house martins nested under the eaves. This move from Dale House to The Haye also ensured the children were surrounded by real country life away from the smoke and fumes of Industry.

The furnishings of the new home were more elaborate than for Dale House, with guest rooms intended, at the outset, for the many visitors who were already coming to see the bridge, as well as for the many Friends who were given hospitality and those who came to see the Coalbrookdale Works on business. Accounts were kept of the acquisition of extra plate, china and glass for this increased hospitality in the new home.

There were also new additions to the family as Francis was to have a brother Joseph born 1785, a sister Hannah in 1786 and finally another brother Richard who was only an infant when tragedy befell. In the last months of 1788, Abraham, Francis' elder brother, became ill of scarlet fever at Sunniside where he was staying with his grandmother to receive tuition at a nearby small school, and after a short illness he died. This calamity was to be followed by a greater one, as Abraham, their father, caught the same disease early in 1789 and after some weeks of illness he too died.

Abraham's wife, Rebecca, was also ill with an infected throat and could not look after her husband, so Sarah, his youngest sister, living at Sunniside with their mother Abiah, came to nurse him. She at once caught the fever and was also very ill indeed, whereupon her friend and companion Susan Appleby went to help, and it is from a letter which she wrote to her aunt in Durham that the details of this sad time are known.

Rebecca was now left to bring up her young family alone. Richard Reynolds, her brother-in-law, helped her, as earlier he had her mother-in-law Abiah, in similar circumstances. Richard had, providentially, just decided to retire from Ketley and moved again into Dale House, then empty and belonging to the Coalbrookdale Company, just as Abrahan became ill, leaving his sons,William and Joseph to run the Ketley side of the business - William residing at Ketley Bank and Joseph at Ketley Hall.

Rebecca was left badly off as Abraham had been obliged to spend his own money on building the iron bridge as the subscriptions made for the erection proved to be inadequate; he had also purchased the Manor of Madeley and other land. It was decided at once that Rebecca should move from The Haye into a smaller house, called The White House, on the edge of the Sunniside deer park, and so be nearer to the rest of the family. There was an immediate sale of horses and farm animals and machinery together with a large amount of furniture, including two thousand of Abraham's books. It is sad to read the names of his horses, which poignantly underlines the end of the happy family life.

Rebecca became a partner in the Company after Abraham's death, joining Abiah, Samuel, Mary Rathbone and Sarah. They were guided by Richard Reynolds who also had his own family interests to consider, namely the children of his first wife Hannah Darby. These children, William and Hannah Mary were now grown up and William took on, together with his half-brother Joseph, the Ketley side of the Coalbrookdale Company that same year. This was the reason Richard Reynolds had decided to move back to Dale House just prior to Abraham's death. He engaged Richard Dearman to come from Birmingham to conduct the day to day running of the Company.

These moves all took place in that fateful year period 1789-1790, William taking over Ketley Bank, Richard's house, and Joseph Ketley Hall.

For Rebecca to take responsibility was not perhaps too difficult for Friends, as they had the always accepted view that in the community the two sexes had an equality of station in the finest sense, which had from the beginning created a maturity of outlook on life.

The White House was situated on the bridle road to Little Wenlock, a pleasant house facing south at the top of the west bank of Coalbrookdale. The deer park lay in front to the south across a small terrace, surrounded by a high iron bar-and-chain fence made in the Works. These animals aroused great interest in the children living in the vicinity.

Adjoining the rear of the house, there were considerable buildings along the roadside, and here probably was the school room which Abiah had instigated for the instruction of the Darby children and the families of Friends and dependants, and which it is likely Rebecca's children were now to attend.

The eldest girls, Ann and Mary, however, were soon sent to the well-known Quaker girls' school initiated and run by the Tukes in York, their names being listed there in 1790.

Francis as a child was to have the small room over the garden door facing south looking across the deer park to the distant view of the far side of the Severn Valley, wooded as it had always been, and from where, below the continuously rising smoke from furnace and foundry, there was a night of crimson glow. Francis had evidently been happy in The White House as he never appeared to wish to leave, even when later able to do so.

His two older cousins Samuel and Edmund, the children of Samuel and Deborah Darby, were sent to Thomas Huntley's school at Burford, and here Rebecca decided to send her sons Francis and Joseph when old enough. She wrote to Samuel to ask him to be kind and look after his cousin Francis as a new boy.

It was an excellent school at Hillside Academy and Thomas Huntley and his wife Mary took great care of their pupils. She cooked delicious biscuits, which she also sold to the travellers on the coaches which stopped near the school, (this being the origin of the Huntley and Palmer biscuit business).

Rebecca also sent Joseph to join his elder brother, but sadly he caught measles and died, being buried in the Burford Friends' Burial Ground.

Rebecca wrote constructively and carefully to her children, encouraging them to do well in their lessons and to conduct themselves responsibly. She thought that Francis should be careful not to try his eyes too greatly by his fondness for drawing, - he was artistic and liked to do so. Sadly, however, there are no examples of his work, except perhaps a spirited depiction of a house in pencil on the side of a document.

After his school days, Rebecca decided to send him to the Becks of Dover for his apprenticeship. There he was taught the expert conduct of business, and also placed in a suitable environment amongst Friends. Sarah Beck, a well-known Quaker minister, had been acquainted with the older members of the Darby family.

On his return to Coalbrookdale, there is evidence that Francis undertook a little farming at the Haye, and lived in a few rooms there while he did so. However, on his sister Ann's marriage to Barnard Dickinson, a nephew of Deborah Darby and a trained farmer and agriculturist, he let them have the Haye in 1805, where they were to remain for a few years.

Francis travelled on occasion during these years with his Aunt Deborah on her shorter ministerial journeys but not at a distance, and she was to help him when he became anxious to marry Hannah Grant even though her parents did not wish her to live at a distance from their home at Leighton Buzzard in Buckinghamshire, situated between Aylesbury and Luton. John Grant's ancestors had, by tradition, come south to England after the unsuccessful 1745 Jacobite rebellion and he still used the family crest of a boar's head on his silver and plate. Hannah, his wife, was the daughter of the redoubtable Mary Brook of Hogstyland. Adelaide's gift for writing was probably inherited from both her great grandmothers, but it is very doubtful whether either of them would have approved of her subject matter.

Leighton Buzzard was an ancient Market Town mentioned in the Domesday Book and divided from Lechlade by the River Ouse. The chief feature was the Market Cross, dating from the early 15th Century - a two storied building of arches surmounted by a pinnacle with fine biblical statues. The streets were narrow with some thatched houses still standing between those of later date. The Church, with a tall steeple, was built of ironstone and its surroundings were frequently mentioned by Adelaide as the place where Matilda and she, when at Leighton Buzzard met their young cousins and friends in these pleasant precincts. The stained glass windows attracted Adelaide, likewise the music, which would frequently be heard from within during the services and choir practice.

The Grants had a substantial house in a large garden in which was a shrubbery and a temple - an ornamental feature which was the scene of confidential conversations between the sisters, their cousins and friends, when staying with their grandparents. John Grant was a successful corn merchant who had been able to enter banking and he owned land in the neighbourhood, to which he often rode, sometimes taking Matilda and Adelaide with him. It was at the time of the building of the first railways and he was able to sell some land for this purpose, enabling the girls to witness some of the early construction of the track - an exciting innovation and one in which their father's business was to have a part in the making of the rails, having laid tracks for horse-drawn loads many years before.

THE DARBYS OF COALBROOKDALE

ABRAHAM I = MARY SERGEANT
1678-1717 1678-1718

(1) MARGARET SMITH = ABRAHAM II = (2) ABIAH SINCLAIR (NÉE MAUD
d. 1740 1711-1763 1716-1794

RICHARD REYNOLDS = HANNAH
1735-1816 1735-62

WILLIAM REYNOLDS = HANNAH BALL
1758-1803

5 CHILDREN

MARY = JOSEPH RATHBONE
1748-1807 1746-1790

ABRAHAM III = REBECCA SMIT
1750-1789 1752-1834

ANN = BARNARD DICKINSON
1779-1840 1781-1852

JOSEPH 1806-60
MARY 1807 = CHARLES STURGE
SARAH 1808-35
BARNARD 1809
REBECCA 1810-28
HENRY = 1) DEBORAH DARBY
1812-86 2) SUSANNAH HADWEN
SAMUEL 1814-1840
FRANCIS 1816-1901
HANNAH 1816 = JOSEPH STURGE
CHRISTOPHER 1818-1904
WILLIAM 1822

FRANCIS = HANNAH GRANT
1783-1850 1783-1860

MATILDA FRANCES
1809-1902
m. 1839
ABRAHAM IV
1804-78

ADELAIDE ANNA
1817-99
m. 1852
HENRY WHITMORE
1814-76

HANNAH = WILLIA
1786-1859 TOTHIL

WILLIAM
1819
JOSEPH
1821
FRANCIS
1823 =
JANE DIGBY
SARAH
1824 =
COL. MUNRO
REBECCA
1826

SARAH
1752-1821

SAMUEL = DEBORAH BARNARD
1755-1796 1754-1810

RICHARD = MARIA SORTON
1788-1860 1792-1860

RICHARD SORTON
1812-1883
MARIA LOUISE
1814-
CAROLINE ANNE
1815-
ABRAHAM MAUDE
1817-1910
WILLIAM HENRY
1819-1882
REBECCA SARAH
1832-1908

SAMUEL = FRANCES WILLIAMS
1779-1808

FRANCES
1806-11

MARY = REV. PRYCE OWEN

HUGH PRYCE = MARY OWEN

EDMUND = LUCY BURLINGHAM
1782-1810 1782-1870

ABRAHAM IV = MATILDA FRANCES
1804-78 1809-1902
CORBYN 1805, Died Young
SAMUEL MAUDE 1806-07
ALFRED I = REBECCA CHRISTY
1807-52
ALFRED II 1850-1925
MARY = REV. JONES
1808-73
DEBORAH = HENRY DICKINSON
1810-55 1812-1886

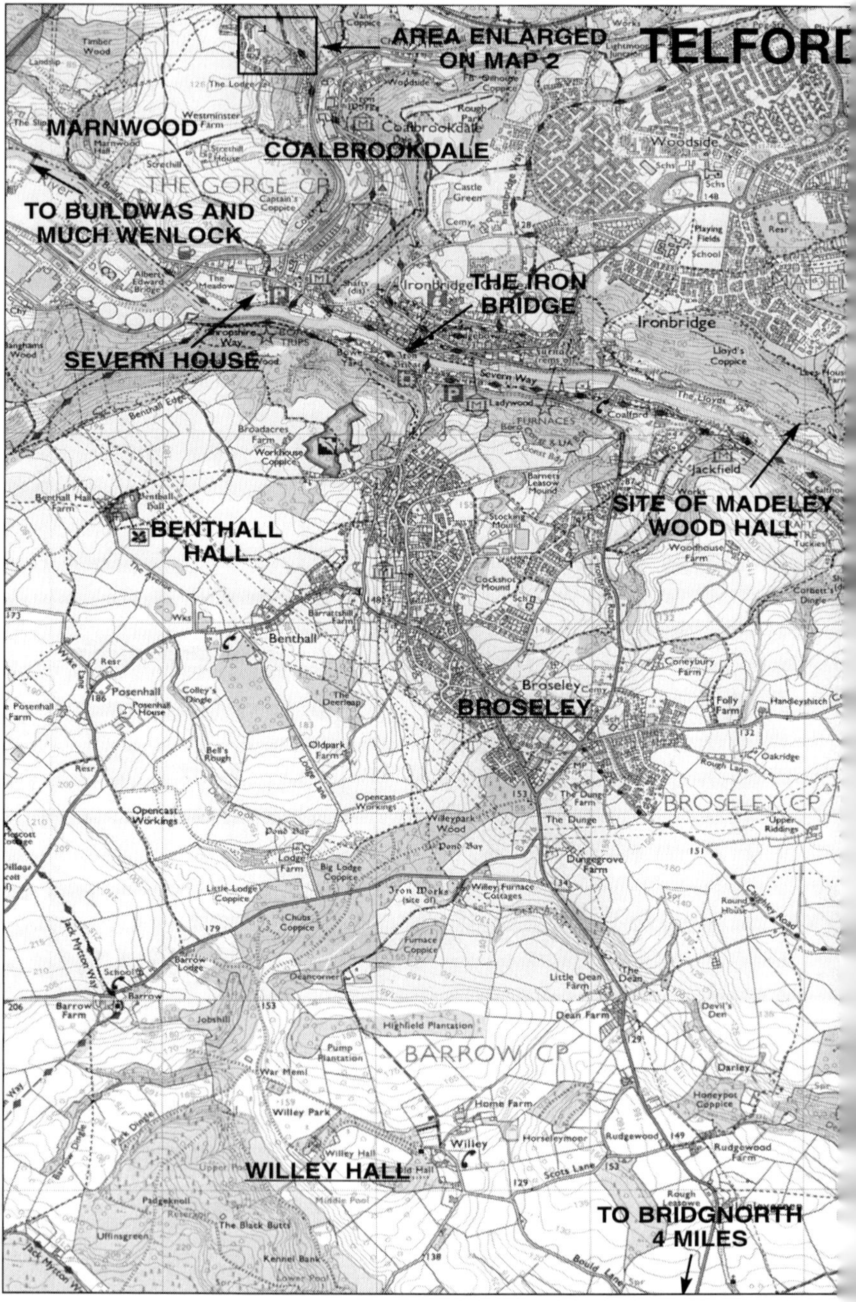
AREA ENLARGED ON MAP 2
TELFORD
MARNWOOD
COALBROOKDALE
TO BUILDWAS AND MUCH WENLOCK
THE IRON BRIDGE
SEVERN HOUSE
SITE OF MADELEY WOOD HALL
BENTHALL HALL
BROSELEY
WILLEY HALL
TO BRIDGNORTH 4 MILES

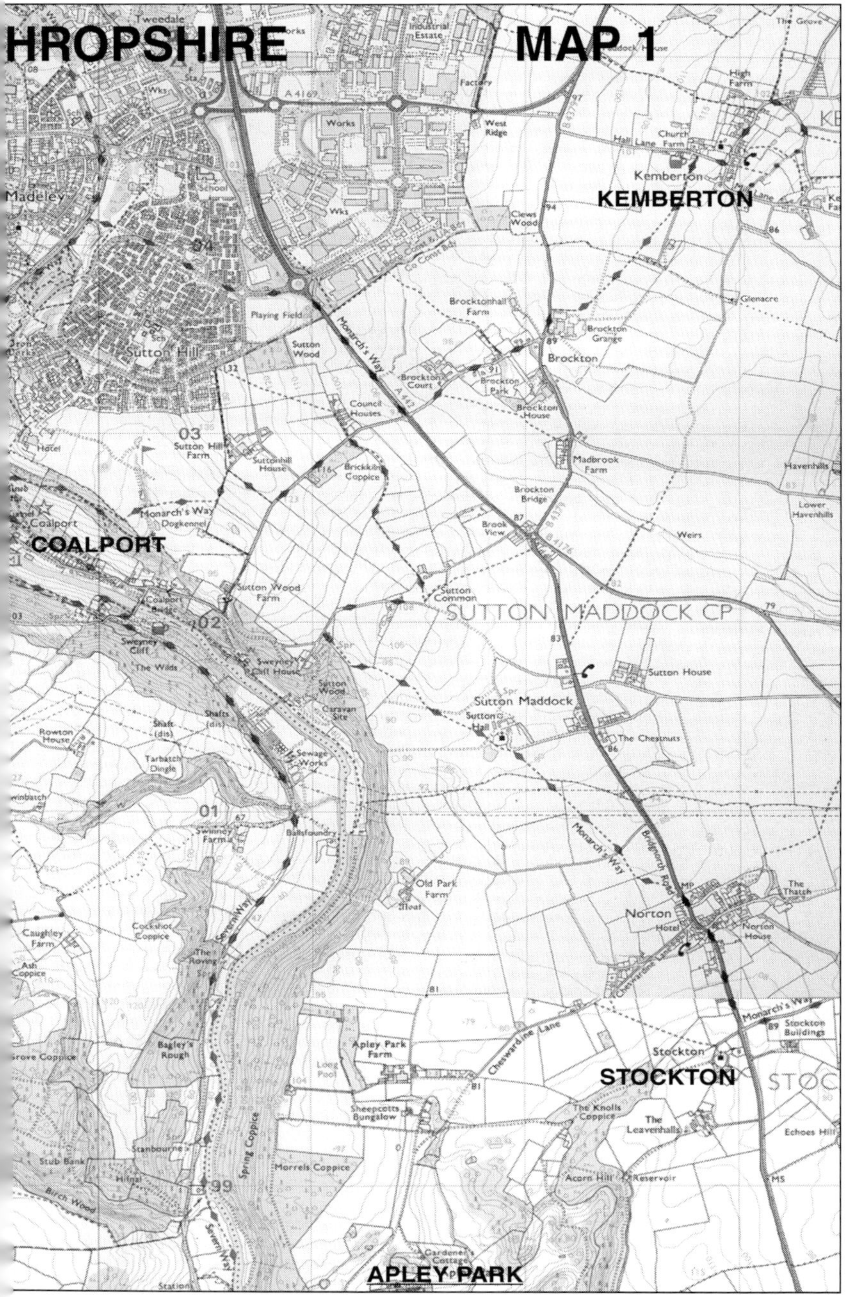
HROPSHIRE
MAP 1
KEMBERTON
COALPORT
Sutton Hill
Madeley
Brockton
Monarch's Way
SUTTON MADDOCK CP
Sutton Maddock
Sutton House
The Chestnuts
Norton
STOCKTON
Apley Park Farm
Spring Coppice
APLEY PARK

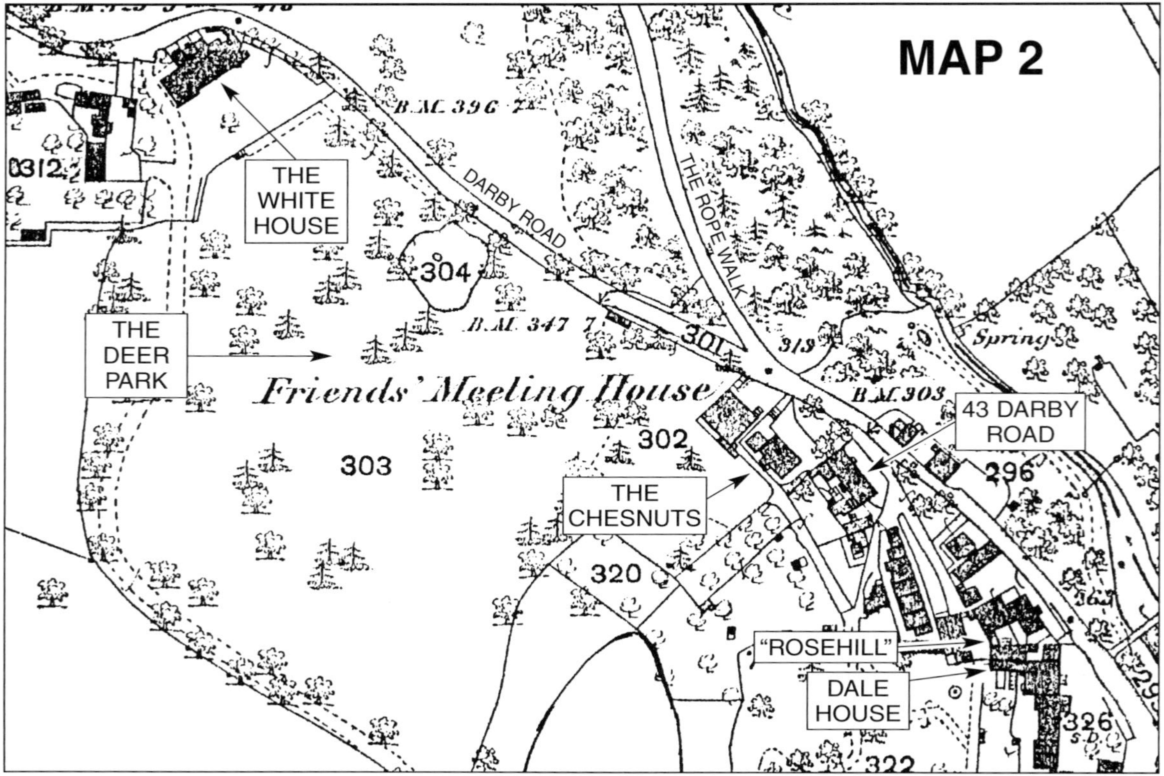

This shows the area at the north end of Coalbrookdale indicated on Map 1. It shows the properties in Darby Road as they were in the 1880s.

Introduction

by Emyr Thomas

Rachel Labouchere died on 22 March 1996 leaving her Foreword to Adelaide's *Journal* unfinished. It is impossible to complete this in the way in which Rachel would have done, but the following comments are added to supplement some of the matters which Rachel might have dealt with, if she had lived a little longer.

Rachel outlined the circumstances surrounding the birth of Francis Darby, Adelaide's father, at The Haye overlooking the Severn Gorge, and, following the death of his father Abraham Darby III, the removal of the family from The Haye to The White House in Coalbrookdale.

Rachel also refers to Francis Darby's aunt, Deborah Darby and her two sons Samuel and Edmund. Deborah Darby was married to Samuel Darby I, who was a younger brother of Abraham III. Rachel Labouchere likewise refers to William and Hannah Mary who were the children of Richard Reynolds by his first wife, Hannah Darby, a daughter of Abraham Darby II.

It was the descendants of these three related branches of the Darby family, i.e. Abraham Darby III, Samuel Darby I and Richard Reynolds, with whom Adelaide was familiar and who feature from time to time in her *Journal* (see family tree of the Darby family, p.xii-xiii).

By the time Adelaide started her *Journal* (1833) the Reynolds family had become slightly detached from the main Darby family. This was because the Coalbrookdale Company, which in the 18th century had controlled the enterprises at Coalbrookdale, Horsehay, Ketley and Madeley Wood had been split into two parts in 1794. Thereafter, the Darby family operated the works at Coalbrookdale and Horsehay, while the Reynolds family became responsible for Ketley and Madeley Wood. Although related, the Reynolds family followed a different path.

In Coalbrookdale, it was the children of the two brothers, Abraham III and Samuel I, who controlled the company during the 19th century. The company had been managed since 1794 by Richard Dearman until his death in 1804. Management was then taken over by the son of Samuel I, Edmund Darby, who had been trained in the Works by Richard Dearman. Edmund proved himself to be a dynamic and imaginative manager, so the future of the company seemed assured. Tragically for the company and for the family Edmund died of food poisoning while staying with an aunt at Melksham in Wiltshire in the summer of 1810. He was only twenty-eight years of age.

What happened next is difficult to understand. Francis Darby, the eldest surviving son of Abraham III was already involved in the Works and would, by Darby family traditions have taken over the management. This did not happen and it was in fact Barnard Dickinson who was chosen to undertake the task. There are a number of possible explanations. One is that Francis himself was disinclined to take on the responsibility. Another possibility lies in his unpredictable temperament. In the years to come he was to demonstrate a certain volatility of character and it is possible that this was already evident in 1810. This raises the possibility that the decision to appoint Barnard Dickinson may have been made by Sarah Darby who was a surviving sister of Abraham III and was, not only the principal shareholder, but was also the dominant personality within the family.

Barnard Dickinson had no experience of the iron industry. He was a farmer and had been trained as such, but he was married to Ann Darby, who was Francis' elder sister and this seniority may have been a factor in his appointment as manager. He took over the Works in 1810. Francis continued to be involved, although presumably in a subordinate capacity. Although unpredictable, he also had an artistic streak in him which became evident some years later, when under his guidance, the company developed a world renowned eminence in decorative ironwork.

By the time Adelaide was born in 1817, the pattern of the family in Coalbrookdale was set for the next 20 years or so. At the head of the valley, on the higher slopes was The White House, where Francis and his wife Hannah (neé Grant) lived with their two daughters, Matilda (b. 1809) and Adelaide (b. 1817). Adjoining The White House was Sunniside, the house built by Abraham II in 1750/51, in which lived the elderly Sarah Darby, sister of Abraham III and the last survivor of the third generation of the Darby family. She was accompanied by Susannah Appleby for whom Sarah was in the process of building The Chesnuts (sic).

Below The White House, and Sunniside was the deer park and below that was the meeting house, built in 1808 with money provided by Richard Reynolds. Next to the meeting house was The Chesnuts. Although built for Susannah Appleby, this fine property was, at the time when Adelaide started her *Journal* (1833), occupied by Lucy Darby (neé Burlingham) widow of Edmund Darby, her two sons Abraham IV and Alfred, and her two daughters, Mary and Deborah.

About a hundred yards below The Chesnuts was the property now called Rosehill. This was originally built in 1738 by Richard Ford and was extended and modernised in 1791 for occupation by Richard Dearman. At the time of Adelaide's *Journal*, it was occupied by Richard Darby, younger brother of Francis Darby, his wife Maria (neé Sorton) and their children, Richard Sorton (b. 1812), Maria Louise (b. 1814), Caroline Anne (b. 1815), William Henry (b. 1819), Charles Edward (b. 1822) and Rebecca Sarah (b. 1832).

Next to Rosehill was the original family home, Dale House, built in 1717 by Abraham I and improved in 1776 for Abraham III. This was the house closest to the Works and the tradition had been established that this was the home of the manager of the Works. Consequently, it was occupied from 1810 to 1838 by Barnard Dickinson, his wife Ann (neé Darby) and their large family. Barnard Dickinson moved in 1838 to a new property which he built for himself to the east of Severn House (now the Valley Hotel) called, rather obviously, Eastfield. Severn House was occupied by his son Henry Dickinson, who in 1841, married Deborah Darby, daughter of Lucy Darby (neé Burlingham) who had been living at Dale House since 1838 when Barnard Dickinson moved out.

In 1817, the year of Adelaide's birth, an incident occurred which affected the career of her father Francis Darby. He had visited Park Gate (probably on the Wirral) where he bathed in the sea and returned home very ill. It was thought his brain was affected, for which he was blooded. He was removed by his parents-in-law, the Grants, to Leighton Buzzard where he was installed in Linslade House, a nearby country house where he stayed for a year. He was diagnosed as having suffered a brain haemorrhage, and although he made a full recovery the episode may have affected his position in the company. Some years later, when his father-in-law John Grant, proposed to leave his share in the Leighton Bank to Francis, the partners in the Bank made clear that Francis was not acceptable on account of the Linslade incident.

There was, however, no reoccurrence of the illness and the family settled down to a happy, almost idyllic life at The White House. The two girls, Matilda and Adelaide, grew up content in each others' company.

The geographical relationship between the White House, the Chesnuts, Rosehill and Dale House at the north end of Coalbrookdale, above the Coalbrookdale Works is shown on the map on page xvi.

PRIVATE JOURNAL OF ADELAIDE DARBY
BORN 10th AUGUST 1817

1833

Comment

Adelaide Darby started her Private Journal on 7th October 1883 when she was only 16 years of age. The first four entries cover the last three months, October to December that year. Having first recorded where she lived (The White House, Coalbrookdale) and established that she had always been "as happy as other people", she recalled that during the previous summer she and her sister Matilda had spent two months at Leamington and that she had also spent some time at Leighton Buzzard in Buckinghamshire, her mother's family house. This was a familiar feature of her life. Her family was sufficiently wealthy to be able to travel from Coalbrookdale and to spend up to two months or so each year away from home staying at places like Birmingham. Leamington Spa, and Leighton Buzzard. Whilst at Coalbrookdale, some of her time was occupied in visiting other members of her family living close by who were about her own age. In particular Louise and Caroline Darby aged 19 and 18, and Hannah Dickinson, aged about 17 years.

From the first few entries in her Journal, Adelaide appears as a rather earnest young lady with her Journal designed "entirely for an account of progressive mental improvements". Later on, however, the Journal was used to display other less worthy aspects of her character. For the time being she was content to record the books she was reading and her steps toward further education, which included French, History and Geography, but not Arithmetic!

Friday 7th October - *On this day I began my Journal which I hope to be able to continue. We have resided all my life at The White House, Coalbrookdale. It is an agreeable situation and I suppose I have always been as happy as other people, indeed I think rather more so. During the summer we have been for two months at Leamington,*[1] *which we enjoyed exceedingly, and I at Leighton.*[2]

I have been much interested in reading "The Young Christians; or familiar illustration of Christian Duty." It is a very nice book and was the occasion of my beginning this Journal, as it much recommends the practice of keeping one.

Saturday being very foggy we did not go beyond the gardens till the afternoon when, rather later than we ought, Matilda and I took a long walk over Stret Hill[3] *into the Shrewsbury Road, then home through the wood, which we accomplished in an hour.*

Monday 27th October - *I spent the morning preparing a long letter for Bonneau.*[4] *Matilda and I went to ask Louisa and Caroline*[5] *to take a walk, but found them going with Aunt Maria to the Bridge, so we went over Severn Hill by ourselves. In the afternoon I sketched a view of the Rhayader Mountains in Emma Reave's album and did a little to my band in the evening. The day was pretty satisfactory, but I found no time for reading except our "Conversations on Chemistry".*

Wednesday 29th October - *Louisa, Caroline and Hannah*[6] *drank tea and we have been very busy forming a Budget.*[7] *If it is carried on with spirit it may be both amazing and instructive, but I rather fear the powers of the members to execute so great an undertaking. Last evening we went to Severn House*[8] *to Dinner, but a description would seem better suited to my pocket book than to be placed in a book designed entirely for an account of progressive mental improvements.*

Tuesday 27th November 1833 - *I think my greatest failing is a sort of indecision of purpose by which I lose much time and do not get on with reading as much as I should like. I have this moment finished the first volume in Miss Taylor's "Contribution of 22" with which I have been much pleased. It is the first time I read it regularly. I get on very slowly with the "Theatre d'Education"; indeed I do not get on with French as I should wish. I should like to read fewer novels for when we do not read them we read something else. We have just done "The Heart of Midlothian" and the "Bridge of Lammermoor". They are both good I think, in their place, but if I had my way we should only read them at spare times and in the evenings. But how can Matilda know I think so when I have never told her.*

Sunday 1st December - *The plan which I should like to pursue at present would be this, to rise about 7 these dark mornings and to work, or else read, in "The Scientific Dialogues" till breakfast time. Then to do my lessons which consist in preparing my French for Bonneau, which, if a little is done every morning does not amount to much. Then to read some French History, Geography ought to be in some way included, but I think I have things more important to attend to than Arithmetic.*

Such should be my employment till it is time to go out, or if anything should prevent that, then a little relaxation either in the form of work or of lighter reading, may be resorted to. After Dinner, either work or Drawing and the same with reading after tea. All this seems very little yet so bad an economist of time as I, that I can with difficulty do it. I have read very little more of the "Oriental Annual" or the "Theatre d'Education", but Matilda and I have read two volumes and half of Scott's "Tales of a Grandfather" with which we have been much pleased.

Monday 16th December - *On Wednesday Mrs Hartshoane came to dinner and stayed till Thursday. On Tuesday Mr Bonneau gave me his last lesson. I* *have done very little indeed this last week except a quantity of plain work and several beginnings of poetical effusions which have had no conclusions.*

NOTES

1. Leamington Spa, on the River Neame, had been given the title of 'Royal' by King George IV and had become a very fashionable watering place by the 1830's. The elegant pumproom built in 1814 was a fine building. Francis Darby and his family evidently visited the Spa from time to time and Adelaide's descriptions of the weeks that they spent there and which she so much enjoyed included a picture of such functions and of excursions made to Guyscliffe and other nearby beauty spots. The chief hotel was "The Royal" that had been opened by a Mr and Mrs Williams where they sometimes stayed for a few days before moving into rooms in one of the fashionable new parades, or streets, usually for a stay of a few weeks, which had been the case when Adelaide began to write this Journal, at the age of sixteen.
2. Leighton Buzzard in Buckinghamshire, not to be confused with Leighton in Shropshire, near Coalbrookdale.
3. "Strethill" is the hill situated south of the White House, between it and the River Severn. It was the location of Strethill Farm/Meadow Farm. It was then owned by Abraham Darby IV of The Chesnuts.
4. Mr Bonneau was presumably a French tutor engaged by Francis Darby for his daughters' further education.
5. Louisa and Caroline were Maria Louise, aged 19 and Caroline Ann, aged 18, the second and third children of Richard and Maria Darby. Richard was Adelaide's uncle who lived at "Rosehill" (see map).
6. Hannah was Hannah Dickinson, aged 17, who was the ninth child of Barnard and Ann Dickinson. Ann Dickinson was Adelaide's aunt. Louisa, Caroline, Hannah and Adelaide were therefore first cousins.
7. The "Budget" is believed to be a local Essay-reading group.
8. Severn House (now the Valley Hotel, Ironbridge) was a mansion built in 1757 by George Woodwin the leading coalmaster of the time. It was acquired by Sarah Darby (sister of Abraham III) and left by her will to the Dickinson family. In 1833 it was occupied by Henry Dickinson who became probably the most influential of the eleven children of Barnard and Ann Dickinson.
9. Charles Henry Hartshorne, born 1808, was an academic. His father, John Hartshorne, belonged to an old Shropshire family engaged in the Iron trade who lived for a long time in Broseley and Bentall. Charles was educated at Shrewsbury School and then at St Johns College, Cambridge, graduating in 1826 and became an M.D three years later - he accompanied the Earl of Guildford to Mount Corfu; he also travelled in Italy and on his return to England he was Ordained as Curate of Bentall, a small but fine church near to the ancient manor house of the same name. He subsequently became Curate of Little Wenlock, a living in the gift of the Foresters of Willey. Charles had married Mary Margaret, the youngest daughter of Francis Keswick, principal Librarian of the House of Commons. Little Wenlock was within walking distance of The White House and the Darbys were to see a great deal of this family to the advantage of both Matilda and Adelaide.

1834

Comment

Adelaide started her Journal for 1834 with a description of a week's visit to Birmingham between 11th February and 17th February. We don't know whether she had stayed in Birmingham before, but the impression is, that although she may have known a few people there through her family connections in Leighton Buzzard, the visit may have been a sort of introduction to the Quaker families in Birmingham.

Adelaide, and her sister Matilda, accompanied by their father, Francis Darby, travelled by stage coach, the "Salopian". Stage coaches which until then had been the predominant method of public travel were approaching the end of their existence. The building of the Grand Junction Railway in the mid 1830s completely usurped their function, except, for a time, as feeder coaches. The people they met in Birmingham were mainly, if not exclusively, from Quaker families. Prominent amongst these were the Lloyds who were so numerous that the young impressionable Adelaide described them as "an interminable people" The Lloyds of Birmingham were relatives of the Lloyds of Dolobran and were descended from Sampson Lloyd who moved to Birmingham from Dolobran in the early 18th century (see Raistrick, *Quakers in Science and Industry*, pp.119-121).

Another family mentioned were the Dearmans who were concerned in the Eagle Foundry, Birmingham. A member of the family, Richard Dearman, had been appointed as Agent-Manager of the Coalbrookdale Company from 1791 until his death (at Rosehill, Coalbrookdale) in 1804. A member of the family, Charles Dearman, appears to have been very attentive to Adelaide. She seems to have "cordially disliked" him and referred to him as "the detestable" Charles Dearman. (It has to be remembered that these are the private judgments of an adolescent teenager!)

Others referred to were the Sturges (related through the Grants of Leighton Buzzard), the Cadburys who later established the great Bournville factory, and the Crewdsons of Crewdson's Bank (see Raistrick, *Quakers in Science and Industry*, pp.74 or 331).

On her return to Coalbrookdale, Adelaide suffered an attack of scarlet fever which put her out of action for a while. Shortly after, "grandmama" became ill. This was Rebecca Darby (1752-1834) the widow of Abraham III, builder of the Iron Bridge, who had been resident at The White House since 1789/90 when, on the death of Abraham III, the family had been obliged to move from The Haye (see Foreword by Rachel Labouchère, p.vii). She was 82 years of age and sadly she died on 23rd June 1834, whilst Adelaide, with other members of the family were enjoying a picnic on The Wrekin, the nearby hill.

During July there was a General Meeting at Coalbrookdale with a considerable gathering of Quakers. This was followed by the customary month's holiday in Leamington. The intention had been that this would be followed by a visit to Oxford, but Adelaide had an attack of jaundice and the visit to Oxford did not take place until 16th September, after about a month in Leighton Buzzard where Adelaide convalesced.

Two days spent in Oxford are a mixture of admiration, awe and even reverence and matter-of-fact observation. From Oxford they went to Woodstock and Blenheim Palace which clearly impressed Adelaide immensely. They stayed overnight at Burford, and then travelled via Cheltenham, Tewkesbury and Worcester to Kidderminster where they spent a miserable night. They arrived back in Coalbrookdale on 20th September, clearly delighted to be home. From the Iron Bridge they noted the Coalbrookdale Company's Warehouse "rising in turreted and embattled rivalship of those convincing and cemented proofs of the March of Improvements". This is virtually the only record which exists of the date of the building of the Severn Warehouse.

On 12th October, Adelaide noted that the Dickinson family had been away at the General Meeting at Hereford and that while they were absent "Mr Cecil Forester took advantage of their not being here to pay a round of civility." Mr Cecil Forester was the Member of Parliament for Wenlock and had been returned as Tory member for that constituency following the passing of the Reform Act if 1832. Adelaide's remarks may perhaps be dismissed as nothing more than mischievous comment, as the Dickinsons were clearly accepted fully as loving and agreeable members of the Darby family (Hannah Dickinson was of an age with Adelaide and was part of the "young set"). On the other hand she may, perhaps subconsciously, have been commenting on differences in lifestyle which were taking place within the fourth of fifth generations of the family, i.e. her father's and her generation.

Barnard Dickinson had retired as a manager of the Company in 1831 having sold his shares to Abraham IV and his family. He had always been a plain Quaker and he and his wife Ann (Francis' sister) had become recognised as ministers in 1824 and 1830. Francis and his family, by contrast, had adopted a more worldly lifestyle and had broadened their horizons by comparison with some of their contemporaries. Francis' accounts show that he had developed a taste for books, silver, Coalport china and the purchase of pictures. Pride of place at the White House was accorded to his collection of paintings which occupied three rooms and were shown to visitors with great pleasure. By the mid-1830s he had acquired a coat of arms which appeared on his silver and porcelain. In short he and his family lived in style as a man of property. In politics, he was a Tory and it was hardly surprising then that Cecil Forester as a Tory Member of Parliament should call on him as a matter of civility.

Francis' brother Richard on the other hand who lived with his family at "Rosehill" followed a different lifestyle. He had a more earnest personality. He was a Whig in politics. He took an active part in public life and local politics. He was involved in the campaign for the abolition of the slave trade and was active in the anti Corn Law league. Perhaps this earnestness showed in his social life, because parties held at "Rosehill" were usually described by Adelaide as 'dull' and 'stiff'.

Although she was only a teenager, Adelaide was conscious of political events which occurred around her. On 5th October there is a first reference to Mr & Mrs Gaskell who were political supporters of Cecil Forester. They appear again in December when the General Election was called. Cecil Forester was again the Tory candidate and Sir William Summerson was the Whig candidate. The result was declared in January 1855 when Cecil Forester won by 94 votes.

Tuesday 11th February - *We set off about 8 o'clock by the "Salopian" very much elated at being permitted to go by this coach. We had a beautiful day, but we both took colds with us which we have brought back. About 2 we arrived at Birmingham. We had persuaded the coachman to take us to Dee's (Hotel) where while waiting for a cab, Mr Francis Lloyd introduced himself. (I afterwards found he was attending the preparations for the Yeomanary Ball on Friday of which he was one of the stewards).*

We were very kindly welcomed in Frederick Street to dinner, Papa leaving us directly.

Wednesday 12th February - *Our colds were both very bad, but we went to the Meeting (it was Monthly Meeting). We called at Bingley with Mrs Lloyd where we saw Priscilla and Mr Thompson and Mr Edward Lloyd, a son of Charles Lloyd (they are an interminable people). We are engaged to dine at Bingley on Saturday to our great surprise. Samuel Charles Sturge brought Charles Lloyd to dinner. Mr Charles Lloyd at Birmingham and Mr Charles Lloyd at Leamington are certainly different people. We went to tea at Samuel Sturges to meet Mrs Matravers who is a delightful woman, and who is placing her little boy, who is deaf and dumb, under Mr Dupoafai's care. Sophia Sturge and John, Joseph and Edmund are all staying in Frederick Street till Southfield is completed for the bridge's reception.*

Thursday 13th February - *Went with Cousin Mary (Sturge) to the Deaf and Dumb Institution to call for Mrs Matravers who was going with John Sturge and ourselves to the Botanic Gardens which are very beautiful. Caroline Matravers dined here, the rest of the Sturges and Mrs and Miss Lloyd came to tea. Henry and ? and Mrs James Lloyd came in after, the latter is very much* *like Cousin Barnard. He had told Charles Sturge he was coming to tea with his mother and sister, and Mary had taken a great deal of pains to get all the Sturges as Charles cannot be at home till late on Thursday. He says they will see more of the Lloyds while we are in Frederick Street than in a twelve month at any other time.*

Friday 14th February - *This evening we drank tea at Captain Moorsome's upon condition that if our colds were worse we should send an excuse to Bingley tomorrow. We only met John Sturge.*

Saturday 15th February - *Went with Henry in the morning to see Anderson's Birds at the Library. We were delighted. We were admitted through the instrumentality of Cadbury and Co. We met Little James Cadbury there though Henry said the birds had been there half a century and he did not know why James Cadbury could not go at any other time. After a shopping expedition we returned to Frederick Street to dress and at 5 o'clock with Caroline Matravers as a chaperone we set off for Bingley. There we met Miss Emma Lloyd, Miss Pearson, Priscilla and Frank at dinner. Many more of the never-ending Lloyds were expected but none came to dinner, but at tea there was an accession in the persons of Mr Charles Dearman, Messrs Charles James Lloyd and Mr Edward Lloyd. At tea, I got between Mrs Lloyd and Frank, and Charles Dearman scarcely ever left me a minute from the time I was introduced 'till I left Birmingham. I cordially disliked him and Mr Frank Lloyd too, who I got rid of in the music room and I comforted myself by elicitating a great deal of Leamington news from Mr Charles Lloyd. Charles Sturge came to fetch us home.*

Sunday 16th February - *Henry came to breakfast. After meeting we saw D. Benson. Mary Bain came to Dinner with the boys from Camphill and Henry and Mr J? and C Dearman. After dinner in came the Sturges, Mr W. Moorsome and Isaac Crewdson. The room was quite full and Henry, said Isaac Crewdson must mistake it for one of his own parties for he always asked all the riffraff. of Manchester in a first day. Caroline and Agatha Pearson came to tea with Charles Dearman, the Detestable. Some of the Sturges came in after tea and a nameless oddity from J. Southalls. It was not much like Sunday.*

Monday 17th February - *Went to see Isaac Sturge's Chemical Works with Mrs Matravers, S. Dearman and the Proprietor. Papa came for us at 1 with Uncle Richard Darby and we are now arrived at the Dale. There is a feeling of desolation and a solitariness here, but we have so much to look back to that it seems as though we must have been absent more than a week.*

Tuesday 8th March - *The second day after our return from Birmingham we both complained of sore throats, Matilda soon had an eruption and Mr Webb*[1] *said it was Scarlet Fever. We have been kept cooped up here ever since, a very sad termination to our gaiety. Grandmama has been so ill that Aunt Tothill*[1a] *came for a week, she went on Tuesday and Aunt Darby went with her as far as Birmingham to see Mr Sturge who has had a bad cough and cold but is now better. I finished the 3rd Volume of "Harry and Lucy" but I have particularly* *disliked reading much. I am so much better today that I have done some French and have begun to read Crabb's "Life" to Matilda, I have begun Goldsmith's "History of England" marking the dates from my little History of the English Kings, also a number of the Library of Entertaining Knowledge containing Pompeii.*

Sunday 18th March - *This morning we went to Meeting. Cousin Joseph Dickinson[2] came up after dinner.*

Wednesday 21st March - *Mr and Miss Wilderspin came to The Chesnuts to put the school to rights. Mr Wilderspin left in the afternoon and Miss Wilderspin drank tea with us. On Friday next is the "Budget"[3] Day. Miss Wilderspin has been here re-organising the school for 8 weeks until the 'Chesnuts'[4] were obliged to go to Worcester to the General Meeting there. Mary Sturge has another little boy; and Henry Dickinson[5] is settling at Gloucester as a Chemist where Sarah[6] is gone for a little while. The season is so mild that Matilda and I had some May in our hair today.*

Friday 20th June - *It is a long time since I have been able to write in my Journal. I have not been engaged more than usual but contrivance is always necessary to fulfil anything which we do not perform at a fixed time. Louisa and Caroline[7] have long been expecting to see Miss Horne[8] who was at school with them. She arrived with Cousin Abraham Darby on his return from the Yearly Meeting. We are rather pleased with her. There has been a good deal of visiting since her arrival.*

Sunday 22nd June - *A Wrekin party[9] is planned for to-morrow. After meeting this evening Sarah asked us to come and see Grandmama[10] who we found much altered. Mr Webb[1] called here to-day and gave us a very unfavourable opinion of her, he thinks it hardly probable that she will survive another winter. She spoke very affectionately to us though her voice was exceedingly weak and difficult to understand.*

Monday 23rd June - *The account of Grandmama[10] this morning was not at all improved and we sent to Uncle Richard Darby to know if they intended to join the Chesnuts party to the Wrekin which as they had no intention of giving up we went also. The morning was a little cloudy but it cleared up and we had a most delightful day. It was Cousin Lucy Darby's party and besides the Chesnut people a Mr Ashworth had been persuaded to stay with them over the momentous occasion. All Uncle Richard Darby's family and most of the Dickinsons who are just come from school and ourselves were there, I forgot to include Sophy Horne who was a host in herself. We were in exuberant spirits and the slide had good service. Mr Ashworth is a very detestable personage. On our return which was not till late in the evening, we were met by a note from Mama sealed with black and we were indeed dreadfully shocked to find that our dear Grandmama[10] had peacefully breathed her last in our absence about 5 o'clock, a time when we had been giving vent to our high spirits in most obstreperous mirth. The revulsion of feeling caused by this sad intelligence was more than I can describe.*

Sunday 6th July - *Sophy Horne,[8] Mr Gulson Reynolds[11] and Richard Sorton Darby[12] dined and Mrs Reynolds and Hester Pinter came to tea. Uncle and Aunt Tothill[13] left yesterday, the Lloyds on Wednesday, and one by one almost everybody. A letter from Leighton to-day says we must fix about going to Leamington.*

Tuesday 15th July - *Henry Newman and Mary Bruin have arrived to be our lodgers at the General Meeting; to-morrow will be eventful.*

Wednesday 16th July - *It is over and like a fading dream. The morning Meetings passed without anything particular and were adjourned to 5 in the evening. The Newmans and J Hadnen and Mary Bruin dined with us and C Barford, D Lloyd, S Lloyd, Mrs Hartland and a tribe besides came to tea after the Meetings. I Pumphrey and Bevington Gibbings wished the women Friends to come into the mens Meetings and appeared very affectionately and beautifully. A tribe of the Burlinghams[14] came up with us, Henry Newman returned to supper and Somers Harford and Joe Dickinson followed. They, myself also, were in high spirits and we finished a serious though a very agreeable day in abundant merriment. It is not I think quite so nonsensical as formerly which is an improvement.*

Thursday 17th July - *All the Harfords came to Dinner with Mr and Mrs J Bradley and Mr and Mrs Burlingham, Jo Dickinson came to tea. We had a delightful day. Tomorrow everybody will be gone, I am ready to cry this evening. J Gulson Reynolds[11] came to tea and predicts rain and thunder.*

Wednesday 23rd July - *Today we arrived, after a most delightful journey, only hot from Birmingham. Leamington is fuller than I ever saw it before.[15] We have rather a nice house, 19 Upper Parade, not as amusing a scene as we had before but sufficiently so when wet weather does not oblige us to remain within. We dined at "The Regent" which is now very well conducted by Mr Abraham Alexander. We went to the Atheneum this morning and bought two stupid books back with us so I have been reading one of the standard novels which Papa brought with him. It contains Vathea, 'The Castle of Strantol' and 'The Bravo of Venice'; the last is translated from German and if it was true would be most interesting and wonderful - totally different from Cooper's which I had read over again though both make their "Braves" not to turn out Braves.*

Friday 25th July - *Mrs Charles Lawford and Mrs Deverel were at the Pump Room; the former called yesterday when we met the Baileys (all from Leighton).*

Sunday 27th July - *A wet day which on a Sunday absent from home is very unpleasant. We have been reading Miss Edgeworth's "Helen" altogether the last day or two of which is a most pleasant way of doing the most pleasant thing for it is one of the most delightful books I ever read. Helen is such a beautiful natural and good character and yet not one which you feel is quite too exalted for imitation. All the people are to the life.*

Sunday 10th August - *To-day is my 17th Birthday though I can hardly realise the idea that I am so old.. It really does seem such a little while since I used to think well I shall be 13 soon - I wish it was 17, and now those inesteemable years are passed for ever without having been improved as they ought. I have now the thoughts and feelings of a woman with the information and knowledge of a child which is rather mortifying, but perhaps it is not yet too late - I will not commit good resolutions to paper - the perpetration of a few good deeds would be so much more satisfactory. During the chief part of our visit here I have been very far from well with a bilious attack which has made me stupid and yellow to a degree.*

Monday 11th August - *To-day I am much better. We are expecting Papa this evening and on Tuesday next we leave for Oxford which we are to visit on our way home.*[16] *I do not expect to enjoy it very much as nothing looks 'couleur de rose' in an attack of jaundice. I am now reading Lady Blessington's "Repealers" which is full of interesting information and I note politics, but I do like this. I have made a curious jumble of our doings and must conclude with the Promenade Ball where Papa took us on Thursday - most amusing and not at all formidable but rather dissipating I suppose it would be to go often.*

Tuesday 16th September - *We fixed upon dining early at Leighton which we left about 2 and soon arrived at this very magnificent city where I think we have been already very industrious. We took a walk before tea and finding the gate of St John's College open we walked in and the porter persuaded us to go through the garden, which happened to be the one John Lawford said we must see being the best or "most elegant" in Oxford. The College itself is quite an inferior one. We saw the hall where the Juke (sic) of Wellington dined the day of his Installation. It appeared rather small by the dusk light in which we saw it. We walked up High Street to get a guide and returned thoroughly tired and hungry to have tea and some music which was very pretty - I have been asleep since.*

Wednesday 17th September - *Today we have been indefatigable in Lion seeing. First to Christ Church which stands highest for size and beauty. The Library is 140 feet long, and is splendid as well as the hall which is hung with portraits of celebrated men. The windows of the chapel, or rather church, are beautiful and it contains several curious tombs. The shrine of St. Fridesivide 900 years old is in a beautiful state of preservation. Christ Church has no garden, but a long walk under stately elms (I think) amply compensates for the absence of one. Papa, Matilda and I went next to New College where the Chapel is most splendid. The stained glass surpasses everything of the kind that I have seen. Patriarchs and beneath Prophets, Saints and Martyrs occupy each window, the brilliancy of the colours is significant. The 'Large West Window' is beautiful with less bright colours - the lower panes contain the Christian virtues and the upper the Birth of Our Saviour. The garden is large and pretty containing beautiful trees, over the gate is the motto "Manners Makyth Man". I enjoyed walking round it excessively in its silent academic aristocratic solitude. Surely with* *such inducements to study it is not wonderful that Oxford and Cambridge should produce our greatest men. I think the reforming spirits of the present day have done an irrepairable evil in so completely overthrowing that respectful and reverential admiration, which if it was a feeling must have been still a most delightful one with which to wander through those classic shades. Mama went with us to Magdalen College where the Library is not very good, but the chapel (upon which the most pains seems bestowed in all the colleges) is beautiful with windows painted in chiaroscur. At first the absence of the brilliant colours seems half melancholy, but there is an elegance about the whole with which this well corresponds. Above the altar is a most beautiful painting considered the finest in Oxford. It represents our Saviour bearing the cross and is now attributed to Morales the whole of the wall in which it is fixed is splendidly carved in I suppose white stone which adds greatly to the beauty of the picture. The sculpture and carving throughout the chapel are beautiful. The large window is most terrific representing the Day of Judgement and painted in the same dark colours as the others. The Deer Park and the water walk are very pretty and there is a simplicity about the whole which is very interesting. I do not know how I came to forget the picture galleries at Christ Church which are very large and beautiful - the paintings generally are old. From Magdalen College we went to Radcliffe's Library where we saw beautiful specimens of marbles, books and a grand view from the top. We descended to All Souls College in which there is nothing worth seeing except an altar piece by Meng's representing Christ appearing to Mary in the garden. From there to the Bodleian Library, very large and curious. There we saw a copy of the Koran among the old manuscripts and a beautiful picture of Addison's deathbed by Sir Joshua Reynolds and many other splendid old paintings, also some elegant models of the ancient temples in Rome.*

From there to the Theatre which is said to be the largest hall roofed edifice unsupported by pillars in the kingdom. There is a most splendid portrait of George IV by Lawrence - the Emperor of Russia and King of Prussia on each side. The ceiling is beautifully painted to represent canvas stretched over gilt cords. Here was the Duke's Installation. What a splendid sight it must have been. Having done all this we were glad to return to the "King's Arms" and equally so to have dinner. Before tea Mama and I took a perambulation to the post office beyond High Street and from there through the Colleges to the Park, which is very pretty beyond Waddam and Trinity. We have a good view of the Clarendon Printing Office of which Matilda has taken a sketch. I have been too lazy to do so. We had some pretty music this evening.

***Thursday 18th September** - Burford - We were really sorry to leave Oxford after breakfast this morning when we proceeded to Woodstock and Blenheim. They showed us first the China Gallery which I did not much like. The park is most beautiful and the entrance with the bridge amongst the trees. I enjoyed the ride through it exceedingly as we went to the front of this immensely magnificent palace. It is an extensive semicircle, terminated by the Corinthian portico where, after going round through a number of buildings, and arches, we enter* *the hall - it is sumptuous as well as the suite of superb apartments which seem endless. They do end however in the Library in which is a beautiful statue of Queen Anne. The collection of pictures by the old masters is by far the finest I ever beheld, every one of the rooms deserves a description to itself, if I was gifted to do them justice. The French tapisterie is beautiful and most interesting, describing the Duke of Marlborough's battles. The Chapel is pretty. We endeavoured to get admittance into the unfinished flower garden which occupies two acres and the beauty of which, from the window, defies description. The Duke always inhabits it and as it was doubtful when he might come in and whether he would let us see it then, we concluded not to wait. We did not duly appreciate the old flower garden which is very beautiful after this disappointment. The grand extent and stupendous magnificence of Blenheim, even in its present deplorable state of preservation surpasses even imagination. I have been more delighted with almost every new object on our journey than with the one before it, but Blenheim makes you silent in admiration. The country is beautiful as far as you can see anything of the woods of Blenheim, but nearer Whitney it becomes dreary to a degree with its white stone walls and flatness as far as the eye can reach, the horizon edged by Whitch Wood Forest and other large woods and flat country. The reflection of the sun on the white walls and roads makes it intensely hot. Burford is a poor little town which we have been perambulating since three o'clock when we arrived. The church is pretty inside and out.*

Thursday 18th September *- We went to the Priory*[17] *which is fast going to decay in the hands of its present possessor Mr Greenaway. We walked over the grounds where we were told we had no business. They must have been beautiful once though now they look melancholy in the extreme. In the evening we called on Huntley who is most agreeable and kind. We are to sleep here tonight, I do not care how soon.*

Friday 19th September *- Kidderminster - We left Burford this morning and breakfasted at North Leach. It is a nice clean little town. From there to Cheltenham the country is uninteresting till you come near the last. This was a pleasure we had not anticipated spending a pleasant half hour in Cheltenham. On to Tewkesbury and Worcester where we fully intended to stay all night and see the Cathedral and the Worcester-Lions animate and inanimate. It was the great Hop Fair and they could not possibly accommodate us at "The Star" neither could we walk out. So after dining as comfortably as could be expected with the house full of farmers, we set off again to try out fate at Kidderminster where we have taken up very commodious quarters. This is a very respectable looking town and can boast a rather pretty old church (St Marys) which we went to see. We have been favoured with beautiful weather-for our little round which I believe we have all enjoyed prodigiously.*

Saturday 20th September *- Coalbrookdale - Here we are at home! We had a wretched night at Kidderminster - the beds were certainly stuffed with stubble and quills and abounding "par consequence" in vermin, and we were glad* *to leave the "White Lion" for breakfast at Bridgnorth. The whole of the way from Kidderminster to the Dale is a beautiful drive, partly through Wolrych - Whitmore's and Lord Forester's estates. I was very much struck with a change in my feelings as we got nearer home. Going down Broseley Hill, which always seems to belong peculiarly to Shropshire and to be associated with a thousand once most interesting county proceedings, I felt as if the carriage contained all that I cared about in Shropshire. These unneighbourly ideas faded however as we reached our really sweet and beautiful home. We were much struck with a number of diminutive castles and a new red brick ruin, in woeful taste, as we passed Quatford on the other side of Bridgnorth, and when we had progressed as far as the Iron Bridge we beheld the Coalbrookdale Company's Warehouse*[18] *rising in turretted and embattled rivalship of these convincing and cemented proofs of the March of Improvements, which might be extended with great utility over the roads which would be much better for a judicious portion of mending and levelling.*

Sunday 5th October - *We have returned two weeks-two tolerably happy weeks during which I have been very busy. We went on Friday last to Shrewsbury - they are red hot in the election of a Coroner which they have been so foolish as to make a party question. Thursday was an important day when I dispatched a certain letter which I now think would have been as well unsent. Mr and Mrs Gaskell called - Oh, they are such delightful people - Mr Gaskell with all his immense fortune has not half the importance and pretension of Mr Bridges and Mrs Gaskell is the most delightfully simple, girlish creature imaginable.*[18a]

Friday 9th October - *Matilda and I went with Mama to the schools,*[19] *after which Matilda and I went along Cook's Wood*[20] *and took a sketch. In the afternoon Matilda went again to the school and I read nearly all the reign of George III in Goldsmith's "Little English History". This was all new to me and I knew so little about it that I set up the Atlas and the Gazettier to find the places I did not know, which is a tiresome business although a very improving method. On Matilda's return we finished reading Wordsworth's poems and I did a sketch of the lime caverns. After tea I partly manufactured a mat for Grandmama and read an account of the Birmingham Festival which is to be grand.*

Sunday 12th October - *Thursday last was the day of the General Meeting at Hereford on which occasion the Dickinsons, the only young people left at the Dale went to it while all were absent the following day. Mr Cecil Forester*[21] *took advantage of their not being here to pay a round of civility. The weather is become very cold and frosty so we have not been out much, I get on with the Italian as well as I am able, but the very dark afternoons are a great hindrance in drawing. After all it is very pleasant to be settled at home - I do not know how I can ever reconcile leaving such a dear dear place - I am sure going out makes me love home better when I come back to it.*

Sunday 26th October - *Mr Hartshorne*[22] *has sent a great Book upon pencil drawing illustrated with such beautifully discouraging Lithographic engravings.*

I am reading Dr Watt's "Improvement of the Mind" - it is rather abstruse, but though the ideas are really complex they are expressed so single and in such a simple old fashioned style that even a head like mine holding but one idea, can understand almost all.

Tuesday 4th December - *We had a party, that is the Dickinsons by themselves, Rachel Fowler*[23] *came with them, we like her so much, she was to dine at the Chesnuts on Wednesday and we persuaded them all to come to tea with us. We were very sorry she could not stay over the Budget. The Chesnut go to Leamington on Friday which was also Budget day. Cousin William R Lawford came to dinner. As the higher powers were preparing for the evening, I had the felicity of providing, according to my very small ability, mental entertainment all dinner time for my cousin, who grows really handsome.*

Papa went to Shrewsbury. Our Party consisted of Louisa and Caroline[7] *and ourselves as being all the Budget members left at the Dale (Sarah is gone to Gloucester) - Cousin Barnard Dickinson, Miss Turner, Papa and Mama joined us, we had 16 pieces and 2 voted out they were on "the course of the seasons" and "Peaceable Principle of Nonresistance". I do not know when we have had so delightful a Budget. We went to dine at Severn House last Saturday - Mr Reynolds*[24] *is come to see his Mother and brings his usual round of company with him. Barnard went with us and we met only Will Anstice,*[25] *a pleasant evening. On Monday, to our surprise, we received an invitation to tea at Uncle Richard Darby's - we went and found as I anticipated a stupid party*[26] *only Hannah there.*

Wednesday 5th December - *The Reynolds*[24] *and Captain Edmonds dined with us. Friday we met the same at Madeley with Mr Anstice, Will*[25] *and Charlotte. Papa only took me, it was rather alarming as we had the chimney on fire.*

Sunday 9th December - *Oh, what a week of laziness, on Monday came a letter for me answering whereof to Sophy put me out of temper and quietude until Thursday which was the Bible Committee when, being at the Bridge,*[27] *I put it in the Post Office. On that day I was appointed a Collector. I do not know how I shall like it. I read "The Lay of the Last Minstrel" in which I was disappointed. We have a volume of Blackwood for 1830, where there are some beautiful pieces of Mrs Hemans. "The Lady of Provence" is very sweet perhaps more so now to us as we have just been reading of the mahommedan conquests in Gibbon. We have finished "The Hindoos". On Tuesday Mr and Mrs Oven called. On Wednesday, Barnard came to tea - ditto Friday. Yesterday we went down to the Bridge to take the Budget Book*[3] *which is almost full. Mr Smith was not at home so I left the Book - woe betide me if the Contributors knew I had left their productions at a publishers where all the country lounges occasionally. Now heaven preserve Abraham Darby and Barnard Dickinson junr., in good spirits and at home for the ensuing week, they are a hindrance and a bar to good works in an evening. Perhaps it is not well to forestall events, but I have thoughts of an enigma for the next Budget by way of novelty.*

Thursday 13th December - *We went today to Uncle Richard Darby's to one of their stiff parties. My feelings grew frozen and cramped though I had been in exuberant spirits before we set off. When I came home my indignation broke at Louise and Caroline's*[7] *disagreeableness and malhomie more I fear with temper than tact. Matilda*[27a] *says it is partly my fault. Part of the disagreements of the evening were political controversies without end. They expect a dissolution of Parliament*[28] *as well as of the Ministry which was announced on Sunday.*

Thursday 20th December - *I have a leisure hour and have wished for some days to write a letter. Much is happening. Politics, those eternal destroyers of harmony and good feeling - they are carrying everybody away with them.*[28] *Mr Gaskell*[18a] *called next morning and said poor Mr Forester had hardly taken one promise of support all day. Papa was gone to Shrewsbury or he would have given one. This morning we have been to the Bridge.*[27] *The houses are decorated with waving blue banners and Cotes is already on them and we believe Bridges in smaller letters, and Parliament is not yet dissolved! People are all on the 'qui vive'. Today grave faces are seen trotting to and fro on steeds which look the worse for an election's wear and tear already. How different was poor Cecil's twilight arrival this time to the bright October morning two years ago when, flushed with the pride of certain triumph, he came attended by a train of equestrian allies all looking as happy and almost as bright as himself. Louisa*[7] *goes about with a black countenance. Miss Turner is an evidently diverted spectator of a scene into the excitement of which I cannot help entering more than should be.*

Friday 28th December - *Thursday we dined at Dale House - Miss Turner and Matilda and I spent a really pleasant day. Sir William Summerville*[28] *called just as we had left the dining room to dress, but we had a view from the window. In the evening we saw the band come up the Dale in procession and it played very beautifully for some time.*

NOTES

1. Mr Webb was a surgeon from Shrewsbury.

1a. The Aunt Tothill referred to was Hannah Tothill (neé Darby), younger sister of Adelaide's father, who in 1818 had married William Tothill of Bristol where she normally resided (see family tree).

2. Joseph Dickinson (1806-1860) was the eldest child of Barnard and Ann Dickinson (see family tree). He was the manager of the Horsehay works.

3. The "Budget" is believed to be a local Essay-reading group.

4. The Chesnuts was a fine property in Darby Road (see map), converted c.1818 by Sarah Darby from some houses previously owned by the Cranage family. It was then occupied by Lucy Darby (neé Burlingham), widow of Edmund Darby and their two sons, Abraham IV and Alfred who were later to feature prominently in Adelaide's diary.

5. Henry Dickinson (1812-1886) was the sixth child of Barnard and Ann Dickinson. In 1841 he married Deborah Darby, younger sister of Abraham IV and Alfred (see above) and they lived at Severn House (see map). Henry became a prominent and important resident of Coalbrookdale.
6. Sarah was presumably Henry's sister, the third child of Barnard and Ann Dickinson.
7. Louisa and Caroline were Marie Louise, aged 19 and Caroline Ann, age 18, the second and third children of Richard and Maria Darby. Richard was Adelaide's uncle who lived at "Rosehill".
8. Miss Sophy Horne, possibly from the London area, was a school friend of Louisa and Caroline Darby. She seems to have been a regular visitor to "Rosehill". The following year 1835 she was accompanied by her brother who became Adelaide's first boyfriend.
9. A Wrekin party involved organising a picnic at or near the summit of The Wrekin (1334 feet above sea level). It remains a popular activity to this day.
10. "Grandmama" was Rebecca Darby (1752-1834), widow of Abraham III the builder of the Iron Bridge. Rebecca Darby died peacefully while the Wrekin party was taking place, much to Adelaide's dismay (see 23rd June).
11. This entry seems to catalogue the aftermath of the funeral of Rebecca Darby. The Reynolds family were related to the Darbys. Richard Reynolds (1735-1816) had married Hannah Darby (1735-62), daughter of Abraham II by his first marriage to Margaret Smith of Shifnal. They had a son William Reynolds, who from 1794 created W. Reynolds and Company, which operated the Ketley Works and the Madeley Wood Company. Richard Reynolds married a second time to Rebecca Gulson. This explains the continuation of Gulson in the name of Mr Gulson Reynolds.
12. Richard Sorton Darby (1812-1883) was the eldest son of Richard and Maria Darby. He married Anna Wilkinson and moved to Hawkswood House, Sidbury, near Bridgnorth.
13. Uncle and Aunt Tothill had come up from Bristol.
14. A General Meeting took place at Coalbrookdale on 16th July 1834, and the Darby family were very much involved over the period 15th-17th July. The reference to "a tribe of Burlinghams" relates to the relatives of Lucy Burlingham, widow of Edmund Darby who had died young in 1810. Lucy was the daughter of John Burlingham, who was one of the leading master glovers of Worcester. The Burlinghams were a big family.
15. This entry chronicles the arrival at Leamington, a favourite holiday resort of the family, as foreshadowed in the entry for 6th July. The holiday appears to have lasted until mid-August during which time Adelaide contracted jaundice.
16. Adelaide had had an attack of jaundice. The intention was to visit Oxford the following week, but this did not take place until 16th September. It has to be assumed that they went to Leighton Buzzard instead, no doubt to recuperate. They spent an interesting two days in Oxford,16th and 17th September and then made their way back to Coalbrookdale via Burford, 18th September and Kidderminster, 19th September, arriving back in Coalbrookdale on 20th September.
17. This presumably refers to Minster Lovell near Burford. In the evening they visited "Huntley" of the Hillside Academy in Burford.

18. This is the first record of the building of the Severn Warehouse which was built by the Company at the former Loadcroft Wharf on the site of a smelt-house built there at the beginning of the 18th century.

18a. The Gaskells were an important family in Much Wenlock. They were involved in the political life of the borough and its representation in Parliament. Today, their memory is recorded by the existence of "The Gaskell Arms" on the road to Shrewsbury.

19. The Darby family, like other Quaker families, placed great emphasis on good education. School rooms were established by Abraham Darby II between 1751 and 1763 in premises at the rear of The White House. These were left by his Will in 1763 to his daughters Mary and Sarah, who continued the family interest in education throughout their lives. The school was probably moved from the rear of The White House, possibly after 1789, when Rebecca, widow of Abraham III took up residence there. Unfortunately there is no record of where it was moved to although it is known that proposals for building a meeting house and Sunday school were mooted in 1785 (VCH XI p.72 note 74 and SRRC 1487/34/1).

    In 1784 Abiah Darby, widow of Abraham II wrote to Reverend Fletcher of Madeley suggesting the establishment of Sunday schools, and this led to the setting up of Sunday schools in Coalbrookdale, Madeley Wood and Madeley. This was reinforced by Richard Reynolds who built schools in Coalbrookdale, Ketley and Madeley. There may well have been a school close to the Works where the girls school was subsequently built because there is evidence (SRRC 1987/31/9 and SPO 1681/138/8) which shows that Abraham Darby IV purchased "the school house and school yard" from Richard Darby I on 18th December 1830. Although the location of the school cannot yet be positively identified, there is a strong probability that it was on the site of the subsequent Girls' School.

20. The Journal records that Matilda and Adelaide visited "Cook's Wood" to make a sketch. This must refer to "Cocks Wood" which is located at the head of the Loamhole Dingle, north of the area known as the lakehead and on the steep eastern slope of the valley between the brook and the Horsehay road above. This land was acquired by Abraham II as a railhead for the Works in the 1750s. Cocks Wood was a fairly easy walk from The White House.

21. The visit by Mr Cecil Forester is interesting. Cecil Forester (or to give him his full name, George Cecil Wilfred Weld-Forester) was the Member of Parliament for Wenlock (which included Madeley and Coalbrookdale). Politics in Shropshire was unusual in that it was relatively free of the corruption which was a characteristic of politics before the Reform Act 1832. It was a county which returned 12 Members to Parliament, but by the standards of the time there was only one borough (Bishop's Castle) which could be described as corrupt. This was because the representation of the constituencies was practically hereditary in about a dozen families, e.g. the Whitmores in Bridgnorth and the Foresters in Wenlock. In the case of Wenlock, Foresters had represented the borough in the 16th century and then almost continuously from 1678 to 1885 when Wenlock was disfranchised. Similar patterns applied both in the county and in the Boroughs of Shrewsbury, Bridgnorth, Wenlock and Ludlow. The Foresters continued to represent Wenlock even after the upheavals of the Reform Acts 1832 and 1867.

22. C. H. Hartshorne was the curate of Little Wenlock. See 1833 note 9, p.6.
23. The reference to Rachel Fowler is intriguing. It possibly refers to the sister of Deborah Darby, widow of Samuel Darby I. Both sisters were members of the Barnard family of Sheffield. Rachel married Robert Fowler of Melksham in 1790. Their daughter Mary became the second wife of Joseph John Gurney, younger brother of Elizabeth Fry. Rachel would have been an elderly visitor, approaching the end of her life.
24. "Mr Reynolds" is not identified, but it was probably one of the three sons of Joseph Reynolds - either Thomas Reynolds or Joseph Gulson Reynolds or Dr William Reynolds. The most likely of the three would be Joseph Gulson Reynolds.
25. Will Anstice was the son of Robert Anstice, who was a cousin of William Reynolds (son of Richard Reynolds). Shortly before his death in 1803, William Reynolds gave a quarter holding in his company W. Reynolds & Co. to Robert Anstice. Within a few years, Anstice acquired the rest of the company and renamed it the Madeley Wood Company. The Anstice family lived at Bedlam Hall, located near the River Severn, south east of Madeley Green. It was built in 1621. As the family prospered they built Madeley Wood Hall further east in Lower Lloyds, and Bedlam Hall was demolished. The Anstice family became the dominant family at the eastern end of the Severn Gorge, rivalling the Darbys in Coalbrookdale.
26. In her Journal, Adelaide seems to underline the differences between her own lifestyle and that of her uncle Richard Darby at Rosehill. Words like dull, stiff or stupid are used. Of course this can be put down to teenage exuberance, but at the same time, there is no doubt a small degree of truth in the description. Richard Darby was the younger brother of Adelaide's father Francis Darby. As Rachel Labouchere has pointed out, Francis, even as a schoolboy showed an artistic talent and this was to be confirmed later in his career. Richard Darby on the other hand seems to have been more earnest by nature. Instead of taking an interest in the Works, he devoted himself to politics of a radical nature. He voted Whig whereas Francis was a Tory. Despite these differences, the families remained in close loving relationship and constantly visited each other, despite Adelaide's disdain.
27. Interestingly Adelaide describes visits to the "Bridge". This was Ironbridge, but it seems that even by 1834 it had not acquired its subsequent separate identity. Coalbrookdale was still the dominant locality and Ironbridge was still simply a part of it.
27a. Matilda was Adelaide's older sister.
28. The first parliament under the new Reform Act 1832 met in January 1833 under Lord Grey. In 1833 it passed the Emancipation of Slavery Act and the first Factory Act, both momentous pieces of legislation. The following year, under Lord Melbourne, the Poor Law Reform Act was passed. Despite these stupendous changes, the level of expectation generated by the Reform Act 1832 was not realised and an election was called for the end of 1834. Cecil Forester, the sitting member and Sir William Summerville were the candidates, and in the event Cecil Forester won the election by 94 votes (see entry for 6th January 1835). Cecil Forester was to remain the Member for Wenlock until 1874 when he became the third Lord Forester in succession to his brother. Adelaide's lively description of this early election contain valuable comments on the way things were run.

1835

Comment

This was a year in which Adelaide stared to grow to maturity. She had her 18th birthday on 10th August 1835. The year began with a gift from her father of *Dr Walker's Dictionary'*. This prompted her to fill a box with her childhood books so as to discard them. She then embarked on a period in which she sought to improve her education and character. her grandfather, John Grant of Leighton Buzzard, gave her £20.00 to buy books. This was a large sum, equivalent to about £900.00 in today's money.

The year starts sadly with the death on 22nd January of Ann Sorton, mother of Maria (née Sorton) wife of Richard Darby of "Rosehill" where Ann Sorton was resident. The year ended even more sadly with the death at Dale House of Sarah Dickinson, aged only 27. Sarah was the child of Ann and Barnard Dickinson.

During July, Adelaide and her sister Matilda visited their grandparents' home at Leighton Buzzard, with visits to Woburn Abbey and Shenley (now a part of Milton Keynes). On their way home from Leighton Buzzard they stayed at Coventry as guests of John Gulson of the prominent Quaker family. here they met Barnard Dickinson, Jnr. fourth child of Anna and Barnard Dickinson, who was resident in Coventry and had, earlier in the year, (January 1835) been suffering from an attack of quinsy. Back at home in Coalbrookdale, a lot of time was taken up with visiting Rosehill, home of Louisa and Caroline Darby (aged 20 and 21 years), Dale House, where Hannah Dickinson (aged 18 years) lived, the Chesnuts, where the family of Lucy Darby (née Burlingham) lived, (this includes Mary and Deborah who were older, (27 and 25 years) but more particularly, Abraham Darby IV and Alfred, aged 31 and 28 years). From time to time Adelaide and her sister visited Severn House adjoining the River Severn at Dale End. This is now the Valley Hotel, Ironbridge, but it was built in 1757 by George Godwin who was then the leading coalmaster in the district. It was purchased by Sarah Darby and passed by her Will in 1821 to the Dickinson family. It was occupied from 1841 by Henry Dickinson who married Deborah Darby, daughter of Edmund and Lucy Darby. It is not clear who was residing there in 1835. The entry in the Journal for 6th February 1835 suggests that the Reynolds or Anstice family may have been there.

The most important underlying feature of the Journal for 1835 was that this was the year when Adelaide started to face up to the prospect of marriage with all its implications. She became conversant with its prospect as her sister's relationship with Abraham Darby IV of The Chesnuts started to unfold. On 6th February, Abraham came to tea and her comment was "Oh! if nothing comes of that *c'est extrordinaire*." The topic was again discussed on 13th March when she and Matilda had a deep sisterly conversation on the subject. Her first affair of the heart began very soon after her 18th birthday on 10th August. The day before, Louise and Caroline, (of Rosehill) announced that they were expecting a Sophie (Horne) and her brother the following evening (i.e. the evening of Adelaide's birthday. Adelaide had also had a similar letter from Sophie. Whether had been previous correspondence is difficult to judge although there are references on the Journal to a letter from London. James, Sophie's brother, stayed a fortnight after Adelaide's birthday and it is obvious that he and Adelaide had developed a relationship. A week later (17th August) she was even contemplating the consequence of absence from her home concluding, uncertainly, that she could not give up "it" (the consummation of marriage) without great sorrow. James departed on 26th August leaving Sophie to stay on for another few weeks.

Adelaide's feelings were in turmoil. On 31st August, she confided to her Journal "I do love James but I constantly feel that I am not in love." Perhaps it was because of this uncertainty that it was decided that Mr and Mrs Horne, rather than James would arrive to take Sophie home. This they did on 22nd September, calling at Leighton Buzzard on their way home. This suggests that they were known to Adelaide's grandparents and their friends there. It was evident that James was as unsettled by his visit as Adelaide was and he continued to write letters, and then spent a week in Coalbrookdale in October.

JANUARY - *I go on with the Italian and like it excessively. I have just begun "Alfieric Tragedies." Yesterday Papa gave me Dr Walker's Dictionary, it is most useful and I had to find a place for it in my shelf of the bookcase and to do so I filled a box with those books which were my delight how short a time ago. I had a letter which did not please me, and unless Papa did choose to allow me to answer these epistles with his permission and knowledge I will not do so. There is something mean in a clandestine correspondence which I will not be guilty of, neither do I like one who, I would fain respect, esteem and love, to persuade me so to do in strong terms, though it would be proof of attachment.*

Tuesday 6th January - *The Election is concluded and Sir William Summerville is in a minority of 94.*[1]

Saturday 10th January - *Oh, I have got such a bad cold! Yesterday Christopher and Hannah Dickinson came to tea and at dinner time Dick appeared. He has been the last day at Sir Edward Szythels. There was a ball at Acton Burnell and he was invited to attend and spend the day. The Election is finished*[2] *and so charmingly, for Mr Gaskell,*[3] *Mrs Gaskell and Charlotte Anstice were there and the Miss Harrisses. We have finished "Belinda" and it is a most charming tale ending delightfully - Oh, I do much prefer Miss Edgeworth's novels. We have begun "Manoeuvering"" which is amusing and* *what is much better contains the same high standard of morality. These books make you feel better and happier. Grandpapa has kindly said that I may have books to the amount of £20 and I have Miss Edgeworth's novels and Burns which last, except for the beautiful plates, I could wish I had not had. I have fallen in love with the Bridgewater Treatises which everybody speaks of highly.*

Thursday 22nd January - *Miss Turner has left us the last two days to be with Aunt Sorton*[4] *who has suffered dreadfully from inflammation of the lungs. It is not thought that Mr Edwards*[5] *healed her judiciously and it was too late on Tuesday when Mr Webb*[6] *was called in. He bled her in a manner which proved it to be the very last resource and I believe expressed little hope that her strength would be sufficient to rally again after it, but there was no other hope he said. Mr Webb called again this morning, when he did not seem entirely without hope of the poor sufferer's recovery and we were hardly expecting the answer to our enquiries this evening that she quietly departed about a quarter past six.*

Her illness seemed short, but Miss T Winer expressed it was her belief that my Aunt was fully aware of her danger though she said little, indeed she had much difficulty in speaking at all. We have heard no further particulars.

Uncle and I believe Aunt Dickinson is gone to Coventry to see poor Barnard who has a Quinsey and is, I fear, very ill, but of this we only heard a few words from Richard Sorton Darby[7] *this morning and an equally meagre account from Papa. I and Matilda had a little walk; the first time I have been out since my cold. I was surprised to see the garden looking so pretty for the last cold weather was intense. We indulge ourselves with one of Miss Edgeworth's delightful books some time in the day. The more I read of them the better I like her characters and the more difficult do I find it to imitate the purity of motive which she ascribes to them. One thing more, though - I am not sure whether reading novels good and excellent though they be and high as is the standard of moral feeling displayed therein by the best characters - I am not sure whether reading so much beautiful fiction does not rather confuse one's knowledge of real life, and of one's own real and peculiar feelings.*

On Wednesday was poor Aunt Sorton's funeral. It was very small compared with the last and very melancholy it looked to see so few relations. Last Sunday we went to see the last beautiful remains which I see I have not mentioned. There was a peculiar sweetness and a beauty very different from what her fine face presented in life.

Sunday 8th February - *I have done almost nothing this week except going on with Italian really assiduously, but this next week I must do more. We have been reading Coelebs - "Je ne l'aise pas!"*[9] *Lucilla is to me the essence of affected goodness, and Coelebs - oh, he is the height of absurdity and unloveability. I can much better endure the too great, or I should rather say, the unnatural perfection of Miss Edgeworth's models of excellence - because with them I feel a sympathy. I hope it is not because reason is too frequently their only guide - the description of Lucilla gives me the notion of a religious maze - I think there is* *too much description of refinement of motive instead of the simple wish to do right.*

Sunday 22nd February - *'Tis two weeks since I have written. Last Friday week was the Budget[9] held at Aunt Dickinsons.[35] The beginning of the week I was busy getting ready for it and on Sunday I was transcribing the productions. Our Budget was melancholy without Barnard, who we thought might have written a piece for us at which Aunt Dickinson expressed great indignation - was it possible Barnard could write among so many agreeable young women at Leamington? Upon the whole it was a nice Budget.[9] Miss Turner was there with a beautiful piece on "Indolence" which propelled me to read some parts of Thomson's "Castle of Indolence." Oh, Meraviglia![10] Dick was there! with a most unoriginal production on Carbon which we voted in! I wrote a "Day at Oxford", a longish piece which Mama and Matilda had much to do in correcting that I call it a joint production this being more agreeable than confesssing I laid the foundation and the bare walls of the superstructure and they did all the embellishing. Also a little piece of poetry on a bit of Italian which I had in my exercise "cogli le rose e lasci stare le spine" there was room with such a motto for many a fair idea but alas, few were mine.*

On Friday, 6th February, *Mr Hartshorne[11] and Richard Sorton Darby[12] dined, it was a very pleasant evening - Richard stupid and quiet "a ta l'ordinairell" and Mr Hartshorne lively and entertaining, even more than usual. He is deeply engaged with his book but found time to tell us a great deal about the "Bridgewater Treatises" which are good, not only in words but deeds, he sent us the one on the Mechanism of the Hand by Sir C. Bell in which we are very much interested. One evening, Papa read to us "Much Ado About Nothing" - we came to an allusion in his "More's Strictures" concerning the fact that reading and writing comes by nature according to Dogberry[13] "The Wit of Beatricell is almost overpowering here and there Benedict is clever." Oh! I do long very much to read Shakespeare.*

Last Sunday into Meeting came Mr and Mrs Ball[14] with Mrs Reynolds. They have a young lady travelling with them whom Mr Ball introduced as his cousin Caroline Bassett to his cousin Adelaide Darby. We were engaged to Severn House[37] for Wednesday when we met them and the Anstices and Miss Turner. Miss Bassett is an incessant talker with a precision and exactness of diction and an absence of that vulgar material common sense, really unusual. Mr W R Anstice[15] amused himself and the company at her expense without her in the least perceiving it. After tea we went upstairs into the music room where Charlotte played and sang with Will, altogether very agreeable. The Anstices are so clever, Charlotte is a sweet girl - a charming beautiful creature. I should think young ladies with pretensions to beauty so considerable and so nearly equal had seldom met in so small a party. I will say that Miss Bassett is not particularly bewitching in person or manners. She hath not tact nor that nice discrimination to catch the manner of discussing subjects and propounding propositions - also she appears to consider herself old and clever enough to lead the conversation at least in such a young party as we were upstairs - she discussed cards, dancing and Mr Joe Reynold's failings in great style. Mrs Owen came and spent a really sociable evening, telling us a great deal of country news some of it not very creditable to the actors.

This day I have spent chiefly in writing this long account of my feelings and proceedings. I had a letter from London today - highly absurd - well I do hope I do right. Abraham came to tea and supper was as good as a play. Oh! if nothing comes of that "c'est extraordinaire".[16] *Cousin Lucy and people come home on Thursday. Mama goes to Leighton,*[38] *I grieve to say, soon. Last week a sad account came from Birmingham - poor Eliza Sturge's baby died 2 days after its birth and its mother followed it on Thursday so like poor Helen but the consolations in this case were indeed great, she was fully prepared and had beforehand expected this termination. Poor Joseph Sturge*[17] *is greatly to be felt for, but he bears his loss as a Christian ought. Papa set off for London today (Monday 23rd). May he see nobody. It was desperately windy, but I did the collecting and called to bid Miss Turner goodbye and to take her the poetry. I was sorry to see her for the last time. On Thursday last the Chesnuts returned bringing with them their precious little dove Caroline who looks very much better for her residence amidst gaiety and frivolity. Mary Darby is not, I think, very much improved - poor Louisa is perfectly lame and Mr Webb lays his injunction upon her not to stir from her chair.*

Thursday 26th February *- I was up late to find a deep snow - what will not energetic spirits do. I was of these on this occasion for after reading a chapter - no part of a chapter of Mayor, I set off through storm or shine for the Bible Committee. I really went on not expecting to arrive safe - but so it happened that I did; delivered its money and saw Mary Darby puzzled beyond measure just as Mama arrived with George, Edmund and the carriage - I like to name things according to their value and Edward's was amazingly increased a few hours after when a ham fell upon his head and we reflected how much worse it might have been than even "an ugly cut" proved. Well I went with her to Smiths and Wheelers and then to call on Mrs Reynolds, whom we found poorly with a very bad cold which she caught in going home on Sunday. She gave me a sweet cup of violets. Then we called at Aunt Dickinsons*[35] *to invite and then at The Chesnuts*[34] *where all was alright and smooth only Mary "un peu fatiguée". Then home just in time for dinner and after I was tired and did just nothing at all but read "Ormond" - till Hannah*[18] *came and I very much enjoyed having her with me. Oh! "elle est belle, elle est aimable, elle est charmantes". We talked and planned till midnight and this morning she departed just before Mr Smith came (the drawing master).*

Then when I was purified from the turpentine, I went to call on Louisa and much to her discomfiture went upstairs at Uncle Richard Darby's[36] *orders - we talked nothings till I went to "Next House" (Oh, Louisa is better) - and to my sorrow and surprise Aunt Dickinson refused to let Hannah*[18] *come again - I trust I have not offended either. Insomuch as Hannah lent me a print to copy of Mr Beverly upon whom she informed me she dotes and delights in him yet was notwithstanding willing to resign him to me I think she is not displeased "avec moi".*

Thursday 12th March - *We went to drink tea at Uncle Richard Darby's*[36] *and had a pleasant evening - Aunt Maria showed us some antique dresses of her ancestors and let us array her in them. When there is a Fancy Ball given at the Dale we are promised the beautiful silks to appear in by Uncle Richard Darby. Oh! he was in such glorious good humour that one would have thought he had gained an Election. On Friday we had the Budget here,*[9] *but it was a small one. We went to Miss Griffiths in the morning and the carriage brought up poor Louisa*[36] *as we came back.*

Friday 13th March - *She has hardly any power of walking, at least her ankle is made worse by the smallest exertion. Mary Darby was too nervous to write or to meet us all. Deborah,*[34] *Louisa, Caroline,*[36] *Hannah*[35] *and ourselves constituted the little Budget,*[9] *it was rather large the - 'in' papers I think there were 14 and some very good. On Saturday (14th) we went to the Chesnuts to tea - they were quite alone. When we came home I and Matilda had a great deal of very interesting conversation about the attentions of a certain gentleman to her. She told me all her feelings and expressed a wish to discourage him in a civil way and I actually believed her, telling her all my observations on the matter and troubled my poor little brains to chalk out the most effectual plan of action for her, for one 8 mortal years older than myself and full 8 times better skilled in the female art of saying one thing and doing another, or perhaps I should say feeling one sentiment at one time and one totally opposite at another - but I am telling my tale wrong - on Sunday we went to Aunt Dickinsons*[35] *to meet Mrs Reynolds and Samuel Waring and there we found Abraham and Alfred Darby.*[34] *We had a pleasant evening and in the innocent mischief of my heart I contrived that Mr Abraham Darby should walk home with us, the next day we walked up to Little Wenlock and on Tuesday Mary and Deborah*[34] *came to drink tea with us. It was after this visit that we had so much of discussion upon feelings deep and still.*

They had a great party at The Chesnuts[34] *on Wednesday to which we went. After giving more advice than I should have thought I could have put together and resolving with infinite difficulty upon a delightful scheme of action for myself, which was to put all straight that had ever become askew, I had the pleasure to see the former sent to the winds - borne away on the wings of imagination - along with the romance of a first love. I, a fair lady, do inwardly say man be better worth trusting than woman! Very angry was I; but let it sleep in the shade - Thank Heaven I made no work for repentance by outward wrath but alas for the evil feelings within!. On Thursday I despatched a letter to Mama and at night Papa came home. He is not well and dreadfully dispirited. On Monday week he goes to fetch Mama till then what shall we do with him?*[19]

***Sunday 29th March** - Papa has been in very poor spirits the beginning of the time of Mama's absence, but he is now better every way. Having to stay downstairs the best part of the afternoon and all the evening we have done but very little. In Italian I have finished Goldonis "La Lacondierall" and Lorenson and the "Chronicle of the Conquest of Granada" are finished. We have begun "Spencer's Faery Queen" - some parts are very pretty, but I rather wonder at its great celebrity. Yesterday Papa went to take his place in "the Wonder" for Monday and in his absence we refreshed ourselves with some of Mrs Edgeworth's pretty popular tales. Tomorrow Papa goes, to return the latter end of the week, with Mama - had I the musical box it should play "Oh, Joyous Day".*

***Monday 30th March** - Today we drank tea at The Chesnuts*[34] *and stayed till 10 - 'twas my fault for Deborah had a game at chess too much. For Tuesday we had planned a walk to Buildwas which the rain frustrated so all our cousins came to tea with us instead, but we did walk to Buildwas next day and went to Uncle Richard Darby's*[36] *in the evening, where we met Hannah and enjoyed it a good deal. Richard Sorton Darby*[7] *drank tea here on Sunday, excepting which we had no company. I hope we shall soon be settled again for really we have done nothing. In the morning we went down to the Committee which was very well attended, Miss Anstice was there and so agreeable. Mary Darby hath a bad cold and is incapacitated from going out.*

***Tuesday 7th April** - We went to tea at Aunt Dickinson's*[35] *to meet the officers of the Bible Society who have got their accounts wrong. On Thursday 9th April, Papa went to Shrewsbury and during his absence Jane - the notable Jane broke one of the beautiful jars in his dressing room.- Ministers are out*[20] *- Sir Robert Peel and Jane are to be pitied.*

***Sunday 12th April** - Many people go this week to Worcester and in consequence the Budget is put off. After dinner today Joe Dickinson came up how he is improved! So agreeable and almost at the threshold of refinement 'tis said some fair lady has brought about this wondrous change, but of her name "je l'ignore."*[21] *What have I been doing? Why, reading a little of Leo X and a little of Spencer, and expecting a letter which arrives not. I should not have thought that this week would have given me so much internal fidgeting, externally to be concealed, as is the case. Really, one's feelings are very incomprehensible - to be consistent is human nature's hard way.*

***Tuesday 21st April** - Last Sunday I walked down to Severn House*[37] *in a bitterly cold east wind though I was wrapped up more than strict adherence to the etiquette of apparel for April admitted. I found great difficulty in accomplishing two chapters of Leo Xth in the afternoon and a bad sore throat,* *changing on Sunday for the most dreadful oppression of the chest I ever experienced, has since confined me almost wholly upstairs.*

Thursday 30th April - *Is it possible that it is the 30th? the month has flown away inconceivably fast notwithstanding last week was very long and uncomfortable. Yesterday came the "Court Magazine" full of pretty tales for last month and this, also Uncle Richard*[36] *and people - all save Louisa came to dine with us and Mr Webb*[6] *coined the party. He and my good Uncle had a warm discussion on the subject of dissent from the Church which Mr Webb maintained was more frequently entered into from interested motives than any other. It was an illiberal sentiment, but I fear there was great truth in it.*

Sunday 5th July - *Here (at Leighton*[38] *there is little to say. This morning was very wet but evils generally bring some good in their train, and the ground is so wet that the Reeve cannot come to walk in the shrubbery and demand our escort all the evening. Mary Reeve is very ill. Matilda and I are just now very interested in the Natural Histories of Enthusiasm and Fanaticism. After Meeting and reading we had a most pleasant walk in the shrubbery and enjoyed an animated and, I hope, enthusiastic conversation partly on the subject of what is meant by enthusiasm and which we settled to be extravagance of ideas on some subjects which sets them out of the orbit of their relative importance with regard to other subjects and partly who is and who may not be thought enthusiastic.*

Monday 6th July - *This has been the treat of the Lancasterian School boys*[22] *- I do hate such things in themselves, but there are generally some redeeming concomitant circumstances. Josiah Wheeler was there busy and absurd as possible. Peter John Bassett too more agreeable and less concealed than ever saw him before. Grandpapa and Matilda quite in their element - which is not mine!*

I like an atmosphere more ethereal and butterfly. I got up by 6 'ce matin' and did some needful mending. After breakfast I did the flowers, finished the Ceramble Oakwood and did a little more of Cheddar than a little of Alfieri. A few pages of Fanaticism before dinner. We set off for Circuit immediately after and stopped until rather late. I enjoyed a long walk excessively with Peter John Bassett in the fields ostensibly to see the children play, but we wandered in imagination to Constantinople, Italy, Scotland, Switzerland - I know not where we went not. We walked home and Peter stayed and spoilt all the good opinion I had formed of his good sense by an half hour's eulogy on Morrisons pills.

Wednesday 8th July - *It is getting towards 1 o'clock, but I am not the least sleepy, for in truth this has been somewhat an eventful day for me and tonight I have been sufficiently occupied to drive away all thoughts of sleep. The first thing I heard this morning of the outer world was the arrival of two letters at our room door, one from Mrs King and the other one that I had to answer speedily. I do not know who to be angry with - because I want a little to see him myself and yet it is tiresome - I have partly written my letter, but as it need not go yet I shall not finish it till it has undergone Matilda's inspection. I ought by all* *means to go to bed, but Mary has favoured me with a long candle and though I have got to comb my hair I mean to finish the sublimary concerns of this day. We went to the Lancasterian school*[22] *this morning. I hate such things and all belonging thereto, but I believe this is a paragon of good management. On our return we found Mr Joe Bailey - oh, so improved, a perfectly good agreeable fox hunting farmer - who came to fix a day for us to go to Shenley and 'tis to be this day week. Peter John called too to engage us there for Friday. We went up to see Catherine Lawford and the Reeves came in after tea. If this is not gay for Leighton, I don't know what is. I fancy I may go home having made 3 boy conquests during my absence - well, 'tis a great satisfaction these may be won and nothing hurt.*

Monday 13th July - *We have been today to Woburn Abbey. The old family portraits were striking and Canaletto's painting splendid. Oh! the pictures were beautiful and the rooms - the ceilings - the gold and the silk hangings - I have seen nothing at all like thereunto since Blenheim. And the flower garden - the hot houses and the Chinese Dairy. Grandpapa went with us and does not seem tired. Sophia Wiffen went over the house with us and the housekeeper, who is a curiosity and withall somewhat entertaining and agreeable. Then Mr Forbes - but shall never come to an end. After breathing this atmosphere of perfumed luxury and inexpressibly enjoying a carriage dinner in the evergreen ride, Grandpapa took us to Apley, a charming village a few miles further where dwelleth Richard Howe and his brother John. Absurdities which bore you without being amusing, but first I should have said we went to Froxfield where the Wiffens received us most cordially and were all that was civil, formal and kind intentioned. Ida is really a very pretty child. From Apley we went to Woburn to buy Mama some garden tools at the other Wiffens - It was fair day there, and all bustle and rag-tag and bobtail. We came again through that paradise of a park with its magnificent trees - abbey - deer and swans all to watch. We came home and had a walk in the shrubbery which did not seem however the less agreeable for all the grandeur we had been in, except a few bright recollections dimly beaming on memory's tablet. Thoughts are mostly dull and melancholy and now it is time that my material hand should leave off writing of these halls of splendour and my imagination should now aspire to visit them in dreams.*

Wednesday 15th July - *We have been to Shenley! - I went expecting to enjoy it, but in truth my ideas went more near the reality of pleasure that I should have experienced had not some degree of fear for consequences crept in. We met Mr and Mrs Kitelee and Aunt Betsy - had some charming music and Plotters sweet effective singing. I came back from Shenley not quite pleased with myself and yet with all prodigiously amazed at the folly of others. Mary's voice is not yet above a whisper - how flattered Mr Clode must be - Mr Joe Bailey is really a splendid specimen of the high degree of masculine intellect common in this part of the world. Whether he is most conversant in hunting foxes or in dressing hares I cannot take upon me to decide and his taste has really attained a pitch of* *refinement so high that he doth know an harmonious waltz - and unaffected gaiety of heart was a most delightful change after so long viewing that stiff picture of pompous still life, Peter John. The rest of this week I expect to be bored to death - I am promised Shenley sympathy.*

Thursday 16th July *- This hot morning down came Peter John to ask us to tea there and we agreed to go - Emma and Mary Reeve were there and Miss Brown a young lady possessed by the demon of shyness to a most inaccessible extent. We had rather a better even than I expected before tea looking over Maria Darton's drawings and a portfolio of Peter John and some really well done horses of Frank's. After tea we walked in the garden and were literally forced by the gentle compulsion of so many wishes expressed to sing for them. When we came back home we found William Allen how agreeable he is.*

Friday 17th July *- It is truly marvellous that I am still alive. This afternoon Grandmama has had all her Saturday school girls at a tea and bun treat on the grass before the Temple. After being utterly knocked up with the heat I was refreshed by a little walk and with describing the pretty Shenley dresses to her; when we were taken forthwith to a horrid Temperance Meeting where we sat up in the platform and heard to admiration all the stupidity that these good and zealous supporters of total abstinence from fermented liquors pleased to put forth, I was soon in my own land of waking dreams far off from temperance societies and all such horrid engines of ennui. 'Twas "tremendously" hot and I was amused by seeing two little damsels with splendid fans in the gallery above us.*

Saturday 18th July *- The Reeves came of course today - I liked them better than usual. Finished a letter to Mama, I don't know whether I have said that we are going to Coventry on Thursday next. This evening we called on Mrs Wilson and on Monday to hear their self acting piano and then on to Catherine Lawford who is really a very nice girl. Surprising it was that rain came on as we returned. Peter John came to ask us to write in his album which we shall be happy to do if time is.*

Monday 20th July *- Drank tea with Catherine Lawford - she is a nice creature. John Lawford came in for the first time since he returned from Hastings. Oh, he is another modification of the bore species, really people should come here to study this order in Natural History. Grandpapa went to Bedford where there has been a trial about the Market Tolls, that is there was to be, but the Judge thought it would take too long to be brought in this evening and Grandpapa will be obliged to go there again tomorrow.*

Tuesday 21st July *- We made our farewell calls on the Reeves and Ann Bassett. I am really sorry to go, we have so very much liked our visit here. Grandpapa and Grandmama have been so excessively kind to us as I never remember them before. Well tomorrow I shall be too busy to write I daresay - we went with the Reeves to Linslade and I really liked Emma so much. These are last words at Leighton.*

Friday 24th July - *Angels and Ministers of Grace defend me from ever more taking up my abode in the utterly lifeless establishment of John Gulson Esq., in the city of Coventry., Here we are set down to vegetate in this soul depressing soil for a whole week! Merciful Heavens! I am sure I shall be withered and dead at the end. It does not do exactly for me to be in a desperate hurry to get back home, so I must take it easily. Oh, I look back upon Leighton as an Elysius, on Grandpapa and Grandmama as the kindest and most indulgent of beings, on Emma as a most sweet and refinedly agreeable creature and on Peter John as a treasure of amusing liveliness. The young ladies here are very singular in their modes of amusing themselves and their neighbours. Last night I literally cried with the feelings of desolation though on our first arrival I rather was disposed to laugh at them here. Last Wednesday I like to look back to. Grandpapa was very poorly in the night and he gave up all thoughts of going with us. Mr Forbes came to dinner - oh, the very delightful man that he is. So thoroughly Scots and agreeable. After tea Reeves called on us and I had a last walk and a few sweet last words with my sweet Emma. Then Peter John called and Frank and we went early to bed. On Thursday morning we got up at 5 and were in the carriage by 6 - Grandpapa quite gave up going and we were instructed to the care of John who took us safely and very fast. We enjoyed the journey excessively and it may be believed did not want for conversation. Oh, what long hours of recollections were awakened on the well known road to Shenley'. Pretty Shenley, it looked so sweet and unruffled in the early morning.*

Friday Evening - *Well, I am getting on a little better here this evening. We have had a party to tea which I fancy is a marvel from the novelty it appeared to all who took part in the preparations. This morning Barnard*[23] *called and took us to the Railway Office to show us an extraordinary Toad preserved in spirits which was found in a solid stone by the railroad men. He also showed us his plans for this stupendous undertaking and a model of some curious Bridges which are forced to be built askew and which appear to be Particularly difficult and rebellious to mathematical rules. Barnard*[23] *came to tea (dear creature that he is; he seems a binding link to the living world) and the Cashes and Southerns. Anne Southern is here but she did not honour the party with her presence - her sister Hannah seems as agreeable as a passé and faded flirt can be. We had a game at La Grace, and I kept up 115 which we thought pretty well after playing in a circle for a long while. I always get on best with the gentlemen of a party and I do think John Gulson Junr. immensely clever and not at all conceited nor disagreeable in the least; Elizabeth is very comfortable in her own opinion of her own intellects and appears not to think appearances or agreeableness of much moment. Anne is a very sweet beautiful creature with far less talent than any of the rest, but evidently turning what she possesses to good account. She is a very striking proof of how very much more agreeable inferior abilities can be than the high and mighty attainers of a lofty and, to all appearances, barren elevation where the common people - the greater part of the mass do not think I am so stupid as half the people I meet with can only look up with eyes not* *dazzled with excess of light, but fearful lest the grave mass of ice should freeze up all their brilliancy - Miss Rachel defies the powers of my pen, I must leave the, to me, inaccessible heights of such excess of talent and such uncommon indistinguishable intellect, for eyes and hearts that can pierce higher and further than mine, and to imaginations gifted with a brighter sun to shine.*

Monday 27th July - *We have really been working hard today, up before breakfast, in the morning walked a distance to sketch a pretty church at Stivichall then on to Lord Craven's beautiful heap Crombie Abbey, a splendid place, with most magnificent family portraits. Barnard came to tea.*[23]

Wednesday 29th July - *Can it be that the week here is almost gone and that tomorrow I shall be back at the Dale. After breakfast we finally finished the sketch of Stivichall church and I went to the top of the battlements with John Gulson Jr. Elizabeth is not well today and did not come with us. We had a splendid view all over the county. Drank tea under the Mulberry Tree and Roger Merrick came.*

Thursday 30th July - *Anne and I had spent half the night in sweet converse and we had engaged to get up very early, which we did, to go to the Railway before breakfast. It is a vast work, a stupendous undertaking, such deep excavations and such prodigious embankments spoiling the face of the country in a merciless manner. The lovely Sherbourne Valley (where John Gulson took me through the wet grass much to the surprise and indignation of the rest of our party) will be quite spoiled by the frightful work of human tastelessness. They divert the course of the Sherbourne to make it pass under a skew bridge. We walked to see the Bridge over the turnpike road which we passed under as we came to Coventry (with what different feelings did I now see it) and we went home by the fields, Barnard returning with us to breakfast. After we had put the finishing stroke to our packing operations we went into the garden to walk about and enjoy the brilliancy of the bright sunny morning. Gulson came into the garden to tell us Alfred Burgess was arrived - now it was most curious that when Anne and I were talking last night I said I should be particularly sorry if Alfred Burgess was to come just before we left, it would be so tantalizing just to see him for a few hours. Anne laughed at the very absurdity of the idea as there was not the least probability of his coming so we were amused to a degree at his arrival.*

Alfred Burgess went with John Gulson into the vinery where Anne and I presently followed them as I was determined to see all I could of him. He is perfectly accessible, passably handsome and surprisingly agreeable. We had some grapes and discussed the causes why so many have shrivelled under John Gulson's scientific care.

Then we talked of florists and botany - of Barnard's insensibility to the beauties of flowers, though he goes into Sherbourne for his own pleasure to find plants rare and valuable as botanical specimens. Petted and took leave of Flora and while I was kneeling under the Mulberry tree to play with her beautiful ears, Elizabeth put her head out of the window to beg they would not keep me out in the sun any longer - I was sorry to leave the scene of so much enjoyment, but how could Mr Alfred Burgess stay another minute after such a summons. In the house we found the rest of the Gulson party and Mr Goodhall a very rough and offhanded being - Papa came all too soon for I would willingly have had a few hours with Alfred Burgess who I would fane know; it is most probable he will soon obey Elizabeth's summons of return by falling again at her feet. My sweet Anne, may she find one as worthy of her. Ours was a tearful part my heart felt torn in a thousand directions.

Tuesday 4th August - *For the first few days after our return, or rather the first few hours I should say, I did find this place most oppressively dull. Dear Mama we find quite well I am sure 'twas more than I was. We took a walk over all the old places we had left in their spring loveliness - the moon was bright but there was a chilliness of feeling outward and inward in the air - at the heart truly different to the cloudless skies and sunny interchange of bright thoughts in which I had participated so happily at Coventry.*

Sunday 9th August - *The novelty of being at home has worn off and our long absence seems like a brilliant fairy dream of yesterday, almost too bright and happy for reality - I hope I am not superstitious but I cannot help remembering how often a bright gleam precedes a day of clouds - there is something of the very essence of happiness so fleeting, that the very nature of enjoyment makes it so soon gone and gone for ever. Rachel Fowler has been spending two days with us, she is a sweet creature so truly loveable and so improving is her society. Louisa and Caroline*[36] *came yesterday to tell us that they were expecting to see Sophie on Monday with her brother.*[24]

Monday 10th August - *Today I am 18 and thankful I am that the day is now over. I am now quite alone and it is after 12, but I must sit up to enjoy a little journalising and the delights of communing with my own heart in this perfect silence - must I go over the events of this eventful day? I will for the end has been so far more agreeable than I had ventured to imagine that it is now sweet to think of the oppressive day. On Sunday I had a letter from Sophie saying that she and James would not arrive until evening*[24] *and I felt as if I had just had a sudden reprieve, and that this day would never end. Rachel Fowler came with us from Meeting to tea yesterday - Mr Bayliss, Abraham and Hannah Dickinson came later. They departed, I had an indifferent night and rose earlier than usual.*

Dear Mama came in soon with her over pretty birthday gift. Breakfast was over and I went with Fanny Edwards to do our Bible Society collecting. While I had plenty to do I was tolerably happy - though the evening did seem a time greatly to be dreaded - I read a little without understanding a syllable of the astronomical mysteries with which I chose to puzzle my brains. Dinner came in due time and Papa requested, as a particular favour, that I would change, my frock being the old I had worn at the Archery Meeting - he remembered too that it was my birthday and I could not object. As reading did not do I tried work after dinner - Mama and Matilda were both upstairs and I thought rather injudicious in their kind consideration that I should meet no awkwardness unexpectedly. I got into a fever of uncomfortableness - an agony of expectation - they went down in due time and I went to sleep over my astronomical difficulties. I dreamed of all modifications of trouble and awoke with a start at hearing, so I fancied, horses and vehicles, a great armament. It was the Dale Company's steeds going to their fields for the night, I shall never forget the horror of that startled wakening. We went forth to water the gardens before tea - I made a grand effort to dress myself and Tilley first[28] - it was over. Tilley went a walk, heaven knows where and I began to copy all kinds of poetical rubbish into my book of originals seeing my powers of doing anything better seemed gone. Toward 8 o'clock Mama persuaded me that a meeting in the garden would be far less awkward than one in the house and I walked with her till 9 when it grew so entirely dark that we were obliged to come in. James arrived-not till past 10 - I cannot go over the evening - it was made up of nothings, but not of disagreeableness - if my life should prove a cloudy one 'there is to be a gleam of sunshine first I do not doubt now - There is a joy in meeting.

Tuesday 11th August - *Well this is romantic, my candle has gone out (the fact is I dropped it) so I am writing by moonlight, but Mama like an enemy to romance as she just came in as I was going on most happily and dispelled the lunar influence with her candle and I must own it is a great convenience. It is most unmaidenly, I suppose, to say that I do enjoy this season to which I looked forward with so much terror. But no it is that I really do. it enlivens me and I do very much enjoy it - this meeting I did such a bold thing. After walking about the gardens with James I went with Tilley[28] and him to Uncle Richard to ask Sophie to come to tea. She came, dear creature that she is, and we took tea out of doors also had a delightful walk in Cook's woods.[24a] Tilley[28] says she feels now more than reconciled to part with me and I feel a degree of satisfaction and a quiet approval of my first feelings which is almost heaven upon earth. I am happy - almost too happy to last long I fear in this world. Oh, may Papa's vanishing good humour stay its wings awhile.*

Wednesday 12th August - *Today has passed very tolerably. Oh, I should have thought it such an insupportable ordeal if I could have foreseen. First James went with us all to Meeting, after which we went a walk in the wood and saw in the distance Sophie, Louisa and Caroline.[36] I made James turn back for which I was particularly sorry afterwards as it would have been so much better to go on and not to mind. After dinner we went to Broseley and Willey (pretty desolate place it is), round by the Hay and then, oh awful, to tea at Uncle Richard Darby's[36] - it passed off very well, however.*

Thursday 13th August - *The Anstices and Mrs Edmonds dined here. We had a most pleasant party. Mrs John Anstice is very agreeable and simple in her manners. John Anstice is so improved.*[25] *I expected a most formidable season but it turned out so much better than I anticipated. They took very little notice of James, that is, not disagreeable notice, and he did not behave conspicuously.*

Friday 14th August - *We were asked to take tea at the Dickinsons*[35] *this evening, but we had arranged to go to Shrewsbury and thither we went much to my satisfaction.*

Saturday 15th August - *After dinner today Richard came to take a ride with James, Sophie and Caroline joined them. We had half engaged to meet them at the top of the Wrekin, but the plans were rather confused and they went to Wenlock while we proceeded to the Wrekin, and up to the top we went. It was a most charming evening and it is so sublime to be alone on a mountain when the darkness of the night is gathering. It was nearly 9 when we reached home and very cold. We found the party long since returned and rather amused at our blunders which were truly extraordinary. This week has flitted past, like a bright bird still sailing pleasantly in the clouds; like a dream, half sadness and half smiles. I do feel a degree of satisfaction very agreeable, but I believe doubts will enter. I am sure they must into everyone's mind in their transitory sphere where nothing appears stable and secure. I feel rather unsettled and this may account for my writing a little incoherently at times. People here behave very well I must say. They laugh not at all and I really do not in the least care now.*

Sunday 16th August - *Abraham and Alfred drank tea here much to James discomfiture. I had rather they had not come but it was to be. They behaved very well to me. We went twice to Meeting. Aunt Dickinson*[35] *has engaged us to go there tomorrow evening.*

Monday 17th August - *I have had to undergo hearing Papa read some edifying passages from Don Quixote this evening. It was rather awful but by seeming rather to see, hear nor understand you may listen tolerably. Tilley slumbers unquietly - she sleeps but not the free and sunny sleep, that lightly on the brow of childhood lies. May she be happy - happy as she deserves to be. We have had a walk in the Dingle and had a pleasanter evening on the whole than we expected. Sophy was there; she comes here to breakfast tomorrow morning. I trust I am doing right. I know not what absence might effect, but I do feel now that I could not give it up without great sorrow (luckily no imaginative person will ever read this to enquire "It!' What?). Oh for a glimpse of the future and yet I would not take it without power to drown the glimpse in the waters of oblivion supposing that I did not like the picture.*

Tuesday 18th August - *Dear Sophie came to breakfast and spent all the morning with us, very delightfully, we went to Apley after dinner and Uncle Richard Darby followed us with their party, but we only met for a few minutes on the terrace. We went on for tea at Bridgnorth. It is a beautiful ride from*

Apley. I never saw the country looking finer and it was charmingly cool and pleasant coming home. James pronounced it decidedly the most beautiful part of Shropshire he had yet seen. I believe he doubted our possessing such scenery.

Friday 21st August - *Mr and Mrs Reynolds dined with us today. They are very nice people. Sophie called this morning whilst Louisa was having her drawing lesson. Tilly has a sore mouth for which she thinks it advisable to remain in bed - so I had a charming morning with James and Sophy all to myself. I enjoyed it immensely though I do think Sophy must be rather deteriorated in points of talented conversation, she appears so much more accessible to my capacity than she was when - when-1 was a year younger. How shall I settle down quietly and properly to improve myself when James is gone? I shall miss him amazingly.*[26]

Sunday 22nd August - *Went to Meeting twice, very praiseworthy. We had no company but Barnard*[23] *is come! One of the deer got out.*

Tuesday 25th August - *James goes tomorrow by 'the Wonder'.*[26] *These two weeks have passed how rapidly.*

Wednesday 26th August - *This day year was the Archery meeting and the day of our speedy departure from Leamington. Well, I am much happier now, and I do feel a quiet satisfaction which I think I may trust would not be permitted were I doing wrong. I was really melancholy last night I thought I should miss James so much, but I fall back very easily into my old habits again and I have really enjoyed some quiet hours with Mama and Matilda for Papa went to Newport.*

Sophie, Louisa and Caroline[27] *came up with us from Meeting and took a walk, after it was stupid work having to task one's brains to entertain them whereas I generally had only myself to amuse. Sophie says I don't half look sentimentally pale and interesting.*

Monday 31st August - *We have been taking tea at Uncle Richard Darby's*[36] *and tomorrow we meet them at Mrs Graham's - one could bear to live constantly with Sophie so that it is delightful to see her so often, but to see Louisa and Caroline diurnally is to suffer stagnation of ideas. I do not feel happy tonight. Sophie seems much softened by her continuance here so this society must be more refined than what she is accustomed to - I cannot ensure unrefined people and I know James rather likes what he considers good-hearted roughness - shall I be happy with those he will prefer? I am sometimes ready to demur as to whether I have not gone too far to recede before I was old enough to form a correct judgement. I do love James but I constantly feel that I am not in love.*[26] *Well, it cannot be undone for I should be using him cruelly. I do feel that his happiness depends in some degree upon me and I shall not be miserable in the employment of making him happy. Happier I think I may venture to hope I shall be than if I had continued to live at home or in forming the most brilliant connexion I could expect in these parts. It is washing day and I have been busy past description.*

Tuesday 1st September - *We have been to Mrs Grahams to tea and I have had a lecture on the subject of formality and inaccessibility. Mr Webb had his eldest son (the Hope of the house) we found here on our return. Tilly says I sat as if I was thinking of my own beauty - Tilly*[28] *knows how to mortify when it is good for me. What a galling accusation!. I had hoped I was superior to such a very paltry consideration, but I plainly feel that I am not superior to much indignation at being accused of it. Mr M Webb gave us rather an interesting account of his visit to France, the diligence and the white horses so universal there. I had a letter from James this morning pretty enough to have made me behave better in the evening.*[26]

Thursday 10th September - *Well if I had anything to write about except the sorrows of this cold and chilling world I would endeavour to make my Journal a brighter record, but I have had a desperate cold every since Sunday with such a sore throat and such inflammed eyes and such utter loss of voice that I have been neither able to write, read, work or speak and wretched it is to be without these natural occupations for if as Dogberry*[13] *says the two first come by nature I am sure the last two do, to female capacities at least. Notwithstanding all prohibitions I have had a book hidden that I could feast upon whenever I was left alone and I have finished "Cowper's Task" - it is a task and I am glad it is done though I do like a passage here and there and Lord Bryon's 'Manfred' which is sublime and how visionary.*

I tell everybody that I have been nursing myself and knitting a garter all the past week, but I have thought much and more deeply than I ever did before, as it seems to me - thoughts such as one does not babble to all the world. I have seen very little of Sophie, malicious spirits have been very busy with my good Papa. The most sapient legion makes mischief proportioned in magnitude to his new name. I have been writing part of a letter to James but I think it will hardly do - Troubles are thick about and what sort of a web the fates are spinning for me is more than I can tell.[26]

Monday 13th September - *I am getting well at last 'tho I am not yet allowed to venture out this fine weather. I had various visitors yesterday and I was allowed to come downstairs for tea, first time since Tuesday.*

Friday 18th September - *Sophie came up this morning while Mr Smith was with Louisa and Caroline.*[36] *Owing to the things that have been said it is fixed that Mr and Mrs Horne shall come down to fetch Sophie home instead of James.*[26] *At first I felt a little disappointed though I know it is for the beet. But, oh, how formidable will it be.*

Sunday 20th September - *They are all gone to Meeting but my cold is not yet well enough for me to venture, of this, I am particularly glad. Last night Papa and Tilly*[28] *went to Shifnal to try if they could persuade Mr and Mrs Horne to come on that night, but they were much too tired. Sophie came to breakfast and a few minutes before 10 the carriage drove up. I did not find it* *so difficult to behave well as I had expected. I have had a very affectionate letter from James - not perhaps one of the best I have had, but I believe it is not what Rose Eylon would think of - not that I set up to be like her. Far be it from me I had been so busy with Italian and fancy work and Charles V the beginning of the week that I positively have had no time for my Journal, not being allowed to sit up at night in my room without a fire - really colds are tiresome things. The Dale looks best in Autumn, I hope I shall not have to leave it then. I read Cowper's "Table Talk" yesterday, it is very clever.*

Sunday 27th September - *I thought I could have written before, but I have been busy about one thing and another all last week. Mr, Mrs Horne and Sophie went away on Tuesday morning, intending to call at Leighton on the way. Dear Sophie, she was quite melancholy at going. I recollect I went on with my fancy work on Tuesday 'til after dinner when we had a walk in the wood, almost expecting to meet Sophie. After parting with one's friends it is so difficult to me to collect my thoughts to read or even meditate seriously. I have said nothing about their visit which was really agreeable though I do not know that I ever dreaded a visit more.*

Mrs Horne is very kind, very talkative, and she certainly is agreeable, but so minus mind! If ever I get into any of the difficulties young married ladies find, those which excite admiration and in whom uncommon prudence is required, she would be the last person I could consult as to conduct and proper behaviour, but while I have my dear Mama and sister, need I fear! but then there are cases in which the immense distance that will separate us might prevent all communication between us until too late - but I will not anticipate evil, I believe James would never be unreasonable. Last Monday they all went to tea at Uncle Richard Darby's,[36] *but my cold was not well enough for me to accompany them so I wrote to James and scolded him a little for they had told so much of his being unsettled that I was thoroughly frightened.*

Sunday 4th October - *Such a bright beautiful week with sunny mornings for sketching which we have improved. On Monday we went to Mr Pritchards to see Lady Corbett. She is much altered, but was kind and ladylike as usual - her fascination is now that of pensive sorrow and melancholy sweetness. Poor Sir Andrew they were deeply attached. Papa went to meet her on Tuesday as she went to Acton. She talked much of her loss - for five and forty years, she said, Sir Andrew never thwarted her in anything so that now she felt herself spoiled and alone in the world. On Thursday the Gaskells*[3] *called - Mrs Gaskell looking so pretty with her bright eyes of blue as the convolvulus in her hair. Mr Gaskell seemed as though this session had been a fatiguing one, but he too is grown amazingly handsome with his jet black eyes and hair and foreign complexion. Will there be an election? Mama tells me that there is a co-operative - Reform Bill passing which is to undermine all conservative power.*[29] *Cecil Forester told Papa that birds were better this season, that he was 2 inches taller* *than his brother - most polite and sociable was he and most amusing is the delighted self-importance of the Lord of the house of Darby at the condescension of the heir presumptive of Willey. Oh, this is an absurd world'. I had a letter from James on Tuesday which I stay at home this morning to answer for he is wishing to come, which will not do yet at all - neither do I wish it - Oh! my feelings are not which they should be, but having gone to far to recede I will not write about them may heaven guide and protect me and as I have really felt as if all that has passed was in the inscrutable direction of an infallible power, I trust it may be for the best.*[26] *We go tomorrow to dine at Madeley Wood.*[30] *Is not this charming - we shall have our new Chalis for the occasion.*

Tuesday 6th October - *Yesterday we met the Gaskells*[3] *and Mr Hartshorne*[11] *with his friend Mr Whey, who is a little inaccessible man with a sharp nose and a mind full of angles. Mr Hartshorne and Dr Forester have been disagreeing about his long absence from Little Wenlock - everybody is talking about it.*[31] *The table being filled Charlotte did not come into dinner and to my astonishment Dick Anstice appeared like an apparition in the Drawing Room after what he called an impalement in the Yellowroom. He is very agreeable - one of the bright spirits of the age - but in person so fallen off as he is not in the least handsome now. Charlotte was looking pretty and agreeable, but Mrs Gaskell's unaffected beauty has a very eclipsing effect on Charlotte. Mrs Gaskell was dressed in a chaly with a running pattern of fuschias and silk, a bandeau of rose coloured velvet with a band and scarf to match, she had a sort of lace canezous with a pink bow and her usual chain and brooch and a buckle to match this. I never saw such splendid hands, they are like a fairy model in papian marble. Mrs John Anstice's drawings are most beautiful. A wet day only a little walk.*

Sunday 11th October - *What have I to say for myself and my proceedings this week past! A good deal has happened and is happening, this does seem a more active life than was mine last year. On Wednesday Louisa and Caroline*[36] *came to tea and with our sketching and talk about the comet, the Gaskells*[3] *etc., we got on pretty well. Mr Bayliss came up too, he has been several times lately and I like him excessively. What was our consternation when Louisa asked us to go there the very next evening just as we thought the purgatory of their company was drawing to a close. It was a desperately wet night and my most kind Mama stipulated for us that if it rained they must not expect us, but the sun shone bright and clear all the morning, but it turned to rain and we were compelled to go and be half killed with ennui - the dog and Rebecca, the Gallery of Portraits, and parish scandal! At last Uncle Richard Darby made his appearance having been all day with the revising Barristers at Wenlock and told us a good deal about the proceedings in which he is deeply interested.*[29] *He hates Mr Gaskell with a most unchristian hatred. On Friday our spirits were refreshed by some delightful intercourse with the thinking and reasonable part of creation. The Hartshornes, Mr Whey and Mr Edmonds dined with us and we had a* *very charming evening. Mr Edmonds was very unmanageable, but he always did tease me so it is nothing new.*

I wonder whether I shall ever leave off the bad habits of people after a few minutes conversation. I did not like Mr Whey at Madeley Wood adhere I thought I had seldom seen greater and more unaffected talent. On Sunday night there might have been a long description of Mr Whey's talents and excellence if Meeting had not come in the way and afterwards came a letter for me from James. At the beginning of the week I wrote to tell him he must not come before Christmas, to which injunction he is wholly insubordinate and writes to tell me he will be here about Tuesday.[26] *Papa when he heard it made a vast explosion of pent up offences taken in the summer visit, but it ended as storms have been known to do before without doing more mischief than giving me a headache. Tilly*[28] *and I had a long walk in the evening. I felt it an opportunity of knowing my own mind and a pretext for giving up all my present prospects - but opposition is a grand thing for curing a little fickleness. We talked and understood each other and I decided to be guided by circumstances. I was dreadfully frightened and literally shed tears of terror.*

Monday 19th October - *The week is over and passed like an Elysium, I hardly know why I have kept no notes of the flying minutes - I told James all my feelings and made him think me the most changeable of beings but it was best I believe to do so - now I have changed again - he left this morning.*[26] *I have been truly miserable. It is very miserable to conceal one's feelings after - having been used to have love and sympathy proffered instead of having to seek them. James and I spent last week very quietly - went literally nowhere - the mornings were fine, used to sit with my work or drawing and he talked or read, and then we had a walk or a scramble. We read some parts of Popes "Homer" and compared it with Cowper's translation.*

Friday 23rd October - *Tilly,*[28] *H Graham and Mrs Little's boy drank tea - it was very boring and I was afflicted with a very bad humour. I write in my Journal because there is a fire at night - it is pleasant before Mama comes to dispossess me. Poor dear Mr Hartshorne! he is going.*[31] *Decidedly I shall always feel unfriendly to Dr Forester, it does seem so wrong but we have had the merits of the case discussed this most stupid of all stupid evenings till I am half sick and cannot for the dear life find another description - bad luck to the Goose of Willey, when are we to hear the last of it! I am very cross tonight but I behaved so well and I have done my hair in a twist, not a plait, oh it is so becoming, and we have been practising positions. Dear Tilly,*[28] *there is nobody like her after all - how she does know all my thoughts and feelings except a handful too deep for words.*

Sunday 25th October - *How different are one's feelings, morning and evening! I could almost believe the sun of the bright day melted some frozen sensibilities and made evening the hour of thinking, feeling, loving - in my nature at least. Yesterday morning was beautiful and we went forth with our sketch* *books and sketched some of the lime rocks at Lincoln Hill, oh! it was so charming. Papa went to Shrewsbury with 'Legion' and oh, the detestibility!*

He is engaged to meet the Hartshornes on Thursday. I bethought me, though it had been raining, I should like to give the deer some acorns - I filled a basket and penetrated through the paddock which was very like a bog, to the walnut trees where I found a remarkable moth as it seems to me amongst the dead leaves, it came home in the basket where I hope it will be good natured enough to live till Thursday when Mr Hartshorne will tell me what it is. Papa went to The Chesnuts to tea, very remarkable! The Hartshornes are really going, I am inexpressibly sorry and I think so will everyone else when they are gone.

"Mankind value not excellence till time has stolen away the proffered good". Mrs Reynolds and her brother, Dr Ball, were at Meeting today[14] *- cold and rainy and uncomfortable it has been. In the afternoon I stayed at home and read Mrs Cornwallis, a dear book that is. Abraham has a desperate cold - when we drank tea there a few evenings ago he would come up with us and eat a supper of toasted cheese.*

Wednesday 28th October - *I had a letter yesterday, James had a most cold journey. Mrs Reynolds and her brother made a round of calls after Meeting, we went to see Louisa and Caroline*[36] *and met them there. In about half an hour they came up to us with Joe Gulson Reynolds! It was a glad meeting full of bright recollections - the gay flower show - the merry day at Stanton Drew - the tea drinkings out of doors - they were pleasant days. It is an agreeable thing always to me to see two people flirt and mean nothing at all except to make the present moment glad, but there - they should both be young and beautiful. I will not be plainer, things amusing enough in a drawing room are terribly stupid told or written afterwards.*

Thursday 29th October - *The Hartshornes and Richard Sorton Darby came to dine - they stayed all night. How ill Dr Forester has behaved - his relations at Willey do not take his part. Mr Hartshorne, poor man, is really to be expelled, I fear at least he seems quite resolved to go. They are nice people much as I used to dislike them and I shall be grieved if they go.*[31]

Friday 6th November - *Uncle Richard Darby and J. Gulson Reynolds dined 'avec nous' - it was a glad meeting - I think he liked to see us again. I do not know how to judge his intentions as he flirted with me all evening and hardly spoke to Tilly.*[28]

Saturday 14th November - *This is the first night that we have had a fire oh, what an indescribable luxury fires were often not lit until the first of that month regardless of temperature. This morning had a letter from James, very very annoyingly wanting to come here next week. I wrote directly and hope it will have the desired affect of persuading him to stop till Christmas. Last Thursday Uncle Tothill arrived on business.*[32] *We are delighted to see him. We drank tea at The Chesnuts*[34] *this evening going very early as the gentlemen were* *all going to some troublesome vile registration. While they stayed we had a merry evening - Uncle Tothill[32] seems to put everybody in good humour with themselves and their neighbours. Mary and Deborah Darby went last week to Birmingham and they returned tonight - it was rather droll but they seemed very well pleased to find a party assembled to whom they could count their conquests over again.*

Frank Lloyd is proposing for some Gloucester heiress, so Mary and Deborah tell us - Lyell grows very interesting about peat mosses and moving bogs, more especially they are Irish bogs on Earl Moira's estate which had just moved and overwhelmed I do not know how many acres of cultivated country. Poor Lord Milton has died of typhus fever, married but just one year - imagine poor Lady Selina so young to be a widow, so soon to be a Mother. I am writing with my feet in water that was hot when I began but as it is now 12 I shall go to bed. On Monday Papa and Tilly[28] are pressed for a concert at Bridgnorth - on Tuesday I joined their party but Mr Jones disappointed us and no horses came on time.

Sunday 22nd November *- Now this week has flown away. On Sunday Uncle Tothill[32] dined here and we came out of the dining room so late that the postbag had gone, so I could not send my letter. Monday morning I went early to do my collecting and then met Tilly[28] in the wood and we proceeded on our way to the Bridge. It was a beautiful morning. Poor Sarah is really very ill and at last they appear sensible that something must be done, indeed it is quite time for she seems fast growing worse.[33]*

Wednesday 25th November *- I am left at home on a November morning almost enough to make me feel half melancholy. I intended to do a great deal this week now that I have finished "the Budget"[9] - alas, for good intentions, made to be broken like lover's vows. Be it known that Mama, having no fire in the study, cannot stay in the dining room has locateth herself and Bessy and a whole ocean of lumber in our apartment.*

Saturday 4th December *- We have been to Uncle Dickinson's[35] this afternoon to hear of Sarah.[33] Poor girl she is much worse, too ill for us to see her and there seems little hope of her recovery - poor Hannah!*

Sunday 13th December *- I have been almost too busy all week to write in my Journal - what a week of mourning it has been. Mourning for ourselves who are left to weep that we may not go with the departing The Sunday following my account Webb and Thursefield met and did not despair of dear Sarah's life being long preserved to her friends. We saw Joe after dinner and he had been very much shocked but said the danger was not immediate and we continued under that impression. I called on Monday morning with Mama - they would not allow that Sarah was worse although she had passed a restless and distressing night.*

We were dressed and on the point of setting off when Louisa sent a note saving that she wished to let us know that Sarah[33] was much worse, but the account from Dale House was not so unfavourable as to prevent our being greatly shocked the next morning when we heard that our beloved cousin had very peacefully expired that morning about 4 o'clock.

Tuesday 15th December - *My Uncle came up after breakfast, they had been much prepared by Mr Thursfield for the change. In the evening we went down and found my aunt very calm and resigned. Poor Hannah we did not see. She has been unremitting in her affectionate attentions to Sarah, and she is quite worn out with fatigue and grief. Mama stayed to tea. We went up to see the remains of our lovely and beloved cousin - and her expression was one of great suffering. On Thursday we went down again as Hannah really seemed to wish it - we stayed tea and endeavoured to assist in the mournful preparations. It was a most gratifying though a very sorrowful visit. The dear form of her we might not see again was placed in the coffin and now there was the rapture of repose in the placid smile. "She was lovely in life" said my dear Aunt "and she is lovely in death". They allowed us to help them and to see all the letters (some very beautiful) as if we had been members of her own family. Dear Hannah is sweetly resigned and commands her own feelings for the sake of others, in fact the whole family, as far as there was assembled, afforded the most beautiful picture of calmness and resignation under this most afflicting dispensation that I ever witnessed. It was a moral luxury to sit with them and the feelings seemed afterwards softened and refined. We returned early with my Uncle and Christy and found Mrs Lucy Darby and Michael Sorton Darby at our house. Oh, it was such a revulsion of feeling - they were deep and warm in political dissension. Until today, Sunday, we have not been out again. It has been the funeral - most melancholy and impressive. There were three Ministers who spoke most affectingly - Samuel Lloyd, T. Burlingham and Richard Barrett. The funeral was large and very affecting it was to see all the brothers with dear Hannah - poor Joseph, of all the brothers he appeared the most affected. May the scene of trial be productive of some good effects. it must have been a solemn and impressive day to all. Papa and Mama went to meet a large company at dinner and we went to tea, which seemed less agreeable than a quiet way of spending the evening at home as one is not prepared for gaiety or something approaching it after such a scene of sorrow and mourning., Dear Hannah bears wonderfully! the day of the funeral she was almost unnaturally calm and tranquil. Mary Sturge could not come. It was very affecting to see once more and talk to poor Lucy Bailey - we must always think of her with gratitude for her great attention to Grandmama - since then she has known much sorrow and it has altered her. It was delightful again to meet John Sturge who took us just where left us and I was enchanted and it proved to me more than any other Circumstance how much I am altered since those Birmingham days.*

I could now talk to him, John Sturge, with real pleasure and I found myself capable of enjoying "the feast of reason and the flow of soul". He talked to me as if I was a rational being and I opined he was surprised to find me so. That was a happy visit but then how different were all my feelings - I would rather have listened all day, I do believe to the prosiness of Mr C Dearman and his professions of admiration and happiness in my society than to all the wit and fascination of John Sturge. It has been a day of sadness not unmingled with clashing sentiments. After tea we had a meeting in the other parlour when Samuel Lloyd spoke at some length very impressively. John Sturge described dear Sarah's character beautifully in a few words - among other things he told me his sister Priscilla Southall had said she thought Sarah the most entire exemplification of Jane Taylor's "Now" that she had ever known. It was striklingly true - and one of the last times we saw dear Sarah she read to us the letter which contained the account of this talented and beloved one's death and its peculiarly affecting circumstances. Was greatly surprised last week to receive a letter from James with a Paris postmark. He is there with Sophie and I have been writing a letter today that it might be in time to reach him there.

NOTES

1. See note 13th, 20th and 25th December 1834.
2. The parliamentary election of 1834/35 which was won by Cecil Forester. There had obviously been a celebration at Acton Burnell, a manor approximately six miles south of Shrewsbury. Acton Hall adjoined Acton Burnell Castle, where the first English "Parliament" was held in 1283 in the reign of Edward I. Perhaps this indicated that the Darby family was beginning to become assimilated into the 'county set'. Strangely, Barnard Dickinson, who was very much a plain Quaker while he was manager of the Coalbrookdale Company, purchased Rushbury Farm)later Manor Farm) only seven miles from Acton Burnell in 1824.
3. Mr and Mrs Gaskell were mentioned from time to time, particularly in relation to Parliamentary elections. They seemed to have been involved in the local political scene. The Gaskells were an important family in Much Wenlock. Today their memory is recorded by the existence of "The Gaskell Arms" on the road to Shrewsbury.
4. Aunt Sorton was Anna Sorton, mother of Maria Darby (née Sorton) wife of Richard Darby of "Rosehill".
5. This refers to Mr Edward Edwards, the surgeon of Coalbrookdale who lived at the house now known as no. 43 Darby Road.
6. Mr Webb was a surgeon from Shrewsbury.
7. Richard Sorton Darby (b. 1812) was the eldest son of Richard and Maria Darby of Rosehill. He had health problems and developed other interests not associated with the Coalbrookdale works. He married Anna Wilkinson and moved to Hawkswood House, Sidbury, near Bridgnorth.
8. I must not take it easy.
9. Publisher's note. There are many references in the Journal to the Budget. This name probably refers to a local history Essay reading Society. In the Quaker stronghold of Street, Somerset, there was one such called "The Village Album" where folk gathered regularly "from the middle of the 19th century" to read each other's essays (which were subsequently bound into

volumes). Also in North London (Edgware, etc.) A Quaker essay readership society still continues called "The Portfolio".

10. Adelaide was showing off the foreign languages she had been learning. Oh, Meraviglia (Italian) Oh, marvel.
11. Mr Hartshorne was the curate at Little Wenlock (see page 6, note 9). Although Coalbrookdale is within the parish of Madeley, the parish church of Little Wenlock was nearer to the White House. Mr Hartshorne was a member of a much respected local family and was a well known academic. Although the Darbys were Quakers, they had good relations with other denominations. In the light of subsequent events the influence of the charismatic Mr Hartshorne may have been profound.
12. See note 7 above.
13. Dogberry was the pompous, overbearing, but good natured constable in Shakespeare's "Much Ado About Nothing".
14. The Ball family had been involved in Coalbrookdale from the mid-18th century. One of the nine shares in the Company held by the Goldney family in 1738 was held by Hannah Goldney who married John Ball. Later, in 1789, William Reynolds (son of Richard Reynolds) married Hannah Ball who was his first cousin. Thereafter the ball family remained an important part of the Reynolds family. The relationship between the two families was further cemented when Joseph Reynolds' daughter Rebecca married Joseph Ball, her second cousin. This part of the family eventually succeeded to the lordship of the Manor later in the 19th century. By then they had become a long-established Madeley family.
15. William Reynolds Anstice was the last steward of the Manorial court of Madeley.
16. This was the first mention of the relationship of Adelaide's sister Matilda and Abraham IV who were married four years later in 1839.
17. Joseph Sturge later married Hannah Dickinson on 14th October 1846 (see Adelaide's Journal 20th September 1846).
18. Hannah Dickinson who lived at Dale House, the "next house" referred to in Adelaide's Journal, where Adelaide found that Hannah was not to be permitted to repeat the late night/early morning experience of the night before.
19. This was an early indication of the failing health of Francis Darby which was to make his life a misery before his death in 1850.
20. Sir Robert Peel's administration after the election on December 1834/January 1835 only lasted four months. Adelaide's Journal of 7th April 1885 records the event in passing. Sir Robert Peel was succeeded by Lord Melbourne.
21. Adelaide does not disclose the name of the lady thought to have brought about a change in the outlook of Joseph Dickinson, eldest of the Dickinson children and manager of the Horsehay works. The affair did not last, because in 1842 he married Lucy Midgley of Castleton, Lancashire.
22. The Lancasterian schools operated a system of education pioneered, in 1808 by the British and Foreign School Society, (See Arthur Raistrick, *Two Centuries of Industrial Welfare, p. 57).*
23. Barnard Dickinson, who was at that time resident in Coventry.
24. Sophie and James Horne.

24a. Cook's Wood refers to "Cock's Wood", which is located at the head of the Loamhole Dingle, an easy walk from The White House (see page 20, note 20).
25. John Anstice was a partner in the Madeley Wood Company and a brother of W. R. Anstice.
26. After two weeks in Coalbrookdale, James Horne was firmly established in Adelaide's affections as her first boyfriend, but was it to last?
27. Sophie Horne stayed on with Louisa and Caroline Darby at "Rosehill" for several weeks.
28. "Tilly" was Adelaide's affectionate name for her older sister, Matilda.
29. The Municipal reform Act 1835 was passed under the government of Lord Melbourne.
30. Madeley Wood Hall at The Lloyds, was built early in the 19th century for the Anstice family to replace Bedlam Hall, Madeley Wood, their previous home.
31. Dr Townsend Forester was rector of Little Wenlock from 1818-41. He appointed assistant curates at Little Wenlock and one of these was the antiquary C. H. Hartshorne between 1826 and 1836. Mr Hartshorne was a popular visitor to the White House. Unfortunately, Dr forester decided that he must leave Little Wenlock on account of his absences from the living.
32. William Tothill of Bristol married Hannah Darby, sister of Francis Darby (Adelaide's father) in 1818. They lived in Bristol. They were affectionately known as Uncle and Aunt Tothill.
33. Sarah Dickinson, third child of Barnard and Ann Dickinson of Dale House.
34. The Chesnuts (see map) was the home of Lucy Darby and her sons Abraham Darby IV and Alfred, and her daughters Deborah and Mary.
35. Aunt Dickinson's was Dale House which was until 1838 the home of Barnard and Ann Dickinson and their children, including Hannah.
36. Uncle Richard Darby lived at "Rosehill" where he lived with his wife Maria and their children including Louisa and Caroline who were friends of Adelaide.
37. Severn House was at Dale End and had a frontage to the River Severn. Today it is the Valley Hotel, Ironbridge. Under the Will of Sarah Darby it was transferred from her ownership to the Dickinson family. In 1835 it appears to have been occupied by the Anstice family. In 1838 Ann and Barnard Dickinson built a new home to the east of Severn House, while their son Henry Dickinson took occupation of Severn House.
38. Leighton Buzzard, home of "mama's" family, John and Hannah Grant.

1836

Comment

For the first half of 1836 Adelaide's Journal is dominated by her problems with Mr James Horne, her first boyfriend with whom she had developed a relationship approaching betrothal. James was in Coalbrookdale over the New Year and left after a fortnight. Adelaide's feelings towards James had become increasingly doubtful to the point where her Journal records "I took an absolute aversion to him". James decided to make a journey across Europe to Jerusalem and this prompted Adelaide to steel herself and terminate the relationship. This was done by correspondence but it was the end of June before the matter was accomplished. The rest of the family were pleased at the news, although Richard Darby's family (with whom the Horne's had stayed during their visits) were concerned that it would be a great disappointment to the Horne family.

A Private Journal is by its nature concerned with personal matters and is not therefore a commentary on other events taking place at the same time. However, passing comments give tiny clues to those events. On 24th January, Adelaide notes "My spirits rose as they did when I heard Mr Gaskell had a majority." Mr Gaskell was one of the family's political friends. That month there had been an election for the Wenlock Council at which the Radicals had been beaten. Mr Will Anstice had been made Mayor and amongst the new councillors was Mr Richard Darby.

In similar vein, on 8th July, Francis Darby read a reference in a paper to Countess Burgstall which prompted Aunt Ann Dickinson to recall that Count Burgstall had visited Coalbrookdale in her young days and Francis Darby then remembered that the Count had greatly admired his sister.

This trivial conversation throws a very small light on the way in which Coalbrookdale had developed. At the beginning of the century Coalbrookdale had reached a pinnacle of achievement and was therefore a place of pilgrimage for visitors from central Europe who were anxious to find out (and to copy) how things were done. Count Burgstall was just one of these. Although Coalbrookdale had much to offer, the process was almost certainly reciprocated. Central Europe was far more advanced in decorative ironwork and there was probably an exchange of information. This was a sphere in which Francis Darby, with his artistic temperament was particularly interested, and as a renaissance took place in the fortunes of the Company after Barnard Dickinson stood down as manager in 1831, Francis Darby appears to have taken a prominent part in leading the Coalbrookdale Foundry towards a new and revolutionary market in decorative ironworks. The foundry started producing art castings in 1834 becoming the first (and the pre-eminent!) foundry in England to do so.

Unfortunately, Adelaide's Journal, by its nature throws little light on important developments like this.

Coalbrookdale was not the only place where great progress was being made. The Madeley Wood Company under the control of the Anstice family was also expanding its Works. The first of the great blast furnaces at Blists Hill was blown-in during 1832 and a second one in 1840. This spelled the end of Madeley Wood Company's original furnaces at Bedlam which ceased to operate about 1839/40. By then Bedlam Hall, formerly the home of the Anstices situated near to Bedlam Furnaces was demolished and the family moved to the newly-built Madeley Wood Hall at The Lloyds. Precisely when this took place is at present not known but on 18th September 1836 Adelaide describes a delightful evening with the Anstice family and their guests at Madeley Wood Hall.

There were two visits to Leighton Buzzard during 1836. On the second of these in September Adelaide witnessed the later stages of the construction of the London to Birmingham Railway which went through her grandfather John Grant's land near the Linslade tunnel.

The Journal ends abruptly towards the end of October 1836.

Friday 1st January - New Year's Day - *It is long since I wrote much in my Journal for I have been very busy to spare moments in writing a history of my life. Dear Tilley,*[22] *if she should ever see it, it will account for much she cannot understand and I know she will have an interest - young and blooming in the most buoyant health. I feel it strange that I should scribble thus, James is here, it has been a dark task for me to go on with it and suffered more in tense anguish of mind. I took an absolute aversion to him, but these are maiden fancies. I will conquer them if I can, I am resolved.*

Sunday 24th January - *I have still been busy with this life, I mean that which I have been writing and recollecting so much so that my Journal has stood quite still and all deeds, good, bad and indifferent floated away unrecorded - here forgotten but their report is borne to heaven. Well, time passed on as it ever will and James stayed a fortnight and departed. My spirits rose as they did when I heard Mr Gaskell had a majority.*[1] *But a truce to this nonsense. I have had a great deal of miserable foreboding - letters from Mr Horne to Papa about my being married - "Sur le champ" - and another from James to tell me he should go abroad. Well, one must he prepared to meet the world and its troubles. "A ce moment", anyway. I shall take leave home and go to all that interests me immediately. Oh! I am really very happy that James will soon be out of the country, I wish the Chesnuts could think he had been refused.*

Sunday 31st January - *Plainly it is my duty to make this stubborn heart of mine either to take upon itself those duties which I have almost promised to perform for the sake of one I do not love or else decidedly and even now, far as it* *has gone, to say I cannot, and I will not think of it more than when it comes to this. I think such a breach of promise is almost a crime, and more I fear still do shrink from the world's harsh constructions that world which I despise so utterly. These thoughts were most forcibly in my mind last night as I was sitting alone with no companion but the moon, and I said to myself "then I must cease to hope for any circumstance which may set this hated prospect on one side". Since in human probability none will happen and I must, yes I must decide cheerfully to take for my companion through life one whose tastes, feelings and sympathies are as far removed from mine as Alpha and Omega, for my companion probably through many more years - Oh, the tedium of looking forward. But my meditations did not go so far, I stifled the gathering tears and ran out of the room. it was only to meet Papa on the stairs - how much easier it is to appear just as usual to anybody rather than to him. The moon rose cloudless and beautiful but when I sat last night with so many sorrowful forebodings, the sky was overcast and there were light masses of cloud driving across the face of the Queen of night, I gazed and fancied there was a resemblance to my own in the sorrowful countenance which may easily be traced on her disk a few nights before the moon is at full and so it has been with me - my existence was first happy and bright as that young moon, how soon it is overcast and through how many clouds has it to steer. The moon was there alone with the stars in the blue and distant expanse like an ocean-hung on high, but what an unruffled orb. There was a calm, a placid smile over all the heaven - like the true earthly happiness - hope will not forsake youth. I thought of the simile I had drawn between the moon and my fate and I went to bed with a heart tranquilised.*

Last Sunday I had a letter from James from Calais - a pretty letter just the thing most young ladies would like to receive; once I believe I used to like them - I have it now to answer since my knight of the sigh and the plume anticipating the day of conjugal obedience tells me "we must answer each other's letters directly". Must and directly forsooth! This is being betrothed, well I would not be a Beatrice quite and the thing must have an answer - plague upon plague - but it is not now with me to say no so I may as well quiet my conscience and my fears thus by thinking of it as a great billet only sorry it should be the adieu of such a dear sweet knight what a precious catalogue of the sighs and sorrow of a fine gentleman.

Saturday 6th February - *Yesterday Mr and Mrs Hartshorne called and left with us a kind of Journal, or as it is called "Decameron Cambriorum". It was kept by Mr Whey and Mr Hartshorne on their Welsh tour in 1834 for Miss Hartshorne.*

Sunday 14th February - *I feel very matter of fact this fine warm morning and with much sorrow of spirit do I read the good resolutions of a week ago I have done very little this whole uninterrupted week, as I have not felt industriously disposed - in the morning it has been too cold to inhabit the dining room.*

On Monday when I was really a good deal alone and had a nice morning (for the typhus fever had prevented my going round the district - poor little Henry Fox died of it on Wednesday).[2] *I wrote a letter to Emma, not having written to her before since my return from Leighton in the summer.*

We sojourned a space at Wombwelle Menagerie[3] *on Tuesday where we met many of the natives curious as ourselves. Verily the beasts were marvellous animals a tiger most beautiful and the lovliest leopards, well this is not such a mat appellation for such fine soft skins moving about with so much lightness they are very catlike - the elephant is a sublime beast. On the whole they were undeniably fine specimens of animals, human and beast.*

Sagacious Cousin Abraham[23] *breakfasted here on Wednesday as he had some business with Papa and other gentlemen. Men of business seem to think a moment of precious time devoted to speaking civilly to your ladies such a dreadful waste of capital, seldom have I felt in a more awkward position. They brought a detailed account of Mr J Wilkinson's resignation and the proceedings of the Committee and the Beaconites*[4] *in which at this time of general excitement one cannot avoid feeling some interest. I should be glad to understand it more clearly, but I cannot think either side always conduct the controversy in the most christian spirit. 'tis 1 o'clock, I have not sat up so late on principle (of getting fat) for many a night, but the effect of a wee drop of Papa's evening potation of Brandy and water is very supporting.*

Henry Dickinson and Mr Bayliss came to tea on Thursday and gave me a lesson of chess. They had two well contested games and Henry won both. Today is poor Ann Morris's funeral[5] *- it is a most lovely morning and the poor little boys are to be pitied.*

Sunday 28th February - *Mr Hartshorne*[6] *preaches his last sermon at Little Wenlock today, they dined with us last Thursday and it was very melancholy to think we should not meet again. Richard and Louisa*[24] *joined our party. I began the week with marvellous resolutions of industry - Monday I walked to the Bridge and on Tuesday was really industrious and in the evening had some chess with Mr Bayliss not established as Master in the art - not the science. Friday night the intelligence came that Mary Sturge*[7] *has a little girl and is doing well. Grandmama has been very unwell with an attack more like croup than anything else - the account today is better. There is another awful conflagration in the paper today which has almost destroyed the seat of Charles Ward Esqre in Derbyshire - there is a long account of the intrepid presence of mind displayed by the whole family - you feel a wish to know such uncommon people.*

Sunday 6th March - *Last night I told Tilley*[22] *- dearest Tilley who sympathises in all my variations and transmogrifications of feeling - that I was quite sure I should be wretched if the present prospects for me were realised and I did feel that my mind was undergoing a change.*

Sunday 13th March - *The determination is taken and the letter written which as it sometimes seems to me will make the world look very cold. My great fear is that sensible people who judge a young woman by her conduct will consider one as a heartless flirt, and feel towards one who can thus change her mind all the contempt such conduct justly inspires. I speak of the affair as if it ended, though in fact only one preparatory letter is yet finished - in doing it I feel much sorrow in being compelled to give so much pain when I think I might have lessened it by deciding sooner, and I see much difficulty to be surmounted further on - "mais ce n'est pa le premier pas qui conte". Mr James Horne has not that steadiness of religious principle required in a world like this as a safe guide. He would be ever swayed by the opinion of those whose standing and fashion he could rely upon - much ascendancy might be gained over him by a superior intellect willing to flatter his vanity with delicacy. I feel vividly the danger of trusting to any one whose principles of simple right or wrong are not founded on those pure precepts implanted in the cradle and which the after study of the Bible should render firm and decided it must undoubtedly be a trial to the other sex in mixing indiscriminately with the world to preserve the mind in its sentiments of justice and generosity and the heart uncontaminated by surrounding selfishness. This must be very disproportionate - to anything we are ordinarily called upon to resist but not the less careful should women be not to trust their happiness with those who do not possess that plain sense of rectitude which render the assistance of God will ever prove a safeguard well able to set this world's follies and temptations at defiance. I believe these considerations had the greatest weight with me in coming to this very important determination. Mr Horne's manner had been so much changed during his last visit that the uncomfortable task of overcoming any affection I once felt for him was almost wholly done for me without an effort on my part. I have not been so really happy for months - I am anxious to separate the quiet satisfaction of having done what I felt convinced is my duty from the exquisite pleasure of anticipating years in my happy home.*

Sunday 20th March - *Elizabeth Gulson came to us on Friday - she is a very interesting young woman. Her circumstances and my own are similar and yet how different! In June she will be united to one who is the chosen of her heart, approved by her own taste and judgement and that of her friends. Last week we heard of the death of poor Joseph Anstice*[8] *- He had been long prepared for the change and his amiable and highly gifted wife says in the most beautiful of letters addressed to his afflicted family "this account will pierce you to the heart but it is what I have been long looking to". Mrs Joseph Anstice bears her loss with the utmost fortitude and Christian resignation. The funeral was most affecting, one clergyman was so overcome that he could not finish the sermon. At King's College everyone appears greatly to feel this loss sustained by all his friends and mankind in general - this is the melancholy end of such brilliant prospects and so much genius.*

Tuesday 29th March - *I have today been enjoying "Leonora" and the beautiful letters from Caroline to Julia at the end of the same Volume. Miss Edgworth's books always incite me heart and soul to improve my mind that I may one day deserve such friends as she describes should they ever fall in my way for I verily believe that they do exist, pure and perfect though they seem beyond the common lot of humanity. Alas! how many precious years have I wasted without almost the ambition even to attain excellence - still at 18 it does not, I hope, seem too late, but did ever a young lady permanently change her mood of thinking and her standard of judging from simply reading a book?*

Sunday 17th April - *Oh, such delightful weather, such charming at my garden - the prettiest little round bed scalloped out by me and Tilley*[22] *only. I have had no letter and for some days was rather perplexed as Mama is called to Leighton and my task would be formidable should Mr Horne either write or make his appearance during her absence.*

Sunday 24th April - *My Uncle Tothill*[26] *and Mr Reynolds of Bristol arrived and my Uncle spent the evening with us and with Abraham,*[23] *Alfred and Joe Dickinson. Oh, I wish to be a man to taste thoroughly the excitement of business (I have also wished to be one for the delights of a sealife and the glory of one in the army). My Uncle has the faculty of making every capacity its real extreme - it was an evening I especially enjoyed.- the unceasing flow of pointed anecdote, Abraham's vastness of ideas and Alfred's minutiae of detail - Railroads, the Beaconite division*[9] *- the Steamboat projection*[10] *to America, Temperance and Abstinence causes*[11] *- perhaps this does not sound amusing, but proved indeed.*

Monday 25th April - *We do not go to Leighton till tomorrow week. It is impossible to experience much settlement of occupation before. How we are creatures of habit, our room is being cleaned today and I sorely discomfited.*

Friday 29th April - *I have been reading the account of Lord Bacon's "Novum Organon Scientiarum" - I like his ideas on the Idols and Prejudices of the human mind. The long expected letter from Mr Horne arrived yesterday dated Rome. From the fact of not receiving one for so long I had been more than ever convinced of having done quite right in refusing one who seemed disposed to take it without further effort - but here it seems that a letter from Florence I never received! In the present epistle it is evident that Mr Horne's attachment is firm and my influence over him appears great enough to induce him to cultivate his intellectual faculties in his present most propitious situation now that he finds it probable he may be rejected for want of them. Although he tells me he is improving himself there is certainly no evidence of increased ability in the most ineloquently long descriptions of Rome etc., and I should have been more disposed to believe that his mind was so improving and making continual endeavours to attain excellence were it not for one or two poetical ideas and reflections lugged in by the ears which I know to be notions so utterly foreign to the usual tenor of* *his mind that I am inclined to think they and the whole epistle are written only with a view to please me and not to depict truly the state of his feelings.*

Friday 13th May - Leighton - *Here we have been established for more than a week. I think it was this day week that I had another letter dated Rome, it was the answer to mine which had not been received before. Mr James Horne goes directly to Jerusalem and other great scenes in the Orient - and therefore during the time which must elapse before his return to Florence requests that I will reconsider the matter. Although at first I could not help feeling impatient at the state of doubt in which an affair must be left on my account, I should wish were finally settled, yet on the other hand I have felt tempted to look upon the three months as a respite from a disagreeable business. I have written frequently to my dear Tilley*[22] *- I miss her extremely but I feel the advantage of being thrown upon my own resources and obliged to form my own conclusions.*

Tuesday 17th May - *Cousin Abraham came here on Saturday and did not leave until early this morn. At home I do not very well like him but here it was really a treat of no small dimensions to have somebody with an intellectual capacity who is also somewhat nearer my own age - Oh, it is trying when all around you, who are young enough to enter into young feelings, are too frivolous to be companions in your best moments. The mind turns on its own resources and lives to itself in a way not good for it. I took the "Physical Theory" into the Shrubbery intending to puzzle myself in its mazes. Samuel Reeve has been here giving us interesting particulars of the Yearly Meeting - it was a stormy time in which charity seemed to take its leave. Luke Howard thought the controversy would continue so long as women friends were allowed any part in it. People mutilate the Scriptures as Friends do by taking a passage abstractedly in their extempore sermons and considering it in a manner which the whole context would contradict. As to publishing the proceedings, although Friends may be prohibited from taking notes during the sittings, it will be hard to prevent those who have good memories afterwards. For his part, Luke Howard hired a shorthand writer to be sure of correctness, and then if any Friends would be ashamed to see what he wants to say in print he had better be quiet - Ann Jones was most unruly in the Mens' Meeting.*[11b]

Thursday 5th June - *We are come back to our dear home and every day in going back to my old pursuits and my beautiful little garden which Tilley*[22] *has made a very paradise in my absence, I feel more and more how rightly I have estimated my own heart and its powers for happiness.*

Sunday 29th June - *Papa came yesterday, we depart on Wednesday. Since I wrote last the weighty business that has so long discomfited me is, I hope, rightly concluded. I had a letter from Miss Horne on Thursday telling me her brother is still in Rome and wishing to hear from me. I thought much about it and decided it was wrong to lose such an opportunity of settling an affair which grows more and more discreditable - the longer the finale is put off. Besides, this letter* *contained the wish to hear from me in the form of a message from Mr James Horne and extraordinary as it did appear to me that after begging so much for a few months reconsideration he should now have changed to wishing it done directly, the path for me seemed plain to write and tell him my determination which I did the same day. I was away from home and utterly uninfluenced.*

Since our return, Matilda and I have been busy,working some pretty trifles for Elizabeth, Barnard (Dickinson) told me on passing through Coventry that she will be married this week - may she be happy. Oh, it does seem a risk for any woman and yet it is surely the will of an All Wise Father, but it is not a command. I never experienced such exquisite pleasure in the beautiful scenery around us this summer, we have had some rain which has made all of such a glowing green.

Monday 30th June - *The presents are packed up to depart and Sophie's letter which has been such a difficulty as it rejoices the heart to have surmounted. I am now confined upstairs with a sore throat and have every symptom of the Measles coming on. Mary Sturge (bad luck to all meddlers) sent Charles home as he was unwell - the evening when the measles appeared, Louisa and Caroline*[24] *came here to tea and they, as well as myself, are now rather poorly. I have been reading the "Black Dwarf" and do not as yet feel the depression of spirits said to be usual. I must mention the opinions of wise people on my past conduct - now the path has been cleared! Papa was asked by Joe Dickinson*[27] *if in verity Adelaide had said no, and when acquainted with the truth, every house down the valley became possessed of the same invaluable commodity.*

Papa went to London last week where he met Dr Simm who expressed his great satisfaction that it was indeed decided so, for he said Mr James Horne was exceedingly unsettled and he had greatly wished we could know how little prospect there seemed to be that the young gentleman ever would settle to anything. Which was the greater fool in these matters, whether father or son the good Doctor really did not know. Dear Mrs Reynolds has been with us since yesterday and cannot but approve what has been done. I read to her all the last letters, and my last she thought quite what it should be, the first she thought rather pettish. Uncle Dickinson[25] *is glad because he thinks it so unfeeling of the betrothed to leave his destined bride merely to follow his own pleasure in other lands, and my Aunt is glad because for some reason unknown she does not wish either of her nieces to marry at all, and Henry*[25] *is glad because he once made himself eminently ridiculous in a political debate with Mr James Horne in which neither understood the main points of the subject in dispute. And Hannah, dear girl, is kind enough to be glad that I am going to stay at this dear place. Uncle Richard Darby's*[24] *family are en masse very sorry because it will be such a great disappointment to the Horne's. The Chesnuts*[23] *are all very glad for no reason whatever that they are pleased to give - I cannot tell why but I dislike their exultation of voice particularly. And now let all the Minnows (tritons in their own estimation) say just they will I should be perfectly happy - if I had not the measles - When could man ever call himself happy without some alloy and how much better when this is bodily - not mental. To feel thought unfettered and the intellectual energies uncramped by one's constantly recurring and miserable idea - Oh, it is worth some suffering to feel as I do now.*

Thursday 3rd July *- I am still kept upstairs and sorely against my own inclination, but the thought of measles is gone and I have nothing but a common cold - Dear Mama is unwell too and so is Papa and I believe "tout le mond" has had colds. On dit c'est 'affire' - ma chere Maman dit that I have had mental anxiety enough to account for this cold! It is strange I can feel so very happy, as I do, however I am much afraid of turning out into an unsentimental heroine - I am not well and have grown exceedingly thin - upwards of a dozen grey hairs have been pulled out of my cranium and appetite fails.*

Tuesday 8th July - evening *- It happened some weeks ago that Aunt Dickinson was taking tea with us, and Papa was reading a passage in the paper which appeared rather interesting - it was a letter from Sir Walter Scott to the Countess Burgstall*[11a] *who had been a scotch lady, a sister of Mrs Dugald Stuart and had sat for the portrait of Di Vernon - that my Aunt suddenly remembered the said Lady's husband paid a visit to these Iron Works in her young days and Papa said that the Count had greatly admired my Aunt and the end of these recollections was an order for Captain B Hall's books from which the letter was extracted. We are now reading said book in the evenings and are much amused and now and then interested by it. It is an account of a sojourn in Syria at the Countess's castle of Hainfeld - a strange old place inhabited by this singular and yet most delightful being. A very interesting part concerns Duke John of Austria and his Ironworks - he has done almost incredible good in Austria and is a most remarkable man.*

Sunday 10th July *- Miss Wilderspin*[12] *is at The Chesnuts*[23] *very much what she used to be only rather colder and less exuberant in her spirits. We only saw her one evening.there for they have kept her at home exclusively. She sang some charming songs and gave me the words, she has suffered much from ill health since we met before and now seems to have some alarming consumptive symptons. Seldom indeed do we see much entire devotion of all the energies of a most active mind to one grand object - her knowledge of human nature is great and her memory extraordinary. She has now an Infant School for the higher classes at Cheltenham, under her own exclusive care - Mr Wilderspin*[12] *is going to America in about a month. I have done a great deal in our pretty garden and we have walked out every evening. During our woodland walks we met a lady and gentleman, very attractive to our curiosity, but I fear I cannot find a romance thereon. NN, he was reading a MSS to her had this is the vacation at both universities.*

Sunday 11th July - evening *- At Meeting yesterday we had two most impressive sermons from Anne Jones,*[11b] *she is Alfred Burgess's Aunt - she and her* *husband took tea with us this evening and we found them both very agreeable. You seldom see a lord of the creation submit so obediently to the guidance of a superior mind in his wife - they have travelled a great deal and Mrs Jones gave us many most interesting accounts of America; the abominable roads threading among old stumps of trees had been appalling even to her, but the splendid tints of the woods in Autumn repaid for much. No American tree turns at once to the dusky brown which prevails here, but the deepest shades of red and yellow mix beautiful with the evergreens planted by the hand of Nature on the Alleghenny mountains. The fireflies shooting like sparks in the twilight or falling to the ground like tiny stars were she said especially pleasing to English eyes. Delighted as you must feel with the simple eloquence of this good Lady's descriptions, yet it is very perceptible that her talents are not only those of conversation and in the communion of mind with minds you feel that you have to do with one of iron firmness and strength which it may be both limited mercy for failings. They dined a week since with dear Elizabeth*[13] *in her new home. Anne is still with her.*

Tuesday 19th July - *I have been overpoweringly busy in the construction of a muslin garment today, our rulers of fashion are going back to the tight sleeves and to make them is almost as tiresome as to wear them. Yesterday we called on Mrs Owen and took tea at Severn House - Our Arms, that is Papa's,*[14] *are the great theme of discourse at present so that I am indeed wearied with or and azure reversed and per cheveron battelle - Mr Burke, the Commoner man, finds the Darbys, these renowned Darbys, however, have no right from the Herald's College to bear any arms and they will not give what we have been used to so the perplexities form quite an epoch in domestic politics.*

Everybody has gone to Swansea and Uncle Richard Darby's[24] *family going soon to Liverpool will leave us quite by ourselves on the hill top. I remember the time when it would have been a source of real sorrow to be left at home when all the world here had departed this way and that, but I hope that it is not from an unsociable spirit that I certainly feel very glad every morning to think no calls are to be paid nor any to be expected in all human probability and it is pleasant to trudge about our garden with my frock through the pocket hole without having to look for observers.*

Sunday 24th July - *Mr and Mrs Egremont*[15] *came here on Friday had took Tilly back with them for a week. I missed her dreadfully the first evening, but I know she will enjoy herself and it is better for us to be occasionally separated. We enjoy being together the more and for my part I think learning to be independent increases not only convenience but affection and happiness. I have been very busy in my garden which I always find the surest preventive to dullness. On my walls grow one or two tufts of that pretty insinuating ground ivy named by myself and others equally unlearned, and very beautiful it looked in the Spring but the hot weeks after killed it in that dry exposed situation, and very untidy I had thought the withered heap but it was not until yesterday that after* *nailing up a great ungovernable rose bush I pulled one dead mass down, but to my sorrow and astonishment I found the exquisite nest of a dear little willow wren I have seen hopping about. I made a hole at the back of it for there was no penetrating at the tiny moss wreathed entrance and I supposed the little birds had flown when to my sorrow I found one warm egg among the feathers. With much ado and half a forked stick I put it in almost the same place, but I fear the old bird will not like it, if they return I shall think such a phenomenon an event in natural history.*

Friday 5th August *- Last evening was one of immense enjoyment. Mrs Owen*[15a] *called last week with her friend Mrs Burroughs and after spending a morning quite in the old way, invited us to dine at the Vicarage. We went yesterday, they were without company and very agreeable - little Mary grows into me of the prettiest children I ever saw. Mrs Burroughs plays beautifully and treats in the way of painting it may be supposed were not few. There is a dead stag in the dining room with an old wolfish sort of dog beside it - really like life itself, nature I mean.*

Mr Owen[15a] *took Papa to see a sketch of Etty's which we were not favoured to see, but as we went upstairs Mrs Owen Peeped into the painting room and we followed Oh, it was a pleasure to be shown Mr Owen's beautiful beginnings for the finished pieces are but few in comparison. With very great kindness he showed me his etching closer and the principles of his art - the plate where the etching was drawn in a greasy substance, I believe, and then taken off with aqua fortis on paper, but I am not clear how. Oh, for one of those universal knowledge people who can clear your ideas and make you thoroughly understand that which you have a few confused notions about. In figures, animals, landscapes, distance - Mr Owen seems alike successful but the human figure is his chief forte. We left my dear Tilly*[22] *there and I felt really glad to part with her where I could not but be certain she must enjoy being. I felt very "exaltée and couleur de rose" as we rode home and formed numerous plans of extraordinary industry in drawing and painting and in other things also to make room for these primary objects and I began very much to wish for such a room and such an apparatus for dabbing in this and that colour and my admiration of Mr Owen's industry and genius had risen to a great height just as we passed the sulphurous coal hearth's blowing flame and smoke full in our faces and alarming me for its effect on the horses. After this adventure my admiration and fears cooled together and it occurred to me that a clergyman certainly ought to do something more than paint. Perhaps it might have been desirable if I had thought whether indeed I do anything better myself with sufficient perseverance to make it worth while. I have been appointed Minute Secretary to the ladies' Bible Association and I hope with fear and trembling I may be able to manage the arduous office Fanny Edwards is determined to give up. Hannah and herself are both young to undertake these posts of honour and exertion. We took tea with the Edwards*[16] *at the beginning of the week - they are really nice agreeable people - very unaffectedly happy in their splendid new room. Fanny played a good deal for us - music is such a delight to me, but I believe if I had played I might have been even more superficial than is now the case which need not be. Tilley and I had a joint letter from Sophie last Wednesday and a very nice one it is only I am discomfitted to hear her brother has never had my last epistle but if he is satisfied without I am glad, but thankful I obeyed Mama and kept a copy of it, as I really do not see why I should take any more trouble about the matter than to send him the said copy.*

Tuesday 9th August - *Somewhat curious last Sunday brought me a letter from Mr James Horne acknowledging receipt of my missing letter on his return from Sicily. Satisfactory to know he feels little more than mortification about the matter. The happiness of having it all decided and myself out of it is I cannot tell how great - the letter is perfectly civil yet I do not feel the less cause for thankfulness in having thus escaped what I can hardly picture.*

Friday 19th August - *My dear Grandparents are staying here - they are both so well for their advanced age - we have seen a great deal of Abrahan Darby*[23] *since grandpapa has been here - I never did see anybody take such pains to be witty.*

Tuesday 24th August - *We have been to Uncle Dickinson's*[25] *where we met Mr Cooper and two of his daughters, Mrs Bartlett and Mrs Reynolds. There was much interesting conversation - a great deal about the wrong feeling to which total abstinence, or at least belonging to the total abstinence Society, generally leads.*[17] *From thence we went to the scientific assembly at Bristol and the probability of our being propelled by galvanism instead of steam.*[18]

Sunday 18th September - *We depart for Leighton on Wednesdav next. It does seem very soon to be again fidgetted away from home. Last week we dined at Madeley Wood*[19] *and had a most delightful evening such a one as is calculated to make everything at home look gloomy and unamiable. It is really beautiful to see a family living under rather peculiar circumstances so entirely guided by love and consideration to one another, so exceedingly fond of Mrs J Anstice's fine baby as well as its Mama, and all so apparently happy together. We met only Mrs Reynolds, Mr John Pritchard*[19a] *and Mr Gabriel Poole in addition to their usual family circle. Now for a little amusing thing - Mr Gabriel struck me directly I saw him as very much like Mr James Horne, whose memory I really did not think I had abhorred so much. He took me into Dinner and I did not at all understand my introduction. I believe there might be need to set me at ease which with the breeding of good Society he evidently wished to do and his Journey into this strange mining country began matters - then followed beautiful scenery; Devonshire, Somersetshire then hunting in his boyhood in that beautiful country - red deer - fallow deer - Exmoor forest shooting - distance for firing at deer etc., My prejudice against the man's frivolity grew to such a height that I actually overlooked the talent evinced by the most splendid descriptions of some sketches taken among the Alps by a friend of his - a patent drawing board for*

Water Colours and pens made of reeds. When I came to talk over our visit and to discover the heap of new ideas in my possession - I began to question where they came from and whether I was quite right in thinking John Pritchard with his champagne and outlets à la maintenor and Will Anstice with his admiration for the Vale of Llangollen so infinitely superior in point of intellect to Gabriel Poole - whom I had disliked simply because he was fond of field sports and in possession of a very fine countenance and figure, as well as unusually agreeable in gentlemanly manners - I wonder now where I could have found the likeness and am very desirous to do Mr Gabriel justice and to show him that I can appreciate and enjoy sensible conversation, if ever I should have the pleasure of seeing him again. My respect was wonderfully heightened upon another discovery - a discussion arose as to whether a forest is necessarily a place filled with trees or not. Mr Gabriel Poole was quite alone in the opinion that the word simply meant a place for hunting which may have trees in it or not - nearly the same thing as a chase only he believed with some different rights. Johnson's Dictionary should settle the matter and when at home I eagerly took down the great quarto thinking, I confess, that Mr Gabriel Poole was quite wrong, but to my great surprise I found that a forest is an uncultivated tract of land partially wooded and belonging to the King. We had a great deal of music this same delightful evening and I must not forget that Gabriel sings, many think, better than Will Anstice. His voice has not lost the sweet softness of his cousins, but there is great melody in almost the deepest base notes I ever heard. They sang part of the Lay of the Last Minstrel set to music by the late Dr Clarke Du Gard's father) - one of the most splendid glees I ever heard, their voices suited so well. Mr Gabriel sang "My Mother Bids Me Bind My Hair"[20] most exquisitely and several others with Charlotte and Will joining in one pretty song. I cannot tell why I was excited, I could not sleep and everything was miserable the next day, but as we were busy preparing for our Journey I could not regulate overwrought feelings in the shortest way by reading. Tomorrow I must call at Madeley Wood with John. Wesley's life which we have finished; to mend a heap of stockings; to alter the sleeves of one frock and make a pocket hole in another; to shorten sandals; mend a pet pair of gloves; ditto a pocket and sundry undergarments; to make a veil and two work bags.

Friday 22nd September - Leighton - *We arrived yesterday to dinner after a journey which extended to Dunchurch on Wednesday. Papa allowed us two hours at "the Society of Arts" which we enjoyed exceedingly. I do prefer the old Masters to any modern pictures unless it may be Sir Thomas Lawrence's which are admitted into the collection of the deceased's Artists. There are several Mr Owen Murilloy's "Sleeping Jesus" is considered a most exquisite picture, but there is one by Carlo Dolci "Salvator Mundill" that I could have looked at longer with pleasure. There is a lion and lioness by some not celebrated artist that are very lifelike. Paul Brillts "Death of Adonis" was a most elaborate picture - it is curious the number of little birds and insects most minutely finished* *in the trees - and I must not forget a landscape by Hobbima in which the effect of light and shade on a summer evening is perfect. Papa is gone this wet morning by Leamington and today is the book exchange - the Reeves have been here this evening, the same giddy goodnatured pretty young ladies as ever - I feel inclined to sympathise in their nonsense for I am strangely altered since I was here in the Spring. The splendid blossoms and damp luxuriance of Autumn takes away all resemblance to the same place last Spring.*

Sunday 24th September - *I am taking advantage of the hour before the Reeves come into the Shrubbery to write my Journal using a distinguished steel pen which cramps hand and ideas.*

Yesterday we went on a long ride with Grandpapa to see and sympathise in all his hobbies, it is generally expected of young ladies that they should enter into people's hobbies. One thing was really interesting that is the progress made by the Railroad[21] *- the two Contractors are nearly meeting on their embankments through Grandpapa's beautiful fields. It is an immense labour to form this and it was singular to see the order and regularity with which the whole was conducted. The vehicles used to convey the soil are rather like the Renney Waggons of our own country - made very strong and capable of holding about 24 cwt. They are brought along three separate railways and when nearly at the end of the embankment the powerful little horses are urged to a gallop, and each is suddenly released from its load - the animal makes the best of its way off the rails and the impetus given to the waggon carries it to the end where it is empited, the end of it having been slid off before taken back again just in time to meet another train bringing earth from the Linslade tunnel. We went on through orchards and barnyards and all kinds of mud and came home too late for dinner. We had a sweet letter from dear Mama this morning, Mrs Reynolds having been with her and Mrs Owen had called upon her; Charlotte is having good weather in Wales and pressing business has called Gabriel from Madeley Wood and Will set off last week to join the party at Barmouth.*

Saturday 10th October - *That all important period at which we came purposely to assist, viz the Quarterly Meeting, is passed without any broken bones in the crush, nor indeed were all the vacated beds occupied - I went in the expectation of novelty and of receiving profit from what I heard - I was very pleased with John Foster's sermon, the clearness with which he spoke of that divine principle in the heart of every man enabling us to distinguish right from wrong and without which it were indeed useless to read the Bible.*

Sunday 18th October - *This week Tilly*[22] *has a bad cold and I have given offence about a shawl of many colours - it has been monthly meeting - Alfred Bassett and Mama Reeve have both had fevers now convalescent, and Louisa has run a needle into her foot - I think such are all the village annals I can pickup. I beg pardon, I should say the incidents of this gas-lighted market town'.*

Sunday 25th October *- Last Monday we went to Woburn Abbey and rambled about the beautiful grounds with Mr Forbes' permission. Grandpapa was not tired which I confess I was. The Statuary is increased - there is a splendid figure of Locke and one of Erskine both by Westmacott. The park looked lovely, the beech trees were changing colour, the red deer too are more abundant than formerly, and the stags with their thick manes and spreading antlers looked like some newly imported wild beasts to me. We heard today from dear a good report of all except for Louisa.*[24]

NOTES

1. The statement that Mr Gaskell had a majority refers to the fact, noted in the Comment for 1836, p.xx) that there had been an elections for Wenlock Council in January of that year. The reason we know this is that it is referred to in correspondence of Edward Edwards who was the surgeon for Coalbrookdale and lived at No. 43 Darby Road, adjacent to The Chesnuts. (SRRC 1987/56; also Thomas E., note re the Edwards Family).
2. This fact is also confirmed by Edward Edwards. His correspondence reveals that his practice was very busy due to a typhus outbreak - 14-15 deaths in the Dale. (SRRC 1987/56; also Thomas E., note re the Edwards Family).
3. This must have been a travelling menagerie.
4. The Beaconites were a controversial group of Quakers in Lancashire, Cumbria and the west of England who published a booklet entitled *The Beacon* in 1835 which proclaimed the Bible as the one and only authority on religion, and so denying the validity of later religious insights or biblical interpretation. Barnard Dickinson was one of the committee of Quakers who visited Lancashire, He reported that "they were not able to produce the desired effect on those more determined to uphold the views propagated in *The Beacon;* at length some 300 Quakers tendered their resignation. These were again visited but to little effect". Evidently, Adelaide had some difficulty understanding what the controversy was all about.
5. See note 2 above.
6. See 1835, note 31 (p.47) Mr Hartshorne, curate of Little Wenlock and his wife, were very popular visitors to the White House, and may very well have had an influence in the decision of members of the family, notably Abraham Darby IV and his wife Matilda, Adelaide's sister to join the Church of England. Certainly there was a growing affinity between the family and the Anglican Church at Little Wenlock.
7. Mary Sturge was Mary Dickinson who married Charles Sturge.
8. Joseph Anstice was possibly the older brother of William Anstice who had inherited the Madeley Wood Company from William Reynolds.
9. See note 4 above.
10. This is possibly an allusion to the building of Brunel's *S.S. Great Britain* in Bristol. In 1839, three years later, the Company produced 800 tons of iron plates for the hull of the famous ship.
11. At this time the Darby family were in difficulty with the Temperance Society. from the earliest days of the Company, (before the time of clean drinking

water) malting for the making of beer had always been part of the business, run separately by individual members of the family. The "Steel House" in Coalbrookdale was part of the original lease granted in 1714, and was converted into a malting house. It was subsequently operated by Abiah Darby (widow of Abraham II) and was currently being operated by the Dickinson family. In December 1835, a few months earlier than this entry in the Journal, members of the Temperance Society had asked Mr Dickinson to give up his malting business. This became a considerable issue but the result was that by November 1836 Mr Chune (presumably the tenant) was given notice not to work the malthouse and the family refused to collect the money owed for malt sold to the workers.

11a. The passing reference to Count Burgstall is of interest. It may offer a clue as to the way in which the Coalbrookdale Works became the leading foundry in Britain for decorative ironwork. See Comment 1836, page 48.

11b. Ann Jones was acknowledged as a minister within the Society of Friends.

12. Mr Wilderspin and Miss Wilderspin were probably retained as teachers in the school which the Darbys ran in Coalbrookdale. The location of the school is still not known.

13. Elizabeth Anstice - her new home at Madeley Wood Hall?

14. Arms used by Francis Darby.

15. Edward Egremont was the vicar of Wroxeter, a parish about 7 miles west of Coalbrookdale, on the road to Atcham and Shrewsbury.

15a. Mr and Mrs Owen of Little Wenlock may have been involved in the parish after the departure of C.H. Hartshorne in 1836 and the induction of George Edmonds as Rector in 1841.

16. The Edwards family lived at No. 43 Darby Road (originally named Rose Hill the name given to it by Sarah Darby who purchased the premises from Daniel Rose, hence the name). Edward Edwards was the surveyor for Coalbrookdale, having inherited the practice on the death of his father-in-law, Benjamin Wright, in 1794 (William Edwards had married Benjamin Wright's daughter Elizabeth). It was therefore a long established medical practice and became even more established when Edward Edwards was joined by his younger brother Benjamin Edwards in the late 1830's.
In 1836 Edward Edwards undertook extensive alterations to the premises when the house assumed its present rather splendid appearance. This explains Adelaide's description of the Edwards family as being "unaffectedly happy in their splendid new room". Fanny Edwards was a younger sister of Edward Edwards.

17. See note 11 above.

18. This was probably a reference to the "atmospheric" railway being planned by Isambard Kingdom Brunel for the Great Western Railway beyond Exeter.

19. This may have been the first visit to the Anstice's new house, Madeley Wood Hall (see illustration). The evening seems to have been a great success, reminiscent of Jane Austen.

19a. John Pritchard was a banker from Broseley on the south side of the River Severn.

20. "My mother bids me bind my hair" - by Joseph Haydn - usually sung by a soprano.

21. See reference in Foreword by Rachel Labouchère (p.x).
22. "Tilly" was Adelaide's pet name for Matilda, her older sister.
23. The Chesnuts was the house below the White House and Deer Park and next to the Meeting House. It was occupied by Lucy Darby (née Burlingham), widow of Edmund Darby, her two sons Abraham IV and Alfred and her two daughters, Deborah and Mary.
24. Uncle Richard Darby, brother of Adelaide's father, Francis Darby, lived at "Rosehill" with his wife Maria, their three sons Richard Sorton, William Henry and Charles Edward, and their daughters Louisa and Caroline and baby Rebecca.
25. Dale House was next door to "Rosehill", and was the home of Barnard and Ann Dickinson and their children.
26. Uncle Tothill lived at Bristol. He was married to Hannah (née Darby). They had three sons and two daughters.
27. Joe Dickinson, the eldest son of Barnard and Ann Dickinson (note 25).

"Sunniside House" (formerly The White House). The photograph was taken in November 1865 from the Deer Park. The small central portion was the home of Rebecca Darby, after the death of her husband, Abraham Darby III in 1789. The east wing (on the right of the photograph) was built by her son, Francis Darby, c1808. The west wing was built by Henry Whitmore, MP (husband of Adelaide Darby) between 1862 and 1865. The property was demolished in 1960.

1837

Comment

The last entry in Adelaide's Journal for 1836 was on 25th October. There are no (surviving) entries for 1837 and the first half of 1838. The next entry of the Journal is on 24th July 1838. When the Journal resumes, Adelaide's lifestyle and attitude seems to have changed. Much seems to have happened in between October 1836 and July 1838. Perhaps one small clue lies in the last entry for October 1836 - "a good report of all, except for Louisa". Louisa was then 22 years old and may have been ill. Edward Edwards mentions in his correspondence that in March 1837 "Richard Darby is in London with his daughter" (not two daughters).

Another, almost more traumatic occurrence, is implied in the first entry for July 1838. It is clear from this that Matilda, Adelaide's older sister, whom Adelaide adored, almost worshipped, had been seriously ill and was then living in a new room at Dale House. One way or another it is evident that some deeply emotional events had occurred.

On a more mundane level, Easter 1837 saw the opening of the new style St. Luke's Church in Ironbridge. The building of this new church was supported by the Madeley Wood Company. It marked the emergence of Ironbridge as a new community.

Another important event in the life of the Darby family and of the community was the building of Marnwood Hall in the extreme south west corner of the parish adjoining the boundary with Buildwas. This was acquired by Reverend John Bartlett who had been appointed incumbent of Buildwas church in 1822. John Bartlett was related by marriage to the Darby family (he was married to a daughter of William Reynolds) and Marnwood became one of the places the family visited from time to time.

1838

Comment

The Journal for 1838 does not resume until 24th July of that year. Adelaide's mother and father (Francis and Hannah Darby) had left for Leighton Buzzard the previous day taking the stage coach, *The Salopian*, which used the toll road from Atcham (Shrewsbury) - Coalbrookdale, stopping conveniently close to Coalbrookdale at Marnwood (see map). The startling disclosure in the first entry however is of the illness of Matilda, Adelaide's older sister, and that she "lives in the rear room on the east side of Dale House".

There are several puzzling features of this statement. Dale House, built by Abraham Darby I in 1717, had always been regarded as the residence of the Manager of the Coalbrookdale Company. Barnard Dickinson moved there in 1810 on the death of Edmund Darby. That was when Edmund's widow, Lucy Darby, and her family moved out to The Chesnuts further up the hill. Barnard Dickinson ceased to be manager in 1831 and should normally have moved out of Dale House. Francis Darby who was of course the most senior working partner was not anxious or prepared to leave the White House. The next most senior working partner was Abraham Darby IV, but he seemed content at first to stay at The Chesnuts. Barnard Dickinson with his family therefore stayed on in Dale House until 1838. The precise date when he vacated the premises is not at present known, It was probably early in 1838 because, while his new home at Eastfield (east of Severn House) was being built during that year he resided in a house made out of the cottages adjoining the stables.

Two other factors then affected the future occupation of Dale House. In 1827, Lucy Darby had purchased some two acres of garden land and orchard at the rear of, and adjoining Dale House, with a substantial house known as Mount Pleasant.[1] At the time Lucy purchased the property, Mount Pleasant was occupied by Robert Barnard (brother of Deborah Darby) but he died in 1830. It is not known who, if anybody, occupied it after 1830, but it is a fair assumption that Lucy Darby regarded it as a future home if her residence at The Chesnuts came to an end. This was a situation which came closer as the relationship between her son Abraham Darby IV and Matilda (Adelaide's sister) materialised, for under the will of Sarah Darby, dated 1821, The Chesnuts belonged to Abraham IV. It follows therefore that on his marriage to Matilda, The Chesnuts would become their marital home.

By 1838 this prospect had become imminent and it was then that Dale House became vacant. The obvious move was for Lucy Darby to move into Dale House instead of Mount Pleasant and this she did in that year.

Again we do not know when that move took place, but was probably early in 1838. The last factor in the situation is a matter of speculation. Adelaide's Journal records that her mother and father had left Coalbrookdale to go to Leighton Buzzard because Hannah Darby's father, John Grant, was not well and had become feeble. Their daughter Matilda needed continuing care and this had become available at Dale house with the highly responsible Lucy Darby in charge, where Matilda would stay until 14th August when she was due to travel to Bath. This could explain Adelaide's statement that "Matilda "lives in the new room on the east side of Dale House".

The description of the "new room" is also a puzzle. (See illustration "The upper part of Coalbrookdale", 1835 by William Westwood, which shows the end front of Dale House). There is no evidence of external structural alteration to Dale house at that date, and there may therefore have been some internal alterations or simply some refurbishment.

Adelaide had her 21st birthday on 11th August 1838. A few days later on 15th August the family went to Bath for two months to enable Matilda to recuperate. Abraham Darby IV visited thrice during that period. he was described by Adelaide as "my worthy brother-in-law elect", so it is fair to assume that Matilda and Abraham were soon to be married. Adelaide's attitude to Abraham was somewhat strange. It amounted to little more than grudging acceptance marked with resentment. One would have expected the situation to be one of great congratulation. After all, Abraham was the most powerful man in the Company, and, assisted by his younger brother Alfred, he had transformed the fortunes of the Company from the ill-managed operation which Barnard Dickinson had left behind him in 1831 to a thriving and profitable business with a considerable future. In the light of subsequent events one is left to wonder whether Adelaide's attitude was motivated by a measure of self-interest or even selfishness.

The trip to Bath was also notable for the arrival on the scene of Adelaide's second affair of the heart in the form of John Dawson, a Quaker lawyer and an acquaintance of the family at Leighton Buzzard. This however was to end in tears in 1839.

Another feature of the trip to bath was the number of occasions on which the family attended religious services at Gloucester Cathedral and Bath Abbey. The family was moving towards an acceptance of the Anglican church.

Tuesday 24th July - *Yesterday Papa and Mama left us to go to Leighton, Grandpapa has not been well and his increasing feebleness makes Mama anxious to see him before she goes with us to Bath where Matilda is ordered before* *the end of summer (if this cold nipping July can be called 'summer') Dearest Tilly walks very little and has been taken into the garden twice - she lives in the new room on the east side of Dale House.*[9] *Bath had no charms for me when we passed through it and had a wheel to mend three years ago. Yesterday I walked down to Marnwood*[10] *before breakfast to meet the "Salopian" by which Papa and Mama went - it was a most lovely morning, so clear, fresh and warm and I brought home a handful of flowers of the cornfield. I long to hear of dear Mama and I miss her - I have been this evening to Mama's garden exterminating the snails that were taking a stroll and watering the roses - how happy one is among flowers.*

Tuesday 8th August *- I have been spending a very pleasant and uneventful evening at Dale House.*[9]

Friday 11th August *- I am really 21 today! As I was reminded by a sweet note from Uncle Tothill*[11] *with my Aunt Sarah Darby's £50 (she left this sum to her nephews and nieces).*[2] *It does seem a great age to arrive at, I would rather have stopped at 18 or 19 - it is strange for me to be with my cousins who are younger than myself. This world is but a passage to a better and my trust is humble and secure that God will assist.*

Wednesday 15th August *- Gloucester. We are only here today but Tilly has borne the journey well. We arrived in very good time at Worcester to dinner and after a great deal of shopping unsuccessfully in search of ribbon for Mama's grey-pigeons-back bonnet, I went with Papa to the exhibition which is closing, but a few pretty pictures were left, a sweet Lucy Ashton and some water colour paintings. Then to Mr Whitings and then to the Cathedral where we saw the monuments by Nolleskins, Chantray, Roubillac, Westmacott. It is a splendid Cathedral and we went to morning service which was most impressive - the chant and responses and the grand tones of the organ - magnificently solemn. We are here the day after the races and the city is dirty and gray in the extreme. The cathdral is undergoing preparation for the musical Festival and did not appear to advantage after Worcester. Outside it is beautiful as we saw the fine tower and west window gilded by the setting sun. Papa and I walked down to the Spa and Wharfe afterwards.*

Thursday 16th August *- Petty France - Badminton - this old seat of the Dukes of Beaufort is about two miles from this clean but ugly village. The park is very extensive, full of elms with innumerable deer. The sporting establishment appears to be an immense scale - the house is old with splendid pictures and carvings etc.*

I was most struck by the fine series of old portraits from John of Gaunt, the founder of the family, downwards and two pictures of the beautiful Duchess of Rutland, one by Reynolds and the other a copy by Smirke (?) from the one afterwards burnt at Belvoir, and above all the most beautiful a full length portraits by Sir T. Laurence of Lord Leveson Gower,[3] *taken when he was*

Ambassador to Russia - a most angelic creature only that Laurence flattered the originals sometimes to desperation. The gardens were beautifully laid out and in them was the fair and solitary inhabitant of the great Castle, the Lady Georgina, the Duke's daughter. I nearly forgot a magnificent cabinet of Florentine Mosaic valued at £100,000 which Mr Beckford[4] was ready to worship. It was given to the third Duke of Beaufort by the Cardinal Albertoni with a white marble sarcophagus of great beauty.

Monday 20th August - Bath - *We came here on Friday and were soon comfortably established on the North Parade, but I do not like Bath. We have engaged a German Master - a most formidable, handsome, good natured old man, and I hope to make some progress in the short time we shall devote to it, but today we have had a treat of no common kind - After infinite trouble Papa obtained a ticket for Mr Beckford's[4] house and while the eccentric professor was taking his morning drive we were permitted to see those beautifully decorated apartments eloquent (in the language of flowers and pictures) of the author of Vathek's[4] taste and genius!*

And there stood we in the private apartment of a man whose strange character has ever been invested with the romantic excitement which eastern magnificence lends to the imagination. There were the flowers he had just placed, the books he had just closed - the pictures, every one beautiful and not one whose place you could wish altered. The vases of gold and gems on ivory; the exquisite bronzes and sculptures placed wherever they added beauty to the general effect without ever giving the idea of a lumber-room (a thing oftener done than those who love knicknackery may think). The crimson hangings and crimson blinds imparting a most un-English glow to the high rooms reflected in the most stupendous mirrors. Yet all was in such perfect keeping, all subdued and beautiful, you could not call it gorgeous, and every harsh outline, every glaring due was softened by the magic of taste's unerring finger. Tomorrow we go to the Tower.[4] I am very unwilling to have the glowing picture spoiled by the recollections of this wizard as we afterwards saw him on our return - simple and uninteresting in appearance - the very reverse of my fancied picture of the gorgeous visionary - the unbelieving genius.

Thursday 30th August - *We have been here two weeks tomorrow and are as happy as possible with plenty to do and with dearest Tilly improving. Papa left us on Tuesday for we do not know how long - knowing nobody here our way of life is very invariable. Mondays and Thursdays I have a music lesson from Mrs Alexander a nice good natured person and I practice on Mrs Hubbard's piano every morning. After breakfast, Mr Eulenstein gives us German lessons. Uncle and Aunt Tothill[11] are coming tomorrow - this will be a treat. We had a call yesterday from Mr T. Reynolds[12] who offered to make himself useful in anyway he could and took us this morning to see the beautiful tessellated pavements on the Roman Villa - discovered in the excavations for the Railroad.[13]*

It is a wonderful discovery and uncovered without any injury to the principal rooms - the largest floor seems to represent Orpheus playing on his Lyre in a circle which may mean the enchanted beasts and bears great resemblance to the signs of the Zodiac. It was hot and very dusty!

Tuesday 4th September - *I am writing at midnight with the most glorious full moon shining in at my uncurtained window and with all the household, but myself, in the land of dreams, and I - curling my hair in visions as vain as ever visited sleep. The Tothills*[11] *arrived and with them Abraham Darby. Abraham Darby wanted the Post Office and I went with him with all the complaisance in the world though I certainly wished him - in Heaven - it was a long way too, a broil over the North Parade bridge and back by the Southgate Street bridge. On our return, Mama was writing and when we sat down she began to tell Abraham Darby the perplexing nature of Papa's chapter of Madeley civility. What can possess my Sister! I was sitting in the obscurity of a white veil, but as I departed to take it off Mama said something about telling Papa and in the midst of an exhortation not to take that course, I threw back the veil and met the great blue eyes of my worthy brother-in-law elect fixed with rather a displeased expression on mine as if they would read my very soul. I had made tea and went to look at the lamps just lighted - after 5 minutes (good tea requires to stand 10) I turned to look at my companions - Tilly, lay on her sofa with a German volume. Mama sat in silence with her work; Abraham Darby sat amongst the tea things with Bentley before him now and then smiling audibly, and that man is to marry my Sister, the lovely, the unparalleled. I grew taller as I looked at him from behind the muslin draperies - there was no intellectual tastes no high intellect that compensated for eccentricity of manner and appearance. Suddenly he rose and I was obliged to laugh off my detected observation of the interesting group, as I crossed the room my cousin kissed me - it was a very brotherly salute but a very illtimed one - I smiled my sweetest and sat down to my tea table duties thinking there was never a more artful minx than myself.*

Thursday 6th September - *Mama has taken me to the Abbey this evening - it was an unlooked for indulgence and a greater satisfaction than I expected. The sermon was excellent and I came home with more serious thoughts than usual, alas how soon to melt away! Abraham Darby was more than commonly at home and therefore expressing my amaze to the most sympathising of mothers, and then I sang all her favourite songs till midnight!*

Sunday 16th September - *Very sweet letter from Grandpa today. Very long walk with Mama and Tom Reynolds.*[12] *By great good fortune the evening meetings are suspended and I can go to Church and hearing Mr Law, a man whose eloquence and deep feeling and simplicity and, to all mortal perception, deep religious experience must surely have sent away his congregation better men and women for the time at least.*

Friday 5th October - *Friday no Saturday morning - Papa came last week a few days after Abraham Darby, and the same house held them tranquilly for three days when the latter was expelled in an outbreak of which I wonder I can write with patience. I will not dwell upon it or I shall get vexed again; suffice it that Abraham Darby departed at 8 o'clock on Saturday night and the despotic head of the house has been in such contrition since. On Tuesday, we went to Bristol to the Exhibition at the Institution which is very fine indeed. The "Plague of Athens" - dreadful death and despair itself - the foreshortening of one of the heads beyond everything I ever saw Nicholo Poussin! Some exquisite Carlo Dolci's, one head of our Saviour with the Crown of Thorns, entranced me 'til I was faint. We called at Mr Reynolds*[12] *and saw only Jane, then to Redlands. Oh, what a host of recollections rose at the sight of all those well known places and when we stopped at Millers and wandered among the glorious Dahlias and the dear rock work, I felt absolutely turned to stone for want of someone to whom to express the weight of recollections. A pleasant dinner at Redlands where Mama and I went with fear and trembling - verily we have all wonderful elasticity of spirit! Found dearest Tilly pretty well. The next day "while the wind set fair" (as Miss Kemble*[5] *would say) we all went to Frenchay and found the natural result of doing without expectation of a fine day we had to go to a Beer shop where the horses rested, which was what we could not do for the place had contained a club-dinner the day before and the tobacco and fermented liquors vied with each other in perfume, so we walked to a pretty little churchyard full of flowers and then on the road for some distance and reached home in wonderfully and able demeanour to find no dinner preparing and the lower rooms let to a Bride and Bridegroom. Yesterday, we went to Prior Park - glorious and magnificent - such a day and such a place. We are reading Fanny Kemble's*[5] *"American Journal" at which Mr Meyler opened wide his fine black eyes when I asked for it unblushingly, and everybody seems to dislike it - there is slander and vulgarity of words not ideas, and very unfeminine language often, but there are exquisite passages, and a degree of originality and simplicity rare and delightful.*

Thursday 18th October - *We have had such a succession of company as I seldom remember and having been left by ourselves to enjoy it, we did so fully. My Uncles, with Dr Tothill*[11] *called while we were shopping and being deeply occupied in among the velvet shawls at Crocker & James, it was not for some time that we heard of their arrival.*

Saturday 20th October - *Cold and wet. Papa is come and we are all in the turmoil of packing. Yesterday when dressing to go out for the last day's shopping Mr Dawson*[6] *called and Mama, having resolved not to be frustrated, left me to amuse him desiring me to follow them and after some conversation about relative tastes regarding houses in town and in country, I went for my bonnet and we went to Hatche's and found Mama. Mr Dawson left me there and went to the Roman pavement being the most indefatigable lion hunter I ever beheld.*

He came to us in the evening and towards half past ten thought of departing with sundry hopes of meeting us, no me, at Leighton soon whereas Mama opened her eyes and when he was gone began to express serious alarm. Now I am coming to the interesting young lady points - does Mr Dawson[6] *mean anything or nothing, or how does he usually behave to young ladies? and above all, what shall I say? Just now it would be a sore trial not to say no! but the time will likely come when the absence of sisterly companionship at home will make the home view gloomy. And though I could never love this good little man as I have often fancied myself loving, yet certainly it might be like a rescue to place myself under the protection of one so very amiable and honourable and whose simplicity and humility has remained undiminished by being looked up to from his boyhood almost, not only by his own family, but by their great circle of connections, I don't like this family, but his better than the Vicar's or than Taff's (Alfred Darby) and I think him more cultivated and agreeable than either.*

Tuesday 24th October - Cheltenham - *Here we are at last established for one comfortable night in the most magnificent of hotels "The Queens" now, clean house. It was a gloomy morning to bid adieu to the dear old aristocratic city of Bath. The inconvenient length of curls that fall to my paper now maybe mixed with grey, and wrinkles deep upon the forehead and oh! what changes deep and sad may have come over this heart before I see Bath again. It was a day without sun or wind or dust in which you go on congratulating yourself that you escape the rain which came down like a deluge tonight. A pleasant day for travelling but not for seeing a fine country, and fine, very very fine it is between Painswick and Cheltenham - the road winds along the side of a hill wooded, then as you descend a little it opens on the sloping side upon the most splendid and extensive view of wood and plain with Gloucester in the mists.*

Wednesday 25th October - Star & Garter - *A bright morning for the gay Montpellier after so much rain as plastered the carrige with mud before it got to Pittville, which is beautiful. Went out to buy glove ties and bought a paper gold and white for the new room. Lord Northwick's house and I think most of the Cheltenham Lions in this past season. Beautiful day and drive to Worcester! Tilly not so well, very tired tonight.*

Sunday 28th October - Coalbrookdale - *Here we are at least in all the felicities of a Sunday here with Alfred Darby and Willie to dinner. I have rejoiced in what few relics of Bath we have with us, but the Dale Company's boats have not yet had the civility to bring our magnitudinous box which contains a silk petticoat I shall want for Friday, and the German books - my screen is like a picture from halls & better times and I work at it with all diligence and delight. I have just finished the lines "Glide on, glide on, my fairy bark!" which I think rather pretty & love dearly because they were written 'con amore' at Cheltenham after midnight.*

Monday 29th October - *A most glorious young moon in the cloudless heavens making Orion's starry belt look dim, a charming fire, an owl hooting and Tilly asleep - what a catalogue of agreeable preparations for a solitary vigil.*

Saturday 3rd November - *Uninterrupted & by the fire, perfectly happy. Last evening was one of intense enjoyment. Mr & Mrs W.R. Anstice with Charlotte and Mr Anstice dined here & Mr Bartlett met them. C. brought her music and Mr W. his voice in the finest state of perfection. They liked my little Piano and gave us a treat indescribable. Verily it is worth while to marry an Anstice, it improves them all so incredibly. Will is beyond measure agreeable and clever and interesting now - and the lady? - why, very pretty & unaffected and perfectly unassuming - and to all appearances perfectly happy, loving & loved, but the maiden gladness gone! - & yet with all so very young looking that you feel tempted to call her Miss Helen. But C's spirits were such as would have thrown most English girls into the shade and very delightful & very lovely she was but yet you feel the striving after effect - as Lady Davenant said of Churchill, there is a spark indeed - but you hear the click of the tinder box. Oh, what work have I cut out for years and every day tries my temper as it flies away leaving me so little time for that mental cultivation which is such hard work for my poor brains & which they so much need. After all it is much more the faculty of finding directly whatever I want in the mental storehouse than the faculty of amassing in which I am deficient.*

Sunday 13th November - *Very bad cold. Papa and Mama gone to Leighton. Miss Turner is at Coalbrookdale and spent last evening with us. Abraham Darby came too. The Chesnuts*[14] *returned on Friday - melancholy accounts Miss Turner gives of Louisa.*[15]

Thursday 23rd November - *"Dear me," said Papa in the plenitude of a well-dined individual's amiability, "what a comfort it is to have butter enough! they have such fine butter at Leighton! and we did all eat so much - upon my word, they know what good living is at L. - Mrs Grant is very particular, tho' sometimes - dear, she's an oddish person! On Sunday we had a hannet of mutton and Mr John Dawson dined there - nice man, too, in his way, I dare say - as Lawyers are - but very formal at first - have you ever seen him?"*
"Just seen him."
"Oh, at Bath, yes - well, he's coming to see me in three weeks, he says & Grandpapa was so very urgent for him to come - and I said I hoped it would be when my wife was at home (I poked in an acquiesence) I shall be glad to see him, I dare say, for he's a clever man, a very sensible man, no doubt. Well, we had a hannet of mutton at the bottom &" - a pause - I remarked upon the excellence of Bedfordshire muttons, but after adding - "& such a dessert as you never saw, I declare Grandmama had 15 dishes" - his thoughts evidently wandered to something else and I never heard what it was that had induced him to begin upon the dinner, I was actually turning faint and red - red as a peony - but long ringlets are quite indispensible with this awkward accomplishment and very

foolish it was, for what occasion had I to take this visit in any way to my own account.... yet I did.

Saturday 7th December - *Mama is come back tonight bringing two agreeable pieces of intelligence - that Mr Dawson is really coming by the 28th and they expect me to go very soon to Leighton, also that they give Mr Dawson intentions at Leighton and two letters from Reeves confirm the same. It has all turned acid and I wish I had time and wit to recount the reasons why. During the two weeks we have been left with Papa all has gone more smoothly than I could even have imagined possible. Our friends were kind in giving us invitations and Miss Turner came sundry times to see us. Well, we went last week to the stupidest Dale party at Uncle Richard Darby's.[11] NB - Alfred Darby was there and deeming it unsuitable to address one word to me. Sunday took us to the Chesnuts[14] where there was noisy laughter enough and obstreperousness that nobody paid any great attention to a rather capricious young lady who chose to be a silent member for that evening. But certain it is that I went cross at having to go and came home cross with the evening. Well, Papa stayed over Wednesday to go with me to Marnwood[10] and I came back so enchanted it cost me a sleepless night, which caused the walk to the Committee next day to knock me up which occasioned a bilious headache the day after. Dear paying for pleasure or rather perhaps for an ill-regulated mind! We met Mr and Mrs Panting who are the most delightful people, good as well as charming - her husband is very handsome and very silent.*

Also was Mr Gwithers[7] and his sister - he is the new Curate for the unvisitable part of Mr Edward's Parish - splendid eyes - and talents it is said and I can believe for he has something of the eccentricity of genius - plays on the piano beautifully and sings as well as his pretty little sister yet Miss Turner described him exactly when she said that he does not move like a gentleman. His sister is very lively when alone with her, but a mouse when the gentlemen returned; she amused me by asking if Mr Frank Harris was a married man. This last and Walter Eyton were all at our party. Mr Frank Harris to my unfeigned amaze was pleased to talk a great deal to me - he led me into dinner over the slowly manifested resolve of Mr Gwithers[7] to do the same - Miss Gwithers was sitting by me and throughout the evening Frank Harris took and made opportunities of marking the unassurable distance between me and the young lady I was talking to.

I did not like this but he highly amused and flattered me and I found in the course of the evening that I must respect two qualities I never suspected that he possessed - his very good abilities and good feelings especially towards the poor in his own neighbourhood. But he did what I thought kinder than all this - he encouraged and made way for me to talk to Mrs Panting, who is a delightful woman upon very intimate terms with him. I found I did enjoy entering into the feelings of that clique for the county and as Mr Harris put on my shawl and led me to the carriage he observed Mr Panting's carriage having just driven off

- "This is like waiting at the Opera, Mr Darby's carriage stops the way!" and as I observed that was a pleasure I had never had, he said how conveniently it might be had now by going up per railroad. I recollected the changes of a settlement in town and recoiled - oh, how my heart clung to Shropshire and a country home! Mr Harris is married - that is well - but otherwise I should have wondered less at his attention to myself or was it to the well-paying Iron trade? My candle is expiring.

Sunday 16th December *- I have been reading the prefaces and first three chapters of Babbage's '9th Bridgewater Treaties'*[8] *- some parts make me angry with the man's self sufficiency and petulance and in others I cannot but respect the depth of his vast reasoning faculties and the might and power of mathematical science. The aim of this first part seems to be to prove that Whewell has given countenance in the Treaties to the opinion that the intense study of mathematical reasoning is unfavourable to religion. Verily Dr Babbage is in some sense a proof of the truth of the position for there is an asperity and conceitedness about his expressions favouring more of the angry man than the humble Christian.*

Undoubtedly, the deductions of highly cultivated human reasoning are wonderful, and very thankful we should be for the possession of powers that should add to our happiness and usefulness, but there is here an exaltation of human reason and human learning with such an absence of that pervading spirit of Christian humility and love which I think very beautifully characterises some of those highly gifted productions that I think Babbage says do not pursue this subject far enough. The book is insidiously written and worded, but I think the temper of it makes it very safe - I mean to finish it for the sake of the soul expending views it opens to silence which my ideas had all the disrespect of ignorance.

Friday 28th December *- The Chesnuts*[14] *and Henry and Hannah came for the evening - Willie played and Papa brought his newly arrived bindings and his gong. Alfred Darby poured the coffee for me, because he could not help it and afterwards talked occasionally for the same reason! I don't know what to make of it! Letter from Mr Dawson,*[6] *he is to be here on Friday - heaven send that I may behave well and as it is most for everybody's happiness. If he has no intentions may there be as now "little to remember and nothing to regret". I am behaving very well to Alfred Darby, but in truth I have little opportunity, in inclination, to do otherwise.*

NOTES

1. S.R.R.O. 1987/17/7-8 and 1987/33/6.
2. Under the terms of the Will of Sarah Darby, dated 27th January 1821, of which William Tothill was an executor, there were a considerable number of pecuniary legacies including £50.00 apiece to Adelaide and her numerous cousins on attaining the age of 21 years.

3. The Leveson Gower family had a Shropshire connection. Granville Leveson Gower, second Earl Gower formed a partnership in 1764 which became the Lilleshall Company, a rival of the Coalbrookdale Company in the development of the East Shropshire Coalfield. Nine generations of the family were chairmen and principal shareholders of the Lilleshall Company through to modern times.
4. William Beckford 1760-1844, author of "Vanthelk", collector of works of art and curios, creator of fantastic decorations. An eccentric. At the end of his life he lived in almost complete seclusion at Fonthill Gifford in Wiltshire. Beckford's Tower remains on the north side of Bath.
5. Kemble, Frances Anne (known as Fanny) 1809-1893. Shakespearean actress.
6. Mr John Dawson, a grocer's son but also a lawyer. A Quaker and a regular visitor to the Grant household at Leighton Buzzard. Despite a very formal nature, he and Adelaide formed an attachment, but this was extinguished very firmly by Adelaide's father, Francis Darby on 5th January 1839. This was an act which Francis deeply regretted afterwards.
7. J. N. A. Gwyther (not Gwithers as in Adelaide's Journal) was vicar of Madeley 1841-59. In 1838 he had been appointed curate. The new church of St. Luke in Ironbridge had been consecrated in 1837 but it was not until 1845 that St. Luke's was assigned a parish comprising Ironbridge, Coalbrookdale and the westernmost parts of the parish of Madeley. Prior to that Mr Gwyther was curate, as Adelaide put it "for the unvisitable part of Mr Edwards Parish".
8. Charles Babbage 1791-1871 known as the Pioneer of the Computer. He was Professor of Mathematics at Trinity College, Cambridge 1823-39. He developed Analytical and Difference engines based on research sponsored by grants from 1823 onwards. These engines are directly relevant to today's electronic computers.

   In addition to being a scientist and mathematician he was a leading social figure, philosopher and militant reformer. In 1814 he married Georgiana, youngest daughter of William Whitmore of Apley. He spent a great deal of time and energy in Shropshire working for the Whitmores in parliamentary election campaigns. There are exhibits relating to him in Dudmaston Hall, Shropshire (National Trust).
9. Dale House was built in 1717 by Abraham Darby I. It was situated close to the Old Furnace and was traditionally the home of the Manager of the Works. In 1838 it was vacated by Barnard Dickinson who had been manager of the Works up until 1831/32. Dale House was then occupied by Lucy Darby (née Burlingham) who had previously purchased two acres of land at the rear of Dale House. (See Comment 1838, p.66).
10. Marnwood was situated off the toll road from Coalbrookdale to Buildwas and was a stopping place for the stagecoach from Shrewsbury. Marnwood was occupied by Rev. Bartlett, the incumbent of Buildwas Church.
11. Uncle Tothill was William Tothill who was married to Hannah, sister of Adelaide's father, Francis.
12. Tom Reynolds was probably one of the five children of William and Hannah Reynolds (see Family Tree of the Darby family).

13. The railroad at Bath was one of the early wooden railways pioneered in this country. It was built in 1731 by Ralph Allen from Combe Down Quarries past Prior Park, Bath.
14. The Chesnuts was situated below The White House and the Deer Park. It had been the home of Lucy Darby and her family. (See Comment 1838, p.66).
15. Louisa was one of the children of Richard and Maria Darby of "Rosehill". She had been a close friend of Adelaide but had become ill in 1836 and was probably suffering her terminal illness.

Francis Darby (1783-1850), above left, was the eldest surviving son of Abraham Darby III (who built the Iron Bridge). In 1808, he married Hannah Grant, above right, of Leighton Buzzard. They lived at The White House, later renamed Sunniside House (see page 64). They had two daughters, Matilda (1809-1902), below left, and Adelaide (1817-99), below right, the author of this journal.

1839

Comment

This was an eventful year for Adelaide. The year started with an explosive end of her second affair of the heart. Mr Dawson, the suitor, was interviewed by Francis Darby and unceremoniously rejected on the grounds of "differences of age and religious sentiment" which Adelaide refers to as a pretext. Perhaps Francis held strong views that his daughter should "do well" in her marriage and could not contemplate her husband being the son of a shopkeeper? The occasion caused a great deal of heartache although it is difficult to comprehend what Adelaide's real feelings were. She expected to be married at an early age because being of a reasonably wealthy family she was considered to be very eligible. By modern standards the whole process of becoming a suitor and then being accepted or rejected seems to have been a rather strange and formal ritual. It certainly did not start with two people falling in love. Romance seems to have been an incidental irrelevance, to the extent that the feelings of the prospective bride seem to have been largely discounted. Adelaide was to experience a number of such rituals.

The prospective marriage of Adelaide's sister Matilda to Abraham Darby IV, unlike Adelaide's own marriage prospects had been following a much smoother course. They had become engaged on Christmas day 1838 and they appeared before the Monthly meeting of the Friends in June 1839, the wedding being fixed for the 8th August following. In preparation for the wedding, Adelaide with her mother and father went shopping in Birmingham and whilst there witnessed the aftermath of the Chartist riots which had taken place a few days previously.

Chartism arose out of the discontent of working people with the result (or rather, the lack of result) of the Reform Act of 1832. People had thought that the passing of the Act would ease their condition, economically as well as politically. In fact, wages became no higher and the cost of living no lower. The working classes remained very badly off. There was much unemployment and a good deal of "sweating" by bad masters in small businesses.

The Charter itself was mainly the work of Feargus O'Connor, a fiery Irish barrister. A petition in favour of the Charter, which contained six main demands, was presented to the House of Commons on 12th July 1839, and the House rejected the motion to go into committee to consider the petition and the Charter. On the 15th July riots broke out in Birmingham, described by the Duke of Wellington as the worst he had ever seen. These events caused a considerable debate within the family. Hannah Dickinson thought it was wrong to fire on the rioters whereas at the other extreme, Francis Darby was in favour of using small shot, although even he demurred from the use of ball cartridges.

All this was in marked contrast to the warm celebrations being prepared in Coalbrookdale for the wedding of Matilda and Abraham Darby IV which took place on 8th August 1839. There was to be a ball in the newly-built warehouse (now the Great Warehouse) with a triumphal arch proclaiming "Prosperity to the House of Darby". In many ways this was a further tribute to the Bridegroom, Abraham IV, for it was thanks to his efforts, and those of his brother Alfred that the Company had been brought to a state of prosperity and was about to experience its best year ever. The financial ability of the Company to build the Severn Warehouse (1834) and the Great Warehouse (1839) was thanks to their management and technical skills. Over nearly 150 years the family had maintained a reputation as fair and benevolent employers. That is not to say they paid their workmen more than the going rate, but although they became moderately wealthy as a family, they first made sure that a proportion of the profits was devoted to the benefit of the community in the form of housing and the provision of schooling - in fact in 1838/39 plans were in hand for the building of a schoolroom and a house for the teacher.

Thanks to Adelaide and her Journal we have a vivid description of the wedding and its subsequent honeymoon which lasted until the beginning of September. To modern eyes, it seems strange that the bride's sister accompanied the bridal couple on their honeymoon, but again, it is thanks to Adelaide's literary skills that we have been left with a graphic description of the Cowes Regatta, and of the Isle of Wight and the Solent before Victoria and Albert built their home at Osborne House.

After her return to Coalbrookdale Adelaide embarked on another affair of the heart, this time with a Mr Joe Bailey, seemingly a cousin through the Leighton Buzzard connection. Inevitably the result was the same.

Friday 4th January - *My mind has been in a whirlwind and I have had to look calm and happy! 'Tis a fortnight since I journalised - a fortnight that has had thoughts, feeelings and shocks crowded into it - enough for a half year, but it is so - the epochs in our existence are not marked only by the lapse of time. The fiat of Destiny said that I was not to go to Leighton - it also said that on Friday (this day week) Mr Dawson was to arrive to dinner at 5. He came - I did not go into the library until I was dressed for dinner and there was something very reassuring in the cool manner of our meeting - that is to say Mr Dawson and I. Friday passed and Papa made arrangements for Mr Dawson's going over to the Horsehay Works next day. We went on very smoothly and I went to bed in much doubt about the necessity of so much feverishness as Mr Dawson's rather over-strained compliments to my music occasioned.*

Saturday 5th January - *Alfred Darby came to take Mr Dawson directly after breakfast. I was summoned to bring my work downstairs for Papa was going out. Mama busy and Mr Dawson just returned. I went with great tribulation, I had just finished my music lesson. They were all in the room, but I was soon left - for the space of half-an-hour - it was a half hour of nothings, but nevertheless I resolved not to make myself similarly useful again. Papa came in after a time and took Mr Dawson for another walk, poor man, he was evidently rather tired or happier where he was.*

Abraham Darby came to tea and then for the first time Mr Dawson was pointedly and particularly attentive to me. He was not careful to avoid observation and in the very openness of his admiration I was flattered and thinking it evident that Papa at least did not object from his careless manner. I bethought myself that if I could get over many things that were displeasing to my taste alone I might be happier with a man of Mr Dawson's refined and generous feelings and great superiority of character than with any of the sundry flirtations that have crossed my way already. On Monday it was my great collecting day and I went to Eastfield[1] after. As I was coming home I saw Papa and Mr Dawson within a dozen yards of me, they did not know me and I went on and they went to Severn House. Hannah and I had missed - I found her at our house - Abraham Darby had breakfasted here and offered to take Mr Dawson over the Works. Tuesday they went to Shrewsbury. When I came down before dinner, Mama was called away and I found myself in a tete-a-tete with Mr Dawson, the very thing I had carefully avoided for some days. I like to keep the conversation in my own hands upon these occasions, but I began, most foolishly, after a silence of a few minutes to ask if he had seen Papa's picture - he had and said "I like it but do not be offended, it is not like your Papa but there is a look that reminded me of you and urged me to have my picture painted so that he could hang it in the Drawing Room in Albemarle Street." I laughed and said something about preferring to paint a picture to sitting for it. Mr Dawson was not to be got away from his present crochet and I, poor goosy, for once did not know what to say, but he persisted in asking me to sit for my portrait to which I replied, "Why you know if Papa ordered me to sit for him I must and to sit again for you think what a plague it would be." Mama came in and I blessed her for it. After breakfast on Wednesday, Papa read a letter from his book binders and Mr Dawson came up to me with some casual observation about a Secretary for my numerous correspondence - then added in his subdued voice "shall you take a walk today, perhaps you would allow me the favour of accompanying you." I observed that it was Meeting day and I must go to represent the family - "After the Meeting then" he said. I smiled and took myself off - it was Monthly Meeting so I stayed longer as I wanted to put off the hour that I saw coming. To make it even longer I walked half way to Eastfield with Hannah and came back thinking if I could make up my mind to like Mr Dawson my chance of happiness with one so amiable was as certain as could be. On the broad walk I met him looking much discomfited so I contrived to convince him I was tired, and by turning resolutely I confined our walk to a small part of the garden. Finding no loophole of escape I patiently waited what was coming and being in rather high spirits contrived to talk and to misunderstand as long as I had a pretext for so doing - at last he went back to his favourite subject of the picture "but if I had the happiness of hoping that the original might even be mine I should care less about a likeness, only you can tell me if I may venture such a hope."

It was a very important question, but I do not know what either of us said further - I do know that I had given no answer when Edward came out to tell me I was wanted. I went down to find the Morning Room full of company - Mr Bartlett was there with two tall nephews, Mr Eric Prideaux and Mr Stradling. Miss Turner had come with Henry to give an account of a slight accident my Uncle had met with that morning from his restive horse, and to excuse their party for this evening; herself and Richard excepted. They soon departed. Miss Turner went upstairs to Matilda and stayed until nearly dinner time.

I remained doubtful that Mr Dawson had had any opportunity of speaking to Papa and as it was my wish to put off his proposal for a few years I considered long how I could manage this. When I went down with Matilda I found Mr Dawson alone with Mama and I certainly saw that his gravity and embarrassment had increased, but I felt awkward myself and sat down with Aristophenes in my hands about which they were talking. Mr Dawson said to me in his softest lowest tone "I will leave that for you if you will scratch out my name." I was struck by the deep melancholy of this voice, but Mama was by and I began to protest that I could read it in no time and that it was very ungallant of him to give away the authoress's own copy with her hand-writing. I read about six pages without knowing a word that was in them and then Miss Turner came. Mr Dawson never spoke to me during the evening, still it never occurred to me as a thing within the verge of possibility that Papa had refused him. When Miss Turner was gone, I was in the hall and Papa seized my hand and said "Why, Ada, are you quite a fool!" and led me into the library to sustain half-an-hour of such animadversion as I had seldom heard, even from himself. I would now allow but that Mr Dawson was a very sensible man and that I was pleased with him, though he is a fright and a grocer's son. Mama was sent for to bring me to reason. Papa protested that I could not like Mr Dawson and it was impossible he would ever give his consent. Mama made matters no better for, to my surprise, I assured Papa that I had not known Mr Dawson long enough to be attached to him, and what he had said ought to be sufficient for any daughter - that he would not give his consent. Difference of age and religious sentiment!!! were accordingly fixed upon as the best pretexts for this most unmanly and despotic refusal. I was told I was to come down to breakfast next morning and to behave with a little spirit. That night I never slept. It was the strangest feeling to be sensible of thoughts, going over every word and look of the last few days, and to be utterly unable to control that current of woe. Tears there were none - I could control them and my eyelids tell tales if they shed. We met probably for the last time, and a glance told that we were both wretched - his last request was that not a word should be mentioned of this unfortunate affair and he hoped I was not offended with him. At half past nine the carriage took him away. I went to the Committee in such a state of mind as it is difficult to describe.

Sunday 6th January*- I went to Madeley Wood*[2] *in a perfectly unexcitable spirit - Dick Anstice*[3] *was there and I would not talk to him. The grand piano was very fine and Will Anstice's 'Freeze, freeze, though bitter sky' brought the first tears that my eyes had known. I liked nobody there, John and Will Anstice and Helen excepted, and I came home to find that during Matilda's tete-a-tete with Abraham she had extracted the fact that Papa had told him what he had promised not to tell - another sleepless night!*

Monday 7th January *- I am a great deal happier today. Time, and a short time too, does wonders, after emotion of any kind nothing seems to restore my mind to its natural state but a few days of quiet ordinary occurrences and a good night. I had a great mind to beg I might never hear Mr Dawson's name again though on the day of his departure a thrill of discomfort was sent to every muscle, I did not express it, so by tacit consent everyone now drops the subject which is a much more agreeable way of getting rid of it. I hope Mr Dawson is as happy today as I am - not free from vexation any more than myself, but after all it was a silly scheme, to think that two people would be happy knowing so little of each other's habits. Yet I am thankful I did not know more of his noble nature, but though much has passed I would fain forget, it is my fervent prayer for his happiness with some amiable woman better suited for him than I. Mama coldly observes that there was a great deal of apparant calculation that I should do honour to his house and look well at head of his table.*

Friday 11th January *- Abraham Darby is just returned from the Great Western Railway contest in London.*[4] *It is decided in favour of Brunell and the Directors - everyone is talking about it and Mr Russell Gurney's speech. Very cold weather has set in at last.*

Tuesday 12th February *- Papa set off suddenly for London, taking Leighton in his way. I was much vexed but had long looked for it and I feel confident that Grandpapa and Grandmama will not let the communications he means to make transpire.*

Wednesday 13th February *- Smythe Owen's hounds drew off at the Wrekin meeting and at about 12 while Mama was gone to Monthly meeting, I was startled from the piano by a barking very near and a "Tally-ho" in the distance - they lost the fox as usual in this very bad hunting country and were very near to coming into the Paddock to search for it. I am not sure if I should resist hunting if temptation came my way. Captain Edmonds rode up amongst the red coats and left a note of invitation for us to dine there the following day - how especially fortunate! No difficulty about refusing! Miss Turner dined with us. Abraham and Mary*[5] *came to tea.*

Friday 15th February - *Very busy dissatisfactory day with my music. The hounds had spoiled one morning and the Committee another. Abraham Darby to tea, ditto Saturday. Sunday Mrs Reynolds came to tea and Abraham Darby - pleasant evening. Today Papa is come home in most happy disposition. Grandpapa and Grandmama very kind and very reasonable. This morning I stole a volume of Dean Swift, amused but on the whole more disgusted.*

Sunday 3rd March - *It was a dark moonless night with thick clouds drifting in masses along the gloomy sky, and now and then, here and there, a star. The mighty oaks bent their leafless tops to the night blast that rushed and howled through the dense obscurity. How darkly the huge heads of the Scotch firs stood out against the eastern horizon lurid for a space with the glare of the furnace fires. I stood and looked out from my window and many and strange thoughts came rushing like the night wind through my brain. All this must pass away! - the very stars of heaven must fall from their places, but I, this mysterious spirit must live for ever in glory or in woe for ever! Oh, strange unfathomable principle of being - the soul will never be dissolved - has it then always existed! How and where has it been embodied or has it rested quiescent - a living spirit - but in the repose of unconsciousness. Memory has no light for another existence - strange power that in its capriciousness conjures up a thousand senses from this earth's past. And will all this be too forgotten? Somebody shut a door, I started - Mama and I had been putting away the clothes - Abraham and Tilly were downstairs. Papa was going down after some question he had had to ask Mama. I had been just five minutes waiting till he had finished.*

Thursday 4th April - *I wish I could sit up all night, but it was Committee and I have had a hard day's work - I believe it is past midnight, but I have broken the tiny spring of my little French watch.*

Thursday 10th April - *This morning Papa went to London by the Railroad*[6] *and later the post brought discouraging news that Grandpapa was ill - Mama is in much anxiety - gentle and kind as ever, dearest Mama. If I am ever a Mother may I be in most things such as she has ever been.*

Sunday 13th April - *This morning a much worse account called Papa and Mama to Leighton leaving little hope that they would be in time to see our dear and venerated relative again. On Monday Grandpapa was well and went to Circuit to choose his cattle for the fair - Tuesday he went out to sell them and became ill, a violent bilious attack with fever. We can only pray that dearest Mama might see him once again in life - by this time she is there, dear kind Grandpapa. Abraham Darby is here and is very kind and gentle now we are in trouble.*

Monday 14th April - *Thank God a better account, though very ill our beloved relative not worse.*

Saturday 1st May - *A letter from dearest Mama with the welcome intelligence that Grandpapa was better. After dinner on Friday Papa began to talk about the pleasure of keeping carriage horses, and then said he meant to go to London about his diamond ring and would set off on Sunday - suddenly he added "You shall go with me! We shall only be away three days and Matilda will do very well - you would like to see poor Grandpapa?" I agreed I would but he was going on to London, whereupon he agreed to leave me at Leighton Station and he had written to Mama before I had well recovered my amaze. I did not like to travel on a Sunday, but it was not right to refuse such a plan and Hannah, dear kind creature, had offered to stay with Matilda. Saturday was such a day of business that I was well nigh exhausted and the next day we set off - I thought it required a little courage to go by STEAM[7] for the first time and to dine with 50 people but sufficient for the moment is the evil thereof and no difficulty occurred. I liked travelling by the Railway excessively and did not complain of the tunnels. At half past five I was at the Leighton Station to meet Mama and Edward Lawford. Papa went on leaving me to wonder at the altered face of the country. Dear Grandpapa not so much altered as I expected. Monday I called upon the Lawfords and saw a good deal of the Reeves - compelled to tell them what Eliza calls "the Dawson affair" - I was vexed and frightened but it was really owing to Mr Dawson's own folly.*

Thursday 27th June - *This is a world of trouble! There are different allotments and widely different spheres of action, but verily all is vanity and vexation of spirit. Yet that was a fine idea of Channings that difficulty is man's element - in truth I can vouch for its being woman's too. Mama has been at Leighton and we have been quiet - they are altering the Library and Papa has plenty to do. We lived out of doors almost entirely and had delectable weather in our literal bower of roses: A great deal of thunder but pleasant air. I am in disgrace at Leighton - Mr Dawson has told them all having added thereunto that he could speak with certainty to the improbability of my ever marrying a Friend if I did not marry him. The consequences are a letter of good advice from my dear Grandmama and a great deal of annoyance from Mama I fear. She saw Mr Dawson at Leighton, rather distant and in her opinion very unlikely to renew his addresses - Grandmama think otherwise. I could not go to Leighton at present with his practice of being there every Sunday, I did not know that Mr Dawson had written to my Papa or that he had answered it - Mr Darby to Mr Dawson he had no objection to waive the objection as to age but there remained others and he begged to hear no more on the subject. Mr Dawson says it was not treating him as a gentleman. Dearest Tilly passes the Wednesday's Monthly Meeting - she will be married in 6 weeks and then I am to go with her.*

Sunday 14th July - *Tilly did pass the Meeting and very well, both said the few words they had to say - but it is a barbarous ceremony,[8] I have no great opinion of any man's humanity who subjects a young and timid woman to such an ordeal and after all such an unsolemn one.*

The Drawing Room is found to be decaying, consequently the sphere of Papa's building and altering labours is vastly increased. The books are all scattered, I have been reading some of Lord Orford's books. Alas! that such a mind should have been so misguided - upon the whole, I should think his work is calculated to do more harm to men than to women, though at first I thought I should never lose the impression of ideas I heartily wished I had never read.

Thursday 18th July - *Yesterday we spent in Birmingham - Papa and Mama and I - shopping. We had no idea of the dreadful state of things there on Monday night. The Chartists ransacked many of the shops in Moore Street and the Bull Ring, setting fire to several.*[9] *I never saw any place look so desolate or more crowded with ill-disposed faces. It was Meeting Day and we found Cadbury's full of plain bonnets. Succeeded to admiration in our purchases and came back well satisfied to be safe with dearest Tilly. Great blame is due to the Magistrates that with a body of the London police, a detachment of the Dragoons and the Rifle Brigade in the town, nothing was done for an hour and a half to check the rioters who dispersed at the first charge of the Cavalry without waiting for the dreadful conclusion, being fired at. The Dickinson's are affronted at not being asked to Matilda's Wedding Breakfast and it is mighty awkward to be asked for an invitation.*[10]

Sunday 21st July - *Everybody is talking of the Birmingham riots*[9] *and it is amusing or at least interesting to hear the various opinions of people on the resistance or non-resistance principle. Hannah and Papa grew quite warm on the subject. It seems the rifles have never fired upon the Chartists though they were on the point of being ordered to do so at Holloway last week when a few of the Cavalry dispersed them like so many sheep. Hannah thought it very wrong to fire - Papa wondered the people did not fire from their houses, adding he would have done so with small shot to maim and keep the fellows quiet for a week or so. Papa agreed that a fusillade would have sent them to their work long ago and a mercy to them I believe in the long run, but he still demurred about ball cartridges.*

Friday 26th July - *I am very sleepy - I have sat up every night this week to read Victor Hugo's "Hunchback of Notre Dame" - a long novel for 11p! but I was very sorry to have read it, it was that sort of intoxicating thing that could not be left unfinished - one feels compelled to follow the dreadful scenes that no mind could picture, but one that has witnessed the last half century in all it's revolutionary horrors.*

Tuesday 30th July - *Dreadfully stormy night - rain ever since St. Swithin's Day - we had a good fire this evening in the middle of summer! Last Saturday they went to pay calls in the rain, on their return, Mama and Tilly were radiant, they had seen the Vicar! Looking much older and more untidy and as far as I could discover much less interesting than of old. He enquired after me and answered all Papa's expression's of disappointment at his long absence with gravity very nearly perfect. Yesterday after my collecting I went down to the Bridge* *with a heap of commissions. I was very late and much tired. Just as I reached home after a long debate as to whether the garden or the lane were best, and a final preference of the latter, I beheld two pretty horses that I did not know - one with a side saddle. I went over the circle of those I knew owe a call when suddenly Mr Edmond's great dog came to me and began to lick my hand. I was appalled, which way should I go in. I thought of the garden door but it was shut. Old Will was holding the horses and he said the door was unlocked when woe I heard the Vicar's voice in the unfinished library but it was too late to turn back. Edward opened the door at my ring and I disappeared upstairs and before I was dressed they were gone.*

Mrs Edmonds and the Captain are at Cheltenham and on their return go to Ireland. I like the Vicar so much and am so much in the way of talking to him that I should never be able to alter - then if he thought he had such encouragement I believe his Irish notions of honour would almost oblige him to propose again.[11]

Friday 2nd August *- I shall be very glad now when the eighth is over and passed. Nobody can imagine how chaotic my thoughts have been for the last few days - I would give anything for an hour or two's hard work - German metaphysics or Latin verbs. Sudden return of the most glorious summer weather. On the 8th there is to be a magnificent present of meat to the men in the Dale, 250 sheep provided; Mr Chune gives an evening party in honour of the occasion and the Dale people have planned a dance in the new warehouse. Three cannons are in readiness. When Papa talked over all these preparations, he came to the conclusion that it was quite right to ask his nephews, did it on the spur of the moment and, of course, was very sorry for it afterwards when the delighted acceptances arrived.*[10]

Thursday 8th August *- This day at last is over. The long-looked for and the anxiously anticipated, is passed so propitiously that we all felt thankful. Need I say that she looked most interesting and lovely the pale fair bride. and in truth it was no common bridal. Few slept this morning after day-break for the thunder of the cannons and the rejoicing music that came on the sunny air as of glorious an August morning as ever dawned. Such a marriage had made the country one wide festival - sheep had been given away - a dinner in the new warehouse decked for a ball in the evening with flowers and bright devices - some of the mottoes we heard were very pretty. The initials of the bride and bridegroom intertwined and underneath "Prosperity to the House of Darby" and a Latin motto of which the sense was "They deserve all we can do and more than all." There was something to me so inexpressibly touching in such proofs of attachment from assembled hundreds all wearing one face of joy and all wishing benefits and blessings for their master and his bride. Such a day was never seen in Coalbrookdale! The sky clouded just as I had gathered the orange flowers and the rain poured at 11 o'clock. We went down in it and found such a crowd as my Uncle Dickinson observed would make work of difficulty for the order* *keepers. The Meeting House was full to overflowing except the reserved seats. We went in, Papa, Mama, Mrs Lucy and Alfred - Abraham and his bride - Joe Dickinson and myself - Richard Sorton Darby; Hannah Darby; Deborah Darby; Hugh Darby Owen.*

The four bridesmaids were delightful. Matilda was dressed to perfection, all white with the loveliest bonnet and the most bewtching scarf, and I am of the opinion that all her 4 bridesmaids appeared to advantage as well as the "dejeuner a la fourchette" which was elegant in the extreme. But so soon came the last goodbye and never did I feel so sorry to leave my own dearest Mama. The sun shone and again it clouded and a little spiteful rain fell fast as we went off through one throng of people from our house to about half way up Lincoln Hill. The cheers of congratulation were deafening and so was the cannon. While banners floated and handkerchiefs waved and roses were thrown into the carriage as it passed under the triumphal arch of bright flowers and here we are at Birmingham at 2 a.m. "New Royal Hotel" No. 27.

Saturday 10th August - *The Dolphins, Southampton - Living so fast as we do in these steam-puffing times it does not do to miss a day - I have scarcely had time to remember this is my birthday and that I am really 22! Can it be? It is but yesterday I was only 17 and thinking it would be dreadful not to be married long before this - and though I see Matilda very happy I am thankful to be at present sufficient unto myself. Yesterday we went by the earliest train to London - Gay, magnificent London! overflowing with associations not one I think I can truly say - agreeable to me. We walked from Osborne's Hotel, Adelphi to St Paul's Churchyard with Mama's spectacles and Matilda would not ride, she was tired of course, but not too tired. The streets and the buildings far surpassed my recollections 11 years ago, and yet I did remember something of them and less did I marvel that its inhabitants soon think there is nothing like their own metropolis. We set out this morning in the most splendid sunshine for the Southampton Railway and had the pleasure for the first time of travelling with a very nice person, an old lady - so very gentle and elegant in manner, at Basingstoke the railway ends so we proceeded quietly on in the carriage. "Take us to the head Inn" said my brother at the next stage and "can we have beds?" said he when we got there! It was odd we did not see the sea at Southampton, but such being the case dinner was ordered and the carriage unpacked and we established ourselves to dress in my little room.*

Suddenly a knock - my sister's maid went "I want to speak to your mistress". "Sir you cannot, I am brushing her hair." "Miss Darby, you're dressed though." "She'll do then!" I went out comb in hand - I am careless on these points. "We've done a pretty thing" said Abraham. "What" said I "have we left the brushes at the Adelphi?". "No" replied he, "but we've stopped short of Southampton - this is Winchester".

How much we laughed and with how much circumlocution we comunicated our mistake to the good people of the Inn I shall not stop to describe, but being there we dined and persuaded Abraham to take us to look at the Cathedral! Just while the horses were getting ready and we spent a delightful hour - I must attempt some memorandum of all the very interesting things it contains. First, the view up the columned arches is very beautiful terminated by a "restored" screen with a beautiful window above it is seen - the organ not being in its usual place - and looking down from the altar through the splendidly carved stalls is very striking since as our interesting guide observed "We are the longest in England".

They have beautiful carving by Gibbon and an Altar piece, the Raising of Lazarus by West, which that great Master considered his chef d'oeuvre. We went through with a clever antiquarian and his son - an interesting and amusing boy educating for the church I should think - they showed us the tombs of William of Wykham; William Rufus; St Swithin; and Bishop Fox who died of fasting in 28 days, he was attempting to follow our Saviour's example of fasting 40 days - they show a wonderful and disgusting sculptured skeleton. Queen Mary and Philip of Spain were married there, we saw the Chapel and the comfortable old velvet chair in which she sat. In boxes above they have the bones of the ancient Saxon Kings. We saw several pretty monumental tablets by Chantry and Westmacott. The old warden seemed to consider the Cathedral part of himself or his property and at 6 o'clock we were quite sorry to hurry awav from so much that would have repaid long examination.

Well pleased with Abraham for his blunder, we now went over the beautiful country between Winchester and Southampton - one continual variation of park scenery with cornfields and then dense plantations of fir trees and dwarf oaks. We descended to the sea and soon were comfortably established at "The Dolphin" and Abraham and I walked down to the pretty beach and pier. It is a beautiful place.

Sunday 11th August - *In the morning we went to Church with the servants, I am always glad to go but I do not like to fall in with charity sermons. This was for an infant school by the Rev'd Mr Fairfax and very good it was.*

Mr Reynolds is here - he has a yacht at Cowes and has been stopping at Southampton for the last month. Walked and wrote to Mama. Abraham is not well and they did not find out that the Quaker Meeting is at 3 till it was over.

Monday 12th August - *Mercy on us all, what a day we have had! Abraham had arranged for us to go to Cowes by steamer, but before breakfast he met Mr Reynolds on the beach and changed his plans. We set sail in a beautiful boat much like a yacht, and after much diverting of plans our course was straight down to the Needles - then round the lovely cliffs with nothing before them but sea and sky - we all began to feel very miserable and were put ashore at Freshwater Bay where we bought curiosities and played with the Newfoundland dogs till Abraham came with provisions which he and the servants found difficulty in* *procuring from the influx of people who had just come - as the boatman observed, to that poor public house and eaten up everything except the lobster shells and cheese rind! In great glee we returned to our dear boat and felt no more qualmishness. We went on to Cowes and arrived at half past 8 and were very glad of mutton chops and tea. We were pronounced good sailors and the trip was 60 miles, and I cannot find words to describe the enjoyment of it!*[12] *We go to Portsmouth tomorrow, though Abraham says if they knew at home they would give him a certificate for a lunatic asylum.*

Tuesday 13th August – Ryde - *This morning we found the sea almost becalmed so Abraham thought it best to take us to Ryde rather than to try to get to Portsmouth, so quite by accident we came to the gay Regatta. The pier was crowded and the little boats decked with flags, oh so beautifully. We steered in amongst them just as the first gun was fired and away the boats went over the glassy water. Matilda was rather tired and we came to the Inn where we had a delightful view of the pier and the sea. Abraham and I went on an unsuccessful hunt for lodgings, came home and found that Benjamin had got them elsewhere. We dined and were tempted by the company and the brightness of the day to the pier again - saw the "Terese" at a distance and Mr Reynolds in her, in his sailor's dress. We found it was extremely dear to find a house, at 8 guineas a week a little cottage was engaged and we came back to find Tilly buying lace in quantities. The most exquisite brass bands were playing all day, the sun shone and so did the dresses. After tea we sat in the open window as the dusk came on and watched a puppet show - fantocini - a sailor dance that I would defy anyone to dance without laughing. Many other absurdities followed and the most magnificent fireworks I ever beheld or dreamed of in fairy tales - Abraham was quite amused at our delight. Everyone disposed to make merry after a Regatta and I have been watching a dance of the sailors from my window.*

Wednesday 14th August - Motville House - *This we all agree has been the pleasantest of all delightful days. After breakfast it was not convenient to go directly to our house so thought we would go to Portsmouth in the steamer and return same way. With speed we equipped ourselves and started for the pier head but not before I said to Tilly that there was a voice in the next room like Mr Dawson's. As we reached the stairs to leave for the pier there were two figures in deep mourning going out, followed by Mr Dawson between two young looking women also in black. They did not see us and Matilda ran back to her husband to take care of her, but I went to the window - it was a French window over the portico with an astonished man cleaning it half open - I sprang through and saw the black party out upon the beach - it was surely, certainly Mr Dawson - what a narrow chance! I went to Tilly and we soon forgot all disagreeables among the gaieties of a great steam packet party. There was the milliner and the milliner's girl - young ladies prettily dressed and older ones talking, a Sir Mulberry Hawk and companion going to the races at Portsmouth.*

We stuck twice in the mud - off we flew at last through the white foam and soon we stood still on the deck amongst an infinity of little wherries, all telling us we could not land without a boat. Abraham chose a sailor for his beauty and, in my opinion, was cheated in consequence.

We asked him to take us down river among the shipping, it was good news and down we went it was half past eleven. We were happy among the waves and close to them for the boat seemed to float like a cockle shell - our fine vessels of war - the wooden walls of England, mostly dismantled and lying useless but in good repair and ready within a fortnight for any service. We hoisted a little sail and we went on past Gosport and the bakehouse where sea biscuits are made by steam - ahead of us was Porchester Castle[13] *used as a prison ship for the French and Abraham asked if we could go nearer. Our sailor offered to take us to see the "Britannia", the finest vessel in service at present, but Abraham had an engagement to be back at Ryde by 3 o'clock. We came back finally but were too late. We tried to see the Britannia, but were told it had been painted and we could not proceed.*

To our great joy then we tried the Victory. No difficulty and up we went without much trouble from the ladder, but oh! to see Tilly climbing into a man o' war. We stood upon the very deck where Nelson fell - on the very spot - in the little room in the cockpit where he breathed his last - oh, there was glory in all around that vessel, she had borne the fire of Trafalgar. The order in which the arms were arranged was extraordinary to me who had never beheld anything like it, and never do I think I had a greater treat. Afterwards we went to look at a strange vessel - a pirate and slaver taken off the coast of Guinea - so wonderfully fast sailing that there was no vessel in Porsmouth could cope with her. She was taken by a little frigate with a truss of hay in her main chains which made the pirates take her for a merchant vessel. The prisoners were a strange crew, darkly discontented. There was the mournful music of a little Spanish guitar under the deck, and a graceful Spanish boy sat cleaning a sabre in the middle. When we think of the affection of sailors for their ships, well might they be discontented at losing her by such an accident. But it was a strange feeling to be in the midst of such wretches. The old sailor who went over with us seemed to feel vast pride in having captured her "on the 14th of April". It was a most interesting day and not the least delightful part of it was the voyage home. We were not splashed, tho' often on the point of it for the little boat went up and down with every wave. We landed on the pier about 5 o'clock, well pleased at the prospect of dinner.

I have failed to make honourable mention of the Royal Yacht - it is very beautiful and interesting from having been used by the Prince Regent. The old Steward spoke of his royal master with all deference but with no shadow of affection.

Thursday 15th August - *A wet day! - we had no plans but to rest today. The Duchess of Cambridge*[14] *came last night at 10 and we walked down to the* *pier but she was not there. No pleasure I verily believe is continuous without some counterbalancing pain. This morning I ran a needle into my ankle thanks to Miss Griffiths and it broke off without my being the least aware of it till after dinner. I turned faint and Matilda fetched Abraham, and he said it was so deep it must be cut out, and I became very much frightened and faint. At last Abraham sent for a surgeon. It was very painful and I behaved very badly. He was very much amused evidently at the trifling nature of it and suggested that it would work its way out in a few days. However, after expressing a great doubt if it was in at all, it took him a quarter of an hour to extract and. then came forth so long -.I was very sorry to give them so much trouble - rather sorry too to be faint to be laughed at. I am better now but must go to bed.*

Friday 16th August - *This morning it was very fine and with a beautiful breeze, we sailed up to Cowes in the Emma Jane for our letters. They had sent them off and we found them safe here on our return - very good account of Mama. We were very much interested in going to the spot where the Royal George is sunk. I never knew the circumstances before; they had laid the vessel on her side as much as possible to do something to the keel after a voyage, kaulking I think it is called - the guns were altogether on that side, the portholes were open and the wind rising suddenly they filled with water - the soldiers rushed down to their guns and the weight became overpowering - the vessel turned over and went down instantly, drawing down those who threw themselves overboard in the whirlpool of her own descent "brave Kempenfell and his 800", - all perished. They are now devising means to blow up the vessel and get to the property by diving,in which Abraham is much interested - it is about 50 years ago, they say. (I think it must be more). We sailed round the Blenheim and the Benbow two frigates of 74 guns lying off Portsmouth. The men were performing their ablutions on deck.*

Sunday 18th August - *Yesterday Abraham was very unwell, and so was Matilda in sympathy, and we did not go out much. I spent the morning shopping, saw the Duchess of Cambridge - Today I have not been to church, for Benjamin brought word that there was so little room that I was afraid to venture. Lovely day - we penetrated along the beach beyond Appley House.*[15]

Monday 19th August - *Nothing particular today. Abraham and Matilda not well yet, but we had another charming walk on the beach after tea.*

Tuesday 20th August - *This morning early we were on the pier and embarked on the beautiful steamer going round the Island with a very numerous party. As far as Freshwater Bay, of starved and qualmish memory, nothing was new to us. It was a most beautiful morning and Black Gang Chine*[16] *looked very fine from the waters. Then follows the lovely shore of the Under Cliff studded with sweet cottages and villas that seemed sleeping in the sunshine on their mossy beds. The coast was beautiful all the way back to Ryde but just as we came to the harbour lights a gale of wind and rain came on as it were in the very path of sunshine.*

The steamer presented a very usual assemblage, I suppose, of odd people. A bridal party, like ourselves - a bride and a cross old maidish sister, and a happy-looking inattentive husband - all very fat and short people - a very magnificent lady and her retired tradesman of a husband, she had been very handsome and was very graceful despite airs. A little odd man with two younger ones under his care one tall and much like Barnard and handsome, all that one could see of him among curls and a straw hat attached by a string to a coat button - he submitted magnanimously to the monkeyish diversions of his companion.

An elderly gentleman and two rather elegant daughters who put the straw hat aforesaid grievously out of countenance by a casual query about Black Gang Chine. A fair bride who was ill all the time and her very attentive and most beautiful husband. He had the most splendid eyes and eyelashes that mortal may hope to see. Some old ladies from Wicklow and a family of worthy shop-keepers I imagine and their hideous eldest hope. A great black dog who was amiable to everybody with sandwiches, and numerous other less agreeable neighbours - too numerous to mention. None of us were quite ill, I did not feel the least, but several on board were. I enjoyed it comme ca.

Wednesday 21st August - *Another walk on the pier this morning, we were to have gone to Carisbrooke today but the Duke and Duchess had taken all the horses. It was very amusing to see so many that we had parted from - pale and untidy yesterday, very bright and splendid this morning. It is rather difficult to know how to take a part half-smile of recognition when you cannot be quite sure if the smile is a shopman or the son of a peer. Abraham arranged that we were to dine early and then take a sail; and a very delightful one it was - in the "Water Witch", one of the pretty Ryde yachts. The boatman was very intelligent and very proud of his little boat, he won the prize last year and told us very many tales of boat racing. "Lord Belfast," he said, "used to live very much at Ryde, and was fond of the water from a baby. They were boys together and used to go out in little vessels of his lordships own contriving, which generally ended in a "douse" for both of them. Lord Belfast's yachts are still the fastest vessels that can be, he says, but their extravagant owner has run through all his property. We went to the place where the Royal George sank and saw all the preparations of old hulks full of gunpowder to blow her up. Our boatman's father was in an Indian vessel not far from her when she went down, so rapidly that although they crowded all sail they could not save one man. She sucked down two small vessels with the whirlpool of her descent. It was 58 years ago the day before yesterday. The Benbow is to sail tomorrow. Oh, it was melancholy to see the noble frigate for after all there is something noble in a ship of war with all her well arranged powers of destruction and to think how many brave hearts that now throbbed with the woe of leaving those they loved, might never beat again under the cliffs of their own merry lands. She is supposed to be going out for the suppression of the Portugese slave trade and the pirate of these vessels, "a wicked looking thing that Spanish slaver in harbour, Sir" - There flew the little blue* *flags the signal of departure and great battle there appeared on board the Benbow - and the evening sun and evening gale were on the frigate and on the boats full of the sorrowful countenances that went for a last farewell. It was very touching to hear those mourning, mothers trying to quiet the sobbing infants of our British soldiers. A Merchant brig sailed out of port before us with Danish colours - she was going home.*

We were to go to Portsmouth tomorrow Thursday August 22nd. Coalbrookdale two weeks today, weeks how full of thoughts and the dance of new ideas. It was a very cloudy morning when at 8 o'clock Matilda came into my room and found me asleep! A gleam of sunshine convinced us we might venture to our boat after breakfast and away we flew from the pier on the most foamy waves Matilda and I had ever encountered. Very lovely everything looks. We danced over the waves and I gained great credit by sketching "the Commodore" (Lord Yarborough's yacht)[17] standing up in our little "Water Witch" as she jumped about with an occasional splash for her freight. The yacht gained additional interest before we returned and I was very much rejoiced at my sketch. All the Cowes yachts were collected and every boat in Hyde went out this bright morning, for it was said the Royal George was to be blown up but in this we were all disappointed.

First then we landed at Portsmouth on the floating bridge, a sort of succession of rafts which sink with your weight to the level of the water. - but we are past being frightened at the prospect of a "douse" now. We went straight to the docks and a large party were soon collected - not particularly intelligent. The docks cover 120 acres - we saw all the processes of turning and cutting and boring for all the vast quantities of blocks and pulleys and paraphernalia used in ships. All done by the steam engine for the complicated machinery. I did not take very great pains to understand it for it would be of little use to me but I did take great trouble to gain some general idea of the management of vessels and the uses of their different parts and by an increased facility in sketching them I can estimate the amount of my <u>new ideas</u>. We were a long while amongst sawdust and hulk prisoners and hot iron and machinery, but it gave one great respect for the English Navy and great confidence in our vast resources - by the way, Matilda and Abraham do not half enjoy the patriotic enthusiasm that I feel continually for they seem haunted by the horrible in War, and by wonder that such things can be. And it is quite right, I know, to feel so, - but yet, how is it possible to help that thrill of joy that tells even a woman's heart that her hand could plant her country's Standard amid fire and smoke, if it were for that country's glory. We went over the Victoria - a beautiful vessel of 110 six-pounders, unfinished. I threw a piece of wood off the highest deck into the water and it was made diminished to a <u>splashing speck</u>. We were in our boat again, and among the gay party of yachts and skiffs, - dancing about on a more flowing sea than ever. The Duke of Cambridge[14] left the Pique frigate just as we came out of the harbour and the royal salute began firing. We were close to Lord Yarborough's yacht[17] *by the time His Royal Highness came up in the Pique's longboat. We went on board with several officers - we saw him shake hands with Lord Y*[17] *and directly the little canons of the yacht went forth their volleys of smoke and tiny thunder. The Yards were manned in the Pique and three other vessels - a very pretty and indescribable sight.*

They all fired the salute and were very close to the Blenheim - they had music on board - coming beautifully over the water and its warlike melody gushing by fits as the wind passed by. When we came to the Benbow just getting under weigh - we were so near that every order was audible from the clear strong voice of the first Lieutenant. "Every one upon deck" and the little boats were deserted and fell back with only the man at the helm. Then the shrill whistle that sent all the men up the ropes and then the lowering of the enormous sails. There she stood, oh, how beautiful, like a gigantic bird just spreading her wings on the pathless ocean. Last of all came the anchors, wet and clay-ey from the water and with the spirited stirring voice of music on her decks the fair frigate sailed as the English colours were raised to her mast heads. An officer leaned over and waved his hat to a lady in one of the Yachts whose handkerchief answered his as long as we remained in sight. Was there one heart in all that crowd that did not give good wishes to the noble vessel? Many a prayer followed her and, I fear me, - many a tear. We watched her during the evening just as it was getting dark, the dusky sails were just visible over the trees.

Dearest Tilly was quite knocked up after it all - but I hope she is pretty well again tonight. When we came back to the pier it was studded with banners and gay as when we first saw it. We met the Duchess's party full - she is not handsome exactly but agreeable and very condescending in manner. Abraham and I have been walking a long way since dinner but it was too dusk for me to see well. The fireworks at Portsmouth have been beautiful. The night very dark and the wind quite lulled after being so "fresh" all day.

Friday 23rd August - *We have been in our boat to Shanklin Chine and very lovely it is. Matilda and Abraham have been planning for the rest of their journey, and the thought that by this time two weeks I shall be really not with dearest Tilly has been almost overwhelming. I am melancholy too beyond the power of telling at the thought of leaving Ryde for I am attached to fifty things that have become rapidly familiar, but more than all to these,blue, blue waves, that sunny foam. Shanklin is beautiful, and we had the loveliest of days. It is a sort of break in the vast rocks of mouldering sandstone which forms a natural glen or dingle at the head of which falls a perpendicular waterfall from a great height - the brook wanders on thro' the trees till it comes to the sea, so wide extending and so blue! God has made this earth almost a Paradise if man would but enjoy it and let it be enjoyed. We came home watching the last traces of the Benbow as she again spread her sails and went down the channel. I went down to the* *beach again before breakfast this morning and when I saw her again with all her sails furled I felt as if it were a friend at a distance.*

The sunset was such a one as I never beheld elsewhere, - except in Claude's magnificent embarking of Cleopatra on the Cydmes - oh! it was magnificently indescribable. The moon was full and no cloud near her as her light became gradually visible when the golden flood of light upon the rippling waters melted away.

Saturday 24th August - *This morning being one of our last, oh! sorrow of sorrows was to be spent partly in shopping. After sundry purchases, I went down to the pier and sat down in the first covered seat to sketch the Castle. It was rather gay (tho' so early) and I was quite alone but not at all frightened. I had plenty of time for my sketch and then Abraham and Matilda came and we went home soon after, leaving him at the Reading Rooms. In the evening we had a sail to Spithead - very charming. Dearest Tilly was quite tired and overdone and I was very uncomfortable for her.*

Sunday 25th August - *I have been to church today to my very great comfort, how often do I let these opportunities pass which are always as it seems to me of such benefit for want of a little determination. I was very melancholy when I thought how long it might be before I could go again. How beautiful are the prayers of the English church! and the sermon that followed was worthy of them, so dear and so homecoming - from the text "It is good for me to have been afflicted", &c. I felt that a great deal of it might have been for my own peculiar experience and at the same time that there was not one heart that could not remember afflictions mercifully sent but not valued as they might have been. The chanting of the children (orphans of sailors) was most beautiful. The Te Deum Laudamus is exquisitely solemn - so accompanied. In the evening walk to the beach Dearest Tilly better but still suffering occasional pain.*

Monday 26th August - *We have been in a delightful open carriage to Carisbrooke over a most splendid country, rich in woods and cornfields. Carisbrooke*[18] *is a lovely ruin crowded with company not particularly in accordance. As I mounted to the keep by an almost inaccessible path, it abounds with sweet peeps and corners for sketching, but we had not a great deal of time as all our packing had to be done. After tea I went forth alone to buy Tilly a parasol and to get her some change in which process I had some laughable adventures.*

Tuesday 27th August - The George - *On as bright a cloudless morning as ever shone on a bright spot of earth, we left dear, dear Ryde in Saunder's pretty boat which he is trying to have as his own. It was the most foamy sea we have ever encountered and we were a good deal splashed in our enjoyment. First of all then we went to the biscuit baking - oh, the wonderful magnitude of everything in these great places. "Are the ladies of the British Empire, Sir?" asked the sentinel. The password "Yes" seemed all required, and after waiting for more visitors a most important Jack in Office came to take down the name, calling* *and abode of every gentleman. "Three ladies with your Sir? Be particular as to the quantity, please. Now you may go - all I have to tell you, is this. Do you touch nothing and not give nothing to nobody." The first room contained casks of salted pork and beef. It was one of a series 101 yards long and quite filled with provisions. All is done by steam engine. The flour is kneaded and rolled and the biscuits marked and cut all by machinery of no very complicated description.*

Having express orders to the contrary they gave each of us a piece of biscuit very hard it was, like bread - all crust; we concealed it and in like manner our intelligent guide expressed himself extremely obliged for Abraham's remembrance of him. We walked back to the boat. They were firing at a mark from a hulk near the docks and we were in time to see the balls dancing and flashing along the water. Then there was the band of music and the launch of the new steam frigate very interesting. She was crowded with ladies. The masts were put in and we saw the whole. We sailed on to the rafts where we landed, really sorry to part with Saunders when he came to bid us goodbye. He told us that on Saturday they fired 48 pounds of powder as an experiment upon the Royal George and the explosion shook all the little boats so that if their original plan had succeeded, many must have been upset. Providentially, the water had got into a pipe leading to the great quantity, a ton I believe, and therefore the scheme failed, and will fail for the present, as this week the tides run too high for the divers. We ordered dinner and left Tilly on the sofa. A. took me to the ramparts which interested me excessively as I was in a degree of ignorance I often find most inconvenient. I shall know now that a ridout and a bastion mean only detached or projecting portions of the offensive or defensive ramparts. We saw the soldiers on parade and heard the splendid band and saw all the beauty and fashion of Portsmouth. Came back to dinner at 4 and took Tilly a walk after. We are just opposite the Lieutenant Governor's house where they have had a party this evening a great deal of beautiful music.

Wednesday 28th August - Brighton, Albion Hotel - *We left Portsmouth this morning soon after breakfast and saw the last glimpse of the Isle of Wight in the distance - shall I ever see dear Ryde again? We admired the beautiful country after we had passed Havant excessively. Rather hilly and beautifully wooded very delightful altogether. At Arundel we stopped to see the beautiful Castle of which we have not heard much and I had no expectation of being so much gratified. It is old Saxon architecture of the time of King Alfred and more striking on entering than any Castle I had seen. The ruins of the old Keep, etc are excessively picturesque, and the views are beautiful from all windows.*

The Baron's Hall contains the most beautiful stained glass I almost ever beheld. The great window represents King John signing the Magna Carta and the smaller ones are by Eggington & portraits of the Howard family. The library is beautiful. The bookcases round it are of mahogany in the most magnificent Gothic. The pictures in the great drawing room are very old portraits, except the present Earl of Surrey by Hayter. The Fair Geraldine's Early Surrey disappoints me, tho' the face was very intellectual. Abraham and I went up to the top of the Keep where there is a very magnificent collection of owls from Hudson's Bay - the view splendid. Worthing seems a very pretty place with beautiful open sea and a delightful beach. From thence to Brighton the road lay for the most part along the coast and the sea sparkled beautifully. Notwithstanding the abundant accessories of dust, sun and wind, we enjoyed it exceedingly and came to this very gay, very magnificent place in good humour with everything. We walked about and are now as comfortable as possible in this most splendid hotel. My little room overlooks the beach and the waves are dashing in with a noise and magnificence I could never have imagined at Ryde. I am really sorry to go to bed, for the moon is very bright on earth and ocean.

Thursday 29th August - Brighton - *A wet day, the first that has clouded our projects for some time. We walked on the splendid pier and the very uncomfortable beach for some time - malgre tout! Afterwards we took a drive on the cliffs.*

Brighton seems a very gay, very magnificent place, full of racket and carriages on a fine day - I should not like it. The only pleasure in these places seems to me to consist in dashing about and knowing everybody, and I do not think this is much to be coveted. I shall be glad to go on tomorrow.

Wednesday 4th September - Coalbrookdale - *What a throng and whirl of conflicting thoughts and of sorrowing emotions. My own little room all in the silence, and such silence.*

Oh, God! the heart thou hast given to man needeth deep and perpetual schooling! My dearest Tilly! this night so often pictured is even come but I little thought of the stunned feeling that would come with it, little of the pent-up thoughts that have but this narrow space - to be poured forth in. I will try to arrange my chaos of ideas by going over all that we have done since I journalised at Brighton.

Friday we left Brighton for London and Abraham took us to the Green Dragon - very bustling and very dirty, very disagreeable. On Saturday we started as soon as we could for Leighton - they had a note saying we should be with them by the 11 o'clock train. When we were about half way to Euston Square the Great boxes were left behind - the servants had been sent on the night before and Abraham's wits were not used to such contriving. He would not go back - first we were to be sent to Leighton without him. Then to wait at the new hotel in Euston Square. We went there - it was not yet opened and the rain fell in torrents. Abraham took us back again. Oh, the beauty of a quick decision. Back to the Green Dragon. We went, and Matilda was dreadfully tired. We went at last by a later train and were at Leighton by 5.

Grandpapa had been quite upset by our non-appearance and by the bells ringing! Sunday he was better, and to Monday. The Reeves called and Mrs Lawford and Catherine. Tuesday, market-day, and we three were sent in to the "best parlour". Matilda and I busy drawing on some little card racks for Grandmama. The door opened and Mr Bailey[19] *was announced. I thought Mr B never made such a quiet entre.*

Saturday 7th September - *I have been very busy since I came home. First, there was all my music departed and I was very anxious to practice it up again. Good temper returned the day following, and I am now very proud, or thankful I ought to be, that I have been able to take such firm resolutions against all* ***fretting****, that tho' dearest Tilly's presence has been bitterly missed, I have very much succeeded in banishing all selfish regrets.*

Tuesday night, 10th September - *I am too sleepy to write much but my mind is full of thoughts and I would give worlds for somebody to tell them to. For the first time I begin to realise what I once heard Sophy*[20] *say - that it has made her quite ill having no-one to tell her feelings to. Yet I am very happy in the belief that dearest Tilly will be very happy in her pretty new home.*

Thursday 12th September - *I ought to be happy! Papa and Mama very kind to me dearest Tilly so near to us - plenty of agreeable occupations and no need to trouble myself about any of them more than I please - the rudest health that can well be imagined - such as it is worth while to have purchased at the expense of complexion.*

Sunday 15th September - *What an interest dwells with that which we have seen. The Pique sailed from Portsmouth on Friday with the Hon. Mrs Paulett Thompson for Canada. We have had a little party today to meet Abraham and Matilda only Mr and Mrs Anstice,*[3] *Mr Webb*[21] *and Joe Dickinson.*[22] *Rather pleasant comme ca have not seen things quite so couleur de rose today - the first thing this morning when Mama came into my room - "My dear," she said, "Papa has had a letter from Shenley - Joe Bailey*[19] *is coming the 30th of this month, Monday." "Is he coming on purpose?" "No coming to Ludlow, I believe, but - you know we have not a bedroom, therefore I say he might be put off, but no! he's a favourite of Papa's, and he is to come and go to Abraham Darby's."*

I went down with a very uneasy mind. Now what on earth am I to say? Papa suspects nothing and I must not let my wise cousin propose to him if I can help it. I must contrive some convenient little opportunity - and yet it is almost impossible when you know just what people are aiming at to help mystifying them which I know one may do till some kind interrupter comes to the rescue. But upon the whole a more turmoiling business never befell me; and partly I believe because I know I have been very foolish. But it is really very unreasonable to expect young ladies to stop to consider whether their minds are made up to marry or not to marry every agreeable young man who may choose to be flirted with. I wish nevertheless that this were the only scrape I had flirted myself into or rather that of all others I had behaved better in this. And yet he has become such an anticipated part of a visit to Leighton that I should miss him there grievously. Mr Joe Bailey is acting under the very probable mistake that I shall have a large fortune - unhappily, nothing here will undeceive him. He is as little fitted as I am to live upon nothing, and nothing in my humble opinion can he have. Mr Bailey has good estates, but them I know, no matter how, that they are mortgaged heavily, and I do not believe he can give his son anything. I have no notions myself of living upon these unsubstantiables of life - love and good expectations - and I am sure it would be most melancholy to see that giddy boy compelled to lay aside his bachelor gladness of heart in the vain endeavour to dash in good society.

Sunday 22nd September *- Most glorious moonlight night! They have sent us Major Mitchell's Expeditions in Australia. Did not know the Aborigines were so dangerous. Mr Cunningham, who accompanied the first Expedition into the interior, was murdered by them. The geology of the island very curious but not much explored. Tomorrow we are going to Market Drayton to see Mr Bainbridge's collection of carved lumber. Verily, the more I think about it the more am I ignorant which way to turn or twist myself out of this scrape with my Cousin. I really did encourage him to pay this visit most foolishly, most thoughtlessly for something to say, as one might have talked to a girl of one's own age.*[19] *If I could help it he should not propose at all, but if he persists in stopping until this is accomplished, I shall wish it had been done at first. Monday was the grand collecting day, and after I found Matilda at our house - walked down with her and found Mr Joe Bailey had arrived. In a moment the idea of what Papa might say came into my head. I had just time to make my escape from the garden gate and give Matilda the trouble of another walk up the hill, which was a source of great compunction. When we met some hours afterwards, Papa's eyes opened rather wide that he knew me so well, and I felt that smile of extreme happiness boded me no good. I do not know that I ever suffered more than that day between the real pleasure that it affords every woman to feel that she is the all absorbing idea in the mind of one by no means disagreeable to her - and the pain of showing that this ought to be discouraged and the absolute fright as to what Papa might make of it all, as he was evidently annoyed and surprised in no small degree. Joe Dickinson*[21] *called in the evening - what he made of all the nonsense he heard I cannot tell! By the next day, Mama informed me that I had put Mr Joe Bailey quite in his place and I had some compliments on my discretion. Still he seemed fully aware of the value of time and but for Papa I should have had some difficulty in avoiding an explanation. Very cross indeed Papa was, and he and Mr Joe Bailey took a long walk. In the evening, we went to Matilda's. I contrived to have but little to do with Mr Bailey till after tea when he brought a book round to my side of the table. It was a great stroke of policy, that - I really wished then to set his mind at rest by an explanation, and I knew there would be no other opportunity. I feared many things - him speaking to Papa - or his stopping after our return from Liverpool. So I made it*

apparent to everybody that I rather wished to avoid his attention by going as far as possible and at the same time it was quite needful that I should sit near the candles and rather away from everybody else. I thought I had made a screen of myself between him and Papa but he chose to lean over the table that he might see me and I was frustrated. There was a good deal of nonsense over the poetical effusions in that silly book and at times we both joined in the conversations going on. Abraham put on his Scotch plaid and so did Tilly, and when the buzz became general Mr Bailey said "Mr Darby told me something this morning that surprised me."
"What was it?"
"Something that surprised me very much indeed."
"But what surprised you?"
"Oh, but I dare not tell."
"Oh, but I choose to know."
"I think I said I would not as Mr Darby would be very angry."
"He would never know, you know."
"Oh but indeed, I shall not tell you."
"Oh, but you know you will if I choose you should."
"Why, I believe you are right there."
There was a pause and I got up to look at an ottoman, and in time went back taking care to look as if it were very annoying that the candles were on that table so that I could see nowhere else for my embroidery. I had guessed what Papa had told him and I wished to bid him say nothing about it, so I said with much simplicity -

"But what did Papa tell you?"
"Oh, I dare not tell you."
"Why did you begin then?" - with a smile and very angry eyes.
"I don't know, I'm sure, will you promise not to tell anybody."
"Perhaps I may not."
"Oh, you must promise without perhaps."
"But I don't know what it is, and I may have some great temptation to tell it."
"Well, I'll tell you tomorrow."
"You will tell me now."
"Tomorrow!"
"Tell me now - you see what it is to excite a lady's curiosity."
"Yes, I've known that before, often."
"Then tell me."
"But I may be heard."
"Oh, no, you will not - wait till these are all talking, nobody will attend to you" (I gave the advice very unwittingly and Mr Bailey set them all talking again about something as foreign as possible from what he had to say).
"It was something about you!"
"Why, what business had Papa to tell you anything about me!"

"Aye, there you fly away, I'll not tell you another word - what business had Mr Dawson to tell me anything about you - you will fly - fly into a pretty little passion I'll be quiet."
A pause - when the buzz rose again, I said -
"Go on!"
"You will be angry!"
"Oh, not, I shall not! I am as cool and calm. Now tell me, they are all talking."
"It was about you and Mr .... Mr .... I can't go on, I shall never find words to express myself."
"You do seem likely to be a year about it."

He laughed, and added without much hesitation -
"About you and Mr Dawson[23] *- do you understand. If you do, don't be angry."*
"I understand perfectly" - there was an awful pause, and I began to think that a general conversation would never revive - it did, however, and then I said blushing, I know, but very low and impressively - "will you promise that you will never tell this?"
"Indeed, I never will tell if you wish it - you are very good-tempered, but I was very much surprised, why if I had been your brother, I'd have hung the man!"

I endeavoured to explain to him that my honourable feelings were implicated in its not being known as Mr Dawson had begged I will not tell it - as if I was going to publish the great honour he had done me, which served to rekindle.

They all began to talk and for the first time I saw that Papa's eyes were rivetted with no amiable expression on me and my cousin. All my presence of mind fled, but it returned by the time Abraham had done speaking -
"Abraham" said I gaily, "the same man, was it not, that said to Matilda and I 'young ladies, your father's waiting for you'." The room was in a roar of laughter and in that roar I recovered strength.
"Why, Ada, how young and blooming you must have looked," a tacit compliment to himself as my father.
"Come Ada" said my father "we must go."

Mr Bailey had exalted my bonnet and shawl on the leaf table where nobody but himself could reach them. He came and gave them to me as Mama went upstairs - he caught my hand as I was disengaging my boa and pressed it to his heart. Entranced and feverish I fled upstairs and saw that, tho' amused, Mama and Matilda had no notion of the truth.
"I'll walk up with you, Mr Darby, if you'll allow."
"No, Mr Bailey, we'll not take you up again tonight" - stiff and cross as Papa's crossest look can be - as that under which my heart sank. Not a word was said. In the silence of my own room it was very difficult to collect my thoughts I felt that I was loved as I had never been before - the memory of Mr Horne's[20] *attention stood out in cold contrast. I had never known what it is to be the only object*

in the thoughts - never seen a lover appear so wholly to forget himself (even in his most selfish capacity - that of urging his own feelings when it is pain to a timid girl to answer) to lose thoughts of himself in that one image of her he loves. I did not love him in return quite but I never knew so vividly that my heart was indeed unseared by earlier love. I do not love Mr Bailey but I was miles further from ever loving Mr Horne. When I thought of the power I should have for good over his mind - by no means strong(?) oh, it was very miserable. Should have liked to cry thro' all that long sleepless night - but no - I had neither headache nor red eyelids the next morning - nothing but a hand that trembled as it had never done before.

Mr Bailey met me very joyously - I him very awkwardly, I believe. Breakfast was over. I could not summon courage to go into the morning room and run the chances of a tete a tete. It was monthly meeting (a fatality is over that day for me) - so wet that they could not go out. Mama and I went to Meeting and I went to M afterwards. I told her a great deal but not the scene, I was quite faint with overflow of thought. When I went in at last, Papa and Mama were both there. Mr Bailey brought a cargo of my songs and sat down by my embroidery frame.

He asked me if I sang that of Mr Rulenstein's "are all my hopes then gone for ever?" I went on with my work a good deal confounded.

"Ada" said Papa "attend to this."
He was reading the marriages - "Robert Byton to Miss Watts"
"Aye, and very proper to think of his brother going to marry a printer's daughter one of the oldest families in the country that I should have been proud to be connected with, Ada.

"So have I often heard you say." It was the climax of misery. We all went to dress. I was ready before Papa and Mama had half accomplished their toilettes. Who could scold me if I went down, it was what I ought to do? Mr Bailey came in a few minutes.
"I thought you would never come home this morning - have you thought of what I said to you last night?"

I told him I had been taken by surprise (an abominable falsehood spoken mechanically) - that he would never succeed with Papa. He was sure he should if I would only give him leave to try, what objection could I have? (Oh, the arrogance of the man!) I had objections of my own, I told him - it was quite my duty to stay with Mama at present, she had but just lost Matilda. Oh that was all nonsense, I was sure to marry somebody, and he would not take me away yet. Then there was Grandpapa, he would never forgive me for leaving these good Quakers.
"Well, but that's nothing, the good old man can't live for ever, you know."
"But you know it is quite true."

And all that encouraged him! I never said a word about it in my accounts thereof. He begged me to let him speak to Papa so passionately that I was almost frightened, but I was firm - he was kneeling - you must, indeed you must, give me leave. "I cannot, indeed you must not." He flung himself back in his chair as he exclaimed, but more calmly and resolutely, "At least I must ask Mr Darby when I may come again! If you will not give me your permission I must do it without - if I do not know before I go whether I ever may see you again, I shall go distracted."
Enter Papa amazed and discomposed at finding a tete a tete. "Well, Ada, where is Mama?" Mama came not and I went to fetch her to dinner. Mr Knight came before dinner was over. I went through my lesson mechanically and (what machines we are!) I have never had a better. I was singing when Mr Bailey and Papa came in and my voice never faltered, tho' I trembled so that I could hardly stand. Exit Papa and enter Edward to tell Mama that he wanted to speak to her! I turned round with a face of terror. My lesson was finished and the pause that followed was very awkward.

"May we ask you to play some of your own quadrilles Mr Knight?"

"I'll play if you wish it" he replied, with the manner of one who says if it is particularly convenient that I should. I turned to Mr Bailey for his admiration of a favourite passage, he was standing by the fire and as he assented, intimated that he had something to say to me. I paid Mr Knight some careless compliment en passant and went to warm my hands. "I have spoken to Mr Darby" said my cousin, "what do you think he said?"

"Oh, have you? What?"
"Why, he would not listen to me."

I began to say that I was very sorry that he had done so as I feared if Papa refused him he would do it with less consideration for his feelings than I should have done. I was going to say but the words stuck in my throat and I stopped. "I begged Mr Darby not to blame you in any way and he promised me that he would never speak to you on the subject" - he covered his face with his hands and we spoke no more.
Mr Knight's quadrille ceased and Mama returned.

Abraham and Matilda and Willie came very soon to tea - they were in the wildest spirits - I can feign anything I think, but so could not my poor cousin - We had a great deal of music, when we went upstairs and talked it all over I told Mama and Matilda of the evening before, before I was aware at all that Mr Bailey had rather overdone his part in (as I really believe) his wish that I should not be annoyed, he told Papa "bona fide" that he had not said a word to me. That evening we were busy preparing for our journey. As long as I had fire or candle I did not go to bed but human nature can bear but a certain degree of misery and I slept for an hour or two before it was time to rise and prepare. How far I enjoyed that trance-like visit to Liverpool may be imagined - the memory of it is as an evil dream. Henry Darby[24] *showed us everything - Cemeteries, public buildings, zoological gardens, docks, foggy days and foggy feelings - we were back on Saturday.*

Tuesday 22nd October - *It was about two weeks before my mind recovered its tone - the first was full of feigned and fitful spirits - then came a bad cold and an excuse for being melancholy. Gradually, I came to myself. Mr Bailey scarcely proposed to Papa - according to Mama's account of it - (for Papa has hitherto kept his promise religiously of not telling me a word). He asked if he might come again when we returned from Liverpool and Papa said "What do you want to come again for?" He blushed, and becoming embarrassed, Papa said - "If it is on my daughter's account, I must give a negative at once - you would have saved yourself pain and trouble if you had told me this when you first wrote to me." Be it forgotten! I have gone back to all my old occupations. We have been to the Chesnuts this evening for the first time since the eventful one. Edward Pease, the member's father, there, a most amusing clever, delightful person.*[25] *I realised for the first time that with such vivid appreciation and enjoyment of talent, I ought not to marry a mere fox hunter (Mama would add fortune hunter!)*

Tuesday 29th October - *Mr Reynolds (Bristol) has been dining with us, Uncle Richard Darby and my brother and sister. He is very amusing - looks older and as if he had suffered from illness, but as cheerful as ever. He is certainly very clever, but I almost think Joe Gulson is much so in a widely different way. He has the faculty of making all things interesting, even steam and the corn laws. He expressed some surprise that public granaries are not established here to prevent a famine, and he told me that corn may be preserved in them for 26 years without any trouble of turning the expense of which A, has raised an objection. One of Frederic the Great's wars, he believed the 7 year war, was concluded very abruptly. He was told that Maria Theresa wished for peace - after expressing his disbelief, he wrote down his conditions then and there, and gave them to the Empress's peacemakers, saying - "send me some people here if she really wishes for peace - let them be neither diplomats or lawyers and it shall be arranged." A peace was concluded without further preliminary; consequently the granaries had just been filled in some instances and when, 20 years afterwards, one of these towns in Flanders, I think, fell into the hands of Joseph of Austria - the corn in the magazines was found as good as ever. The method was to place lime slightly wetted beneath, around and above - forming I suppose a kind of cement (a nutshell, Mr Reynolds said) impervious to the air and disposed to absorb the damp. Bridges - Brunel, the science of building arches. The East India's multiltude of sins. The cotton monopoly - the Waverly novels - the culture of plums - the habits of weasels - nothing really seemed at all without the range of his habitual thoughts. His intellect chiefly consists in a very good memory and an imaginative tendency to embellishment and exaggerations, which makes everything he describes interesting and gives people room to observe with a shrug that many clever men draw with a long bow; perhaps the tendency* *to speculations may be traced to the same temper of mind - speculations which you would think by his account must answer and must benefit all mankind and by which he has contrived to diminish large fortune to less than a fourth I believe, and by which his son (John) seems busy at present diminishing the property of others. I was very much delighted and yet reminded of one of his friends who, being asked where Mr Reynolds might be that morning, said that he had left him talking to someone in Park Street 2 hours ago - very likely he was still there. Few people play with the ball of conversation more energetically, but many are more willing to let others run for it.*

Monday 11th November *- Delightful party at Mrs Reynolds. Mr & Mrs W.R. Anstice,[3] Matilda and Abraham, and Mr Ashworth, who is here under somewhat of a cloud, seeing that he has proposed to a young lady, Miss Wilson, who referred him to her Papa, and he allowed three weeks to elapse without referring - refused, etc. I had to go into dinner with the man, who I have hated always more nearly than a Christian ought, but I cannot say he was not attentive and civil - if he did overdo his part, we should not quarrel with good intentions - they are not always met with. "Will you allow me to ask you to do me the favour to take a glass of wine!" Mr R very agreeable and dear Mrs R. They are going to the Hunt Ball on Thursday. How I do envy them, but I think much gaiety would turn my brain, the enjoyment I feel in it is too vivid - perhaps it might diminish.*

Wednesday 13th November *- Dined at The Chesnuts, Matilda's first party.[26] Mr & Mrs Reynolds, Uncle and Aunt Richard Darby and Willie & Mary Darby. I enjoyed it a good deal, some mistakes in the dinner, as to gravy minus, and side dishes appearing too early. Mr Reynolds did not choose to speak to Miss Mary, who was touchy "par consequence". Never saw him so rude! Very attentive to me (feminine vanity must display itself at a postern or at a grand entrance and I prefer the latter). Just in the very place with which I have many associations not the pleasantest. I was sitting when Mr Reynolds came in and without further mystification said - "I want to sit by you, how am I to manage it?" He did manage it, and the conversation turned upon looking glasses, and Mrs Reynolds admired the one in the back of the chiffonier. "Awkward for manoeuvering" said Mr Reynolds to me with a smile.*

Aunt Dickinson is much worse. Henry has just proposed to Deborah[27] and been refused! He set about it like a young man friend by saying "I think thou love'st me". What else could the goose expect, perhaps indeed he is not very sorry ....

Saturday 16th November *- Dined at Uncle Richard Darby's. It ought to have been very agreeable. Mr Reynolds, Mr Anstice and Joe Dickinson. Mr Reynolds contrived to take me in to dinner and to be devoted for the rest of the evening.*

Thursday 21st November - *To say that I have enjoyed this evening is saying little! My very pen is in a runaway mood at the excited enjoyment of an evening with 14 people all in good humour. But I must go on with the realities of the clouds and the sunshine of working life. Last night my dear Mama complained of being unwell but she went to bed early and I hoped it would all go off, but alas! this morning just as I was rubbing my eyes open, at eight o'clock, Papa came in to my room to tell me that she was very poorly - not half-an-hour's sleep and he was going to send for Mr Webb.*[21] *She did not get any better 'til he came and ordered first an injection of warm water, then some mutton broth with cayenne pepper in it, and some prescription which has been very effective. It was long a matter of doubt in my mind whether I ought to leave her but Papa seemed at length to think we might and with gloom of spirit I went to dress at her particular wish.*

Dearest Tilly was going to Mrs Owen, of which I was very glad, tho' at the moment it seemed rather unfortunate she could not be with Mama. The whole house was cold and my practising prospered, but as practising does when one's thoughts are elsewhere, I felt frozen and dissatisfied with myself - my powers of nursing and everything. When my toilette was finished grey satinette - Tilly's ornaments and that magnificent white scarf of Cadbury's, I was better satisfied with it than I expected. We went and met Mr & Mrs J Anstice,[3] *Mr & Mrs Bartlett, Mr & Mrs Reynolds,*[3] *the Vicar,*[11] *Mr & Mrs Edmonds, Mr Bates. Mrs Wm. Anstice*[3] *altogether delightful, as I said to Papa how seldom we see two people so happy and at ease at their first dinner party, to which he made answer - "Yes, and one seldom sees two pheasants on a dish!" Oh, it was a brilliant evening, the last of these charming parties that have rocketlike gone forth - the last star the brightest. I am so charmed and inspirited by Mrs Edmond's beautiful sketches that I am ready to sit up now and do my best endeavours in the same way. Mr Edmonds did not see me when he first came in. I was standing by Mrs J. Anstice*[3] *and he turned round suddenly, and started as if he meant to drop. I held out my hand and his own trembled as he pressed it. Mrs W. Edmonds came up to me in stateliness and black satin. Mr Reynolds took me in to dinner, and talked some of the most interesting imaginative senses and some of the arrant nonsense that I have often been favoured to hear. He promised me a sketch of the "Therese" if he could persuade his man cook (who has a most extraordinary natural gift that way) to draw one for a lady without turning his head.*

Wednesday 27th November - *Papa had a great deal to say about the extraordinary 'year' - the best ever known to the Iron Works. The position that he ought to take naturally occurred to me, and when finally Mama spoke of the Tothill's and how they spend all upon the education of their children, and Papa began to endeavour to reconcile it to his conscience that I had been very nicely educated it was really more than I could bear, and I went upstairs very hastily to conceal the scorching torrents of uncontrollable or uncontrolled tears from* *whose violence few suffer like myself. I thought how mine are intellects that are particularly intractable and impliable to self cultivation and yet are such as yet might have been of no common order under the influence of that salutary compulsion which most young persons have now the benefit of - music, dancing, languages, how wastefully neglected.*

Tuesday 19th December - *I have been spending four days of great enjoyment with dearest Matilda while Papa and Mama went to Leighton. Quite alone with all our pleasant occupations and interchange of thoughts. I have not been so happy uninterruptedly for four days since we were at Ryde. To find dearest Matilda just the same - oh, it is Elysium! Matilda tells me that such a discipline as ours is of great value in thoughts.*

Sunday 22nd December - *A very wretched day. I never remember a more heart-searching struggle with misery and yet its causes are so little. Papa was angry with me for not going to Meeting on Wednesday, then for saying I did not know it was of any consequence. I refrained resolutely from a good fit of crying last night and I almost regret it - but I had suffered much from the last.*

Thursday 26th December - *We are happier again. Yesterday was such a beautiful Christmas Day that it was enough to spread a natural spirit of rejoicing with its glorious sunshine I heard the distant Church bells and how melancholy they made me feel. How I thought and longed to know how many more Christmas Days would find me precluded from this highest of serious Joys. Feminine timidity I am not overburdened with but yet it arises up along with the dread of eccentricity which I believe is a salutary one for my father's daughter. These things stand like spectres in the way of that which I know to be best for my moral and religious good. Yet I do not feel it so much like a positive duty to leave the society I was born in as it is a matter of preference and affection towards what seems to me a more instructive and animating form of worship. It is only when I think of that holy sacrament so clearly ordered by Our Saviour that I almost tremble.*

Sunday 29th December - *Last Friday Matilda and Abraham dined with us because they were engaged on Christmas Day - a very enjoyable visit we had which I enjoyed extremely and was quite happy when suddenly Papa being alone with me began with the utmost fury to accuse me most falsely of - to say the least of it - an unladylike impropriety, though I cannot say that he made much further insinuation connected with it. I trembled all over with indignation as I simply denied the charge. His look was fiendish! For my poor Mama's sake I did not tell him I would leave his house and live by my own industry, but I went upstairs in such passionate misery of heart as found no relief in tears. Oh, the chaos of thoughts that were silently endeavouring to arrange themselves through those sleepless hours. Fervently I prayed for help and guidance and patience. At first the want of money seemed the grand difficulty, and then I thought over every respectable way of gaining it, and there are few open to women! Suddenly*

I thought of my verses and sanguinely thought I could easily support myself. Of this I am more than doubtful now but I then planned how I could write to some magazine and how I could manage a correspondence, and on the spur of that wretched night I think I may put the scheme in practice.

The next day I walked to the Bridge with Matilda and told her all. Oh, how she sympathised and scolded. I have had another long walk with her today after begging she would tell Abraham and ask his advice. It was - not to leave home without Mama, to bear it at present until, something should occur that would give just and fair ground for such a step - to be perfectly respectful always in my behaviour but never whatever I do to allow myself to be frightened! All this so fully agreed with my own plans that I was charmed.

NOTES

1. Eastfield was built in 1838 by Barnard Dickinson. It was situate in the field east of Severn House (The Valley Hotel - see map). Barnard Dickinson and his family had vacated Dale House early in 1838 thus allowing Lucy Darby to move there. While Eastfield was being built, Barnard and Ann Dickinson occupied a house converted from the adjoining stable block. When Adelaide visited in January 1838 it was but recently built.
2. Madeley Wood Hall was the recently built home of the Anstice family, north of the River Severn near Coalport.
3. The Anstice, Reynolds and Ball families were inter-related in a somewhat complicated way. William Anstice (1781-1850) had received a quarter share in the Madeley Wood Ironworks in 1803, from William Reynolds for whom he was then working. William Reynolds was married to his cousin Hannah Ball, whose sister Susannah Ball was married to William Anstice's father, Robert Anstice! The Reynolds and Ball families were Quakers, although the Anstice family were not. When William Reynolds died aged 45 years in 1803, William Anstice took over full control of the Madeley Wood Ironworks. William Reynolds and Hannah Ball had five children. Robert Anstice and Susannah Ball also had several children including William Anstice who was manager of the Madeley Wood Ironworks. William Anstice died in 1850 and was succeeded as manager by his son John Anstice who had as co-partner his brother William Reynolds Anstice who was a solicitor. Both are referred to from time to time in Adelaide's Journal.
   John Anstice was a popular and generous figure in the community and was remembered following his death in 1867 by the building of the Anstice Memorial Hall in Madeley in 1868.
   It is not at present clear where Dick Anstice fitted into this relationship.
4. The meeting of the Great Western Railway took place at the London Tavern, Bishopsgate Street, London on 9th/10th January 1839. It is described in McDermott's History of the G.W.R. (Vol. I, p.85) as the decisive meeting of the company, when it was decided to proceed with the broad gauge recommended by Brunel and the directors rather than the standard gauge adopted by the other railway companies, and recommended by a substantial section of the shareholders referred to as the Liverpool Party. Abraham Darby IV must have been a shareholder.

5. Mary Darby (1808-1873) sister of Abraham IV.
6. Francis Darby, like everyone else, had very quickly adopted, and adapted to the new form of transport, the Railroad.
7. Adelaide very quickly followed in her father's footsteps in using the Railroad - a very exciting experience.
8. In this period, two years after queen Victoria came to the throne, young Quaker couples were expected to come before their Monthly meeting with each confirming that there was no impediment to their marrying each other and so for their fellow worshippers to give their blessing upon the union.
   Some present-day readers will support the words "barbarous ceremony" in Adelaide's private Journal, while others will shortly realise in these pages that Adelaide is becoming increasingly critical of all aspects of the simple unostentatious Quaker way of life, leading to her resignation in favour of the ordered services, music and hymn singing at the Church of England which greatly attract her.
9. See references to the Chartists in the Comment 1839, pages 78 and 79.
10. The problem was probably one of space. The matter was remedied on 2nd August when Francis Darby extended the invitation to all his nephews.
11. Adelaide does not name the vicar in her Journal. It is therefore a matter of conjecture as to who he was. The vicar of Madeley at the time was George Edmonds a bachelor who became rector of Little Wenlock from 1841-1889. Although they were all the same family it is not clear what the relationship was between the vicar (George Edmonds) Mr and Mrs Edmonds and Captain Edmonds.
12. The journey was anti-clockwise round the Isle of Wight.
13. Porchester Castle was originally one of a series of forts built by the Romans in the third century. In 1120 a castle was built there and over the centuries this became a starting point for military expeditions abroad including the embarkation of Henry V on his Agincourt campaign.
14. The Duke and Duchess of Cambridge were representing the Royal Family.
15. Appley House, Ryde.
16. Blackgang Chine is just west of the southernmost point of the Isle of Wight, St. Catherine's Point.
17. Lord Yarborough (of the Pelham Family) owned the grandest home on the Isle of Wight, Appuldurcombe House between Newport and Ventnor, with grounds designed by Capability Brown.
18. Carisbrooke Castle, originally a Saxon camp, which was enlarged by the Redvens family who ruled the Isle of Wight until 1293. It was purchased by King Edward I as a royal residence. During the Civil War the castle acted as prison to King Charles I who twice attempted escape.
19. Mr Joe Bailey was to be the next suitor for Adelaide's hand.
20. Miss Sophy Horne, sister of James Horne who was Adelaide's first boyfriend.
21. Mr Webb was the surgeon from Shrewsbury.
22. Joseph Dickinson (1806-1860) was the eldest child of Ann and Barnard Dickinson. He was a cousin of Adelaide.
23. Mr Dawson, recently rejected as a suitor to Adelaide.
24. William Henry Darby, son of Richard and Maria Darby.

25. Edward Pease (1767-1858) was a leading Quaker who financed the world's first passenger-carrying railway from Stockton to Darlington.
26. Abraham IV and Matilda were since their marriage the sole occupiers of The Chesnuts. Lucy Darby and the rest of the family had moved to Dale House in 1883.
27. Henry Dickinson (1812-1886) proposed marriage to Deborah Darby, daughter of Lucy Darby and sister of Abraham IV. She was then living at Dale House. Although she turned Henry down, she did in fact marry him two years later in 1841.

Lucy Darby (née Burlingham) (1782-1870), above, was the widow of Edmund Darby (1782-1810). At the time of this journal, Lucy Darby and her family were living at The Chesnuts (page 157). In 1838, Lucy moved to Dale House (page 128). She had two sons, Abraham Darby IV (1804-78), below left, and Alfred Darby (1807-52), below right.

1840

Comment

The beginning of the 1840s saw the Coalbrookdale Company poised to enter a period of prosperity and profitability. In 1839 it had acquired ownership of the Lightmoor Furnaces to add to its existing furnaces at Horsehay and Dawley Castle. That same year the Horsehay furnaces had produced 800 tons of iron plates for the hull of Brunel's *S.S. Great Britain* then under construction at Bristol. The year before, in 1838 the Company had displayed in Liverpool two wrought iron plates, each measuring 10' 7" x 5' 1", claimed to be the largest ever rolled. The Company was clearly back at the forefront of the iron industry. In terms of their wider social responsibility, Richard Darby became a guardian under the Poor Law, and a new boys' school was built by Abraham IV, at his own expense in Wellington Road, Coalbrookdale adjoining the Upper Furnace site.

For Adelaide however 1840 started in a wretched way. A few days before New Year's Day she had experienced a great row with her father. Francis Darby, whilst he could be very congenial in company, even charming, was a man of unpredictable temper. Increasingly, he was subject to bouts of explosive fury. Adelaide suffered one of those bouts on either the 27th or 28th December 1839 when her father accused her of "an unladylike impropriety". (See Journal 29th December 1839). This caused Adelaide to contemplate leaving home, relying for support on her literary skills. Her sister's (Matilda's) advice was not to leave home without her mother. This was very good advice because by the 3rd January, after studying Bentley and Blackwood magazines for that month she concluded that she did not have "the most remote clue to the way of sending a production to the magazines". And so things returned to normal. Before the month was out, her next suitor was identified in the shape of Alfred Darby (Abraham IV's younger brother) who was then 33 years of age and was very influential in the management of the Company. This caused an agony of anticipation but for the time being the suit was not pursued.

There was much toing and froing between Coalbrookdale and Liverpool where the Company had a warehouse. It is not evident what the purpose of these visits were. certainly the Company was building up its presence in Liverpool, where the Company had been involved for the better part of the century. J. S. Kohl writing at Liverpool states - "To see how many things are now made of iron in England, one must visit one of the iron warehouses, as for example that of Coalbrookdale, at this place. Tables, sofas, vases, inkstands and an endless variety of articles fashioned into the most graceful forms may there be seen".[1]

During the summer of 1840, there was the annual visit of one month at Leighton Buzzard and more unusually, a fortnight's visit to the Tothill family at Stoke, Bristol.

Two family funerals occurred during the year - that of Ann Dickinson (Francis Darby's sister) and Samuel Dickinson, her fourth son.

31st December/1st January 1840 - *It is the witching hour of midnight. I have been leaning out of my window with the raindrops falling gently like summer's tears upon my face,listening to the distant church bells as they came fitfully in what was intended to be a rejoicing peal - but subdued in their far-off melody into that deep melancholy which so well accords with our memorial of another year departed - gone for ever as years go in this weary world where the days of men are few and evil.*

Friday 3rd January - *Last Wednesday Papa went to Liverpool and did not return until this evening. A holiday for Mama and me that will leave one bright spot upon the most sorrowful Christmas take it all for all, that I ever remember.*

Matilda came up with us from the monthly meeting on Wednesday. She could not spend the evening with us as they were going to Dale House to hear of Henry's second private interview.[2] *Miss Deborah seems somewhat like Miss Helen, convolvulousy prudent and wary in putting off the evil day of taking a husband but quite without objection to a lover. Mama and I spent the evening alone and after making ourselves most thoroughly miserable by talking over our many troubles and feeling ourselves so bound up in each other that I was almost reconciled to the afflictive causes. We finally began Crichton, but did not find it very interesting. After we went upstairs Mama read me her Pocket book for the last eventful year in the warm curtained happiness of my little room. Then I read some of my pieces to her, with which she was pleased to be pleased (apropos I have got Bently and Blackwood for this month but I cannot find the most remote clue to the way of sending a production to these magazines - I must give up my scheme for the present).*

Tuesday 6th January - *Dearest Tilly with us - so unlike an old married lady! We have been dining at Severn House to meet all the Baches. Very delightful but now I am almost asleep. Mr & Mrs WR Anstice*[3] *and Mr J Stradling there. Met a gipsy this morning when Tilly exclaimed "Why, what would she tell me, I wonder? - she will not know I'm married." The gipsy told her - "You have known trouble, you have had sorrows, but I have them not in store for you" - and she concluded with - "before many days pass over your head you will have a kiss from one that had given the same salute before - one that you love best in the world" - and tho' she never seemed to suspect that M was married, there was not one thing that I heard her say that did not fit into the circumstances. To me she said "You shall have a happy new year and a handsome present - there is a gentleman with the light hair and a gentleman with the dark, you know I tell you the truth, the one with the light hair loves you the* *best, the one with the light hair shall give you the present. Do you beware of the hasty temper and it will be for your good. You have had trouble and you may have trouble but you shall always have luck. This year you will see one that you shall be glad to see. Cross your hand with the silver and I will tell you a letter of his name. I see 'W' under the shilling - if you make a fool of W - W will never make a fool of you."*[4]

Thursday 20th January - *Party at Dale House.*[5] *Alfred Darby coming to his senses. Long and good music lesson this morning.*

Tuesday 20th January - *How is it that we never look at the moon in ought but sadness? There is something so softly sympathizing in that melancholy lustre. Matilda has been with us again since Friday - how intensely enjoyable! Abraham has been to Liverpool and when she came she said she had a great deal on her mind that she should not tell me. Need I add that in 10 minutes I knew it all and it purported that Alfred Darby having seen fit to make her his confidante, many a mystery became solved. Likewise he had persuaded her to think very favourably of him; to believe that he is devotedly attached to me and moreover that he was most impatient to propose to Mama and Papa. When I very coolly asked her how he was to be refused with the most civility, she seemed almost surprised and said with something like disappointment "I never saw you so decided before".*

We have been to Dale House[5] *and it was very agreeable, Alfred talked to me more than he has ever done before - not a thought of a refusal. Matilda went home to make some arrangements, she met Alfred advised him to speak first to Ada, what more she said I do not know, but take it to have been something to discourage him.*

Wednesday 21st January - *I am in an enviable state of mind tonight! I am bursting in ignorance. Mama and I went to Meeting this morning - and I went to the Chesnuts*[6] *where we found Mrs Lucy Darby, Deborah and Alfred, Abraham and Matilda, for me it was an awkward moment, but I put on the highest spirits and they became natural soon. Alfred looked very cross, like a very miserable thrice rejected lover. I was glad when Mama got up to go - Abraham and Alfred are both going to Liverpool tomorrow and Matilda will be coming to tea.*

Edward brought in the tea things and - asked him if Willie Tothill had gone in to Papa. "No Ma'am" came the laconic reply "That was Mr Alfred Ma'am". I trembled internally and went on reading without knowing the sense. Presently the Library door opened, Papa sounded such a peal as I have not heard issued for long and the departing went forth without a word. There had been time for nothing but a refusal surely! At last Papa came in and began to talk a lease of the Pit House coppice and then about the history of the Liverpool warehouse so I thought if Alfred had proposed it must have been amongst other affairs of business. I think Papa must have refused him and mean me to know nothing about it.

Yet I hardly think he would refuse him at once - I am in a perfect fever but will not attract Mama. The primary person in these things ought to be first consulted and if parents are paid the compliment of being asked first, they ought to leave the decision to their daughter's judgement when they are at years of discretion. The next day Alfred came up to tell Papa about the Liverpool warehouse and that was all!

Sunday 3rd May *- Since this day week my poor Aunt Dickinson*[7] *has been almost given over. In all human probability she never can rally again. I have been twice to sit in her room, she is most kind and affectionate and fully prepared to go - very patient in her suffering. Such beautiful weather; the nightingale making night melodious and the cuckoo as happy all day as its reiterated two notes can make it.*

Sunday 10th May *- Yet I scarcely thought when I was writing the last that today I should have been attending my poor Aunt's funeral.*[7] *She died on Tuesday morning after a night of continued suffering during which my dearest Mama stayed with her as always ready to assist in trouble. True it is that few may have a Mother like mine to lose, or few to be in a position of such bitter desolateness as I should be without her. We dined at the house, 53 in all. The Tothills came and an importation of the Burlinghams, Mr Reynolds, Tom Fowler, very agreeable, Mr Ash very clever and extraordinary, and a very agreeable Norfolk lady, Cordelia Buyer, who told me how much I reminded her of Mary Gurney. Mr Ash's sermon was splendid, he dwelt much on the peculiar doctrine of the inward spirit, but beautifully and very agreeable and the whole very encouraging.*

Tuesday 13th May *- I have been spending a week delightful past description with dearest Tilly! The Tothill*[8] *girls were left with her and I went to help! They are nice girls - charming studies of character and proof of the great value to a Mother of that faculty in the mind that enables us to grasp all the unfolding powers of young human nature to guide and direct its excessive waywardness. I love them both dearly and should like to go and see them at Stoke (Bristol).*

Papa and Mama had a visit from Dick Sorton and Charles[9] *on Sunday and from them they heard the marvellous story of Mr James Horne's marriage.*[10] *The lady was a Miss Slaughter - a cheesemonger's daughter in Southampton. Her father is dead - she had £10,000 and his father gave him £10,000 more, and on the £800 a year they have taken an expensive house on Clapham Common. Rumour says that this universal admirer paid his visits to Miss Pease*[11] *and to his southward inamorata at the same time. The Quaker beauty refused him! I was sorry to hear of it, but yet there is a feeling of satisfaction in knowing that one's judgment has not been deceived. He is very extravagant, quite a scamp says Richard Sorton Darby.*[9]

Sunday 18th May *- Mama has not been well. We went yesterday to Badger*[12] *and a lovely dingle it is. Charming place for a picnic. Swan Rhododendrons - cascade temple! Mr Cheyney has not come to take possession yet. We came home* *by Chesterton and Worfield Church - very lovely that country in the season is beautiful but it is yet very wet.*

Sunday 14th June - *Tomorrow we start for Leighton. Last night I sat up reading Lady Carbery's Peeress - intensely interesting and affecting - I had a long candle but it expired before I came to the end of the second volume. I was too much interested to sleep so when it was broad daylight I went on again for an hour or so. Went to sleep about half past four, woke at 6 and finished the third volume. No marvel I was sleepy today. The world is wild about the Great Anti-Slavery convention, the Queen having been fired at the murder of Lord William Russell.*

Monday 15th June - Leighton - *Arrived here soon after 7 - met Mr & Mrs Oliver at Wolverhampton.*

Thursday 25th June - *We have been at the Quaker Meeting at Berkhampstead - upon the whole much more tolerable than might have been supposed probable. I have been up for two mornings before 6 and had a long walk with Emma to Grove-berry and to Linslade - oh! how lovely everything is at that sweet hour.*

Friday 3rd July - *The Wool Fair - made many calls and went to see the dinner table set out in the tents. Papa came and stayed till Saturday. Went with Grandpapa to buy ducks and to look after the peas, beans, corn, hay and cattle - I enjoyed it very much. Grandpapa was very cheerful.*

Monday 13th July - *Grandmama and Mama went to London to look at a carriage.*[13] *Emma was thrown off her horse on Cossgrove Common.*

Sunday 19th July - *We left Leighton on Wednesday. I had a hasty walk on the Heath with Emma and heard Peter's voice on the other side of the hedge in their garden, but we sped over the style and up the workhouse lane and escaped. Dearest Tilly I was charmed to see - she was almost worth coming home for. I am now beginning to feel settled into my old haunts, habits and occupations. I have resumed the German songs and my music, and we have a charming box of new books from Bulls.*

Monday 24th August - *Tomorrow morning we start for a visit to Uncle and Aunt Tothill*[14] *- I am going with Abraham and Matilda so it will be charming. I have been horribly lazy in journalising, one delightful thing was a party of Mr and Mrs Anstice*[3] *with Abraham and Matilda, the two Mr Edmonds and sweet Miss Driver, Mr and Mrs Egremont,*[15] *Uncle and Aunt Richard Darby, Mr and Mrs WR Anstice.*[3] *Then we went to Wroxeter*[15] *and met the Thursby's and the Jenkins. Next day I went with Abraham and Matilda to Mrs WR Anstice's where, of course, it was a delectable evening. I have had the great enjoyment of a week with Matilda while Anna was with her - I do not think I ever enjoyed any quick pleasure more than I did sitting with her in our bower. Oh I have had a treat of the first magnitude Mr Knight's concerts! Fessani and*

Rubini, Nigri and Puzz. All too delightful only that Mr Edmonds was there and too devoted to be agreeable - thank heavens I am to be away during the venison party this week and shall miss seeing him - Anna is to be my substitute. Poor Barnard[16] *has one of his dreadful sore throats and is in some danger - Uncle Dickinson has gone to him.*

Sunday 6th September - *We returned yesterday from Stoke after a fortnight of much enjoyment, such concentration of the pleasantness of life. I could not journalize because I never was alone - occupying part of the young ladies roof. A sad occurrence met us on our return. After watching the post and fearing daily that poor Barnard's earthly career of vanity and folly would be ended suddenly comes the intelligence of his brother Samuel's death.*[17] *Truly we know not what a day may bring forth. This day week poor Samuel was at Rochdale Meeting. Monday Barnard was so much better that he left him and returned to Birmingham feeling rather unwell, he wrote us on Tuesday to say he was suffering from an attack of Cholera, was in bed but hoped by Sunday to be up again!*

Sunday 13th September - *Wednesday was the funeral of Samuel.*[17] *Papa went with some others so that dearest Tilly came to us; but I was so ill on Thursday that Mama sent for Mr Webb - it is a sort of dizziness that entirely prevented me from sitting or standing.*

Monday 23rd September - *The first of Mr Murray's lectures on Geology tonight. As we came home Henry Darby and Christopher*[18] *illuminated the country with a splendid blue light - dazzlingly beautiful. Henry and Willie*[19] *dined here last evening - these two boys were perfect impersonations of intellectual good humour - not greatly gifted. Dear, dear Willie I wish he was a girl that I might sit down and cry comfortably over his departure.*

Friday 25th September - *Erratics - masses of unfossiliferous rock found scattered all over the known globe. Their nature resembling nothing in their own vicinity - evidence of the deluges as they appear to have been broken off our biggest mountains, and rolled by the mighty rush of water far from their birthplace. The bones of man have been found in the caverns which contain those of hyenas, tigers, deer and cat. This fact kept out of sight by Buckland Lyall because it goes against pet theories and preconceived notions. I have dined at the Chesnuts with Mr and Mrs Murray, most agreeable, fascinating people they are. Mr Murray spoke much of the Jews - he knows them well having been admitted to most of their festivals save the feast of the Passover. "The Confessions of an Opium Eater" a dangerous book - I wish to see it. Mr De Quincey, the author, takes Laudanum at the rate of 600 drops a day and his wife and daughter no less in proportion.*

Tuesday 6th October - *Powers of endurance! We are going to the General Meeting at Hereford. Alas, alas, I am 'en despoir'.*

Saturday 12th December - *I will try to journalize again. I have been to Leighton and enjoyed myself intensely and read 'Master Humphries'. I have never mentioned the Birmingham expedition including the theatricals and great expansion of mind - nor "The Magician" by Leigh Ritchie who half turned my head with admiration. I have had dearest Tilly with me and have been to see Hannah. Papa is reading old Ellison over again to us - how interesting it is and how it brings back the feelings with which Matilda and I read it a few years ago when we never dreamt what those years were to produce.*

New Year's Eve 1840 - *Poor John Sturge*[20] *died last week after a fortnightly illness leaving his sweet young wife and one little boy. How those that diffuse happiness are taken.*

NOTES

1. IGMT Museum Guide No, 2 published 1974.
2. Henry Dickinson was still pursuing his proposal of marriage to Deborah Darby of Dale House (daughter of Lucy Darby and sister of Abraham IV). Although turned down for the second time, they did get married the next year (1840) and set up home at Severn House.
3. See note 3 for 1839.
4. A curious coincidence. Adelaide eventually married Henry Whitmore in 1852.
5. Dale House was the traditional home of the Manager of the Coalbrookdale Company. It was situated close to the Works. From 1810 to 1838 it was occupied by Barnard and Ann Dickinson. They moved out to Eastfield in 1838. It was then occupied by Lucy Darby (née Burlingham), her son Alfred and two daughters Deborah and Mary.
6. The Chesnuts, built about 1815, was situated below The White House and the Deer Park, next to the Meeting House built in 1808. It had been devised in 1821 by the Will of Sarah Darby to Abraham Darby IV. It had been occupied by him and his mother, brother and sisters since then. When he married Matilda Darby in 1839, the rest of the family moved to Dale House (see note 5).
7. Aunt Dickinson was Ann Dickinson (née Darby (1779-1840). She was the eldest surviving child of Abraham III. She was married to Barnard Dickinson in 1805. They lived at first at The Haye (see map) but when Barnard was appointed manager in 1810 they moved to Dale House where they lived until 1838. They then moved to Eastfield but she only lived there for two years before her death.
8. William and Hannah Tothill had five children. the youngest were "the Tothill girls", Sarah Hannah (b.1824) and Rebecca (b.1826).
9. Richard Sorton Darby and Charles Edward Darby were sons of Uncle Richard Darby who lived at "Rosehill" next to Dale House.
10. Mr James Horne was Adelaide's first boyfriend and suitor. (See journal for 1834).

11. The Pease family of Darlington were a distinguished family of Quakers involved in textiles, banking and transport.
12. Badger is a delightful village five or six miles south east of Madeley. There were manorial connections between Badger and Studly Hall and Grange (just north of Madeley). In 1839 it was held by Elizabeth Hawkins Browne, widow of Isaac Hawkins Browne (M.P. and essayist). She died in 1839 and the estate was divided between the children of a kinsman, Robert Cheyney, who had died in 1820. Adelaide visited Badger Hall before "Mr Cheyney" had arrived to take possession. Chesterton and Worfield are neighbouring villages.
13. This was a sign of the growing affluence of Francis Darby. The family acquired a carriage and horses.
14. Hannah Darby (1786-1859) was the youngest child of Abraham III. In 1818 she married William Tothill of Bristol. They had five children and lived at Stoke, north of Bristol.
15. Edward Egremont was the vicar of Wroxeter, which was situate about seven or eight miles west of Coalbrookdale on the road to Shrewsbury. It grew out of the ruins of Uriconium, the Roman camp at the west end of Watling Street where it reached the River Severn.
16. Barnard Dickinson, junior, son of Barnard Dickinson, senior, lived in Rochdale at the time. he was prone to quinsy (inflammation of the tonsils).
17. Samuel Dickinson (1814-1840) was the seventh child of Barnard and Ann Dickinson. Soon after his mother's death on 5th May 1840 (see note 4 above) he returned from the West Indies. he went to see his brother Barnard who was ill at Rochdale (see note 16 above). He attended Rochdale Meeting and then as Barnard was better, Samuel returned to Birmingham but succumbed to an attack of cholera, from which he died on 9th September 1840.
18. Henry Darby can only be William Henry Darby, 5th child of Richard and Maria Darby of "Rosehill" (born 1819). Christopher can only be Christopher Dickinson, 10th child of Barnard and Ann Dickinson, (born 1818). They were of around the same age, the early twenties, although what "the splendid blue light" was is a mystery.
19. "Willie" is probably William Dickinson the youngest of the Dickinson's family of eleven children. He was born in 1822 and was therefore only 18 years old, which may have prompted Adelaide's maternal sentiments.
20. A member of the Birmingham Quaker Family of Sturge. Mary Dickinson was married to Charles Sturge and later (1846) Hannah Dickinson married Joseph Sturge.

1841

Comment

As a background to an understanding of Adelaide's Journal, it needs to be appreciated that during the years when she was growing up, her father Francis Darby was extending his ownership of land in Coalbrookdale so that by 1841 his was the largest landholding in the Dale. This had been a gradual process. The land which he had inherited when he came of age in 1804 comprised Sunniside and The White House, the deer park and a modest number of acres around. In 1816, the year before Adelaide was born, he had acquired Furnace Bank Farm adjoining the eastern side of The White House. In 1827, he had acquired thc hillside on the south side of Sunniside, known as the Whales Back. In 1837 he had purchased 70 acres of farm land on the west side of Sunniside formerly belonging to Richard Reynolds.

Apart from expanding his landownership in this way, he was also tidying up the neighbourhood. In the mid 18th century, a settlement of small houses, housing workers of the Company, had grown up opposite The Chesnuts, along the Rope Walk. During the 1830s he had been acquiring the freeholds of all these properties. By 1841 this process was complete and he then demolished the lot, thus ensuring that the neighbourhood up Darby Road from the Works was predominantly occupied by members of the family, except for people like Edward Edwards, the surgeon for Coalbrookdale and his family.

With the increasing profitability of the Company and surrounded by a substantial land holding, status had become an important issue for Adelaide. Her father, Francis Darby had acquired a coat of arms, and the family now had a carriage and horses with the appropriate stabling. These trappings of wealth clearly affected her attitude to the prospects of marriage. This was a period during which the prospect of marriage to Alfred Darby (Abraham's brother) was advanced but at the end of the year, Adelaide recorded that "I rather think Miss Darby of The White House is of more importance than ever Mrs Alfred Darby will be".

An important wedding did take place however between Henry Dickinson and Deborah Darby of Dale House (sister of Abraham IV and Alfred Darby and daughter of Lucy Darby) on 17th March. The couple took up residence in Severn House (now the Valley Hotel). Later Henry Dickinson was to become a leading figure in the life of Coalbrookdale.

During the year Adelaide visited Leighton Buzzard twice, during the second of which, yet another suitor (Peter) was rejected by Francis Darby. At the very end of the year she wondered whether she would like to be

Mrs George Edmonds who had just accepted the living as vicar of Little Wenlock (having previously been vicar of Madeley).

Apart from the usual social round, the highlight of the year was probably a weeks holiday in the Derbyshire Peak District in September in the newly acquired open carriage.

Beneath this agreeable life of wealth and leisure, there was a deeply unhappy undercurrent. This comes to the surface from time to time in Adelaide's Journal. On 5th April 1841 she confides "in truth no-one knows the unhappiness that has been mine often of late. The depressing influence of home were verily taking away all spirit, all hope, almost all faith ..." Adelaide did not elaborate on this theme, and it can only be conjectured as to the cause, but we know from some notes written by Adelaide's older sister Matilda in 1872 that the marriage between their parents, Francis and Hannah Darby, was passing through a difficult and unhappy period during the late 1830s and the early 1840s ("The story of the Leighton Bank as well as I remember it" – Matilda Darby 16th June 1872). In her reminiscences Matilda described her father as being "rather above than below the common average of intellect until a strange delusion possessed his mind when his health began to fail for his last long illness. His delusion regarded our Mother's faithfulness to him. She must have been about 50 years old and had always devoted to him her whole life and time and thoughts. Papa spoke of this delusion to Mary Page, to Abraham and Alfred before I think we knew of it. But at last before Papa, Mama told me of what he accused her! When I got home my husband then told me how he and others had heard Papa talk about it. As Alfred had heard it from Papa we consulted him what should be done. Papa's manner being very violent we were all doubtful of Mama's safety ..."

It is a fair assumption that Adelaide knew about this marital episode which would have caused her profound unhappiness. It also helps to explain the deteriorating relationship between her and her father, which surfaces from time to time through her Journal.

Sunday 3rd January - *It has been snowing and I am left at home to my meditations. The gift of journalizing is almost taken away, but yet I do not feel quite so vegetable as I did - I am reading 'Bouricane' which Grandpapa has just sent me - mean to write and thank him.*

Thursday 8th February - *Just parted with dearest Tilly after several visits of delightful memory and hope she is coming again next week. The Muirkirk works in agitation*[1] *- he (Abraham) has been much away and I have had many hours of real happiness. Oh, those days before the links that bind the sisters of a family circle are broken - alas, they are gone before we knew how they were to be prized, and yet Matilda and I never were I think so much to one another* *as now. Never was she so dear to me, and not for all the joys that are lost would I have her now unmarried.*

Sunday 30th February *- Dearest Tilly has been located with me the last week while Abraham, good man, has been canvassing the members for the county and Borough inclusive on behalf of the Severn Navigation Company. Deborah is to be married the 17th - 'On dit' Mr Edmonds[2] has bought the living of Little Wenlock.*

Thursday 17th March *- Henry and Deborah's wedding day[3] - well and preposterously over.*

Monday 5th April *- It is very strange how completely I have lost the power of journalizing - I have been spending a most happy week at The Chesnuts[4] - indeed it has done me a great deal of good - for few - in truth no-one knows the unhappiness that has been mine often of late. The depressing influence of home were verily taking away all spirit, all hope, almost all faith which is horrible to think of, but indeed it is only the small particles of these holy gifts remaining that saved me from absolute despair.*

Thursday 15th April *- I went to tea at the Chesnuts on Sunday. Miss Wilkinson was there also Henry and Charles[5] - very pleasant as always - Alfred came after tea and did try to be attentive, but I seem rather to have disturbed his plan with my new dignity.*

Monday 26th April *- Just returned from paying the evening bride visit to Mr and Mrs Henry Dickinson[3] - very agreeable. We start at half past 7 tomorrow for Leighton and it strikes 1.*

Tuesday 28th April *- Came to Leighton, awful hot day. Travelling companions rather agreeable and exalted people. Wrote letters on Wednesday for Grandpapa and Thursday went, much against my will, with Papa to London. We stayed at the Euston Hotel. Saw Martin's "Fall of Mineoch" at the British Institution, Westminster Abbey, a long desired treat, then the Waxwork, quite faint and frightened in the room of horrors. Drove in Hyde Park at the fashionable hours to see the Queen but she did not appear till too late. Dined and went to Covent Garden to see "London Assurance and Beauty and The Beast" was very much charmed, quite new and very exciting to see. Could not have been more delighted but do not exactly wish to go again. Madame Vestrie one of the prettiest women I have seen, said to be 60 but quite incredible - did not sleep much but lay dreaming in my pretty French bed. Friday morning accidentally had a most excellent view of Her Majesty and Prince Albert as they were leaving the Royal Academy - very much pleased - the Prince is not flattered in the print shops. Came home in the evening - Mrs Fry in the next carriage, she claimed acquaintance rather to the apparent amazement of two young officers, our travelling companions, who had been making themselves as agreeable as their foppish fraternity think it in general worth while 'en passant' to* *be. Found Emma there. Papa went back on Saturday - walked with the Reeves in the evening. Frank Bassett going to be married, so is Mr Cassell! to a lady of property and related to Baptist Noel.*

Tuesday 4th May - *There was a poor man killed on Saturday fighting with some Leighton vagabond. I had a very pleasant walk after dinner with Eliza and Emma and on our return the town was all in confusion. The Jury had just brought in their verdict and the man was being conveyed to Bedford.*

Tuesday 11th May - *A Mrs Squires expected, did not come - Callers of all kinds. The Rev Mr Wardle with his own publication on the 'Regeneration of Man' and Major Gilpin with a petition against Lord John's Corn Law fixed duty - Major Gilpin very handsome and gentlemanly and Grandpapa quite as much the latter though he would not sign it.*

Wednesday 18th May - *Dear Grandpapa not more overcome than usual at parting with us but he is now really a very old man - we cannot meet many more times on this side of eternity so far as human foresight can tell.*

Tuesday 23rd June - *Dearest Tilly's birthday - who would guess she is 32. She has been with us today. Charming letter from Mama, Tilly is going to Leighton next week. I think no book has ever expanded my faculties like Carlyle.*

Thursday 15th July - *The Anstices all came to dinner, Mr W Edmonds and Abraham. Dear Charles stayed with me till Saturday - never enjoyed anything more. Went a long walk to Lumhole Pool.*[6] *Next Friday, the 23rd, Sophy*[7] *is to be married to Mr Gaselee.*

Sunday 1st August - *Dearest Tilly returned from Leighton last Tuesday bringing Eliza and Emma and they dined with us on Thursday. Friday we went to tea at Dale House.*[8] *Walked with Matilda and the Reeves - repairs in wardrobe - and preparation for Mr Knight who did not come - have occupied this week and this Sunday evening I go to the Chesnuts*[4] *for a few days and I am most happy.*

Thursday 25th August - *Mr Hartshorne came on Tuesday bringing Charles who has undergone the operation for the cure of squinting, it seems to have been quite effectual. Mr Hartshorne most agreeable, all affectation gone and he is now a very talented clever man without any of the nonsense that used to leave me doubtful what there was really superior in his intellect.*[9] *On Wednesday, 1st September, we started at 8 in the open carriage - lovely weather but quite frosty. At Newport called on Miss Burm - then proceeded to Eccleshall, changed horses and went to Stone. "Stone in Staffordshire" is a nice looking place - then came Cheadle, scenery pretty and very much like our home views but it improved after leaving Cheadle. We then came to the first sight of Alton Towers rising castellated out of the woods - hills tremendous - Mr Ragg's copper works not agreeable - found ourselves landed at the "Shrewsbury Arms" at half past three - ordered dinner and walked down to Alton Towers whence we met a great deal of company returning. It is a strange kind of house covering a vast space - the* *entrance I think very beautiful, up a flight of steps guarded by two magnificently carved dogs. The arms and motto "Prest d'accompli" carved over the doors through which we could see a long hall or gallery full of ancient weapons and armour with banners hanging above. We were not allowed to see the house in consequence of Lord Shrewsbury's absence and the terrible domestic calamity that swept off his daughter and her three sons in the course of a week.*

The gardener, who was very communicative, said plainly that he suspected something was wrong - it looked suspicious that all Prince Borgheso's sons should be taken and his daughter left who cannot inherit. The chapel is beautiful with its stained glass windows and Italian pictures; each side of the altar stands an Angel with golden wings and resplendent habiments, the expression of devotion most beautiful and in accordance with the theatrical georgeousness of Roman Catholic worship. The housekeeper was a Swiss and seemed to tread the holy sanctuary with great reverence. Then the gardens - we entered through an arched gateway, through a thick shrubbery to the front of a pretty cottage - strange and splendid was the scene - opposite was the hill rising gradually from a dingle of bog plants and pools of water lilies to a terrace where flowers and statues were mingled in profusion - then came a range of dome shaped conservatories and at the back a thick wood of pines and larch all beheld in the most glorious setting sun.

On the right the rock was left bare for a light pagoda-ish temple with a lovely view of the other side of the house - the spray of fountains, on a scale I never saw before, fell glittering and silvery against the dark green banks. It was a fairy land and the melody of a Welsh harp added to the sense on enchantment.

The greenhouses contained enormous exotic and beautiful flowers - bread fruit tree, fan palms and feathery papyrus and Mrs Murray's Musac Texalis, Arches with climbing plants twining up the pillars and over the arch beneath which were white Italian vases, taller than ourselves and covered with mythological carvings, £300 each - dined at 6 and now am sleepy.

Next day we went to Matlock to Mrs Cummings at "The Old Bath Hotel" going from Faxley Ilam - odd uninteresting country with great round hills - Mrs Watts Russell's beautiful house, Elizabethan. A sketch of the Countess Mongelet, very very beautiful. Magnificent rooms all in use by rational people evidently. Mrs Watts Russell died a year ago. From Ilam to Dovedale, not far, walked four miles through Dovedale, most beautiful, rather like the rocks at Wick, a deep glen through which runs the Dove dividing Staffordshire from Derbyshire, then to Matlock - tolerably comfortable in a wee corner of the Hotel.

***Friday 3rd September** - Spent the day at Matlock, ascending the Heights of Abraham, splendid views! Then to Mr Adams Museum and bought some little things as relics - shop full of mineral beauties, spare stalactites, vases and carved marble. After dinner Mr Adams took Mama and me to see the spar-turning, pretty and curious requiring great skill. Mr Adams gave me a pretty little winder spool that I saw made. Sketched in the garden by the fountain, in* *the evening finished sketches domiciled in pretty pink and white bedroom. On Saturday we could not start before 12, the rain was so heavy, uncomfortable drive to Haddon - the river so swelled and foaming under the magnificent High Tor that it was not like the quiet Derwent we had stood to admire in sunshine the day before. Haddon Hall, a very curious old place, but on the whole Nash's Lithographic rather cause one to be disappointed.*

Sunday 5th September *- Remained at "Chatsworth Inn" at Edensor, delightful place like everything else belonging to the Duke of Devonshire - Mama went with me to church - beautiful and effecting discussion by the Duke's Chaplain Mr Wilmot. It would be difficult to listen to such truths so forcibly uttered without growing wise and better - I was delighted - walked to Chatsworth for the Duke allows anyone to ramble his park as they please, how I wish he had been at home! Chatsworth affects me like mountain scenery or a sudden view of the ocean. I long to be alone with its vastness. There is a great deal of gilding, window frames, balconies etc. Thousands of deer, sheep and cows. The beautiful Wye winds through the park - in general I hate show houses, but this has so much of the Athenium Temple, the Venetian palace so much linking it with all the brightest imaginings that it is unlike its companions - no that is not the word for I have seen nothing before worthy to be called so - nothing that took my breath away and overpowered me with its splendour. We start early for Casleton so I must enfold myself in the sweetest little french bed a lovely room but the smell of cigars villainous - a special comfort, a large looking glass enough to see the whole human form divine, not having met with one before.*

We started on a fine frosty Monday morning for Castleton. Middleton Dale, rocks like castles very fine but after the two miles it occupies the country becomes of the most miserably bleak - Sterile stone wall description - better for future tourists to drive about a mile up Middleton Dale, then turn back by Hathersage where the road is better. The hills tremendous and the precipes so awful that we walked down the last descent into Castleton where some country festival was held the effect of bell ringing among the mountains was extremely pretty. From the Inn we walked to the Peak Cavern and into it as far as the water, which even I did not wish to cross, being dark and dirty but wonderful. Mr Vallance told Papa he must visit the blue fluor spar mine.

Behold us then this Blessed Monday, the 6th day of September in the year of grace 1841 stopping at the entrance of the Blue John Mine. Narrow and dark the way descended - now steepest and most rugged of steps each holding a tallow candle in a state of nature, a party beforehand having taken all the candlesticks. Down we went through windings and twisting the most incommodious to the human form divine. Papa thinking he was going to perdition I do believe. At last we came to a sort of chamber among the rocks where our guide, a bright-eyed bright-intellected little boy, lighted a rude sort of chandelier which he drew up to a height of 50ft, displaying above, below and around the most magnificent rocky chasm glittering with wet stalactites and looking most unearthly. It was very sublime, but yet it was impossible to help laughing as the great drops of water came splashing down on our upturned visages and as Papa expressed the ultimatum of his wonder and admiration - it would do very well for Drury Lane - devoutly do I believe would he have preferred seeing it there.

We went no further having gone halfway through the mine and is much like what we saw but finer - next we turned off to the blue fluor spar mine - after descending a little the passage became lined with the beautiful marble streaked with veins of the brittle and beautiful spar, it was very lovely - greasy and dirty and intensely diverted I emerged into the light of day. The mine was very warm and we got into the carriage more comfortable than before - a little further on our driver stopped to show us the ebbing and flowing well, a most curious natural phenomenon. In wet weather the water flows about three times in the hour, but after a dry time it is often two hours keeping people waiting. We were most fortunate for it was just beginning to flow as we stopped and in five minutes it had filled a sort of basin or drinking place for cattle. By 10 minutes it had all run off, or flowed back, and the place left nearly dry. How I wished for the power of sketching - there was a pretty girl sitting on a stone above the well with others of the simple-hearted peasantry of this north country and as the water rose she said "there are seven wonders in this world and this is one of them" - people here are less liberal, they talk of the seven wonders of the Peak.

Buxton, where we soon arrived is a nice place, rather pretty, rather gay, but we dined in our own room. The crescent is a munificent donation and embellishment of the late Duke of Devonshire. Stayed the night and on Tuesday morning came to Ashbourne through a pouring rain that grievously prevented our enjoyment of Miller's Dale and some of the finest scenery between Buxton and Bakewell that Derbyshire can boast. It is like Matlock but grander. The Church is a beautiful one and contains some very ancient monuments where the marble Knights and Dames of high degree still lie in state - the little tomb which is more particularly celebrated is one by Banks to the memory of Penelope only daughter of Sir Brooke and Lady Boothby of Ashbourne Hall. The flowing sash and the delicate feet are indescribably pretty, she was about 6 years old and her slight figure is laid on a mattress and pillows slightly bent in the most perfect nature. The hair is bound in wavy masses but the face not very pretty.

Wednesday 8th September *- Came to Lichfield this morning through Needwood Forest in the midst where six roads meet in view of the little white lodge is Mr Harper the Head Axe Bearer of the forest which is crown land. Pretty country and a fine day. Lichfield is a nice town, city I should say, and the Cathedral splendid; Chantrey's monument to the children is so beautiful that a person's expectation can hardly be too much raised. The repose is exquisite the pillow seems bent into the very folds of down under their wavy hair; they are rather fat and so life-like and child-like you expect to see them breathe notwithstanding the undeceiving white marble. After dinner we went to hear the organ* *play - sweet very sweet were its fine tones in the "Plead thou my cause oh Lord" of Mozart. The grand Hallelujah Chorus of Handel and several other chants and anthems. The verger, Mr Null, has taken us under his peculiar protection and we go tomorrow morning to the service. Very good shops here and tomorrow we reach home - it has been a very pleasant tour. Heard the chanting next morning in the cathedral and reached home by 6 - a wet day.*

Thursday 7th October *- Came here to Leighton on Monday and Papa went back next day when Grandmama and I had a long conversation. Alas, the best intentions in the world so often do not good, rather harm! Tilly and Abraham have been kind to us beyond expression, but not altogether judicious, exceeding their mission.*

Preparations and the arrival of Sarah Grubb, Mrs Impey and John Bull, house full Mama and I tabernacled at the Langfords who had gone to Brighton. Thursday the great meeting, Mrs Grubb electrified everyone by her anathemas at the Quarterly Meeting - she could see the bites of the old serpent! Yet was it all in the spirit of charity that she was probing deep in the wound even as that was but an unskilful physician, who would apply outward patching and plastering, a more agreeable woman too than might be expected out of the gallery - after dinner everyone departed.

Took a walk before breakfast with Emma to the field of Mr Hayters where the ploughing match was to be. Met Peter and sent him splashing through the mud with a message to the ploughman - that they would be late. After meeting, Grandpapa, Grandmama and Mama being all gone into the field I thought I could not do better than see the cattle from the garden, so went in with Emma and Charles. Major Gilpin's fat ox. Mr Hayter's Durham bull - sheep, pigs, cows, oxen, all as fat as possible. Saw Lord Charles Russell and Mr Hayter - Lord Charles very, very shabby and undistinguished looking - went home and found they had been to the ploughing field and stuck in the mud.

Friday 8th October *- As we were sitting after dinner a note came with a black seal and the Stratford postmark - it was from Miss Lawford announcing the very sudden decease of my Aunt Kitelee, we were all very much shocked. She was quite well early on Thursday morning and had been at Church the day before; about 12 she had a fainting fit but no danger was apprehended until about 6 in the evening when they sent for Mrs Bailey who did not arrive in time to see her mother alive - she breathed her last after 10.*

Tuesday 19th October *- After breakfast was informed Papa had had a note from Peter requesting an interview - sick Fidgetty day! Walk with Emma (no Peter) and Charles - packing 7 o'clock he came - their conference was not very long. Papa was pleased to say that I was old enough to judge and speak for myself and Peter had better see me - but Peter opened the case thus "I wished an opportunity to tell thee of my attachment to thy daughter and to ask thy consent, if thous canst give me any encouragement to hope I shall succeed" - Papa shook his head but expressed respect for Peter and his father. Might he come to* *the Dale, No - Papa said. If Papa could give him no encouragement it would only be a greater trial to his feelings to see Adelaide, and at this point the heartless booby fled I call it ill usage! How does he know that I am not much attracted to him - does he suppose that a young lady's Papa is the person to know the state of her feelings? Oh! the shabby way of sneaking out of a refusal.*

Wednesday 20th October *-We have been to the Exhibition - Maclise's picture of the enchanted palace where everyone is sleeping for 100 years. "Trial of Effie Deans" Finished with the theatre, "The Hunchback" Mr and Miss Bandenhoff, she is very pretty - a good passionate actress. Sleepy now!*

Thursday 28th October *- Behold on the Sunday following our return, a letter from Booby Esq., properly enclosed in one to Papa. Two mortal days and part of a night devoted to answering the monkey properly, but it is comforting when such a thing does not need thinking twice about. Abraham helped me with the pleasurable observation that I knew amply sufficient of him to decide.*

Friday 3rd December *- A marriage de convenance would be consistent conclusion for such an unromantic girlhood as mine! Rachael Foster came to stay till Saturday, when behold enter the bodily presence of Alfred Darby who has been paying us Sunday evening visits of late. On Sunday evening he and Abraham started on some London business and I had Tilly all the week they have been away and I in an unpleasant state of suspense! Now on 7th December it is over! I have not quite refused him! I believe I shall though but whether I shall be sorry?*

Saturday 18th December *- Dearest Tilly has been stopping with us since Thursday - my new appendage did not pay me a visit on Monday - vanished with its Mama to Liverpool - It's an odd beginning! what will be my name by this time in 1842!*

Tuesday 21st December *- Behold my appendage is returned this day and hath not been to see me. I will let him go on for a while to see the extent to which his incivilities will carry him. Tomorrow I am to meet the gipsy and hear who I am to marry at last - I am really sillier by far than at 16!*

Friday 24th December *- Last Wednesday evening another visit from Alfred what can I do? They all tell me I shall kill him if I refuse him - I do not love him, hardly like him in many respects but I cannot be an assassin.*

Wednesday 29th December *- I cannot marry that man. I suppose I must see him tomorrow evening and pave the way for telling him so. It would be very awful to live at Little Wenlock without a carriage, but surely Mr Edmond's kind warm heart will not bury his wife alive when he has one. Now people would say I was foolish to refuse my cousin because he has plenty of this world's goods and his wife's position might be pretty good, but I rather think Miss Darby of The White House is of more importance than ever Mrs Alfred Darby will be - therefore, as I cannot love him, and therefore could not influence him much, I am sure I would rather remain as I am, or be Mrs George Edmonds.*[10]

NOTES

1. This is probably a reference to one of the centres of unrest under the Chartist movement. Following the rejection of the People's Charter by the House of Commons in 1839, a National Charter Association had been formed in 1840 to agitate for the Charter by speeches and writing.
2. George Edmonds was the vicar of Madeley. In 1841 he became vicar of Little Wenlock. He was a rich bachelor. Partly at his own expense, he founded the village school and restored the church (V.C.H. XI, p.90).
3. Henry Dickinson (1812-1886) was married to Deborah Darby (1810-1855). They settled at Severn House (now The Valley Hotel, Ironbridge). The Dickinsons had sold their shares in the Coalbrookdale Company to Lucy Darby and her family in 1831. The marriage between Henry and Deborah brought the Dickinsons back into the mainstream of the Darby family. Under the marriage settlement Henry was to receive £1,000 a year after the death of Deborah (which took place in 1855).
4. The Chesnuts was the home of Abraham Darby IV and Matilda, Adelaide's sister.
5. Henry and Charles were the sons of Richard Darby of "Rosehill".
6. Pool at the head of Loamhole Dingle and the far end of the Rope Walk.
7. Miss Sophy Horne was the sister of James Horne, Adelaide's first suitor.
8. Dale House, close to the Coalbrookdale Works was the home of Mrs Lucy Darby, and of her son Alfred and daughter Mary.
9. See note 9, 1833, page 6.
10. Alfred Darby was rejected for the second time. George Edmonds was the vicar of Madeley who had recently become the vicar of Little Wenlock.

Dale House was traditionally the home of the Managers of the Coalbrookdale Company. It was built by Abraham Darby I in 1717. It was occupied by Barnard Dickinson and his family until 1838. Then it was occupied by Lucy Darby and her family from 1838 to 1858.

1842

Comment

If at the end of 1841 Adelaide thought that she had seen the end of her affairs of the heart for the time being, she must have been disillusioned. The affairs with Alfred Darby, George Edmonds (now vicar of Little Wenlock) and Peter (from Leighton Buzzard) reappear in the Journal during the early part of 1842.

On 26th March she records a discord in the relationship between the family in Coalbrookdale and the family in Leighton Buzzard. This arose from the fact that John Grant (Adelaide's grandfather) had established a Bank at Leighton Buzzard in partnership with a John Bassett. In his Will, John Grant had declared that his share in the Bank should pass to Francis Darby, but during his last illness, he had made a codicil stating that the share should pass to Abraham Darby, not Francis Darby. This was at the instigation of the Bassetts, the other partners. Adelaide's mother, Hannah, was outraged and being of a disputatious nature (as was to be demonstrated later) she demanded that the codicil should be cancelled – but her father refused. She wrote to Abraham Darby who in turn wrote to Francis Darby to disclaim any knowledge of the change and to reject it. Francis accepted the explanation but was understandably indignant, to such an extent that he avoided visiting the family at Leighton for the rest of the year. The repercussions of this incident continued until the reading of the Will in 1843.

The highlight of the year was an "expedition" by the family to the Lake District and to Edinburgh during July, graphically described by Adelaide in her Journal. By a coincidence, on the return from Edinburgh they met Joseph Dickinson, eldest son of Barnard and Ann Dickinson, and his new bride, Lucy Midgley, whom he had married at Rochdale on 14th July.

In October 1842 just as the family were due to return from Leighton Buzzard to Coalbrookdale, John Grant became seriously unwell and died over two months later on 29th December 1842.

Sunday 2nd January - *New Year's Eve we dined at Severn House. Mr Reynolds and his "cadeau of Le Paravent", Mr & Mrs and N Anstice and Mr John. Charming evening! I have had one other evening with Alfred and can only say, as Dryden did of the ungifted stage manager 'let him alone! let him alone! and he'll do worse yet.' He was supremely disagreeable - I had a good opportunity of judging too, for things were going very disagreeably at home, but then it is for life! and I think it would be but leaving one cage for another. He has neither warm heartedness nor that gay happy temper nor sparkling wit which* *are all fascinating to me. I can never love him and I will not marry him though I should have to subside into a temporary 500 per annum.*

Wednesday 5th January - *There is a spell over my refusal! Yesterday I walked to Eastfield and thence with Hannah over part of her district. She told me first of her brother's prospects of marrying Miss Midgley*[1] *and then asked me about my own! It seems that the report is very general but whether it has come from the servants, or is only a revival of the old one which I heard of very much just before the proposal I cannot tell. She exhorted me to think of it - I came home very much out of humour. Turning a corner of the works a piece of grit flew into my eye, stuck into the upper eyelid. Came home after calling to see Abraham who has got a dreadful strain in his back and cannot stir. Eye worse, went to bed as it made my head ache - could not see Alfred of course, so he stayed and enchanted Papa and Mama! Not been to see me today as in duty he ought. After tea found speck in eye and got it out. We are to call at Little Wenlock this week, I have got a cold, but intend it to get better this time as I am going, refusal or no refusal, - I wonder who would make the best husband? I am almost sure Mr Edmond*[2] *would be the kindest and most affectionate. I know I like him the best and I am going to see him!*

Thursday 6th January - *Alfred has been here this evening - quite angelic tried to refuse him - told him my excessive dislike to consideration of this kind. Hoped I should see him very happy with someone far better suited to make him so than I should be - but what can one do when a man says that his whole interest in life centres in oneself - alack a day! I am going to bed. I know if I could like him that I should be foolish to refuse him, but then he was angelic tonight, and he is often very disagreeable. Mr Edmonds would be 10 times as passionate but not so devoted. I suspect he would be much more in the "I think you love me a little" style than in the "You are all the world to me" - and yet I do not know - his eyes have a wonderful genius for saying the last.*

Wednesday 12th January - *It is decided and without any offence taken and I verily believe without at all lessening me in his esteem. I am much relieved but have the headache and must go to bed. Papa to my surprise exclaims about the £60,000 lost!*

Friday 28th January - *A lovely morning, the first for very long. Papa came in and asked if he should send for horses to go to Little Wenlock. Mama quarrelled with the roads, which in truth in these parts were a sheet of ice and was no way inclined to go - 'malgre tout' we did go for I was much disposed to venture though to say truth I was glad when the exploit was over. Mr Edmonds I must say made the exploit as easy for me as he could.*

Saturday 5th February - *Charlotte Anstice and I had a long chat over the fire - she seems very happy - she gave me a great deal of good advice, was not at all pleased with me for attempting to bring my mind to consider at all about the Alfred affair. "Whatever you do, Ada, do not throw yourself away upon the* *idea of its not signifying who you marry. Your life has been a peculiar one and I would rather you made up your mind not to marry at all at present. There is nothing agreeable in being married itself nor anything advantageous without love. How could you promise to obey a man you did not entirely love?...."*

Wednesday 16th February - *Mrs Anstice and Charlotte called this morning and then went to Matilda's and I went with them. She had been shopping with us again and Abraham did not return till night. Charlotte very pretty in black velvet bonnet and feathers and scarlet Indian shawl and ermine muff. My cold rather better. Now Papa is quarrelling with the very flippant wit of Horace Walpole in his letters to Horace Maine &c.*

The recollections of the Court of George I and II are very amusing and new. We are reading Frankenstein. I am very disappointed. It is the most deliberately woven texture of disgusting impossibilities conceivable! There is no revelling in the wild richness of an imagination that loves the supernatural - but a sage walking forth with demons, the work not of incantations but of a most barbarous pair of hands. Frankenstein is a student of Engoldsladt who forms a human monster and finds the means of endowing it with life. It goes forth and gains a literary education through a chink in the wall of its hut which joins a cottage where a delightful family of French exiles have taken up their abode - when this thing appears to them they flee in terror, and he assumes at last all the malicious manner of hunchbacks and betes in general.

Thursday 17th February - *Last night I sat up after my Journal reading Frankenstein. It was warmer than it has been and the fire being somewhat large for such near approximation I removed into bed. I heard a bell from time to time from a distance and the secondary train of thoughts which usually accompanies one's perusal of even interesting stories, was employed in accounting for the sound. At last it rang longer and I knew it for the Dale bell. Still I went on and finished the wild story and just as the bell ceased I had finished the fiend's farewell promises to light his own funeral pyre. I put out the candle and looked out at the window was it the force of fancy that had brought such a realisation of Mrs Shelley's picture! - At the back of the Scotch fir beyond the pool rose columns of thick white smoke lighted up in the darkness by a mass of fire that shot up in sparks higher than the ridge of Lincoln Hill. I rang for Anne who came and satisfied me that it was the old pattern shop - by 2 o'clock it was almost over - Abraham and Alfred came home when the flames were highest. No accident and no damage beyond the destruction of timber left in the pattern shop.*

Sunday 13th March - *Mama goes this week to Leighton - I am going to be left with Matilda for four days. I might have gone with Mama and seen my friends at Leighton or I might have gone with Papa to London and seen "Acis and Galatea", and perhaps Adelaide Kemble, but as neither very much wished for me, I judged it to be most wise and pleasant to remain. Everybody very* *distressed at the murder of Sir I MacNaughton and the loss of 8,000 men in Caboul.*[3]

The other day we saw in the paper the death of Sir W Anson's second son - on board the "Isis" off the coast of Africa from the effect of a fever, aged 23. Very melancholy, he had the sweetest disposition in the family, or as they thought in any family.

Sunday 20th March - *They have been four happy days with Tilly and her dear husband is good nature itself to chuse to have me to the exclusion of his brother. Mama has brought back a catalogue of grievances for me, and I don't know whether Grandmama will have me again at Leighton.*

Saturday 26th March - *Among other disagreeable intelligences from Leighton, Mama brought an account of certain new articles of partnership at the Bank whereby Abraham's name has been substituted for Papa's at the wish of the Bassetts as they said which after it had been so long promised seemed rather a hard case.*[4] *When Abraham heard of it he was very wrath and refused to have anything to do with it - he did not want the thing, and it was very unjust to throw an appearance of underhand dealing on him. Mama wrote and he wrote and this morning brought a letter to Papa explaining the circumstances - of course his surprise and indignation were great. Abraham has been to him this evening and I am glad to say he is quite exonerated in Papa's eyes.*

Thursday 14th April - *Last Saturday the things for the Mansion House Bazaar*[5] *finished, the note to Miss Gurney composed, and the whole off my mind. There were about £10 worth of work, and the same in a box of berlin castings. Coalbrookdale I mean, which Mama and Abraham sent. Bull's box of books went back at the same time so that I was left with grand lack of occupation. Pulled a frock to pieces and moralized upon the vanity of human wishes. Mr and Mrs Harte are stopping at the Chesnuts, charming Americans - the very best specimens that race could see, I think. I have been spending "Quarter Day" with Matilda and them and was almost reconciled to losing Tilly in the pleasure of going to see her. Was obliged to come home this evening, they were going to Dale House and three Grahams were coming to see us, Miss Barrett is with them a pretty girl with the most lovely blue eyes.*

Monday 18th April - *This world has some agreeables - I have been to Apley, and today to Wenlock Abbey with Tilly and Mrs Harte, she is the sweetest person that ever crossed one's path in a sunny day! This evening they have been with us. Mrs Harte plays most beautifully - her execution is wonderfully rapid and brilliant, like her conversation, and her musical memory so perfect that she seems to remember and pick up every pretty little air that falls in her way, and with all never was mortal so entirely devoid of everything in the remotest degree like presentation or vanity or display. Mr Harte is almost equally delightful in a quiet way - they are very charming people and though not always very warm in the expression of any sentiments I cannot like and dislike by halves.*

Tuesday 19th April - *Mr and Mrs Harte left today for Birmingham but they are coming back. Abraham and Matilda went with them on their way to Worcester. They have left me some nice American novels, "Hyperion" and "The Green mountain Boys" by Judge Thompson but they pale their ineffectual fires beside such genius as Bulwers.*

Thursday 26th April - *Dearest Tilly came up after dinner with Mrs Harte whose husband has returned to bestow a little more attention upon his sails; and behold she (Tilly) asked me to go with them the next day to Liverpool. I had permission, and of course was very happy! We had lovely weather and passed Thursday there very delightfully. Shopping in Bold Street with Henry,*[6] *who was our humble and very obliging servant. After cemetery went to Abraham at the warehouse; he took us down to see the docks and across to New Brighton, delicious sands - charming place to spend a quiet time. Should like it very well for a honeymoon retreat provided always that I marry with the prospects of wandering to my heart's content over this beautiful world. After lunch and a race to catch the steamer and a delightful return we went back and inspected the warehouse which is very handsome. Mrs Robinson*[6] *at the head thereof. Then Henry*[6] *took us over the custom house - superb - and the Town Hall, magnificent - and run up to the top of the last, even up to the lion's paws. Then after that it was I believe that we went back to Abraham and he took us back to the Waterloo and told us to sit on the sofa and be quiet till it was time to dress for dinner. We let him depart in the good conviction that we were going to do as we were bid - then we went and did some more shopping and were just dressed and ready when the three gentlemen came to dinner - iced cream and iced water and all sorts of luxuries. Then Mr Robinson*[6] *persuaded us that there was going to be a lecture on Mesmerism by Dr Braid, and that we should enjoy it. It was very wonderful. In a few seconds by some imperceptible influence exercised over them, the patients were thrown into a trance-like sleep. They stood still, and if an arm was lifted up it stiffened. They became more and more insensible until the cataleptic state was produced in which a pistol fired close to the ear produced no emotion. Two paralytic patients submitted themselves to his hands and were soon put to sleep, and three gentlemen, two of whom had been mesmerized before, the third failed entirely. The last scene was a young lady who came in apparently asleep and in the most spectre-like manner glided on to the platform; she was very pretty and assumed the most graceful attitudes at the wave of a diabolical-looking black glove. It was very mysterious and wonderful, but very clear that there was no deception.*

Thursday 16th June - *Set off for Leighton where Papa did not stop*[7] *- found the Bassett's paramount. Pleasant walks with the Reeves.*

Friday 24th June - *Went to tea at the Reeves, charming long walks over Groveberry and by Lebburn, a new way. Tuesday Abraham came for us, Papa not chusing,*[7] *and Wednesday we came home.*

1842 - LAKE DISTRICT EXPEDITION

Monday 18th July - *Waterloo Hotel, Liverpool. Left home this morning at 9 oclock - "en grand seigneur", from the Whitmore Station Halt.*[8] *A pleasant cloudy day, in Liverpool by 4. Went to the Mechanics Institute which is full of curious things and more than full of visitors.*

Tuesday 19th July - Bowness - *Wet day. Went to show Mama the Warehouse, then did some shopping and saw the print of Rayter's "Coronation!" picture the Duchess of Sutherland must be a splendid creature, and looks as if her beauty and her jewels were both things of course. From Liverpool to Lancaster we came by the railroad, all new to Mama and me and after Preston the country is pretty - Lancaster Castle is grand. Walked up to see it and the splendid view from the churchyard. After Lancaster it rained provokingly, the country is beautiful but I think not at all fit to follow Wales and Derbyshire. We went from Lancaster to Milnthorpe and thence to Bowness, which looks over Windermere.*

Wednesday 20th July - *This morning we explored Windermere; went a little way on it and admired it as much as the cloudy weather permitted. It began to rain again just as we started - beautiful drive to Ambleside along the banks of the Lake, six miles - thence we had to take horse and a drag, and great preparation for the hills, which are certainly awful. Rydal Water and Grasmere are lovely and they follow mountains above - mountains lost in the clouds. It brightened delightfully as we came near Helvellyn in which I was disappointed - beyond it is the vale of St John - Saddleback and Skiddaw which are real mountains. We were glad to reach Keswick after this long 18 miles (I have forgotten to say how lovely Thirlmere on Leathes Water is at the foot of Helvellyn). Windermere is to Derwent Water what Llangollen is to Beddgelert, a quiet, beautiful introduction to the really sublime. Tho, dark purple rocks and beautiful green Islands upon whose thick foliage the evening sun shone beautifully made me think Derwent Water far lovlier than anything we had yet seen. Windermere is prettiest from Lowood just below Elleray the seat of Professor Wilson and it was pleasant to look at the scenery which must have inspired many a bright thought in the benevolent and joyous musings of Christopher Worth. But oh, Skiddaw and Derwentwater, they are worthy of each other and both magnificent. We are not comfortable here, Keswick is a poor place - with a pretty church though - of pink granite from Penryth. The Inns do not look on the Lake which is a half mile off, but it is a most sweet walk and along the banks where the boats are moored and where Captain Henry allows people to walk through his plantations. There is a seat among fir trees at the end looking down precipitately on the lake towards Castle Crag, oh! it is delicious, I could sit there for days, but one longs to be alone with the rock and the wave, things that hold not man's dominion. The Inn so full that we are disposed of in a lodging house adjoining.*

Thursday 21st July - *Glorious day at Keswick, drive round the lake and up to the Bowder stone in Borrowdale. Not a cloud on Saddleback or Skiddaw - sundry walks to the lake and verily a sail upon it with Papa in the evening round the great island under the protection of the most encouraging boatman in the world.*

Friday 22nd July - *This morning we left Keswick soon after breakfast and were delighted with the first part of the drive to Cockermouth by Bassenthwaite lake and valley. It is thickly wooded and altogether greener than Derwentwater but the precipitous heights of Lord's Crag on one side and Skiddaw on the other prevent its seeming tame after. Then the country grows uninteresting though it has all the advantages of glorious weather and from Cockermouth to Wigton it does not greatly improve though we see Skiddaw and Helvellyn at one time in the distance. From Wigton we went on to Carlisle and soon saw the blue Scottish mountains beyond the Solway and a vast wide extent of country totally different from anything we had passed before. Carlisle is a very interesting old city - went to see the Cathedral. The jail and courthouses are fine buildings of the red stone usual in this country - I was sorry there is no vestige of the celebrated old gates remaining. Carlisle was destroyed by the Danes and remained in ruins until William Rufus built the walls and restored it. They are continually finding old Roman remains in digging among the broken debris of a city which has seen such various fortunes.*

We stayed and dined and went to call on a certain Mrs Scott who enters with great interest into the antiquities of her fine city. She showed us a piece of Cumberland silver which is found in considerable quantities among the lead. After dinner, left Carlisle and went on to Longtown, and, the evening being beautiful, resolved to cross the border and sleep at Langholme. Most interesting drive between these two places. Just after Longtown past Netherby, the beautiful seat of Sir James Graham, among woods with the Esk flowing clear and sparkling over its stony bed, which the dry weather has left often very visible. We passed through the very scene of Lochinvar's elopement with the bride of Netherby - one almost expected to see the Netherby clan, Fosters, Fenwicks and Musgroves "racing and chasing o'er Carnobie Lea." Then came the thick, luxuriant woods of the Duke of Buccleuch and immovable crossings of the Esk and we found ourselves established at Langholme which partly belongs to the Malcolms. There is a monument in honour of Sir Palteney Malcolm.

Saturday 23rd July - Toosonce Inn - *Today I have seen things I have longed to see ever since I was old enough to delight in Sir Walter! We left Langholme this morning and followed the windings of the Esk along a hilly but good road over the wide moors of Eskdale to Mosspaut, a country inn where we changed horses, through Teviotdale the country grew very lovely. I had no notion of the clear beauty of the dashing views of which Scott loved to sing. The Teviot runs to Hawick, and at Hawick we began to plan our sightseeing. "Horses to*

Selkirk" said Papa, "except you will go all the way to Melrose, we want to see Abbotsford."

At last we reached that scene of countless interests and associations. It is not a fine show house, but who expects mirrors and gilding in a place which Sir Walter Scott gave all his cash and genius to decorate. The hall is full of armour and relics seen through the bright stained glass, and above and along the ceiling are the coats of arms of each Scottish Chieftain. Oh, it was intensely interesting - the chimney piece is designed from an arch in Melrose Abbey. There are the enormous keys of the Tolbooth in Edinburgh. In a pretty little breakfast room is a painting of the wild castle on the sea coast of Berwick which is the original of Wolf's Crag. The dining room is small and rather low with a beautiful oak ceiling copied from designs at Melrose. There is a beautiful head of Queen Mary after her execution which Sir Walter said gave him a better idea of her beauty than anything - it is placed like the heads of John the Baptist and the handsome Duke of Monmouth. There are sketches of Mickle Mouthed Meg being offered to the prisoner who stands debating with the hatter before his eyes, and of the dish of spurs. The tables are of sort of oak, the gift of Buccleuch. There is a little ante room containing his greatest treasures. The silver broad sword presented to him by the Celtic Society, Prince Charlie's gold spurs, Napoleon's pistols, the eagle Sir Walter picked up on the field of Waterloo. Rob Roy's gun, the claymore, a seal andrea ferara, his own pistols - and interesting relics without end.

The drawing room is pretty and has portraits of himself, Lady Scott and Miss Anne Scott (by Raeburn) who is extremely handsome in a Spanish dress of red velvet, and black mantilla fringed with gold - she is like Miss Margaret Rathbone. The little water colour picture of Mrs Lockhart standing with her hand on Maida is very pretty. The picture of the present Lady Scott's mother, quite a common-place handsome fine lady is strangely out of keeping.

With the rest - the Library is as it should be in the house of such a man the best room. The present Sir Walter in his uniform is over the fireplace. His figure is perfection and he is certainly very handsome but there is something strange and against one's feelings of what should be in knowing that this retreat of poetry and literature belongs to the dashing Colonel of the 40th now in India with his regiment, but they are expected to return and live here in a year or two. In this beautiful room are the chairs of boxwood and the Italian vase and table given to him by Lord Byron - the ebony cabinet and Dugdale's Monasticon which were George IV's gift, extreme comfort as well as elegance in everything. The last room we see is the study with its beloved shelves and the beautifully contrived staircase where as he told the Duchess of St Albans he could run down from his room and write for hours in the early morning and no-one any the wiser. I should have liked to be left in that room to have a comfortable cry over the last sad scene - when the pen fell from the great Magician's hand. In a glass case are the very clothes he then wore - his own mallet and wood knives and hatchet and gloves - I like his son for one thing, that he will have everything left in the state it was at his father's death the broken windows are not mended. From Sir Walter's desk one may easily understand how he imagined he saw the shape of Byron. The housekeeper seemed quite to understand the great interest of the place and gave us plenty of time. It is a very heavy style of architecture for the size - a cottage castle of Scots gothic. I had a treat of no commonkind at Melrose Abbey where I hoped we should have stayed to see it by the light of the glorious harvest moon, it is the most beautiful and perfect ruin I ever saw and this too sanctified by the genius of Scott. There too they tell us the niches that he admired, and show his simple monument to Tom Purdie. The tracerie and carved figures are wonderfully preserved. It was despoiled by Oliver Cromwell and John Knox. To our lamentations over it, the Scots boy who showed it with great intelligence observed - "Gin ye harry the neests - the craws ill soon flee away."

On we went to this lone wayside inn on the moors, passing the best view of Abbotsford which the larches will hide in a year or two. Also Galashiels and the pretty place of Mrs Scott of Gala. As the moon I could only console myself in the good well-furnished room over the tea and toast by thinking how few and far between are the people who would in their hearts care for "staying to view fair Melrose aright".

Sunday 24th July - *Went on the two remaining stages to Edinburgh, a most magnificently situated town. At Tushie Bridge, the old landlady counselled us to "go to McQueen's Hotel", sending her compliments to him and directions to tell us everything worth hearing and seeing - we asked her about Borthwick Castle. "Aye," she said, "ye'll haw seen it frae the hill - an old ruin - it were a gran place when Queen Mary came there". We pitied the unfortunate Queen and she replied "she war ill used, but she wanna gude, she wanna gude, but your English Queen were always a muckle deceiver". When we got to McQueens, he informed us the old lady at Rushie Bridge was the original of Meg Dodo - Sir Walter liked to talk to her. She hoped we had approved of Abbotsford.*

"Ye'll hae read Jennie Dean's" she said. We went to a Presbyterian kirk with the service - or rather no service of which I cannot say I was pleased - the sermon was good and on the uncertainty of time which we should all remember but prosy to a degree. The Scots accent, too, is far more agreeable in the lower classes than in the higher - Yet all the people are freer from affectation than in England, there is no spark of that servility which implies - "I will cheat you the first opportunity" - but they are quietly civil at all times out of respect for themselves much more than to you.

Monday 25th July - Edinburgh - *We have admired the magnificent views and monuments of the Calton hills, and Mrs Forest's beautiful groups of sculpture. It is wonderful the amount of talent Scotland has produced from her* *peasant population and yet their intelligent countenances and contemplative attitudes when an Englishman would be asleep or only lazy, should make one cease to wonder at their love and pride in their splendid country and in their imperishable writers - Tam O'Shanter is very good in the sculpture, so is Mazeppa, and in a different way Cuddie Headrigg - and Burns resting from the plough is beautiful. From the Castle Hill is a beautiful view opposite we saw the Scottish Regalia with some difficulty by means of a soldier. I admired the ancient Crown of Bruce very much with its uncut stones of great value. There are two sceptres besides with Cairngorms of great size at the top. On a separate plateau are the collar and sparkling diamond star of the Order of the Garter sent by Elizabeth to James 6th in a much more modern ring, which I forget the history, unless it came with the collar but containing a ruby of great beauty. Then we went to see Mons Meg of historical memory and to the wee room where James 6th of Scotland and First of England was born. Then to Holyrood where the interest is indeed great in its half-ruined magnificence. It was indeed interesting to stand in the long picture gallery hung with barbarous likenesses of the Scottish Kings and remember that there Prince Charles held fine balls in '45. I suppose be had also Queen Mary's rooms, curious very, with their antique beds and proof of her industry. There is a sweet picture of Rizzio, the dark stain on the floor, and the secret staircase are very awful.*

There is a fine painting by Sir David Wilkie of King George IV in the Highland dress in the room that was fitted up for his reception and court. The rooms inhabited by Charles I and his attendants are also shown. It is a sort of refuge for exiled princes and nobility, as no-one can be arrested there; the privilege extending I believe over Salisbury Crags. We ascend a little way in the evening, far enough to see the ruined hermitage which was the scene where Jennie Deans was met by the ruffian Robertson, and lower down is the cottage where she dwelt - at St Anthony's well we had some of the clear water, which has the same rainy taste that it all has here. We saw also the picture of the Royal Institution, a very fine building in, I should think, the Egyptian style. There are some of Ettyle, the finest I had seen. Three - Judith raising her dagger before she strikes Holofernes - Judith running from the tent with his head - and Judith's slave listening at the door of the tent. They are very large and life itself There were a number of students taking copies, fine intelligent boys. The other pictures were by the Old Master but not the finest of their productions. We went to some tartan shops and were struck with the dearness, the great civility and sympathy Mama's Grant plaid researches met with.

Tuesday 26th July - *We left Edinburgh this morning, to my sorrow - it is magnificent! The scenery about Selkirk is beautiful with the Yarrow and the Ettrick flowing through it - we stopped there for dinner and Mama and I walked on. An old man overtook us and we asked him something about the rivers and admired the country which made him happy directly. "It will be the bonniest place in Scotland - I mane the South. I dinna ken the Highlands maybe the* *mountains will be higher." And so it was, lovely in the extreme, with the beautiful woods of Bowhill stretching far away. We were not permitted to stay at Hawick and at Langham fell in with a fair and were obliged to go on in the dark through that beautiful part of Liddesdale and Netherby, in moonlight it is true. Longtown is a comfortable place.*

Wednesday 27th July - *Went to see Netherby - a pretty old place that belonged to Viscount Preston who forfeited it in '45. It has since been given back to the family. The oak carving is beautiful but since Sir James has been in office the family are very little there. From Carlisle to Wigton, where we found the difference between Scots and English tempers, the driver waxed wrath, and when he had cooled upon his first offence, he said we had made a great mistake not to take 4 horses and go straight to Keswick instead of to Cockermouth, finally persuaded Papa to take a pair of leaders from Cockbridge and took us over a dreadfully hilly road. When we came here Mrs Hill's Inn was full and we were put into wee lodgings. By the lake we met Joe Dickinson and his bride she is very agreeable and rather handsome.*[9] *We called upon them at the Inn after. Miss Grubb her bridesmaid and her brother were with them.*

Thursday 28th July - *From Keswick to Bowness. Went to see Glen Rothay as it is now called, William Balls, a small pretty place in excellent taste. It has been much enlarged and contains some nice rooms. The views of Rydal are lovely. Lady le Fleming's waterfall and the brook at Ambleside. We went to The Crown at Bowness, Cloudesdale's very comfortable. Explored some of the pretty walks about Windermere.*

Friday 29th July - *Tried to have a row on the water but Papa would not go far, very lovely weather but the wind had changed, there were really waves. As we came here called to see Levens, a most curious old place! It is all kept up in the best possible taste of centuries back by Colonel Howard, who must be a most amiable man by the account the servants gaveof him. There was very little about Mrs Howard through whom the property comes. She is of the Netherby family and both descended from the Bellinghams. There are the most curious clipped yew trees in the garden and the most charming old gardener. "I had been brought up with hothouses" said he, "and when I had seen the yew hedges I vowed I wouldn't stay a fortnight, but however, Colonel Howard came home and when I had once seen him we never parted - two and thirty years, and never a cross word, Sir!" There is a dais in the hall where they mostly prefer to dine. The antique style is well preserved and united with a very tolerable degree of comfort. Patchwork bed-picture of Anne Boleyn, very pretty; she had light auburn hair. We are settled for the night at Lancaster - the Assize week and not very agreeable.*

Thursday 4th August - *Very white day in my calendar. I went to the Committee where by the way I was at the very head of affairs, Hannah being at Westbury making preparations for the bride's reception and Mrs B having* *company. Called upon Mrs Williams, saw them both so amiable and so agreeable. Went to Mrs Reynolds to meet Mama. Miss Stradling was there, she is grown quite handsome. Spent the rest of the day with dearest Tilly, took my drawings and was very happy. Sent my last song to Mrs Cunningham this morning - I watch the result quite alone, there is no clue whatever to discover the author so that no harm will be done. I don't suppose they will accept it but perhaps they will be civil in their sheet "to correspondents". Going to copy Wolf's Crag for Abraham, very proud and happy.*

Thursday 18th August - *The weather is powerfully hot, exhausting and yet delightful. I live in the arbour almost. Mrs Adey has sent me a requisition to work for a Missionary bazaar. I am drawing a little from Sydney Cooper. After tea I took Prince, who grows very amiable and not quite so fractious as in his puppyhood, and sat under the fir tree with the moon looking hazy and golden, and not a leaf stirring. I did not get on with "Guy Mannering" between the dog's caresses and the evening's beauty. We hardly think it safe to stir beyond the gardens for the country is in a dreadful state and daily nearer and worse.*[10] *There was a Chartist Meeting yesterday and today the Colliers have struck work. At Preston the Military have fired on the mob and the loss of life has been considerable, and in the Potteries - dangerously close - they have burned and pillaged the houses of Magistrates and Clergymen in a frightful manner. Trentham was considered in danger. So formidable an insurrection has not been known for years, and the sanguine and hopeful look at each other and say "Where is it to end?". Plentiful and cheap as provisions are through the mercy of Providencey the poor creatures having neither work nor wages cannot buy any and trade is in such a state that if they all returned to their labours tomorrow there would be employment for but an inconsiderable number. People vilify the Corn Laws and Sir Robert Peel and the Parliament just prorogued for grouse shooting, but can Christian men exist who, having given all their energies to understand these difficult questions and knowing that certain changes are needed, who could possibly for small and selfish motives look on and see their fellow creatures reduced to misery in their power to alter. Papa has been to Bristol and returned poorly, there is a great deal of typhus fever about. There is to be a great sale at Clifton of Mr Adraman's effects a failure so ruinous the Dale Co. is likely to lose all the £3000. About September 4th the bridal party from Westbury dined here. Met Mr and Mrs Anstice, and a few days after we met them and Mr and Mrs I Anstice at Matilda's. She and I had very pretty dresses, which is all seems worth recording. This is a stupid world, not at all worth keeping a journal of.... We go on the 20th to Leighton.*

Tuesday 20th September - *We came to Leighton.*

Wednesday 5th October-29th December - *We were to have left Leighton on Monday. I spent a very pleasant evening at the Lawfords, Papa came that night and the next day Grandpapa was taken very unwell. On Wednesday night* *he was so much worse that Mr Otley said Mama must not leave him, and Papa returned without us. Thursday was not much better and Dr W sent for. His opinion was very unfavourable. The symptoms were high fever and great weakness and pain in the chest. After a fluctuating illness of some weeks, Grandpapa died on December 29th.*

NOTES

1. Hannah Dickinson was referring to her eldest brother, Joseph Dickinson (1805-1860) who was resident in Rochdale (having at one time been the manager of the company's works at Horsehay). There was a prospect of his marrying Lucy Midgley also of Rochdale. The marriage took place on 14th july 1842.
2. Mr George Edmonds, vicar of Little Wenlock and previously vicar of Madeley.
3. This incident took place in the First Afghan War (1839-42) and was a massive humiliation of the British Army. The British had occupied Kandahar and Kabul in 1839 and had placed Shah Siyah on the throne. This was resented by the Afghans. Insurrection broke out and the people of Kabul murdered the English residents in the winter of 1841-42. A weak British Commander, General Elphinstone, negotiated a humiliating treaty with the Afghans and began a retreat in the depths of winter. Despite assurances the retreating force of one British regiment, four native regiments and thousands of camp followers were massacred. Only one horseman, Dr Brydon, survived to bring the news to Jalalabad.
4. See background to this incident, Comment (page 129).
5. This was probably in aid of the Anti Corn Law League which had been formed in 1839.
6. Henry was William Henry Darby, son of Richard Darby, and therefore a cousin of Matilda and Adelaide. He appears to have been in charge of the Coalbrookdale Company's Liverpool interests. Mr Robinson who was in charge of the warehouse became a partner with Abraham, Alfred and Henry Dickinson in the Ebbw Vale Ironworks.
7. This was in protest at the decision of John Grant to remove his name from his Will in regard to the Leighton Buzzard Bank. See Comment (page 129).
8. Whitmore, south west of Stoke-on-Trent, was a Halt on the Railway from Birmingham, via Stafford and Crewe to Liverpool.
9. See note 1 and Comment (page 129).
10. The Chartist movement sent a petition to the House of Commons in 1842 purporting to be signed by three million persons (actually about a third of that number). The government refused to accept it, and so Chartist agitation continued.

1843

Comment

John Grant, Adelaide's grandfather died at Leighton Buzzard on 29th December 1842. The reading of the Will in January 1843 caused the problems foreseen in 1842 about the Leighton Buzzard Bank (see Comment 1842 - page 129). Adelaide's Journal glosses over the problems other than to comment that "the trouble was infinite".

Writing much later (16th June 1872) Adelaide's sister Matilda recorded

> *"- - - after his death his Will was read out to us all. - - - I do not remember ever hearing a word from my father on the subject; but my mother was very much annoyed. Abraham had to leave immediately after the reading of the Will to attend an Ironmasters' Meeting as Manager for the Dale Co. Mama said to me that John Bassett had called and expressed to her his sorrow that the Will had been such as it was, then I said if Abraham gives it up for Papa it will be all right. The impression on my mind was that she thought so too, and this I wrote to Abraham who returned to Leighton and in accordance with our views wrote to John Bassett that he wished to decline in favour of Francis Darby his father-in-law for whom it had been intended. But John Bassett told him that he would never enter into partnership with Papa and that John Grant was quite aware of this and of his reasons. Abraham asked to what did he object. He said that Papa's state when he came to Linslade was too well known and would be prejudicial to the Bank if he were admitted into partnership in it. But he accepted Abraham's resignation eventually and allowed Grandmama herself to retain her husband's share for her life, she supplying for that time the capital."*

This incident underlined two truths - first, that after the treatment of Francis's "brain haemorrhage" at Linslade House in 1817,[1] there were continuing doubts about his temperament, and secondly (perhaps more importantly), his wife, Hannah, had an interfering and overbearing character, which refused to accept even the sanctity of a Will, and to demand the substitution and execution of her own views - a characteristic which was to produce devastating results less than a decade later.

In her Journal for May 1843 Adelaide describes in great detail what can only be described as an attempt at matchmaking by Mrs Egremont, wife of Edward Egremont, vicar of Wroxeter (seven or eight miles west of Coalbrookdale), and a friend of the family, between Adelaide and a Mr Maude (possibly Mrs Egremont's brother) and a naval officer, Captain Russell. There followed an elaborate charade which demonstrated how difficult it must have been, within the manners of the time, for a young lady to negotiate the hazards of meeting prospective suitors, and avoiding fortune hunters.

After reaching her 26th birthday Adelaide had the pleasure of another visit to the Isle of Wight followed by a memorable trip to mid-Wales. The year was rounded off by spending December, including Christmas at Leighton Buzzard.

Thursday 5th January - *The week passed strange and dull and dark, and Mama, Tilly and I had a sort of happiness too in being altogether. But the rooms were so still and had such an intensity of mournfulness, and the sacred remains in their marble beauty so coldly impressed the heart with their nothingness, and Nurse Iredale guarding them with her noiseless step and dark visage looked so like a living "Lucy Ashton's Nurse". We were very busy, too, Matilda and I, with our black preparations. At last the day came, wet and cold, and oh! so many people. Grandmama insisted on walking in the procession and she did it with Papa - then Mama and Abraham - Tilly and Emma Lawford - I and Mr Grant, and afterwards the Lawfords. Mrs Ivy came to the funeral and beautiful and consoling were her words both at the densely crowded meeting and to us after. We were all glad when the day was over. The morning of the 29th, Mrs W Grant gave birth to a little boy - very few hours after the death of the oldest member of the family this little heir to his name was born.*

Wednesday 11th January - *Papa and Abraham stayed a few days for the transactions of the overflowing amount of business they find. Mr Grant came down on Saturday to read the Will - on Tuesday A. sped off declaring he could stand it no longer - 'twas impossible to please all. He gave up the bank from the first and so did GM and she changed her mind again and gave her name to it and the trouble was infinite.*[2] *This day Wednesday 11th, Matilda and I went to the opening of the church. Mr Melville preached and we were delighted. We were in Emma Lawford's pew and Lord C Russell was there and called here afterwards, and Miss Inglis - she is a most charming woman.*

Thursday 12th January - *Papa took Tilly to Birmingham to join her husband, sorry to part with her. Mama and I installed in our own room.*

Saturday 11th February - *Papa and Abraham went to London about proving the Will.*[2] *Papa came here on his way back, stays till Monday.*

Friday 31st March - *Dearest Tilly came by herself - I am charmed to see her but I find I am to go back with her. Grandmama is quite ready to part with me.*

Friday 7th April - *(Note: there was on this day in her Journal a long description of Peter's proposal and her refusal). Told Grandmama perhaps it would be best for me to settle the matter myself and at 11, Peter was put into the room. As he would probably not be allowed many minutes, he would begin by assuring me that the sentiments he expressed in his letter were unchanged and his* *attachment unabated were such as time never could lessen, and he trusted in time that they may be reciprocated. I told him that my sentiments had been fully expressed then and that they remain unchanged, that I should regret to say anything unkind but that be must be aware it was in such a case more considerate to speak decidedly as I felt. I rose then and said "we part then friends, I hope?" "Certainly, quite so." We shook hands, this time my hand was not kissed and he departed.*[3]

Tuesday 11th April - At home - *Pleasant journey and pleasant reception. Yesterday morning we spent in making calls. Everybody very kind and gracious and sorry we were going. When I came in I found a letter long indeed from this booby flame. Abraham was gone to Woburn and when he came back I took counsel with him and sent the epistle of only 4 sides back with nearly these words "AAD returns the enclosed to the writer as it would be wrong to retain such a letter in justice to him or to herself". She has already informed him that it is entirely out of his power ever to encourage the sentiments expressed.*[3]

Tuesday 18th April - *Everybody gone to the Worcester Meeting. I have been tonight to a very pretty little concert at the Ironbridge arranged by Mr Wildblood, very spirited of such a young man.*

Monday 24th April - *I have got a cold, and so has Mama. Papa went to Cheltenham last week and we went to see Mrs Reynolds. I have worked in the garden prodigiously and practised immensely and am making a set of under garments with my own hands, and am reading "Rob Roy" with great admiration and Dryden's "Virgil", a present from Miss Turner, with great labour. Miss Turner is come to pay Aunt Maria a visit. The Duke of Sussex is dead and Mr Dawson was married on the 20th.*[4]

Saturday 29th April - *I heard yesterday for the first time that Papa was not content with leaving the matter to me, had desired his factotum Thomas Graham to write to Mr Bassett - was vexed.*[2]

Tuesday 16th May - *Was washing day and had been altogether uninteresting when about 4 o'clock Mrs Egremont arrived in great spirits and begged for me for a week, or as she said, 3 or 4. Marvellous it was that I was permitted to go - Papa said it should be left to me and I said I should like it of all things, and even though Mr Maude was there I was allowed to put my things into a bag and to go with Mrs Egremont. When I was in the carriage she said - "I dared not tell Mr Darby that I have two naval officers coming to dinner today but you will not mind". We were very late for dinner and I went downstairs with Janet and she introduced me to "Uncle Tom" and Captain Russell. At dinner thought Captain Russell very gentlemanly and agreeable. After dinner they danced and in the second quadrille persuaded me to join with Janet - managed pretty well.*[5]

Wednesday 17th May - *Mrs Egremont's birthday. She did not come down to breakfast. The gentlemen went to shoot rooks at Longnor,*[6] *it was rather wet.*

Louisa and I practised songs together. Mr Maude came in and would be sang for, then it rained, and Mrs Egremont was not well enough to talk, so I went with Louisa to discuss plants, etc. After luncheon they gave me a lesson in dancing and I soon understood the figures, etc. The dinner, then dancing, and I managed tolerably. At the end of the quadrille he put in a gallope, a sort of waltzing whirl with his arm around his partner's waist and a squeeze at the end which offended my dignity, but which I thought it better to take no notice of. Miss Atrier was next tried in the same way - she took great offence and would not speak to Captain Russell and all next day ran away from him. He was very saucy to her and I found my place far better to seem perfectly free from surprise or offence or emotion of any kind. Mr and Mrs Egremont tiffed about the violincello. That same evening came a round game and a game at "fright" at which they persuaded me to join - vingt-et-un is amusing. Captain Russell set a chair for me next to him and was certainly very attentive. He played on the guitar too, most beautifully. Most fascinating person there but when I took counsel with myself on my pillow I thought Mr Maude's heart the best worth winning and the most likely to be retained if ever won, and as for Captain Russell I was not altogether pleased with him for the dances.[5]

Thursday 18th May - *The gentlemen enquired after their partners and went to their own occupations and I to the schoolroom as Mrs Egremont was not downstairs. Mr Knight came and a note for me from Mama, which I went in to the drawing room to answer. Captain Russell sat on the sofa mending his guitar. It is awkward not speaking so I said "have you broken another string, Captain Russell?" "Yes," he said, "great nonsense keeping a guitar in such a hot room, beautiful strings, these," and Captain Russell really got up and brought the guitar to me.*

"I brought them from Naples, look how clear they are. Do you want a pen?" - and he arranged the writing materials for me and mended a pen - "will it do?" "Beautifully, thank you." When the note was done, it was a fact he lighted the paper for me, and then I took the note to Mr Knight. Mrs Egremont and Mr Maude were going to the Scarth's to dinner, and Captain Russell had begged for dinner at 5, that the children might have a dance. We had not much time and were rather late, Captain Russell the latest of all. The whole tiff of the violincello was discussed between him and Mrs Egremont - he scolded her. Afterwards came a country dance with all the children and then they came to bed and candles arrived and I played at chess with Mrs Egremont and Captain Russell played upon his guitar. Then we became greatly puzzled - what to do with the long evening he had contrived for us? Well, at last we thought of "blind man's bluff" and "forfeits" and it certainly was very merry but I was very unlucky for my satinet rustled so that I could not stir. Louisa was in great spirits and Mrs Egremont at last became so much amused that she ran about with us. The "forfeits" were rather cramping and Captain Russell asked me to repeat with him and then stand on a chair and kiss flying which Louisa and I managed right after three attempts. I did not look vexed or pleased, but I said I had

paid my forfeit quite well. The Captain was in the middle of a sailor's song when the other gentlemen came back and encored it.

Friday 19th May - *Was Ted's birthday and unfortunately wet. Captain Russell was very cross all day. Mr and Mrs Maude went to look at a house at Harnage yesterday and Mr Maude said to his sister - "What ails Russell, he is very flat, and was yesterday in our ride?" "Well, we all have our troubles." Went to Charlton Hill*[6] *to buy some pigeons. Nothing would satisfy Mrs Egremont but another game at "blind man's bluff" in the evening, and Mr Egremont blind-folded. Mr Maude danced with me and I began to think he was really very attentive. Mr Egremont looked on and thanked his stars he was not in such a romping dance. Captain Russell improvised another dance at the end changing partners which he went through with me first, but that was only a pretext for having Miss Atrier in his possession for with pride I do say the squeeze was not repeated. Miss Atrier ran away and tore her gown and Captain Russell laughed into fits. Mr Maude ran half over the house after my candle squeezed one hand while he presented it with the other.*

Saturday 20th May - *A great many letters were read and written and the gentlemen were all in the drawing room, Captain Russell not in good humour again. Ink bad, blotting-paper bad, pens horrid, finally drew up the blind, which, as Mrs Egremont observed he must know would not be pleasant to a woman her age. Went to Shrewsbury after lunch. "Where's Miss Darby?" said Captain Russell, with a very impertinent smile. I do not know why, but he began to laugh at Mr Maude and me this day - I curtseyed being close to him - "You see how anxious I was that you should not be left behind" - with a smile wickeder than before. "Thank you, Captain Russell" I said then, "I think you might have known where I was!" "That's very right, Ada" said Mrs Egremont "a most just reproof." We had a most amusing drive, Mr Maude was inside and Louisa teaching him Welsh.*

Monday 22nd May - *Louisa and I went for a walk after breakfast. Captain Russell and Mr Maude waylaid us and went with us. Mama and Matilda came for me - went to call at Marnwood as we returned and Mrs Reynolds came to tea. Home certainly did seem rather flat.*

Wednesday 24th May - *Papa and Mama went to Leighton, and I went to Mrs Reynolds. Mr and Mrs Anstice were at dinner and Mr and Mrs Bartlett*[7] *brought Mr Edmonds and Barnard was there and John Edward, who is going to leave the country.*

Thursday 25th May - *I came away from Severn House. Mrs Reynolds brought me home, and at the stables behold! a carriage with a blue lion crest. "Mrs Egremont is at The Chesnuts" said Benjamin, "and there is a note gone for Miss Darby." When I came in, Tilly said "Mrs Egremont is come to know if you will marry Mr Maude or Captain Russell". "Not Captain Russell," I said in amaze. "He admires you, I believe" she said, "but now go to Mrs*

Egremont." When Mrs Egremont was able to speak, which was not for a long time, she said "Tom has had no sleep since you left Wroxeter. Indeed my dear you quite won his heart, and he is so very much afraid that you preferred Captain Russell to him that he has made me come over today, when indeed I would rather have done anything else".

I said that I was very much surprised, for I never should have supposed it likely that two such men as Mr Maude and Captain Russell would have wasted their time in thinking of a girl educated as I had been and entirely unused to society. "I wish" said Mrs Egremont, "that I could convey to you the delicacy and sensitive feelings of my brother - he was pleased, I believe, with that very freshness and that you had not been hackneyed like the women he is continually seeing, but his fear of Captain Russell is extreme." I said "I would be quite candid; if Mr Maude and Captain Russell were each to say 'I want a wife and you shall be that woman if you choose' I believe it would be Captain Russell, but I would not marry either without knowing them much better, and cannot tell that I would marry either then." Mrs Egremont commended my truth and said she should have said the same herself at my age, but her brother would make far the best husband for many reasons - the main one, that he had more sensitive feelings. But I said "Whoever thought of Captain Russell but Mr Maude. I am sure he never paid any serious attentions indeed I did not know either of them did". "Well" said Mrs Egremont, "they do say that ladies require a great deal of attention now, but you know that if you had wished for the Severn they would have brought it to you - at least Tom would." "But surely not Captain Russell?" "I do not know about Captain Russell, I could tell you of such a long list of girls he has flirted with and meant nothing that I cannot tell you what he means." "I hope you do not put me on the list?" "No, no." "I acknowledge I thought at first Captain Russell was inclined to flirt with me and talk nonsense, but I never yet was flirted with in that way and I never will." "You are quite right, my dear, the day you left he asked me to invite Louisa Jenkins. I don't believe he has ever thought of you since and I have never heard him mention you. I don't believe he would ever marry an Iron Master's daughter for not having family himself, he looks for a good connection, and in that respect Miss Darby would not do." "Does Mr Maude realise what it would be to marry an Iron Master's daughter without fortune or connections or the habits of Society?" "Oh yes, all that would not matter to Tom though it would to Captain Russell. I must tell you that Captain Russell dislikes dark hair. I never heard what he thought of you, I should have heard it all some time ago, but of late he keeps out of my way and tells me nothing." I laughed and said very innocently "if Captain Russell had had any serious intentions of proposing, he would have been here himself already and consulted nobody - you have surprised me very much, Mrs Egremont, very much. I thought whilst I spent that very pleasant week with you, which indeed I enjoyed excessively, that Mr Maude and Captain Russell were both remarkably gentlemanly, and agreeable men, but I never supposed it likely that I should ever see either again, and you will not think me uncivil to say that this was a matter of perfect indifference." "My dear, you have the feelings of a perfect gentlewoman, however, I think you will never see Tom Maude again if I am to take this message about Captain Russell." "But" I said! "whoever thought of Captain Russell but Mr Maude himself, I am sure I never, did." "No, just what I said Tom must needs poke at Russell when nobody else thought about him, but it is his sensitiveness dear fellow."

Then, would we go to the Wrekin to meet a large party? Abraham said we might do as we pleased so we left it to the chapter of accidents. Mrs Egremont went to call on Aunt Marie and I went to put some flowers into the carriage, and meanwhile Mrs Egremont said to Tilly "Do you think Tom's fortune would be as much as Ada would expect, you know he is not a rich man, would your Papa make them any allowance, does he to you?" So Tilly smiled not, but made Ada's fortune about double what it will ever be, and Mrs Egremont's eyes opened and she became oh, so civil to me it was quite incredible. When she was going she said "Well, I am not to tell poor Tom that you like Captain Russell better than he?" "No not that certainly." "However, you are not engaged?" "No, I am not engaged, anybody may know that, for it is true."[5]

Friday 26th May - *Mr Maude called having been on the Wrekin alone. He was gracious, very, but a little condescending. Did not stay long. In the mornings Tilly and I went to Severn House and told dear Mrs Reynolds all. She advised me to gain time. Could I be happy with such a disparity of years, and as soon as I saw Mr Maude again, I was sure I could not. It was a very wet day. Sunday Mrs Reynolds dined at The Chesnuts, and was glad to hear that I was going to refuse decidedly.*[5]

Monday 29th May - *Just as we had our bonnets on to go out Mr Maude made his appearance. He brought an invitation for tomorrow to the Wrekin - again. We declined as Papa was coming home but Mr Maude said he would ride over in the morning and persuade him to let us go. I begged he would not take the trouble - he begged I would not speak in that way. "If I fail in persuading Mr Darby, I shall have made his acquaintance which I greatly desire to do. It is my wish to let you know as much as possible of me, Ada, but I am at a loss how to manage it, can you tell me!" He brought me some songs that I had left, and I said "Will you give my love to Louisa, Mr Maude?" "All my intimate friends call me Tom Maude, may I beg you to do the same?" I bowed and went on "and tell Louisa I will send her the songs I am copying for her." Well, it was the most difficult case in the world as I could not refuse him without implying that he stood committed more than was really the case, and he might say he was refused without having asked. He stayed two mortal hours and left me with the anticipation of seeing him the next day for certain. Papa came home in the evening - I told him Mr Maude was coming and wished to* *see him and he wondered what for, but he did not seem to fancy that I had anything to do with it.*[5]

Wednesday 31st May - *Mr Maude called but Papa did not choose to see him and I was gone to the Bridge and knew nothing about it. This has been a most eventful half-year to me - I have been, I trust, learning wisdom at a great rate, and it has been strengthened by hearing Abraham's views about me from Matilda. He thought Ada's ever achieving an advantageous match more than doubtful. It is very difficult for a beauty to attract a really superior man, Abraham says, he is apt to be afraid to penetrate the good qualities lest he should be taken in by the pretty face. Between Abraham and Captain Russell I begin to understand many things. I am not exactly sorry that I never set my wits to accomplish fascinating the Captain - in the first place I do not think I could have done it in a week and in the second I do not know that I could perform the task of teaching him constancy. But I know now that there are really noble minds and good and brave men in the world who do not bore - about the corn laws, and I know too that while I can only charm fortune hunters and fox hunters, I will not marry. Mem: to abstain as much as possible from charming much. Abraham said that my first affaire, Mr H,*[8] *was unlucky because his character was generally known and since every fool of the same sort thought he might try. Abraham was wrong because I am sure some of them knew nothing of him but the same love of admiration and of gaiety and of eclat has led me, how many times, into being amiable to the wrong man.*[5]

Thursday 15th June - *Last evening the Committee of the Mechanics Institution gave a Concert and tea party, and I went with Abraham and Matilda, and was delighted.*[9]

Sunday 2nd July - *We all, Papa, Matilda and I have influenza. Papa saw Mr Webb, who bled him and pronounced him in much fever.*

Tuesday 4th July - *Oh, how we were alarmed! Mr Webb and Mr Rowland met at our house and then went to see Matilda. Mama went to hear Mr Webb's opinion and it was so decidedly unfavourable we thought our darling in so precarious a state that I was terrified! I never knew how dearly I loved her and how much she is at the end of every pursuit - of every thought. He said it was Bronchitis and if the Inflammation could not be subdued and prevented extending to the lungs consumption would be the termination. I had to be with her and she was not to know of Mr Webb's fears - it did me good, but I shall never forget it.*

Sunday 16th July - *Dearest Tilly was out yesterday for the first time. Thank God she is getting better, though as weak as Mama was almost. I have been with her constantly, and for three days Abraham has been out. Throughout Mr Rowland has not taken so unfavourable a view, and we think Mr Webb need not have frightened us so very much. It is three weeks tomorrow since we first* *became alarmed seriously. Now all is as sunny as the weather and poor Abraham happy again I think she is almost as dear to me.*

Sunday 6th August - *Just as everybody else got well, I began to be ill. It is three weeks ago tomorrow since I sat out late in the evening with "Madame d'Arbley" and a white frock. When I came in my hair was straight with the rising fog - it was only 9, but even July does not authorise these things in this cold part of the world. Well, I have been very ill, but it is going off and I have nothing but great weakness now. I suppose the fever occasions that. I am going with Abraham and Matilda to the Isle of Wight next week, I hope, but the Tothills are coming this and Mrs E Lawford. I want to feel stronger, for I am not up to amusing everybody. I almost think I have had the Influenza twice, but perhaps the first time was a bad cold. Mr Rowland has been very kind.*

Wednesday 9th August - *I shall be 26 tomorrow.*

Friday 18th August - *We set out at 4 o'clock in the morning, very foggy - hot and dusty in the middle of the day. Established in the evening rather tired but glad to have accomplished so much.*

Saturday 19th August - *Came over in the steamer to Ryde. All day house hunting. We could not be certain about the one we preferred and we took a ride to Red Cross by Sea View, proved to be a cottage too small, and rather inconvenient the distance. By the evening Mr Wallis sent word we might have Montague House, but it was so late we stayed at the hotel until next morning. Had a delightful little sail.*

Sunday 20th August - *Settled ourselves in a most comfortable abode, old furniture, but very clean - charming view of the sea, and a piano. Garden with flowers. I went in the evening to St James' Chapel where Miss Chester has a seat. Very interesting Sermon for the Church Missions in India by a Mr Weitbrecht, a German who has been 11 years in Bengal.*

Monday 21st August - *Went to the library and shopping in the afternoon, we had a sail beyond Cowes, amongst the Yachts - The "Karifa", Lord Wilton's, is a great beauty. We were in a pretty little boat, Saunders*[10] *is in attendance on Lord Seagrave but is coming back tomorrow.*

Tuesday 22nd August - *Wet, wet. Saunders took Abraham out as far as the Nab light but it blew tremendously. Between Nourmahal and the Piano and some Netting I am thoroughly happy even on a wet day.*

Wednesday 23rd August - *Went over to Portsmouth and walked about the fortifications. It was wet and windy but very delightful, we came back wrapped up in a sail.*

Thursday 24th August - *Tilly and I sat on the beach most of the morning, very delightful. After dinner we sailed to the Nab light. Mama writes that the Tothills have suddenly been recalled by the dreadful accident to my Uncle.*[11]

Last Monday he received a kick from his horse at Shirehampton[11] and broke the thighbone so near the joint that they fear he will always be lame. It is very sad.

Friday 25th August *- Rather showery. Walked on the pier and I took a tepid bath in preparation for bathing in the sea. While Abraham went to a Corn Law lecture (which by the way the Wise Authorities here would not permit to be given) Matilda and I had a most pleasant ramble.*

Saturday 26th August *- It rained when I had my bonnet on for bathing and after breakfast Abraham set sail for Alum Bay and I was not very sorry. The wind was high and Matilda and I were both ill, not very usual for us - I was very faint the first time and half asleep when Abraham and Saunders were talking, and a great wave came all over me thanks to the steering - the salt water running most refreshingly over my neck roused me up to see William mopping in great indignation. We dined at the Inn and rambled over the rocks near the Needles and then had to be carried back to our boat through the surf. We went out beyond the Needles and saw real great waves, but the coming back running before the wind was horrible. I was so sick. We got in sight of Ryde just as they were firing the sunset guns. The sickness soon went off but we were very tired - I had a very good night.*

Sunday 27th August *- Went twice to St James' church. Tilly went with me in the morning. 'Tis indeed an oasis in the desert to hear such a clergyman. Beautiful fine day.*

Monday 28th August *- Very wet in the morning early. At 12 we heard the guns fired at Cowes and the Royal Squadron of steam vessels came in sight. After tantalising a vast assemblage of her subjects on the Pier by going to Spithead, her Majesty came round and finally landed in the Admiral's boat, we saw her very well. She is fatter and far happier looking than in London. They went to St Clare's castle - Colonel Harcourt's and returned in half-an-hour. The Queen wore a straw bonnet with lilac ribbons and feather and a black velvet shawl. Prince Albert was in uniform and very pale. The reception not very enthusiastic but then everybody was very wet and cross, though the rain had ceased.*

Tuesday 29th August *- Dearest Tilly took cold from wet feet on the pier, and this evening we went out in a boat beyond Cowes and a foggy evening made her cough very much. Saunder's boat was six minutes before Yachts or any competitor in the Regatta today. We passed the little "Water Witch" in much exaltation. She was hired by Captain Claxton.*

Wednesday 30th August *- Went early over to Portsmouth. Walked on the ramparts saw a regiment pass and heard their beautiful band. Then through the Dockyards, very pleasant day but fatiguing and Tilly not better.*

Thursday 31st August - *Very hot! The weather has become all at once overpowering. Tilly only went out for a little while. I went on the Pier and on the beach and studied some new waltzes that are very pretty.*

Friday 1st September - *Memorable 1st September. Tilly and I went to hear Grisi and Mario and came back with our heads half turned. They have the most splendid voices that may well be imagined. She is a most magnificent creature and he is the handsomest Italian I have seen. There were Brizzi Pillotti and Mr Lavenibut they were nothing. The Dowager Countess of Craven and Lady Wharneliffe were there. I never was so charmed or so excited by a concert and Tilly little less.*

Saturday 2nd September - *Abraham took us to Ventnor on the coach, enjoyed it immensely but very hot, and very amusing - altogether there has been more to enjoy and to remember this week than ever I recollect stuffed into the same space of time; oh! I am very happy happy enough to set against much misery and make the balance even. Reading "Barnaby Rudge."*

Sunday 3rd September - *Hot enough to bake cakes still. Went twice to St James'. Found Abraham killing crickets in the kitchen when we came home.*

Monday 4th September - *Went to Ventnor on the coach, very pleasant - very hot and very amusing. Delightful sail in the "Water Witch", we stopped again at Ventnor, but it is so hot that I think we shall not take up our abode there. There were several butterflies making the best of their way to the shore. Saunders said the north wind had blown them off the Sussex coast.*

Friday 8th September - *Letters yesterday decided that we should return - how blue and beautiful everything looked in the lovely weather. Crossed to Portsmouth in the boat. The Queen has disappointed Portsmouth by returning straight to Brighton after her visit to Louis Phillipe. The Yacht had just come into harbour and we sailed round her - very pretty for a steamer, extremely rapid and gilded and sparkling. Hot and dusty, got to the "Victoria!" about seven.*

Saturday 9th September - *Started by the 10 o'clock train, two pleasant gentlemanly travelling companions. Called upon Grandmama and dined there. Peter going to give up the Bank and to leave Leighton for which the fates be thanked.*[3] *Reached home at about 10. Found Papa gone to Bristol about game, and Mama intending to go into Wales next week.*

Monday 11th September - *Papa came back in the night of Saturday, party of Christy's at meeting. Mr William Christy and his son called this morning, a long call. Went to the library and chose some books and joined Mama at Eastfield. Dearest Tilly not very well, but she spent part of the day with us.*

Tuesday 12th September - *Mr Rowland says Matilda will be better soon, bilious attack, often an effect of the sea. Bid her goodbye upon our little tour. Shrewsbury to Welshpool, quite new to me. Colonel Wingfields and then Rowton*

Castle, the Bredon hills very picturesque. Great fair at Powis Castle, very fine place, very large trees, garden fruit and flowers rather "en mass" but very beautiful. Curious Indian relics - a knob from Tippoo Sahib's chair, gold inlaid with gems, very valuable.[12] *Wonderful old velvet bed in King Charles II's room. Castle red stone, walls I should think 2 yards thick, giving one thoughts of all sorts of secret passages. Several pretty water colour pictures by Lady Powis and her daughters. People all very obliging and seem very much attached to the great family in their neighbourbood. Inn "Royal Oak" and very comfortable.*

Wednesday 13th September - *Lovely morning, walked before breakfast. Last evening I forgot that we went into church, fine old structure, carefully preserved. The ivy hangs inside in a long string from the ancient roof. There is a fine view all round from the churchyard, the Castle and Mr Clive's new church, and Mr Pugh's place, Llanerchidd. We went to look at the monument.*[13] *Mrs W erected for her daughters, a plain stone sarcophagus railed around. "Sacred to the Memory of Frances Ann, aged 7 years" - she died in 1811.*[13] *Mr Owen has had the tomb very nicely restored. "Here lies the grief of a fond Mother.*[13] *Well, about 10 o'clock we left Welshpool for Newtown, 14 miles and we see the house where the Williams live. Papa met and spoke to Mr C Williams at Welshpool. At a distance Montgomery Castle visible. Newtown to Llanidloes 18 miles. To the Devil's Bridge 20. This was a very memorable stage, the road winds amongst the wildest mountains of the Plinlimmon range where the Severn and the Wye take their rise in tiny streams. Grey slaty rock comes out here and there, but the hills are covered to the top with greenish brown heath and sheep walks, all the Duke of Newcastle's.*

When we reached the steep descent to Hafod, that is to the Inn on the Devil's Bridge, the hills began to be covered with little oaks. From the "Hafod Arms" where we stay the view is splendid and very extraordinary. The fall of the Rheidol is among the rocks below, which rise into wooded hills on each side. We went down below the Bridge, an extraordinary fissure between the rocks, the lowest bridge that's left to commemorate the legend of the old woman devil, cow and dog that is said to have been thrown over by the Monks of Ystrad Florida Abbey. The water has worn away the rock in a fashion that must delight Lyell, and rushes below the fissures deafeningly. We went through the little oaks to see the falls of the Mynach, they are most magnificent, the finest I ever saw, 210 feet. Intelligent guide, people all Welsh but speaking tolerable English.

Thursday 14th September - *Went to Hafod. Very fine scenery, the house Moorish and exceedingly picturesque. I should have thought its light arches and fairy architecture of questionable taste among such wild scenery and high mountains. The pictures are beautiful Claude, Rubens, a little Eve Home by Moralez, &c &c. The Duke of Newcastle is going to sell Hafod to an Indian Millionaire. In the church is a sweet tomb with three figures by Chantrey, to the memory of Miss Johns the only daughter of the former proprietor she died suddenly at 26*

- now they are all dead, Mrs Johns last, and her remains were brought to be interred in the family vault on the day when the Duke first arrived to take possession. In the evening we came to Aberystwyth, the rain having compelled us to dine at the Devil's Bridge. It is now beautifully fine again and I hope it will last. The drive is splendid, over a mountain nearly all the way, no fence to prevent the view.

***Sunday 17th September** - We have been till now in our little room at the Belle Vue and very comfortable, in Aberystwyth. Lovely weather, we like this place very much. Fine open sea, pretty bay and harbour and fine bold Rocks. Marine Parade gay and pretty, beach full of wonderful pebbles and pieces of seaweed. Went today to Church and heard a very good sermon from Mr Hughes. It was a Charity Sermon for the Infirmary. In the afternoon went again to hear the Service in Welsh, it is a singular language full of th's, and sounds that ours has not at all, but not quite unmusical and capable of great solemnity.*

***Monday 18th September - Dolgelly** - We came here after breakfast, the drive more lovely than ever, then we went to Mannan, Sir Robert of Vaughan's up an immense long hill. Fine outline of Cader ldris but too misty to ascend. Nothing but Welsh, it is quite difficult to make ourselves understood.*

***Wednesday 20th September** - Came from Dolgelly to Welshpool. To breakfast at Mallwyd, lovely waterfall and river, the Dovy. Very bad horses from Cans Office, myself frightened and everybody else much more. Lanerchidiol.*

***Thursday 21st September** - Came home to dinner, called on Mrs Dugard, she has been ill and at Cheltenham. Dearest Tilly much better.*

***Saturday 23rd September** - Venison Party, Mr and Mrs Joe Dickinson, Abraham and Matilda, and Charles. Very pleasant the Dickinsons stayed all night.*

***Tuesday 26th September** - Mama went to Leighton.*

***Saturday 14th October** - I have prospered most astonishingly in Mama's absence - she came back this evening to my great joy. Tiff with Abraham and Papa but all over, I hope, quite done with. He called with Tilly this evening. Emma is going to be married and to Sampson Lloyd of Birmingham! I was very much surprised! good match, I believe and hopes though Abraham laughs. Most sweet letter from her. Alfred dined at the Chesnuts today I was very glad. We are going, I believe, to dine with the Edmonds on Tuesday, I hope it is correct. Mama quite well - I am going to Leighton in December.*

***Tuesday 17th October** - Very pleasant dinner at Wenlock. Met Mr G Pritchard, Miss Clarke, Mr & Mrs Bingley, Mr & Mrs Birds of Preston, and old Captain Edmonds. Mr Bingley a very agreeable person - Grisi in a passion - lives in London, was at Persiahio concert; great talk of altering the road, Papa* *"en grand signeur". Mr Edmonds a little attentive and tolerably sociable. Dearest Mama not well and the place like an icehouse.*

Saturday 21st October - *I went with Papa to Shrewsbury and Miss Pritchard took my measure for the "thunder and lightning!" cashmere. Walked through the market myself, saw the Hills and Mr Egremont from P and L's, where I went for a bonnet ribbon for Mrs Bartlett. To my horrors Papa chose to call at Wroxeter and to ask Mr Egremont to dinner - "thank you, we have a friend with us Captain Russell is here yet, Miss Darby". Mrs Egremont was not at home. I saw only Janet beside Mr Egremont but they were very happy to be civil.*[5]

Thursday 2nd November - *Yesterday I went to the Chesnuts for dinner. Mrs Reynolds, JG Reynolds, J Reynolds, Uncle Richard Darby, and Charles, Henry and Deborah. Very delightful day. Mr Reynolds gave us much profitable advice for Paris if we ever get there. Englishmen going "en garcon" not very well treated there at present.*

Mr Reynolds was once, 2 years ago, in a theatre, when an English uniform came upon the scene. He was probably the only Englishman present, and the whole audience turned their eyes upon him crying "a bas les ecrivisses". He asked a man in the same box if he was right in supposing himself an object of aversion, and he said "they do indicate you, but keep your seat and take no notice; it will pass." Tilly and I blue tartans, and "success de toilette".

Sunday 19th November - *Willie Tothill has been here the last week,*[14] *the Chesnuts his headquarters. He is just the same dear amiable creature whose very soul seems to move in a melody, but though very young for 24, he is advanced in knowledge of the world. He has lost his shyness without any of that rare purity of thought so distinguishing in him.*

Thursday 7th December - *Came to Leighton Friday, Papa and Mama stayed this one day - the alterations at the churchyard.*

Tuesday 12th December - *Fair day. T Reeves has come home and claims graveyard. Tuesday week the good people had hurdled off a path from Wagstaff's house to the meeting house garden as they thought right, I suppose. On my return from a walk with the Reeves, AR sent a message to Grandmama about it, and in the afternoon she went up through the market with me and pronounced her approval of it. Wrote a note to SR who was ill in bed, but came next morning and all was settled. They are to build the wall and Grandmama is to move her own door.*

Thursday 21st December - *The Quarterly Meeting, horror of horrors! Thank Heaven every horror must have an end. I was not turned out of my room nor did I have a drab coloured companion in it. Cousin Dorothy, and Mrs Hester were here, Josiah Foster and George Stacey, Collins from Northampton and a host of people that I did not know.*

Saturday 23rd December - *Went to call upon Miss Andrews and then came home and found Eliza had called. I knew that Mr Lloyd was here and was glad of an excuse to see him so went on the Linslade road. Met Charles on horseback - "You will find them all further on" - "Is Eliza there?". "Oh yes, you'll not be in the way, I'll go back with you." The horse stepped in a puddle which benefitted my frock not much. "Oh no" I said "Good Morning." "I beg your pardon" - whether for the splash or the proposal I did not enquire, but he rode on. Well, Mr Lloyd is tall and quiet and grave and slow and a Lloyd and I don't know yet whether he can smile - rather proud in manner, and yet how can that be? Emma very sweet and pretty - they must love one another on the principle of being opposite.*

Invitation from Mrs Egremont to spend Christmas at Wroxeter. What can that mean? Replied. After dinner Mrs Bailey called and gave me the most gracious invitation to Shenley - Wolverton and the Queen's passing by. The Baileys all there - "how was it we did not see you?" "We came in the evening by the 7 o'clock train." "Somebody told Joe you went up on Monday, and Mr and Mrs Darby, and he couldn't think how it was he hadn't seen you. He was there all day on duty, you know."

Sunday 24th December - *A Xmas Eve like May, so mild. Emma brought Mr Lloyd here, do not like him much better.*

Monday 25th December - Christmas Day - *Eliza called for me very kindly, and we met their whole Party on the Linslade road. Very amusing walk, tried to please Mr Lloyd, and he certainly is a well-informed superior young man, but what a quiet contrast to Emma's brother and brother-in-law. They seemed fond of each other and I think they will be happy.*

NOTES

1. See Introduction, page ??
2. See Comment, page 142.
3. These were the final acts in the proposal of marriage by Peter, of Leighton Buzzard (see Comment 1841 page 119) whose surname was not revealed, but who was referred to by Adelaide as "Booby Esq."
4. Mr Dawson was the suitor rejected out of hand by Francis Darby in 1839 (see Comment 1839, page 78, and note 6, page 76.)
5. See Comment, page 142.
6. A small village, 2 miles west of Eaton Constantine, between Coalbrookdale and Wroxeter.
7. Mr and Mrs Bartlett of Marnwood House. Mr Bartlett was the incumbent of Buildwas Church.
8. Mr James Horne.
9. This must have been in Liverpool.
10. The Boat man.

11. William Tothill. Shirehampton is between Bristol and Avonmouth.
12. Robert Clive of India married into the Herbert family of Powys Castle. The Clive Museum at Powys Castle still contains a collection of Tippoo Sahibs' "treasure" (National Trust).
13. This was a visit to a family grave. Adelaide's grandfather, Abraham III builder of the Iron Bridge, had a younger brother Samuel I. He was married to Deborah Barnard and they had two sons, Samuel II and Edmund (Abraham IV's father). Samuel II married Frances Williams of Welshpool in 1803. They had two daughters who were first cousins of Abraham IV. The eldest was named Frances Anna who died in 1811 aged 7 years. It was her grave that the family visited on 13th September 1843. The other daughter Mary was born in 1807 and it was she who inherited her father's estate. In 1825 Mary married Reverend Edward Pryce Owen of Wellington and it was he who was referred to in Adelaide's Journal as "Mr Owen" who had the tomb very nicely restored.
14. Willie Tothill was William Tothill, eldest son of William and Hannah Tothill of Bristol.

The Chesnuts (sic), Darby Road. Built by Sarah Darby c1818. Home of Lucy Darby and family until 1838/39, then the home of Abraham Darby IV and Matilda until 1851. Subsequently it became the vicarage for Holy Trinity Church, Coalbrookdale.

1844

Comment

This was a year in which Adelaide only spent about six months in Coalbrookdale. The building of the railway had made a great difference to the travelling arrangements for the family. As a result, Adelaide spent about 5 months in Leighton Buzzard and about a month with her mother and father on holiday in and around Dover.

Adelaide was as much at home in her grandmother's home at Leighton Buzzard as she was in Coalbrookdale. She may even have felt less restrained amongst her friends at Leighton. Unfortunately she rarely attaches surnames to them so it is difficult to trace the relationship. The two central families were the Reeves and the Lawfords (who may have been related to the Grants). The closest friend was probably Emma who was of the Reeves family, but there were also a sister Eliza and a brother Charles. The other family were the Lawfords, William Lawford and a brother refered to as E---. They had a friend Carry Deverell who during the year married a Mr Cowie and departed on the "Oriental" to Calcutta for a life in India. Frank and John Bassett also turn up in the Journal together with a Miss Osborn, Miss Benson and Mr Riplin. Emma Reeves was married during the year (14th November) presumably to Sampson Lloyd. Of significance was the fact that she was married in Church, and not in the Meeting House. There were to be other examples of a drift from the Friends to the established Church.

Two other events were refered to in the Journal for 1844 which were to prove of great significance. The first (25th March) was the purchase by Abraham IV and others of the Ebbw Vale Iron Works. The second was the expanding interest of the family in Liverpool (17th July). The family had long had connections in Liverpool and maintained a warehouse there under the management of William Henry Darby (son of Richard Darby). Liverpool had of course become a leading port and (although it is not clear how it happened) the family acquired interests in the maritime industry. Abraham IV had become an enthusiastic advocate of Free Trade. The year 1844 therefore became a significant year for the Darby family - the year in which the family's interests which had always been centred on Coalbrookdale and Bristol began to extend to Liverpool and South Wales.

Saturday 6th January - *Emma came to tea just as of old. She is not a bit changed. We were standing over the fire discussing her wedding when something made her say "When you are married.......... "My dear, how often am I to tell you that I shall never be married." "Nonsense."*
"I have given you a dozen sensible reasons why........."

"Give me one."

"Why, it is time we went down to Grandmama, but I'll give you my best - I don't like the sort of men that like me and those that I like don't like me - there" and taking up the candle.

"Ada!" she said with energy and "con espressione" - "is there anybody here that you could like? Anybody that I know? Perhaps you wouldn't tell me, and yet - do."

"I would tell you directly, dear, but there is nobody."

Wednesday 10th January - *My dearest Tilly came this evening, the good man brought her and went away after tea to Quarterday. She looks very well - I hardly knew how I should delight in having her.*

Wednesday 16th January - *I have lost dearest Tilly after a delightful week in which we saw things through the same spectacles wonderfully. "J'ai grand envie de pleurer" - but there is no use. Yesterday Mr Lawford took us all over the farm. Heard of the decease of Maria Fox, which is affecting to Grandmama. Dearest Tilly went alone by the 10 o'clock train.*

Monday 22nd January - *I went with the Reeves on the Linslade road - Louisa came for me and then I cried over her troubles past with great folly. Had on a new cap red roses.*

Saturday 27th January - *Phoebe called and Grandmama sent me out with her and she told me how Miss Andrews had told her there were three young clergymen, Mr Hart, Mr Munnings and Mr Feliz looking out for wives, and they must have £2000. Phoebe told it Miss Osborn without the names, Mr Hart is paying his addresses to her and she told him. He and his columnated brethren put on the cap directly and scolded Phoebe for making mischief with their characters - she said she had mentioned no names but with great self denial abstained from saying they must have felt its truth as they knew the portrait.*

Monday 29th January - *Met Emma, Mrs Barrett and Mr Kiplin as I was going to Prices, said I would come and meet them on the Linslade road. Just as I crossed the canal bridge a great drop of rain fell in one eye, it was followed by another - and no umbrella! I turned back to fetch one and met Mr Barrett.*

"Dear me, are you afraid of the weather?" "Yes, don't you see my velvet bonnet?" "Oh, I'll fetch an umbrella don't go, I'll run all the way, besides they are all this way, and I must fetch umbrellas for them." "Oh no, thank you, come if you like but I must go for mine." So we went back together, and he said after a while - as I thought - "My father-in-law is really ill today." There were some carriages passing from the Abbey and I was looking at the coronets so I said - "oh, how sorry I am to hear it". "Can't come out, obliged to be on the sofa." I said "Is it the gout?" but it was lost in a load of hay that went by. He saw it was an enquiry and answered at hazard "He says it was eating Stilton cheese

at supper." "I am very sorry, how often he has been ill lately." "Why yes, he does not seem strong."

"I don't think he takes proper care of himself, I see him out in all weathers." "I dare say you do, but did Stilton cheese ever make you ill?" "No, probably it is a luxury I never met with" - and he went his way! and I went mine.

In the afternoon Carry[1] *came for my velvet pelerine, quite full of Mr Maude, whom she is sure really did propose in the letter. Miss Osborn knows all about it I gave her a great deal of good advice not to marry him; he is very weak "on dit".*

Tuesday 30th January *- Alas, yesterday deprived us of a dear, kind friend, whose loss can never quite be repaired to us - dear Mrs Reynolds.*[2] *She had only been ill one whole week and her friends were unprepared within a few days to part with her. It is a grievous loss! It was a bad cold apparently that she sank under, for her strength had long been greatly reduced.*

Wednesday 31st January *- The first really winter's day in this unparalleled season, snow, wind and frost.*

Sunday 4th February *- After meeting this evening, snow deep and threatening more, I chose to go to see Gilbert, who is very ill, and Emma came with me. I called at the Post Office and Frank Bassett gave me a letter for Grandmama, which turned out to be for me and misdirected, and a very dismal account from home, for they have all been ill, dearest Mama extremely so - but better. Cow ill in the road, myself frightened "un peu".*

Tuesday 6th February *- This evening as I was putting in the finishing shades of my dog's cushion EL*[3] *came in and said "They are going to walk, will you go with them?" "Oh, yes," I said, and Carry came in an hour after for me. I found they included the Miss Andrews and their brothers. We had a charming walk over the fields to the farm. The A's are a nice happy party - Mr Stevens very clever, his elder brother rather handsome - but not over gifted, I think. It is not often we see the sisters have the best of it as to sense, but so it is here. After, went on the Linslade road. Yesterday was St Paul's Fair, and Carry's birthday - she was 19. The Meeting House and C is Copyhold property*[4] *- Grandmama has never admitted to it, and before she can transfer it, it is needful she should "take it up at Court".*

Monday 19th February *- This morning Louisa called for me to walk out, Mr Lloyd was with them she said on the Linslade Road. So were Charles and Mr Kiplin to whom I stipulated to be introduced. Charles came back to meet us when we got in sight, which I had feared, might divert them a little, and we followed rather slowly because I had to be told how Mr Lloyd had made orations to the brother and sister on the enormity of the approaching baptism. "And as for himself" whispered Charles, "he's nothing that I can find out - he's an 'anythingarian'," Mr Lloyd not being far off. It began to rain so fast that we were* *all glad to go over the fences into the wood and we got there first. I went very graciously to meet Mr Lloyd and shake hands with him when he said "I should apologise for my cigar only that I saw Charles walking with his close to you." I said "Oh, I like the smell of cigars rather." "So he appeared to be aware," said Mr Lloyd "your veil must be quite fumigated." I stood in utter benumbedness of spirit - there stood Mr K who had heard the scene with Mr Barrett, and to be taxed in this indirect fashion with not having kept up my dignity, and the boy standing by - it was insupportable! and from Mr Lloyd too who I gave credit for such gravity, and who said it all so much as a matter of course, that the smile round Mr K's mouth seemed almost out of place. C to my great surprise came to my rescue, though I had no great cause to thank him for the first scrape nor for turning it on Mr K. "Kiplin" said he "let me introduce you to Miss Darby - Mr K - Miss D"- we bowed. "I hope, Kiplin, you won't catch cold this morning you've such a nice colour and it's such a lovely day." I tried to say something about nobody catching cold such weather and walked further in the wood as nothing takes away awkwardness better than moving, but the laugh was contagious although smothered and all joined but Emma, while Eliza turned the subject by a timely supply of lollypops. "There were 250,000 more letters on Valentine's day passed through the general post" said Mr L, "I should not have thought there had been 250,000 fools with nothing else to do." Somebody thought it must have been 250,000 pair - he smiled and said "but a thing that's never heard of in good society, really" - and you did not think there were 250,000 of Her Majesty's lives deprived of the advantages of good society? - Emma brought him to call on Grandmama in the afternoon - he is vastly agreeable though I think I showed the most Christian spirit in forgiving him.*

Sunday 17th March *- Oh, the cold east wind. I have had a stiff neck but it is roasted nearly well again. I have hardly seen the Reeves all the week till yesterday. They have had Mr Lloyd and his youngest son with them. George II in from Liverpool, and I think they do not fully appreciate the abilities of the young engineer who talks of comfort in the air of "Polly put the kettle on." Went on the Linslade road today - met Charles and Louisa - the hounds meet at King's Wood tomorrow, would we go? I hoped Charles was not going to risk his precious neck now. What if he should break it - somebody would be found, he supposed to take his place. Eliza asked him how he felt when he came to fairly proposing - "Very much as if I were going to be hung." "Did you not think it was a pretty expression in the President's daughters," said B, "there was a question in his soul for hers." I demurred, and so did Charles - Eliza said it was too poetical for him, and that as for me she supposed I doubted if there was much soul in such matters generally. I was energetic in my defence (I believe the thing seemed to me affected). "There's a precious deal more art than soul required for success" said Charles. In the evening we were laughing over it. "I am afraid you will think it is to be an Art Union" said Eliza.*

Wednesday 20th March - *Eliza scolded Charles after she informed me, for she thought, such speeches would sound very ugly if he got the habit of them - "I am; sure this lady of yours would not like them if she heard you." "But she never will hear me," said Charles, "there's the Art of the thing."*

Monday morning Catherine had wrote to invite me to go on the Heath with them to see the Hounds. Of course I went, it was a glorious morning. Miss Benson was with them, a quiet girl, but clever. Mr Lowndes pack invited to hunt the Oakley country. Mr Ashfield and Mr Woodman overtook us walking on the Heath. Charles and Mr Bodger and William Lawford leading their horses. We were advised to go to Stock Grove and under the park palings, we took up our position. The Hunt came down the hill by Baker's Wood beautifully. Mr A had said "Scarlet coats, horses, dogs or men - which of the four has the power to bring you out so early, ladies?" "Oh, Mr A" said Catherine, "what a question." "Why, you are come to see all four, Mr A" said I, "and so are we." Major Gilpin led them and looked splendid. Phoebe was ready to lay any wager, she said, John Bailey close to us. I did not look just then, but doubted, and he was not there, it seems. Mr Clode was, and looked altered. It was very exhilarating to watch them beat the covers and then gallop off to the first. An old shepherd stood by and gave us tales of Miss Loraine Smith. The whole field went off to Bow Brickhill wood, failing to find a fox before. There were four ladies on horseback - Catherine fell in a gorse bush, and I went next day to enquire after a scratched forehead, and WL gave me the whole history of the fox hunt to the horror of Mr Wiley who fairly went off the field in clerical stiffness. Walk with Phoebe in the Close - Mr Felix has proposed to Catherine and been refused. Mr Monins is going next week. He is paying assiduous addresses to Carry, so is John Bailey to a fair Miss Gertrude Lucas of Newport.

Thursday 21st March - *Yesterday I went with Grandmama to her house and then to call on the Reeves and was sent a walk with them. We were waiting in another room for Louisa when Charles came in. Nothing was quite right but that is not uncommon. After Meeting today Eliza said we must meet on the Linslade road we have a mountain to tell you. Charles said "It's all off between me and Carry."*

Sunday 24th March - *Met Charles yesterday on horseback, rather subdued but not broken hearted.*

Monday 25th March - *Letter from Tilly this morning, Abraham is become one of the purchasers of Ebbw Vale and Sirhowy.*[5]

Thursday 28th March - *I went with Grandmama about various things all the morning till after 1.*

Friday 29th March - *So hot, had to go to the expense of a parasol. Singing class. Grandmama to book exchange and then a walk, Linslade road with the Reeves, Miss Clarke not come. Charles was hunting all yesterday and with Mr*

John Bailey who has sent word to me that he comes to the breakfast at Major Gilpin's on Monday on purpose to meet me. Charles said it was highly probable I should be there, indeed he would bring his sisters and he knew he could bring me. Now if I get in any scrape for going, nobody will pity me, but I think it is all nonsense and Mr John Bailey is so fond of flirting that he loses no opportunity. Went to gather white violets with Mrs E. Lawford and the Lee &c. &c. Grandmama drove to Mrs Harrison's in the evening to hear about the Quarterly Meeting.

Monday 3rd April *- The Reeves, Mr Kiplin and I did really walk "straight as the crow flies" - over hedges, ditches, styles, double rails and a brook to the Grange - right merry was the expedition! The Major came out to meet us and said would we have breakfast. We have warned Charles to say 'no' though he vowed the Major would be delighted. Did he not say at every public dinner that the ladies were the life of his heart. Well, he took us into the field through the garden, and Mr John Bailey was there of course. We took up our position Mr John Bailey rode up and paid his compliments - the Major came and told Charles to go about a mile further on, which seemed like two but I was tired. They turned out the stag "enlarged him" over a hedge, 20 minutes more then the hounds came up and "now we're off". He said "Goodbye" to me "but I shall see you again" - mysterious words. In the evening there was a lecture on Electricity at the school to which we went. Experiments were many - a cannon fired by electrical agency which frightened Miss Osborn into hysterics - the dissolving views were really pretty and the lady had recovered when the laughing gas finished the business and she fainted.*

Wednesday 3rd April *- Mr How of Aspley came to tea to meet a certain Francis Marriage who asked me if I was Alfred Darby's wife - it was worth an empire! or at least I deserved a niche in Westminster Abbey for keeping my countenance as well as I did. I said Abraham was married to Matilda, but there was an Alfred - "Is he still alive?" - "Yes!" and I was grave still.*

Sunday 7th April *- Met with friends in the Close, one who had a celebrated Sculptor as Uncle. Tuesday next is to be the Great Easter Fair. On Wednesday Mr Grant came - very agreeable, as ever, gave permission to have the Malting pulled down - said, malting puzzles me. The Executors ought not to let such things be - droll scene Saunders and Mr Grant "Your bond and delivering up your deeds would be sufficient security without a Mortgage I should say". "Ay, but where's the lawyer would tell me that tale? they'll never let a thing be without a Mortgage it brings so grist to their mills".*

Monthly Meeting took place on 11th April and next day I walked with the Reeves and had tea there. The following day was the Bible Meeting. Mr Grimshaw arrived to tea, a most agreeable man he is - Mr F was Chairman, he spoke excellently and sensibly and with the most perfect ease to himself. Mr Pym called after breakfast on Friday - oh so agreeable and oh so gentlemanly

- it is a marvellous thing to see a private gentleman of £5000 a year devoting his time to an object like this. Mr Wilson and Mr Adey came and I went to the Reeves and found them all at breakfast. On my return I found Mr Grant talking to Mrs Fry - he knew a Mrs Shard who accompanied her in visits to prisons and much desired to know her method of addressing sinners. On one occasion Mrs Fry was addressing a group of very hardened female convicts describing what women should be in society - a being to ameliorate the sorrows of humanity.

Monday 22nd April - *Papa and Mama are coming tomorrow. I have only a week longer here. Today have been out on Carry's pony*[10] *- in the Ledburn fields across the railway to the turnpike, then over the cornfields and out at Circuit Moors to Linslade by the beeches and over the heath - delightful cantering and verily came down the town in the same fashion, how I enjoyed it but how stiff and aching I am it were equally vain to tell. On Thursday Papa went to London - I cut out the grate paper and a plague it was (this was to place in the grate for the summer).*

I had another delightful ride on Friday, alas! I don't know how home is to be supported. Louisa and I have been quite determined upon our morning walks and the dogs have taken to joining us. On 1st May we came home - bought a bonnet in Binningham.

Monday 12th May - *Dearest Tilly has been here all last week - Abraham at Ebbw Vale. It is very dull here but beautiful; I have taken to cultivating my flower garden with great energy. Charming days with Tilly.*

Friday 21st June - *At home almost two months - awfully quiet. Hardly a shower of rain since the beginning of April - grass as brown as the rabbits. I have worked in the garden, read a little, practised a great deal and made good resolutions enough to add a great sad piece of mosaic to the pavement below - I ought to do a great deal in these quiet times, but instead I seem to require double sleep and get thin too. German progresses diligently at the present time. Chrissy is married*[6] *so is Mr Ashfield. Last Tuesday Tilly and I went to the Mechanics Institute tea drinking - they had a little concert with Mr Knight playing the piano and a Mr Gough was there- who sang very nicely.*

Wednesday 10th July - *Papa and Mama went to Leighton to bring Grandmama and I went to dearest Tilly. Abraham in Wales. Not well - little influenza and a bilious attack - Mr Rowlands black draught. On Friday Grandmama arrived - she bore the journey well indeed.*

Wednesday 17th July - *I went with Abraham and Matilda to Liverpool to see the launch of an iron merchant vessel, Mr Horton went with us. He is very agreeable. All together at the Clayton Arms seeing that the races have quite filled the other hotels. Henry Darby very affaire and very handsome. Next day was the day of the launch when Tilly was to christen the vessel under the guidance* *of Mr Blaine. The bottle of Champagne tied to the figurehead - she on a platform underneath - wind blowing strong from the sea and the string much in the way, the bottle broke not until the mate drew up the ribbon and christened the vessel just as with a thunderous lurch she slided into the sea - by the euphonious name of the Richard Cobden! I was on the deck of an iron steamer unfinished with Mr Horton and a great throng of people.*

Then came a public déjeune at which 200 people were present and some of the Liverpool aristocracy - Mr Ewart's family, Mr Reynolds, Sir Arnold Knight and Henry Ashworth who made a speech on free trade, and Abraham another.[7] *Great diversion it is to be in the midst of toasts and expected to join in them too. Mr Shipton and a great train of Young Ladies were there. We then went on board the John Horton and all through the docks and finally to Mr Blain's to tea. Mr Edmond Ashworth was there and his wife, who was a Christy, rather agreeable people for quakerism thrice dyed and trade every inch. Right glad to go home and to bed. The next day, Friday, went shopping and called on the Richard Rathbone's and at Allerton. Dressed for dinner at Mrs Hadwin's - a very handsome dinner - she is a sister of the Ashworth's, Mr Edmund Ashworth is really affected and a great bore and yet I do suppose a favourable specimen of his class. Grand hot house of orchidaceous plants - pretty greenhouses, pretty garden, pretty ponies and pretty damage to satin shoes seeing them all. Then shells and Henry Darby great on the subject of bear hunting. Mrs Fowler called in the course of the evening with her son Robert, who is very tall, handsome and 15 and going to be drilled into all quaker affectations at Tottenham.*

Saturday 20th July - *Little more shopping. Fish market and came home. Sorry to say goodbye to Mr Horton at Shifnal. His sister is going to marry a Mr Edward Brockbank of Carlisle.*

Thursday 25th July - *Called at Eastfield on Christopher*[6] *and his bride, then went to Benthall which is to be sold*[8] *- old fashioned, out of repair, very dull and miserable to live in. Next day the Eastfield people came to tea - she is rather pretty and he very attractive. They have heard of my Uncle's safe arrival in America after an eight day passage - he went with a certain good friend Anne Jenkins at a very short notice to the amusement of all his friends and the great wrath of his sons.*[9] *On Saturday I went to the Chesnuts to tea to meet Eastfield and Severn House, Miss Turner and Rebecca and Charles - the heads of the house being in London. Russian Bagatelle and a pleasant evening.*

Thursday 1st August - *A letter came to tell me that Carry Deverell*[10] *is going to marry one of the Cowie's, an East Indian millionaire. He must sail for his return to Calcutta by 3rd October. She seems perfectly happy in accepting this "very advantageous offer" and I hope she will find it all that can be wished, but it is an awful distance from her friends and I suppose he was a stranger until very lately. She says at the end "you will be shocked to hear that no hope is given of Mr Reeve's*[11] *recovery.*

Saturday 3rd August - *Grandmama had letters with the sad account that poor Mr Reeve is indeed gone.*[11] *Yesterday morning he breathed his last after lingering for some days in an insensible state. Mrs Barratt was safely confined last Tuesday but Mr Lloyd brought Emma away the day before, her father was so much worse.*

Monday 5th August - *We left home with Grandmama for Leighton - Papa, Mama and I. Dearest Tilly was left alone to my great sorrow. I called at Mr Lawfords and was introduced to Mr Cowie. Carry*[10] *looks happy and he is certainly agreeable and gentlemanly and being very rich what could she do otherwise - the idea of the voyage must be an adventure highly agreeable at her age. After staying at Leighton we go then to Dover via London - in general it will be very dull and stupid I suppose, but there will be a good deal to see. Next day we stayed until the middle of the day that we might call upon the Reeves - they are indeed much to be felt for and greatly overwhelmed, having been less prepared for the blow than might have been expected. Mrs Lawford and Carry*[10] *and Mr Cowie were all going to town we had the same carriage and I enjoyed it very much. Mr Cowie is certainly very good tempered and perfectly English in his tastes, said goodbye at the station. In the evening went to the Chinese exhibition a great collection of lumber of various degrees of ugliness. Then to Madame Tussauds.*

Wednesday 7th August - *The fatigue of sight seeing in so great that it is well there is some pleasure in remembering all we have done. First we went through the picture galleries - The British Institution now full of the ancient masters and the National Gallery, Westminster Abbey and Hall, the Cartoons etc. In the evening Papa took me to the Haymarket to see "Taming of the Shrew" - in the after-piece Celeste and Webster danced the Polka.*

Thursday 8th August - *Walked in the Parks and a little shopping - we then started for Dover and Brighton Station. Travelled with a bridal party, very agreeable sort of people. It is a wonderful journey, the railway runs between the cliffs and the sea. We stayed at the York Hotel tolerably comfortable but the house so full that my tabernacle is made in the dining room, upon the sofa. On Friday we were established at 24 Waterloo Crescent. Charming drawing room - 4 windows, the sea, the Castle and the Pier; it is entertaining when the steamers come in and people land in little boats - Dover is a nice place. Spy glass in the window - Flora, a dear little tiny spaniel left by a family gone to Boulogne, she is domiciled with us affectionate and pretty. My 27th birthday on 10th August was forgotten, thank the good genius of maiden ladies. Took the bit between my teeth today - went to Warren's Library and enquired about a dancing Master. To Church on Sunday morning and to Meeting in the evening, there is really not a soul that we know, horridly dull.*

Monday 12th August - *Mama went with me to call on M Delplonque - I am to have lessons every day - rather a formidable individual - French every* *inch of him - very good tempered too he seems and yet likely to be minded. I am to have my first lesson on Tuesday evening, first figure. It was very wet again on Wednesday could not get beyond the pier - another lesson advanced to second figure. Thursday was finer and we went to the Castle, grand old fortification, third figure for the dance lesson. On Friday drove to Kurnsey - a place of Mr Fector's going to be sold - small in the Abbey style - river running through the grounds all very pretty. Lesson was the perfecting of the three figures with the violin.*

Saturday 17th August *- Mama and I met the bridal party we travelled with at the Bazaar, they are nice people. The bridesmaids and I became very good friends, they live near Teignmouth, she has a brother in the Navy and knows Portsmouth well. Went to Trinity Church on Sunday evening. The day was most beautiful and crowds of people came to enjoy the beach and the castle walks. We drove over on Monday to the Earl of Guildford's at Waldershore - it is a large old place, red brick and stone with magnificent trees in the park. Lord Guildford does not allow it to be shown not even the gardens, but we walked through the park for two miles and joined the carriage again at the end of a little path through turnpike and corn fields. Letter from dearest Tilly - poor Abraham met with an accident last week in the wet weather he slipped over a deal plank and dislocated his little finger, getting better but was most painful. Some of the Christy's have been there en route to North Wales.*[12]

Tuesday 20th August *- Went to Shakespeare's cliff - views beautiful and precipices magnificent. My dancing lessons go on with tolerable success every evening, but he is "au despoir" that he cannot teach me the Polka properly in time. This evening Papa took me to the Theatre - they have the company from the Princesses Polkamania it is a clever little farce and prettily danced. Next day I went out on horseback with Mr Fackham, who took the greatest care of me - we went by river and Kurnsey and finished with a gallop along the Marine Parade. It was beautiful!*

After shopping on Thursday we went upon the heights and Mama rambled about to my amazement, we came down through the shaft, I was stiff to begin with, by evening when my lesson came I was fairly cross too. I took my lesson on Friday morning - Monr Delplonque is resolved I shall dance the Polka and gets angry because I cannot do it at once, it is not an easy dance. When I was ready to drop, as most people would with a succession of hopping and standing on one leg, I had to go home and dress for riding.

We went to Walmer Castle[13] *- Papa and Mama in a fly - I with Packham. He brought me a much larger horse, more spirited but delightful. We went over the castle - little rooms, yellow beds, papering and painting done by Government, the former all red passion flowers. Her Majesty's bedroom was pretty and convenient. The walls are so thick, like walking through a passage to get to the* *windows. It is strongly fortified but the moat is made into a garden. Mrs Fry is staying at Walmer so we called on her.*

Kent is a fine fertile county with splendid crops. On getting home I was very fatigued, such an extremity of aching weariness and yet so pleasant I would not for anything have missed it. After writing to Tilly I went to the salt water baths and enjoyed one immensly.

Saturday 24th August - *We never have unmixed pleasure - this morning they woke me out of my sleep to tell me dearest Mama had been taken ill - a bilious attack and she continued sick and in bed all day. I stayed with her until evening and then went out to fetch her some medicine and to have my last lesson - at last the Polka was managed tolerably! Dearest Mama - was better next day so we stay on until the day following. I went to Church in the evening of Sunday, a very good sermon from the text 'Be not overcome of evil but overcome evil with good'.*

We left Dover by the 11 o'clock train for London on Tuesday, a fine but dusty day, pleasant people in the carriage, a family party from Hoddesdon. We reached Leighton for tea. It is Carry's wedding tomorrow,[10] *her trousseau is beautiful, but it was melancholy to think how far off she is going and to see her sweet blue eyes full of tears among her white satin and orange flowers. I walked with Emma in the afternoon, she is to be married in about three months.*

We came home on Thursday - very green and quiet it looked - dearest Tilly so much better for the seltzer water. We went to the Chesnuts on Friday to meet Mr Reynolds of Bristol and John. Aunt Tothill has sent me the most lovely pair of Honiton cuffs. On Saturday Tilly had a Wrekin Party[15] *- Dale House and Mr Young, themselves, Mr Ransome, myself and Uncle Richard Darby's family. The Dickinson's could not come. It was a pleasant party considering the materials!*

Thursday 12th September - *With Papa and Mama to dine at Madeley Wood. Mr and Mrs Robert Eyton*[16] *and Mrs Gabriel Poole, Mr Reynolds and Mr Edmonds. Mr Poole's voice is even improved from what it was 8 years ago, he sang Wilson's songs beautifully "Welcome Royal Charlie - Ah but ye've been long a'coming - He's o'er the hills that I lo'e weel". Then "I dreamed I dwelt in marble halls" from The Bohemian Girl also "An Oxford Chorus", a hunting song and "The 4-leaved Shamrock" - Lovers, and Mr Poole's handsome face, which is ten times handsomer since his marriage, is expressive and benevolent enough to do justice to the beautiful idea in that sweet Irish legend. Mrs Poole is a pretty woman with a simple animated manner - 5 children in 6 years! but they seem the happiest most satisfied pair and worthy of each other. Mrs Eyton seems good natured but a most remarkable person - I thought her quiet at first but in the drawing room after dinner she talked immensely, unaffectedly it is true but with some resemblance to a housemaid. It was a delicious evening - a breathing place in this flat wilderness.*

Sunday 15th September *- I am sympathising with half our little world in a bilious headache this morning what accompanies the arrival of plums and pears - so I am at home. Dale House, Severn House, Charles and Uncle Richard Darby have been almost a week at Liverpool for the sailing of the iron vessel. Tilly and Abraham came to tea - rather stupid but yet a great deal that was enjoyable.*

Tuesday 24th September *- We came to Leighton, Papa returning home next day. Called on poor Miss Lawford and also the Reeves - Cousin Dorothy and Mr J Edmonds ,Mr and Mrs Yardley arrived for the Quarterly Meeting. On Thursday a host of disagreeable people came, but among them James Atkins - a treasure to anybody fond of gardening - he knew the name of every plant we came to. The Yardleys are excellent people who really go about doing good - their sojourn in Greece afforded much that was interesting though they had great privation to undergo. They travelled from Athens into the country where there are no inns, so had to take provisions with them or to buy a kid which would be brought from the flock and roasted whole as their property. Some of the poor Greeks were able to read, but had never seen a Bible in the modern Greek and were unacquainted with the history of creation and redemption of man to which they listened with intense interest pressing the treasured book to their hearts.*

Friday 4th October *- Called on everybody and then went with the Reeves for a last walk, meeting Charles and Tom Stone on the heath, we walked over the heath to Linslade, Dew berries and woodbine, the last of the year and a nosegay of forget-me-nots. When I came home I found the Mansfields had been calling. Papa came at 4 and Mr E Lawford returned from seeing Carry*[10] *sail on the "Oriental".*

Thursday 7th November *- Committee, and went with Abraham and Matilda to dine at Madeley Wood - charming visit. The Kings there, she in crimson velvet and hearts. On the Monday following dearest Tilly had a cold - Papa had asked Mary Darby*[17] *to tea, she came a marvellously dull person only waking to be spiteful. Frank Dickinson is going to be married to a Miss Stevens*[18] *and Hannah has gone to Birmingham to prepare his trousseau! Mama has a copy of 'The Diary of Lady Willoughby' - it is fiction and is around the 1638 time of Cromwell.*

Thursday 14th November - Emma's Wedding Day[19] *- Gran had written they were to be married at church and that she was horrified accordingly.*

Friday 22nd November *- Uncle and Aunt Richard Darby, Rebecca, Charles, Mr Rowland, Abraham and Matilda came to dine - it might have been worse. On Monday Papa took me to Mr Knight's concert at Bridgnorth. There were Parry, a host in himself, Miss Hawes whose voice is wonderful, the two Miss Williams - "Oh, come you from Newcastle" is a pretty ballad and the dear old Mermaid's Cave was sung most effectively. The Parrys and the Pritchards*[20] *were there.*

Friday 6th December - *Uncle Tothill and Frank came to breakfast, then I went to Severn House - dined with Tilly and Uncle Dickinson[21] and Hannah went to tea so did I. Russian Bagatelle and a pleasant.evening. Frank is very agreeable talks well but looks younger than he is - my black satinette and rose coloured ribbons.*

On Saturday dearest Tilly stayed with us all morning whilst I was packing and making bonnet cap - we go to Leighton on Monday. We left at quarter to 8 - bitterly cold stopped in Birmingham to call upon Emma[19] who looks not well, but happy - arrived at Leighton after 7. Papa and Mama went home on Thursday. Snow, Grandmama does not go out, everybody has a cold except me and I am so well it is marvellous. On Friday Grandmama had a fall in the garden when alone, she was frightened and hurt her knee.

NOTES

1. Carry Deverell, probably a friend of the Lawfords.
2. See note 3 for 1839 (p.108). It is difficult to identify this particular member of the Reynolds family, but she may have been resident in Bristol.
3. Possibly Mr E. Lawford.
4. Copyhold tenure of land was the normal tenure of land held of a manor. Transfers of copyhold land were effected by a mediaeval procedure before the Court Leet or Court Baron usually held before the Steward of the Manor.
5. The lead in acquiring the Ebbw Vale Ironworks appears to have been taken by Abraham IV. He was joined in his initiative by Henry Dickinson (of Severn House) and William Tothill of Bristol. The other partners were Joseph Robinson who was manager of the warehouse in Liverpool and Thomas Brown who was the local manager. The works comprised four blast furnaces at Ebbw Vale, and another at Sirhowy, situated in the next valley, north-west of Ebbw Vale.
6. Chrissy was Christopher Dickinson (1818-1904), 10th child of Barnard and Ann Dickinson of Eastfield. He was married at Luton on 16th May 1844 to Sophia Browne of that town. They moved to Stoke-on-Trent where he later became Mayor of that Borough.
7. Sir Robert Peel was the Prime Minister of the day and headed a Protectionist government but this was split on the issue of Free Trade and the Repeal of the Corn Laws. Politics apart, manufacturers like the Darbys of Coalbrookdale spoke out for Free Trade as did Abraham IV on this occasion.
8. This refers to Benthall Hall (built c1580) on the south side of the River Severn, opposite Coalbrookdale. Benthall, one of the first places to be industrialised, lies to the west of Broseley. The Hall was acquired in 1852 by George Maw when Maw & Co. began to make tiles in the parish.
9. This episode involving Barnard Dickinson who was then aged 63 and a widower (his wife Ann, née Darby, having died in 1840) was the subject of some hilarity and a cause of outrage and embarrassment to his family. Barnard, an eminent minister, had during 1844 taken to accompanying Anna Jenkins on visits to Birmingham, Ireland and the North Country. His journal states "I

found my dear friend was feeling the prospect of crossing the Atlantic with strangers. I therefore proposed to go with her if she did not object, she acknowledged my offer but could not press such a thing." They left Liverpool on the Hibernia in July 1844. Obviously his sons felt this was unseemly.

10. Carry Deverell was a friend of the Lawfords of Leighton Buzzard. India at that time was under the control of the East India Company and obviously the Cowie who she was to marry was an employee of that Company.
11. Mr Reeves was the head of the Reeves family who were close friends of the Grants at Leighton Buzzard.
12. In the light of subsequent events, this may have been a significant visit.
13. Although Adelaide does not elaborate on their visit to Walmer Castle, it might have been of some significance to her father as a Tory supporter. At the time of the visit the Duke of Wellington (Prime Minister 1828-30) was Lord Warden of the Cinque Ports and enjoyed relaxing in the Keep which was converted for the use of the Lord Warden in the 1730s.
14. It is not known whether she was related to Elizabeth Fry.
15. The Wrekin is a hill, 407m high, north of Coalbrookdale. It was a traditional practice to climb the Wrekin and to enjoy a picnic at the top, with its fine views over the north Shropshire plain.
16. The Eytons were a very old and illustrious Shropshire family, based at Eyton Hall, north of Wellington, Telford.
17. Mary Darby was the sister of Abraham Darby IV. She lived at Dale House with her mother Lucy Darby. In contrast to Adelaide's somewhat vitriolic comments, Mary Darby was becoming highly regarded within the Coalbrookdale community for her conduct which was felt to be consistent with the traditions of the Darby family. She was to become known as "the Queen of the Dale". Adelaide was probably aware of her growing reputation and may have felt that it was a threat to her position as "Miss Darby of the White House". Subconsciously she may have resented the situation.
18. Francis Dickinson (1816-1901), 8th child of Barnard and Ann Dickinson was married to Sarah Ann Stevens at Plaistow, Essex on 15th November 1844.
19. Emma Reeves of Leighton Buzzard was a close friend of Adelaide. She married Sampson Lloyd.
20. John Pritchard was a banker from Broseley. The Pritchards were to become close friends of Adelaide.
21. Barnard Dickinson had returned from America in August 1844 (see note 9 above).

1845

Comment

At the end of 1845 Adelaide confided to her Journal that the year had been "passably happy". Certainly by then she had recovered from the emotional crisis which she had experienced at the beginning of the year. This was caused by a note she received on 23rd January that Mr Joe Bailey was going to marry a Miss Chatmore. This was a dreadful shock. Joe Bailey was an early suitor who had been refused by her father, but over the years she had cherished the hope, however distant, that one day she would be his wife with a "degree of certainty of happiness that good nature and good talents for society would confer". This was a bitter blow and it took her some time to get over it.

Once again, as in 1844, she spent many months at Leighton Buzzard. During May there was great excitement with the organisation of the Bazaar at Morley's Hotel, Trafalgar Square. This was the National Anti-Corn Law League Bazaar. The ladies of the family had been working hard to prepare work for a stall. The Coalbrookdale Company had also made a special effort and displayed for the first time art castings, which included statues of Goethe, Napoleon, Wellington and Benjamin Franklin and other decorative cast iron exhibits.[1] The Corn Laws were repealed in the following year, 1846. This was followed by a fortnight in Birmingham where they were entertained by the Lloyds. Much of July was devoted to a gathering of Friends for a General Meeting at Coalbrookdale. This included two members of the Christy family whose friendship had been consolidated during the Bazaar for the National Anti-Corn Law League. Later in August and the beginning of September they had a holiday in Leamington, but for the rest of the year they spent most of the time in Coalbrookdale (except for a visit to Leighton Buzzard for a Quarterly Meeting).

During her description of social life in and around the Dale, Adelaide included a very brief reference to another episode which was of greater significance (Journal 13th October). She said "it has been rather a stormy time beforehand and talk of giving up the Dale and Mama and Matilda at sparring matches - - -" The talk of giving up the Dale seems rather curious in view of the increasing profitability of the Company. It may however have arisen from the fact that a few months beforehand (1st August 1845) the Company had finally acquired the freehold of the Coalbrookdale site from Joseph Reynolds.[2] This meant that for the first time, Coalbrookdale represented a considerable financial asset rather than a short term lease which it had always been before. Fortunately any talk of realising that asset seems to have evaporated.

Of much greater significance to the family was the reference to increasing antagonism between Adelaide's mother (Hannah Darby) and Adelaide's sister, Matilda. Within the next few years this friction seems to have polarised into a position in which the father (Francis) seemed to favour Matilda and the mother (Hannah) seemed to favour Adelaide. The consequences were to prove devastating.

Friday 4th January - *I went to dinner at Mrs E Lawford's and she gave me a bundle of Carry's letters to read from Gibralta, Malta, Alexandria, Cairo and Aden - very simple like herself and interesting to those who know how she suffered much on the voyage, but is now safe at Calcutta.*

Monday 6th January - *Eliza and Miss Clarke called for us they were going to explore Linslade House which is being repaired.*[3] *On Friday went a long walk and in the evening went with John Bassett!! to a Phrenological lecture at the British School and on Saturday the man Droffuose came to examine my head - wonder what he will say.*

Wednesday 15th January - *Saw Her Majesty's bonnet as the train went by at 45 miles per hour, she sat ungraciously with her back to us. Mr Droffuose brought home his discoveries in my head - some wonderfully correct, but the intellectual part quite wrong, quite. Ten days later we went again very loyally when Her Majesty returned from Stowe, we saw her bouquet of horhouse flowers, that was something. Gran has dreadful dreams which with her giddiness seems to me unfavourable. Tilly at work for the great Anti Corn Law Bazaar in London, I am going to do a little.*

Thursday 23rd January - *This morning came a note from Mrs Bailey to say that Joe Bailey is going to be married to Miss Chatmore.*[4] *Grandmama told me with that dreadfully examining face of hers - probably she only examined if the curls hung lower than usual, at any rate I smiled and said "Is he indeed?" - I felt as if a thunderbolt had fallen notwithstanding for about 5 minutes. I was surprised as well as a little unhappy - I always thought it pretty certain that if I became possessed of sufficient fortune and Mr Joe Bailey not married, that I should be his wife and have that degree of certainty of happiness that great good nature and good talents for society would confer. He was married, as least the same thing, and the last link between me and the world of balls and music and society so dear to the heart of woman still lively and once handsome was severed for ever.*

I might have married a thousand times better than Joe Bailey, but just then I should have been content to marry him. They are ill words 'might have been' and no woman of strong feeling should use them if she wishes to preserve her happiness - I hoped she might not be as pretty as myself. When Mr Dawson was to be married I was truly unhappy having lost the heart of a sensible man, and this through my own fault - I had refused him myself because his letter was not as romantic as Mr Joe Bailey's would have been and by marrying Miss Smith he was proving that fortune was not his object - I saw he had loved me for myself and that it had taken 4 years to forget me, but when his marriage was in the paper I had to go to bed with a dreadful headache. Perhaps I had more nearly loved Mr Joe Bailey than any other being my own age and though his family is not desirable he had some pretensions more aristocratic than some of my admirers who had more money - then he was in the Bucks Huzzars - then he had been taught love (?) making at Eton. However, it is not so bad as losing Mr Dawson as I did not look foolish or to be pitied and above all I cannot blame myself. On hearing he was to be married I was petrified with surprise and mortification which was almost wicked because I never meant to marry him. However, I behaved so well I was consoled in the strength of my own seeming-good desire. In two days I really wished him married and happy and he thought I did so from the first.

I felt very malcontent with life and thought I had been sent in as a shuttlecock for fortune to play with. Of the three respectable gentlemen who might be encouraged to repeat their proposals - Mr Edmonds[5] is a saint but so dreadfully old and buried alive also not rich; Mr M[6] is old and jealous. I tried for half an hour to reason myself into thinking I should be happier with Alfred Darby[7] than at home, that it would look well in the papers if nowhere else, but then the Quaker Wedding and my sons, if I had any, sent to a Quaker School. Oh, I will be Miss Darby still with my free thoughts and midnight hours - they are worth something.

Sunday 26th January - *Charming reunion in the close. Mrs Ashfield introduced me to her eldest brother, very agreeable. This does seem to be a splendid match of Mr Joe Bailey as Miss Chetwode is beautiful, amiable and 18, will have a thousand a year and drives a pair of Shetland ponies - her father, Sir John Chetwode's son and very much respected. The girl's Grandmother was a beauty Mr Ashfield saw her at the Opera the same night as Queen Caroline was there, very vulgar looking. I then told the story of Lord Eldon and the wig and it did very well. Mrs Ashfield was beautifully dressed in a very light satin with gymp. On Tuesday evening Eliza and Louisa came to tea and brought the Irish Dragoon. The following week was rich in diversion - Miss Ashfield and Mrs Woodman began to give parties in honour of Miss Cowie to which Mr Ashfield and the Reeves were invited - Cross questions and crooke and all sorts of absurdity.*

Easter Monday 24th March - *Last Wednesday I tried Carry's pony in the close and on Thursday went with it to Mentmore and a gallop through the Wing Park. On Wednesday, 2nd April the Egremonts[8] have been calling and paying civilities to the Iron that is turning to Gold at such a rate. Very droll. There will be a dinner visit and a pale pink silk for me.*

On Monday, 7th April Mr Lawford took me on horseback to see the hounds throw off at Liscombe - the Young heir and his family are there, fair, pale and amiable looking about 19. The Marquis of Douglas - grown fat and foreign and like Mr Beckford - Viscount Sugden, three Barons and Anderson the great horse dealer. We went into the field the stag turned out just in front of the house - the most beautiful horses I ever saw - Charles Reeve rode up and told me over again who everybody was. Next day I went to meeting and then back to look after Grandmama who has a stye on eye.

Friday 11th April - *Fanny and I went foxhunting and were in at the death of two. Mr Lowndes came to King's Wood. Miss Cowie was there so was Charles and Mr Lawford and the Major. When Gypsy ran off with them it was charming - never thought I looked well on horseback before. On the 16th went to a steeple chase at Mentmore*[9] *- saw it beautifully. A saddle turned, was tired and teased with it. On the 19th Mr Dawson*[10] *came to Leighton, met in the street - Grandmama was gracious he extremely so. Grandmama asked him to call, he came in the afternoon and I came in before his departure. Oh how little he has altered, glad I was to see him. We returned home on 2nd May, Mama and I alone as far as Birmingham where we met Papa. Called on Emma. The last two weeks at Leighton were delightful, several charming rides.*

Wednesday 7th May - *Matilda, Abraham and I set out with many last efforts for the Bazaar,*[11] *established at Morley's Hotel, Trafalgar Square, which we visited next day, found a great deal to do in order to be open by 11. Mr Moore has placed our fancy work in a little stall which he wished us to take with a Mr Johnson as Steward. Arranged with Mr and Mrs Dickinson to go to the Opera "Don Giovanni" and "The Ballet of Ondine" - the Queen was there, Mrs Treacher dressed us, Tilly in a little cap and I in a wreath of acacias with a white rose and green grapes. Next day to the Bazaar again, introduced to the Christys. There are all sorts of things at this Bazaar - carpets, shawls, cloth, dresses, a Shetland pony, farming implements - the Coalbrookdale stall*[11] *and the Sheffield full of iron and steel. Berlin work of all sorts and drawings - good and bad dolls, a post office and a refreshment stall with a refreshment room for those wearing the Freetrade favours, very amusing.*

Saturday 10th May - *Rather a flat day as to selling, but we left early for Kingston. Miss Christy came to town and Mr Richard and we returned together to Woodbines*[12] *- so clean, so cold, so overwhelmingly kind. The Christy's are a fine study of character - not overdone with sense perhaps but amiable in the extreme - Mr Henry Christy reported of Miss A--- B--- the least agreeable by degrees the Mama is quiet and rather the gentlewoman which he never seems to be himself. Mr John Christy suffers from rheumatism, by far the most clever of the sons. Rebecca is a very fine girl, distinguished in manner and elegant in dress. Her sister Elizabeth rather pretty, rather high and Quaker-like. Wandered over the beautiful grounds laid out by Capability Brown.*

Monday 12th May *- Bushey Park, Hampton Court and Claremont*[13] *- the last a very pretty place, shut up 14 years after the death of the princess. We looked about and our kind friends drove us back in their carriage to the Esher Station by 12 - dressed and were in the Bazaar by 1. Next day with Mrs Moore and Mr Johnson to study the Rock Harmonium in the upper boxes. On Wednesday they saw the Government collection of geological equipment etc, in Craig's Court under the care of Mr Phillips - his son showed us all kinds of curious things in the Laboratory. How arsenic is detected by the slight stain left from its exhalation. Smelt Prussic acid - there were plans of Ebbw Vale and a geological plan of the Salisbury crags. The Royal Academy is full of portraits - one pretty thing by Landseer "The Shepherd's Prayer". The National Gallery is as splendid as ever, Abraham enjoyed it. On the 15th called on Mr Grant who was not at home - walked through the parks and came away to Leighton in the evening.*

Friday 23rd May *- Spent a most pleasant week with Matilda at Leighton without much incident - Tilly sat for her portrait. Today we came alone to Birmingham and I am left with Emma for a few days. Mrs Lloyd of Bingley*[14] *called on 26th May and engaged us to dine there on Saturday - must write home as I intend to stay until the beginning of next week. Went to Frederick Street in the evening, met Mr and Mrs Edmund Sturges - very bad weather. Emma and I walked to the farm on the 27th May - introduced to Miss Roltea, very agreeable, and to Mrs Alfred Fox, old Mrs Lloyd's daughter. Next day Emma and I made arrangements for her party - went to Frank Dickinsons for a nosegay, saw his wife*[15] *- then the party at six - Mr and Mrs James Lloyd junior; Mr I and Mr WR Lloyd from Bingley; Mr George Dixon and Mr Lancaster who Mrs Lloyd had been calling an Indian and had expected to see arrive in paint and feathers - he is from Bombay, very agreeable music-mad and keeps a monkey - a clever man too and one who excels in sifting out all there is to sift in one's intellect.*

Thursday 29th May *- Emma*[16] *and I set out to call at Bingley, met Mr WM Lloyd who took us to the Society of Arts to see the distribution of prizes to the students at the School of Design, Lord Calthorpe in the Chair. Went to tea at "the Farm" in the evening, which was an opportunity for comparing notes in tastes - Wordsworth we did not love - Byron we agreed in admiring against our judgement. Mrs Hemens he likes as much as I do, a rare masculine admission. Cowper he liked and I did not - Tennyson we agreed. Mrs Lloyd ill with rheumatic gout sat in her chair dispensing old-world ideas in no amiable spirit. Mrs Alfred Fox too appeared a clever woman but with ideas contracted to that uncompromising sphere of journal quakerism which wonders at every thing beyond. Next day Mrs Fox and Mr G Lloyd, the Papa, same to tea. I am reading "Heros and Hero Worship" - the hero as a poet - Shakespeare and Dante is most interesting.*

Saturday 31st May - *Went to dine at Bingley - Emma and I had walked to the Cemetery in the morning - the Bingley party included Mr Robert Lloyd and his sister from Hagley Terrace and Miss Hart who is clever - Mr Tom Lloyd showed us a cargo of Mexican idols and helmets with Parrot's feathers red, blue and yellow and a splendid collection of minerals, silver ore etc, and Mr WR Lloyd produced his researches in antiquities, impressions of brasses and models of Apollo from Pompeii. Mr Robert Lloyd is a clever oddity - I like him not.*

Sunday lst June - *Too late for Mrs Capper's funeral so we went to Church both times - Christchurch in the evening and the large church in the Bullring in the morning. My cold is come on again and very tiresome, Mr Lloyd got me something for it but it made me sick, or was it Emma's Gooseberry pie? On Monday Emma and I went to call and take lunch with those at Hagley Terrace, Mr R Lloyd came in to observe he had been half round Birmingham thinking of the goodness of providence in constituting the human frame so as to bear heat and cold and retain itself the same even temperature by evaporation. As we came home Emma told me of the romance of Miss Hart and her cousin Nehemiah - she had not been to Birmingham before his death. In the evening Mr SJ Lloyd took us to the Town Hall to hear the organ - magnificent and overpowering. The "Gloria in Excelcis" of Pergolesi and Bellini's "Come per me sereno" were lovely, and the Irish airs were very pretty and I am half ashamed to say I liked some of the Donizetti (selections from Don Pasquale). Next day dearest Emma and I walked about shopping and at one o'clock I bade goodbye to them, persuaded Mr Lloyd not to go with me as he much desired to do, but Papa had permitted me to go alone and I much desired so to do. Train delayed by accident - the Dale green and beautiful but dull in the extreme.*

Tuesday 10th June - *Cold troublesome all week. To cure it I took some Paragoric lozenges and then lay talking to Matilda for hours, Abraham in London and this morning my voice nearly gone. Next day took some blue pills and Jame's powder, staying in bed - voice wholly gone! By the 15th June the weather was glorious - Mr Rowland looking grave, myself silent in bed studying patience and Dr Arnold - mustard poultices and linseed tea and quills - the sun has kissed all the colour out of the rhododendrones, they blossom white.*

On 8th July the Tothills and Anna Rebecca Tregellis arrived for General Meeting. JJ Gurney also here, his son is to marry out of the Society and a cousin of Bessie Gurney is to marry a second son of the Chevalier Bunsen. JJ Gurney had a public meeting in the evening which Papa and Uncle Tothill attended, also Miss Tregellis - whom I like very much. They are very lively, pretty and accomplished and as simple as possible. Joe Dickinson and Uncle Richard Darby came up in the evening and the latter was eloquent on the merits of the "narrow gauge" or S. and B. Railway. The Tothills are pulling Stoke (their house) to pieces and going to live for half a year at Hillside. On Thursday Miss Tregellis went to dine at Severn House, we had a pleasant walk in the morning with her and Uncle Nathaniel who is clever, intelligent and quiet - after dinner we set out for a drive to the Wrekin and were caught in a most pouring shower, but no one caught cold.

Sunday 13th July - *Papa chose to have asked Mrs Burlingham, her daughter and "brother Gregory" to tea - Mary Darby came too and was not very agreeable. We have most pleasant days, duets etc, and all "couleur de rose" and my young friends do not appear dull. I see that I have not recorded a party when the Grahams came to tea - Papa gave it in honour of a Mr John Maude Ogden who came and was very attentive to me to my very special annoyance - he is a great talker and teller of tales - not without abilities but very silly and tiresome. Miss S Graham was here a Miss Armistead and Uncle Richard Darby's party, Rebecca and all. Well the said Mr Ogden called again and is now coming to the cattle show at Shrewsbury. "On dit" he wants a wife - do not wish him to propose for me. On Saturday we dined at the Chesnuts and met Uncle and Aunt Tothill.*

Tilley invited us to tea on the 15th, she had two of the Christy's and Uncle Richard Darby's party with Henry just come home - Russian Bagatelle. Abraham began to show us how to play and wished me to choose partners, so I asked cousin Henry to choose them for me - my galaxy of beauty looked all that I could wish. Miss Tregellis in dark with white satin scarf and the Tothills pink borege with short sleeves and pink satin ribbons (I was in white muslin brodia and rose ribbons with the mechlin lace) the Tothills left for Eastfield the next day. Papa went with Abraham to Shrewsbury on Thursday and asked the Christy's[12] *to tea with Matilda, they are agreeable and gentlemanly and quite without Quaker awkwardness, Mr Alexander Christy I really like.*

Friday 18th July - *Miss Tregellis and I spent the day sketching. The Tothills came up in the morning and we walked down with them and encountered Mr Ogden and Henry Dickinson who talked for half an hour over the hedge and asked us to go with them to Apley, we then met Uncle Richard Darby and Basil Rathbone who repeated the invitation. Matilda has also made similar plans but she did not wish people to say she was a match-maker. However, Abraham asked Anna and me to go. The "Apley Day" on the 19th was charming and very well arranged, consisting of about 20 people.*

On Sunday we had a very pleasant dinner party with the Christy's, Abraham and Matilda - Mr Ogden came afterwards, he pays some attention to Anna. I like the Christy's for one thing and almost nothing else - they appear to dissassociate me from my people - an amiable gratification. The following day, Monday, the Christy's and Anna left.

Tuesday 22nd July - *We dined at The Chesnuts to meet Mr and Mrs WR Anstice,*[17] *Mr Basil and Henry Darby. Mr Basil Rathbone improves on acquaintance - he has beautiful eyes and is clever. Some man, a member of the Willoughby family, wrote Longman requesting to be put in possession of the* *remainder of the MSS of Lady Willoughby's Diary, Mrs Rathbone did feel that to be a compliment, though she had no idea of attempting so decided a deception as the book has proved. I stayed all night at The Chesnuts, Papa going to London next day.*

Went over the works on Friday, 25th July to see the Atmospheric pipe planning which though dirty and smokey beyond conception I was glad to have seen - it is a wonderful thing to have affected - so different an undertaking in short a time - not very profitable I believe thanks to Mr Cubit and Mr Saunders. Joe Bailey is really married.[4] *Her name is Emily Hyacinthe Anne. I hope, really hope he will be happy and yet I believe I should have been as well pleased if it had not been, I am sure it is wrong because I could not marry him myself - probably never could let him have been ever so patient to wait.*

Sunday 3rd August - *Dearest Tilly has been here all the week. She and Mama are of the same mind concerning the Titmouse. I am sure it never occurred to me here that he was at all likely to propose. Time will show - I would rather not think because he has too much of the Quaker spirit in him, which to me is dreadful. I have been reading 'Sybil' and like it very much. Novel readers aver that the love story wants interest and political economists are put out to find their researches crossed by a love story, so poor Disraeli pleases but few, and perhaps I owe some of my satisfaction with him to a wet, wet day when dearest Tilly departed and all would have been very triste only for these brilliant pages. This is a wet summer indeed.*

Wednesday 13th August - *We - Papa, Mama and I came to Leamington, the wet summer having put aside all thoughts of a longer expedition - Dearest Tilly and Abraham came on Saturday and the former stayed with us more than a week, during which Mama went to Leighton. Two weeks later I felt inclined to state that there is nobody we know or it would be pleasant. I am having charming rides with Edgerton exploring this lovely country and thoroughly happy - oh, how strangely altered in 10 years! Mrs Treacher has sent me a lovely dress - would I might ever have an opportunity to wear.*

Thursday 9th September - *Tomorrow we leave Leamington. Many charming rides I have had on a love-of-a horse - Chesterton Windmill*[18] *is a place everyone should see. Yesterday to Princethorpe*[19] *where there is a convent. Papa and Mama went in a phaeton and bought some things from the bazaar they have. I was sorry to have missed the Lady Abbess in her black veil, but not knowing people were admitted, I did not stop, but enjoyed the ride back through the fields by Offchurch - very pleasant.*

Monday 22nd September - Leighton - *We were at home a fortnight then came here today for Grandmama's Quarterly Meeting - while at home I had a little music, a little toilet preparation, a little visit from dearest Tilly. It has been a pleasant visit but we return home on Wednesday 8th October. First there was the Quarterly Meeting, we brought Miss Nicol, Benjamin Frebohm and the*

Yardleys and a little man named Shevrell. Miss Nicol just what I expected but prejudiced and enthusiastic and Irish. A Gurney can do no wrong even John Henry in this mercenary match with his cousin. Mr Frebohm is wonderfully eloquent and gifted, a German by birth - family visits Johnson's song - some man going to many a young wife his first having been dead but three months - John Yardley said he would be willing to let him have two if it would keep him quiet in the Yearly Meeting! It was a great dose of Quakerism but on the whole they were favourable specimens - the next day came the Cattle Show and many freaks worthy of this place. The Ploughing Match - Miss Roberts and I in a ditch and Mr Lovett helping us out, good opportunity of admiring his blue eyes and flaxen moustaches. Drive home with Mr Bailey in his dog cart - heard how his son threatened to hang himself the first wet day after his marriage on the banks of Derwentwater, began to think I was right glad not to be Mrs Joe Bailey. The Duke was there and Mr Shelley and a great Turk man and Mr Bouverie. On Wednesday, 8th October we went to Leamington and stayed at "The Regent" all night, it seemed so like coming home!

Monday 13th October - *Matilda took me with them to Apley and I dined at the Cave after - Rachel Fowler is at the Dale and coming here - the dose of Quakerism seems like to go on but no matter. They departed the next day and I went with Matilda and Abraham to the Mechanic's Institute tea party, some really nice singing - Miss Taylor favoured the company with several songs and a fit of hysterics. There was a man named Allen, a moulder in the Dale, who really sang very well indeed - he and a Broseley genius - Glover and another sang "The Red Cross Knight" - the mass shall be sung and the bells shall be rung - it was beautiful - Mr Hill not a very good Chairman.*

At the beginning of November Wilson[20] *gave one of his entertainments in Shrewsbury and Papa went to it and met the Egremonts - some way or another all old feuds were forgotten and a few days after Papa and Mama went over to Wroxeter, had a most gracious reception after Mrs Egremont's own peculiar manner. They asked the Egremonts to dinner and they came 6th November and met Mr and Mrs J Pritchard,*[21] *Janet was with them. Mr Knight*[20] *gives a concert next week, Papa will take me dining at the Pritchards*[21] *first. The same people gave a concert in Shrewsbury the next evening and Mrs Egremont invited me to go there and stay at Wroxeter On Sunday, 16th November, the great Quaker celebrity, Lindley Murray Hoag attended - he deserves his fame as a most beautiful and spirit stirring preacher of the Gospel - the evening Meeting was crammed. Brockbank dined here and went with us. The following Tuesday evening Uncle Tothill came - it has been rather a stormy time at the company meeting with talk of giving up the Dale. Mama and Matilda at sparring matches. It is difficult enough to walk carefully!*[22] *What a pity it seems when people with so much good in them spoil it all with temper and nonsense.*

Thursday 20th November - *Mr Knight's concert at Broseley*[20] *- Papa took me and Matilda and Abraham - we all dined at Mr John Pritchard's*[21] *- very very charming, with Dr Rowley and his daughter, two nice boys and a Miss Jackson and Mrs Gordon. All the world was at the concert, we had Madame Daler who is wonderful and very beautiful as is her playing, also Mademoiselle Schloss who has fine German voice and is a fat German person - Herr Goldberg sang "Meme Nezzist am Riene" with great feeling and spirit and the two Miss Williams and Parry (the inimitable Parry). It was a nice Concert. With two notes I have got off my visit to Mrs Egremont*[8] *and am rather glad.*

Tuesday 25th November - *Dined at Little Wenlock to meet the Pritchards,*[21] *Miss Pritchard, Miss Yate, Mr and Mrs Anstice and a silent oddity, Mr Eastwick - an agreeable party and Mr Eastwick fascinating. Mr and Mrs Pritchard invited me to pay them a visit in the Spring which was, I am sure, very kind. I go to Wroxeter tomorrow for the rest of the week - may Mr Maude not be there*[6] *- I pray it more than most things of so little consequence. I shall enjoy my visit here extremely, I came on Wednesday and Mr Maude is NOT here, but Captain Russell is!*[6] *He came to dinner today and stays. A charming creature, Miss Walford is also here - very pretty and quite unaffected with the world - she is teaching me the Polka.*

Thursday 27th November - *We had an amusing morning with Captain Russell's guitar and his matrimonial speculations with Janet. We then walked with him half way to Harnage. Mr and Mrs Egremont went to Oriston to dinner. In the evening as we were dancing there came a ring and Louisa exclaimed "There's Uncle Tom"*[6] *- I am too angry to write any more. Friday was wet and drizzly. After luncheon we danced and then Mr Maude and Ned rode out. Captain Russell reappeared at dinner.*

Sunday 30th November - *The finale came sooner than I expected. Before I was up Capsy brought me a note from Mr Maude which at first I thought a joke of Miss Walford and Louisa and perhaps le Capitaine - I replied kindly but firmly, but half fear with too much kindness. We were up late and the 3 gentlemen late. Mr Maude's note was written in the drawing room last night as he used the seal always kept there.*

Captain Russell left before breakfast. When Mr Maude came down (I had written my note in pencil and sent it up by Capsy) looking very pale and wretched as was proper he announced his intention of going to Harnage. Papa took me away from Wroxeter on Tuesday, 2nd December and we called at Leighton[23] *on our way home - went to see the monument to Mr Kynnersley.*

New Year's Eve - 31st December - *Old 1845 is finished within an hour, Thank God for a year even so passably happy! Abraham and Matilda spent Xmas Day with us but I was reminded of days that were - when a Merry Xmas and Happy New Year seemed a mocking wish.*

NOTES

1. Trinder, The Darbys of Coalbrookdale (1991), pp.53, 54.
2. SRRC 1681/138/10.
3. Linslade House was where Francis Darby recuperated for a year after his brain haemmorhage in 1817 (see p. ??).
4. Joe Bailey was an early suitor for Adelaide's hand. He was refused out of hand by Francis Darby. His marriage to Miss Chatmore in July 1845 was a dreadful shock to Adelaide (see Comment above).
5. Mr Edmonds was the vicar of Little Wenlock and a standby candidate for Adelaide's hand in marriage.
6. Mr Tom Maude was a brother of Mrs Egremont of Wroxeter (west of Coalbrookdale). He and Captain Russell were possible suitors for Adelaide's hand in marriage.
7. Adelaide was consistent in refusing to contemplate marriage to Alfred Darby which otherwise would have been a good match.
8. Mr and Mrs Egremont of Wroxeter (west of Coalbrookdale) seemed rather over anxious in pressing their friendship.
9. Mentmore is a few miles south of Leighton Buzzard.
10. Mr Dawson was an early suitor for Adelaide's hand in marriage. He was inexplicably turned down by Francis Darby, a decision which he later regretted.
11. The National Anti-Corn Law League (see Comment above, p.172).
12. The Woodbines was the home of the Christy family in Kingston-on-Thames. By all accounts it was a splendid house. It has since been demolished. Some panels of hand painted Chinese wallpapers rescued from The Woodbines by Rachel Labouchere are on display at "Rosehill", Darby Road, Coalbrookdale (I.G.M.T.). The Christys were a prominent Quaker family related to the Fells of Cumberland. Their name is best known through their introduction of turkey towelling into Britain.
13. Claremont is in Esher. The gardens were started c1715 and involved some of the greatest names in landscape design such as Vanbrugh, Bridgeman, Kent and Capability Brown.
14. Bingley in Birmingham was the family home of the extensive Lloyds family.
15. See 1844, note 18 (p.171).
16. Emma Reeves from Leighton Buzzard.
17. William Reynolds Anstice was a solicitor and a partner, with his brother, John Anstice, in the Madeley Wood company.
18. The windmill at Chesterton is about 4 miles south of Leamington.
19. Princethorpe is about 5 miles north-east of Leamington.
20. Mr Wilson and Mr Knight appear to have been local empresarios.
21. Mr John Pritchard was a banker from Broseley. Mr and Mrs Pritchard were to become close friends of Adelaide in the 1850s.
22. See Comment 1845 above (p.172-173).
23. Leighton is a village between Wroxeter and Coalbrookdale - not to be confused with Leighton Buzzard. The Kynnersley family were distinguished lords of the manor. The monument to Mr Kynnersley is located in the village church, next to the manor house.

1846

Comment

As Adelaide moved into her late 20s, her social life expanded somewhat and became more sophisticated. A notable extension came with an invitation to stay with Mr and Mrs John Pritchard at Broseley. As an industrial town Broseley was in decline, but at the same time a measure of gentrification was taking place. The Pritchards as Bankers were part of this process. Another place prominent in her social round was Wroxeter where Adelaide was a regular guest of the Egremonts.

July was taken up with visits to London and to Ebbw Vale in Wales, where Matilda and Adelaide became godparents to children of Mr and Mrs Browne. Mr Browne was the manager of the Ebbw Vale Works, in which Abraham Darby IV was a partner.

At the end of the year Adelaide remained unmarried, having finally rebuffed (once again) Alfred Darby's proposal of marriage. Not only was she unmarried, but at the end of the year she was invited by Louisa Egremont of Wroxeter to be one of her bridesmaids in her marriage to Captain William Russell. This was a blow below the belt (no doubt unintended) as Captain Russell had been one of Adelaide's suitors, and Adelaide cherished the possibility that he might remain on her list of 'standby intended'.

Sunday 17th January - Leighton - *I came here on the 6th, dearest Mama stayed a week. I have been once to tea with Emma - she goes tomorrow. I am working diligently, the companion to Mamas Ottoman and reading "Damascus" to my old lady and reading a host of things to myself.*

Saturday 14th February - Valentine's Day - *Abraham came a few days ago and we have had two pleasant evenings at Mrs Ashfield's - Tilly's visit was one of tears and smiles to me - I love her better probably than any created thing and therefore feel it the more when she scolds me. Grandmama wished me to have my picture taken in miniature and I had been sitting in white. Catherine Lawford is really coming home with me on a visit which I do not think will be very pleasant. On Friday, 6th March went to Mrs Andrews, danced all the evening, sang the "Light of other days".*

Wednesday 1st April - *Papa, Catherine and I came home - prosperous and unadventurous journey - met Mr Bailey and Kitley at Wolverton and called on the Lloyds in Birmingham. Emma's baby very charming. The next morning dearest Tilley came up before breakfast, Miss Christy is at present with her - Catherine and I called at The Chesnuts.[16] On Friday the Chesnuts[16] came to dinner with Mr Oliver and in the evening arrived Mr Henry Christy, a little to everyone's amusement.*

Saturday 4th April - *Snowed all day - so did Sunday, but Catherine and I went to Ironbridge Church in the morning, we had a rather prosy sermon from Mr Wolfenden and met Mr R Anstice*[17] *who, wonderful to relate had recovered his powers of speech - I had not heard the sound of his voice these ten years. In the evening I went to Meeting. Monday it snowed again, Papa went to Shrewsbury and Henry Christy called.*

Thursday 7th April - *Catherine and I went to The Chesnuts*[16] *to dine as the Christy's go tomorrow, met Alfred and Mary. Alfred played on the Jew's Harp and we had the Russian Bagatelle - Mr R Christy and I came to a difference about Warburton. Next day the weather cleared, Christy's left - Abraham to Quarter days and Matilda came to us. On Thursday we went to the Ironbridge and during our absence Mr and Mrs J Pritchard*[1] *called. Mama had never been well since I came home and this day the affair became serious and she went to bed. The Pritchards*[1] *sent an invitation for us to dine at Broseley and for me to stay a day or two and it was accepted.*

Good Friday 10th April - *We three went to Buildwas Church.*[2] *Mr Bird preached a most excellent sermon. Abraham returned on Sunday and Catherine and I went again to Buildwas - Mr Bird promised to call on Catherine but would not come to dinner.*

Thursday 16th April - *Page, Catherine and I went to Mr John Pritchard's.*[1] *Mama much better but not well enough to go. We met the Miss Younge and Mr Smith - the party stopping in the house, also Miss Pritchard and Mr Gordon.*[3] *Mr Baugh, a young man staying with the Pritchard's and Mr Wilton the curate of Mr Forester. Plenty of music, plenty of singing and altogether a pleasant evening. Mr Smith is a Barrister on the Midland circuit as yet have nothing to do, very quiet, gentlemanly and handsome - but not perhaps overwise. The Miss Younge's are Irish, they were left orphans early and Mr Nesbit, whose widow was a dear friend of the Pritchard's, was their Guardian - they are visiting the Hunts of Felton having been at school with Miss Hunt in Warwickshire. On Friday we went to Astley*[4] *on horseback after luncheon and had a great deal of amusements. I was on a horse I could not manage so thought of Mr Pritchard and he gave me a pony which was offended not liking me as much as Mr Smith. We went - the pony and I into three ditches and one hedge I came home on Miss Younge's horse. Met Mr Gordon who returned from Linley*[5] *with us to dinner, no one else but Mr Baugh.*

Saturday 18th April - *A lovely morning we rode to Benthall over Tickwood to Buildwas, then to Wenlock Abbey*[6] *which Lady Granville and a party were surveying. How charming it was, my horse was so perfect, everybody in such spirits, Mr Smith so useful and handsome and poetical. Then we went over that beautiful country by Willey through the preserve home, through the park where Miss Younge and I rode races, which I won. Met Mr Bates, dear old man - We went to dine at Mr Pritchard's, the three Edmonds, Mr and Mrs W R Anstice*[17] *and Miss Bache - our party were six - all very kind to me and charming music. On Sunday Catherine came just as Mr Smith was reading to me the history of the attack upon Louis Phillippe*[7] *- she went to church with us, good sermon by Mr Forester. They were to walk to Linley*[5] *in the afternoon - Catherine and I returned in the carriage, I was very tired and half dead with the shaking of my horse the day before.*

Monday 20th April - *We all dined at The Chesnuts*[16] *to meet the Tothills and Miss Bache - Catherine and I had been collecting fossils and hearing from a Wesleyan Minister of the changes of the days from the old Quakers. On Wednesday Mr and Mrs John Pritchard*[1] *and the Miss Younge's called - I was in some wonder which cavalier would be in attendance but I expected Mr Gordon*[3] *was gone to Oxford and that Mr Smith would be the happy man, but Catherine put all doubt at an end by lifting up her handbag saying "There's Mr Gordon". All the pictures, all the library, then the kitchen garden, the ladies in their habits - Mr Gordon hardly spoke to me three times, well, no matter they are all really very silly for sensible people. In the evening we went to Horsehay.*[18] *On the 23rd Catherine and I dined at The Chesnuts*[16] *to meet the Edmond's, Mr and Mrs Pritchard,*[1] *Mr E Bartlett and Mr John Anstice*[17] *- a charming evening we played at "Knights of the Whistle". One day last week Papa took Catherine and I to Tong Castle*[8] *and on to Apley.*

Wednesday 6th May - *Abraham, Matilda, Catherine and I to Shrewsbury for the Bazaar - Lady Charlotte Lyster was still in great beauty. Mr and Mrs Joe Dickinson there and Mrs John Midgeley,*[9] *also the Misses Younge and we sat for a few minutes, probably for the last time in this world! The Bazaar cleared more than 1100 pounds. Next day Catherine left us, Papa took her to Birmingham - Mama is far from well. On 11th May we went to Admaston*[10] *for four days. By Thursday Mama was much benefitted I am thankful to say. The house full of people but we have not been in the public rooms. Mrs Gwyther, her Mama and baby there. On Saturday 16th May Miss Praeger*[11] *arrived, I rather like her.*

Saturday 7th June - *Mademoiselle stayed two weeks with me, then one with Matilda - she was a curiosity and rather impertinent - she certainly taught German and singing well - French she refused to speak because I had not specified it in my letter. NB to specify in future all things. Mrs Egremont*[19] *came at 12 o'clock to fetch Miss Praeger, Captain Russell and Louisa with her - they are said to be engaged and have been since last summer, before my Autumn visit, but that Mrs Pritchard refuses to consent to it at present. We almost finished "Undine" and I learned to copy the German characters with some facility. Miss Praeger was fascinated with dear Abraham, they had two pleasant dinner parties.*

Monday 15th June - *Mrs Egremont*[19] *invited me to go to Wroxeter tomorrow. Until after post time today it seemed a doubtful point, but at last Papa* *allowed me to go and we remained good friends too, so I have been writing to Louisa.*

Thursday 18th June - Wroxeter *- I came here on the 16th and am much better - this hot weather - hotter than anything that anybody could remember - had made me almost ill. Dearest Tilly has been in her bed for several days. It is charming here. Thank God we have no Mr Maude!*[12] *On Tuesday evening when I got here to dinner there was no-one but Captain Russell. He is not going to marry Louisa it seems, nor anybody else either, according to Miss Praeger. I hope the other scandal may not gain ground but I cannot tell. She is most imprudent though I do not believe one syllable of evil and he, like most men, saying everything they think, gives great room for people to wonder. "Il etait trop attentif a moi" - but it meant nothing and he was really rougher, more from before the most than ever I saw him. Mrs Edwards was very foolish. He was expecting a Mr George Richards who had been on board his ship for five years as chaplain, so he fled very soon and we spent the evening rambling over the fields.*

Wednesday morning came my first interview with Miss P, her indignation great at the things they had said of us in the drive to Wroxeter and of Mr A such a good natured man. I never heard what and so did not believe much of it. Mr and Mrs Perry called this morning - while they were here Miss Burton arrived - not exactly pretty but very unaffected and clever and very amiable. Mr Rocke came to luncheon, that is dinner - for their plan is to dine at one - now and afterwards we all walked to Mr Stubbs. The Stubbs are from home and the Egremonts have leave to go where they please, over those lovely grounds. We stayed there until Miss Burton's horse came for her and then walked slowly home. Mrs Egremont had gone in the meantime to Shrewsbury whence she was to bring back Macaulay the handsome young gentleman who was so attentive to Mrs Egremont and to me at the circus.

Before we went to Mr Stubbs, Miss Lodge had been summoned to give us all an essay on the Art of Lovemaking, she having now a love affair with Mr Williams, one of the romances of Wroxeter. She came and read to us Byron's Dream, at least Miss Burton did. When we came home, Macauley was in the garden, he sprang over the fence and rushed up to me, we shook hands without any further introduction.

At 12 o'clock, Louisa, Macauley and I went to Longnor.[20] *It is a lovely place. Miss Burton was drawing for the Romances of Miconium in a beautiful library surrounded with oak bookcases and comfortable easy chairs and sofas - and then the most beautiful carved oak ceiling. Luncheon being announced Miss Burton contrived very cleverly to arrange Macauley and Louisa at each end of the table where they ate and talked and quarrelled and made it up again in the most ludicrous manner. Mr Macauley hinted at reports concerning naval captains (I should not have forgotten that at Mr Stubbs we found a fortune-telling wheel and that Louisa and I spun it round to the same thing, a sailor Captain with a cockade) and Owen Rocke said in his quiet drawl "I hope you won't fight for him, at any rate." Macauley remembered this and his jealousy fed upon it till he grew quite pale. Louisa has a great deal of quietness and roguishness. She is very graceful and looked particularly well. After luncheon, we walked to the Rookery and Miss Burton and I contrived to get quite away and leave Louisa with her little adorer. I found Miss Burton a very charming person, very full of life and disposed to be amused with everything, but without a spark of ill nature. When we got back Captain Russell and Mr Richards were arrvied - Mr Richards[21] is a handsome, agreeable man of imperturbable silkiness of manner - they appear very much attached to each other and certainly two men more unlike could not well be found. We had a droll evening - poor Macauley was so angry at the sight of the Captain - Mrs E E? hoped Mr M? had made himself agreeable - "very much so" I said no doubt, "though Miss Burton and I did not see much of him." Captain Russell laughed.*

Mr and Miss Burton rode over in the cool of the evening and stayed until quite dark. Captain Russell and Mr George Richards[21] were going at the same time - we were all out. Macauley half wild with delight that he was getting rid of his tormentor. "We might as well take some of these girls back with us," said Captain Russell. "One apiece, George." "Miss Mary, will you go?" said Macauley. Miss Mary made no answer. "Miss D?" said Captain Russell, "Will you go, I'll be chaperone." "Not half such a good one as I made this morning, besides I think it is going to rain." They departed and we sat talking until rather late.

Friday 19th June - *Macauley departed after breakfast, but there was nothing very tender. Last night he squeezed Louisa's hand, and then mine most cruelly because I laughed, and we threw the roses we had been wearing at his candle when we were safe on the landing above. Rather romping days but bright days too, how bright in the waste of wilderness of such a life as mine. After Macauley was gone, Mrs Egremont quarrelled with Miss Praeger, who by the way, was very disagreeable and Miss Praeger's departure was fixed for tomorrow. Mrs Feade sat discussing a tour into Wales and I copied music and sat with Mrs Egremont listening to her fears as to the extent of her patience. Captain Russell and Mr Richards came very late to dinner, and Papa arrived for me before dinner was done. There was a curious scene with some roses of Captain Russell's which finally he sent to Mama. Mrs Egremont bestows some tears upon it.*

Wednesday 1st July - *Osborne's Caledonian Hotel, Adelphi. We find ourselves established here very comfortably, and dearest Matilda recovered the fatigue of the journey before bedtime and wonderfully. Mr Browne[13] was here to meet Abraham. He is rather a nice agreeable person and we are to go into Wales to see them whether from here, from Leighton or from home is a little uncertain.*

Thursday 2nd July - *We stayed resting most of the morning and then Abraham took us to walk in St James Park and in the evening he took us to the Opera. Oh, the changed coat is a blessed thing for us. We had the Semiramide with Grisi as the Queen of Babylon. Assure - Fornasari Oroe Lablache and Arsaces, Mdlle Saughioli, a moderately pretty woman and a fine voice, one act of Lucia di Lammermuir for the introduction of Castellan and Mario. The scenery is very beautiful and both were in splendid voice. Then a little divertissement of Bacchantes with Lucille Graham as Prima Donna and Perrot, and this very long Thursday concluded with Barrota ballet of Lallah Roohk.*

Cerito is a lovely Lallah Roohk and Louise Taglioni is the Princess of Bucharia St Leon Feramorz and Perrot Fadladeen - The scenery is splendid - the storm in the desert is quite awful. I never saw dancing more splendid the whole affair is gorgeous! Mr J Browne with us.[13]

Friday 3rd July - *I slept this morning till 11 o'clock, then Abraham took us to the Academy where there are some beautiful pictures - Mulready's "Choosing the Wedding Gown" and Landseer's "Peace and War" and Papa's two pictures by Frith and Maclises celebrated "Ordeal by Touch" - Afterwards we went to the Panorama of "the battle of Fobreon which the Duke of Wellington has pronounced to be very good. It conveys a dreadful idea of the slaughter of thousands without being at all disgusting.*

Saturday 4th July - *Shopping in Regent Street all the morning - Alfred Darby arrived to dinner and we went in the evening to the St James Theatre, "The Ethiopian Serenaders" which was nothing particularly agreeable though the melodies were some of them pretty in their simplicity.*

Sunday 5th July - *Abraham was not well and stayed at home until evening - Alfred Darby went with Matilda and I to St Martin's church! will marvels ever cease. In the evening walked in St James Park. Sir Henry Duckenfield preached a very excellent practical sermon.*

Monday 6th July - *We went to call at Mr Grant's, found them at home and saw all the children. Mrs Grant is tall and rather quiet and agreeable, not exactly pretty but yet with nice features. Abraham took us then to see the valuable old pictures exhibiting at the Pall Mall Institution. Alfred Darby came to dinner and we all went to the Hay Market to see Mdme Tuillon in the "Black Domino". She is very pretty, but the band was very bad and either that or Anber himself made the music by no means melodious. There was only Miss P Horton besides Mdme Tuillon as a singer and their voices are wiry after Italian ones. In Borough politics we had Mrs Glover as Mr Thompson - Webster as Farmer Thompson and Buckstone as the editor of a newspaper. Alfred Darby finds great fault with the love scenes and lovers - the ladies act their parts much the best - it is a little amusing.*

Tuesday 7th July - *Sir John Soanes Museum - Hogarth - a sweet little Rysdael - and some pictures by Henry Howard very pretty indeed. Wonderful antique bronzes down to the cellars and lighted by mirrors. Then the Chinese Collection. Abraham and Matilda went to the Princess's afterwards and we went to bed.*

Wednesday 8th July - *We are here for one more day - Abraham wanted to stay over the Harratt affair. It seems very provoking to him. As we go tomorrow and perhaps to see "Rachel" tonight I must pack.*

Friday 10th July - *We did go to the French plays on Wednesday night - did not see "Rachel" - Dejazet - and Laport - in a Conte de Fies and gentle Berard, also the Ethopian Serenaders. The Queen was there and looking rather pretty, and Prince Albert and the Duchess of Kent and Prince Leiningen and a very lovely lady-in-waiting, Lady Augusta Bruce. Tomorrow we go into Wales I believe.*

Saturday 11th July - *Abraham again set out with his "family" - we went as far as Ross. Matilda and I went twice to Church and Abraham went once - it is a pretty place, Ross, and a very nice church.*

Monday 13th July - *We set out again from Ross, dined at Abergavenny and played with a dear little Newfoundland puppy - about 7 o'clock we reached Ebbw Vale. It is a pretty house and grounds - the neighbourhood barren and ugly in the extreme. There are five little girls and the baby to whom Matilda is to stand Godmama. Mrs Browne is rather a grand lady. "Your visit was almost unexpected Mrs Darby this time, it was a very short notice, but I am always happy to see you."*

Miss Jones is a rather excitable invalid, not particularly agreeable. Mr Browne makes up for all the rest being unpleasant - he is very gentlemanly and delightful.

Tuesday 14th July - *The morning was rather warm and Mrs Browne not inclined we should go out, so we did not until evening came and then we went to tea at Sirhowy - Mr & Miss Williams - Mrs Browne's father and sister live at Sirhowy and keep house for anyone whose pleasure it is to go there. The garden is pretty, and the house, which was undergoing repairs, shows that Somers Harford comprehended what is comfortable. A Staffordshire - Mr Barke, dined with us today, and his son - I imagined they were from Wales and could not comprehend the decided Shropshireisms that I recognised - "I wrought Abergavenny at such an hour" and "Nor Mr Darby I don't know how you "eat your pudding furnaces but this is the way I eat mine"*

Wednesday 15th July - *We went up the mountains at the back of Ebbw Vale House, the views were certainly lovely towards Victoria - my sore throat which had been several days very troublesome becomes worse and worse and prevents me from enjoying myself. Tomorrow is the great christening. I have had a letter* *from Mama today with melancholy news from Leighton - she says that poor Miss Barrett has died from scarlet fever after about ten days illness and that Peter had taken the complaint.*

Thursday 16th July - *The baby's christening turned out to be a christening of six. In Wales they leave these things until there is a large party, "saves expense" as an old Welsh Innkeeper strove to enlighten us. Miss Williams was second Godmother to all. There were two Miss Jones' and a Mr and Mrs Williams, and a Mr and Miss Hughes and a Miss Helms of Bath to divide the honours - Mrs Browne to my great surprise asked me to stand to one of the children - I could not well refuse though I think people ought to be first baptised themselves - Mr William Hughes and I had the honour of leading in little Elizabeth. He is an exceedingly nice young man. Oxford and slightly Puseyite perhaps - he is a clergyman. Twenty-four of us sat down to dinner and we had a dance in the evening. I danced with Mr William Hughes, a very graceful partner and for an Oxford clergyman a good dancer. He was much more attentive to me all day than I wished, though I liked him - very much. He knows the lovely Mrs Mountjoy Martin and he and his sister have been evidently accustomed to good society - The fair Miss Helen, who I like moderately had an hysteric fit or a fainting. Mr and Mrs Irvine are among the nicest people there - the Doctor and his wife. The whole affair was very amusing not solemn in the least or approaching to my ideas of what a christening is designed to be. Mr Reece the Cwm Cellyn clergyman came in to some condemnation from Miss Hughes for writing in the registers at the communion table.*

Friday 17th July - *We came away. Matilda had had quite enough of it!!! It was not altogether easy to be "assez discrete" for the occasion. We dined at Raglan and walked about the beautiful castle and then came on Ross by 10 o'clock at night.*

Saturday 18th July - *We reached home. Poor Benjamin, he is never to drive the carriage again, and they have engaged another coachman. When we were coming from London he could barely sit upon his seat and we were in some danger.*

Tuesday 21st July - *We went to tea at Dale House,*[22] *the first time for several years. It was desperately stupid. Abraham and Matilda were there and Sevem House.*[23] *Maclises Illustrated Edition of the Irish Melodies is beautiful and I had never seen it at leisure before. Oh, I was so continuously thankful that I was not going to be the Mistress of that house!! pretty books are not all one wants. Abraham has altered the Chesnuts very much and they are still amidst bricks and mortar - they have now sundry pretty pictures and a new piano. These things are nice very, I do dearly love Abraham and Matilda though they are not always easy to please in small things and this is my fault, no doubt, heaven knows how seldom I stop to think enough about making myself agreeable.*

Wednesday 22nd July - *Papa was very ill in the night - Mr G Burd called with a large party and walked in the garden.*

Thursday 23rd July - *Papa was well enough for us to come to Leighton.*

Monday 27th July - *Rode out on Gypsey with EL? - we have lovely weather but very hot - Papa stayed in London until yesterday evening - this morning he left for home.*

Tuesday 28th July - *EL? took me out again with WRL? over Heathe - it was very charming.*

Thursday 30th July - *The Lloyds of Lake Street gave a picnic in Wandon woods about 6 miles from here. we were a party of 32 and very pleasant - a day "fait expris". There were the Woodmans and Miss Cowie, Mr and Mrs AA? and Louy, the Andre's Fanny and Charles and Louisa and Mr Kiplin - Mr Allan a new partner of Mr Ashfields - MT Edward Ashfield and his little boy - Mr and Mrs Lawford and all the Lake St Lloyds, except Mrs Lloyd, Miss Burness and her brother - Mrs Reade, Fanny's friend Miss Gorton and Mrs Robert Deverell, Mr and Miss Deare. There was a long table fastened into the ground under the tall trees and we sat upon the moss - dried by a week's burning sunshine. We had dinner and champagne in abundance then we walked about the wood and some of the party encountered a violin and got up a quadrille on the turf. We had tea in the same place and came home in the cool evening.*

Friday 31st July - *I rode with Catherine and WL? by the Brickhills and Woburn, a charming ride.*

Wednesday 5th August - *Another ride with Catherine and WL?. We went to Soulberry and Stoke and across the country to Stock Grove and the Warren, where we had a charming gallop, Gypsey kicking up her heels so that I half expected to go over her head. WL? has heard from Mr Gore and he enters soon upon his situation in Shropshire, very soon.*

Friday 7th August - *EL? took Mama and me out intending W? to drive us to circuit but we went instead to Mentmore and saw the Stables and Kennels and the garden and the shooting box - some of the horses are magnificent and immensely large and strong in consideration of Major Rothschild's weight 17½ stones. Mr SS Lloyd is here.*

Monday 10th August - *We went in the morning with EL? to Circuit. It was the evening for Grandmama to go to meet her teetotal school at the Temperance Hall and we took the carriage after she had done with it on to the Heath. When she came home she seemed rather tired and poorly.*

Tuesday 11th August - *Grandmama was taken ill with the English Cholera so generally prevailing - it began in the night and though she got up today she was so ill with spasms as to be obliged to go to bed again. Papa came in the evening - we are going into Devonshire.*

Sunday 16th August - *We have been under great uneasiness about Grandmama. The complaint continued some days and when Dover's powder had in some degree removed it there remained a stupour and constant sleepiness with some fever said to be very unfavourable. We were wise enough to let all our possessions go by the boats, only keeping what we wanted for our journey into Devonshire. "L'homme propose et Dieu dispose" Papa returned home yesterday as Mr Otley gave no hope that Grandmama would be well enough to let Mama go at present and at the same time he did not fear an immediate change for the worse. Dr Witt saw her yesterday twice. He did not give us much hope, he said indeed that there is everything to fear.*

Monday 17th August - *Dr Witt recommended injections of new milk warm from the cow as Grandmama was quite unable to keep anything on her stomach. This was tried with the best effect for it appeared to remove the tendency to fever which no doubt proceeded from weakness. Today Dr Witt was quite surprised as the change for the better - she is to take nothing for some days but a tonic of steel when Mr Otley will allow it. We were awakened this morning to know if Missis might have some fried bacon and bread - it quite agreed with her and she goes on eating and recovering.*

Friday 28th August - *We could not get away before this date. The Wednesday before, Abraham brought dearest Tilly to us and we all returned home together. Papa met us at Birmingham.*

Thursday 10th September - *I have been very busy arranging my "things" and Miss Fletcher and Madame have both been busy for me, feminine garments are so transitory in summer time. Dearest Tilly was with us almost a week, a charming week and among the numberless improvements at the Chesnuts,*[16] *the piano to me is the greatest. Tilly takes lessons now of Mr Knight, makes charming progress and I have lessons with her. "On dit" that I am to marry Alfred Darby, ditto ditto Mr Edmonds. Apropos the E's? have been to London and Paris, c'est a dire. Mr and Mrs WE? and the dear old lady at 92 has been up the dome of St Pauls. I have been reading Memoirs and letters of Mrs Grant of Laggan, and Dicken's and most entertaining of all, and then we are so tired of partridges between Alfred Darby and Captain Russell. I was extremely astonished to hear of the last - And the more I think about it the more I wonder - he is forever one of those men who do what nobody expects and then he is punctilious - but then Papa had made no acknowledgement of the fish - none in the world beyond words - and yet came six birds. Then did Papa put six bunches of grapes in the basket and sent back by the Cockade for which he has had no answer. The new carriage is very pretty - a clarence blue and drab in excellent taste. And at the C? the departure of bonny Benjy has been the signal for a change of horses. Abraham now has his own and a coachman from Lord Forester, the perfection of a man.*

Monday 14th September - *The Chesnuts[16] and Mr Blake. He is a vain, good natured rattling man of perhaps 45, clever too, and has seen a good deal of life. He came to our house and pronounnced Papa's pictures very good ones of the sort, and increasing in value every year. Told us a multitude of stories in the evening at Chesnuts[16] - he hates the royal family with a most disloyal hatred - they are all heartless and unfeeling. The Prince Regent and the Dukes of York and Cumberland were most wicked, they gambled to an extent that made their resources quite insufficient and then had recourse to the Jews. They borrowed upwards of 2,000,000 and a half from Jews on the continent and at length became troublesome for their money. The Princes sent invitations to them to come on board a vessel lying off Hamburg and said to have been in command of the Duke of Clarence - they had unexpectedly obtained the means of paying the money and would be glad of meeting the accommodating merchants, to restore the borrowed bills and give them a banquet on the occasion. The catastrophe seems almost too horrible and treacherous for belief in the 19th century. The Jews suspecting nothing came out in boats and remained expecting that the princes would receive them. In the meantime the Captain and crew contrived to make their escape, the vessel was swamped and the unfortunate victims all perished. But a short time since a book containing an account of this diabolical affair was in course of publication it was purchased by royal command at £500 a copy. The lady who eloped years ago with Richard Gurney is a Mrs Muskett - Mr Muskett is not living, he committed suicide. Mr Blake does not know her daughter, the present Mrs John Henry Gurney, but he seemed to think she might be happy not withstanding the mercenary nature of the transaction.*

Tuesday 15th September - *We went to call at Little Wenlock. Mr and Mrs W. Edmond have been to Paris. Mr R Anstice has taken up his abode there apparently - he has taken and is Mr Edmonds curate.*

Sunday 20th September - *Joe Dickinson and his wife dined with us. Joseph Sturge is at Eastfield[24] today, Hannah[25] is to be married about the 14th of October.*

Tuesday 22nd September - *Mama and I came to Leighton for the 2 - we found Grandmama quite wonderful, sitting up downstairs to receive us.*

Wednesday 23rd September - *Papa left early - a Mrs Grey Hester came and later Thomas Edmonds with Miss Rebecca came to tea - I was dreadfully ill all day and so sick that I thought there was no chance for me but cholera, however, thank God, it went off with a good night.*

Thursday 24th September - *Grandmama was persuaded to remain in her room and only see a very few - there were some Sewels of Ipswich and the Yardleys.*

Friday 25th September - *Mrs Hester did not leave until this morning - the cattle show - Phoebe and Jane Andrews and I walked to see the ploughing -*

where later on Mr Ridgway contrived to be thrown over his horse's head and to break an arm. He had refused some large offer for the horse from Meyer Rothchild. Mr Bayley called upon us. Mr and Mrs Joe Bayley were gone to Chilton to meet her brother just returned from India on a short leave of absence from his regiment - told him about poor Mr John Brookes whose death has not been so affecting but it seemed a branch of the family not much known to them. His farm is in an awful state from the disease among the cattle - it is the old disease that made them all lame some seasons back.

Saturday 26th September - *Mama and I took courage and went to London for a morning's shopping in Regent Street. We found no sort of difficulties and prospered exceedingly. Yesterday evening came the intelligence that Emma Lloyd*[14] *has a little boy - both doing well though nearly a month sooner than she chose to expect.*

Friday 2nd October - *We came home on Wednesday. Yesterday was the Committee. Today has been "tres mauvais temps" - Alfred Darby has been asking for an interview, and truly if he is now a pupil of Mr Blake (like his two young noblemen) I must say his improvement in "affaires du coeur" is beyond everything. The thing was' thus - After a very wet morning I went down to Matilda's for a little practice. As they were at dinner still, I took the "Bourgois Gentilhomme" and amused myself with his absurdities until the rain came again, and Matilda also under an umbrella to look for me. We went in and practised and Abraham and his brother came in - Abraham went out - I stayed until darker than I intended and then Matilda said she would go with me. Alfred came with us - I had no idea at first that he had anything to say. I had walked with him miles in town and he took no advantage of the opportunity - but there was a hesitation that at last alarmed me. Ho, how fast I talked! I told him all the history of Grandmama and all the Bassett troubles - I never stopped till we were at the gate almost and he would only walk, oh so slowly, I never walked so slowly up that hill except with Mr Edmonds once. Then Alfred said "Ada" - dead pause - "Will you give me an interview of half an hour this evening?" "Oh, no, indeed I cannot, it is of no use." "It is indeed." he said, and then looked as far as I could see, aggrieved he rang the bell, and I said "I hope you are not offended." "By no means." "But" I said, "do come in now, Papa would be so very glad to see you." I thought poor Papa did not at all deserve to have any of the blame. "No" he said, "not now, but is it quite hopeless that I may be allowed to come?" "Oh, yes, indeed it is" I said, "pray do not ask me" I gave him my hand and then asked Matilda to come in - neither could, of course. I was very disagreeable! and I suppose it is so silly to refuse him. But why should I marry at all? God knows I would refuse a Dukedom to know that one noble heart was indeed mine. Still, I know it is great folly to speculate on that very vague probability.*

***Sunday 4th October** - I did not mean to tell anybody what passed that twilight evening but the next day I found that Matilda knew it all - he had told her after going down the hill through the dirt at an awful pace. He told her furthermore how much depended upon Ada's decision - how he had thought of this so long and could not bear to give it up, and had hoped and couldn't live at the Dale and give it up. I went there to tea last evening and met him who was "assez desagreable", but he endeavoured to be amiable and Matilda and Abraham think he might succeed if he knew how, which is almost a mistake. However, I suppose in general we might all of us do anything if we knew how.*

***Tuesday 13th October** - Tilly has been with us almost a week. Wilson's concert at Madeley tonight, the first concert in that very nice room. Abraham came home just in time, he and Alfred and Matilda were together. Papa and 1, thank heaven, quite in another corner, with sweet Miss Jackson and a young man with hair like melted flax who was agreeable notwithstanding. Alfred looked certainly one of the most elegant and interesting men in the room - and as Eugene Sue would say, a profound melancholy gave lustre to his eyes. So I sat and tried to like him, and to think something might be made of him. Matilda says he has not been well and that I am coquettish. Still, I remembered - Matilda's last waking words had been one night "If he has another interview, tell him by all means that it is hopeless. Do not leave him a hope as you have done before."*

***Tuesday 17th November** - I have come to a dark page in my life! Oh, mon dieu, how dark! Is it to colour all the rest with it's own shade! 1, who thought myself iron and steel to feel what I have felt! - Last Friday, my Uncle Tothill and Willie, and Abraham and Matilda and Alfred Darby came to dine. Uncle Dickinson too came to tea, so that we had not much music. Alfred certainly tried to be agreeable and I tried to be proper, and oh, how glad I was to say goodnight - he felt like a cloud in my path and in my own heart, also, there came a ray of sunshine of most deceitful April brightness, sending all such clouds far away. The next morning at breakfast a note from Louisa Egremont. "My dear Ada, I am actually engaged, I have given the cold shoulder to your admirer Macauley, now I have to look upon Captain Russell as my future husband, I have been attached to him for many a day. Will you be my bridesmaid, we shall be married the end of the year." I felt stunned.*[15]

***Thursday 19th November** - There are pleasant things left in this blighted world after all and of such was yesterday's party. The Dugards and the three Edmonds . We had charming music. The Edmonds were very severe on the Wroxeter marriage. Gertrude Dugard spoke of it and I confirmed it. I looked very well in my pink satin, which was a mercy. I never felt good looks so precious before and I suppose people would have thought it absurd to suggest that Captain Russell was ever anything to me but a bad match. I can hardly understand myself - I suppose that the elasticity of the human mind is very great always. I felt when first this thunderbolt fell, as if there was no more hope or* *happiness for me in this life and yet - in a day or two the mere fact of being resolutely in tolerable spirits and talking a good deal did me good. I remember the first thing I hoped was - as I could not go at once abroad, nor go into a convent, nor take prussic acid - my hope came to be that after many years I might live with Abraham and Matilda, the world forgetting by the world forgot. Now I begin to hope many things - I had so thoroughly made up my mind to terribly small means that now and then I have felt almost comfortable in thinking of the comparative luxury that I may expect.*

NOTES

1. The Pritchards were an important Broseley family. At the beginning of the 19th century they were lawyers, but by the 1840's they were firmly established as bankers. The Bank they established was taken over later in the century by Lloyds Bank. The Bank which has been constructed at Blists Hill in the Ironbridge Gorge Museum is a replica of their Bank in Broseley. (VCH10).
2. Buildwas church is about 2 miles west of Coalbrookdale.
3. Mr Osborne Gordon (1813-1883) a native of Broseley, was appointed Reader in Greek at Christ Church, Oxford in 1846. He was a prominent divine in the University until presented to a living at Easthampstead, Berkshire. His epitaph was written by Ruskin. (VCH10 p.258, DNB)
4. Astley Abbots, a village north of Bridgnorth.
5. Linley Green, east of Willey.
6. A nice ride, but hard on the horses, west of Broseley covering about 7 miles, returning later via Willey, a total of well over 10 miles.
7. Then King of France. In 1846 he was involved in a project with Spain which caused deep resentment in England. He was deposed in 1848.
8. East of Shipnal near to border with Staffordshire.
9. Joseph Dickinson's mother-in-law. He married Lucy Midgley on 14th July 1842.
10. Admaston Spa was built in the late 18th century. It was north of Wellington. It is now residential development.
11. Miss Praeger must have been a tutor.
12. Mr Egremont's brother and an unfavoured suitor for Adelaide's hand in marriage.
13. Mr Brown was the manager of the Ebbw Vale Ironworks and one of its partners.
14. Formerly Emma Reeve, Adelaide's close friend at Leighton Buzzard.
15. Captain Russell, a naval captain was a friend of Adelaide's at Wroxeter. He was thought to be a suitor of Adelaide's at one time, but nothing seems to have come of it beyond flirtation.
16. The Chesnuts was situated below the White House and the Deer Park, next to the Meeting House. It was the home of Abraham Darby IV and his wife Matilda, who was Adelaide's sister.
17. Mr Richard Anstice was a member of the Anstice family who were interrelated to the Reynolds and Ball families. They were regarded as "relatives" of the Darby family through William Reynolds (1758-1803) who married his

first cousin Hannah Ball, and who passed on his shares in the Madeley Wood Ironworks to his nephew William Anstice. The latter had sons including John Anstice who lived at Madeley Wood Hall and William Reynolds Anstice who was a solicitor, and was the last Steward of the Manor of Madeley.

18. Horsehay Furnaces, 1½ miles north of Coalbrookdale, established by Abraham Darby II in 1754.
19. Mrs Egremont was the wife of Edward Egremont, vicar of Wroxeter.
20. Longnor is a village, near Eaton Constantine, west of Coalbrookdale.
21. Mr George Richards was the guest who had spent 5 years as Chaplain aboard Captain Russell's ship (p.186).
22. Dale House, built by Abraham Darby I in 1717, is close to the Coalbrookdale works. In 1846 it was occupied by Lucy Darby and her son and daughter, Alfred and Mary.
23. Severn House (now the Valley Hotel, Ironbridge) was the home of Henry Dickinson and his wife, Deborah (née Darby).
24. Eastfield, built in 1838, was situated next to Severn House. It was the home of Barnard Dickinson and his family.
25. Hannah Dickinson married Joseph Sturge.

Rosehill, Darby Road (formerly The Grange), built in 1738 by Richard Ford. At time of the Journal, it was occupied by Richard Darby (1788-1860), uncle of Adelaide Darby, and his family.

1847

Comment

The year 1847 started for Adelaide with an emotional crisis. This was occasioned by the marriage on 5th January of her friend Louisa Egremont to her standby prospective suitor Captain William Russell. Although her relationship with Captain Russell had never really developed, it is nevertheless clear (with hindsight) that Adelaide fancied him and would have married him if matters had worked out favourably. She had not considered Louisa to be a rival and therefore her marriage was a devastating blow exacarbated by the fact that Louisa had invited her to be one of her bridesmaids. It took Adelaide a long time to recover from the shock.

As had become the custom Adelaide spent several months in Leighton Buzzard with trips to London to visit the theatre and the Royal Academy. Her father Francis Darby, was amassing a considerable collection of pictures and books for his gallery and library at The White House. Abraham Darby IV (Matilda's husband) was doing the same at The Chesnuts.

Adelaide reached her thirtieth birthday in August 1847 which she described as rather like "attaining to middle age". Certainly she might have regarded herself as being "on the shelf", especially with so many of her friends, relatives and acquaintances becoming married, both in Shropshire and in Leighton Buzzard. Even her long term suitor, Alfred Darby, became engaged to Rebecca Miller Christie of the Woodbines, Kingston-upon-Thames.

As she moved into her thirties, she seemed imperceptibly to be standing more on her own two feet and making her own decisions. Notably she decided to undertake the vows of baptism, something which she said "I have so long desired". In some ways this was almost predictable. For years she had been friendly with the Hartshorne and Edmonds families - C. H. Hartshorne was curate of Little Wenlock from 1826-1836, and he was succeeded as Rector from 1841 by George Edmonds. Edward Egremont, with whose family Adelaide was friendly, was vicar of Wroxeter. Increasingly Adelaide had become involved with established society in Shropshire, and perhaps unconsciously she drifted towards their way of life. By this act of adult baptism, Adelaide signalled her allegiance to the Church of England, and departure from her family faith, that of the Religious Society of Friends (Quakers).

January - *I had no notion what I was to feel! I hardly thought myself capable of it - oh, that night when I wrote gaily and prettily to Louisa congratulating her and accepting her invitation. I shall be occupied myself resolutely all day*

- we had walked over to Marnwood[1] *and then I had been busy gaining permission to be bridesmaid and I would not allow myself to think - but when it was done and I was alone - oh, how utterly alone - forever in this world, I was almost terrified at my own misery. In that hour I was almost wicked enough to long not to be a Christian - and why? - for the sake of ending my days with prussic acid - coward both ways, I should have feared a death more painful and I feared, oh, what a long life, not perhaps as yet quite half over, a life that seemed like a tomb without the rest of a tomb. I dreaded the next day and every day. Should I be able to be so cheerful that no-one should suspect a shadow in my path, and could I ask God to help me to deceive everybody? Oh, Russell, Russell, you have thrown away a happiness of which you never knew! that is my deep comfort, no-one does know!*[2] *And I once thought I cared about Joe Bailey! I care about society, and balls.*

Sunday 3rd January *- Tuesday is the day. Abraham and Matilda spent Xmas day with us and very charming it was. Allen brought the Carol singers in the evening and Papa let them come in. How soon some bitter things pass away - I do not know whether my mind is more strong and stony than the others or whether its impressions are more written upon sand but I am again happier than I ever expected to be - and already, and with the prospect too of Tuesday. I do not always* <u>*seem*</u> *only* <u>*to be*</u> *happy.*

Tuesday 5th January - Louisa's wedding day *- I was very ill the night before - it turned into slight dysentery and I was terribly frightened. I saw myself on the bed and almost fainted, and then prayed most fervently that I might be able to go and not be faint. I had nothing that was good for me, but so that I could go I felt rather more than resigned to die afterwards. It pleased God that I was better - "and am no like to die." I have a rather confused memory of being up early and looking better than I expected in white and pink - and the morning was damp and warm, the carriage windows covered with steam more outside than in, and I tried to be very agreeable. A few minutes after ten I went into the drawing room at Wroxeter. Mr Egremont came to meet me and Janet, the room seemed to have a great predominance of men - very young men - There was a graceful - well, brideswoman by the fire, and Janet gave up her place to me beside her. She was a Mrs Owen I found after, one of Captain Russell's sisters. He had forgotten the licence and was gone to Shrewsbury. Gradually the room filled with pretty girls, some pink, some blue. Louisa had all the twelve she decided on - Mrs Moorsome came in and spoke to me and introduced her lovely daughters and then Tom Maude came. I told Mrs Owen who all the people were that I knew and she was very agreeable, and told me how she was now living with her husband in Montgomeryshire, and how they had done wrong in being so gay at Wall the week before. "We were all up so late last night and they have a Mr Reece here who tormented my brother to death. Poor Russell, he was very low too." At that moment William Russell came in ready dressed for his part. There was a cluster of beautiful girls by the door and Owen Rocke* *talking to them, but Captain Russell passed them all and made his way to me, he shook hands almost affectionately. There was no malice between us, and why should there be - then he gave his hand to his sister and passed on to Mr Beckwith.*[3] *I looked at Louisa Walford when she came in, she had been pale before, but she grew paler then - poor girl, from my very heart I pitied her. After a long time the room was cleared of all but the bridesmaids and Mr Egremont. Mrs Egremont came in and kissed us. At length, Louisa came in, white satin covered with lace and with a long lace veil fastened with two beautiful silver filigree pins and the wreath of orange flowers and white roses. She looked very elegant. We followed her - her four sisters, the two Moorsomes, Miss Lloyd, Miss Howe, Miss Walford, Miss Thursby, Miss Beckwith and myself*

Few brides ever had a handsomer set of bridesmaids. Perhaps the three youngest Egremonts had the least pretensions. I know from several little things that I looked very well and more brilliant in complexion than usual. Louisa and her father and Captain Russell took their places and Mr Beckwith began the beautiful service.[4] *We were arranged round - Louisa was all smiles and very happy. When we rose from our knees, poor Miss Walford was in tears. I thanked God that mine will always keep. I went to insert my name with many others. I kissed Louisa and I turned to shake hands with Captain Russell. Yes, and to give him the brightest smile. His beautiful eyes were filled with tears - there was the dream now true. Then we sat down to the dejeuner returning from the church. As we went, Capsy and two other little lady's maids pinned our rosettes in the church, they were prettily made of orange flowers and satin ribbon, and those for the gentlemen had silver leaves. I was in the neighbourhood of a Mr Merest the Rector of Wem and Mr Dryden Corbett and Lily and Mr Maude was not far off. Then we drank the health of the bride and bridegroom, and Captain Russell hoped to see us all at Harnage*[5] *- promised us a hearty welcome, and hoped we should always find him and Mrs Russell agreeable. Mr Reece gave the health of the bridesmaids, thanks to them for looking so well and being so useful. Owen Rocke would not return thanks for us, Mr Maude did with the air of a man whose wits are "au courant" in such things. He concluded by hoping that this wedding would bring others, indeed he was instructed by the bridesmaids in returning thanks for the honour done them in this toast to propose another - the single married and the married happy. When the health of the bridesmaids was drank, it was rather troublesome, the work of bowing and it is a remarkable fact that Captain Russell drank it collectively except to myself. I was at some distance and Mr Merest said "Captain Russell is bowing to you." As soon as I turned, he said "Miss Darby, I have much pleasure in drinking your health." Then Sir Henry Edwards would have a bit of cake put through the bride's ring and wondered which of us he should dream of. We disrobed Louisa of her lace and satin, and I am not sure but that this was the most picturesque part of the affair. She gave us each some relic of her dress, and then we attired her for travelling. She kissed us all and we went downstairs. Mrs Egremont* *chose to take leave of them in her bedroom - because she knew they would forget her, she went out of the way on purpose, however, they did not. I was left some time after the rest and Mr Maude was of course attentive. He confessed himself proud of his nieces, which proves at least that he is discerning. They are very sweet girls, handsome and clever, and highly educated, as unlike their cousins as possible.*

I have not given my list of the bridgroom's men. Mr Reece perhaps, Dryden Corbett, Sir Henry Edwards, Mr Lloyd, Mr Kinnersley Gardner, Mr Thursby's son, Owen Rocke. Mr Howe, Mr Maude and Ted Egremont - Mr Stubbs and Mr Merest. As we were standing over the fire afterwards, Miss Moorsome and I agreed it had been a happy day. I said I was so glad to hear this wedding was a settled thing - it had been so long talked of.

Wednesday 20th January - *I wrote all of this historiette of the wedding in scraps of time. Dearest Tilly has been here ever since while Abraham went to Ebbw Vale and Quarter Day and Momus knows where. I rode out on his horse now we have a deep snow. Things fell into the even tenor of their way soon after "the 5th" and I was very soon well again. This has been a most fatal winter - J.J. Gurney by a fall from his horse which he survived only a week. The day of the funeral, poor John Reynolds died after only 24 hours illness of some terrible internal complaint which caused most awful suffering. They say it was the breaking of one of the bowels. Sir William Anson's death too we see in the paper.*

Sunday 24th January - *Fog, snow, frost - we have never seen the sun shine all this year until today.*

Saturday 20th February - *Yesterday was one of those days when there is a great deal done. It was lovely sunshine - Abraham not yet returned. Papa bien affaire, thinning Cock's wood.*[6] *It was arranged for us to go to Leighton next Monday, so Matilda with her rare good nature took me to call at Harnage.*[5] *We missed the road and had some adventure but at last we arrived and found Louisa very amiable, very elegant and supremely happy. It is a pretty place on a small scale - but more the love in a cottage style than I had imagined. The drawing room very pretty, but not, as Miss Moorsome told me "perfect". Captain Russell came in after a while. Just the same, or nearly so as he used to be, but appearing to greater advantage in his own house. He and Matilda were charmed with each other. Louisa is perfectly simple and happy. She looks young enough to be his daughter and hardly takes the lady of the house upon her as yet. He must love her. They both look extremely happy, and from the bottom of my heart I rejoiced in their happiness and thanked God for it, and not less than that I could rejoice. How much we alter in a few weeks, that is, the fresh poignancy of some feeling alters.*

Captain Russell is all that most women would require in a husband, but as only one wife can have him in Great Britain, it is a comfort that he has chosen one so fitted to make him happy, and now I am favoured to see that the world is wide, and I intend to be moderately happy in it too, if people will let me. I do not think I must marry but there are many ways of making others happy without marriage.

We went on to Shrewsbury after the call at Harnage, dined at "The Raven" in great state and dignity - did some shopping and called on Mrs DuGard, who was charmed to see us. We were at home by seven and very glad to have prospered so well in our adventure. Thank God it is done! and so well done! Miss Walford is going to leave Shropshire - Mr W. Edmonds has been calling here we found with a Sir Francis Blake out of Yorkshire, a connoisseur in books and pictures. Abraham writes from Ebbw Vale that he has met Miss Hughes who enquired after us and said she had been advising her brother to apply for the Curacy of Coalbrookdale which she had seen advertised.

Monday 22nd February - *We came to Leighton. Called on Mrs JS and took lunch with them. She is very pretty and agreeable in her own house. Mama and I left cards for Mrs SS Lloyd.*

Saturday 6th March - *In the morning I had a charming ride with Mr Lawford. Mama was not well yesterday, not quite so today - myself rather cross and sleepy and difficult to be revived even by Florence and little Paul. Dickens is very interesting in "Dombey and Son" and in places witty as ever - his cold collation of a "dead dinner laid in state" is capital, so is his "middle-aged men with grey hairs here and there among the black, as if the steps of Time had splashed it." About nine o'clock a bustle in the street as we three were sitting alone and then a bell too much of the nature of a muffin bell to have alarmed me greatly, but Mama got up, paler even than she had been, and said "the fire-bell!" We opened the door into the street and Bailey was standing by the paling. He said "Mr Claridge's ricks!" and pointed to the light shining on the curly white smoke over the Bell chimneys.*

I went with Phoebe into the close. It was a magnificent sight but very shocking yet there seemed a most special providence in the strong west wind that blew the sparks and pieces of burnt hay still red over the fields - straight in the only direction where they could do no harm. There were seven stacks of beams all on fire together, flaming and flaring like great bonfires, masses put together on purpose to burn. They were a long time forming lines of people to the water and there was no show of good feeling and willingness to work hard, especially among the men, the women worked until very late. I went again with Mrs Lawford and Fanny so near to the leeward of the fire that we felt its heat. Bushell has a little farmyard in the North End and there the fire broke out first but happily it was seen in time and was almost out when the second alarm was given. Had not this been subdued the destruction amongst those wretched thatched houses must have been very terrible. Mr Lawford's little engine from the wharf did good service. - then one came from Woburn and by 12 o'clock Mr Lawford and the Coopers stopped underneath our windows to tell us all danger was over, though some of the beams burnt until daylight.

Monday 8th March - *It is a time of disasters. This morning Mr Lawford was thrown from his horse at Stourbridge and broke or displaced a small bone at the side of the knee. He was brought home in a gig by a good farmer and has suffered great pain for some time but all are thankful it is no worse. The bit broke and fell out of the horse's mouth going at full speed over a ploughed field, and Mr Lawford threw himself off seeing a ditch where he knew the horse would leap and unseat him. Papa came at night and while he and Mr Otley were talking we were again frightened by the firebell! This time it was as far off as Mr Fountain's, near Wing - but three ricks were burnt and a hovel with a poor cow. Papa caught a terrible cold last night and has been in bed all day - Mama rather better. They have taken up some people on suspicion connected with these terrible incendiary fires.*

Thursday 11th March - *Papa and Mama could not go until this morning, both being so unwell. I went to the station with them, a bright frosty morning which would do anybody good.*

Sunday 14th March - *I have felt very much alone in the world and moreover was not at all well for two days after Mama went. Yesterday Mr Edward Lawford Jnr took me out riding as far as Newton Longville. It was a very pleasant expedition and romantic in so far as neither he nor I knew the road - but had to find it through long lanes with extensive views in the Bradwell direction. We fell in with a camp of Gypsys which my pony would on no account pass, so Mr Edward threw his bridle to the prettiest gypsy girl in the world and led my pony with a great deal of coaxing past it. Then as we were returning quietly by Stoke "Gypsey" chose to fall down on her knees and I, having no sort of notion what was going to happen, came off ignominiously over her neck. I had a dreamy notion of twisting my foot out of the stirrup and finding myself sitting in a heap in the road and considering whether I should stop there or get up which I decided for the latter. I scrambled up again very valorously, was quite astonished when Edward asked if I were hurt. "Gypsey's" knees suffered very little which was a mercy.*

Alas, Mr Edward remarked it was a mercy my habit had not hung on the pommels, and I thought so too, though I could hardly help laughing at the recollection of the uncomfortable Wroxeter story.

I have been to see Mr Edward Lawford today, "Uncle Edward," and he is truly kind, but bids me in future ride the pony with a shorter rein. I said it was very kind to say anything about the future for I did not expect he would trust me with her again - "Bless you," said he, "If you had not looked at the pony's knees nobody would ever have known - I once did some such thing, and Bailey never found 'it out because I gave him the horse as if nothing had happened."

Wednesday 16th March - *Miss Inglis called yesterday and has taken away Mama's scarf - bought it and the collar. Grandmama continues feverish about the education bill. She thinks the church is going to be made supreme and regards* *the church as something wicked, mysterious, terrible, as I regard the Jesuits, somewhat - Sunday we called to see poor Mrs Lawford, she cannot be long in this world as far as human foresight can go.*

Thursday 18th March - *Went to the Ashfields to tea - Mr Allen and by accident Mr Felix, who was very agreeable. There is something not aristocratic about Mr Allen, though he has divine blue eyes and some knowledge to use them.*

Wednesday 24th March - *Poor Mrs Lawford died this morning. She had been quite unable to swallow anything for two days, the paralytic attack having been on the throat, neither could she speak, but to the last almost she could write and was quite resigned, indeed anxious to be released. It is the Fast Day ordered by the Queen's letter as a day of repentance - the Famine in Ireland etc.*[8] *It is 15 years since the Fast Day when the Cholera was so alarming. Yesterday Mr Trower called here. That same Wednesday 24th dearest Tilly and Abraham arrived. He went on to Town and she stayed until the Saturday and then met him by the Express at Wolverton. How I did enjoy those three days.*

Monday 10th May - *Papa and Mama came to Leighton.*

Tuesday 11th May - *Papa went to London and took rooms for us at "Cox's Hotel", Jermyn St., where we came on.*

Wednesday 12th May - *Went to the Exhibition*[9] *directly where we met Abraham who stayed with us at the National Gallery while Papa went to his tailor's. The Modern pictures are very good this year, Etty's "Joan of Arc" and Standfield's "Carrara Mountains". And Landseer has a few very fine and curious pictures. There is one of Van Amburgh in which the Lions are done marvellously lifelike. At night, Papa took me to the Haymarket to see Mrs Nisbett in "The Love Chase." She is prettier than ever on her reappearance after the death of Sir William Boothby.*

Thursday 13th May - *Went to the Coliseum and to the Zoological Gardens which took up the chief of the morning, then in the evening we drove to Hyde Park which was the prettiest sight in London.*

Friday 14th May - *Had my hair cut at Clarke's and then we returned to Leighton. Called upon everybody and settle all the multifarious accounts of Irish knitting. Have £14 beside the Duchess's £6 and £2.18 for Mama, in all £22.18.0. At night we packed up.*

Saturday 15th May - *Reached home and found dearest Matilda had been very ill from what appeared like an attack of Irish fever. She and Miss Christy had been talking to an Irish woman. Miss Christy went home with Alfred, of which I am glad.*[10]

Sunday 23rd May - *In bed for the best of three days, with a stiff neck of awful severity. The weather so warm that it is very unpleasant.*

Friday 28th May - *This is comfortable new ink! - The weather is like August. I have been leaning out of the window for half an hour and watching the clouds and the moonlight through the oak branches - there is no nightingale, only a corn crake, the dismallest thing.*

My rose, my Russelliana is coming to flower - it is trained so beautifully, and every time I look at its buds the tears come into my eyes. I say to myself that I do not repine or regret nor wish one thing otherwise, but oh! I am so much older![2]

Monday 7th June - *We are established at Christie's Hotel, St James Street. I am with Abraham and Matilda. We started, upon a thought of last night at 7 o'clock this morning. There was a dreadful accident, a collision at Wolverton on Saturday evening. Seven people were killed, and waiting for the inquest. Everybody looked grave and gloomy. We passed Leighton and Mr Theobald without a word. This is a nice hotel and a very gay situation. Tuesday we went over the Exhibitions again, and I bought a shawl of Madame T. In the evening we went to hear Jenny Lind in "Roberto le Diable." "Meyerbeer's music is in parts very fine. Her voice is exquisitely clear and like a nightingale, her acting the perfection of nature and simplicity. She has a sweet smile but not exactly pretty.*

Friday 11th June - *We left town by the railway after having gone to Oslers in Oxford Street to see Ibrahim Pacha's chandelier, 18-ft high. It is one of the prettiest glass shops. We travelled with a Staffordshire Ironmaster, a Mr Williams and another man named Fryer; a third man was a great talker and a great bore, but we laughed very much more than is common in a Railway carriage. We left London at 5 by the Express and were in Leamington by 8. We met Mama and Papa very comfortably established at "the Clarendon."*

Tuesday 14th June - *Mama and Matilda and I returned the Dowager Lady Corbett's call - she came to see us on Saturday; her daughter-in-law and Miss Corbett called while we stayed. They were very agreeable and Lady Corbett must have been very handsome. Late in the evening Papa and Abraham came from London and from Frome.*

Wednesday 15th June - *Lady Corbett (The Dowager) came to spend the evening, oh, she was very amusing. Lady Moncrieffe was speaking to her of Halston and telling her that the Shropshire people did not like a Manchester cotton spinner coming among them all. "Why, perhaps not," said Lady Corbett, "but I am told he is pretty well married, this Mr Wright." "He's just married to my Grand-daughter," said the Scotch lady drily. "Then," said Lady Corbett, "he must date his pedigree from the day when he married your Ladyship's Grand-daughter."*

Thursday 16th June - *Abraham and Matilda left us, to our great sorrow and an hour or two after Mr and Mrs Hartshorne*[11] *came to spend the day. I* *should have said first, however, that Sir Andrew Corbett called, and Mama and I found him gossiping with Papa on our return. He is a fine looking man and very good-natured, but manifestly rather weak, perhaps. Mr Hartshorne came in the best possible humour, he was charming as he alone can be sometimes.*

Friday 17th June - *Mr Hartshorne took us to see Mr Russell's pictures, they left by the 3 o'clock train.*

Saturday 18th June - *We came home.*

Friday 2nd July - *I had an invitation from Mrs Egremont the day we left Leamington, and I answered it that I should not be at home in time, dated from Leamington. By some means, however, she found that I am at home and asked me again. It is to meet Mr and Mrs W Maude, and I shall go early in the week. Papa has not allowed us to be very happy since we came home, yet for me things might be much worse as I will not quarrel.*

Saturday 3rd July - *Mr and Mrs John Pritchard*[12] *called here. She is charming as ever and looks very interesting in her deep mourning for her mother. Mrs Anstice was confined the very night of the day we called, with a little girl - the first.*

Monday 5th July - *Papa took me for a few days to Wroxeter. I was a little surprised at being allowed to go but he made no objection except for a few fits of tears for I do not know about what. I found Mr and Mrs W Maude and Miss Thorsby there. Mrs Thorsby came to fetch her daughter the same evening - not a pleasant person but very handsome she has been. Mrs Egremont came into my room and consulted with me about what I have so long desired - my being baptised.*[13]

Tuesday 6th July - *After luncheon today, Mrs Egremont*[13] *ordered the church to be left open. She is very kind about a thing she so much approved. She said the church was often ordered to be opened and that Andrew Wetherby being a tax gatherer it would occasion me much annoyance if he knew what we were about to do. Mr and Mrs W Maude went with us and dear Lily. Mr W Maude was truly kind, the same ceremony had been performed for him after he was grown up at Cambridge because he could not be matriculated until after, therefore there was less remarkable in the thing for him and to Mrs Egremont. Mrs W Maude appeared much to prefer such a service to Infant baptism. I had read over the Baptismal service the night before, after Mrs Egremont left me, and I prayed fervently that I might do what would please God - yet I think I was hardly prepared for the solemnity, the awful impressiveness of the vows I took upon myself - To renounce the flesh and the Devil seemed not so hard, God helping us, but the world and its pomps and vanities seem at times so dear and bright. It is always difficult to me to know exactly what is meant by the world. God* *never meant us to live as hermits and to renounce doing good in the world - no, it must be the folly and weakness and wickedness.*

Wednesday 7th July *- Mr Scarth came to dinner - In the morning we went, Mrs Egremont, Mrs William Maude, Jane and I to call at Mrs Henry Hill's of Berrington.*[14] *The lady has just had twins and Mrs Egremont was not admitted. Both are boys and the oldest as appears at present, will be Lord Berwick. It is a brick parsonage house with a handsome portico, an avenue of woefully thick limes leads to it, and there is a fine view towards the Wrekin. Thence we went to the Scotts of Belton*[15] *out from home - a curious old low house - a glass door opening upon an open vestibule place with benches, like the entrance to an old Welsh Inn, and fine standard roses "et voila tout". From there to the Vaughans of Chilton,*[16] *Vaughan was at home - the flower garden very pretty, though the lady said she had been too busy with parsnips and cabbage to attend to the roses. She has been distressed about the scarcity though thank God it has visited Shropshire so lightly. She is not young and perhaps never handsome, but amiable very, and good I should think. Now I have time for Mr Scarth, yet not much to say of him except that he is good-looking, good-natured, and better bred than I had expected. Mr William Maude and he speak to each other as William and Jonathan, and all seemed like brothers - another surprise.*

The Russells were expected but they came not. Captain Robert Russell is still with them and a great invalid - a great nuisance, said Mrs Egremont. "Captain Russell is so good-natured," said I, "he would do anything for a suffering relation." "It is not good nature, it is Principle; when you are my age, Ada, you will read character better. William Russell would do anything, not matter how disagreeable or painful to him, if he knew it to be right."

In a walk with Janet, I asked her about Louisa's marriage. She said she was surprised, because Captain Russell was more attentive to Lily than Louisa, that he had proposed, however for Louisa, a year and a half before, but it was "put aside" then. Then it came on again, said Janet, and they were married. They seem not at all on intimate terms.

Thursday 8th July *- I came home. I do not know that I am happier for being baptised.*[13] *Since the rite is performed, I feel its insufficiency except as an act of obedience to God's will.*

Thursday 15th July *- Mama had a letter this morning from Mrs Dugard - Elizabeth is about to be married to a Mr Peters of Radnorshire, very agreeably. I am sorry for JE? and for her - no doubt it cost her a heartache. This evening Abraham came home from London where he has left his brother, gone truly to propose for Miss Christy.*[10]

Friday 16th July *- Yesterday, in the afternoon Mrs Egremont called and Mrs William Maude and Janet. They stayed 2 hours and ate strawberries and were very amiable. They called on Lily but she was out - gone to Bradley. The Russells* *were to have come but Captain Russell appeared to have thrown cold water upon the plan in various ways and finally had been unable to come or would not. This is odd - but perhaps one had better not want to know all about every odd affair, besides I am thinking of other things. Mr Hodgson has been today to see Papa. He put him to great suffering with the catheter, I believe it is called, and My Uncle Darby said it ought to have produced very little. Hodgson said he found no stone, which he wished he had.*[17] *He was very kind and quiet in manner, but said not much. He and Mr R stayed to tea - they say the same thing must be done again, but if there is no calculus, it seems useless to give suffering. We are all sick and miserable tonight thinking of such dreadful things - God grant us all patience and energy. Papa is rather comforted himself to hear there is no stone, I suppose he does not know that there may be things less curable. Alfred Darby writes that he has seen Mr Christy - was going to Woodbines and did not expect to be home for a week.*[10] *I am afraid if that poor girl marries him she marries misery and yet I so much wish him to marry somebody that I know not how to wish to hear she will not have him.*

Wednesday 21st July - *Papa is somewhat better I believe. Mr Hodgson seems to have done him good. Mrs W Edmonds gives a large Wrekin party*[18] *next Tuesday and I go with Abraham and Matilda - I hope it will be fine. There are many invitations from these parts and I hope Alfred Darby will be there - Miss Christy has it "under consideration" no doubt she will have him - he would not speak to me on Sunday. Dearest Matilda has been with me two days and very happy because of this petite affaire.*

Apropos of something or nothing about Alfred Darby I told Matilda of my solitary real predilection - she was not at all surprised - but said she and Abraham had been certain that Christy was in love with me. I do not know if I was wise to tell her just yet - it has rather opened a fast closing wound.

Tuesday 27th July - *Mrs William Edmonds Wrekin*[18] *party. I went with Matilda and Abraham. There were about five and twenty people - glorious weather and all very agreeable. They asked Mr and Mrs Henry Dickinson and Mary Darby, it was a little droll, they did not prosper very well. Miss Webb came with the Anstice's and I was surprised to find her at once so ladylike and clever. She is very lively, still handsome and far above the average of women. Miss Emery is an agreeable elderly lady who dressed very well and looks quite on the contented side of life. There was a host of rather dull clergymen, Mr Wilton of Broseley at the head, Mr and Mrs Stoneham - Ketley people at the end. Miss Pritchard came and brought a Miss Colley. The rest of the Pritchards and several other people were kept away by the Elections coming on. Abraham has been requested to stand for Wenlock but declines - he might have come in on the Forester interest - times change indeed.*

Tuesday 3rd August - *A rick of hay on fire at Strethill*[19] *and the Bailiff woefully hurt. Tilly and I walked over after tea and found the men pulling it to* *pieces and the fire engine playing upon it and a hundred people about, and Abraham telling everybody what to do and everybody doing it directly. His brother arrived very cross, very fussy and very well dressed, a most remarkable contrast. He put every soul he spoke to in a fuss and made them not know what they were doing. I was very thankful not to be Miss Christy that special moment. Poor Griffiths is better today, Wednesday, and the hay was not all burnt. They say it was quite dry but the grand manuring had made the grass so full of sugar it fermented and they did not make chimneys enough.*

Thursday 19th August - *Charles Reeve*[20] *was married to Fanny Deverell. If they are but happy I shall have a high respect for matchmaking or at least assisting. The same day Mr Bassett married Mrs Satterthwaite at Warwick. It will be no matter of surprise to me if these last (for whom the gloss of life must be so worn off and tarnished) are the happiest.*

Sunday 22nd August - *I am to pay the Dugards a visit at the end of this week. Elizabeth's marriage is to be on the 27th and I go to stay with Gertrude afterwards. We have still lovely summer weather. Tilly and I make progress with our music. We never spent a happier summer, I think. Papa gets much better and is rather amiable. I think I made no mention of my 30th birthday, but indeed it seems like attaining to middle age. Alfred Darby is really accepted I believe, - half married. It will be a really agreeable fact that people cannot say I am to marry him.*

Wednesday 29 August - *The Cattle Show. Mr Kiplin and Louisa appeared in the ploughing field, I should think as fiancees. Mary Jane was in her White Satin as a bridesmaid.*

Friday 1st October - *Called upon Mrs Bassett, Mr Hopkinson was there; we went to see his carriage and the garden after tasting the wedding cake. Madame is a very agreeable lively person, and perfectly happy in her new position.*

Sunday 3rd October - *Mr and Mrs Christy are at Dale House, therefore Matilda beat a retreat and she and Abraham came to Leighton last evening. They stay till Tuesday as Abraham goes to London tomorrow, they called at the Bassetts today.*

Wednesday 13th October - *We returned home rather before we were expected - travelled alone quite without let or hindrance. Found Papa gone into Cheshire to see some place on sale. He came back rather ill. The household upside down - the cook gone for applying a blacking brush to the underfootman's face. Myself with a horrid cold and quite hoarse.*

Tuesday 19th October - *Mama and I went to Leighton ("la petite village") to enquire about a cook. We had Wright's horses and one of them was taken ill - while we got out they changed the animals at Leighton, the one that had the fit having recovered but the man thought it best to ride home on the other. He* *put them into the carriage and changed the head harness! They took fright the moment the blinkers were off - broke the pole against the low wall and upset the carriage after knocking down George and going over him - he escaped however with one bruise. Mama and I walked about a mile when we met Mr Thursfield, who took us home in his carriage.*

Friday 5th November *- Mr John Pritchard took me out malgre the rain which was small but rather determined. We rode nearly to Bridgnorth and then turned home by Stanley - the loveliest of rides - the place might suit Abraham.*[21] *It is now let to General Davidson. Miss Tyrwitt is now engaged to a son of Sir William Joliffson, and the beautiful Miss Bridgeman is to marry Lord Albert Conyngham. We went in the evening to dine at Mr Pritchard's. They were quite alone and we had some delightful duets and singing.*

Saturday 6th November *- My last day, but Mr John Pritchard insisted as it was beautifully fine that I should ride with them to Bridgnorth and that Miss Baugh and I return with the servant which we put into execution most successfully. Dearest Matilda sent her carriage and people for me about 3 o'clock, and I spent the day with Abraham and Matilda and went home in the evening.*

Friday 19th November *- I have had a stiff neck for two days - dismal. We hear of the calamitous want of money and of failures everywhere.*

NOTES

1. Marnwood was the home of Reverend John Bartlett, incumbent of Buildwas parish church. He was married to a daughter of William Reynolds.
2. This was an emotional *cri-de-coeur*. Captain Russell, a naval captain, was introduced to Adelaide when Adelaide was invited to spend a week at Wroxeter by Mrs Egremont. At the time Mrs Egremont's intention appears to have been to make a match between Adelaide and Mr Tom Maude, Mrs Egremont's brother, but this manoeuvre misfired. Instead, Adelaide took a shine to Captain Russell, and although their encounters are well recorded in Adelaide's Journal, they do not appear to have been more than an exciting episode. Matters do not appear to have progressed to a position in which Captain Russell was considered to be a suitor. It may be that Adelaide was inhibited in this matter by the attitude of her father who considered that Adelaide's marital prospects were a matter primarily for him to consider. Whether through reticence on the part of Captain Russell or failure of Adelaide's feminine wiles to communicate her inner feelings to him, their liaison was allowed to simmer undeveloped. Clearly however, Adelaide cherished inner hopes which were dashed by the decision of Captain Russell and Louisa Egremont to marry.
3. Mr Beckwith was the parson who conducted the wedding ceremony. Mr Edward Egremont, Louisa's father, was vicar of Wroxeter, but as father of the bride, he had other duties to give his daughter away, and so it was left to Mr Beckwith to conduct the service.

4. Curiously, there is no specific mention in the Journal of the name of the church. Louisa's father, Edward Egremont was vicar of Wroxeter and the ceremony would therefore have been at the parish church, a beautiful old church, constructed predominantly from the stones of the Roman town of Uriconium from the ruins of which the village of Wroxeter had emerged.
5. Harnage is a village on the opposite side of the River Severn from Wroxeter. As the crow flies it is only just over 2 miles distant, but by road it is only accessible by crossing the river at Cressage or at Atcham, several miles in either direction.
6. Cock's wood, just north of Coalbrookdale, was originally held on lease by Abraham Darby II from the Forester family. The lease passed under Abraham II's will to his widow Abiah and then by entailed interest to Abraham III and his heirs. In this way it came into the ownership of Francis Darby. It was originally acquired and used as a railhead for the first wooden railway built in 1751-52 from Coalbrookdale works to the coalmines in Little Wenlock, and continued to be used later by the Company as a source of timber.
8. The devastating potato famine took place in Ireland in 1845.
9. The Exhibition would have been at the Royal Academy, Piccadilly. Francis Darby had for some time been making a fine collection of pictures and books for his gallery and library at The White House, Coalbrookdale. His pictures included a number of Dutch flower pieces and still life, and some good modern landscapes of the day.
10. Alfred Darby had been dancing attendance on Adelaide for many years. Adelaide had rebuffed his several proposals of marriage. This she did for the final time in October 1846. Thereafter Alfred paid increased attention to Miss Christy, of the Quaker family firm at The Woodbines, Kingston-on-Thames.
11. See note 9, p. 6.
12. Mr and Mrs Pritchard were Adelaide's friends from Broseley. See 1846 note 1, p.196
13. The Journal only refers to Mrs Egremont in connection with Adelaide's baptism. It has to be assumed however that the baptism was carried out by Mrs Egremont's husband, Rev. Edward Egremont, who was the vicar of Wroxeter.
14. Mrs Henry Hill would have been married to a member of the Hill family of Attingham Hall, Atcham (about 2 miles north west of Wroxeter) where Lord and Lady Berwick resided. Berrington is about 2 miles from Attingham Hall on the south side of the River Severn.
15. Betton, near Berrington.
16. Chilton is about a mile west of Atcham.
17. Francis Darby's health had been deteriorating during the 1840s. It is not clear what the ailment was, but the entry in Adelaide's Journal for 16th July suggests that he was having painful bladder trouble.
18. The Wrekin is a hill, 407 metres high, to the north of Coalbrookdale. It was a tradition (and still is) to walk to the top of the hill for a picnic and to enjoy the view across the North Shropshire Plain.
19. Strethill is to the west of Coalbrookdale, between the White House and the River Severn.
20. Charles Reeve of Leighton Buzzard and Fanny Deverell, sister of Carry Deverell, who married Mr Cowie and left for India.

21. Mr John Pritchard of Broseley was Adelaide's riding companion. They rode as far as Stanley just north east of Bridgnorth, the location of Stanley Hall referred to by Adelaide as "the place might suit Abraham". This was indeed in Abraham's thoughts as The Chesnuts was becoming too small for his increasing art collection. Very unfortunately, Stanley Hall was offered to Alfred Darby who jumped at the chance, thus thwarting Abraham's plans. This was to have serious consequences in two year's time.

Madeley Wood Hall, the Lloyds, near Coalport, was built by the Anstice family in the early to mid 19th century, to replace Bedlam Hall (their previous home), near the Madeley Wood furnaces.

1848

Comment

Adelaide's Journal for 1848 is dominated by an account of her travels first to the Lake District in April, with a visit to Cheltenham in May and June. This was followed by an extended tour of the continent, during July and August, with Abraham Darby IV and Matilda. Their travels through Belgium, the Rhineland and Switzerland were most diligently recorded and described by Adelaide.

The fact that they were able to undertake such journeys indicates that the family belonged to the wealthy middle classes which had become firmly established by early Victorian times. In the four years leading up to 1848 the following was the income received from the Coalbrookdale Company by Francis Darby (Adelaide's father):

	£	s	d[1]	Present day equivalent £[2]
1844	5,901	7	6	274,455
1845	7,323	15	0	323,164
1846	12,471	1	4	523,532
1847	12,668	14	3	484,424
1848	9,558	5	9	411,280
	£47,923	3	10	£2,016,855

During 1848 Francis Darby was able to acquire additional acres at Castle Green and Lodge Farm. In total his land holding amounted to 437 acres making him the second largest landowner in the parish. Abraham IV had a similar income from the company and he owned 161 acres at the neighbouring Strethill and Meadow Farms. As a family they were therefore well able to afford extensive continental holidays.

During the year Adelaide's marital prospects were never far from the surface. She received two proposals of marriage, one from Barnard Dickinson, Jnr. and the second from William Tothill. Both were first cousins and were therefore rejected on the grounds of close relationship. Adelaide herself even contemplated the possibility of marriage to Osborne Gordon. He was a native of Broseley but was making a name for himself in religious affairs at the University of Oxford. Adelaide felt that if he were made a Bishop he might be a possibility (in fact, he became vicar of Berkhamstead and never did "make Bishop".)

Towards the end of the year another ecclesiastical candidate appeared on the scene (at Mrs Egremont's, of course) in the person of Archdeacon Beresford.

Friday 28th January - *I am not yet at Leighton but hope to be soon. Abraham I am sorry to say has been ill for weeks with inflammation of the liver, at least that is the name Mr Hodgson gives to his singular malady. As he has had it before I trust it will soon be well. I met Alfred there today and had an opportunity for the first time to congratulate him. He looked quite disposed towards me.*

Friday 4th February - *We had a droll party the night before last, all Dale people. Alfred Darby had only returned from London but sent word he would come with his sister. Papa was better than sometimes. Our Romeo was dreadfully cross - to me he spoke not at all but sat with his thumb in his mouth occasionally, like Patience, numbering his injuries. I had the comfort of looking particularly well for 30 and half, but it seems very foolish of Alfred. He is in really triumphant position with respect to me if he chose to take it so. He is going to be married first and the lady receives his address with joy and gratitude. What would he have? It was the same day that he passed the Meeting. He has not yet got a house but is going to reside near London, that is a certainty - and a great blessing.*

I should have no objection to marry Osborne Gordon[3] *for anything that I have ever seen to the contrary but I know very little of him. And as a connection it is dreadful - would need a bishopric in possession to make it tolerable. He is four and thirty.*

There has been an insurrection at Palermo and the insurgents have bombarded the town. All the English were allowed time to go on board the war steamers lying off the shore, and there we are told in the Times a Mrs Bardhouse died from the effect of terror. If, as we think it should be JJ Gurney's daughter,[4] *it is most melancholy. She went to spend the winter at Naples being out of health. She had lost a baby since they went but was better herself.*

Wednesday 8th February - *I came to Leighton, Abraham bringing me. It was a most agreeable journey to me, and Grandmama is very amiable.*

Sunday 20th February - *Here 12 days. Last Wednesday Mama had redirected a packet for me saying no doubt it might be patterns. It was a Valentine quite splendid to behold, with an embossed border round a sheet of what the bonnet makers call white aerophane - a large lyre made of flowers, the strings of silver; midway down the strings floated a small cloud whereon sat a small baby holding up the torch of Hymen. It was a most elaborate Valentine and contained also a proposal of 4 pages of folio, and this from my cousin Mr Barnard Jnr!!!*[5] *I don't believe I thought enough about him to mention in my Journal that he paid a long visit at Severn House and called upon us twice.*

Appeared to expect to be asked but Papa not being well enough, there was an end of it. We thought him paying attentions to Mary Darby. Papa did say after the last call - "If Ada wishes to marry Barnard, I have nothing to say against it," but I thought it all nonsense. I do not know that any offer was ever made to me in a more graceful gentlemanly manner - in a manly style he comes to his point quite untroubled with any real love to make him awkward. I suppose from knowing rather more about him and the tree of the knowledge of good and evil than ought to be - it was that I felt nothing but positive disgust, as for proper gratitude it was out of the question, but being such a near relation, I wrote as kindly as I could understanding all as I was intended to understand it. Some way, as we have never done anything but spar and wrangle, I think he must have felt puzzled, paying compliments to my beauty and talents, how he came to stumble on just the thing I do not possess was - unlucky. Oh, those muddy eyes - well, I can't marry Osborne Gordon[3] if he asked me, but his are eyes that have a haunting power in them, though they are not beautiful eyes.

Sunday night 5th March - *This last week great things are done in France - Louis Phillippe is a fugitive in England![6] It seems the French desired some changes rather resembling our Reform Bill and a grand reform banquet was ordered. Guizot advised not to interfere but the King would not be controlled and very late he informed the Parisians that it should not be. The troops were summoned and the people revolted. They attacked the Chamber of Deputies - where the Duchess of Orleans took shelter with her sons. The Ministry resigned and Louis Phillippe abdicated in favour of a Regency with the little Count de Paris as King, but it was too late - a Republic was proclaimed with a provisional government - our old friend Lamartine for foreign affairs and Arago something else.*

The Mob attacked and sacked the Tuilleries - burnt the throne in the grand quadrangle, made bonfires of satin and velvet hangings - ladies' dresses and bonnets - smashed the mirrors - ransacked cellars. An officer of the troops of the line had his horse shot by accident - thinking it was the signal for attack he caused his men to fire. In the struggle about 500 fell, and this was the beginning of such dreadful work. The National Guard all fraternised with the people - the Municipal Guard followed - all the royal family fled of course, the King with 5 francs in his pocket so that the officers of Vincennes had to make a collection for him.

Sunday 11th March - *What a marvellous woman Grandmama is - tired often at night and with memory not quite as good as it was, but reading at 87 aloud with a voice as clear and strong as a girl's. She has a very expressive voice in speaking - with the sight of but one eye she writes oh, so neatly. She would be shocked ever to have perpetrated such a page as this. With no teeth, she speaks without lisping and eats quicker than a dragon on a march.*

Friday 17th March - *Dearest Tilly came today to my great comfort, and consolation, oh how we talked! Alfred Darby has taken a house on Clapham Common from Betts the Brandy Merchant, but a grand place, I believe too.*

Tuesday 21 March - *Abraham and Matilda took me to London for a day or two. We started in a snowstorm. Snow went off; went to Mr Bretts, beautiful things - almost fainted, but conquered. In the evening to Franconi's where we were very well amused. The horses not so good as old Ducrow's, the acting better - music better and the food far better. That reminds me that on Monday Abraham and I went to tea at Miss Ashfield's - met the 2 Andrews, Catherine and Phoebe and Howard and Mr Allen who played at chess with me. He is a good-natured, not unpolished but not very clever. Wednesday we went looking over the British Museum where I was very much pleased. The old Sculpture is so beautiful and every imaginable part of Natural History is so well arranged. In the evening to the Hay Market to see "The Wife's Secret" a clever playtime, "The Commonwealth" Mr and Mrs Charles Kean. He is a fine actor, rather too much rant, perhaps, but when we consider how little he owes to personal appearance and how annoying a certain business of voice is, one feels that his power must be great Holt was very handsome as the cavalier brother and Mrs Keeley wonderfully clever as the maid. It was very hot and we only stayed half through the after piece.*

Thursday 23rd March - *Shopping and then to the British Institution - some nice pictures - To Mr Bretts where Tilly bought a dog, dined at 4 and started back again (to Leighton where Abraham and Matilda left Adelaide).*

Sunday 2nd April - *Weather quite sultry today, a thunder storm; after it, and almost after dark I went into the Shrubbery and the most beautiful gothic windows of the church were lighted up. I stayed under the cedars listening to the last hymn and thinking how in truth or in spirit I was, or longed to be, a worshipper there. I truly believe that God's salvation is free and given to all without reference to one or another sect so that we are all of the Christian church.*[7]

Tuesday 11th April - *Last Monday Mama came here, an immense pleasure. Everybody is kind here but as I care for so very few it is rather a desert of affection. We went about quietly shopping and calling for the weeks and talking a great deal, for our world at home is full of events. Abraham and Matilda have really resigned their "birth right memberships" as they call it!*[8] *This upon the subject of tythes, I believe, and Matilda wished to go with her husband. When Mama came she told Grandmama this and of course we have had sighs and sorrows multiplied - yet not so much as might have been expected quite.*

Thursday 20th April - *Set out by myself from Leighton. Tolerably pleasant people in the train. At Birmingham made a porter take my things and find me a nice carriage and then went into the refreshment room where after a while Mr Robinson and one of his brothers appeared. Having been fed we started again. Mr Robinson had discovered a shawl of mine and requested to have a place in* *the same carriage but the porter had told him no - that a lady had taken all that carriage. He came back much amused and asked permission to have the place I had taken for him. At W?[9] met dearest Abraham and Matilda past Stafford and Lancaster and Preston to Kendal. Oh, it was a long way to Windermere, 210 miles for me, they said - safe at Low Wood and very comfortable.*

Friday 21st April - Good Friday - *We did not go to church being much limited for time. To Croft Lodge which is a very pretty place with lovely gardens and a boathouse. Splendid views all over the widest part of Windermere. Thence we went on to Keswick, dined on bread and cheese and beer at a tiny public house where the horses rested. Drove to Barrow Falls with fresh horses from Keswick. The Bowdler Stones and up the pass to Borrowdale then round the Lake on the other side and back to Keswick by the Vale of Newlands. We are a very pleasant party and it is something to find four people who all understand each other.*

Saturday 22nd April - *To Ullswater through Patterdale - lovely scenery - this quite new to me. Dined - walked. Back to Low Wood by Patterdale and had beer and water and amusement at the "highest inhabited house in England," - the hill is awfully steep coming back - quite precipitous!*

Sunday 23rd April - *Matilda and I went to church at Ambleside - After dinner and after a very charming walk which preceded it we went a drive to Rydal Water and round the other side of Windermere on the Hawkshead road and a lovely drive it was all full of gates and difficulties and then the prettiest of peeps of far off houses, beautiful with lake and mountains and sunshine. We missed the afternoon service at Mr Redmayne's pretty church so walked in the grounds of Croft Lodge and they too are charming. Mr Redmayne is very original and nice - rather poetical, but with a strong sense of the humorous, learnt perhaps from A very clever and claiming to be quite self taught yet without the vanity and display so common to self taught geniuses.*

Monday 24th April - *We drove down to Bowness, leaving Low Wood with much sorrow. Went upon the lake to Mr Curwen's Island and to a summerhouse beyond on the mainland. Wind strong coming back. Abraham wrath and rowing with might and main. Mr Redmayne the aggressor much distressed and singing as some Lancashire witch had sung "the light of other days". Tilly and I much splashed and much amused. Had lunch and were in the train in time. I was obliged to go home as it was too late.*

Tuesday 25th April - *One day at home.*

Wednesday 26th April - *Abraham took me to Birmingham. Saw Alfred for a few minutes good spirits but very fidgety - he is to be married on the 10th. Went on alone. I met with a very agreeable Mr Rose whose nephew had left only the day before for the Lakes, he has taken a pretty house, Borwick House,*

Hawkshead, Ambleside. Believe Mr Rose lives somewhere near Daventry, got in at Weedon. Found Grandmama entertaining a party of people who came to poor Mrs Poulter's funeral, hardly knew her illness was dangerous. The Norices of Berkhamstead were there - having remembered that she is Mrs JRs sister it seemed like black ingratitude not to mention that he had been with us - did so - found I had made a great, great blunder - they had heard from him the day before he had never said that he had been away from Malvern and his wife. I grew quite hot and cold but concluded not to make bad worse by telling him and Mrs Norke not to say anything about it.

Sunday 30th April - *Abraham and Matilda gone to Cheltenham where I am to follow. He has had a low fever, the Doctors say and must be cured some way.*

Thursday 4th May - *I left Grandmama for Cheltenham. With Abraham and Matilda for seven charming weeks. Too happy to keep a journal so I must write one now. I went alone Hughes meeting me at Birmingham. Found Mr and Mrs Abraham in a charming house, 8 Lansdowne Terrace. They had seen my old friends Mr William Hughes and the Brownes - the last called with a small Mr Pearce, who we did not cultivate. Then Abraham consulted Dr Hooper about himself and his malady was pronounced to be inflammation of the mucous membrane of the stomach, a very tedious complaint I fear and not much better yet. Dr Hooper a very handsome man and very agreeable - was Lady Connie's doctor. Lady Connie had the house before ourselves. The 10th came Mr Alfred's wedding, Abraham and Matilda went and very elegant her dress was. It was a vulgar affair they say. While they were away Mr and Mrs Charles Hertford called and took me out to drive. All this time I had a dreadful cold and cough, taken that one day at home going to see Chinese Goose. There was a charming riding school involving new habits and at length horses for both of us! Tilly conquered all her fears and difficulties in riding "Brunette" being a horse and Mr George Reeves, a riding master both "born on purpose for her". Very amusing those rides were! The Miss Underwoods and Miss Macgregor went out always and I gained leave to take Abraham though gentlemen are not always permitted. The Owens[10] came to Cheltenham and we were a good deal together. Hugh and Mary Owen[10] I do like very much, she has a good proportion of vanity they say but she is charming and so handsome. We dined twice in Suffolk Square, the last time to meet a large party, and then Miss Owen got up to dance, very pretty it was. I had been taking lessons from Mrs Furlong and danced tolerably with Hugh Owen and a young Mr Coghill, a Yorkshire Baronet's son.*

I rode out often with the Owens, one expedition we went to Tewkesbury. The day after the party Hugh and Mary left for Apley Castle. The Owens and Frasers and Major Burns all came to dine with us one day.

I read "Jane Eyre" and "Tancred" and "Angela" and "Lancartine's Histoire Des Girondius" a little, and Mr Reeves and I talked over the novels to a large extent now that my riding does not need such constant looking after. Finally Grandmama gave me 60 guineas to buy "Sentinel" and Abraham conducted it for me. Mr R?[11] *was to bring him in a week. He is a darling horse.*

Tuesday 20th June - *We left Cheltenham for Stoke (Bristol). Rode to Thornbury and to Blaise Castle. Dined at Mrs FT?*[12] *one day. Met the Harford's and Mr and Mrs Core-Langton, Willie and Sara Hannah went with us, to Miss Morgans and the Mamma of one, she was Viennese, and a young Mr Morgan came after tea. Miss Morgan played beautifully. Mr Morgan flirts well also and took me down to the carriage. Willie was very attentive certainly but avancons. Mrs FT?*[12] *had told us he was in love with me but we hardly believed it.*

Friday 23rd June - *Saturday and Sunday were the two longest days I ever knew. Monday came Mr GR?*[11] *and Sentinel. Tuesday I was to take a ride with him and Tilly we went up the Wrekin. Now I had been used to talk so much to Mr R*[11] *(the name is rather an ill-omened one for me) that it did not at first occur to me that when there were no other young ladies it was possible that M? might take exception and perhaps I myself be a little annoyed. So however it was and after rather amusing myself with a long chapter of poetry and nonsense in which he did not quite propose to me - have had since to sit in the dust and the ashes for the impropriety of my conduct, and to be told that the naughty child is not to go to Cheltenham and to hunt in the winter.*

Monday 3rd July - *Came a letter from Aunt Tothill announcing Willie's*[13] *very long attachment to me and about one o'clock he arrived himself - it was objected to as being a first cousin and I was obliged to see Willie all tears and misery, all devotion, and to speak comfort and rejection at the same time. He would have no dinner and fled instantly. I felt cold as stone, although I was so exceedingly sorry for him. I really could not care about him. Women are very contrary animals, we associate an idea of protection I believe with that strength of will that so often makes us miserable afterwards, and here was nothing but tears and useless regrets.*

Tuesday 4th July - *Mary and Hugh Owen*[10] *came to stay at the Chesnuts*[21] *and I went to stay with them.*

Tuesday 11th July - *We set out, Abraham and Matilda and I with one portmanteau and two large square boxes for the expedition into Belgium. Left home at 4 o'clock in the afternoon by the Express and by half past eleven we were at the "London Bridge Hotel" half dead with sleepiness. I remember Mr Robinson brought in Murray's guide and we found an "Omnibus Basket" sent by Mr Curling, and then we went to bed and slept profoundly till 9.*

Wednesday 12th July - *Went to Ackerman's for drawing materials and by a little absurdity missed seeing Mrs Alfred Darby, who called by appointment, therefore it was a sad case of delinquency. Wrote to Mama and to Willie and* *bought a shawl in Regent Street. Mr Spencer Curling, Consul to His Netherlands Majesty came to dinner and to be introduced to us. It is a comfortable hotel.*

Thursday 13th July - *11 o'clock left London by a steamer for Margate. Dearest Tilly was rather ill but we had a lovely day, so smooth that I think she ought not to have been. I enjoyed it very much. There were a great many people on board. Margate is a very ugly place, green shutters cockneyfied. We went to Deal by the South Eastern Railway, a very slow one. Mr Curling made us most comfortable at his house. There are no ladies but he and his grandson Mr Tryon have a great faculty of letting women feel at ease and at home in their house. It is full of curiosities of all lands, rather like Bingley. Some pretty little bits of carved ivory and shells and birds and Indian ferns, and a great stuffed Albatross looking really like the ghost of a bird to frighten Ancient Mariners.*

Friday 14th July - *We spent the morning writing to Mama and Mary Owen and sitting upon the Bastion looking at the boats and ships with a telescope. Mr Curling's house is close to the sea, beautiful open sea and a fine day making everybody feel lazy and happy, the dog included. We had an early dinner and left for Dover at 5 in a pretty little open carriage. The road was very familiar to me, I wondered what had become of Packham and the pretty black horse I used to ride with him. We expected to have been established at the "Dover Castle", "Mrs Diver's," and went for some shopping accordingly, and walked on the Esplanade sending Mr Curling and the carriage on to make arrangements, and "en passant met" Mr Henry Christy, very civil, very cockneyfied, and signifying very great surprise to see us. Mr Curling came out of the Inn to tell us how he had engaged very nice rooms when he found that our steam boat for Ostend, "The Garland", was to leave the docks at 12 at night instead of by 6 in the morning as we had expected. Tea and supper together, toilets made, and we went on board and took our berths. It was fortunate we did for the place was soon full of ladies, babies and hommes. I slept with a consciousness of who came in and out until 2 o'clock, when the place became so hot that I followed Miss Thesiger's example (she was in the next place to me on the sofa) and went on deck. It was cloudy and mild, a nice breeze in our faces, but the ship going very smoothly. She was a fine boat with two large chimneys. Dearest Tilly came on deck about an hour after when everybody became ill in the 'cabin, and she also, I am sorry to think. It was more blowing as the day dawned, before we had a great deal of lightning. We were obliged to land in the boats at Ostend. I was not ill at all, Miss Thesiger and I the only two, I think, who quite escaped, for the sea is very rolling in the Channel.*

Saturday 15th July - *I never shall forget the delight of the charming coffee and eggs at Ostend at our breakfast about 6 o'clock. "Hotel Allemagne". The Customs House people only just opened our boxes without annoying us in any way. Ostend has nothing interesting about it. We left for Bruges in a very comfortable fly, very large and cosy, the harness partly of ropes, but the horses magnificently strong and sleek clean. Dressed and dined at the Table d'hote at "Hotel* *de Flamande," we were quite ready for dinner at that hour considering the time of breakfast. How the Dutch do eat! They would make about 10 courses of the things at an English dinner and expect you to eat each thing. The cooking is rather greasy and oily but I do not dislike it. I forgot the country between Ostend and Bruges but there is little to see or describe except from it's total novelty to ourselves. It is flatter than anything I ever saw with wide dykes and fine crops of corn and beans and flax. A paved road very noisy and for the most part trees along the sides. It is very wide and sandy at the sides when to the great comfort of passengers the vehicle has to turn off the stones to pass a load of hay in a wagon that looks just out of an old dutch picture and horses also. The women dressed in bedgowns and wooded shoes and most primitive caps and now and then a bonnet. I was struck very much with the good care they seem to take of horses and donkeys, the last are really fine animals. Bruges is a most curious old place, very Moorish in many of the buildings. We went to the Palais de Justice where we saw the famous and magnificent "chimney piece" carved in oak dated 1329. In the middle is a statue of Charles V, Maximilian and Charles le Nardi with their wives on each side. The chimney piece itself is black marble with white marble bas reliefs, the carving is above and reaches to the beams upon which the carving is a little way continued. We saw the antique council chamber of the Magistrates and then went to see the Public Library at the Hotel de Ville. This was built 1377, a very elegant building. We saw the room of torture in the days of the Inquisition, it is now part of the library. There are some fine pictures, 2 portraits of Marie Terese, 1 of Van Dyke's Charles II and many more. It is impossible to understand the people here who mix French and Flemish in the oddest manner. At the Hotel most of the waiters speak English and all French. Now and then a femme de chambre can speak neither.*

Sunday 16th July - *We went to High Mass at St Sauveux's the Cathedral. One's sensations are exceedingly strange in a Catholic Church for the first time during mass. The music is very fine. The church altogether exceedingly magnificent in shrines and pictures and chapels with candles burning but the profusion of angels and golden crosses and little pictures and ivory virgins seems almost like a curiosity shop. The large pictures are fine, Van Cost is a favourite artist. I was more pleased with Notre Dame (Onser Vrouw). The tombes of Charles the Bold and his daughter Mary the wife of Maximilian are magnificent, the effigies of copper gilt and reposing on black marble slabs. At the sides are golden geological trees designed with great taste and supporting the richly enamelled coats of arms which record the long list of duchies which the young heiress brought to the house of Austria and bestowed upon her grandson Charles V. Also there is a Virgin and Child sculptured in white marble by Michael Angelo, very beautiful. Some beautiful pictures, an adoration of the Wise Men by Teghers. Dined at the "table d'hote." Sunday no fish and an influx of bourgoisie, they behaved very well, really elegantly. After dinner and a siesta and journal proceeded, then we walked up to Notre Dame again and saw a very interesting spectacle - the service for a catholic funeral. The singing was very exquisite and* *the whole extremely striking. The coffin is brought in covered with black cloth, and being a higher class funeral, two wide strips of white silk were placed over it in the form of a cross. Stands of large candles, 12 in each were placed on each side,a large silver and gold cross elevated at the feet. Then the magnificent service proceeded with the flinging of incense and sprinkling of holy water. The coffin is then carried out of the choir into the body of the church and another part of the service I suppose goes on - the cross is laid upon it and the holy water sprinkled over it and over the people. It is then carried to the hearse. Afterwards Abraham and Matilda and I walked a long way and came to a beautiful avenue a little way from Bruges and we turned into a lovely garden belonging to the Societe Philharmonique. We found a very good military band playing there and all the fashion of Bruges assembled, I should think a hundred people sitting in parties round small tables talking quietly and with great propriety, enjoying the fine evening and the music. They began with sacred music and then went on to Polkas and Waltzes and long pieces from operas, as if it was not Sunday. The people of Bruges appear extremely well off and there is nothing that seems vulgar to a foreigner. Wrote to Mama to go tomorrow.*

Monday 17th July - *Went again to Notre Dame for the Morning Mass, and then to the Hospital where there are some famous pictures by Hans Memling - he was several years in the hospital and cured there of wounds received in battle, and he painted these pictures for the gallery at the Hospital out of gratitude (1479). We went to a pretty little chapel by the Hotel de Ville, called La Chapel du Sang de Dieu. Returned for the "table d'hote" still at 1, and at 4 left Bruges by the Railway for Ghent. "Hotel de la Poste" - not so clean as the "Flamande" at Bruges but very agreeable situation and pretty rooms. Ghent is a fine place, large and very modern compared to Bruges. We are in a large square - the "Place d'Armes", with beautiful lime trees. Went with a Commissionaire to the Convent of Beguin Nuns, the order of St Elizabeth. The Mass was beautiful in chapel and afterwards one of the Sisters took us through the kitchens and private apartments, she spoke very good French and said they were extremely happy. There are 600 Sisters and they have one young English girl, a daughter of Protestant parents. The garden was pretty. Every Nun provides for herself, they go into the town when they like and see their friends. They have their own fortunes and the rich ones pass their time working for the poor. The Nuns without fortunes work for themselves.*

Tuesday 18th July - *Three Churches with our bon Commissionaire.*

Wednesday 19th July - *Concert Rooms and Theatre of Ghent - all under one roof, splendid decor with gold and white and fresco painting. By railway to Antwerp, awfully hot and dusty. Crossing the Scheldt delightful, it is a fine river, so wide that we crossed in a large steamer. Walked about the place after the dinner or rather tea.*

Thursday 20th July - *The Cathedral and Ruben's Descent from the Cross - there is also an altar piece by Rubens. The Cathedral has been much spoiled by the ravages of the French mob in Robespierre's days. It is now in process of being restored very beautifully. Afterwards we went to the "Musee" and were indeed delighted. We came back to a solitary "table d'hote" at 5. Afterwards Abraham and Matilda and I walked on the fortifications, it was quite late as we came back through a noisy suburb of the town but everybody seemed orderly and well-behaved.*

Friday 21st July - *Our sightseeing began with the Church of St Jacques, the only church which quite escaped the ravages of the French. Rubens is buried there with all his family.*

Then we drove to the Cathedral again where a military mass was being celebrated with splendid music and voices, it was the Anniversary of King Leopold's I accession and the church was filled with soldiers and the town authorities and spectators. A review was to take place in the Grand Platz opposite to our hotel and for which we hurried back, our rooms all looking to the front. It was a fine sight, like a picture by an old master as to colour, but I do not think the discipline was good - the horses were not fine, the men undersized and the uniforms excessively ugly, which one regrets to think that the hat has been transplanted to England.

In the evening we went to the gardens which were full of gay company and the band of the Rifles was playing charmingly. At the "table d'hote" was an English party, a Mrs Williams with a son and daughter, we found that they came from Shrewsbury, and Mrs Dugard. It was droll to meet in Antwerp.

Saturday 22nd July - *We have been shopping a little and now are about to depart for Bruxelles. Hot journey and a horrid shaking carriage. Dearest Matilda was quite knocked up and made ill. We are at the "Hotel de Flandre" too and do not like it, we think we ought to be at the "Belle Vue."*

Sunday 23rd July - *The Cathedral here has not very much in it except some wonderful old tapestry which is only hung on state occasions. We went over the magnificent Palace of the Duc d'Aremberg, the richest subject in Belgium. Dined at half past 4 at the "table d'hote" rather on a grand scale. Afterwards we drove to the Jardin Botanique which contains the most splendid collection of tropical pines and palm trees, really trees. The house where they grow is about 4 times the length of that at Woburn and the trees twice the size. Fan Palms and Bread fruit and the tree from which is obtained the palm wine. A large Macaw, 50 years old. We went to see Mr Green's balloon ascend and were so fortunate as to be near it, enough to read his name upon it. The little parachute descended very nicely. Then we drove in the Place Verte, the Hyde Park of Brussels, a very pretty sight it was. Many pretty faces and dresses rather elegant, the carriages were fine also, but with rather too much silver ornamentation for London taste*

- the horses are heavy and clumsy. At night there was a very grand thunder storm, one flash of lightning I really thought the most vivid I had ever seen.

Monday 24th July - *Left Brussels at 10 and found the air so cooled by the thunderstorm that Matilda preferred coming on to Cologne rather than stopping at Liege or Aix, about 160 English miles took us from 11 o'clock to half past 8. At Verriers we dined very comfortably, expecting to be searched, but some way or other our baggage escaped altogether even at Cologne. Between Liege and Aix the country becomes very pretty, not unlike Wales, but with a Castle now and then, and there are wild forest tracts, that look as if banditti might still exist. Cologne is very old and very dirty and the grave and untidy germans do not appear to advantage in comparison with the lively Belgians. Part of the way we travelled in a 2nd class carriage to escape a terrible family of French with 2 children - no, they were Germans escaping from Paris and dirty in the extreme. The 2nd class was cooler and pleasanter in every way and we met with an interesting Irish man. It rained in torrents at the end of our journey. "Hotel de Cologne" not very good.*

Tuesday 25th July - *The Cathedral of Cologne is celebrated for the tomb of three Kings, the Magi who carried the gifts to the Infant Saviour. The shrines are most valuable, that of St Englebert who built the Cathedral is shown first and is of pure silver and gold, also a sword and a dagger and some church ornaments covered with precious stones. The shrine of the three Kings is seen by candle light and the jewels and the antique cameos and intaglios are beautiful. There is an Oriental Topaz which is as large as an egg and garnets of wonderful size and every conceivable precious stone of large or smaller size. The tomb of Marie de Medicis had been deprived of it's brass entablature by the French. The outside of the Cathedral is in process of renovation and already it is very splendid. The inside is rather spoiled by quantities of modern stained glass and gilding and colours upon the carved stone columns. In the church of St Peter is another fine altar piece by Rubens - The Crucifixion of St Peter, the head is downwards and the effect of the whole wonderful and terrible. Mr JP Weger's house and collection of pictures is allowed to be seen. It reminded me of Mr Beckford's. There is a Cuyf with a Red Cow, magnificent. It is a beautiful gallery in the Moorish taste. He draws beautifully himself. Curiosity shops and Eau de Cologne included, we have had a good day's work. Tomorrow we leave for the Rhine which from here disappoints us rather, but everything seems dirty in this curious old town after Belgium, the people stupid and the cooking greasy.*

Wednesday 26th July - *We travelled by the steamer to Coblentz and took up our quarters on the Ehrenbriestein side at the "Hotel der Weise Rosse," very nice and clean and good. The Rhine is magnificent, it is a succession of most interesting old castle ruins with a tradition to each and fine rocks of volcanic origin but not so high as expected until we came to Ehrenbriestein.*

Thursday 27th July - *Visited the fortress, it is very strong and would resist a long long siege. After we found a man who could speak French we got on very well but the want of German is great here. He showed us the weak side of the garrison which seemed quite impregnable and the canons taken from the French, also the place where Frederick the Great had a seat made that he might survey the magnificent panorama afforded at the top. It is tremendously steep and precipitous naturally and fortified all the way. The garrison seemed full of troops wearing the handsome Prussian uniforms, they are smaller than the English but far handsomer than the Belgians, grave but very good tempered and polite and quick in understanding foreigners. I am glad that we are generally in alliance with Prussia for I have seen no soldiers before so able to contend with English ones, indeed they are very superior in manners and education to privates in our own country. "Table d'hote" at 1. They gave us Sanlier, I can eat it. Nice Swiss gentlemen at the dinner, they could speak French and a little English and we got on very well, they liked to talk to the foreigners. They have a grave quiet look and quiet eyes. I am surprised to see how brilliant English eyes are in comparison. After dinner we went to the Castle of Stotzenfels - the same of which we saw the Diorama at Cologne. It was offered for sale some years ago for £80 of English money, the Corporation of Coblentz bought it and gave it to the present King then Crown Prince of Prussia and he has modernised it and made it habitable although not perhaps more in character with the scenery than before it's restoration. Queen Victoria paid a visit there when some rooms were fitted up for her very beautifully and Jenny Lind gave a concert. There is a great deal of curious armour, Napoleon's sword and Murrat's Sobigakis, a lovely little garden with a fountain. The views are lovely up and down the Rhine. We rode up on donkeys. A young American girl and her brother went over with us. We had travelled with them by railway from Cologne to Aix. They have been over England and Scotland, in Paris through the last troubles and were going on through Switzerland to Italy and Syria. There is not much to see at Coblentz, we leave tomorrow by the steamer at 8 o'clock.*

Friday 28th July - *Went to Biberich by the steam packet, the scenery is indeed fine. We had breakfast on board the boat and afterwards a "table d'hote" on the deck. The day was as fine as possible, the same Americans were with us and really found them agreeable, the journey by Railway to Frankfurt very tedious, 25 English miles in two hours. We are very comfortable at the "Hotel de Russie" and very glad to have escaped the "Hotel d'Angleterre" where Mr "Knickerbocker" wanted to take us.*

Saturday 29th July - *We drove out for some shopping in this very nice town. There is not a great deal to see here. The "Hotel de Ville" with portraits on the wall. Dannecker's beautiful statue of Ariadne, the museum containing it is in a most untidy garden and the statue is in a small room into which glow lights from rose coloured and amber glass. A very charming "table d'hote". 'A very agreeable Spaniard who we had met in the museum was also at the dinner, also* *an English party who had been travelling for three years, still very English. We went in the evening to an out-of-door concert at some gardens here. The band was beautiful, it was the band of an opera house or theatre, almost all violins, numbers of people were sitting out.*

Sunday 30th July - *We went this morning to an English church. It was very pleasant to be again at one. Only back in time for the very early "table d'hote". Met the same English party.*

Monday 31st July - *We travelled through a lovely country bordering I believe upon the Black Forest to Heidelberg. I cannot describe the magnificence of the ruined castle. It was four times bombarded and sacked in the 17th century and is now of course dilapidated, not so much from time as the mischances of war. I see that I wrote of Frankfurt before the day there was finished. Sunday evening we went to the opera. The performers are not I suppose much known to fame but yet the acting and the music were both delightful. The band and the beauty of the choruses were perhaps better than often in London, the opera was Norma. This morning we went to the Chamber of Deputies, met Miss Porter again, and saw the pretty Jewesses who throng to the Assembly, it is a very handsome room. We went afterwards to choose some of the pretty cameos made of stagshorn. The English people are a Mr and Mrs Isham and a Mrs and Miss Wood, they know the Owens[10] very well and were at Rome in the winter they spent there.*

Tuesday 1st August - *We have been all day sketching about the Castle, 3 times we have been up to it on donkey, in carriages or our own feet.*

Wednesday 2nd August - *This morning we got up very early, before 6, and we took a carriage and prepared to ascend to the Konigsthule, the mountain behind the Castle whereon there is a tower from whence we have splendid views. We had a pair of nice strong grey horses and the most good tempered driver who made us understand his german and himself our english. Some hundred yards up the hill we had a pair of brown ponies added to the others. The views were 'lovely and clear fresh morning with the bluest sky and the brightest greens. We were again at the inn by 10 and took luncheon and packed and rested ourselves and then left by the RR for Strasbourg. We find the 2nd class carriages much cooler being often lined with horsehair and therefore we go in them and Mr Curling in the 1st class therefore we had time this day to study Murray and Matilda said that we should be annoyed at the Douane at Strasbourg and that it was better to leave our boxes at Offenburg. Mr Curling chose to go on and was cross so at Oppenheim we parted, he going on to Kehl, the nearest station to Strasbourg and we to Offenburg and few miles further on the road to Basle. When there the people could not speak anything but German so in our trouble and with their good nature they sent for the Landlord of the Inn who explained all in two minutes. All was left at the station except a bag and a basket containing night caps etc, and we went back to Kehl incumbered with Mr Curling's luggage which was left at the Douane and which he chose to go to fetch although* *as arranged it might have remained as "baggage non declare" and for a fee (which Abraham paid) have been permitted to stay at the Douane until our return next day.*

It was a melancholy change into the French territory - Tricolour flags and "Liberté egalité fraternité" are not pleasant sights to English eyes. There is something about the people too, far more inflammable. The town was full of French soldiers and very strongly fortified. Handsome rooms at the "Ville de Paris" where Mr Curling was waiting for us.

Thursday 3rd August - *We were again rather early, it is much better in these warm countries. Went out with a commissioner to see Strasbourg. We saw first the Protestant Church where there is a splendid monument to Marechale Saxe Maurice of Saxony. The figure of the Marechale in the centre and a female figure representing France kneeling and with one hand putting back that of Death, a very finely imagined figure opening a tomb beneath, on the other side is a figure of Hercules in sorrow and a little angel in tears. The banners of France stand on one side and those of Austria, England and Bohemia are broken on the other, also their cognissanses the Eagle, the Lion and the Panther are prostrate. It is of Carrara marble. The coffin of Verd antique and beneath there are beautiful wreaths of cypress in bronze, I believe the artist is French and named Pigale. The Cathedral is the highest and most light in tracery of its tower perhaps of any that we see. In this dry climate the red sandstone of which it is built appears durable, and its colour has a beautiful effect. We went into the crypt, 1000 years old and looking quite fresh. There is here a wonderful clock doing more than ever any other clock did - to show the age of the moon and the days of the month seems a small thing for every quarter of an hour a different old man walks out and strikes a bell, at 12 o'clock two little angels add to the rest, one striking a bell for the last quarter, I think, and the other turning an hourglass, a figure of Time strikes 12, then the 12 Apostles walk out and when St Peter appears the cock at the top flaps his wings and crows three times.*

Strasbourg is a nice place and full of its peculiar fine wire ornaments yet we felt very glad to be again among the Duke of Baden's amiable people. We went after the "table d'hote" to Offenberg where we are very comfortable, a little country place where Mr Phachier acts as landlord and wine merchant and general benefactor. Beautiful partridges for supper, a charming walk and iced champagne.

Friday 4th August - *The neighbourhood of Offenburg is lovely, we had a charming walk and magnificent breakfast. When we were going away Mr Phachier gave a beautiful bouquet to each of us, he is the kindest man and the most gentlemanly ever met with in his station. Went on as far as we could by rail road and then I think 9 miles by Diligence - this took about 3 hours, the hills very steep, the road through the black forest part of the way and then the beautiful views of the Rhine and Basle in the distance. We were taken for the* *party of Mdme La Comtessa de Sidone and have charming rooms in consequence at Les Trois Rois.*

Saturday 5th August - *We remained all day at Basle hoping to meet with Mr Pritchard's guide, at length we arranged to go during the night to Berne by the Diligence. Mr Curling terrified at the idea of such energy and has arranged to go to Lucerne and quietly wait for us and I believe after all we shall not go there as we have more to see than can be done in the time.*

Sunday 6th August - *The Diligence journey was an awful fatigue but better in the night than in the day. The coach was quite full, a young German student changed places with Abraham and went into the coupee which Abraham pronounced very cold. The supper at the little Inn about 11 o'clock was most amusing. The distance was 61 miles and it was 7 o'clock next morning before we reached Berne. I never shall forget the first sight of the Alps, tired as we were and with our eyes full of sand the sight was perfectly inspiring and wonderful. The peaks of eternal snow are beautiful and sublime beyond description. Abraham and Matilda went to church to hear Mr Timperley but I fell asleep in the process of dressing and was left to rest in peace. We dined at the "table d'hote" and Matilda and I then walked out and met with a guide who indeed proved very good and honest so far. He was well recommended from the "Faucon" and has a book full of testimonials. He went with us to Thun in the evening, we had an open carriage and find it delightful. Thun is the most picturesque town imaginable - the beautiful Lake and view of the Bernese Alps.*

Monday 7th August - *At half past 8 we were in the "Bateau à Vapeur" to go down the Lake, most smooth and blue and lovely and before us the Shreckhom and the Jungfrau covered with snow and round the end of the Lake rocks and pines and the most picturesque wooden houses. Open carriage to Interlaken where a second breakfast and deposit our baggage, and proceed in the carriage. Interlaken is a real paradise among the mountains. We have again met our very agreeable german who helped me to buy apricots and then told us this best route when we travelled together in the Diligence to Basle. He travels chiefly on foot. From Interlaken to Lauterbrunnen the most wild and beautiful valley among steep rocks covered with firs and the river rushing over stones and pieces of rock, the road winding between. The valleys widen continually with slopes covered with green turf so soft and thick as a park. The children bring fruit and flowers and it seems very nice and pretty until the begging grows tiresome. Still the Jungfrau with her beautiful peaks of most unsullied snow. We walked from Lauterbrunnen to the fall of the Stanbach. The rocks here 9,000 feet high and the torrent falls over where they are not perpendicular but overhanging from the top, much of the water loses itself in mist before reaching the bottom, you see the wind blow it about and feel it fall in rain, the rest runs into the river we had followed up the valley - Byron in the Journal compared the fall to the tail of a white horse and it is not a bad comparison. The Stanbach translated means the*

Dusk fall, it is most beautiful. From Interlaken to Grundelwald we proceeded in the carriage, across the Wengern Alps is grand but very fatiguing, 14 hours on mules. This was almost enough for the faculties the first time here. The river through the valley is singularly black and dirty, its source is the great glacier of the Grundelwald opposite to which is our Inn, "der Adler." The heat in these valleys (though we are 4,000 feet above the sea) is intense. The neatness of the little Swiss farms is beautiful very, every inch of land is cultivated and the grass and potatoes and hemp and corn most flourishing, they were carrying a second crop of hay in nets and depositing it in barns. The cows live higher up the mountains in houses just like those for human beings. We had tea and honey and mutton chops and Fricandeau de Gveau and then walked with our guide to the great glacier at the foot of "le grand Eiger". We scrambled along many miles I suppose without the least fatigue and tasted a piece of beautiful clear ice. Saw and heard 2 avalanches which we thought very fortunate, they were about 7 miles off, I should have guessed 2 - one loses all sense of distance very strangely here. The Alpine flowers are beautiful. We got up early to avoid the heat so I am going to bed after watching the moon set behind the grand Eiger.

Tuesday 8th August - *We got up at half past 4 and found 3 nice horses on which we set out to visit the glacier of Grundelwald. The road was indescribably difficult - precipitous and stony. We had to walk several times and at length came to a stable where the horses were left and we proceeded on foot. The glacier very rugged and covered occasionally with debris of sand etc that made it look dirty, was beneath us, and our path was so narrow in the rocks above that at a distance as we saw afterwards, it was hardly visible. At length we came to the ice itself. The guides cut steps for us with their axes and laid down 2 planks across ice chasms otherwise impassable. In places we were carried, Matilda and I; but I found on returning that it becomes possible to walk upon the ice with only a little help. We ascended far enough to see the beginning of the river, the black water rushing along at a great depth among the rocks in a channel it has worn in this never melting ice. It was all very very grand and magnificent and our heads stood it pretty well. I have rather an advantage in being always able to enjoy precipices. We were back by half past 12 having started at 6. Had some dinner then a little rest, and started at 4 for the ascent of the Faulhorn, certainly the most magnificent in views imaginable. The panorama of mountains was indeed grand and we visited some mountain chalets where the peasants live with their cows and goats. It was getting dark and cold and cloudy as we got to Scheidegg where we were to sleep after a day of great exertion certainly but the loveliest weather. Nice people at this elevated Inn and everything nice except the beds, it was quite a chalet. While we were having tea the wind rose and burst open the windows and blew out the candles. In the night the tempest became awful with thunder and lightning and torrents of rain which came into the rooms at all points. Of course some of our things were the worse, yet on the whole we agreed that the worst part was to be kept awake when we were so tired.*

Wednesday 9th August - *We left Scheidegg and made a most beautiful tour through the Valley of Rosenlani etc by the fall of Reichen back to Meringnen. Rather a less propitious day, at the end we were in Scotch mist. Stopped to look at a vertical saw worked by a water wheel, nice old man who showed us his chalet and gave us black cherries. Dined at the Inn near Rosenlani, we ascended to the glacier of Rosenlani, the loveliest thing ever seen, its ice caverns are of a soft bright blue and the pure white is also exquisite. I believe the river is the Reichenbrach which takes its rise from this glacier, fine St Bernard dogs at the Inn at Rosenlani.*

Thursday 10th August - *From Meringnen to Grimsell on horseback, started at 5. The waterfalls magnificent beyond anything imaginable. The falls of the Aar came soon after our halt at Guttanen. We are here for the night at a height of 7,000 feet or more above the level of the sea. The "table d'hote" the best filled we had seen. There were a great many Americans and very agreeable men they were.*

Friday 11th August - *Started about 7 from Grimsell, even when the fog of last night had cleared and we could see the fine lake it was still dreadfully cold, like November. The little Hotel was very comfortable, the beds nice and warm, the landlady the prettiest woman I have seen in Switzerland, we met the same party at breakfast at half past 6 as at supper the evening before. Our course was now a very wild and desert one. We passed by the Lac du Mort where was the great battle between the French and the Austrians in 1799. Then over the Gallenstock mountain previous to which we stopped at a little inn to feed the horses and sketched the Glacier du Rhone which stretches down the side of the mountain. Then over the wild Furchalf and wide wastes of snow where we walked and slid. The road was not so much among precipices but it was very bad, among large stones and pieces of rock where the poor horses tumble about woefully after we had left them being soon tired of riding. The flowers were beautiful. Very hungry by the time we got to the "Hospital" famous for trout and cheese and wine (view d'Asse). We went on as far as Wasen to save an hour tomorrow. The road over the St Gothard and the Pont de Diable too fine to describe now I am so sleepy. Stopped at a little chalet on the Gallenstock which supplied bread and cheese and wine not over good, and there we met three very agreeable Englishmen and a German, young and very handsome and dressed in a style so picturesque that he looked quite ready for the stage. They seemed almost bewildered to find themselves in such a place, there was one long table, a bench and stool, we could see the light through walls and roof, Urick called it the "Hotel d'Angleterre."*

Saturday 12th August - *We have had a long fatiguing day and lovely ride, 36 miles. The poor little mountain horses though very strong were almost knocked up although we walked a great deal of the distance but we could find so little for them to eat. We left Wasen early right glad to get away it was so dirty and proceeded here by the Sustine mountain, a most magnificent pass with much more* *accessible roads than many. We stopped at a clean little inn where there was not much to eat and unhappily nothing but a little hay for the horses. Urick made a beautiful omelette for us and gave us cheese toasted with honey, he is invaluable. The road was made I believe by Napoleon when La Vallaise was added to France, in places it has fallen into ruins and is only practicable as a bridle road. The valley of the Sustine pass rises on both sides of the mountain most lovely, finer than the vale of Hasli where Meyringen is situated.*

Sunday 13th August - *Left Meyringen and had a charming drive to the beautiful Lake of Briens where we took a boat and rowed to the fall of the Giesbach, a most lovely cascade or rather succession of falls of the clearest water, like crystal. We disembarked and climbed up the very steep ascent more than half way to the beginning of the fall, in one part the rock overhangs so much that we are able to go behind the fall and see it foaming down with great noise, lower there is a pretty little bridge on which we stood, and I think it looks lovelier here than anywhere. There is a nice Inn where we had fruit and cake and wine then we again descended for the Bateau à Vapeur which conveyed us delightfully along the beautiful Lake of Briens to within a short distance of Interlaken. Dined at the 'Table d'hote' at 4 and went to the English church. Interlaken is a lovely place and the moon tonight is magnificent.*

Monday 14th August - *Left Interlaken at 6, at Tratigen we dined, at Kandersteg we mounted on horse back (I had a mule for the first time and vicious thing it was, but very sagacious and safe among difficulties). Beautiful views of the Stockhorn and the Blumeus Alps but these were left behind. Then we began to ascend the Gemmi, this takes about 6 hours. it is very fine and romantic at the beginning among firs and beautiful Alpine scenery. Then it becomes wild and barren in the extreme. At the top we had some rain. There is a wild desolate lake almost at the summit. We had to dismount in descending the mountain becomes so very steep. It is a long and most precipitous winding descent. We had set out rather later than Urick intended and in consequence we were in the dark nearly. Tremendous rain came on and we and the guides and the horses took safe shelter in an overhanging cleft of rock. The lightning was brilliant and after the rain had passed, the moonlight on the high rocks above us was lovely, though we did not see it rise before we were safely at Losche. "The Bins de Loches" are famous and dirty, 20 or 30 people all in one great bath where they stay from one hour to eight, the water is a warm spring and not disagreeable.*

Tuesday 15th August - *All night it rained and a beautiful morning was the result. We went on mules as far as the beginning of the Simplon Road. Thence in voitures and a Char Bernoise, dined at Lion and are to sleep at Martigny, a close marshy place with a very unhealthy reputation where they have shut up the windows of our rooms because of the gnats or mosquitoes. We had opened them again when Urick came to shut them because of the "petites mouches". The scenery is lovely in the direction of the Tete Noir and also towards Lion.*

The large green frogs we have seen for the first time and also immense moths like hummingbirds.

Wednesday 16th August - *We left Martigny on mules and the magnificent scenery of the Tete Noir did not disappoint me. It is not quite as wild as the Gemmi but extremely beautiful and grand. We met with some disasters, a thunderstorm which nearly frightened the mules out of their propriety and wetted us thoroughly. We had the mules; one, however, put into a char-a-banc, in which we came to Chamoni, a long narrow valley skirting the tremendous chain of Mont Blanc.*

Thursday 17th August - *We are all writing in the Salle where there is a good fire, for it is very cold. The weather continues very bad. We have seen the summit of Mont Blanc but once. Germans, French, Swiss, and some, I am sorry to say, indifferent specimens of English who sat close around the fire, keeping everybody else cold, were confined to the house nearly all day, towards evening we went out, Matilda and I as far as the Casade de Pelerins - very wet, very dirty, very rainy, under the guidance of a little girl of Savoy, also very dirty, very troublesome and very extortionate. Our money was almost all Prussian and we were very thankful to meet Abraham and Urick on our return or we should have been obliged to take the little imp back to Chamoni. Wrote to Gertrude and Miss Owen,*[10] *the evening finished still raining. Urick says that it is necessary to feel the weather very cold in these regions before it becomes fine and that it is not yet "assez froid."*

Friday 18th August - *This morning got up at 6, on Mont Blanc not one cloud! It is a most glorious mountain, grander than anything that I have ever seen. We breakfasted and set out on fine large mules to the Moatanvert. It is a very precipitous ascent and rather difficult for the poor mules. The views glorious all the way through a wild rocky pine forest with the snows of Mont Blanc on the right and to the left the valley of Chamoni and the Brevent and Flegere mountains on the opposite side. Higher up the Glacier du Bois Tres Sale. here is the source of the little river Arveron which falls into the Arne, the larger stream running through the valley of Chamoni and rising I believe in the Col de Balme. At 'the Pavilion,' a dirty looking inn, we left the horses and proceeded to the Mer de Glace - it is an immense tract of rocky ice, whiter than the lower part, the 'Glacier du Bois.' We had not time to cross it which is indeed a fatiguing affair. The mountains here are much more broken than in the Oberland, they are sharp and pointed and inaccessible in the extreme. The Aiguille Vert is 13,000 feet above the sea. as we descended the day remained clear and beautiful. We met almost all our acquaintances of the Hotel who would hardly believe that we had accomplished so much by 10 o'clock. The extreme point of Mont Blanc with the Dome du Conte and the Grands Mulets remained perfectly clear and white against the deep blue sky. We had a "dejeuner a la fourchette" and proceeded in a char-a-banc as far as Bruneille on our way to Geneva. The road is very* *hilly and beautiful. I think the height of Mont Blanc is more impressive the greater the distance. The rivers become very pretty being larger than those about the Rhine and twisting about trees most gracefully. At Brunneville and before we perceived the people in a good deal of excitement, the National Garde had been enrolled and the poor men about to be sent into Italy where affairs are very serious. Milan has surrendered to the Austrians and Charles Albert it is thought has betrayed his people to the Emperor of Austria.*[14]

Saturday 19th August - *Left Bonneville by 6 and arrived early at Geneva. The difficulty of the Passport was a very small one, we passed almost as easily as if it had not been safe at Baste with the boxes. Geneva is the loveliest place and the Hotel seemed a palace after roughing it among the mountains. We made excursions among the Jewellese and sat watching Mont Blanc from the little garden promontory called the "Isle of Rousseau," where there is a bronze statue of that dismal man. The day was most brilliant, the lake like sapphires and not a cloud on the mountain from morning to sunset. An Englishman we met at the 'table d'hote' said we were very fortunate, he knew Geneva well and had had an illness there of a month's duration and he never saw Mont Blanc all the time and it is not often that the atmosphere is so clear. After dinner which was at the more civilised hour of 5 we went upon the beautiful lake and stayed till after dark and it was almost difficult to distinguish the stars of the sky and the starry lamps on the prows of the boats. There was a band playing very spiritedly in another vessel and fireworks let off from some of the private pleasure boats. It was like fairyland or some land seen in dream - I mean some lake. The boats too are extremely pretty with their little red awnings.*

Sunday 20th August - *Left Geneva with some sorrow as early as 8 by the steamer for Vevey. Sunday is always so much a fete day that it was full of gay couples. Never lake was so beautiful before! It's blue is so intense! Vevey is charmingly situated and the Hotel is very good and grand, its gardens reach to the lake where there were baths and boats. We dined there and I sat among the Oleanders and orange trees and figs and roses watching the lake and the mountains. We could not stay because there is hope of the Rigi if the weather permits. But as we drive up the steep road to Bulle we saw Chillon and its Castle very plainly on the banks of the Lake. Also, Clarens on the opposite side. Lausanne we had passed in the boat. Bulle is a clean nice place. Tonight a little rain. Gruyere cheese.*

Monday 21st August - *From Bulle to Fribourge where we stayed at the Zueringer Hof for the 'table d'hote' and went to hear The organ, the finest I suppose in the world, it's power and sweetness is indeed extraordinary. We heard some airs from the Freysschutz, the human voice and the notes of birds are wonderfully imitated upon it, also wind and thunder. Fribourg was a stronghold of the Jesuits until last year when they were expelled in the small civil war of which we heard much. General Dufour was at the head of the Protestant division. In* *the evening we went on to Berne, saw the Bears there and some rifle practice. We were at "the Couronne" and liked it better than "the Francon." It is cleaner. Amiable English gentleman there who thought Abraham was in the Navy.*

Tuesday 22nd August *- All the way from Berne to Lucerne. Beautiful scenery but a burning day and as we were up at 4 we are desperately tired and sleepy. The "Hotel de Cygne" is opposite the beautiful lake and most lovely it is. We went to see the beautiful sculpture of which Thorwaidsen made the design and Ahorn the finished work. The Monument to the Swiss Officers who fell at Paris in 1792. It is a grand design - a dying Lion sculptured in the rock itself. It is reflected in a little lake and surrounded by beautiful trees.*

Wednesday 23rd August *- We left Lucerne very early by the "Bateau à Vapeur" which leaves at 5 o'clock. It was a lovely morning, we breakfasted at Weggis and then went up the Rigi on horseback. Urick and two guides with the horses. It is a very beautiful ascent. We met many people coming down and some Germans who told us we ought to remain all night on the Rigi for the sunrise. Nobody then had any doubt about the weather. After we had arrived very near the top where we ought to see on the Zurich side of the mountain the clouds began to gather about us and there was very little of the valley visible. We were very glad to arrive at the Inn and in a few minutes there were clouds all around us. A solitary Englishman remained at the Inn and we found him very agreeable as to our cost we stood in sore need ultimately of society. Urick came in looking very unhappy, the weather was very bad he said, horses could not go to Zurich - we must have chaises a porteurs and descend in one hour and a hard day's work it would be. The weather might clear. He rather advised our staying for tomorrow's sunrise. This was at 10 o'clock in the day I suppose and rather a melancholy prospect. However, we resolved to stay. Our 'table d'hote' at I was of 4 people, then the rain began and they were obliged to shut the shutters on that side of the house. Afterwards I went to my little room with a French novel out of the little Salle Library. It was very cold and I made myself happy in the little bed, the wind and rain and darkness continuing. At tea-time we met again, our Englishman joined us - very quiet and gentlemanly. A horde of German adventurers arrived very cold and comfortless. The "Livres des étrangers" for some years past gave as much amusement as could be found in such trying circumstances. They are full of miseries about the weather.*

> *"Misguided by Murry I mounted the Rigi,*
> *Expecting the clearly marked mule path to see,*
> *But the one that I chose was ne'er mounted by any*
> *Except by one Donkey - that Donkey was me."*

There was a little Library where we English established ourselves and the stove being lighted on that side, it was comfortable.

Thursday 24th August *- The morning was "affreux." Snow and wind in the night without remorse. We were obliged to give up going to Zurich and to* *resign ourselves to be carried down the mounts in two chaises a porteur. It was so dirty that we were very glad to be out to it, though the motion is not pleasant. Our English friend arrived at Lucerne by the steamer in the evening. Urick took us to Kussnach and thence in a voiture to Lucerne. In the valley we were out of the bad weather and rain but it still was very cold. Kussnach is a little village celebrated in Tell's history. I believe he shot Gessner there according to tradition. We were all quite sorry to part with Urick but it was not necessary that he should go on to Basle. "Le Cygne" was full of Italians - very handsome, too happy in appearance to have suffered much in the troubles of their country.*

Friday 25th August - *Lucerne to Basle was a tedious affair but the country is very pretty - the distance 18 Steander or about 64 miles. This was to be performed by one pair of horses, and only one a very good horse. We left Lucerne very early by 5 and it was quite dark when we got to Basle. One of the poor animals fell down on the slippery stones and we got out to make our way on foot to Les Trois Rois and thanks to the assistance of a very gentlemanly stranger who spoke French and English we arrived there about a quarter of an hour before the voiture. They gave us good rooms all very charming at "the 3 Rais" notwithstanding the desolation of our arrival. We stopped to dine at Otteu a poor town and rather dirty but where we found a very clean Inn and a very civil and clean Landlord who spoke good Swiss-French, and who told us that every Swiss is a soldier from 18 to 60 if his services are required for the good of his country. The little boys were beating a rappel for their own amusement. The "dejeuner a la fourchette" was beautiful there were "pigeons aux truffes." We had not a very clear view of the Rigi and Lucerne mountains from the last pass which is rather celebrated, I believe. Lacufelfingen.*

Saturday 26th August - *Basle to Strasbourg by the Railway. Along the very flat country we saw the Alps again - the Bernese chain quite distinctly. The day was clear and the sun so powerful upon the snow that I think the mountains were visible further off than usual. Our boxes were not even looked at but passed without the least inspection at Strasbourg. We met again the very agreeable American, Mr Ward, who was at the Grimsel and he went by the packet as far as Manheim. He showed us a lovely scarf worked in gold and silver which he brought from Damascus and he was as kind as if he had really known us a long time. There were some very disagreeable English on board. Manheim and Mayrene appear two nice towns and at Manheim there are beautiful trees and walks but we had no time except to eat and sleep.*

Sunday 27th August - *We were roused very early by the embarkation of two steamers full of Swabian troops, sent, we were sorry to hear, to Schleswig Holstein against the Danes. Our bateau à vapeur and theirs ran races all the way to Cologne. This is a beautiful part of Cologne almost all the way. There were many people on board. An Ambassador - French, they said, going from Naples to Brussels with all his family, carriage and everything; and a Russian family* *with a great house of a carriage and two pretty children, very troublesome and very clever, and there were English also, and as usual I am sorry to say not the best specimens, and a Dutch family from Amsterdam who had been staying at Baden, they spoke English - the son and one of the 3 daughters - very well, and it added much to the pleasure of our voyage. At Frankfurt they told us there is again much political excitement. It was too late when we got to Cologne, and Cologne and the "Hotel Cologne" as dirty as ever.*

Monday 28th August *- We stayed in Cologne to go again to the beautiful Cathedral, it has been greatly improved since we were there. The scaffolding inside was taken away and the beautiful stained windows the gift of the King of Bavaria are arranged in their places. They are very beautiful for modem glass of this kind, but the Cathedral contains also some fine ancient windows far more magnificent in colour. The subjects of the new gifts are in the principal part of the windows. 1 - The Preaching of St John; 2 - The Birth of our Saviour; 3 - His Cruxifixion; 4 - The Day of Pentecost; 5 - The Stoning of St Stephen. Underneath are separate figures of the prophets and evangelists. We went also to see 2 models of the Cathedral as it is to be when finished. Then from Cologne to Aix. We travelled with 2 pretty German girls who were charmed with Abraham's Indian dressing gown and were very agreeable speaking, one of them very good French. Aix is a very pretty place with rows of lime trees along many of the Streets. Our Hotel the Grand Monarque we found most comfortable and the eatables were charming. It is the hottest place I have ever been in, I think.*

Tuesday 29th August *- We went into the beautiful church at Aix. It is small but lovely. Aix la Chapelle is full of remembrances of Charlesmagne. We left about 1 for Antwerp, it was very hot and crowded and a very slow railway. Did not reach Antwerp until after dark and then we lost Tilly for about 5 minutes, very amusing afterwards. It had been the fete of Rubens - an anniversary of his Birth or Death or some great event and we were in time to see the Cathedral tower lighted up with different coloured lights, very pretty indeed it was. There was so much smoke that it looked exactly as if the tower was on fire.*

Wednesday 30th August *- This morning we went to see once more the magnificent Rubens pictures in the Cathedral. The celebrated "Descent from the Cross," the Altar piece which the French called the Bouquet de Rubens representing the Ascension of the Virgin surrounded by little angels and beautiful women and the elevation of the Cross - a confused picture painted soon after the return of Rubens from Italy, and when he was quite young. It was a treat to see them again. Seebrook went with us also, we went on board "the Antwerpen" by 10 where I am writing. She is a fine large steamer and very steady. The weather could not be better.*

Thursday 31st August *- Still on board the Antwerpen. Dearest Matilda not ill, nobody ill, she and I have a cabin to ourselves and it is most comfortable. Landed at Blackwall.*

Friday 1st September - *We went out shopping in the morning then to "Bromfield"[15] to call on Mr and Mrs Alfred Darby. The place difficult to find but rather pretty, a second edition of Tickwood, but Abraham says not so good a place. She is very gauche and not pretty and no style, but I thought that he looked happy, and I do not see why she should not make him so. We left in the evening for Leighton, Grandmama much altered, memory failing and her health altogether in appearance much weakened.*

Sunday 24th September - *Matilda and Abraham have I am thankful to say decided on not being of those amphibious mortals who are neither of one thing or the other. They go now to church always - to Little Wenlock. I long to go too but am not certain about timing it best, I will not go until the membership is resigned.[7]*

Mr and Mrs Alfred have been here, dined at the Chesnuts,[21] Severn House,[22] Dale House[23] and John Howard and myself. It was very droll, Alfred Darby did not come in until late, very cross. There was a fire too at the Bridge, and Mary Darby ran into the dining room nearly favouring Abraham with hysterics. Abraham offered 'Sentinel' to Alfred as a carriage horse, he gave no answer but called a few evenings after about it. Abraham said the horse was mine and not to be sold now. The fact was we had decided to keep him on the farm. I have had a great trouble about 'Sentinel', be carried me beautifully for about 2 weeks. We went one evening to Admaston and a boy struck him with a whip. This only made him fly 50 yards and quite in my control. He behaves as well as a horse could. He always had a trick of turning round but was quite tractable when shown that he must proceed. At last he became at first ill-tempered with Devey and then refused to go to Bradley with me, he did go but behaved ill, very. The next day he was punished for the same wickedness and ran away with Devey who hoped he was conquered. I took him out in the evening and had to fight with him just the same. He threw himself round under Brunette's feet and frightened her and her fair mistress. I was never to ride him again.

Since then I have been out on Brownie but was very glad when Abraham promised to send 'Sentinel' to Strethill, for I love him even now better than anything else that ever went on 4 legs. Devey was sent to Cheltenham but Mr Reeves had nothing that he liked. About the same time Sarah Hannah's horse became unsafe and had to be returned. I used to lie awake at night and imagine 'Sentinel' being punished and finally in a knacker's yard. He may get usable again but for me I fear it is doubtful.

Wednesday 27th September - *Mama and I came to Leighton. We found Grandmama rather altered and Mama was a good deal struck by the change of memory. Thursday was the Meeting and the agricultural day also and the wettest of days. All the people were gone by evening which was a mercy.*

Sunday 1st October - *Mrs Bassett came down yesterday to ask me to dinner and I went, for what else could I well do to meet Mr ES? There was also a Mr*

Thomas Corder, a clever good-tempered rough young man and Alfred Bassett. I think these last had been in Australia together. I am afraid I put an end to all my hopes of being Mrs ES? or being asked to be, by calling Clapham Common a vulgar locality. The dinner was worth recording as a Sunday dinner in a Quaker family - talk of German dinners being large!

Fish, 3 great Soles at the top and a great boiled eel at the bottom surrounded by fried ditto, a boiled leg of mutton and a huge pigeon pie. Having dined as I thought, Mr Bassett said "Would thee take pigeon pie, we have only a goose coming!" Pudding pies and a great trifle however did come. Mr Bassett now gives plenty of wine and he substituted by mistake some whisky for hock which was called very good.

Sunday 15th October - *When Mama reached home she found dearest Matilda recovering from a sudden terrible attack that had all the symptoms of Asiatic Cholera. She had awful cramps and spasms of the stomach and fainted for the first time in the hall where she was standing with Mr and Mrs John Pritchard*[18] *who had been calling on her. She fell on the marble slab and cut her face and hurt her finger. They were ten minutes bringing her to life again. Thank God after 24 hours she was out of danger, the laudanum and brandy having saved her life I suppose and Mr Rowland was most attentive but she was as weak as a baby and only now beginning to get strong.*

Sunday 22nd October - *Last Tuesday there arrived twin sons to the house of Bassett, Mrs JB doing very well. Thursday pleasant little party at Miss Lawford's. It is Ash, near Whitchurch, where the Bensons are living.*

Monday 6th November - *I am going home on Thursday, I am very glad to get away and to see Mama and Tilly. Grandmama is very unhappy, poor old lady, and she is so altered.*

Friday 10th November - *I came home. Abraham came from London the night before to take care of me home, very kind of him. The new speculation in furs much admired.*

Tuesday 21st November - *These have been pleasant weeks at home, but I have been near recalled to Leighton. Grandmama having met with a wound in her ankle which confines her much to the sofa. Matilda is better but not very strong.*

Wednesday 6th December - *Charades at the Schools,*[17] *the acting capital. Dr and Mrs Kennedy very kind and attentive to everybody, he found me charming partners, I danced first with one of Huesdale' Corbett's sons, a dear little naval officer, then with his brother Lionel, and then with two grown-up boys, nice dancers. One a favourite pupil of Dr Kennedy's and very agreeable. It was a cram especially the supper. We left about half past 2. Everybody I suppose in Shrewsbury at all presentable was there.*

Tuesday 19th December - *Went to Mr Pritchards,*[18] *Abraham and Matilda and I, for Mr Bates birthday. Matilda had a very severe cold all the week before, Abraham was out, and we nursed her well again and very pretty she looked in canary satin and blonde. I wore the gift of diamonds as a bracelet and black tulle. However, I think it is not now distinguished, all the three Miss Rowleys wore it.*

Friday 22nd December - *A long planned expedition of Matilda's to Wenlock. We were to have gone with Mr GE*[19] *on horseback, but the day before a frost set in, and the courage tailed of many, not mine however, for I thought it very different going for the amusement of riding on horseback and going in the state of a carriage purely to see schools which I have no proper taste for. It was a monstrous bore and Mr GE*[19] *a great deal to answer for. I will not go to Wellington I will say there are three things for which I have no proper taste - schools, children and the matron's place in a carriage beside Mr GE.*

Saturday 23rd December - *I am come to Wroxeter for a week, very very pleasant so far. Archdeacon Beresford arrived this evening. Mr Richards here when I came but left.*

Sunday 24th December - *Excellent sermon from Job XXXI - what then shall I do when God riseth up and when he visiteth what shall I answer him.*

Monday 25th December - *It was a delightful sermon and most solemn communion. Then we walked afterwards in the clear cold air and then came the little annual fete at the Sunday school. Mrs E*[20] *had a fright in the evening - the death of a poor woman, Jenny Jones, of cholera, but it is to be hoped it will not spread.*

Tuesday 26th December - *Mr & Mrs Burton came to dinner, and Mrs and Miss Walford, and Captain Scott. There had been much fun about Captain Scott who Mrs E*[20] *really seemed to wish me to marry, and to doubt not he would be ready to do so. I thought him one of the greatest fools. Charmed to see Miss Burton again and Louisa Walford sang some of her prettiest songs. She is somewhat altered.*

Wednesday 27th December - *Went to Shrewsbury in the morning to bring back Miss Walford, then Maynard House and Mr Richards came to dinner - we have been dancing until very late.*

Thursday 28th December - *To Shrewsbury again, Miss Walford and I and Mr Beresford. Went over St Mary's and St Chad's the last to look at Evan's new window, copies from the Antwerp Rubens - the descent from the cross. The Hursby's to dinner. Mr Beresford did the kindest thing, he made Mrs Hursby civil to me - ie he is a great star with her and he happened to be particularly attentive to me. Yesterday Mrs E*[20] *told him exactly how I am situated in matters of religion without mentioning my name of which he had not the slightest idea. He said that in such case it would undoubtedly be the higher course of action to go over to the Church. That our duty to God is higher than our duty* *to our parents, at the same time the motive of not hurting the feelings of a parent was good and amiable, he would not judge it to be displeasing to God, he thought we would counsel waiting to see if God would not open a path - I do not know how much longer it might have been, if Mrs E*[20] *had not turned round from the driving box and said "Sara, when will you have the pig killed?" - how we did laugh!*

Friday 29th December - *Mrs Maine and Miss Taylor called to lunch and a young Mr Maine, very handsome, who took me in to lunch and was very civil. Mr Archdeacon was puzzled - it appeared after that he was engaged to Miss Taylor. We took a walk and again met the Burtons on their way to Wroxeter, we went on. Mr Beresford read me some beautiful lines written on his return down the Rhine after the death of his wife. In the evening to the Ball at the Thursby's. I danced 4 or 5 times and played at Chess with Mr Richards and then talked to Mr Beresford all the rest of the evening.*

NOTES

1. Francis Darby's account book, 6th January 1849 (I.G.M.T.)
2. Present day equivalent calculated by reference to Bank of England criteria.
3. Osborne Gordon was an acquaintance of Adelaide's at Broseley, but was making a name for himself in religious affairs at the University of Oxford.
4. Presumably Joseph John Gurney a leading Quaker.
5. This would have been Barnard Dickinson (1809-1896) 4th child of Barnard and Ann Dickinson. He was eight years older than Adelaide and left Coalbrookdale in 1831, so Adelaide had not met him recently, although he had paid a long visit to Severn House and had called at The White House twice. He was however a first cousin of Adelaide and therefore a dangerously close relative.
6. 1848 was a year of revolution in France. In February riots occurred in Paris. Louis Philippe escaped to England. He died in 1850 at Claremont, which Adelaide had visited in 1845.
7. Adelaide had been baptised at Wroxeter in July 1847. She hesitated to break all links with the Society of Friends, so she took refuge in ecumenical thinking.
8. Abraham IV and Matilda were the first members of the family to join the Anglican communion. There had been a dispute about the poor rate. The previous chaplain had performed his duties gratuitously, but with a change in the living, the Poor Law Commission directed the Union to appoint a chaplain and it was agreed that he should be paid. Barnard Dickinson who was a guardian of the Union refused to pay. Whether this was the issue on which Abraham resigned his "birthright membership" is not clear, although Adelaide seems to imply that it may have been.
9. No doubt W was Wolverhampton.
10. Hugh Darby Owen was a relative. His father Reverend L. Pryce Owen, formerly vicar of Wellington, Shropshire, had married Mary Darby, daughter of Samuel Darby II. Their son Hugh Darby Owen married another Mary. He was a shareholder in the Coalbrookdale Company.

11. Possibly Mr Reeves.
12. Presumably Mrs Francis Tothill, wife of Francis Tothill, 3rd child of William and Hannah Tothill (see family tree).
13. "Willie" was William, eldest child of William and Hannah Tothill (see family tree). He was a first cousin of Adelaide and therefore, like Barnard Dickinson (see note 5 above) a dangerously close relative.
14. 1848 was a year of revolution in Europe. There was a rising in north Italy against Austrian domination.
15. Alfred and Rebecca Darby were living in Clapham.
16. "Sentinel" was the horse purchased at Cheltenham with 60 guineas provided by Grandmama, Mrs Grant.
17. Shrewsbury School known as "the Schools".
18. Mr John Pritchard was the banker in Broseley who was a friend of Adelaide.
19. Mr G.E. was presumably Mr George Edmonds, Rector of Little Wenlock.
20. Mrs Egremont, wife of Edward Egremont, vicar of Wroxeter. She seems to have occupied a great deal of her time in match-making.
21. The Chesnuts was the home of Abraham Darby IV and Matilda, who was Adelaide's sister.
22. Severn House (now the Valley Hotel, Ironbridge) was the home of Henry Dickinson and Deborah (née Darby), who was the sister of Abraham IV and Alfred.
23. Dale House was the home of Lucy Darby (née Burlingham) and her daughter Mary Darby. Lucy Darby was the mother of Abraham IV and Alfred.

Severn House (now the Valley Hotel, Ironbridge, Telford), built by George Goodwin, Master Collier, c1757. Bequeathed by Sarah Darby to the Dickinson family. During period of the Journal, it was occupied by Henry Dickinson.

1849

Comment

In her entry in the Journal for 19th January, Adelaide states "This year, 1849, begins badly for me with a romance full of trouble and discomfort". She did not exaggerate - of all the romances that Adelaide experienced, the one with Archdeacon Beresford caused the greatest agony and heartache. She met the archdeacon at the home of Mr and Mrs Egremont at Wroxeter - where else! The Egremonts were incorrigible matchmakers. Beresford came from Ballyhaise near Dublin. What he was doing in Shropshire is not clear from the Journal, but he seems to have been given the impression by the Egremonts that Adelaide (and possibly a Miss Thursby) were ladies with a "fine fortune". Adelaide was certainly captivated by the archdeacon. She soon discovered however that apart from the Egremonts, nobody else seemed to think that it was a good idea for Adelaide to uproot from Shropshire and go to live in Ireland.

Extricating herself from the situation in which she was in proved, however, to be a long and painful process. The archdeacon pursued his proposal of marriage with great perseverance and Adelaide had to refuse him several times. On 14th March she set out a masterly and final rebuttal of all the archdeacon's representations. Sadly this last letter was not sent and the love affair "terminated in reproach and bitterness".

She passed a great deal of time at Leighton Buzzard, and then from June to August she spent her summer holidays with Abraham and Matilda at Dover. By the time she returned to Leighton, grandmama's health had deteriorated to a point at which it was thought fitting to move her to Leamington, where she spent the rest of the year. Adelaide and the family joined her there for much of the time, but she returned to Coalbrookdale at intervals, where she found herself elevated to a position of some stature in Shropshire society. Her Journal records details of her experiences at the fund-raising service at St Chads, Shrewsbury, where she was responsible for one of the "plates", for the Infirmary, followed by the Hunt Ball. Both events had had to be postponed for the Thanksgiving day for the abatement of a devastating outbreak of cholera which had afflicted urban areas of the country during 1848. It was this outbreak which prompted the passing of the Public Health Act 1848, the first attempt to deal with the need for sanitation in urban areas.

Monday 1st January - *I came home. Abraham and Matilda coming to fetch me. It has been a curious visit and I am glad to be at home to arrange my ideas.. Mr Beresford and I parted with a promise not to forget each other. He did not* *propose for me and yet it was nearly the same thing. I liked and admired him very much but could hardly believe that a man of such good family would think about me. The last 2 days he contrived tete a tete walks.*

Tuesday 2nd January *- I went with Abraham and Matilda to Mr J Pritchard's to dinner, and I to stay until Thursday. How glad I was of this total change of ideas - for the time it did me good and until I came home again I was very happy, happy in thinking of Mr Beresford as a brilliant creature about as near perfection as this world was likely to afford. I found Miss Lucy Davenport, Mr Moore of Larden and Osborne Gordon[1] staying in the house. General and Mrs Davison of Stanley[2] and Mr Bates came to dinner.*

Wednesday 3rd January *- A ride on horseback with Mr John Pritchard, Miss Davenport and Mr Gordon. At dinner, Mr & Mrs and Miss Waine, Mrs, Miss and Mr Bull. A droll day. Miss Davenport is the most entertaining creature.*

Thursday 4th January *- Came home. Snow. Walked with dearest Matilda. Stiff with riding and cold and dead asleep and utterly tormented by doubts as to the wisdom of my preference for Mr Beresford. Abraham does not like the Archdeacon and would not trust him, thinks him sly - and was Abraham ever wrong? Certainly nobody ever amused me so much in so short a time. He delighted in my sympathy and appreciation I believe. He told me all about himself with a vanity that at the time struck me perhaps too little. I never thought whether he was handsome or not and was rather surprised to hear that he is positively ugly, I can but pray to God to take care of me. With so little to make me happy here, it seems better to give up the hope of being more so, and yet it might be less so. In Abraham and Matilda and Mama, I have much to leave - it would be banishment.*

Friday 19th January *- Mary Owen[3] writes, "I heard you were well employed at Wroxeter kittling the Archdeacon" - still, I do not think I can bear the great risk of going to Ireland. It is a painfully absorbing subject, if I could only think that Abraham would like Mr B, and that Mr B would like Abraham. I should be happy. Mama and Matilda would be sure to like him and he them.*

This year, 1849, begins badly for me with a romance full of trouble and discomfort, one in which also I have not the happiness of saying I have a good conscience and have acted wisely, discreetly, prudently. The Old Journal ended with the Xmas campaign at Wroxeter. I came home and in process of time many small missives came from Mrs Egremont. Matilda and I arranged to ride over there to call on Mrs Russell one fatal Monday. Sunday there came another note enclosing one from the Archdeacon, he had arrived, and asked me to fix a time and place for an interview. I knew that I was coming to Leighton and I dreaded Mr Beresford coming first to Papa. I really meant fully to marry him, I thought I loved him. I knew that I admired his talents and for anything I knew to the contrary he was a fair, a very fair match for me. I knew him rather vain, but of this by and by. Matilda was against me about going to Wroxeter. Abraham was against me. Mama thought as I did, that the plan having been made before it was less remarkable to go than to tell Mr B to come to the Dale. So Matilda and I went over.

Monday 29th January - *We were later than I had in my notes always said that I would be. Mrs Egremont was gone out and Mrs Russell. The drawing room was easily cleared and Mr Beresford proposed to me. I told him in 2 months he might speak to Papa and in the meantime write to me at Leighton. I believe he was as he afterwards said for the time the happiest of men. Alas, Miss Thursby called. My sister became very angry and Abraham said it was the laird of Cockpan the other way up. It certainly was not wise nor perhaps dignified, yet it enabled me to see what the Archdeacon was. In his letters he never failed to plume himself upon my journey to see him.*

Tuesday 30th January - *Matilda had a dinner party and that same morning Mrs Henry Dickinson and Barnard called and took lunch at our house. This morning as soon as I awoke I began to see how my expedition to Wroxeter had appeared to everybody and my misery was too intense for description. At lunch I was very near fainting. (First time of seeing Mr Beresford since - how little truth can be known in this world.)*

The party was Mr & Mrs J and Mrs John Pritchard and Miss Jackson and B and Mr GB who was very extraordinary and grand. Papa and Mama were there also and great was my agony lest Wroxeter be mentioned and my wild ride there.

Thursday 1st February - *With Abraham and Matilda to dine at Mr Pritchard's. The John Anstices and a great many people I did not know, music charming. Mama and I were to start for Leighton by 6 next morning. Abraham disapproved of the plan much and it was a disagreeable one. I said "I wish I may never have to do anything worse in my life." "Aye," he said, "I wish so too." I was in wretched spirits and that haunted me all night. I began to distrust Mr Beresford and my own judgement. I disliked his style of proposal. He had gone too fast for me.*

Friday 2nd February - *We came to Leighton. In the meantime came 2 letters from the Archdeacon at the Primate's where he had been to his cousin's wedding. The first was very interesting, very affectionate, but it was plain that he thought me won completely just as my faith in him was beginning to waver. I had written to Mary Owen*[3] *and Mrs Egremont, both sent me long, long letters. Mrs Own and Mary said I was throwing myself away fearfully, Mrs Egremont threw doubt upon Mr Beresford's opinions as a clergyman. Mrs Russell wrote that he is all that is excellent in domestic life, indeed both she and Mrs Egremont said he had been a kind and excellent husband, very indulgent to a wife much older than himself. I had got alarmed, my dignity was frightened and offended and the affair was being talked of, so said the Archdeacon,* *in a dreadful manner. I wrote and refused him on the ground that my mother objected and that I saw the same objections also in a far more forcible point of view. 3 letters followed - he went in some degree into his proper place, he wrote a most civil letter to Matilda very different to the first in which he asked Abraham to go and see him at Ballyhaise and to know all about him. I was beginning to waver again for his talents are to be less a snare to my vanity and his gentleness of manner (tho' it may be the softness of a cat and as little to be trusted) is yet to my affections another snare. But Providence surely had ordered otherwise. The 10 days had expired after which Louisa Russell was to return to Harnage and I had written to tell her what I had done and had said in my letters - Do you like the Archdeacon, and does Captain Russell like him, and is it of your own knowledge what you say of his kindness and goodness in domestic life. Captain Russell answered for himself - Oh, how manly and short and conclusive, and yet I felt afraid to answer. It was hard to thank him enough and avoid a flummery he would hate. I doubt if he ever loved me and yet it was plain he thought me worth saving from the Archdeacon. I wrote another refusal and had no reply. A week passed, I was forgetting the thing and growing dreadfully ill with what Mr Otley calls neuralgic headache. I was lying in my bed very nearly insensible from pain when a letter came from Mr Beresford at the Swan requesting an interview. Mama wrote for me that I would try to see him the next day - Tuesday 27th August. Almost the first thing Mr Beresford said was - "this change is what I cannot understand because I know your steadiness of character but I know also your timidity and caution which amounts to suspicion, somebody has been poisoning your mind and knowing you are truth itself I am come here to ask you this". In honour to those who had trusted me I had to deny it all and very hard it was. I saw how well he understood me, I saw too how well he appreciated me - but under and among all still lurked the monstrous vanity which with Captain Russell's help saved me. I felt all the time that I loved him and also that he would not be happy. His cross examination was very clever, "you are as clear as glass," he said, "and yet now I cannot make you out, surely you liked me once and may again." I said "since I have thought steadily over the objections, they appear to me so great that I do not wish to like you better, can you forgive that?" He took the objections one by one to pieces, made mincemeat of them; at last he came to his own age. "This is the only thing I cannot alter, Ada" - I believe I burst into tears, I said "You cannot alter it, why do you make me give you pain thus?" "Because," he said "I must know the truth, however bitter, then this is the great sin, Ada, and cannot you forgive it?" I was nearly choked, I could only shake my head. He added very gently "did you feel this at first?" I said "I suppose I ought if I had really acted with the caution you give me credit for, I should, not have given you all this pain." He was silent, but he still held my hand in his. "Now," I said, "you are thinking that I have treated you very ill, and not one reproach, oh, I would rather you would scold me!" "God forbid," he said, "that I should ever say that of one I still esteem so much and shall always love!" Well, now you perplex me by this turn of affairs.*

Lady Gainsborough, Lord Radnor's daughter, would marry no-one but Lord Gainsborough and he 30 years older, and Lady this and Lady that - - -. I came to myself again. "You are a fine character and it is very hard to resign you for what I think you will find a folly." "Dearest Ada, I would have loved you as well as at 25, I think you would have been as happy. This is one of the bitter things of Providence." I said "you will soon forget it - think how short the time has been." "Years sometimes count by minutes," he replied, "and the world has few like you, I never knew but one, and she was something like you." I said "How is it then the strength of the impression has not been the same?"

"There was less to attract you, dearest my very fair friend, you are very beautiful and you know it, but you will never marry one who will love you better or as I think who would make you a better husband." I remained firm, but I was sick at heart. "I will go to your father now," he said, "and tell him all, may I write to tell you what he says?" "No." "Why, as a friend I might do that." "But you must not go, what right have I to make you more wretched?" "What will it signify how your father treats me after what you have said, I do not care, not if I was shot, or if your Father kicked me out of this house."

"Perhaps," I said, "you would not care much for his answer, but it would do no good, it would not alter me, if you have understood me now you know this." He made no answer, he took me in his arms for the last time with a sad smile and a peculiar one. As soon as I could I escaped. Mr Whitfield and his little boy were in the other room and he very much astonished at my rudeness in running away.

Saturday 3rd February *- Came letters from Matilda and Papa. Mr Beresford had been to the Dale. He had not seen Papa but had written to him - no opinion from Papa, but I wrote to tell him I did not wish to marry Archdeacon Beresford and that it would be useless, any further acquaintance. Having done what I was not particularly happy and thought that perhaps Captain Russell in his estimate did not at all know the unusual miseries that I have to meet at home with Mama. They had had tiffs among the servants and untold discomforts, and I went to bed and cried.*

Sunday 4th February *- Letters from Mr Beresford, telling me what he had done and imploring me to take no steps, if Papa allowed the matter to rest with me, that should prevent him seeing me again. One from Louisa Russell, very angry, but inviting me to meet Mr Beresford at their house either Harnage or in the North and telling me I was lucky to have gained the affections of such a man, and one from Gertrude laughing at him without mercy - full of life and fun and good sense.*

Monday 5th February *- Mama went away early. I took a ride, reading Miss Austin's "Emma", a good book and strengthening to the understanding. Grandmama had been ill yesterday and remained in bed. Mr Lawford and I were in cabinet counsel about buying a horse when a note was brought to me,* *the Archdeacon again. I thought I could not well refuse to see him for "the melancholy satisfaction of saying farewell." but it soon appeared that he had no earthly intention of saying farewell. He had gone to Liverpool and there it occurred to him to come back and try if I would see him. He thought that if Papa made no objection that the Egremonts would not object to ask me there to meet him if I would promise not to object myself, I would not promise. Then Mrs Egremont had been telling him that her conscience smote her, and she thought she had influenced me out of regard for her brother Tom. In the midst of his grief Mr Beresford could not help laughing. I assured him she had spoken most highly of him, then he repeated some beautiful verses to me and I very properly replied that they were beautiful and very like his poetry, and that I was sorry they were addressed to me, and he feared that I thought he wished to lead the life of a hermit and bury me alive in the country, but indeed as to society, I should do just as I pleased and should go as much to Dublin as I liked. One year he stipulated I should live in Ireland and if I did not like it he would then come to England. He was very devoted but yet I thought I should have very little voice in the matter. I began to doubt my influence over him greatly - no, no it will not do. He is sly, he is not quite sincere. I began to see what the prettiest and most refined love-making is worth. It is very nice to listen to, like a novel or a song, with one's pretty self for the angel heroine, but what has this to do with the heart of the lover being a disinterested heart, with his being considerate for the feelings of others and generous towards others. The Archdeacon is in such haste to entrap me into admitting more than I feel, that his professions resolve themselves into caring little for my really loving him.*

Monday 12th March - *Dismally unhappy, dreadful letters from Gertrude and Tilly, people are saying that I did accept the Archdeacon and that he said so too. He went back to Dublin and sent me a picture of myself and a letter containing professions of friendship and attachment, and saying also that he thought himself accepted. Oh, Mon Dieu - this is a terrible passage in life. I have made so many people unhappy and am so sunk in my own esteem. Against marrying Mr Beresford all the world advises me and my own reason also strongly, for I am not bound in honour but it is a wretched business.*

Wednesday 14th March - *Dreadful letter from Mr Beresford. If I should see him, I must explain "could I make any explanation that would restore your peace of mind I would rejoice to give it and could see you as soon as you please. But you must promise not to attempt to alter my determination, we have only to speak of the past and not of the future, and it must be a point of honour between us that this interview does not transpire to any one as my friends would probably think me wrong and imprudent in granting it." I must begin my account of myself at Wroxeter. I never had any distinct feeling that your attentions were serious, I used to speculate upon it sometimes but it appeared to me unlikely. I thought that you would likely to require accomplishments or cleverness in your wife, I knew nothing of you, and I know that it is a habit of your country men* *to be attentive to ladies. The attentions of so gifted a man were flattering to my vanity, I have told you that before. The last day I was entirely perplexed and bewildered, I thought that you took an unusual interest in me and I thought that I liked you but after I returned home, I thought that the whole interview mounted to but little. I came to the conclusion that very probably you were not serious. I remembered again that Irishmen pay a great deal of attention. This showed want of knowledge of your character but remember how short a time I had had to form my judgement of it then. I did not give the time between this and receiving your note, to consultation and reflection as you unfortunately imagined, but resolved to think no more about it. I have explained all I can explain about going to meet you at Wroxeter and you know that I regret it. You know that I slightly objected to Ireland, it was my own thought that I should not like it. You must remember tho I was far from rejecting you that I distinctly told you I could promise nothing unless I had known you longer. I did not attach your important meaning to the permission to speak to Papa. I thought that if I saw you again at all he ought to be consulted first and I requested you not to apply to him until I was returning home, one reason for which was that I might have time for the reflection and counsel which I fear must unconsciously have led you to suppose had been already given to the affair. It never for a moment occurred to me that you could consider I was pledged to anything. That you should have said you thought yourself accepted hurt and astonished me very much. I came here and told all to my mother and she highly disapproved of Ireland, that you were a good deal older than me and of the grown up family. She convinced me of the importance of these objections for I had given little thought to them before. However agreeable I had thought you the liking of one week was not sufficient against these things when put strongly before me. All this I believe I tried to make clear in my first letter. You say that I knew all these objections and considered them as long ago as at Wroxeter but that is a mistake. I never did in the least appreciate their importance at all properly. I do not think I said anything about your family however. My mother said there was an unkindness towards your daughters in specifying it but you oblige me to mention it now because you say that I gave different reasons to you and to my father. I think now that at this period of the affair it would really have been less painful to your feelings if I had referred you at once to my parents as with my mother the objections began but at the time as they gained strength in my own mind it appeared to me unfair to you to do so. Your first letter came and I saw you supposed my affections gained far more than the truth, your second impressed me yet more with the great responsibilities I should have to undertake. Can you be surprised that I wrote to you just as I did? It appeared to me unjust to you and to myself to do otherwise. You insisted upon applying to my father without my consent as I had told you I must in honour towards you withdraw it. One reason you gave me was I believe that the affair had been talked of so much, this occasioned me much regret and annoyance for my different friends began to write to me every day on the subject and perhaps I ought to tell you that with the exception of our mutual friends at Wroxeter I was universally advised against it. I do not mean that I heard anything against yourself, of that I have assured you already, but that I should think of going to Ireland seemed as terrible to all as it did to Mama. Will you think me unfeeling if I add that my friends greatly impressed my mind against encountering a grown up family, they assured me that I did not know what I was doing nor how disadvantageous it is considered in the world and this was true for it is a circumstance of life that I had never for myself had the means of judging. I know that you had said it was of no importance or rather an advantage but could I, after all you had told me of your feelings regard you as altogether a dispassionate judge of the subject. I should not have said all this but that it appears you earnestly desire to know everything that has influenced me. I am not surprised that you thought my letter to Papa unkind with regard to yourself yet entertaining all those views which had been so impressed upon me, I could hardly do other than answer him distinctly. He only sent you a quotation, had you seen my letter you would have been aware that I told him all the advantages of the connection at much greater length, exactly in short as you have told them and written of them to me. You could not then but have been convinced that my parents had the opportunity of judging for themselves and that you really had no right to say that my Mother would not have disapproved or my Father refused if I had not withdrawn my consent. Will you not misunderstand me if I say that if this letter makes the past more clear and satisfying to you I should be gratified by receiving one line from you to say so. I thought your last letter more severe than I deserved, for the kind expressions at the end you have my thanks, and in bidding you farewell let me once more assure you of any sorrow at having caused you pain, and of my most sincere good wishes for your future happiness and prosperity in future."*

Thursday 22nd March - *This letter never went, never love affair terminated in more reproach and bitterness.*

Monday 9th April - *Abraham and Matilda come here tomorrow. Mr Beresford sent me back my letters about a fortnight ago, asking for his own. I sent them all but the last one.*

Wednesday 25th April - *We had the account from Lichborough of the death of Mrs Grant*[4] *on 20th, aged 98. It is 2 months' mourning.*

Thursday 10th May - *Adelaide's cough became much worse. Mama and I came home leaving Grandmama less well that could have been desired and with a cough like mine.*

Wednesday 16th May - *We went to Admaston*[8] *and I was out late and the evening wet. I had been going on pretty well and the cough better but this put all wrong again and Mr Edwards*[5] *was sent for.*

Monday 21st May - *Edward Lawford Jr. came to fetch Mama to Leighton, I was in great distress that I could not go too. Grandmama had inflammation of the lungs.*

Sunday 27th May - *A very invalid week but I am better. Grandmama wonderfully recovered. Mama still there. Abraham and Matilda and I start tomorrow for Leighton and then on I believe to Dover for a little time. Dearest Matilda also took the Hooping (sic) Cough from me and is just recovering, Grandmama no doubt has it. It is a horribly infectious complaint. At Leighton they gave me calomel and aconite to Mr Reeves great indignation and he counteracted it with Hyociannes so that it is perhaps not wonderful I have felt half dead.*

I hope much from the sea. Not one ride on horseback. Abraham intends, I believe, to have the horse from Mr H, it is a very handsome creature. Whether Grandmama will recover is of course uncertain, I think she will for a time, altho' Mr Reeves and many people who write to us think it will be next to a miracle if she could. I do not think I could have lived thro' all this cough and fever and medicine and misery if I had been 88.

Monday 28th May - *Left home with Abraham and Matilda. Set out in the afternoon and slept at Birmingham, great labour it was. Interview with Mr Bull about school mistresses.*

Tuesday 29th May - *Abraham set out early for London. Matilda and Mr Bull sent to see a school. I lay on the sofa. Mr Bull saw us safe into the train, a very nice kind man. We got to Leighton, Matilda and I and Margaret to dinner, he going on to Dover with luggage, beautiful arrangement. Found dearest Mama looking so well and comfortable. Grandmama very much altered the Hooping (sic) Cough has tried her extremely and I think if I had been 89 I should have not got over it. Rather tired but not like the first day. After dinner, and it also being the remains of the Whitsuntide fair, I rode out on the young animal Mr Lawford means to give me. The breaker likes her very much, she is partly Arabian and I suppose will be good and handsome. She is as gentle as possible. I rode about 18 miles and indeed I was tired.*

Friday 1st June - *Left Leighton for Dover. Long long way. Slow train and tiresome children. Milk and barley sugar. The smell of the sea when at last it came was perfectly delicious. Were established in such a pretty little house all to ourselves, 22 Marine Parade. Everything so very clean and delightful and ourselves close to the Asphalt and the Beach smelling of nice seaweed.*

Sunday 3rd June - *Abraham and Matilda went to church but I was afraid to venture. Very hot at present. Ten days later I contrived to catch cold after a thunder storm we had and have been thrown back rather, but becoming very strong and hungry. Charming libraries and piano and telescope. It seems to me we have everything to make us very happy and Abraham goes out fishing. I have been out once in the boat and Matilda went out when it was very stormy indeed. Packhams's horses are improved. We find a chestnut and a grey that we can ride and have been out several times which is charming. Now 'Jim Crow' hats - very becoming'*

Wednesday 13th June - *We went to Walmer, it keeps very cold. Wind always East. Matilda cold and Abraham very cold and I coughing and the fire will go out. At Walmer Castle everybody complaining of cold June. Apple tree in blossom, roses beautiful.*

Thursday 14th June - *Abraham went away home this morning, with him to the station. Little dressmaker from Hazeldines' fits Matilda. Very nicely, came to try on velvet polka for me. In the afternoon went to hear the German Band, it was very pleasant and the music I thought very good as far as it went. Very pretty faces, almost all the pretty dresses were French or German. Letter from Mr Bull who means to be here tomorrow.*

Sunday 15th July - *We have been here at Dover 4 weeks yesterday, not a great deal had happened. Mr Bull had been here and at the Dale, made great muddles and got them right again some way. Mr Robinson*[6] *and Abraham spent a week in Paris and then Abraham was obliged to go home. There had been a fire, also Mr Pritchard wrote to say Stanley*[7] *is to let, and would it not suit his brother! It had been a pet scheme for Abraham to take Stanley*[7] *himself but this made it impossible! Mr Pritchard's letter must be sent to his brother and at present his brother likes the place as indeed anybody must and probably will take it. I was very sorry and Matilda also but it is perhaps all for the best. At any rate it could not be helped but bad or good I do not quite love Mr Pritchard for leaving Abraham no choice. Abraham had returned home about a week and we very happy and quiet with our music and a whole library full of clever novels to amuse us and a little amateur dress, for the lassie at Hazeldines' of course failed totally to fit us.*

They generally go boating in the mornings and in the evenings for it had become very hot and they rode after dinner. Those rides had a sad finish yesterday. We had one pet road, by River and then on the London Road 8 or 10 miles out and in, and the horses were taken by the week. They had behaved very well, and we were saying how we loved them, and how they had improved with us, when, as we were coming home, passing the bridge out of Buckland in a nice canter, dearest Tilly's chestnut suddenly fell, she was between Sir Fretful and the grey, the chestnut rolled over on her left side, I heard dearest Tilly scream, but very faintly and saw the feet of my horse as it seemed upon her and among her habit - I cannot tell how it was, some say the grey sprang over her and some that she fell between it and her own horse, but the horror of half a minute during which I thought I must have killed her was beyond describing. Through the mercy of God we were spared and when I could stop the grey, or rather when she threw herself back with a short melancholy neigh for she knew as well as we did that there was something wrong, dearest Tilly was standing up leaning against the bridge and some good kind man going to her. She said she could not walk her foot had been squeezed under the horse, and they carried her into a little Inn, gentle nice people. She was very faint and I could not make her comfortable on chairs so they carried her into a little back room and laid her on a nice comfortable sofa. It was their own room and the little children crept about in a sort of alarmed sympathy.

There was a rather gentlemanly man with a cigar who spoke most gently to us and went to find a surgeon but none was to be met with. Poor Packham's fright was immense but he got a carriage as quickly as could be and carried her into it and we were soon at home, but the unhappy foot swelled dreadfully. Then he went for the surgeon he thought best, Mr Sankey, who was here in a few minutes and said there were no bones hurt and he would send a lotion. Hughes who had slept downstairs was made to vacate and nothing could be better for such an accident than the drawing room with this bedroom adjoining. She had a very bad night and slept hardly at all, the pain was so great but the lotion seemed good and the swelling and the blackness are I suppose favourable. Packham had been to Margaret and Hughes and they were standing in the greatest tribulation on the steps. Certainly such things bring out the kindness of human nature wonderfully.

Wednesday 18th July - *Miss Ashfield and Miss Howard called bringing a little pacquet from Mama which after dinner took me to the Joint Stock Bank. (A bill payable at 3 days means 6 days and I suppose would remain available any time after. However, they gave me the money because Mr Bassett's signature would not be easily forged.) Mr Sankey comes every day and is very attentive and kind and clever, I think. Abraham came in the evening.*

Thursday 19th July - *Dearest Matilda had a horrible headache at night, the foot remains very incapable and she cannot leave the sofa but Dr Sankey says there is no permanent harm.*

Friday 20th July - *Enter Mr Bull who transfers his own teacher to the school at the Dale.*

Monday 13th August - *We left Dover after 10 weeks, very, very charming to me in looking back. I had some rides and we went out several times with Berry in the Fancy, dearest Tilly became able to do that. Poor Miss Ashfield had not been a week in Dover when she was called away by the death of her brother Mr Edward Ashfield of Aspley. It was very sudden at last although he was ill enough to have somewhat alarmed them. Mr Charles Childe is to be married the 20th, to a Miss Shakespeare.*

Tuesday 14th August - *Came on from London to Leighton after some very pleasant shopping in Town but London is very empty. Abraham took us to Mdme Tussaud's where Mr Rush now reigns in the chamber of horrors.*

Wednesday 15th August - *Abraham and Matilda stayed, and left Thursday morning, I remaining at Leighton. The line is now by the Trent Valley to Stafford turning off from the Birmingham railroad at Rugby.*

Friday 24th August - *St Bartholomew's - Dearest Abraham and Matilda were to be baptised at Little Wenlock Church last Wednesday, she writes me word.*

Thursday 30th August - *Set out for Leamington, Mama and I with Harry and Moorcroft. Mama and I came the Saturday before, looked over many lodgings and engaged some nice rooms at Lloyds, a china shop in the Lower Parade, No 26. Grandmama bore the journey better than might have been supposed likely, but she was very tired.*

Monday 10th September - *Miss Lawford is coming today to remain with Grandmama while Mama and I go home for a little while. We are comfortable here and Grandmama much better for a week of the "waters". On the 11th Mama and I went home for one little fortnight and never two weeks passed so rapidly. I rode out almost every day with dearest Tilly and upon dear 'Gazelle'. One day we called on the du Gards staying at Admaston[8] and dined at the table d'hote. There was a Mrs Price and her grand daughter, Montgomershire people and rather amusing and agreeable, the young lady very French and pretty. Our journey back to Leamington very prosperous. Papa is much better I think and came with us as far as Wolverhampton. Met Miss Davenport at the station at Birmingham. Then Mr & Mrs Lawford who are staying here at 19 on the Lower Parade, very pleasant for Grandmama.*

Wednesday 26th September - *The last day.*

Tuesday 2nd October - *Dearest Matilda came for a few days, a fortnight perhaps. Mary Lawford went away taking Grandmama's maid Mary with her to be replaced by Phoebe, and this a great comfort. It is a great joy to see dear Matilda looking so well. In the afternoon as we were establishing ourselves in Miss Lawford's vacated dominions Lord Leigh called, and Miss Leigh, she is very pretty and very agreeable. He not prepossessing, but probably very good natured.*

Monday 8th October - *My cold has gradually become very bad, and I hope now going way. Wet weather all the week, very wet. Grandmama's old friends Mr Grimshaw and Lady Corbett are in Leamington.*

Thursday 18th October - *We left Mrs Lloyd's in the Lower Parade and removed to 34 Upper Parade, the next house to Lady Corbett's, belongs to a John Parker or Joseph Parker and we have the people who let these three houses Mr & Mrs Proctor and nieces, these people have £1.1. a week for their services, 1/- for brushes, and the house £6.6.0. Grandmama seemed as if she would be more comfortable in a house to herself, besides she was gradually buying everything particularly useless or ugly in the china shop.*

Saturday 10th November - *We have remained at No 34 very comfortably all the time. No events except Lady Corbett's occasional coming to tea and our calls upon her and Mama finding an old school fellow Mrs Fisher, once* *possessed of a very large fortune and now living on the wreck of it left by an imprudent husband. She has a widowed daughter, Mrs Moriarty, living with her and another invalid who I don't know much, and a third very agreeable woman. Sometimes I walk with Mrs Moriarty, sometimes ride with Egerton, and others pursue the great chair in chenille and wool. Grandmama goes out daily in the Bath Chair for the Autumn is a lovely one. Dearest Mama does nothing in particular but everything for the comfort of others. Great thoughts about dresses for St Chads where I am to hold a plate at the Infirmary Meeting, Papa being Treasurer this year but not well enough he thought to act. Mr Burton took all the responsibilities for him and appointed me one of the ladies. Dearest Tilly offered to take me and be chaperone and they said unless on the score of health I could make no excuse.*

Sunday 11th November - *Grandmama announced her intention of going to Warwick. The morning beautifully fine, I to church here. Grandmama quite knocked up when evening came.*

Monday 12th November - *I left by the half past 10 train. Grandmama in bed. The first journey quite alone. At Stafford the confusion awful, expected to be sent to Liverpool or back to Birmingham or on to Shrewsbury or anywhere but right. I put myself and luggage under the guard's care and sat in the ladies' waiting room with my feet on the fender and my eyes on the luggage far off high and dry on the other side of the platform, a black bag and a new black portmanteau. Got safe to Wellington, found dearest Matilda and Hughes waiting for me. My tent pitched at the Chesnuts[19] in very short time where we found Mr & Mrs Edwards[6] come to call. Papa pretty well. Brought down pink satin for dinner. Mary Owen and Hugh[3] staying in the house. They want me to go to the Hunt Ball, Mary and Tilly had heard about it - the latter as if she did not wish to go but would go if I liked.*

Wednesday 14th November - *I had been to see Papa and coming back found Mrs John Pritchard had persuaded Papa that we ought to go to the Ball, that it would be regarded as an affront if we did not, that he would write for a Ball dress from Mrs Preacher to be sent to 'The Raven' by Friday morning, that she would go to Papa and make him write to Mr B? or tickets for us. I felt quite petrified and sick and was sure Papa did not like it, also that the dress could not be had. Mary Owen[3] took the white satin skirt to Shrewsbury to be covered with white tulle for she like the rest of us thought it next to impossible to get the London one. Mary[9] left to go by the train to join Mrs Owen at Shrewsbury. She is come to go to the Ball with Mary and Tuesday being appointed a Thanksgiving day for the abatement of the Cholera, Ball and Infirmary Meeting had to be put off one day and Mrs Owen to spend it in Shrewsbury. I went with Mr & Mrs John Pritchard a ride round the Ercall, I on Sentinel, for I grieve to say that Gazelle has taken to bad ways and comes down. She must go back to Mr Lawford they say. She has grown the ugliest shape in the world with a straight shoulder.*

Wednesday 15th November *- The Thanksgiving day. Went to breakfast with Papa then to church with Matilda and Abraham. In the evening quite late we set out for Shrewsbury, I feeling very frightened. Found Mrs Owen there and Mary and Hugh*[3] *and Hugh Owen Wilson. We had a room to ourselves however - Mrs Owen is very magnificent.*

Friday 16th November *- I felt as frightened as if I were going to be married. Went about 11 to the church, waited until after 12 and after, all the gentlemen going to the Infirmary to join the procession with the Mayor and Corporation the Treasurer and the Bishop. We were put into the Vestry with a good fire and a good luncheon which Gunter had supplied and there came all the ladies in the county - Lady Newport*[10] *looking very elegant and lovely among them. It was rather awkward to know nobody but I did not much mind it. Now the dresses - Matilda's was blue and white striped silk gown, a brown velvet mantlet very rich, and a blue velvet bonnet and feather. Mine a violet and green dress with large pearl buttons, a green mantle that fitted in a lovely manner and trimmed with miniver, a white terry velvet bonnet and honiton veil and feathers and inside were green feathers. At last all being in church Mr Burton introduced me to Lady Leighton*[11] *and to Mr Rocke. Her supporter was Mr Algernon Heber Percy*[12] *of Hodnet. We walked in state into the church with white wands on each side of us. Mr Yardley read the evening service and then the Bishop preached an excellent sermon. Then we four walked out as we had been walked in and were set upon two little raised steps with a comfortable mat to stand upon. Lady Leighton on the right and I on the left each of our gentlemen holding a silver plate in which we held a finger.*

Then the crowd passed out, Mr Rocke was quite unselfpossessed, I soon began to enjoy it. We had men with wands beyond us holding larger plates into which ours were emptied when full. The Vestry was so full that we went into another room to count our money. In the Vestry were an immense number, Mrs Egremont and Janet among the rest. I had to taste the Tankard, proclaim the sum £335, and then set off, the horses looking very pretty and the bells ringing. It was a lovely day. We dined altogether at 6 - Mrs Owen, Hugh and Mary,[13] *HE Wilson and ourselves.*

About 11, the dress having come and the tickets, we started for the Ball. it is a pretty sight, the Hunt Ball, that very simple unornamented room and lighted with little candles, and then the pretty women so well dressed. Lady Scaham was in blue gauze with diamonds in her hair and round her neck. They were very large and fastened on black velvet. I danced with Mr Rocke of course, then with Hugh Owen and then came up Mr Edgerton Jeffreys for a quadrille - he took me down to Supper. After the second quadrille I was standing by Abraham, having set Hugh Owen free to find out a certain fair Miss Ripley who had caught his eye and fancy, when Lord F[14] *came up and made Abraham introduce him. The crowd had rather dispersed and it cleared away further leaving a wide half moon - I should have been frightened if anyone had told me I should be standing in the middle of the Hunt Ball talking to Lord F*[14] *the observed of all the observers, the handsomest man of his time, or one of them. He congratulated me on the Collection, asked who Mr Rocke was, said the ladies are much wiser now than ten years ago when he used to attend Infirmary Meetings and they then wore evening dresses to stand at the door. He admired the music at the church and the Bishop's sermon, but that was a thought too long. I asked after the Queen Dowager,*[15] *he said Lord Howe had written him word that she could not live long, said she was an excellent person, a good woman, he said, no doubt, it was very well she had lasted over the Infirmary Meeting. He asked after Papa and after some other things. I left him thinking he was more likely to speak to me again if I did not bore him. He left I think soon after. He is very handsome and with no disagreeable expression of face. Very graceful in manner, perhaps affectedly so. I think his impediment in speaking is not at all embarrassing, he minds it evidently so little. To bed and to sleep, late enough next morning when we were obliged to get up for very hunger. Mary Owen wore a cerise coloured satin with lace, Irish lace, an antique Berthe on a greek cap with pearls - she looked very handsome, the gentlemen of the Hunt said it was a fancy dress and disapproved of it accordingly. Mrs Owen*[13] *was still more so - blue satin trimmed with antique lace and blue satin hat and a great many diamonds not the most brilliant, she looked very handsome, that is an encore; and danced much with an old love, Bulkeley Owen. Saturday, what remained of it, was spent with Papa.*

Sunday 18th November - *To church and to the school where they have a Mrs Wilson now, who I like not.*

Monday 19th November - *We went to call at Wroxeter - a very good move and very unpleasant as such good moves often are. I felt quite sick as I got near, I remembered how I had been blamed, how it was said I had made Mr & Mrs Egremont quarrel, until the very sheep seemed to look at me from among the turnips with faces indignant that I should venture into that country again. Mr Egremont was extremely gracious, rather perhaps amused, and Mrs Egremont quite her most delightful. They were alone at first, with Mr Barnabas Maude staying in the house, the Queen's Coll. man and he who was prisoner at Verdun.*

Then came in Mrs and Miss Thursby and the renowned Fanny Anne, Miss Hardinge. The Egremonts had a Fanny Hardinge, a cousin of the fair celebrity staying with them, a handsome girl and very agreeable. Then came Mrs and Miss Owen, and the room filled almost. Janet laughed crimson between amusement of the levée her Mama was holding and that the Thursby's should call when we did (we for the first time since that memorable day -, when it is all over now) also perhaps she laughed that the two girls thrown by the Papa as a fine fortune at the Archdeacon's head, should both be in the room together. We had to call at Severn House[17] *and Dale House,*[18] *found Mary able to sit up.*

Came home after dusk. I went in to Papa, put on the ball dress for him to see it, then put it safe way. Got some things I wanted, locked everything up.

Packed up at the Chesnuts[19] *and Tuesday the 20th got up at 4 and set off with Abraham and Henry Dickinson as far as Birmingham. Then on alone to Leamington. Found Grandmama very ill.*

Wednesday 21st November - *Mr Bolton called in Dr Jefferson, both seem to have a bad opinion.*

Monday 26th November - *Grandmama is a very wonderful person indeed. I believe that although not yet allowed to leave her bed, that she is recovering as fast as possible. They feared inflammation of the bowels and applied a blister and turpentine embrocation and she is cured. Mr Bolton brought his pretty wife to see us today, a friend of Mrs Hartshorne's. I have been riding with Edgerton round Stoneleigh, a lovely day it was but bitterly cold.*

Wednesday 28th November - *Mr & Mrs Egremont called, very gracious. He is here to consult Mr Jones and certainly does look ill. Jephson gives all his patronage to Mr Jones. Walked back to the station with them. So cold that the steeple chase is put off. Mrs Egremont asked me to go with her to the January Ball, think it won't be possible - besides, I ought to dance better.*

Thursday 29th November - *Call from Mrs Oddie who is here again and means to bring her husband, then a long walk with Marianne Fisher. Cold but pleasant. She is a nice person and we have wonderful sympathy in our religious views. She joined the church about 10 years ago. She disliked the Quakers very much as I did from not being able to reconcile their rejection of the "ordinances" with the New Testament. Lady Corbett sent for me as I was resting myself very happily in the twilight and in 5 minutes Sir Arthur Brooke walked in. She introduced us and was half merry and half angry about some Miss Piggott who had been teasing her and Sir Arthur for money to build a church. Then poor Miss Lyster and her horrid squint, then a good many jokes at Sir Arthur's expense, how he could be so often at Leamington among so many young ladies and be a bachelor yet. He parried the jokes without taking much notice of them, but seemed rather on thorns as to what her ladyship would say next and no wonder. All this was very droll. She had no suspicion we ever had met before and I don't know that he was certain of my identity, and yet he soon talked to me as I were not a stranger.*

Friday 30th November - *Met Mrs Andrews and Lady Corbett and Sir Arthur all together - oh, it was a wet dirty day. I had on my green velvet mantlet and miniver which Hall was keeping away from the wheels of Lady Corbett's Bath Chair, and she turning me round to see it.*

Monday 3rd December - *Dear Mama went home leaving me not a little overwhelmed at the responsibilities of housekeeping. Went with her to the train, called upon Miss Fisher, called at Reeves and heard of the death of the Queen Dowager*[15] *- long expected but yet sorrowful for how few has this earth to lose so good as she was. I settled the accounts and Mr Bolton came and I wrote a good report in the evening to Mama.*

Tuesday 4th December - *Called up at 5 - Grandmama very ill and Mr Bolton sent for. He ordered fomentations to the bowels but gave me little hope, wished Mama sent for at once. We waited for the half past 10 train. Grandmama poor thing quite gave herself up, only longed to see Mama. I was at my wits end but thought of Procter who promised to go and Mr Bolton and I sat with our feet on the drawing room fender waiting the result, by 7 o'clock she was more free from pain. He went away, I sent the maidens to their breakfast and sat down by Grandmama's fire to write to Mama if Proctor required credentials - She grew quieter and was asleep on Mary's return. Mr Bolton came about 9 and gave every hope if the pain could be kept away. He was most kind and attentive, he came 5 times that day.*

Wednesday 5th December - *Poor Grandmama went on somewhat improving, of course we were still very anxious about her. Mr B*[16] *and I sat up talking, I told him all about our changes of religion and he told me how he hated his profession at the beginning. He knew the Grants, admires Anne, and is Sir Charles Knightley's cousin. Mr Craig has much improved him he says, he does not think he was fit for the church in his young days tho' he would like it now.*

Thursday 6th December - *Grandmama so much better that I went out to ride with Edgerton. Think I never enjoyed anything so much as that good shake after some days nursing and bad weather. Mrs Bolton called very amicably, then Mrs Oddie and then Mr B. I had met Mrs Andrews and found where she is staying.*

Friday 7th December - *Mrs Oddie came to tea with me. I required a little generalship to keep Grandmama in her room one more day.*

Saturday 8th December - *Very wet. Mrs Oddie came for me about 12 and we went to Mrs Torre's, she is a great lady here for dancing and deportment. There is hardly a great lady in the neighbouring counties they say who has not been under her care for finishing, but she was out, said Miss Torre and am to call on Monday. Then went on to the Miss Morrices to call on Mrs Andrews.*

NOTES

1. Osborne Gordon was a native of Broseley. He was making a name for himself in religious affairs at Oxford.
2. General and Mrs Davison were the tenants of Stanley Hall, near Bridgnorth, soon to be the home of Alfred and Rebecca Darby. See note 7 below.
3. Mary Owen was the wife of Hugh Darby Owen, who was a cousin of Adelaide.
4. Mrs Grant who died on 20th April was no doubt a relative of Adelaide's grandparents.
5. Mr Edward Edwards, the surgeon who lived in Coalbrookdale.
6. Probably Mr Joseph Robinson who was a business acquaintance of Abraham's from Liverpool, and also a partner in the Ebbw Vale Works.

7. See note 2 above. The letting of Stanley Hall to Alfred Darby was a severe blow to Abraham. The Chesnuts where he lived was becoming too small for his collection of paintings and his library and music room.
8. Admaston Spa, north of Wellington, Shropshire was built in the late 18th century as a health resort and a place to "take the waters". It is now a residential development.
9. Probably Mary Darby of Dale House.
10. Lady Newport of Weston Hall, Shropshire, seat of the Earl of Bradford.
11. Lady Leighton of Loton Park.
12. Algernon Heber Percy of Hodnet Hall. At the time of the publication of this book, his descendant the present Algernon Heber Percy is the Lord Lieutenant of Shropshire.
13. The Mrs Owen referred probably Mary Owen (née Darby), widow of Rev Pryce Owen and mother of Hugh Owen and mother-in-law of Mary, Hugh's wife. H.E. Wilson was a relative of theirs.
14. Lord F was presumably Lord Forester.
15. No doubt the Queen Dowager was Queen Caroline, widow of William IV who had died in 1837.
16. Presumably Mr Bolton.
17. Severn House (now the Valley Hotel, Ironbridge) was the home of Henry Dickinson and Deborah (née Darby), sister of Abraham Darby IV.
18. Dale House, built in 1717 by Abraham Darby I was situated close to the Coalbrookdale works. It was the home of Lucy Darby (née Burlingham) and her daughter Mary, sister of Abraham Darby IV.
19. The Chesnuts, situated below the White House and the Deer Park, was the home of Abraham Darby IV and his wife Matilda, sister of Adelaide.

Henry Whitmore (1813-76), of Apley, Shropshire, married Adelaide Darby on 15th April 1852. He was the youngest of three brothers (see the Whitmore family tree, page 333). He succeeded his eldest brother, Thomas Charleton Whitmore as MP for Bridgnorth, Shropshire that same year. He remained as MP for Bridgnorth until he resigned in 1870. He had been Lord of the Treasury in Lord Derby's second and third administrations from 1858-59 and from 1866-68.

1850

Comment

This was a pivotal year in Adelaide's life. Her father, Francis Darby died on 20th March and it was this event which sparked what was described by Matilda (Adelaide's elder sister) as "a very painful family affair". Francis died intestate and by all accounts he did so deliberately in order to ensure that his estate would be divided equally between his two daughters, in accordance with law.

There has to be some conjecture as to how this situation arose, but some facts are known. Instructions for the making of a Will had been given to Mr Potts, the family's solicitor, in Broseley. These instructions have survived and are attached to this account (see Appendix A, p.277). We also know that these instructions were made between 1845 and 1850 because the paper on which the instructions were written was water marked 1848. The Will if it had been executed would have transferred Francis' landed estate to Francis' widow, Hannah, and to Adelaide for their joint lives, thus excluding Matilda the elder daughter. The existence of these instructions was disclosed to Matilda after Francis' death and Matilda was "thunderstruck".

The circumstances surrounding the preparation of the "Will" are not known but what is known is that Francis refused to sign it after it had been engrossed for signature and simply asked the solicitor for his bill. He told "several persons that he could not make a Will, and that the law would make a better Will for him than he could do for himself" (letter from Matilda to her uncle, probably Richard Darby, sent in March/April 1851[1]). The first question is whether he was influenced by someone else! This was certainly raised at the time, and although there is no direct evidence, the finger points, almost beyond doubt, to Hannah, Francis' wife. Certainly, Adelaide knew of the making of the "Will", and, although she disclaimed knowledge of its contents, she certainly knew that the intention was that she would be the principal beneficiary. It must have been a considerable disappointment when Francis died intestate. Adelaide realised that she would have to lower her sights in the marriage market down to the "second rate gentry" (Journal, 8th May, p.267 and note 6, p.274). However despondent Adelaide may have felt at that time, she reckoned without her truly formidable, manipulative and ruthless mother.

Adelaide's Journal for 1850 gives scant information about the events which took place in the next six months or so. Fortunately, Matilda placed the sequence of events on record in an account which she set out at Stoke Court, Buckinghamshire, where she was then living, on 4th and 5th October 1852. This contains a coherent and entirely credible description of what occurred after Francis' death. An extract from this account is attached as Appendix B, p.278).

After the disclosure of the "Will", Mr Potts the solicitor struggled to come up with a division of the property which would be acceptable to the parties involved. One of these seemed eminently fair under which Matilda received the Sunniside estate and Adelaide received the Hay estate above Coalport. This was what Francis Darby expected would happen and would have provided a solution to Abraham IV's urgent need for a larger property than the Chesnuts. Sunniside which had been empty for some 30 years, was a large and prestigious house and would have suited Abraham's status as the Manager of the Coalbrookdale Company.

Despite this, Hannah Darby who would have received a life interest in The White House was awkward to the last, and made it clear that her tenure of The White House was going to make life difficult if not impossible for Abraham and Matilda on the adjoining Sunniside (see Appendix B, p.292). Thoroughly needled, Matilda (foolishly and unwisely) threw in the sponge and Abraham and she decided to leave Coalbrookdale to the horror and consternation of the inhabitants of the Dale, and very much to the detriment of the Coalbrookdale Company.

Once again Hannah Darby had demonstrated her unwillingness to accept the due process of the law. In 1843 she refused to accept the terms of her father's Will (see p.142). This time she flaunted her husband's known intentions and substituted her own views very much to her own benefit and above all to the benefit of Adelaide who emerged the clear victor out of the whole distasteful and "very painful family affair".

Wednesday 2nd January - *Lady Corbett came for the evening and was quite her most agreeable, and Thursday Matilda and Abraham left us. It was the most prosperous visit. They were truly kind and did not seem to miss the many omissions - quite couleur de rose all the time, and then, few know how fascinating they can be.*

Sunday 13th January - *Letter from Matilda. She had had a call from Archdeacon Beresford, and Captain Russell, and the Archdeacon had asked after me and expressed himself convinced of my attachment to him!! and she had advised him to think no more about the young lady, and he had said perhaps it might be wiser but when judgment and inclination are at variance it is difficult to be wise. Then he went back to our Leighton interviews and seemed to me to have much misrepresented them - he put the interviews after the refusals and I felt really angry, after such bitter letters on both sides it was so unexpected that he should thus appear again as if nothing had happened. Captain Russell went to order the carriage when the Archdeacon began. I went to church very* *sick and miserable. Miss Fletcher's friendship is now very useful and we have met daily and this afternoon I went with her to her seat.*

Monday 14th January *- Letter from Mrs Egremont from her bed - ill with a bad cold, "At every turn you may expect to see." In the evening Sontay's concert. I went with a nice party - Mrs Moriarty was chaperone. Miss Fisher, Miss Card, and Mr Henry Fisher. We were early, the fear of the Archdeacon rather spoiling the delights of "Rode's Variations" and "Home Sweet Home". Sontay had had a bad cold, caught in the snowstorms in Scotland. As I was passing out Mr Beresford came up to me, and at his second question "How long have you been in Leamington?" I gently impelled Mr Fisher into the passage room, there was a great crowd which was enough apology. We had lost our party and he said, "Won't you go back and wait while I find the carriage?" I said, "I'll wait here, but where is Mrs Moriarty?" How thankful I was to see her. Mr Beresford did not attempt to follow.*

Friday 18th January *- A most disagreeable week notwithstanding Mama came on Wednesday. Archdeacon Beresford called on Tuesday morning and I had given special orders for him not to be admitted, the stupid servants told him I should be at home at 2 but engaged, so he called then and said "I know Miss Darby is engaged but I will wait." Grandma said "Let him come in." He came and when she had finished desert she walked away for her nap bidding me stay where I was!! He was in great spirits I almost think now that he thought he could carry all his own way and need not hurry. He said, "How much that picture is like you, you were naughty to send it back." I said, "You are very good not to be offended at it."*

Wednesday 6th February *- The MC Ball. I went to the Vaughton's to dinner at 7. There was a nice party of 13. Lady Corbett and Mr & Mrs Vincent Corbett, Mr Knightly and Miss Richmond, Mr Fazackerly and Mr Burton. Afterwards came the three Miss Burtons to whose party I could not go. Miss Tollemache in pink and lilies of the valley. At 11, Lady Corbett's Whist was persuaded to end and we went to the Ball. I danced about 7 times - it was more than I expected, knowing no-one and having been very busy all the week with Mrs Tone I managed very well, but Polkas are trying and Gallops more so. The music was good, or at least tolerable, the ladies were very nicely dressed and Major Hopkins looked very happy. Robert Vaughton danced twice with me and Mr Fazackerly and Mr Pritchard the heir of Wroxted Abbey, there was a Mr Middleton too - I did not know the names of the others but Sir Arthur told Lady Corbett the next morning that I had very good partners all the evening. We came away about 3 in the morning. I don't think I ever enjoyed a Ball so much nor assuredly ever had such a headache next day. I was introduced to Miss Glasgow and we made a compact to ride together. Thursday morning we all went round by Stoneleigh, and a charming ride it was. Miss Glasgow took her groom and it was very pleasant. She rides very well but most ungracefully. Lady Corbett* *sent for me there and I was much amused, there was Mr Hobson and a Mr Acton afterwards - very amusing. Mr Acton had been to a wedding that morning, therefore, was not at the ball last night. Lady Corbett said that she never knew that people might not go unless they were going to be married themselves.*

Monday 11th February - *Mama had yesterday a Summons home to do the honours at the house for Mr Hartshorne and she obeyed it this morning. Afterwards I went to Mrs Tone and at night I went with Mrs & Miss Vaughton to the Ball, the last before Lent. I enjoyed it very much. Was introduced to Lady Wale who introduced me to her daughter. I danced with her son a very handsome young officer in the Navy but rather stupid in the Polka. Plenty of partners after that. Mr Pritchard asked me to dance again, with Mr Glasgow three times! the Polka with him is very easy. There was a small Mr Golightly who the Miss Burtons introduced to me. I was obliged to go away without the Polka he asked for. I made grand progress with these young ladies who promised to call again. Robert Vaughton was not there, he is really ill. Yesterday we walked to Lillington Church, the three Glasgows, Miss Vaughton and her brother and me - returned over the fields and styles. The Ball night there was a wonderful meteor - fiery red with a blue tail, burst after a course from west to north with a noise like thunder about a quarter to 11. Of course we were just arriving at the ball and heard nothing of it.*

Wednesday 20th February - *Lady Corbett and Mrs & Miss Vaughton came here, very sociable, quiet and pleasant, people are very good natured.*

Thursday 23rd February - *Mrs Vaughton came in - "Will you go to Lady Wales," she said, "she has just asked me to take you on Wednesday." I said I should be very happy.*

Monday 25th February - *What a nasty tiresome ugly world this is - Lady Corbett and Mrs Vaughton won't let me go to Lady Wales. This is how it is - Lady Corbett sent for me after dinner, Mrs Vaughton was there. I sat down in my place on the stool at her feet and Lady Corbett began. "This is an awkward business. You mustn't be huffed," said Mrs Vaughton, "It's just what I'd say to my own daughter. Lady Wales has been asking both of us so many questions about you that she must have some reason for it -"what is her father?" "He's an Iron King," said Mrs Vaughton. "Has she brothers, no," and to Lady Corbett "She'll have a great fortune, won't she" "Now," said Lady Corbett, "you are not a child but you are here without your own mother, and that old lady's not better than nothing and therefore, tho' you may consider us impertinent, we've had no sleep all night about you, and we've decided to warn you." Well, I said I was very much obliged to them, but need I stay away from the party? No, Lady Corbett said, not at all, go and enjoy yourself, she's among the best society here, make her useful, but don't be caught, she's got 9 children, some of them very well married. "One's married," said Mrs Vaughton, "the 2nd son's engaged to a Miss Prest, and the 3rd, who you danced with, is I think meant for you -*

oh, if you like him, I've nothing to say but that he's of good family and in the first society, he looks soft but that's nothing you know, but he's got nothing, he's in the Navy." "I wish he was with his ship, said Lady Corbett, "I would not have you marry such a tribe for anything, the Cormorants." "We are going to look for Sir John Franklin," and I am to go to Lady Corbett. "Gracious no, you're to stay at home with Lady Wales and keep all the family, where would your father be I should like to know, why the woman asked me about your father's fortune and I said how can I tell you? Mr Darby knows his own property, I don't, and then she calls you my protegee. "I hope it's true, Lady Corbett." "What can an old woman like me do for you, my poor child. I love you for your Mother's sake and old Granty there." "Well, we only wanted to warn you, now go and bring Mr L to see me." Mr L and I stayed until Sir Henry Broughton came in. A note from Lady Corbett, it seems she said "that's Miss Darby." "Why did he go," said Sir Henry Broughton. I should like to have asked her about my relations at Liscombe - your protegee Miss Darby who's to marry a Mr Wale, I'm told!!!

Today she sent for me - "Mrs Wale wants me to take it all on myself, but however she says you'd better not go." "Very well, I'll just do what you tell me." "Sir Henry Broughton is in the Wale set and therefore this report originates there, you had better not be seen at Lady Wale's if you wish to crush the story." I said it's so very disagreeable. "It is my dear, and very hard too that you may not go and enjoy yourself, you're old enough to judge." "Must I call?" "Leave your card, don't ask for Lady Wale, but say to the servants - 'be good enough to give this to Lady Wale', don't go in, she would ask you why you can't go, if you don't go." I left the card and went to Mrs Vaughton she is very ill, I fear. "I wouldn't go, I think, if I was you." Went home and found a small note of invitation - "Miss Darby presents her compliments to Lady Wale with thanks for her polite invitation, and she regrets that an unexpected invitation prevents her the pleasure of accepting it," - sent this note this morning, Tuesday. Lady Corbett says I have done quite right, "Whatever you do, dear, you do well." (what a mistake) "I feel a great interest in you, I pray that you may marry well and as you have a right to do, God bless you, do nothing till your Mother comes, I wouldn't have you tied to the tail of a regiment for the world" - what did she mean?

Friday 8th March - *The Ball at Lady Wale's. Went with Emma Vaughton and the Croxton Johnstones. There were 140 people, 4 rooms beautifully arranged, music and singing first, then dancing. I had danced 2 or 3 quadrilles the last with Mr GM - we were sitting after it when Mr Doyne came in, I was so glad to see him, a polka and to the refreshment room where Mr GW followed - he seemed to have the organ of ubiquity and to be so amazed at Mr Doyne who Irish-man like came up like an old friend. Dr & Mrs Arnold were agreeable very. Tea and coffee first in a back drawing room where we put one's sorties-de-bal and arranged our hair, found Mrs Pritchard there and plusieurs autres. Then upstairs, the front drawing room for music and dancing, the back* *for cards. When we went downstairs the looking glass and toilette was gone the folding doors thrown open and a beautiful supper laid out.*

Wednesday 20th March - *Went to church in the morning. It was a beautiful sermon by Dr Young concluding his discourses on the book of Jonah. Jonah's impatience and love of creature comfort is so like that of every sinner still, in the afternoon I was so profoundly happy expecting Mama and Matilda. Mrs Moriarty was going from home the Monday following and therefore we agreed to walk and I to return and go in a clarendon carriage to the station. How particularly happy we were! Great Heaven, that mortals should be so particularly among roses when just on the eve of the most unexpected blow. I ran into the house fearing that I was late, the carnage had been sent away they said. "Oh, then" I said, "Mrs Darby will soon be here. "No, she was not coming." "Oh, why" "There was bad news". Phoebe seemed not capable of telling me a word more, Mrs Procter, good and excellent woman, was wringing her hands and crying, I ran almost into her arms "Your husband is ill?" I said - no - then Lady Corbett? - no, but your butler is come and Mrs Abraham's maid .... my father, my poor Father, upon whose life we had counted as likely to last for years - he was dead! not ill, not so ill that I was to hasten back and receive his last blessing, but dead, - dead -never to speak to me again! I remember fainting almost and then summoning all my strength to go and tell my poor Grandmama! How she teased me poor thing all that long evening with incessant questions about herself - what was to be done with her and where would she go, the letters I was compelled to write for we had engagements thick and thronging for that week, then the packing and arranging which Leonard did all the practical part and then the journey so long and cold and dreadful! It is not to be described. Abraham sent his carriage for me, very kind Abraham whom I first met in our home of which he who had always been so pre-eminently the head and the guiding spirit was now gone forever! And how my dearest Mother fell into my arms and wept, as we both did bitterly yet not as those without hope! The shock had been tremendous to all, I found, except the Doctors, they suspected Angina Pectoris which he suffered so persistently was not dangerous to life and was indeed lessening. The body - oh, how beautiful in death, was already placed in the shell and rested on the carved bed in which he once took such a pride, and the gorgeous velvet hangings and solemn darkness of the room accorded well with our feelings of what he had loved in life.*

But the sweet expression of that face in death is not to be told, nor the beauty of the features for indeed we hardly knew how handsome he had been. How day succeeded day, sorrowful and sad and people called and we ate and drank and wrote letters to all with the most mechanical feeling of misery and poor Mama sat in such quiet so resigned and yet so desolate, and the poor dog who would go to no-one but her and looked at us all as interlopers. So we went on until the funeral the 26th March, a Tuesday.

The morning came beautiful and we were all ready. There were throngs of people and for the last time we stood round that coffin and shed bitter tears of almost a first sorrow, the first true desolation made by death amongst us. How beautiful he looked, they had taken a cast of his face the day before, there was change but that beautiful look was not gone -never was to go out of our hearts and memories. The snow fell and kept falling, falling till it was so deep so slippery. My Uncles and Abraham said we must not go and we went not. I am not sure that it made the trial any greater to me, I knew that all would be done as well and solemnly if I were not there. I am not sure but that women are best away - we went not. We sat by the fire all three in bitter sorrow of heart yet not hopeless, no - with the fullest sense of the rest and happiness of him who was gone -Requiescat in pace.

They said there were about 2,000 people notwithstanding the weather. The Doctors, 3 clergymen and gentlemen walked first and then the clerks, house servants I think, the coffin, then the the relations who all returned to dinner. We were spared, how cold it was. Mr Bassett was there! Mr Lawford was with us also, Mr Edmonds, Mr Gwyther and Mr Jettar - the 3 clergymen went to the meeting afterwards. Mr Crooks[2] *arranged all. Keppel, Lord Forester's groom of the chambers, came with Carpenters to help waiting.*

Tuesday 9th April *- After the funeral came callers - oh, that is a misery, and yet from some and especially the clergymen a sort of consolation! The Egremonts were kind and Mr Edmonds very and the Anstices too in their way, and Mr & Mrs John Pritchard. There is no Will so everything is divided in three.*[3] *Letter from Mary Owen, she is going to many a Mr Colmore - I fear good in money only - sent his picture, handsome certainly.*

Thursday 1st May *- Miss Lawford wrote word that she could stay with Grandmama no longer than the 25th so on the 23rd I went to Leamington, odd what a chapter of distress it was. I dreamed of .... strange! his beautiful eyes looked so happy and so amused! Strange! that I knew so well by experience that dreaming of him bodes no good that I came down to breakfast thinking something disagreeable would happen. At the station met John Edwards,*[4] *went together to Stafford. Abraham had been to Shrewsbury and got out of the train. "Going fishing" said he, looking at a rod and line. Very fast we talked, and he told me of the Miss Dugard affair. He left at the Trent Valley line and I thought no more of him. I had Edwards, who does not know much about travelling, he took a wrong ticket and then encountering my Uncle Dickinson at Birmingham full of the sorrow of a young French lady, he set Edward to take care of her boxes and par consequence one of mine went on to London! Awful was the trouble! and I gave it up and wrote to Madame who put a dress in train for the Sunday, box came the following day, ditto a letter from JE full of sorrow that he had not come with me and sent a message (to his brother who was in waiting at Wolverhampton) by the Telegraph. I wrote playfully I believe to thank him.*

Miss Lawford propounded that she could stay till Monday - all arranged. Edward arrived again to recall me there was plate to divide.[5] *Oh, what a wretched business, how difficult to please people and behave right and how I stumble from one dilemma to another heaven knows, caring no more for the plate than pewter in comparison with keeping peace, but that was not to be. Back on Monday, this time with my Uncle Richard Darby and Aunt Maria. Edward lost nothing this time. Tuesday morning put Miss Lawford on the train and saw her off and the Vincent C's also. Rich is come to the Leamington station. Got back to find Mr Grant with Grandmama - merger of Tythes to sign he very agreeable, talked of Lord John, Sir Charles Napier, the landed interest, the Navy and free trade without country.*

Wednesday cruel cold letter from the people among the spoons at home, one would think I had done very wrong and wickedly.[5] *Wrote to Abraham as well as I could, finished a letter to Mama and there came one from John Edward - didn't come to see L, but to see me, oh, Heavens, such a pretty letter. Well, I thought it best to send no answer, could get no advice. Almost wish I had asked Lady Corbett but thought she would think me a fool. Went to her this evening and she is going to Lady Wale's who had asked her to bring any friend and Lady Corbett. Talked to me about what a prize I am until I was so sick I wonder I did not think it prudent to carry small basin into the Drawing room where I went to solace myself with the May number of Copperfield.*

Wednesday 8th May - *Yesterday a letter from Mrs Egremont - the Archdeacon Beresford is going to be married, clever, rich and 10 years his junior. "He rated at your rejection even in that" said Mrs Egremont. This was good news, good enough to make me happy for all that day. By the second post a letter from JEB - Did I remember that silence gives consent according to the adage and was he so to interpret having no reply. It was a botheration, but I wrote at night, I trust amiably - I trust not so amiably that he might say in future days he did not know what to understand by it. Mrs J Sparling called and Mr Howard, I was gone to inspect some caskets at Brights for Mary Owen, chose one. Mrs Sparling PPC she leaves tomorrow so I went today - not at home. The world looks very desolate especially after a wet cold day and when one has a headache. But marrying JEB could not alter it much, a house of my own, that would be a comfort, on a small scale though. Very likely a pretty garden, very likely in Shropshire, but it would be a position of the second rate gentry hardly better than my own, I think not quite as good. Then the man, good natured but a bore, not a quiet bore like Joe Bailey who he resembles in some points but a noisy rattling bore rather addicted to talking of himself, I don't think I should be happy with him and I don't think he would attract bright spirits to his house. As the world goes at present it would be easy enough for me to marry a man of small means when I really know what my own position is to be, c'est a dire, if I don't find it an agreeable one. We are in a dark valley now. Oh, to be able to please Abraham and Matilda.*[6]

Monday 14th May - *To the fair I have been!! With Miss Fisher and Miss Croker and met there the Burtons in great force, Mr Spooner and some naval officers - affair with Mr Spooner about some forget-me-nots at Mr Harris's, how hungry we were. Well, after all it was not so bad, there were three carriages full from Stoneleigh and a great many handsome carriages. Everybody in the county and everybody from Leamington. Mrs Willoughby and Mr Frank in windows opposite, the pretty Miss Richmond ditto bowing and smiling and Mr Knightley down in the street grave and annoyed and Mr Bowen with his family and his spectacles in a fly. Then the procession!! - Queen Elizabeth and Lord Leicester and Guy Earl of Warwick in full armour, Henry VIII in black hat and diamonds and feathers. Two Britannias in chariots with Tridents and sailors and emblems of all nations, "Odd fellows and banners, "Foresters" and banners and a capital Robin Hood and Friar Tuck and Little John, all such merrie men in green with black velvet hats and bugles in their belts. Then the forest of Robin Hood and park adjoining travelling upon a char-a-banc which gave way and subsided for half an hour opposite our window adding much to the fine scenic effect. The forest contained a stuffed fox and a live Robin Hood 6 years old and the park a small live shepherd and shepherdess, 2 live lambs and a live dog all reposing on green moss happy and pretty and 2 large stuffed deer. Then followed the Bear and ragged staff the Leicester Arms, and a live bear but a failure, the poor thing walked and was tired. A man carried the staff. After Robin Hood went a train of dogs among them Oscar. There were 5 bands of music, that of the 17th, from Weedon the best Infantry band in the service, and then to behold the Warwickshrie Yeomanry, how they were passing quickly the prostrate forest and park and how the same began to move being mended and how the horses being astonished thereat began to plunge and to kick to the terror of the beholders on the pavement, to the admiration of beholders from windows. Then the Pavilion for the evening Ball. The glory of going thro' the cattle fair and the dust thereof oh, my unfortunate crape - I am dusty still and going to be washed and put myself to bed.*

Wednesday 22nd May - *Mama came bringing Mary Blodwell.*[7]

Saturday 1st June - *Abraham and Matilda arrived, Monday they took me to London and we stayed at the Victoria. Tuesday to Regent Street for shopping. In the evening the Overland route as a Diorama which was excellent. Wednesday the "Home and Colonial School" and a Review in Hyde Park, the Life Guards and the Marquess of Londonderry and Prince George of Cambridge and we ought to have seen the Nepalese Prince but didn't. Mary Owen is in town choosing wedding dress, left a note for me. Thursday called on Mary at 11, Dover Street. Hugh sent us to her at Clarke's in Regent Street, the dresses very pretty and the lace. Mrs Owen is recovering very well from the dreadful broken leg at Malvern, Coly not in London. We went then to the Exhibition and thence to the Medieval Art. At the first our taste was a little spoilt by Mr Wilson's Rubens and Greuses and Sebastian del Piombos and Coreggios. There* *was only one and that by Hanfield of the Witches and Macbeth to be cared about. Waterloo is very unpromising.*

Friday came away early - Took Abraham to the band in the evening, introduced him to Mrs Vaughton passed Mr Howard with a few words. Abraham liked the band.

Saturday 8th June - *Went to the Gardens, Mr Spooner. Abraham and Matilda left at half past 10.*

Monday 10th June - *Met Louise Burton in the gardens where we take the water very diligently. Appointed to meet in the afternoon. Went with Phoebe Lawford to Guy's Cliff. Then to the Gardens, then Lady Corbett and Miss Ashfield and Phoebe to tea. Tired by night.*

Tuesday 11th June - *Went to a wedding, Miss Mollineaux and Mr Arthur Mowbray to Chochrane. By the way, the Archdeacon is really married to a Mrs Bomford, she was a Miss Kennedy, all Irish, they were married in London where Mrs Egremont writes me word. Tom Maude and Mr & Mrs WM and the Tothills were there too on their way to the Rhine - and so we had many escapes. The Pritchards*[8] *were there also, also Mr Osborne Gordon.*[8]

Thursday 13th June - *There was a wedding at which appeared Major Edwards, Miss Chester was the bride and the Revd Mr Powles the bridegroom. The Major looks very young, very self possessed and very handsome. He was in full uniform and wears a beard right orientally. I think it was the day before this that I went to a flower show with the Vaughtons. Everybody was there, it was a wet day. Mr Glasgow was there with the band of his regiment the 4th Dragoon Guards. The Burtons were there with a host of men. Mr Howard was very stiff I thought, wonder what was the matter.*

Sunday 16th June - *The Fletchers are returned in great force. Mr & Mrs John Cooke and Mr Donnington Fletcher and Miss Anne called after church. Mr Fletcher is surpassingly handsome and rather agreeable. Walk with Miss Burton and Emma Vaughton in the afternoon. All the rest of the B's gone bodily to Ashow where Mr H. St. J.H. preaches. In the evening to the Parish Church with Phoebe Lawford who come to tea, and who thank heaven goes back to Leighton tomorrow.*

Friday 12th July - *We left Leamington, Abraham coming for us. Grandmama bore the journey wonderfully - at home very flat.*

Monday 5th August - *All are very busy about the new church which Abraham is to build and to endow and to appoint a clergyman, it really is fun hearing of their coming to be appointed and all failing. One is a wax doll with whiskers, another not enough of a gentleman and a third won't work. I should of all things like Mr Howard to have it but know alas that the very worst office I could do any man would be to recommend him. They say that we must divide the* *property one taking the Hay and the other the Sunniside property.*[9] *M advises me to choose this tho' she says it is against her own interest - it is much against mine, I think I would rather have the Hay.*

Wednesday 28th August - *Went to Abraham and Matilda to a flower show at Badger.*[10] *Met Miss Burton again there with Capt. Annesley also Mrs Thursby and Lily Egremont and the Pritchards and the Rowleys and the Vickers and all the world.*

Wednesday 4th September - *Commenced a strange scene in this strange little life of mine. Mama and I went, taking Sarah who is to be Grandmama's maid, to Leighton*[11] *to the old house. It was very uncomfortable and very cold. Until Thursday we were bien affairees among dust and old letters. The servants did not behave well, but then that was to be expected. Thank heaven to be well rid of the whole affair. Mr Bassett said by a clause in the Bank Articles that it was impossible to remove Grandmama from Leighton without withdrawing her name. Mr Grant came to our aid and it was put straight with a little plain speaking. Mr Lawford wants the old house. Flint will not let him have it. It is a lovely place yet I feel strangely little in the parting. It seems like closing a gloomy page in one's life history and I felt glad to turn to a more cheerful independent state of things where I could see more daylight. I think Mama feels the parting and the returning also to our changed home. We got home very early found Grandmama well, daily weaker in mind, and our kind invaluable Miss Lawford, very glad to see us and to be released from a post of no pleasant duty. The 7th September Mrs Alfred Darby produced a son and heir.*[12] *Great were the rejoicings. Just on our return Egginton had pitched his tent in which there was a dinner given to the men and a dance to the wives and daughters in the evening. There were fireworks from Vauxhall. Lord Newport and Col. Forester came to the dinner and made speeches and stayed and danced and Mr Stevens came and the Frank Tothills came with Rebecca all the way from Clifton. Mrs JB expecting a confinement some time.*

Tuesday 1st October - *Mr Pritchard gave a little fete at Astley,*[13] *very pretty in honour of the small heir of all this racket. The children of Lady Tyrwhitt's School had beef and pudding and beans in the evening. The child was brought in and held up to the assembled small people who gave three cheers, the brat did not cry nor diminish his dignity in the least. There was a handsome luncheon very and a host of people but Dale House*[19] *and Alfred and Severn House*[20] *and the Pritchards rather clung together, I was so glad to see Mrs Stevens and Charles Humphrey again. Astley Dingle is a sweet pretty place and we wandered in it very happily. Mr Stevens is unlike his wife rather shy and reserved and quiet.*

Wednesday 2nd October - *Lord Forester*[14] *and Lord Newport*[14] *having signified an intent of going over Abraham's farm and the Works and to come for him to the Chesnuts,*[21] *Matilda asked me to go and help her and I was very* *happy. Lord Newport is a quiet gentlemanly young man with reddish hair, some sense of his position, c'est a dire he has not the graceful popularity and manner of the Foresters. Lord Forester remembered me to my surprise, he said he had been ill or perhaps he would have come to the fete. He gave Matilda leave to drive through Willey to Stanley. He must have been divinely handsome at one time. It is not quite a happy face but an interesting one. The difficulty of understanding his accent is awful.*

Monday 14th October - *There came an invitation for Abraham, Matilda and I to Willey, also one from the Pritchards for the same day but luckily giving us the choice of two, it is to stay all night at Lord Forester's, and looks rather formidable.*

Tuesday 22nd October - *Mrs Treacher sent us some pretty additions to our mourning. At 7 we arrived at Willey ready dressed, the dressing bell had just rung and all were gone, Eppel said, we were dressed, and so waited in that beautiful library, how beautiful the hall was and all the place.*

Most of the things old but all in such excellent taste. Dr Rowley arrived first, then Lord Forester. There were Lady Suffield, Lady Charlotte and Mr Lyster, Lord John and Lord George Manners, Colonel Forester, and Mr & Mrs Jane and Lord & Lady Newport. Lady Newport takes the head of affairs. There was a small Mr Litchfield, not very agreeable. It was very pleasant and not so very formidable a second time and should not be afraid at all. Lord John Manners is rather handsome and infinitely clever. Colonel Forester handsome and rather agreeable. We had a round game very amusing. Lady Newport is very graceful and fascinating, not exactly pretty for a Forester. Colonel Forester took me in to dinner, Lord Newport Matilda. Lord Forester is very agreeable as far as he can or will speak. The next morning at breakfast how pretty everything looked. The men all went farming. Lady Charlotte departed to her room and Lady Newport and Lady Suffield and we were quite sociable and happy. Matilda and I left about 1 o'clock.

Friday 25th October - *Lord Newport left a note on his way to shoot, it was from Lady Newport to say that she and Lady Suffield would pay their little visit at Chesnuts*[21] *and about 4 o'clock they came. Lady Newport and the Marquis of Granby and Lord John Manners on horseback, Lady Suffield and Colonel Forester in a pony carriage and Mr & Mrs Bridgeman ditto. They stayed at the Chesnuts until quite dark looking at the pictures and various things. Lord Granby is very tall and not particularly handsome. Both brothers have much genius in their faces. Lady Newport was excessively pretty and graceful in a jim crow hat and feathers and what she called a pea jacket over her habit fitting close to the slightest and most elegant figure.*

Friday 22nd November - *The Pritchards and Ernestine de Satz came to luncheon here. The Pope has sent Dr Wiseman to England as Cardinal Archbishop of Westminster. The 5th November was celebrated in London as it* *had not been for ages. All the churches are ringing with denunciations of Popery and the land is in a ferment with meetings to protest against the Papacy.*

Wednesday 27th November - *The Du Gards were coming, but Grandmama was too ill. Mr Rowlands frightened us a good deal but she quite recovered soon. Letter from Mrs Oddie, some man of good fortune and position who was Sherriff of his County asks for an introduction to me - there is no name, one would not have thought that*

"Such motives to a pilgrimage,
A shrine like mine affords."

Wednesday 4th December - *Mama replied that she could say nothing upon such scanty information but that amiable qualities and good position sound well but she did not wish her daughter to marry unless it would add to her happiness in every way. I am very unhappy but marrying would not help it much. The division of Papa's land is a great difficulty. Mr Potts arranged the Works in 3, the debts in 3 and the land, for Matilda to have the Dale and I the Hay, and Matilda to make over to Mama a life interest in the White House and fields adjoining. Now Matilda has given it all up and it appears they thought the division unfair when I supposed this half to be so much the more valuable of the two that I dared not wish for it. indeed, indeed je suis malheureuse from not knowing at all how best to say what I wish done.*[15]

Thursday 5th December - *Mama and I asked to go to Severn House*[20] *but Mama does not go out yet and I could not, for Mrs Dugard and Gertrude were coming. They came, stayed till Saturday and it was pleasant very, a change of ideas. Scotch songs, new American plait and a new crochet edging. Abraham and Matilda not well.*

Monday 9th December - *Matilda came to say they were going out with Alfred looking at estates, Greyhurst etc. I think that I felt the least little bit disappointed. The estates themselves were a sorrow of mind to me because they might perhaps have remained here had things been different, then the old plan had been for me to go with them and they had put off one journey for me. It was like throwing me overboard handsomely with all the property which I know how to manage as much as a baby! Matilda and I had a walk, she said she felt defrauded of her rights but unable to keep them! Yet, as it had been Pap's intention that the property should remain in the family she would think it more honourable in me to make over the Hay to my Uncle when I marry and to marry no-one who would not consent to this. She went. I went home very unhappy. Mr Knight came and gave me a lesson and my Uncle came to tea. Both in that excellent good humour given by the first frost to man and beast. But, through all the pleasures of my new piano, all the jokes, all the histories my Uncle gave of the Cobden visitation, I had one feeling of misery, what could I do about dividing the land? And through bitter tears and most fervent passionate (if that can be) prayers for help, I came to this conclusion. I would have but half the* *rights and just legal half - but Matilda having said that they would not and could not make a residence here I felt no hesitation in changing the half, as this adjoining the place where I should probably have to live is far more agreeable and convenient and confers more independence. I resolved to tell her - I look at the case thus - Papa devised an unjust Will, whether he was influenced or not is not to the purpose now, but as many things prove that he had fully prepared for the sudden death it pleased God to send him we may presume that he did not approve the Will he had made as it was never executed. I do not know that any stain save this Will rests upon my Father's memory and I will not be the means of making it lasting by acting upon it in any way. I will sign no document by which the property is conveyed to me. In short, whatever Matilda does with her half, to me it never can be given because I have been cruelly placed in the wrong. I knew of the intention to make a Will without being aware of its contents and therefore it is presumable that I did know how much I was to benefit from it and Matilda says if I knew anything it was dishonourable in me not to tell her because Abraham laid out an immensity of money on Strethill and the fields he rented of Papa in the expectation of coming to live here. I look upon the production of that Will as the most unjust thing to me.*[16]

Tuesday 10th December - *Mr Potts came in as I was practising in a far happier state since my conclusion about the property. I tried to tell him how I felt about it and my firm resolve only to have just the half. He tried to assure me that my sister thought nothing of it*[17] *- did not wish for it and he went away I hope resolved to make an equitable division. Called at Dale House*[19] *(Mrs Lucy has lost a sister) and at Marnwood.*

Monday 16th December - *Abraham and Matilda returned Saturday evening, bad colds. The estates not yet decided. Bill Hill, Grayhurst, Silwood all out of the question, but a pretty place, Stoke Court near Windsor, to be bought if can be for £30,000. Mrs Oddie Mama wrote to at last to pay us a visit after Xmas. My long letter of explanation did not go.*

Wednesday 18th December - *A. has bought Stoke Court for £29,000. I felt at first very sorry, very unhappy. Matilda is very amiable and very kind but fixed which I did not expect to part with her share of the property here and she says it is me an obstinacy like Grandpapa and the Railway to refuse to have it. I don't know what I ought to do but au reste I am so glad when things are so far couleur de rose.*

Friday 27th December - *Such a beautiful day after the snow. Mr Potts came to the Chesnuts and they sent for me. He has arranged for me to take, with the Hay and the whole of the freehold property, M's share of the debt. This makes it somewhat less unfair, it is about £7,000. We are much happier than we were, ie I am.*[18] *I pray that all may now go right and the truth prevail. The neighbourhood is in consternation at Abraham and Matilda's projected flight from Shropshire. After I came home from Mr Pott's the Jettars called, also Mr* *and Mrs W Edmonds, and in the evening I went with Abraham and Matilda to dine at Marnwood.*[22] *Mr Reynolds was there, and Mr Edward Bartlett and Miss Bartlett. She is a nice girl and plays very well. The Mama had much to say about her dear JE, and I said I hoped both her sons were well. - "Do you know them both?" "Yes, I have had the pleasure." "Have you been long in Shropshire?" ...... It was a pleasant evening, very. Now this morning there came an invitation from the Pritchards for me to go with Abraham and Matilda to dine on Thursday - I said I would go.*

New Year's Eve *- Old 1850 is dying, going out in the sighs and groans of such a west wind that I cannot hear the bells ringing anywhere. Oh, to know what is yet unknown in 1851 strange delusion, strange fancy when it is hidden in such wisdom, such mercy. This day last year to have known all that was coming, one would have prayed to lay down and die. A year of years. So many heads of families gone to their long home of rest. My dear and lamented and ill-understood father, then his early friend Mr Anstice within a fortnight of poor Papa. Suddenly also Mr Moseley, more recently Mr Russell and his son-in-law Mr Bailey just before his - Oh, year of years and further off and higher and more widely felt the loss, the great and good Sir Robert Peel, the Duke of Cambridge and Louis Phillippe.*

12 o'clock *- he is gone - old year of many sorrows to me and others to be for ever as many years in one. Exeunt omnes.*

NOTES

1. Copy in possession of the Ironbridge Gorge Museum Trust.
2. Mr Brookes was a senior manager at the Coalbrookdale Works.
3. This is the first indication in the Journal of the conflict which was about to engulf the family. Francis Darby died intestate having let it be known that "the law would make a better Will than he could."
4. John Edwards was a servant at The White House.
5. The dividing of the family silver was the start of the ensuing discord.
6. These thoughts were the result of Francis Darby dying intestate. Until then Adelaide had regarded herself as the Darby heiress and had probably been encouraged in that view by her mother who felt that Matilda had already been well provided for by her marriage to Abraham Darby IV who had for many years been the Manager of the Works. She now had to contemplate sharing the estate with Matilda subject to her mother's continuing interest during her lifetime. She realised that that might reduce her marriage prospects to that of "the second rate gentry" - hence the prospect of having to marrying "JEB", whoever he was.
7. Mary Blodwell was the lady who attended Francis Darby at his death.
8. The Pritchards were Adelaide's banker friends from Broseley. Likewise Mr Osborne Gordon.
9. The division of the property proved contentious.
10. Badger is a village 7 miles or so south east of Coalbrookdale.

11. Mrs Grant (Grandmama) had been a problem for some time. After the death of her husband, she might possibly have moved to Coalbrookdale to be cared for by her daughter Hannah Darby, wife of Francis Darby. Of course all her friends were in Leighton Buzzard and so she stayed there, and the family increased the frequency and length of their visits there. During 1849 illness suggested that she needed more care. She moved to Leamington (for a time). We do not know whether the question of removal to Coalbrookdale was considered then, but it is possible that Francis Darby might not have welcomed that. Francis died on 20th March 1850 and Mrs Grant moved to Coalbrookdale on 12th July.
12. The new baby, whose arrival was marked with such great festivity was Alfred Edmund William Darby, later to become chairman of the Coalbrookdale Company Ltd, which was registered as a company on 11th July 1881. Alfred II (as he later became known) was born on 7th September 1850. He was followed by two sisters Alice Mary (born 1851) and Alfreda Lucy (born 1852).
13. Astley Green is a small village between Broseley (home of the Pritchards) and Bridgnorth. Presumably the "small heir of all this racket" was Alfred Edmund William Darby, note 12 above.
14. Lord Forester (in 1850) was G.C.W. Forester (1828-74), the 3rd Lord Forester, of Willey, near Broseley. Lord Newport was a member of the Bridgeman family (Earls of Bradford) of Weston Hall, which is at Weston-under-Lizard on the Shropshire/Staffordshire border.
15. This was the crisis point in the controversy over the division of the land. Mr Potts, the solicitor from Broseley proposed another alternative under which Matilda would have the Sunniside estate in Coalbrookdale and Adelaide would have The Hay above Coalport, which she said she preferred under the previous proposal. In addition their mother (Hannah Darby, widow of Francis) would take a life interest in The White House and some adjoining fields. This seemed an eminently fair arrangement, but unfortunately, although Adelaide does not mention it, the accord which had at last been reached, was scuppered by Mrs Darby's unreasonable demands for the White House. This was consistent with the untoward and provocative attitude which she had pursued throughout (see Comment 1850 above, p.260). As a result Matilda (unwisely) took umbrage and after discussions with her husband she decided to forego her entitlement to her share of the estate and she and Abraham decided to leave Coalbrookdale, a devastating decision for the Dale. (For Matilda's version of these events, see an account which she wrote two years later when she was living at Stoke Court, Buckinghamshire, on 4th October 1852, Appendix B, p.278).
16. The second part of this entry in the Journal throws considerable light on fundamental aspects the dispute between Matilda on the one hand and Adelaide and her mother on the other hand. The sentence, "Papa devised an unjust Will, *whether he was influenced or not* is not to the purpose now" raised the question of who influenced him. The Will was drafted between 1848 and 1850 (the watermark of the paper on which the instructions for the Will was written was 1848). This was the period around Adelaide's 30th birthday when her mother was becoming increasingly concerned about Adelaide's marital prospects. There can be little doubt therefore that the Will and its contents

were the result of Hannah Darby's wifely pressure. But Francis refused to sign it!

The second significant sentence - "I *knew of the intention to make a Will* without being aware of its contents and therefore *it is presumable that I did know how much I was to benefit from it ....*" Adelaide may not have known the precise details of the Will, but she was so close to her mother there can be little doubt that she knew the general intent of the Will. Understandably, Matilda regarded this as a major betrayal, especially considering how close the two sisters were.

17. Mr Potts was the solicitor. He realised of course that it was far too late to retrieve the situation. The rupture had already occurred and the decision by Abraham and Matilda to move from Coalbrookdale had already been taken.
18. This was the final act. Everything had turned out in Adelaide's favour, and she indulged in a note of triumphalism.
19. Dale House, built close to the Coalbrookdale works, was the home of Lucy Darby (Alfred's mother) and her daughter Mary Darby.
20. Severn House (now the Valley Hotel, Ironbridge) was the home of Henry Dickinson and his wife Deborah, Alfred's sister.
21. The Chesnuts, situated below the White House and the Deer Park was the home of Abraham Darby IV and his wife Matilda, who was Adelaide's sister.
22. Marnwood Hall is situated off the road from Coalbrookdale to Buildwas. It was the home of Rev. John Bartlett, the incumbent of Buildwas Church. He was married to a daughter of William Reynolds.

APPENDIX A

COPY [Watermarked 1848]

Instructions for the Will of Francis Darby
of Coalbrookdale Esquire

Devises all his Farms lands tenements and hereditaments situate in the Parish of Madeley or elsewhere in the County of Salop *(Except the Hay Farm and the Broad Meadows) to his Wife Hannah Darby and his Daughter Adelaide Anna Darby for their joint lives* in case the said Hannah Darby shall continue his Widow and after the death of the survivor to the Children of Adelaide Anna Darby in tail then to his Daughter Matilda Frances the wife of Abraham Darby of Coalbrookdale Esquire for her life and after her death to her Children in tail if neither should leave Children then to her surviving Daughter in fee with the power to dispose of the same by Deed or Will as she shall think proper. *Devises all his shares in the Coalbrookdale Ironworks to his Daughters Matilda Frances and Adelaide Anna* (subject to the *payment of an annuity of £800 per annum to his wife* during her life or widowhood but in case she should survive her two Daughters without either leaving issue then after the death of the survivor to be increased to £1,000 per annum payable quarterly equally to be divided between them during their joint lives after the death of one of them the share of her so dying to go to her children equally if no issue then to the surviving Daughter and her Children equally. If the survivor has no issue then as she the survivor shall by Deed or Will appoint.
Devises the Hay Farm and the Broad Meadows situate in the Parish of Madeley *to his Daughter Adelaide Anna* during her life then to her Children in tail in default of Children to his Daughter Matilda Frances during her life then to her children in tail in default of Children to the survivor in fee with power to dispose of the same by Deed or Will.
Bequeaths to his wife Hannah Darby all his Household Furniture Plate Linen Books Pictures Horses Carriages and all other effects (except as hereinafter specified) for her own use Bequeaths

to his Gardener John Baston	£200
to William Morris Labourer	£50
to John Hanley Labourer	£50
to Edward Davis Footman	£200 and his Gold

ring set with a Garnet, his Gold repeating Watch purchased from William Baker of Shrewsbury and all his Cloathes Coats Waistcoats Trousers Shirts Handkerchiefs Gloves Boots and Shoes of all descriptions as a mark of remembrance of his services to him when so long unwell provided he is living with him at his decease

to his Nephew Joseph Dickinson £100
to poor old Amelia Edwards of C.B.Dale £30
to Margaret Webb Housemaid £50 and also a years wages in addition provided she is living in his service at the time of his decease and to all his other Women servants who may be living with him at the time of his decease a years wages in addition to what may be due to them.

Bequeaths all his Monies securities for Money debt and debts and all other his effects not before bequeathed to his Son in law Abraham Darby his Nephew Alfred Darby and his wife Hannah Darby In trust to pay all his just debts funeral expenses and the legacies bequeathed by him and if insufficient to pay all he charges upon the whole of his Freehold property and shares in the Coalbrookdale Works before devised. Appoints his Nephew Alfred Darby and his friend John Pritchard Trustees for carrying the trusts in his Will into effect and devises to them his Trust Estates.

Appoints his son in law Abraham Darby his cousin Alfred Darby and wife Hannah Darby Executors and Executrix.

APPENDIX B

JOURNAL OF MATILDA DARBY

Stoke Court,
4th Oct 1852

Since I am much alone I mean to make a companion of this My Journal and to write my recollections of the events that have placed my Husband and me in a position so far away from the home and from all the affairs and the interests of our early lives.

On the ?? of March I was awaked by my Maid Leonard. She said I was wanted at the White House, I asked if the preparations for my Mothers and my journey to Leamington were ready. She said, "You will not go to Leamington today". I felt startled and stupified, could not think what had changed Mama's plan. My husband was in London. I had passed a restless night from a feeling of oppression in my head. I wondered what had changed Mama's plans. Gradually as I dressed Leonard broke to me that Papa was very ill. He had long been an invalid from some disease of the bladder and his digestion was far from good, but I parted with him cheerfully the evening before. A.R. Tregelles and Deborah came to dine with me and they were to go to the White House to see Papa's pictures. I feared it was too late and that he would be taking his evening nap. But he came out of the morning room so kindly and cheerfully that all my fears were relieved. And he showed us all his pictures and took us to the dining room window to see a Fir Tree that he was questioning whether or no it should remain. A.R.T. said, "Wilt thou not pull down Sunniside?" "No I shall never do it. Matilda must do it?" (How I treasure that kind speech in my recollection, for though I have relinquished my claims it is a satisfactory conviction to me that my Fathers last thoughts were not to disinherit me). At last I was dressed, and Leonard gave me a cup of tea, saying with a strange meaning, "You had better drink it before you go down. In the drawing room I found the surgeon Mr. Edwards. I don't recollect how the awful truth was spoken to me that my Father had ceased to live. I went up the hill as fast as I could. Some woman stopped me, "Is it true that Mr. Darby is dead?" I don't think she knew me. It is an awful truth that I confide to my journal but I had a repugnance to Mama's way of expressing her sorrow. My Father lay in his old place in the bed. All his deep colours gone. His fine features were as pale and as clear as Marble, but so sweet a smile was on his face as I never saw in life. It spoke of the forgiveness of sins by the merits of our Saviour's sacrifice and of rest from pain and vanity and vexation of spirit. As I sat upon the couch at the beds foot solemn but sweet and happy thoughts filled my soul with thankfulness that we can know and feel and confide in the arms of Jesus Christ even when those nearest to us are called thro' the valley of the shadow of death. My poor Father's life had not been happy. His marriage had not been congenial to him though I think he was very fond of Mama, but she became snappish with him as his health failed. He had been of violent temper in his days of health and he had an excitable temperament that was happiest in a very quiet life, and this quiet was disagreeable to Mama, who had been an only child and accustomed to see much variety in her Father's house but I think her tastes were not refined like Papa's nor her mind as well cultivated so that she was not a companion to him, but she had a quiet way of putting him in the wrong before visitors that wounded his feelings and made him fall back upon the Society of his inferiors where Mama would not be present. Mama disliked that Papa should consult anyone but herself and if I answered his questions about domestic affairs she always told me of it afterwards. I could write many painful things but I will not confide them even to my journal but set down to knowledge account for my own guidance (what indeed) I am so blessed in my marriage that it is perfectly easy to try to avoid the errors I have seen. A woman should always consider she is a cypher apart from her husband. Every happiness she contributes to him reflects upon herself but every pain she gives him will start up to be a thorn in her own side.

I have written at the time the history of my Father's sufferings, and through that night Mama believed he was improving and she was not at all alarmed when as he sank into Mary Blodwell's Arms she saw the beautiful smile settle on his features. She thought he was playful in the sense of relief from pain for to my journal it is not indelicate to confide that he had been assisted out of bed to the night stool, and his last words were, "This will relieve me very much". Poor Mary Blodwell is dead also. She married John Ashton and made him very happy and about six weeks ago she died suddenly too, from some disease of the brain, which she had been aware of but begged the Medical Attendant not to mention to anyone.

October 5th. The first steps were to be taken my Uncle R. Darby. He sent off our Servant Darcy with a message by Telegraph for my husband. Meanwhile Mama wrote to Ada at Leamington and sent it by a servant who was to accompany her home. We had all 3 left the Society of Friends and our Mourning had to be ordered. I found myself obliged to write to Mr. Crookes for the first steps to be taken for my dear Father's coffin. I proposed that the Friends of the Meeting and the Clerks of the C.B.D. Co. should, after the funeral, have the refreshment usual among Friends at our house. When my husband came, Mama threw herself into his arms and said sobbing that she had no one but him to look to now. Abm. wrote all the letters and procured everything and gave all the orders for the funeral.

When Ada came she was in a state of excitement that did not look exactly like grief but she was very punctilious in the due expression of it, and I was surprised on reading one of her letters to see the expression that she felt herself desolate or words to near that effect as we had lost the head of the family. It seemed inconsistent with the bitter and slighting tone in which she used to speak of him. I was obliged to be very quiet or I got snubbed. I cannot well describe though it can never pass from my memory. The day of the funeral was a very heavy snow storm, so deep the drifts lay that it was difficult to walk. My Uncle Richard Darby and Abraham persuaded Mama not to go and Ada and I were to stay with her. It felt all like a dream. Of course I could not feel the same sort of grief as though my Father had allowed or encouraged me to love him but I did in many things admire him and now the sense of fear with which he inspired me from my childhood was laid at rest in the Grave. I felt that his mind and my own could in some things have sympathised had we ever broken through that crust of fear on my part and reserve on his. I thought now a path of considerable influence and usefulness though of much self denial was opening before me. I pictured to myself how much good might be done in the place and amongst the children. One of the first things that gave the pain was the manner in which Mama said at breakfast the morning but one after the funeral, "Papa offered thee those jars and thee refused them". I knew that Papa did not always mean his gifts to be accepted at once, and I feared he might repent. He had once offered me a tea service of silver and then he said, "Well, we shall see how it will be". This was not many weeks before he died. Mama began to say, "I hope there will be no will". "Papa said to me only a few days before he died, "I have left a paper of what legacies I wish thee to give to the servants. Art thou quite satisfied without a will". And she had said she was quite satisfied. Somehow she conveyed to me an idea that it was greatly to my advantage that there should be no will. Now to my journal I conceal nothing. I did think that my Father had never done justice to my husband's character. I knew that my Husband had been so self denying for the advantage of his own family and also for that of the Dale Co. that I believed the blessing of God would be given to those who worked with him. I thought Mama and Ada had now the opportunity to prove that they did not take the same selfish views. Alas! I was miserably deceived! The first thing Mama brought down was the jewelry. I had a feeling that my Husband was imprudent in expressing his belief that Papa had vast hoards of jewelry etc., and some curiosity about it. He and Ada often wished for the same thing and I had to interfere about a diamond ring and the Watson Taylor plate.

In both these cases I own my husband was wrong to have expressed an opinion as to what he would like and I was mistaken about a chain which I thought was gold and fit for Ada and it was not gold and I know now that she was offended. Then Ada said to me Uncle R.D. has been trying to make mischief between Mama and us two. He has been telling her it is hard for her not to have the White House for her life. I appealed to Abm. before Mama and he promised that we would never distrust her in it. She gave me a great deal of table linen and Ada some and she offered me something, I forget what, but I said give it to Ada for her husband when it comes to her marriage (it was something only useful for a man). Ada said "When I am married my Husband shall buy those things for himself". That speech gave me the pain. I felt she meant me to understand that mine wanted too many things, although I knew he did not really want them. Mama gave me a large Turkey carpet. Then came the taking out letters of Administration. Mama proposed that Abm. should take them out. When Mr. Potts came he said at once that they would not be granted to a Son-in-law. Mama was then to take them out herself. She said to me, As we are only (left) with no minors we can do just as we please. About this time Mr. J. Pritchard said to Abm. that he should be very happy to be of any service to us in arranging about Papa's property. But we did not know there was any need for advice and only thanked him. Then Mama sent Ada to Leamington and after she was gone, She, Mama, proposed to Abm. and me to go up with her to divide the plate. We earnestly pressed it upon her that Ada should be by. At last she consented that Ada should return. The plate was all spread out in the Library, it was a wonderful sight. Mama wanted our servants to go to see, but I declined for I felt it would be painful to have it so soon made a sight of. Mama began to divide it into 3 parts. She said in Daniel's presence that Ada was to have a certain tea service because Papa had bought it for her against her marriage. Then she arranged on 3 tables what she proposed for each of us to have. My quantity was all put out by Mama. Then Mama proposed to get back a bread basket she had given to me and which she made me understand well on Saturday night when she had made an end of dividing. Abm. caused my part to be moved to our house. I am certain he only thought of the risk of leaving about so much valuable plate. I felt very much obliged to Mama and very glad to possess it. It was so very beautiful and I set it out on the table in the Dining Room and asked Mama to come and look at it. She said , "I would rather see it here than in a silversmith's shop". These words struck a strange chill to my heart.

As Ada and I walked to Church she said, "It seems as if Mama wishes to have a third of the Plate and all that she has seen Papa use besides. But the Servants have been talking and Mary Blodwell said to me, "I hope Miss you will have plenty because both Mrs. Darby and Mrs. Abraham have plenty already". These words made me uneasy, but I had added up my share and thought I was well under the third. Alas I had added them wrong, Ada added the lists late at night after Sunday, and on Monday morning Mama and Ada said something about candlesticks that Ada had too many, and Mama said "I shall have those candlesticks". Ada's speech about Mama came full into my Mind tho I don't remember saying anything. Breakfast over Ada gave me her list of and behold mine was far too much. I have the lists in another place. "Abm. we have got too much plates" I said and he became in earnest at once, and he saw that it would be right to deduct for a present of plate given to him by my late Father before our marriage. I was to drive Mama and Ada to Wellington. I felt very much annoyed nay indifferent for I thought they had used me unfairly and Mama said if I were to have made the division right at once I must have had <u>much more time</u>.

Then I saw she had been displeased at A's moving <u>our</u> share of the plate on Saturday night, I felt in a tempest of indignation because I was in a false position, and I thought Mama took advantage of it to make me give up more than was fair, and I fear I said so. I did not feel dutiful, nor patient, nor resigned to be placed in the wrong and by my imprudence and indignation I fear the foundation was laid for much that I afterwards suffered. Ada had told me that her acquaintances at Leamington said children alone could <u>inherit</u> land. I looked in Coke upon Blackstone and found it so. Mama said sometime after, J. Boycott wished the Hay to be sold and "it ought to have been sold long before".

I thought Mama had no power to sell. I told her that the law gave my Father's land to his daughters as joint heiresses, and that she had a claim of Dower on one third of the inherited land. I brought the book

"Blackstone's commentaries" for her to see for herself and I reminded her that she inherited by Grandpapa's will all his land and property for her life, and that Papa had never had any of it. She told me the next morning that if Papa had known the law was so, nothing would have prevented him from making a will. "In the will he had made he had left me for my life all his landed property in the Dale and the Lodge Farm and the Coppices and when I said I don't want all these, he said don't say a word for thee shall have them, they will give thee power. I don't think of Matilda, she is provided for, I only think of Ada and thee". I was thunderstruck, but I said to whom did Papa leave the Hay. She said, "I had rather thee heard that from the Lawyer than from me". For I had said that the will could be found from the solicitor who had drawn it up. I went to the Chesnuts and laid my head upon my arms on the dining room table and wept long and bitterly. I could hardly believe that my Father had left me nothing. When it was through the hard task of thought and hand that my Husband had increased the value of Papa's property more than one third, and had paid out the Dividends which had enabled Papa to pay for part of the land he had purchased (he still left upon it a debt of £9,350 or nearly so). Alas! I had reason to fear Mama would deny all she had been saying, and would yet use it to annoy me whenever she wanted something from me. I wrote down what she had said, and Abm and I went up and read it over to her, and she said, "thee hast got it nearly right, only I said 'I could never have prevented him from making a will'. Oh how I felt to love every tree and shrub of my childhood, and how I deplored what appeared to me the <u>folly</u> of turning my Husband away from the Dale. I wrote to Mr. Potts asking for the instructions Papa had given for his Will but I got no answer for a long time. Meanwhile I made a very foolish offer of compromise to Mama that she should let Abm. and me live at Sunniside and improve the property till the debt was paid, and that then Ada should have it paying a consideration for the improvements. Ada objected to do this, but she said the only thing that could make her like the Dale as a residence would be our living at Sunniside. Mama said the same and this misled me. I proposed the garden and carriages should be all one. I thought this would give Mama and Ada much more comfort than they could afford alone, and would not be unpleasant to Abm. I hoped Mama had only been in a pet with me, and that if I was henceforth very reasonable all would be well. But one day, Mama said, "Do you mean to cultivate your garden in the Wood? Are you wishing for some cabbage plants?" I thanked her and thought I saw that she wished the gardens at least to be separate. I said, "You don't like to have the gardens all in one". She said, "I should like always to give directions in Papa's Garden". This seemed hardly an answer because she was to give directions in all if she pleased. I said, "Perhaps, Mama, you don't quite like us to live at Sunniside'.' She said "I don't object to that so mind thee don't say so, don't put any of thy nasty constructions upon it". I went into the White House. Ada was alone. I said Mama does not seem' satisfied about the Gardens." Ada replied, "You cannot expect her to be satisfied with merely a town Garden." I said, "Would you like to buy my half share of the land altogether". She replied, "I would rather sell you mine". From that time I gave up serious thoughts of living at Sunniside. Mama and Ada went to Leighton.

I think it was in September, Mrs. Alfred Darby had a son, and their great rejoicings were made. Abm. and I took a very active part in them. But whilst Mama was gone Mr. Potts at last sent me the copy of instructions he professed to have received from my Father for his will. It was without date. It left all the property in land in the Dale with the Lodge Farm & Coppices to Mama & Ada jointly for Mama's life then to Ada and her children, if she died without having children it was to come to me. The Hay Farm was left at once to Ada and her children, if she left none, at her death it was to come to me. The property in the Dale Works was divided between Ada and me and we were each to pay Mama an annuity of £400 per an. We, i.e. Abm. and I first sent Mama an offer to carry this out. She declined saying she was sorry that the law made her a Partner in the CB.D. Co. if she were considered a troublesome intruder there. This was of course at an end. Mr. Potts made for Mama a point with Ada and I that the personal property in the White House should all be given up to Mama. I tried another arrangement which Mr. Potts proposed. Ada was to have the Hay, the Lodge Farm and all the land to the left of the road going thro' the Dale towards the Severn. I was to have the property round Sunniside and the White House, and Sunniside and the Paddock and garden belonging. I was to build a cow house and sundry repairs for Mama. It seemed to me to be prudent to know what they were. I took Hinley with me to the White House to receive orders. My rental was very small and Mama would need so much of it that I saw I should never pay my way. Besides Ada said, "I am glad we have made a division at last, that we can agree about". I saw she did not like it in her heart. I proposed to Abm. to let me give up my whole right to the land. He consented. We told Alfred. He advised us to give it up. He said we had better have done so as soon as we heard of the Will. I sent my directions to Mr. Potts. He was sure Ada would not consent, but I did not find any difficulty though she was ungracious about it. Mr. Potts saw us together. Ada said, "Do you not give this up because you are placed in a situation in which you could do no other?" "I give it up freely of my own will". Mr. Potts had said to Abm. it would be only just if Miss Darby had the whole of the land that she should pay my third of the debt. Abm. said, "Mr. Potts, remember that suggestion should not come from either my wife or me". When all was over between Ada and me and she was very cross certainly and asked me if I should not repeat what I was doing. Mr. Potts said, "Allow me to say that I think Mrs. Abraham ought not to pay any of the debt". Ada said sharply to me, "I did offer you this". In truth she had said, "Perhaps you ought not to pay the debt then". I had made no reply. I thought it did not belong to me to make any because though this land would have been my own, the third in the Iron Works belonged by law to my Husband, and he would have to pay the third of the debt. No more was said about it. Ada seemed particularly annoyed about it, I thought.

At the end of 1850 when Matilda made her dicision to forfeit her entitlement, she and Abraham started to look at advertisements of estates. They visited three in the Home Counties (Gayhurst, Bill Hill and Silkwood) before deciding to purchase Stoke Court in Buckinghamshire.

Abm. asked me to get up at seven o'clock and go down with J.R. and himself to "Stoke Court" built by a Grandson of William Penn who had embarassed his affairs by a passion for building and furnishing. The house was said to be very complete.

We found it better than we hoped. We liked the neighbourhood and the land, though there was less land than A intended to have. Before we started home by the Express on Saturday night J.R. met us again at the Railway. The deposit money was paid and Stoke Court was my Husband's property supposing the title to be good. J.R. managed the purchase very cleverly. Perhaps he talked about it a little more than was convenient. Exactly one year after my Father's death I signed the Deeds, there were 3, one for Sunniside which was found to be entailed by my Great Grandfather first to all the descendants of his eldest son my Grandfather, and then to those of his second son, my Husband's Grandfather, another for the Hay Farm, and a third for the purchased property. Ada and my Husband signed it also.

And in April we left the Chesnuts for ever as a residence; but I did not know then that it would be so. When Mr. Potts called at the Chesnuts with the deeds, Abraham took me also up to the White House. We were shown into the Library it was just as Papa used to keep it. Grandmama had been brought to live with Mama at the White House about the end of June after Papa died. She had a serious illness just at this time. Mr. Rowland said ossification of the Heart was beginning, and this very morning as we went up to sign she was believed to have lost consciousness, and to be dying. I was sitting alone by her bed. Mama had left the room. Suddenly Grandmama opened her eyes, I kissed her and she said, "My dear I have had a hard struggle but it is over now, and I am spared a little longer".

On the 1st of May was the opening of the Great Exhibition in Hyde Park. It was gorgeous and astonishing. The Queen was received with vast acclamations and she seemed proud and pleased as a woman at her husband's triumph. It was to Prince Albert's courage and patient firmness that England owes this national triumph. Everything in all England was made subservient to the Exhibition. Noble and peasant alike flocked to see the rarest and best from every country collected in a Glass palace which was raised in one year and is now being re-erected at Sydenham as a monster Green house for the recreation of the People of London. To spend days at the Exhibition was a great opportunity of cultivating ones taste. Lace from France struck me as especially beautiful. I admired it beyond that of Brussels. Curious heavy Spanish black lace was also there. The English lace is all made by machinery or nearly so, and is very cheap, but for articles of luxury, cheapness should not be the only aim. An ornament in bad to worse taste is dear at half-price. In printed muslins England succeeds better, but her real strength is in machinery to conquer the rugged difficulties of the mine or to till the earth or to weave plain useful fabrics. In all that is tasteful and ornamental she is far behind, except her jewelry and silver plate. These were very fine and often in good taste. But the English have no cheap good taste, and yet expense has little affinity with elegance, simplicity suits it more, but except those who have foreign blood in their veins or those who are dressed by their French Maids, English women are tawdry and untidy. They put colours together without any consideration, or burden themselves with odds and ends of ribbon and ornament.

The Egremonts Mr. & Mrs. and Lilly and Pauline came to us the day before, they were nearly our first guests in our new home. We had no curtains yet, and no pictures hung up. But we tried to make them welcome. Mr. E's Tory sentiments would not let him go to the Exhibition. We left them all here on the day of the opening, and there I saw Ada with the John Pritchards and attended by Mr. Osborne Gordon. She was constrained and when I asked her to come and see us, she said she depended upon her Friends' arrangements. This being the case, I invited all the P's. Mr. & Miss G.P. also. From our places in the Gallery I could see Ada all the time, and we met once again. She looked proud but unhappy. What could she be doing to accept obligations from the P's who hope she will marry Mr. Gordon rather than remain quietly at home.

Mrs. Egremont and Lilly and Pauline went with Abm. to their great contentment the next day, it was the Guinea day and the Company highly satisfactory to Mrs. E. only she came home with much to say about Ada. She was certain Mr. Gordon thought himself accepted, and she wondered and remembered that his Father was a dealer in horses and drank himself into bad repute, and she thought the son bold and pushing. Well they went away and Mrs. Lucy Darby and Mary and Henry Dickinson and Deborah came. It was perhaps rather a painful visit on both sides. A.R.J. was with them. They were rather disparaging to our new home, but it is some people's way. Alfred and Rebecca came next, they were much wrapped up in each other and took long walks and searched out the place by themselves. They were not thoroughly cordial. Uncle and Aunt Richard Darby came at the same tine and he was really kind, thought Papa would have liked the house and that the trees in Gray's Walk were as old as those Scotch Firs I loved so well in their gloomy grandeur at Sunniside. This place is far more cheerful.

People begin to call upon us kindly. I feel it as an ark of refuge from much that was painful, yet we have felt together, my husband and me, that we were banished from our patrimony. I believe nothing short of the pain of Papa's will and the way we were told of it and the way Alfred and Henry Dickinson instead of sympathising with us, studied to make what advantage they could of our going, nothing short of these things I believe would have broken our many ties to our Birthplace. The place where I first met my Cousin Abraham's bright blue eyes and happy smile bringing a new sunshine over all my little world and lifting me above all the troubles that beset a schoolgirl on her first introduction to society. I was only 15 then, my 30th birthday passed before we were married, yet in all the trials of those varied years I never quite lost my faith that he loved me, and that some day I should be his own.

Thos. and Hannah Graham and the Robinsons came to see us. I cannot describe the disapprobation of H.G.'s manner, but what it meant I cannot tell. I took no offence, and it passed away, and we parted amiably. Next came the Pritchards all four with their Man and two Maids, and Ada. It was painful. Abm. could not meet Ada without pain, and she was ill at ease.

A little before Xmas fixed for the consecration of the Church at Coalbrookdale. It was a strange season of mingled satisfaction and trial. I could not take my Husband to the White House, and I begged to be taken in at Dale House and they allowed it and invited Friends to meet us. Ada appeared at the school and at the luncheon gaily dressed and escorted by a young gentleman who I found to be Mr. Henry Whitmore. Everybody was talking about her and would she marry him. But all petty feelings were to me down on the occasion. Mr. Bull's addresses and Archdeacon Warings carried all before them, And Gunter's luncheon was very good, although I don't know that it pleased some people. Alfred and Rebecca behaved very oddly. She never said a word about hoping to see us at Stanley. And both Alfred and herself went away before luncheon. He did not return in the evening.

Mrs. Egremont and Lilly and Pauline and Mr. & Mrs. John Anstice and Mrs. Stephens and Mr. & Mrs. Bartlett were at dinner. Mrs. Stephens said Ada was engaged to Mr. Henry Whitmore, or she would not have appeared in public with him. I had observed a difference in Ada's letters, a species of indifference is perhaps the true description. Since there had been a time when she appeared desirous to make me forget all that had passed. I asked Mama. She said she knew nothing, if there were any engagement, she did not know it.

I was to spend a day at the White House. Mr. Henry Whitmore came in by the Garden door like an habitue of the house. He was carefully dressed in white buckskins, a blue neckchief and large pin. His manner was gentlemanly. He reminded me of others of Ada's admirers, perhaps most of J. Horne tho' he is not singularly handsome. Ada persisted that she was not engaged to him, indeed that he had not proposed to her. She was then discussing some questions about going with Mrs. Sparkes to the Ball at B'North, also she was going to a Ball to be given at Ludlow.

Mrs. Egremont wrote to me from Stanley, full particulars of Henry Whitmore's appearance at the Ball and announcing himself as Miss. Darby's accepted lover. I suppose he had made it a condition that she should not appear at either Ball and a bad cold furnished an excuse. I remember nothing particular thro Jany. towards the end of Feby. I obtained Abraham's leave to invite Ada to stay here for her shopping in March. I was amazed at the illtempered look with which she greeted me at Euston Station, where I had waited for her. She behaved with great hauteur in the dinner parties that I gave and said that Henry Whitmore might have accepted my invitation for this week as perhaps he would have been useful, but you do not want any help. She sat by Mr. Brown at dinner. I said to her, one day that I would tell her a secret, that a large party wanted Abraham to stand for Monmouthshire. She said Mr. Brown told her that. Her manner was so unfriendly and often impertinent that I could not feel any wish to meet oftener than duty would require of me. She never lost an opportunity to make a fling at me, and one day she said, "If I were married to a man like Abraham , I should cry every day of my life". At length my eyes were opened. I saw instead of the sister I had loved, a selfish woman, desirous to make me useful and to compel me by taunts to do her bidding. Yet I believe I was very civil, and Mr. H. Whitmore I found rather kind, though he might be proud of his old family. He seemed to me very interfering in Ada's purchases and in her money matters, but that was not my affair. I asked Mama to come and she did so. She was not very amiable, not the same as she would be without Ada, but I began to see that Ada's has been the influence to my discomfort which I thought had been Mama's.

APPENDIX C

A letter from Matilda Darby explaining why she and Abraham left the Dale following the death of Francis Darby

(See note at end. Presumed date April 1851)

My dear Uncle,

I have hesitated to tell you a very painfull family affair, but if I do not explain it to you, the reason of our leaving Coalbrookdale must seem mysterious and very inconsistent with our past lives, and connected in business as well as by esteem and regard my Husband might suffer in your opinion. As you know, my Father left no Will. But my Mother told me that he had made one leaving the whole of his landed property in Coalbrookdale, and the neighbourhood to herself, and to my sister on the ground that I was married to a Husband amply able to provide for me. I asked how Papa had left his estate at the Hay and Coalport, and Mama said, "I would rather thee heard it from the solicitor than from me".

I applied to the solicitor who drew up the Will, and he sent me a copy of the instructions he had received from my Father. They agreed with what Mama had told me, and also directed that the Hay and Coalport should be left to Ada, and her children if she had any were to have the whole of his property both landed and personal. But if she died childless, and I survived her I was to have it. For my life I was to have half Papa's property in the Ironworks and to pay Mama £400 per Ann. Ada to have the other half and to pay the same. All the personal property was left to Mama except the shares in the Ironworks.

The solicitor added that Papa declined to execute this Will after it was engrossed, and sent to him for his Bill; he seems to have said to several persons that he could not make a Will, that the Law would make a better Will for him than he could do for himself. It was thro' the most generous feelings of nature that Papa, I believe, came to make this Will in the first instance - as he believed himself to have prevented my sister's marriage to Mr. Dawson at the same time that I was married.

It was in Sept. that I received the copy of the Instructions Papa gave to Mr. Potts the Solicitors at Broseley. I hesitated much what to do, but I had before seen some reason to believe that Mama and Ada did not wish us to live at Sunniside. Abm. and I offered first to give up to Mama all our interest in the land in the Dale and to Ada our interest in that at Coalport and the Hay, and we offered the annuity in the Will to Mama if she should give up her third in the Ironworks, and to give her all the other personal property. Her reply was in writing, "I am perfectly satisfied with what the Law gives me, though I am sorry it should make me a

Partner in the Coalbrookdale Company, if I am considered a troublesome intruder." She continued, "I shall be willing to agree to any arrangement between Ada and you to divide the land between you." I told Ada if she pleased, I should like to have the Hay Farm. But she said, "No, you have talked about rebuilding Sunniside and laying out a great deal of money there", and Mama added, "what can we do with Sunniside without the lease of the Whale's Back". Then I said no more, and in due time received from the solicitor the copy of the proposal which I enclose. Abm. and I agreed to it at first, but about the end of Novr. I went up to enquire about the Cow House to be built, and took up with me a Builder to receive orders. Mama wished to have a Barn, Cowhouse, appleroom, tools shed, and, as the old walls at the back of the Kitchen Garden were not strong enough, they required to be rebuilt or strengthened, and new pig styes to be built, besides which were pointed out to me many repairs required. However, Mama said, "I do not want much spent upon this as it is only for my life that it will be wanted".

When I had time to reflect upon my position it was thus. One third of Papa's shares in the works i.e. £16,000 was to be given to me, and one third of the debt £3,860. Abraham was tenant for the land at Coalbrookdale and I knew that he lost by it at the rent. I think the rentals of the property assigned to me was £210 out of a rental of £900 or £1,000. But the most difficult part of my position was this. Mama had declined to take Sunniside, the paddock, the vinery and gardens, and had chosen the fields all round so that we could not well have lived there, and yet must have kept them up, or done an ungracious thing in discontinuing them; whilst I reflected how to manage to pay a part of the debt and to pay for the alterations and repairs wanted, a conversation with my sister accidentally showed that she felt herself to be making a sacrifice in giving up the part of the property allotted to me. I asked Abraham to let me give it all up now, as he had advised me to do first when I told him about the Will. He readily consented and indeed I believe he felt like myself best satisfied to do so. It seemed to me prudent to ask Alfred also and he said the same and only regretted that I had tried any compromise. Then I wrote to the Solicitor to prepare Deeds to that effect. He asked Mama for the Title Deeds, and had an interview with Ada and me together. I told Ada that I was most satisfied to give it up, that it would be of very little use to me as we did not intend to continue our residence here, and that I thought the whole of the rental might be useful to her, as I doubted whether the income from the Ironworks would continue as large as it had been. She objected at first to receive it, but finally consented. The Solicitor had, previous to Ada's coming, said to Abm. "I think if Mrs. A.D. resigns everything except the share of the Ironworks, she ought not to pay any of the debt". Abm. said, "Pardon me, but no such suggestion ought to come from my wife or me." However, when Ada had consented to take the land (Abm. was gone away before she came). Mr. Potts said to Ada, "I think your sister ought not to pay any part of the debt". Ada turned to me and observed, "I said the same to you". I replied, "Are you quite satisfied that it should be so?", and she answered, "It is like buying the Hay for 3,000£s."

But I thought it best not to object to this. Ada then said to me, "Are you sure that you give up this land willingly, and not because you felt yourself placed in a situation in which you could do no other." I assured her that I gave it up freely and of my own accord. Which I am afraid was in one sense not quite true, because except that Papa had once promised it to Mama and Ada I should not perhaps have done it. It took a long time to draw out the Deeds, and to our great surprise Mr. Potts told us that Sunniside and five acres round it purchased at two separate times by Abraham Darby is entailed first to the descendants of his son Abraham whether sons or daughters, then to the descendants of his son Samuel in the same way; and this entail was not cut off at the same time as the entail of the Hay Farm. On the 20th of this month we all signed the Deeds. I have an abstract of them but this I think you will not care about. Ada agrees to give Abm. and me the nominal value of 10/- such portion of land as the Ecclesiastical Commissioners may want.

[*Part of the letter is missing at this point*]

....District, only we shall not have as much money to spend in the ornamental part of the Church. I have told Miss Lane and the other teachers that they must take more pains than ever to do right, and though we are going to live at a house Abm. fortunately met with near Windsor Abm. will return from time to time to Coalbrookdale.

The children at the school have been very happy and busy making some shirts, which they hope you will condescend to accept. I am very sensible that the sewing needs many apologies and that in the fronts especially the Elder girls have been too ambitious.

My kind regards to Mrs. Bull and your amiable daughters.

If you will forgive my silence and permit me, I will write to you again from Stoke Court. We begin to remove there next week. It is a painful transplanting to me.

Miss Lane knows nothing of this, at least not from me.

Abraham IV and Matilda left the Chesnuts on 10th April 1851 (see Adelaide's Journal entry for that date, and also Matilda's Journal dated Stoke Court 1852). If that is correct this letter was written at the beginning of April or the end of March 1851.

End of Appendix C.

1851

Comment

This was the year in which Adelaide's life changed dramatically. After the events following her father's death in 1850 she had started the new year having inherited virtually the whole of her father's estate, contrary to his intentions. The only negative aspect of this situation was the departure from Coalbrookdale of her sister Matilda and Abraham IV. This caused some shedding of tears but she adopted a hard nosed attitude to the situation and took the somewhat hypocritical view that it was somehow wrong that her sister "should appear to think that a course of conduct would have been practicable for me to adopt whereby they possibly might have stayed." (There were of course any number of courses of conduct that she could have taken.)

Adelaide was taken under the wing of her friends Mr and Mrs Pritchard of Broseley. John Pritchard was a banker in Broseley (now Lloyds TSB) and was part of the process of gentrification which had been taking place there. It was the Pritchards who arranged for Adelaide to go to the Great Exhibition in Hyde Park. Later in the year she visited Dudmaston, one of the homes of the Whitmore family. It was after that visit that two of the Whitmore ladies were entertained at The White House and then Adelaide accompanied them to a Bazaar at Arley Castle, Worcestershire. In this way Adelaide extended her presence into the upper reaches of Shropshire County Society and even of neighbouring Worcestershire. She was then 35 years old and was recognised as a mature, and wealthy, young lady. In October she was invited to stay at Dudmaston and it was there that she met Henry Whitmore of Apley Park to whom, after due and somewhat extended formalities she became engaged to be married. It is difficult to know how far love came into the process. She was wealthier than Henry Whitmore and Rachel Labouchere who transcribed Adelaide's Journal and was herself a descendent of both the Darby and Whitmore families offered the opinion that Henry Whitmore needed the money to further his career in politics. Whatever the truth, Adelaide was able to confide to her Journal the following year (18th January 1852) that "God is very good to give me such intense happiness".

Friday 10th January - *Mrs Pritchard's children's ball. A very pretty sight it was. Matilda danced in the Country Dance, Abraham also and capitally. I danced a good deal. All the Gordons were there and Mrs Stevens and her two nice-looking nephews Henry and Alfred Humphrey. Went in the mourning with a net for the hair made of steel and black bugles. Almost everybody in white.*

Wednesday 22nd January - *I went to dine at Mrs John Pritchards "toute seule". There were the Sparkes and two daughters, the WRE's (he sang divinely), Mrs Alfred Darby heavy in silence and equally heavy in speech, he had a cold and came not, Caroline de Satze - oh, "si belle, si belle" - Osborne and Pearson Gordon, Mr Browne and Mr Johnstone - the former very tall and conceited and entertaining, the latter entertaining and little and very agreeable. I wore the scarlet net with a gold thread and tassels.*

Sunday 2nd February - *Poor Prinny died, I must say it is a great sorrow, the poor thing had not been well for a fortnight perhaps, but only ill and refusing food for three days. He drank water immensely, appeared to suffer no pain but was sick for three days and would not eat. Papa was so fond of the dog and the dog so fond of him and of us, that we shall never love another so well. When I came home from church I carried him out of his bed to the kitchen fire, he could not stand and after warming him we put him in his bed again. When Morris came to give him some gruel I went to tell him not to disturb the poor dog. We looked at him and he breathed twice and died so quietly that Morris would not believe it. He was so affectionate and all day long with me that it is quite silent and melancholy without him.*

Monday 3rd February - *This is a time of dismals. A poor little girl was burnt at the school, she is buried today. Sir Francis Lawley is dead suddenly.*[1]

Friday 14th February - *There is a tide in the affairs of humanity. Mrs Sparkes sent me an invitation to an evening party and to go with Mrs Alfred. While I was debating what to do Mrs Alfred called and gave a very handsome invitation, in addition I was to go to Stanley to dine and sleep, and she would take me with her to Bridgnorth where otherwise she was going alone (she gave a different version to other people but that I did not know in time). I said I would go, Stanley is a nice place, inhabited certainly as it never was before. Mr Blake and Mr Robinson were there. Mrs Sparkes' party was a ball and rather pleasant, about 30 people. I danced a good deal. Mr & Mrs Kettle and a droll little girl, Mr Cooke (who sings the Great Mogul and who is engaged to Miss Carr the daughter of a mad Papa), Mr Matheson, Mr & Mrs Hayes, Miss Rowley and 2 brothers, 2 Miss Bests, a Miss Whitmore (cousin to Apley), Mrs Hart, sister to Dr Merriman who has taken the Schools and Mr Moseley of Leynton in Staffordshire who plays divinely on the harp, she had a nice agreeable son with her from Rugby and 3 daughters the eldest engaged to a Mr Peel. It was really pleasant, we danced in the dining room with a good floor, lemonade in the hall and singing and music between the dancing in the pretty drawing room. We returned to Stanley about 1 o'clock. Breakfast next day at 9!!! I came home with an awful headache. Mrs Sparkes gave me no time for a white dress so I went in black tulle and camelias for which I sent to Willey but they came from Mr Pritchard's at last, they were very lovely. Mrs Alfred projects a ball or a carpet dance on the 26th.*

Tuesday 18th February *- At the Chesnuts, teaching Abraham and Matilda the Polka. They go now very soon to Stoke Court which is a grief.*

Friday 21st February *- To dinner at Severn House. Mr & Mrs Alfred Darby, Mrs Lucy Darby and Mary, Uncle and Aunt Richard Darby and Rebecca, Abraham and Matilda and I. Abraham has let his farm at Strethill to Henry Dickinson - the part which they made over to me for one year. Tuesday 4th March is fixed for Mrs Alfred's Ball - but who can tell. Grandmama is very ill tonight, it is influenza in which we have all shared through the house. I hope for the best but after 90 there is more fear than hope. Abraham and Matilda are not yet gone, will not go just yet.*

Sunday 9th March *- After being so ill all the week that we hardly expected her life from day to day, Grandmama is to the surprise of us all and of Mr Rowland's also, a little better. Tuesday the Ball came off at Stanley about 40 - magnificent rooms and supper and chandeliers. The grand piano in the entrance hall and violins and flute also. I do not think the affair was badly done nor yet that it gave quite so much pleasure as might have been expected from so much expenditure. Mr & Mrs Stevens were there and 2 or 3 nieces and 2 or 3 nephews, Mr & Mrs Sparkes and their two pretty daughters, very pink and pretty. Three of Mrs Alfred's brothers and two cousins, Miss Christies with their gouvernante, a conceited unprepossessing person and fair specimen of the tribe of plant. Mr & Mrs Kettle, Mr & Mrs Pritchard and Mr P, 2 Miss Thornes and*

(Note: gap in text)

Thursday 10th April *- Matilda left us today. Very melancholy were the weeks that are passed and little to tell of them. I have shed many tears in my life but none so bitter as now. Sad indeed it is to part with one once so dear and still so dear. Hard indeed that they should resolve to go but harder than all that she should appear to think that a course of conduct would have been practicable for me to adopt whereby they possibly might have stayed. They were to pay a visit at Roderick House and then proceed to their new home. Great was the change from past days that they both should go without a word of invitation - Abraham without ever saying goodbye or I shall hope to see you.*

Janet came to spend a day or two with me and Mary Darby came to dinner. By the way that same woman has told stories to my sister, I cannot rightly tell what but she has shown dissension and I truly believe has told what is not fact.

Friday 11th April *- I meant to have taken Janet to Stanley but Mrs Alfred's brother died and we could not call. So we went to Albynes, Mrs Stephens was not at home. Drove back through Willey, it was very cold. Walk with Rebecca.*[2] *It was not very entertaining but with heart and soul unnerved it was all of use and kept me from thinking. Mr & Mrs John Pritchard and my Uncle and Aunt Richard Darby and Rebecca came to dinner and we had some music. The John Pritchard's are going up for the Exhibition and they asked me to go with them.*

It is a large party and will be very pleasant, I am sure. I had been sorry with sufficient means to have no opportunity of seeing this great sight.

Mr & Mrs John Pritchard called to say Mr Petterson has a room for me. Letter to tell us that EL's match is quite off with Miss Benham and that James Fletcher has the curacy of Willey and Barrow under the Hon. Mr Bridgeman.

Wednesday 16th April - *Letter from Matilda the first to us both, very kind. They are in such confusion and have sent away Mrs Frost at once.*

Good Friday 18th April - *Mama and Uncle Richard Darby have been all week arranging the clothes, melancholy work in my dear Papa's dressing room. It appears that Matilda told my Uncle of the entail upon the property which I think was not particularly kind or necessary.*[3]

Monday 28th April - *Very cold, snow on the hills. London is in a great ferment shoals of people. Matilda said before Easter it required more time to drive thro' the streets than usual. Carried on the negotiations for my Uncle to have Mrs Egremont's lodgings at 280 Regent Street. She wrote most accusingly of them, dirt, noise, fleas, and bad cooking, and after Easter they asked for these 10 guineas a week! So he resolved to go to Shaftesbury Terrace, Pimlico. Mr John Pritchard procured my ticket, No 9000 and many more gentlemen's tickets sold, they are two guineas. He is most kind, offers to do anything for us, says we ought to make Wills after the lesson we have had.*

Tuesday 29th April - *Left home for London at half past 11. With Mrs John Pritchard to Wolverhampton where we joined Miss Pritchard and Miss Baugh. Arrive at Paterson's by 10 o'clock, Mr John Pritchard joined us. Very comfortable and clean and quiet is Paterson's Hotel, 46 Brook Street.*

Wednesday 30th April - *Glad to have a day before the Exhibition. Interview with Mrs Treacher's dressmaker, lovely white lace bonnet and flowers - silk lace cloak, the prettiest thing with a hood. Went to Mr Saul's to see Mr Gordon's picture a small sketch and good likeness mais un peu en bon point. Then shopping to Hill's in St James Street and a shop of charming French bijouterie and flowers and millinery. Harding's in Piccadilly and then to Mrs Hill's, a wonderful French dressmaker - who I like not. Walked after luncheon and were caught in the rain and took shelter under Mr Hudson's portice. Saw Lady J Manners.*

Thursday 1st May - *Inauguration of the Exhibition. We set out at about half past 8 and were informed there had been a double line of carriages from 5 o'clock the whole length of Piccadilly to the Exhibition! So with much difficulty got to the Albert Gate and walked from there. The first entrance to the Building was most grand and imposing -from North to South a third of a mile in length and filled with the most magnificent statues and foundations and then the Queen's throne with its blue and gold canopy. We had very good places in the nave, and JB Reynolds joined us and we saw Abraham and Matilda who had seats in the* *gallery. At half past 1 the Queen came with a flourish of trumpets and then 'God Save the Queen' and the Hallelujah Chorus on the organ and a full choir of singers. The Archbishop offered up a prayer and the Queen pronounced the Exhibition open at which point a Chinese in full costume advanced to the Throne and made a profound salaam to the Queen and Prince Albert who laughed and acknowledged it.*[4] *Then the procession formed up and walked round the building. The Court were in full dress. The Queen pink and silver brocade and diamonds. She had the little Prince of Wales with her in Highland Costume. Prince Albert in FM uniform, the Princess Royal is very plain. She had a wreath of wild roses very like a ballet dancer and a lace dress. The Duchess of Sutherland*[5] *and Lady Dour followed, the maids of honour - of the men there is not much to say. The Duke of Wellington and Marquis of Anglesea walked together and were cheered very much. The Queen bowed very gracefully to her subjects as she passed. The Chinese came on alone looking very solemn. Lord J Russell*[6] *is indeed a fright maigre. It was cold but the sun shone. No accident and no untoward event. Saw Mr Reynolds, Mr Y Mrs I Tothill, Uncle and Aunt Richard Darby and Rebecca. Had a great fight to get at the throne after the Queen was gone the crowd was so tremendous and the French people by no means the most civil.*

In the evening to Covent Garden Italian Opera, the Huguenots - Margaret of Valois, Castellan, Valentine, Grise - her love, Mario - The Page, Mdlle Augres. The Count de Nevers to whom Valentine is married until happily he is shot, terrified. Augres' voice is very beautiful, a contralto and by no means so fine people say as Alboni's. Mario's acting and singing as it always is most enchanting and he is handsomer than ever in a dark velvet and gold dress, gold spurs and hat and red feather. The ladies' dresses were ugly I thought from the long square sleeves hanging loose from the shoulder almost to the feet but no doubt it was right for the period. We had a pretty little box holding 5 just opposite the Royal Box. The Queen came looking better than the morning with the Princess of Prussia - she is become red and brown like a little Hottentot.

Friday 2nd May - *Exhibition again. These 3 days at a guinea are very precious with our season tickets. Mrs Egremont and Lily, Pauline with Abraham. Yesterday Matilda was quite done up and left the dinner table faint - Saw Mr Bridgeman who condoled with me on their leaving.*

Things to remember - Rudolph of Hapsburg, inaugre a Bruxelles 1848, a colossal white statue, in the nave where is also the "Dome with the Eagle slayer"[7] *- Also the Amazon on horseback attacked by a tiger, a bronze from Munich. In the galleries jewellery from Garrards and Hund and Roskill, a diamond and ruby spray worth 19,000. It is very beautiful, when close you can see it forms a rose and lily.*

Mr Gordon went back to Oxford. He was a capital person as chaperone, knew all the great men and did not mind a crowd. Out of compliment to him the Bishop of Oxford bowed to me and gave me his place in the tremendous crowd at the great diamond - it is so large (a drawing). Mr & Mrs John Pritchard and I walked in the rain to an orange shop, and to Nicholl's, and we were glad to get home and be quiet.

Saturday 3rd May - *Exhibition early in the morning, a great many grand people. Went through the park with Lord Gardner who looks a scamp, very unlike Lady Suffield. Say Lucy Burton who has left a card for me. The rooms of Dresden china and Berlin bronzes more beautiful than can be told. Stuffed animals in the Zollverein, a boar hunt and a stag hunt and two nests of owls, a nest of young foxes with the papa bringing home a partridge. The house where Prince Albert was born, a pretty toy model fort with a village fete going on, the figures dancing - 2 vases in the Russian department with a rich arabesque pattern in gold and brown with medallion pictures upon them that one would value as pictures - the one is an Italian scene with women in Roman caps and handsome brigand looking men lying on the grass as a foreground. To Chiswick - very cold - some rain caused the company to be small. The flowers beautiful, Rose from Lara, Paul and Francis, all Hertfordshire. The Madame de St Joseph is a lovely yellow white rose and a "Geant de Batailles" such a magnificent double deep red one.*

Saw the Duchess of Devonshire and after the Duchess of Sutherland - Lady Blantyre, Lady Constance Gower and and the Marquis of Stafford.[8] *The Bands of the Life Guards the Coldstream and The Blues. Oh, it would have been charming but for the cold.*

Sunday 4th May - *Went to Lincoln's Inn Chapel - heard Mr Anderson who has just got a great living from the Duke of Beaufort. In the afternoon the Temple Church - very magnificent on the plan of Aix Cathedral, I think and too much like a Roman catholic Church. It is gothic with a groined roof painted in frescos and pillars of green marble - the altar gilded and gorgeous. Dr Woodsworth preached a wonderfully long and learned clear sermon with almost as much Latin and Greek and Hebrew as English in it on the text "Thou art Peter and on this Rock I will build my Church". Purbeck stone found in Hampshire.*[9]

Tuesday 6th May - *Went to the Royal Academy. Pictures beautiful - this year, a sunset by Creswick. Stansfield has several sweet pictures and Sir Landseer a Stag - and group of Italian peasants with donkey, etc. Naclisa - Caxtons printing press with Edward VI and Elizabeth Woodville and the beautiful little Princess Elizabeth. Stansfields "Battle Reverede" - Grant has some sweet portraits of pretty women. In the miniature room portrait of Mrs John Ruskin and a chalk drawing of the beautiful Duchess of Argyle, the Countess of Chesterfield and Lady Emmeline Stanhope. To the Opera (Queen's Theatre).*

Wednesday 7th May - *Exhibition. The Sevres China - flower, paintings on enamel after van Huysiom Tapiserie Gobeline and Beauvais, and furniture most beautiful! Rich pink, the rose du Barry is used as a ground even for roses and is beautiful Also pale blue also a pale bluish green. Sofa and chairs Louis XIV* *exquisitely worked in the tapestry of Beauvois. The Gobelin tapestry was framed in two instances and one was ready to say what fine pictures!*

To the St James Theatre clever acting and beautiful dresses as always. Soribe's Bataille des dames - time 1817.

Thursday 8th May - *We go tomorrow to Stoke Court - all!![10] Partly my fault, I fear. Dog Marchant in Princes Street, little King Charles from £3 to £5. To Water Colour Exhibition, Proust, Copely, Fielding, Cox, JM Richardson, Bentley, some beautiful sea pieces and Hunt Fruit and Flowers. To the Italian Opera (Covent Garden) La Donna de Largo, Rossini. Most charming opera.*

Friday 9th May - *Went to Stoke Court, tis very pretty country between the Paddington Station and Slough, passing Wormwood Scrubs and Manwell, and then the view of Windsor.[10]*

Saturday 10th May - *We returned to town to luncheon very poorly with bad cold and stiff neck. Wet afternoon, went to the Diorama of Holy Land and Jerusalem, beginning from Rameses near Cairo and following the wanderings of the Children of Israel. Stoke Court is the sweetest place in the world and the most beautifully furnished.[10] Next day in bed all day with cold but on Monday went to the Royal Academy. Millais pictures in the Peragino and Albert Durer style - Ansdell is beautiful in sheep. in the evening to the Philharmonic Concert - Hanover Square Rooms. Very ill, quite done up.*

Tuesday 13th May - *Great Exhibition for the last time, how grand it is. The organs were playing and it is becoming quite a fashionable promenade. Saw Miss Lucy Burton and Col Forester, he had been at Stoke Court only an hour after we left, said he was very sorry. Mr Gordon in the evening. Archdeacon Vicker's death is very sad and sudden so we did not go to the Opera.*

Wednesday 14th May - *The Flower Show at the Regent's Park. We went to luncheon at Mrs George Barker's, a pretty house it is, and pleasant people and a very handsome luncheon. The flower show was beautiful - the three bands of the Life Guards, the Coldstream and the Blues at Chiswick. The "Victoria Regia" in flower. Mrs Smith was there, the handsome Mr Smith a Barrister, and also Mr Frederick Smith.*

Mr Emery's young gentleman. We enjoyed it so much we stayed to the very end instead of going to see the Hippopotomus and the baby elephant and the Chinese lady.

Thursday 15th May - *Mr Pritchard took me to see Gordon Cumming's collection which is curious particularly the Cape Waggon which went with him everywhere. Then for the last time to the wonderful collection of jewels and wonders at the Exhibition. I think at every visit the place grew more wonderful and vast and beautiful. It was rather a sad adieu to London. The Dog merchant brought me a little black and tan spaniel for which I was wise enough to give £5 but it seemed a darling. Met Mr Broadbent at the train and we proceeded* *altogether as far as Wolverhampton. Little was talked of but the death so sad and unexpected of Archdeacon Vickers. His successor is to be Hayward Cox a man well known at Oxford. The living of Chetton*[11] *is to be filled by a clergyman who was formerly curate there. I was home by half past 10, found Miss Lawford with Mama.*

Tuesday 20th May - *I went to Broseley to settle our account and stayed all night - only Miss Pritchard there and Mr Pearson Gordon. Mr John Pritchard makes my share of the expenses in Town including railways under £30 - it is very little. They are truly kind friends and as we grow older we value real fiends. Fido came, he is very affectionate to me - a beautifully undivided affection he growls at Mama who feeds and pets him, snaps decidedly at Grandmama who teases him, is not at all on good terms with Miss Lawford for numberless kind attentions. He is very fond of gentlemen.*

Tuesday 27th May - *Mr & Mrs John Pritchard and Mr Edmonds dined here and I returned with them at night to the Bank and remained with these dear and good natured people until Friday. Wednesday we rode as far as the five chimneys beyond Wenlock a very pleasant ride and a beautiful view, "Sentinel" behaved very well.*

Thursday 29th May - *Ascension Day. Went to church, a good sermon from Mr Andrew Burn. After luncheon we rode to Bowman's Hill beyond Bridgnorth and back by Worfield. Had tea at "the Wheel". Mrs Mortimer who lives at Broseley Hall has a Mrs Acre living with her and a pretty Miss More.*

Friday 30th May - *Mr John Pritchard and I rode to Linley and over the fields to the Severn where the view of Apley is beautiful. Then back through the woods to Stanley and Astley. Mrs John Pritchard had a party of little girls, very happy they were, a round game in the evening. Miss Lawford came and Fido to bring me home.*

15th June - Trinity Sunday - *Mr Barlett*[12] *preached at our little room in the Dale. They say a Mr Charles Marshall is appointed to the Dale and that there will be a church some time built. Mr & Mrs Alfred Darby dined with us leaving Miss Tregelles for a week with me. It was a wet day and rather stupid.*

Tuesday 17th June - *Miss Lawford left for Leighton. I have Mrs Owen's 'grey' for Miss Tregelles and we will have some rides. The Bible meeting at Ironbridge and a Mr Cane. It was the first Bible meeting I ever attended here. There was much about the Pope in very bad taste.*

Monday 23rd June - *I came to Leamington to visit the Fletchers. Found them both great invalids but as ever very truly kind and Anne met me at the station. I made the journey quite alone with great success. The carriage from Birmingham full of bows and arrows for the Archery meeting*[44] *to be held on 25th and 26th. The shooting was in the Cricket Ground, the targets are arranged in rows and the shooting is at 100, 80 and 60 yards. The ladies wore every imaginable ugliness in the way of green uniform - generally a polka jacket and straw hat and* *some were covered with trinkets won at successful Bow meetings. Louise Burton was there with the Dalys' who leave in a week for Interlaken. Also Mr & Mrs Knightley - she told me her sister Fanny Richmond is in Germany. Mrs Hulme looked very happy and was still acting chaperone. The Croxton Johnsons were there. Wednesday evening fireworks to which we went. Thursday a Ball where I went not. Mr Golightly went with us and came to dinner "sharp six". Mr Dunnington carried a bench about with him for us at the gardens and we saw the fireworks very well.*

Friday 27th June - *In the evening we drove to Guy's Cliff with the Dalys and cool and delicious it was. The old Cave of Despair looked far more horrible than of old. Sir Godfrey Kneller's picture of the Duchess of Ancaster. The room is filled with Mrs Greatheed's pictures and was rather dark - magnificent old oak cabinets in it. Great black Newfoundland dog and a little furry white one about the size of Vick (Mr JT's spotted terrier). Saturday Mr Dunnington went away and I am to stay until Wednesday. Went to dine at the Dowager Lady Corbet's she is in a dreadful state and I really think almost deranged. Hall thinks quite so at times. She went soon to bed.*

The night of the Ball we went into the Gardens with Mr Golightly and Mr Dunnington. It was all very quiet, no-one there but the Miss Storers and their Mama. We sat asking charades - "What letter taken from six makes 9? - and how do you make 9?" Taking a letter from six - letter S. leaves ix (9). "Why are you like a prisoner eating fish?" "Because you are a captivating soul (sole)."

Friday 11th July - *Picnic at the Wrekin and a wet day which was wretched. It was not a picnic after all but a luncheon at the Little Wenlock Rectory - a drive to the mountain and a most determined expedition up it and return to tea at the Rectory. The party from Stanley was Mr & Mrs Alfred, Mr & Mrs Christy and Miss Christy and Mr Dicky - Mrs Lucy Darby, Mary, Major Edwards from Ireland and Mr More and Mrs Harris of Broseley. Mr More is now living at the 5 Chimneys and is going to London for the Exhibition took me in to luncheon which I esteemed a great favour, and talked in gratitude. There is to be a great Bazaar at Arley[13] - Lady Valentia's and Mrs Alfred Darby asked if I would go with her - would rather not. View on the Wrekin best on a showery day - on our return we found Mr & Mrs John Pritchard arrived with Mr Smith - it was a refreshment to see them again and I am again to go there next week. The City Ball to the Queen at Guildhall, Matilda went to it.*

Tuesday 15th July - *I returned again to my kind friends at Broseley and after dinner early we drove to Dudmaston Lodge[14] - Mrs John Pritchard, Mr Osborne and Mr Pearson Gordon went on horseback — it was rather showery but cleared up for a beautiful evening. Dudmaston Lodge[14] is a sort of baby house - the very prettiest "love in a cottage" sort of place with a little entrance hall full of Australian curiosities and wonderful garments from New Zealand and a little drawing room with a little piano and books and a table most elegantly filled with* *ornaments and flowers. Very pretty drawings and paintings in oil and water colours. After tea in a lovely dining room looking upon flower beds through an open casement window we drove to Dudmaston.*[15] *It is the most beautiful place with near views and distant views and a garden of gardens - rock work terraces sloping down to the water and flowers in banks and beds and masses, a fairy land of flowers. We walked through the hall which contains an immense billiard table and a bust of the late Lady Lucy Whitmore,*[16] *a beautiful drawing room - library and the dining room opening into a small conservatory a mass of geraniums reaching to the top. Then back to the Lodge by the Dingle, quite as lovely as Badger*[17] *- there is a large kitchen garden besides - Mr Whitmore*[18] *gives his gardener £200 to manage the whole affair and it is all done by three men and 2 boys. A pretty and most attractive supper - chicken and ham, jellies, cakes, fruits of all sorts and creams. We were asleep in the carriage and home by 11 on a moon light night.*

Wednesday 16th July - *Madame de Satze drove over to Chesterton*[19] *to bring her two boys Ernest and Oscar. We played at battledore. Mr John Pritchard, Mr Smith - Mr Gordon and I until we were very hot and Ernestine tired of looking on only. Then they put up the target and bows and arrows in the garden and Tenniel, Mr Smith's servant, a Maltese man of genius, picked up our arrows and instructed us.*[44] *After luncheon we went to the hill to tea. Mrs J Pritchard and Ernestine drove and I rode, a very pleasant ride it was with the gentlemen. We went through Willey Park, "Sentinel" was very gay. Found Ernestine in bed with a headache from the sun and Mrs J Pritchard looking very pale. She and her two brothers went to see Mr & Mrs Alexander Gordon's farm and I went farming in my habit through hedges and over stiles with Mr Smith and Mr John Pritchard. It was a delicious evening and we rode home most happily.*

Saturday 26th July - *Dearest Mama's birthday. Mrs Grizzle Edmonds came in the evening to pay Grandmama a visit and next day her grandson came with the bundle of precious deeds for her signature. He stayed until Monday evening and certainly did wonders in the way of seeing the country, he walked to the top of the Wrekin before breakfast on Sunday morning. Monday morning I made the exertion myself of getting up at 5 and went away with the young gentleman to Buildwas Abbey and Wenlock and home by Willey Park and Broseley. After breakfast we looked in Dugdale*[20] *for descriptions and I was a little tired. He rode the grey and I "Sentinel". In the evening Mr & Mrs Lawford*[21] *came and Mr Richard Smith went away. He is very clever and gentlemanly allowing for opportunities, and the task of womanising him gave me two pleasanter days than the succeeding ones, but comparisons etc.*

Tuesday 5th August - *Mama sent me with Mr & Mrs Lawford and Mrs Grizzle to Apley Park - Driving along the Terrace it is quite possible to take a carriage by the fields to the Shifnal Road and thence to Apley Lodge and through the Park.*

Saturday 16th August - *We - Mama and I - drove over to Lilleshall*[22] *and went through the gardens, they are certainly very beautiful, not rare flowers but an immense quantity with the best arrangement of colour. We have had quite a walk and valued it. Mrs Sparkes sent me an invitation to stay with them this week and go to the Arley Park Bazaar.*

Tuesday 19th August - *Miss Charlotte and Miss Laura Whitmore*[23] *arrived after dinner and stay with us to go to Arley.*

Wednesday 20th August - *The Bazaar at Arley Castle*[13] *was arranged and prepared by clever and accomplished women and in addition to the usual useless things at fancy fairs there were many drawings and some oil paintings by Miss Davenport very beautiful - and flowers in abundance. Lady Valentia and Lady Winnington had the 2 principal stalls, Miss Cockburn, Miss Somerset and Miss Davenport others. The Moseleys were prevented by a death from taking their stall and Lady Valentia gave it very graciously to the two Miss Whitmores and me, ie she distributed us along the stalls giving her own to me and Mrs Edward Taylor. It was a comedy to be next to Lucy Davenport she sold a great many things and told people wonderful stories and fortunes at 6d with a black Obeah woman standing in the middle of a pasteboard circle. After selling things for three or four hours I was glad to be taken out to see the grounds which are beautiful. People came from Bridgnorth in Barges and there was a band on the banks of the Severn and people dancing on the grass as they do on the Continent. The river winds round the Park and with the fine old trees and very uneven ground there is great variety and beauty of prospect. The Miss Spearmans and Mrs Lowndes came and took my place with some of the Sparkes. There was a handsome luncheon in the great dining room and we could go into the Castle at the back of our Stalls, the tent being against the outside wall of the house and open opposite. The late Lord Mountnorris built the Castle as it now stands but it was never quite finished and has now passed with the estate to another branch of the Annesley family away from the title. The Band of the Worcestershire Yeomanry played on the Terrace and cannons were fired and the bells of the pretty little old church rang and it was a day certainly of much merriment. I was introduced to the Actons who came over the Gatacre. Mr & Mrs Alfred bought a multitude of things and also good natured Mrs Stevens - Lady Ward was also a great purchaser, the mother-in-law I suppose of the young lady of somewhat scandalous notoriety.*

Saturday 23rd August - *During my absence they have made a door from my room to dear Papa's dressing room and very nice it is but I shall be a fortnight getting settled.*

Thursday 28th August - *There was the Flower Show at Dudmaston. I drove over to Mrs Lowndes in the morning and went with her party. Saw many people I knew. The two Miss Moseleys were with the Spearmans and their new brother-in-law Mr Peel, Mr Richards, Mr Merriman and Mr Plumtree, James Fletcher was there with Mrs Cooke and the Hon Mr & Mrs Bridgeman ("bien* *gracious" as also was Lady Valentia) she introduced me to her niece Miss Somerset. Charlotte and Laura Whitmore were with Lady Wrottesley and the 2 little Sparkes. Mr Gwythes and Mr & Mrs J Anstice and Mr G Pritchard. I saw 2 beautiful girls, Lady Londesborough's sisters, the Miss Bridgemans. Mr & Mrs Farmer, née Jenny Bache. There were the beautiful grounds - thrown open and there was tea and buns for 2 little schools and there were running matches and climbing greasy poles for a pig - Old English amusements valued by young England. Lucy Davenport was there and a nephew who let a gate bang in the face of Mr Lowndes - by way of jokes, Lady Valentia's servant ran up and caught the gate in time, and Mr Lowndes said with a smile of imperturbable good temper as he drove up to young Davenport "you can drive up to the stables you need not go round to the front door". I was very late home and it is at least 13 miles.*

***Friday 5th September** - I drove to Bridgnorth for a lesson from Dr Marshall. Like him and his lesson very much. He insists on hard work "power commence" and finds that I know little and that little thought without taste - Poor dear Mr Knight I am so sorry to leave him and have been so long convinced that it was a waste of time to go on with him, "La cie darene". I am to work on some exercises. Mrs Cavendish Will was there from Dudmaston where Mr Whitmore has a large party of beautiful Bridgemans also.[24] "We played" said Mrs Cavendish Wall "a game called Post" one of the party is blindfolded and all the rest agree to name themselves after some post town - they call out "the post is going from Bridgnorth to Shrewsbury" and as they move the blind man is to distinguish who it is by the tread - to see Mr Whitmore[24] trying to step lightly along was 'capital'.*

***Thursday 18th September** - Mr Grant and Arthur left us and I drove over with Dr Marshall to Much Wenlock where Mr & Mrs Wayne had provided a handsome luncheon in the school room. The church was re-opened after being enlarged. There was a confirmation and our Bishop (Hereford) and Dr Hampden preached a sermon. Dr Marshall had with him a little plan of the church which he showed to the Bishop of which he approved.[25]*

***Saturday and Monday 20th and 22nd September** - Mrs Sparkes and I and Aston were mightily busy rectifying Madame Treacher's blunders and bad fitting but the dresses are lovely - particularly an embroidered tulle ball dress over white.*

***Tuesday 23rd September** - Journeyed quite alone and quite safely to Cheltenham.[26] I think I was very brave to come without a maid but had no advantage and brought my things quite safely. Abraham and Matilda did not come for some time afterwards. I went in the garden to gather flowers with Mrs Owen and Hugh.[26] Matilda looked very handsome when she came. I would rather have gone to bed than have had to dress and go down to dinner. I sat at dinner between Abraham and Hugh Owen Wilson - the former appeared cold but then I was dreadfully ill with an awful headache.*

Thursday 25th September - *Tilly and I breakfasted in our dressing gowns - very important was the arranging of the bouquets and the dressing of ourselves to start at half past 10. We went down and found Mrs Owen and Capt W (Wilson). Talked and tried to be very gay and found it difficult, though Mr Owen talked about Owen Roche having gone as a bottle holder to Hugh Wilson.*

The Butler came to announce that Mr Owen was come down.[26] *Capt Wilson and I were sent together in a carriage to imperial Square where we found a room filled with bridesmaids and groomsmen and Mrs Smith fastening on the favours. We had not been dressed above 5 minutes when we were summoned "Mrs Owen's carriage for Miss Darby and Capt Wilson." In the carriage were my sister and Mrs Owen and we drove altogether to the church - Charlton Kings - singularly enough the church where Capt Wilson's father was buried, and this with no property or family connection with Cheltenham or the county. We six bridesmaids were all in white with no colour but our bouquests and our ornaments of which we might wear all we possessed and the effect was better than might have been thought. When we knelt round the beautiful bride*[26] *in her wreath and brussels (lace) veil and white moire antique she made us wait a long time in white satin shoes on that cold stone floor. Mrs Owen was in peach blossom brocade with a blonde bonnet and profusion of antique yellow "point de Venice". Mrs Colmore brocade brown and white and pretty clear lace bodice with scarlet ribbons and a white chip bonnet from Madame F. with scarlet feathers inside and outside. Matilda was very elegant in a blue and white brocade embroidered with china shawl and a blue bonnet with geraniums. Hugh Wilson made the long service very long. The bridegroom looked very pale, John Roche very red, the bridesmaids remarkably composed and cool and then away we all went, throngs of people not all too clean and numbers of policemen to make way for us - quite necessary. Back to Mrs Smith's. The breakfast like all other wedding 'dejeuner', ice and champagne and game. 60 people - one half unknown to the other and walking on "terra incognita" in regard to them - everybody was glad when it was over, even I was, although Capt Wilson told me all sorts of good stories and never flagged. Then the bride vanished from the drawing room with one bridesmaid and Louisa Roche and Mrs Colmore, and I enjoyed some nice talk and I found I was "engaged" to Mr Osbourne Gordon to Mary's indignation and my annoyance. Some of the gentlemen came in and some went with Hugh for his packing. The bride came down in peach blossom moire and stayed listening to pretty things from the gentlemen. When at last she came prepared to go, it was in mushroom coloured velvet cloak with a hood and white bonnet.*

Friday 26th September - *Abraham and Matilda and Capt Wilson left for London by the 10 o'clock train*[27] *- Hugh Wilson and I found the Roches at the station and a very merry party we were to Worcester. I went on with 2 stupid old women and a little boy and two gentlemanly men offered all manner of civilities and attention. I was too late for the train, Hugh and his bride*[26] *came up to speak to me as I was watching my two boxes. I waited until 6 and it was quite* *dark long before I reached Wellington. The carnage was gone and a sort of fly vehicle was ordered for me - it could not get up the hill and I had to walk home in the rain. I got home half amused, half frightened, the whole household astonished to see me - How tired I was and happy to go to bed.*

Monday 6th October - *Janetta and I went to Bridgnorth. We were early rather, for I was to go on to Dudmaston.*[28] *Found Mrs Sparkes and Nora ready for their tour in Wales. Mrs Sparkes ready to go with me. I think I was more frightened than at going to Willey. Mr Whitmore is a fine tall formidable looking person*[28] *- his sister Sophy Whitmore all kindness and amiability, Cavendish Wall, his nephew, very clever and animated. These and Donald Carr were all the party. We walked about the grounds and through the beautiful dingle before lunch and afterwards went on the lake and had a lesson in rowing which Mr Cavendish said I managed wonderfully. I had an immense room with three great windows and a very great fire - it was charming altogether. A beautiful little dinner but Mr Whitmore*[28] *is a little grand and does not exactly place a small woman like me at ease. Played chess with Mr Cavendish who beat me after doing my best and gaining tolerable applause. Sat up very late reading a novel of Bolwer's "Harold the last of the Saxon Kings."*

Tuesday 7th October - *Breakfast about half past 9. Donald Carr arrived looking very handsome and went to play at billiards with his Uncle. Mr Whitmore*[28] *was going to Woodcote*[29] *but news came of the death of Lord Liverpool. Mrs Sparkes and Aunt Sophy went with me as far as St John's*[29] *and then I went home. Mrs Egremont, Mrs W Maude, Janet and Trotty came to lunch.*

Tuesday 14th October - *Arch in wine cellar threatening to fall in. Hilly to mend it for us. Chimneys invalided the next day. Young Mr R Smith appeared one day the rain being perpetuaL he went away after lunch. My Uncle Richard Darby came giving me a sorrowful account of his health and his affairs.*

Friday 17th October - *Set off for St John's*[29] *taking with us a haunch of venison, the other went to Stoke Court but I do not know that it was very agreeable. My third lesson from Dr Marshall. Began Hertz's "chasse aux chamois". Mr Henry Whitmore*[45] *at lunch. Mrs Sparkes went with me to call at Stanley*[30] *and at Mrs Stephen's who gave me some carnation plants. Met Mrs John Pritchard who drove back with me a few miles to Linley - all the people are returned from the Continent very troubled, with the English servants they took with them.*

Wednesday 22nd October - *Took post horses and drove to Dudmaston calling for Mrs Sparkes and Jannetta. Invitation from Mr Whitmore for Mrs H to see the Quatt Schools. The gardens first then Mr Whitmore*[31] *appeared with two delightful Danish noblemen - Count de Pantre and his nephew. He had been summoned to England by the Countess Reventlow on the sudden death of her husband. Then lunch, 3 birds and a pheasant and a side table. Then we* *walked all together to Quatt where the schools are. Very wonderful schools. About 30 girls and 30 boys taught all sorts of things - the boys farming and the girls house work and cooking. Mr Whitmore appears to great advantage talking to these happy looking boys. It was late of course when we got home for we stayed to look at Quatford church built by Moliza.*

Thursday 23rd October - *Coalport - Brosley - Wenlock and Buildwas Abbey. "Recontre" with Col Forester and some ladies, Mrs and Miss Spalding and Miss Anson, he was very civil. Mr & Mrs Edmonds and Mrs Edmonds came to dinner.*

Friday 24th October - *We had a long walk to Lincoln Hill.*[32] *Then to the works after lunch and to Horsehay. Mr & Mrs Marshall and James Fletcher at dinner.*

Thursday 30th October - *James Fletcher came in the morning to lunch and we took a walk - he and Anne and I. J Reynolds came to dinner. We played at Spillicans and dominoes and had a rather pleasant evening.*

Friday 31st October - *Anne and her brother and I rode over early in the morning to Bridgnorth - then lunch - then a ride in which I was frightened and changed Jannetta's horse at the beginning for the pony she rode. We rode to Apley Terrace - Met Henry Whitmore*[45] *at Mrs Clarke's cottage. He led my pony to see the view. Mr Sparkes and I then rode on and met James and Jannetta cantering back again. Jannetta most good-naturedly changed again - home through the park, leaped a ditch - to dress for dinner. Mr & Mrs Hayes - a little curate Leigh Richmond Ayre - Mr Frederick Greenstreet, Dr Marshall and Henry Whitmore. The two last and ourselves remained the night. Dr Marshall's playing is beautiful and his singing is exquisite. Lord Ossleton sang "the Pirate's Serenade", "This night or never my bride thou shalt be" - "Awake lady wake for my bar's on the sea." It was a charming evening.*

Saturday 1st November - *We walked after breakfast to the High Rock - beautiful morning - beautiful views - beautiful bivouac under the rocks during a shower of hail. Stanley is so pretty from there. Our party was Mrs S, Nora, Jannetta, the two children, Henry Whitmore and three ourselves. Met Aunt Sophy returning. Lunch, Mr Whitmore called from Dudmaston - About 4 left - Drove home by Stanley - left James with a dreadful cold at the Willey gate.*

Monday 3rd November - *Henry Whitmore and his brother George called, bringing an exchanged umbrella - it was not a pleasant day.*

Tuesday 4th November - *We had arranged to ride and James Fletcher came over to lunch. I was crossing the hall in my habit when a small black scotch terrier fawned upon it - I said, "pretty creature, is it yours?" to a man like a servant. "No, ma'am, it is Mr Henry Whitmore's." In the morning room was a great parcel of books and a note, I threw it to James Fletcher - "Miss Darby, after this will you condescend to ride with me." "Nonsense, am I to answer it?"*

"Of course not - there is no sort of occasion, send your compliments and thanks, if you like to write you can and I'll give you a blue stamp with which you can send him ten pages." We took our ride and Anne Fletcher sat her pony admirably - James went back to dinner.

Friday 7th November *- James Fletcher came over to lunch for another ride and Lady Louisa[33] and Henry Whitmore drove up just as we were going in. Lady Louisa is very agreeable and nice and gentle - not at all aristocratic looking - Mama would not ask them to lunch, they were going to Willey. We had great fun in our ride which was to the Bannings where Anne Fletcher wished to call. Anne caught cold in her ride and in the afternoon James and I walked to Lincoln Hill[32] very pleasant and he went away after dinner.*

Monday 10th November *- Yesterday went to church, Abraham was there - for the Shropshire Bank & Company's meeting. Note of invitation from him.*

Wednesday 12th November *- Mama and I went for the first time to the Company's meeting. There were Abraham, Alfred, my Uncle, Mrs Edmund Darby and Miss Mary Darby, Mama and me. Abraham gave up the management to his brother and appointed for him £500 a year. The year is not a good one and I suppose nothing better is to be expected.*

Thursday 13th November *- I drove very early to Wroxeter. Janet and Mr Mayne went with me to the Infirmary meeting - met George[33a] and Henry Whitmore[45] on the steps at St Chads (Shrewsbury). We had the pew behind the Mayor and Corporation and saw everybody wonderfully well and the Infirmary meeting is altogether so much more like a theatre than like going to church, that it is natural to look about. We went into the Vestry while Mr Edward Mayne went to look for the carriage. Lord Forester came up to me at once and shook hands like an old friend - "Glad to see you here and in Shropshire - how long have you been here?" "I have not been away." "I heard of you at Wenlock, 'tis said you were only down for a week." (Oh! The mess, Fr' did that) "I have not been away."*

"How is Lady Newport, is she here?" "Yes, she is there." I did not like to follow but meeting with John Roche and his sister who introduced me to Mr and Mrs Walcot.[34] I went a long way to the other end then the John Pritchards came up and at length Lord Forester brought his sister to talk to me, turning away Henry Whitmore by a button. She was very amiable and said almost the same things as her brother, adding much about Tilly's departure from Shropshire. The Roche's were in the vestry too and Mr & Mrs Walcot[34] of Bitterley and the Whitmores. Mrs Egremont and Mrs Edward Hayes and I went in our carriage and in the other were Lily and Pauline, Mr Edward Maws and Mr Maude. It was a very pleasant ball, tho' rather thin. Henry Whitmore[45] came with the Sparkes and asked me to dance the first Quadrille, he took me to supper and danced again with me after. John Roche danced with me and we had some tea and a french bonbon which exploded magnificently and he took me to the

carriage and Mr Mayne danced with me and when at 3 o'clock we went away I was engaged to dance with Mr Egerton Jeffreys which I was glad to escape. Lord Forester came up to speak to me again. He said with comic misery "The room is very thin, the church was gayer than the ball."

Mrs Bridgeman came and Miss Anson was there, she is very plain. We went too early and stayed too late - Must never to be there before half past 10 and to leave soon after supper and to go to the left side of the room not the right.

Friday 14th November - *We walked to Atcham after a 10 o'clock breakfast to see the Meet - saw it all in great perfection. Mr Harnage came to breakfast and then joined the Hunt and Mr Maude also. The fox crossed the river at Wroxeter and the whipper in and Mr Barton ran their horses across and went themselves with their saddles in the ferry boat - all the rest went back to the Atcham bridge. As we returned we met Hugh and Owen Wilson,*[26] *rather stiff and stately and very handsome. He was with the party at Onslow.*

Monday 24th November - *Had settled comfortably to practice when Mr Potts*[35] *and Dr Marshall came in with the deeds for signature - poor little me. Very clear it seemed, how I, Adelaide Anna Darby Spinster gave and made over an acre and a half of land in the fields called Straw's Barn field for the site of a church to be erected also a footpath to the said church - signed and sealed. As we were going to lunch, James Fletcher called to ask me to ride with him, we were going in the carriage but Mama gave it up to me like her dear amiable self - "Sentinel" was too fresh and very restive again. While we were riding George*[33a] *and Henry Whitmore*[45] *called, they stayed some time and left a paper for Lady Barnar's Irish schools.*

Thursday 27th November - *The laying of the first stone of the church is now fixed for 11th December. I had asked Dr Marshall if possible let it not be the week before the 16th, as I wanted to be in Northampton, and now he fixed that very week and observes with the utmost coolness, that he told Mrs Abraham Darby. It was arranged to accommodate her sister - he is a curiosity, told us how he is lucky in finding things, how he found money sometimes picked up half-a-crown at the railway station the other day, one of the police came up and said "What have you got there?" "It is no matter to you, what I've got is as much mine as yours - there's no possibility of identifying money, you know, unless it's marked, now any other property there's a danger of identification but not money!!!"*

Friday 28th November - *St John's, good lesson with Dr Marshall. Jannetta and I rode to Dudmaston. Mr & Mrs Frank Laing*[36] *and Miss Carr and Cavendish Wall there, and Aunt Sophie. Harry Whitmore followed us and rode back with us - only he and Mr Plumtree at dinner. Stayed the night, long conversation with Mrs Sparkes till 2 o'clock in the morning. I said that I did not know enough of him and I told her all of our family difference and at present I have not more than 500 a year - he has 400.*[37]

Saturday 29th November - *Left after breakfast to go to Pattingham.*[38] *Not in very high feather to be agreeable, charming drive with hoar frost on the tree. James Farmer as soon as I drove up exclaimed "is it yourself or an iceberg" it was very cold. Mrs Greestreet has been very pretty, her husband very agreeable, her children a bore - she manages them beautifully.*

Sunday 30th November - *I stayed and went twice to church - Monday I came home.*

Monday 3rd December - *Henry Whitmore*[45] *called but I did not see him - was writing notes to Archdeacon Waring as Mr Edmonds had directed. I wanted Mama to see more of him and I think she liked him.*

Monday 8th December - *Day of hindrance! - Boycott and Wilkes called about the well, no water found. Then old Martha, then Dr Marshall, then Henry Whitmore*[45] *who stayed lunch. Then Mr Edmonds.*

Wednesday 10th December - *Henry*[45] *called upon us. In the morning came 10 clergymen to meet the Archdeacon*[39] *who arrived having lost his gown recovered however by midnight. Hon & Rev O Forester, Mr Bartlett, Mr Mayne, Dr Marshall, Mr Edmonds, Mr Nunn, Mr Gwyther, Mr Jetter, Mr More, Mr Fletcher. The Archdeacon is very agreeable.*

Thursday 11th December - *James Fletcher only stayed with the Archdeacon here. Dr Marshall came to breakfast. To a second breakfast came Mr & Mrs Sparkes, Nora, Janetta and Henry Whitmore.*[45]

Dr Kennedy came after to go with us to the ground and the Edmonds. We walked to the school and formed into a procession. I had to walk with Henry Whitmore[45] *notwithstanding some contrivance so it could not be helped, I made myself as happy as circumstances would allow. Flags and music and clergymen without end and Henry Whitmore laid the stone and the Archdeacon and Mr Forester, rural dean, and Mr Gwyther and Mr Jetter and Mr Ball took parts in the service, Dr Marshall acting as Master of Ceremonies. Walked back as we came and to the lunch - by Gunter, soups and game and made dishes and confectionery and ices. Abraham gave "The Queen" and the Archdeacon proposed his, Abraham's health and Mrs A Darby's, the speeches were so touching that everybody cried, at least I did and Henry Whitmore*[45] *had two toasts given him which he proposed so prettily and gracefully. The Anstices were there - all the Pritchards, the Egremonts, the Thursbys, Mr Bagnall, the Stephens, Dr Rowley and a daughter. Mrs GP, Mr & Mrs JP and Miss Baugh, Mr & Mrs WE and Mrs GE, the Archdeacon, Dr Kennedy - JF dined here. Henry Whitmore, Mrs Egremont, etc called on us and the Archdeacon. Never in the natural history of Fetes was I so tired.*

Friday 12th December - *The Archdeacon left early. Flat and tired. John Pritchard went away with a cold. Abraham and Matilda called upon us. Eppel went into the wine cellar. In the evening Mama and I went to dine at Dale*

House. Met the Edmonds, Severn House, Alfred and Matilda, Abraham was not well and went to bed.

Saturday 13th December - *I came by myself to Cogenhoe,*[40] *most kind reception. Since the glorious fine day for the laying of the stone nothing but fog.*

Sunday 15th December - *Lord Aboyne and Mr Layard arrived, a Mr James clergyman, Charles Hartshorne also - Lord Alwyne Compton and his Uncle Mr Dickens joined the party at dinner. Layard is rather short and thick and clumsy with a great head, thick eyebrows, heavy features, bright grey eyes, not gentlemanly in anything and Lord Aboyne exquisitely so. Lord Alwyne is slight and dark, very fine features, very agreeable, talks nicely and kindly. He came to me across the room and talked without any introduction about french affairs and the feasibility of making slaves of our prisoners of war - there is fear of a war with France. Went in the morning to Whiston*[41] *Church, beautiful late gothic monuments by Nillikins to the Irsby family, Lord Boston.*

Tuesday 16th December - *The day of the Soiree. Drew, copied a thing of Mr Petite, Mr Layard admired very much what he was pleased to call my wonderful command of a pen. Mr Layard gave me his autograph, I must say that he almost offered it to me when Miss Hartshorne was asking him. He is most agreeable and so unpretending and unostentatious. Lord Fitzwilliam presided at the Soiree and we had speeches from him, Lord Alwyne, Lord Woodhouse, Lord Henly, The Hon Vernon Smith, Lord Aboyne, Mr Layard, George Cruikshank, Mr Charles Knight, the cheap literature man and Mr Hartshorne and Dr Connolly. There was a new organ in the music hall or corn exchange and the music was beautiful.*

Poor Layard declared he had been bothered out of his life by a horrid man about bricks and tiles, a Mr Watson. How we enjoyed coming home to supper of oysters, even Lord Aboyne was brilliant.

Wednesday 17th December - *Drove to Brayfield church, lately restored in brown and white stone. Mr Francis is the curate, Mr Smythe the Rector and his brother the Squire. House by Ashby, met Mr Dickens and lady Elizabeth, Mr Woolward and Lord Ashford. Ashby is splendid indeed, avenue like Bushy Park. Lord Alwyne and Mr Lavard went away in the morning - the former in scarlet, the latter away for Newark. At night came Mr & Mrs Francis to dinner and Mr Pidcock - we dined until 12. I must now go to bed.*

Thursday 18th December - *I came home, Mr Pidcock went with me so far as Blisworth.*[42] *The Electric Telegraph and messages. At Stafford Mr & Mrs George Bridgeman, cough very bad.*

Friday 19th December - *Nursed in bed and went to Broseley to dinner. Mr & Mrs Kettle, William Tothill and Mr Brown of Ebbw Vale, Mr & Mrs Alfred, Abraham and Matilda, one of the Christys, Mr G P and Miss P. I stayed the night and Abraham and Matilda, Mr & Mrs Kettle.*

Saturday 20th December - *Mama and I dined at Severn House to meet Abraham and Matilda and Mr & Mrs Alfred - very stupid.*

Monday 22nd December - *Matilda came to spend the day and Henry Whitmore*[45] *came to luncheon. At dinner Abraham and Matilda, Mr & Mrs Alfred, Mr & Mrs Egremont and Pauline and Lily, Dr Marshall and Mr & Mrs William Anstice - charming singing.*

Tuesday 23d December - *Abraham and Matilda went away to Stoke Court. In the evening there came a great many books and a long letter from Henry Whitmore*[45] *to Mama.*

Wednesday 24th December - *She answered it. Christmas Day was not quite happy to me, I could not fix my thoughts upon all that should be our chief delight at the season.*

Thursday 26th December - *Henry Whitmore*[45] *came and Mama gave him her answer and approval and I was persuaded to believe that unless he alters greatly or I alter, I may be very happy as his wife.*

Tuesday 30th December - *Was the Bridgnorth Ball but Henry Whitmore called the day before and gave me his and Lady Louisa's advice not to go.*[43] *The affair was talked of in a way to make it disagreeable I promessi Sposi. Henry was obliged to go as one of the patrons - I had been invited to go to Clungunford for the Ludlow Ball.*

NOTES

1. Sir Francis Lawley belonged to the Lawley family who carried the title Baron Wenlock. The estate was predominantly at Monkhopton (south of Much Wenlock) where Manor Farm (now St Peter's House) was the chief house. Sir Francis had undertaken considerable improvements to the estate and to Monkhopton church prior to his death in 1851 (VCHX, pp.359-60, 363-4, 420-2).
2. Rebecca Darby, daughter of Richard and Maria Darby of "Rosehill".
3. The entail related to Sunniside and some 5 acres of land adjoining Sunniside (including The White House) which was acquired by Abraham Darby II before he built Sunniside in 1750/51. By his Will Abraham II left Sunniside to his widow during her life. It was then entailed to Abraham III and after his death it was entailed to Francis Darby and then to his children, i.e. Matilda and Adelaide. By her actions after the death of Francis, Hannah sought to override not just her husband's wishes but also the inheritance of Francis' grandfather, Abraham II. (This involved barring the entail.) It was small wonder that Matilda would have told Richard Darby (Francis' brother) of the entail, which was a very important matter.
4. A well-known incident. It was not until afterwards that it was discovered that this was an unauthorised intrusion.

5. The Lilleshall Company and its extensive lands in the Coalbrookdale Coalfield were part of the Duke of Sutherland's estates and formed part of his Shropshire estates.
6. Lord John Russell was Prime Minister at the time.
7. Although Adelaide does not mention it in her Journal, "The Dome with the Eagle Slayer" was one of the Coalbrookdale Company's exhibits. The Dome was designed by Charles Crookes, Manager of the Company and the Eagle Slayer was designed by John Bell, the well known designer who also designed "Andromeda" which was subsequently purchased by Queen Victoria and is now in the garden of Osborn House, Isle of Wight. The Company also exhibited an ornamental fountain entitled "The Boy and the Swan" (now back in Coalbrookdale in front of Abraham Darby I's original furnace of 1709) and a set of ornamental gates (now in Kensington Gardens).
8. Lady Constance Gower and the Marquis of Stafford were related to the Duke of Sutherland.
9. Purbeck stone, which has a greenish hue comes from Dorset. It was used extensively in early ecclesiastical buildings, such as the Temple Church, long before Portland stone, also from Dorset, came into use.
10. Although Adelaide's Journal contains only brief references to her first visit to Stoke Court there is a more revealing description of the occasion (see Appendix C, p.289). Mr and Mrs Pritchard's party to the Exhibition included not just Adelaide but also Mr Osborne Gordon. The gossip, disclosed by Mrs Egremont of Wroxeter was that Mr Gordon thought himself accepted as Adelaide's suitor.
11. Chetten is a parish a few miles south west of Bridgnorth.
12. Mr Bartlett lived at Marnwood. He was the vicar of Buildwas.
13. Arley is on the River Severn south of Dudmaston. It is in Worcestershire close to its border with Shropshire. It is the site of a traditional ferry across the River Severn.
14. Dudmaston Lodge should not be confused with Dudmaston.
15. Dudmaston, part of the Dudmaston Estate, now owned by the National Trust, is a house situated approximately 4 miles south east of Bridgnorth on the Bridgnorth-Kidderminster Road. The estate was owned by the ancient Shropshire family of Wolryche from 1403 until 1774 when it passed by inheritance to George Whitmore of Apley. The house was built by Sir Thomas Wolryche in 1695 but was remodelled and enlarged in the 1820's by William Wolryche Whitmore, a Whig MP for Bridgnorth, who was a strong advocate of the repeal of the Corn Laws. His radical views lost him political support in Bridgnorth and so with the passing of the Reform Act of 1832 he stood for and won a seat in Wolverhampton. His cousin, Thomas Whitmore of Apley then represented Bridgnorth as a Tory MP from 1832-1852.
16. The bust of "the late Lady Lucy Whitmore" was of Lucy Georgina Bridgeman, daughter of Orlando, 1st Earl of Bradford of Weston Hall. She had married William Wolryche Whitmore in 1810 and had died in 1840. The bust is still at Dudmaston.
17. This was a perceptive comment. The Dingle at Dudmaston was laid out by Walter Wood who was for many years the gardener at Dudmaston. The

Badger and Dudmaston Dingle were long picturesque rivals. (National Trust handbook).

18. The Mr Whitmore referred to was William Wolryche Whitmore (see note 15 above). He died in 1858.
19. Chesterton is about 8 miles east of Broseley near Badger.
20. Presumably this is a reference to Dugdales Monasticon.
21. Mr and Mrs Lawford were close family friends from Leighton Buzzard.
22. Lilleshall Hall is located some 2 miles south of Newport, Shropshire. The Hall is in the grounds of Lilleshall Abbey, an Augustinian monastery which was suppressed in 1538 as a result of the Reformation. It was the Shropshire home of the Leveson Gower family, created Earl Gower in the 18th century. George Granville Leveson Gower (then Marquis of Stafford) married in 1785 the Countess of Sutherland and was created Duke of Sutherland before his death in 1833. His brother Granville Leveson Gower was created Earl Granville, and it would have been his son, the 2nd Earl Granville who would have been resident at the time of the visit in 1851.
23. This contact with the Whitmore family may have been the result of the visit to Dudmaston.
24. William Wolryche Whitmore had been married to Georgiana Bridgeman, daughter of the 1st Earl of Bradford, so the "Beautiful Bridgemans" were no doubt relatives of his widow.
25. This plan was probably a plan of the Coalbrookdale Church then about to be constructed.
26. Although Adelaide's Journal does not specifically say so, the occasion of the journey to Cheltenham was the marriage of Hugh Darby Owen, Junior, to an anglo-Indian bride. Hugh Darby Owen was an important shareholder in the Coalbrookdale Company as he had inherited from his parents (Mrs Mary Owen (née Darby) and her husband, Reverend E. Pryce Owen, former vicar of Wellington) all the 90 shares (out of a total of 720) allocated to his grandfather Samuel Darby II, when the partnership was reconstituted in 1807. The family had moved to Cheltenham where they were closely related to the Wilson family.
27. No doubt the time of the train was established by reference to Bradshaw's Railway Guide published by George Bradshaw, another of the Quaker entrepreneurs who graced Britain's industrial life.
28. This visit to Dudmaston where she had been invited to stay overnight enabled her to become more acquainted with the Whitmore family. Adelaide found it more frightening even than her visit to Willey where she stayed with the Foresters. Dudmaston was the home of William Wolryche Whitmore (see note 15) but the Mr Whitmore ("a fine tall formidable looking person") is possibly his cousin Mr Henry Whitmore of Apley.
29. Woodcote is a village close to Lilleshall Hall (see note 22). St John's was probably the home of Mr and Mrs John Pritchard in Broseley.
30. Stanley Hall was the home of Alfred and Rebecca Darby.
31. This was probably Mr William Wolryche Whitmore (see note 15) and not Mr Henry Whitmore.
32. Lincoln Hall, south end of Coalbrookdale.

33. Lady Louisa (Douglas) was the wife of Thomas Charlton Whitmore who was the eldest brother (of three) of Henry Whitmore who was the youngest. Lady Louisa was the eldest daughter of the 5th Marquess of Queensbury. Thomas Whitmore was the owner of Apley and was Member of Parliament for Bridgnorth. His wife, Lady Louisa, by virtue of her position and her aristocratic birth would have been considered as the Matriarch of Apley. Her visit to the White House would have been of considerable significance.
33a. George Whitmore was the middle of the three brothers. He was the Rector of Stockton, close to Apley, to which he had been appointed in succession to his uncle, who nevertheless continued to occupy the Rectory at Stockton.
34. Probably Mr and Mrs William Walcot of Bitterley (east of Ludlow), owners of nearby Moor Hall.
35. Mr Potts was the family's solicitor from Broseley.
36. Mrs (Mary Dorothea) Laing was a younger sister of William Wolryche Whitmore.
37. No doubt this was a crucially significant meeting. It was probably part of the "sounding-out" process. Rachel Labouchere, who transcribed Adelaide's Journal, and was a descendant of both the Darby family and the Whitmore family, was of the opinion that Henry Whitmore needed the Darby money in order to advance a career in politics.
38. Pattingham in Staffordshire is just over the Shropshire border east of Badger. It was the seat of the Earl of Dartmouth.
39. This gathering of clergymen was in connection with the laying of the foundation stone of Coalbrookdale Church for which Adelaide had agreed to provide the land (as part of the land settlement (see Journal entry 24th November) following the death of Francis Darby) and which Abraham IV had agreed to endow.
40. The Journal entries for 13th to 18th December contain no obvious explanation for the visit to Cogenhoe, which is a village immediately east of Northampton. The only familiar name is that of Mr Charles Hartshorne and Miss Hartshorne.
41. Whiston is a village close to Cogenhoe.
42. Blisworth is just south of Northampton. It was a station on the railway to Stafford.
43. No doubt this advice was because the engagement of Adelaide and Henry Whitmore had not then been announced. Perhaps there would have been a great deal of speculation.
44. Archery was a popular pastime for women, although later it was superseded by lawn tennis and croquet.
45. Henry Whitmore of Apley was the future husband of Adelaide. This is the first specific mention of him in the Journal, although they may have met at Dudmaston (see note 28).

1852

Comment

The first entry for 1852 (18th January) states that "Mrs Whitmore and Emily came to luncheon". This was a warm-hearted confirmation of the fact that Adelaide was accepted within the Whitmore family, as the future wife of Henry Whitmore. Henry was the youngest of the three sons of Thomas Whitmore of Apley who had died in 1846. The eldest brother who had inherited Apley was Thomas Charlton Whitmore who at the time was Member of Parliament for Bridgnorth. He was married to Lady Louisa Whitmore (née Douglas) who was the eldest daughter of the 5th Marquess of Queensbury. The second brother was Rev George Whitmore MA who was Rector of Stockton, a parish church close to Apley, who in 1848 had married Sarah Deacon of Mabledon Park, Kent (see extract from Whitmore family tree, p.333).

The principal event in 1852 was the marriage of Adelaide and Henry Whitmore which took place on 15th April 1852. Adelaide was 35 years of age. Her marriage was marred however by the sudden death, the day before (14th April 1852) of Alfred Darby who had for many years been the persistent (and rejected) suitor for Adelaide's hand in marriage. He died aged 45 at his home, Stanley Hall, Bridgnorth, of erysipelas. The wedding was attended by Adelaide's sister Matilda who recorded the departure of Lucy Darby and Mary Darby (Alfred's mother and sister) in great distress to Stanley Hall. Henry and Adelaide left for honeymoon in Malvern, returning to a great reception at Bridgnorth.

Adelaide's life thereafter was almost completely transformed. As a member of the Whitmore family she occupied a very elevated position in Shropshire society. Henry and Adelaide set up home at The White House, Coalbrookdale because Apley was already the home of Thomas Charlton Whitmore and Lady Louisa Whitmore, and Dudmaston was the home of William Wolryche Whitmore.

Increasingly thereafter, the Journal becomes more of a daily diary, containing a bewildering catalogue of visitors and guests. Some of these can be identified as members of the Whitmore family which by then had become considerably extended. The family had branches in the Cotswolds (Lower Slaughter and Chastleton), London and Kent, and some of these more distant relatives appear from time to time in the Journal. Amongst other guests who can be identified were the Garforth family. These became close friends. They came from Yorkshire where they owned Wigganthorpe Hall, situated some 10 miles north of York. Although the Journal does not elaborate on the relationship, they must have been political associates of the Whitmore family.

The other big event in 1852 was the parliamentary election in July. Bridgnorth up to then had been represented by Thomas Charlton Whitmore, but he stood down at that election in favour of his younger brother, Adelaide's husband, Henry Whitmore. From that moment on, Adelaide became, not just a member of the Whitmore family, but a political hostess as well.

This involved long stays in London, first at Lowndes Square, Knightsbridge and then at South Audley Street. The hospitality included visits to the leading aristocratic families of East Shropshire (the Earl of Bradford, Lord Newport and the Bridgeman family at Weston Park, and the Foresters at Willey) and neighbouring Staffordshire (the Wrottesley and Lewisham (Dartford) families).

On the political front the year was notable for the short-lived administration of the Earl of Derby, who Henry Whitmore supported (27th November 1852 to 18th December 1852).

Saturday 18th January - *Mrs Whitmore and Emily came to luncheon.*[1] *I cannot describe their affection nor how they took me to their hearts and made me feel to them a daughter and a sister. God is very good to give me such intense happiness.*

Wednesday 19th February - *I went to Stoke Court,*[1a] *my first visit, and to procure my trousseau.*

Friday 23rd February - *Henry came.*

Friday 9th March - *We returned home. Mama had come to Stoke Court*[1a] *on Saturday.*

Tuesday 14th April - *We were all horrified at the sudden death of Alfred Darby!*

Wednesday 15th April - *I was married.*

Wednesday 29th April - *We returned from Malvern. Great reception at Bridgnorth.*

Saturday 15th May - *Came to 33 Chesham Place (Belgravia, London SW1).*

Thursday 20th May - *A little dinner party. Mrs Whitmore*[1] *came to stay with us for a day or two and we had besides Mr & Mrs Colmore and Lady Bandon,*[2] *Mr Creyke and Sir F. Hopkins.*

Friday 21st May - *The Regent's Park Flower Show at the Botanical Gardens, the Roches there, the Thursbys. Introduced to Mr Giffard.*[3]

Tuesday 25th May - *Dined at Mrs Charles Whitmore's.*[4] *Lady Whitmore and daughter Emily, Miss Brownrigg and Mr Brownrigg, Mr & Mrs Bristowe and Mr Wolryche Whitmore.*

Monday 31st May - *Mrs Whitmore left us early this morning. We went in the evening to the Philharmonic Concert. Mr and 2 Miss Garforths*[4a] *dining and going with us afterwards. Beethoven's Sinfonia in C minor No 5. Clara Neville and Spandigl.*

Tuesday 1st June - *The Garforths*[4a] *came to us and we went to the Opera (Count G Grise and Mario in Lucrizia Borgio and Mdme Jullienne in I Martisis).*

Wednesday 2nd June - *Henry dined at Lord Hotham's and I went to Mrs Garforths.*[4a]

Thursday 3rd June - *I went with Maria Garforth*[4a] *to the Corridor at St James' Palace.*[5] *Henry got the tickets for us. Mrs Whitmore comes to town today with all the party from Malvern.*[6] *They dine with us and Sir Francis Huskin and Mr Wynniat and then Henry and I go to Lady Listowel's and to Lady Bradford.*[7]

Friday 4th June - *To Lady Beecher's. Party of 20 or so. Mrs Twistleeton very agreeable, 2 Miss Beechers.*

Tuesday 8th June - *Dinner the same. Mr and Mrs Charles Whitmore and Miss Brownrigg,*[8] *Col. Forbes and Lucy*[9] *and Emily, Mrs Forbes and Mr Wynniat. Afterwards the desert, ornaments being left and a supper of jellies creams and ices added, we had a few more people. Two Professionals who sang and played very well, Mr Durand and Mr Cooke. Lady Laura Grattan, Mrs & Miss Garforth, Admiral Byng and Miss Byng, 2 Miss Blackburns, 2 Miss Sandersons, Mrs Chapel Cure and Miss Ducheene, Tommy,*[9a] *Mr Watts Russell, Mr Hugh Douglas, Miss Chudde, Sir Baldwin and Lady Leighton and 2 Miss Leightons, Lady Beecher and 2 daughters and Mr Beecher. The Isaacs and Hollands and MacInroys, Mrs Foley and her sister. Mr Packington, Sir William Davidson, Mr & Mrs Bristowe, Mrs Fitzroy. We were about 50 and the Miss Beechers sang delightfully.*

Thursday 10th June - *Went to Connaught Place for Miss Sophia*[10] *Whitmore. Lady Louisa*[11] *and Nina and Harry and Emily arrive at 11 o'clock from Richmond, were coming to luncheon. Mrs Whitmore*[11] *asked us to go to Lowndes Sq. We went. Miss Whitmore and I went shopping and then in the Park. The weather cleared a little. In the evening we had the party from Lowndes Sq. George*[11] *and another George Whitmore, Mr James Whitmore, Mr Gatacre and "Sophia",*[10] *and Tommy.*[9a] *We were 12. Henry and I took Sophia back to Connaught Place in the evening and we went ourselves to Lady Dalrymples, a gay party, pretty rooms and very well dressed people, tea in the ante room. Henry met some friends who I liked very much, 2 Miss Gapes.*

Friday 11th June - *Lady Elizabeth Tollemache*[11a] *paid us a morning visit. Then Emily and I went to Mrs Graham Pigot's in the Regent's Park, found her at home and her daughter. Cards at several other places and some shopping. Dined at Lowndes Sq., Mr Gatacre and the Garforths.*[4a]

Saturday 12th June - Chiswick - *Rather cold but not wet. Saw Lord Bradford*[12] *and his daughters. Mr John Cotes and Mrs Wedstn, Mr Fredrick Cavendish and Miss Coleshill, Miss Hartopp. Dined in Lowndes Sq.*

Sunday 13th June - *I did not go out at all, bad cold and cough.*

Monday 14th June - *Mrs Garforth*[4a] *here early, I am much better and going to Lady Ryan's. In the evening went to see Mrs Garforth and Miss G dressed for the Caledonian Ball.*

Wednesday 16th June - *George came. Miss Lucy Deacon's*[13] *death occurred yesterday and Sarah was gone to Tonbridge - George and Henry went to Salt Hill, they did not find Douglas. Mrs Whitmore and Emily came to dinner.*

Thursday 17th June - *We are going to Iver and Lord Powis' Ball.*[14] *The Ball was a very large one, 500 people perhaps. All Shropshire and all Wales and all London some people said.*

Friday 18th June - *Luncheon in Lowndes Sq. to meet Mrs Pigot; and then to Albert Smith's Mont Blanc.*

Monday 21st June - *Lucy, Henry, Colonel Forbes,*[15] *Emily and I went to Beckenham to dine with Mr & Mrs William Whitmore, very pretty place. On our way we called upon Mrs John Whitmore at Clapham.*[15] *We were all at Lowndes Sq. when a telegraphic despatch was brought in for Henry - Cadogan is canvassing in Bridgnorth.*[16] *Went to Richmond and then at 5 in the morning off for Shropshire and to stand a contest.*

Wednesday 23rd June - *George came yesterday and today we were very busy with Emily counter ordering Gunter and sending to about 100 people to put off an evening party for Friday. Then we went to a fete at Woolwich given in the grounds of Sir Thomas Wilson at Charlton, a beautiful place close to Sir George Whitmore's. Bands of music, flowers and Batty's circus.*

Thursday 24th June - *Drove with Mrs Whitmore in the Park. George and Sarah went back to Kemberton.*

Friday 25th June - *In the morning with the Miss Garforths, I mean the Royal Academy, then for luncheon at Mrs Garforths then Emily and I went by the train to Richmond - to Mansfield House and Bute House, Lady Queensbury's.*[17]

Saturday 26th June - *The Miss Gapes and Mr Brooke called, they would have come last evening. Dined with Mrs Garforth.*

Sunday 27th June - *To St James Church, Picadilly, to hear the Bishop of Oxford. Toosie very ill.*[18]

Sunday 4th July - *Friday I dined with Mrs Garforth and met Colonel Forbes and Lucy*[15] *and Miss Graham Pigot. Every other day at Lowndes Sq. Yesterday paid visits and went shopping. Thursday I had news poor Mrs Frank Tothill died a week after her confinement, leaving a third girl.*[19] *Henry's election next week and we all go down on Monday and I had to provide mourning at a moment's notice and handsome mourning too for the election. Shall we ever be out of black?*

Monday 5th July - *Left London. Mrs Whitmore and Emma going to Apley and I to Mama.*

Tuesday 6th July - *Rest at home.*

Wednesday 7th July - *Drove over early to Apley. Breakfast. Procession of the Tenants. The Nomination. Returned to Apley.*

Thursday 8th July - *The Election. Whitmore - 442; Pigot - 360; Cadogan - 283; Majority for Sir SP - 77.*[20] *Returned to Apley.*

Friday 9th July - *I came home, very tired and very down. We went to luncheon at Kemberton and then I with Mrs Whitmore and Emily to the Dale.*

Saturday 10th July - *I rode over to Apley on "Sentinel". They left for London at 4.*

Sunday 11th July - *I went to church at Little Wenlock.*

Wednesday 14th July - *Mrs Edmonds party at the Wrekin, Mama and I went. Tea in the Cottage, more than 60 people and a thunderstorm. Henry in London canvassing for Lord Blandford.*

Sunday 18th July - *I went to church here in the evening. Henry at Leamington with Lucy.*

Monday 19th July - *Henry came home, I was indeed glad and happy. Capt and Mrs Brazier called.*

Sunday 25th July - *Reading "The Household of Sir Thomas More" and the "Maiden and married life of Mary Powell - Mistress Hilton", - 2 nice books. Sarah lent them to me. They are by her governess and in the style of "Willoughby's Diary" but I think very superior.*

Wednesday 28th July - *Henry came to Shrewsbury for the Assizes - HVs on the Grand Jury. Mr & Mrs Forester called. I went with Mama to Marnwood*[21] *and to see Mrs Nunn. A wonderful letter from Stoke Court.*[1a] *Abraham has sold his shares in the Works to his sister. It appears that her money had been placed by her brothers in a building speculation at Liverpool and as this becomes profitable very slowly they could not afford the rate of interest. Abraham is said to have offered her the shares or that he should resume the management here, the former has been agreed upon. It appears that he does not think it unsafe as he leaves his mother and sister's property in it.*[22] *Sarah has been very ill at*

Malvern, terminating, George says, in what the late Lady Pigot called a "mademoiselle Voiture."[23]

Thursday 29th July - *We dined at the Pritchards - 17 - Mr & Mrs Forester Mr & Mrs WH Anstice etc. Music.*

Friday 30th July - *Mr Isaacson came over with his second "fils bien laid." I went with them to call at Marnwood. They remained to dine and Mr & Mrs Nunn came and stayed all night, very amusing Mrs Nunn was.*

Saturday 31st July - *Mr & Mrs WR Anstice called. The Nunns stayed until Henry and I went to Wroxeter to dine and we left them on our way. Mrs Egremont only well enough to appear for a few minutes before dinner. Capt Russell and Louisa there.*[24]

Sunday 1st August - *We drove over to Apley. At church twice at Stockton and stayed to dine.*

Monday 2nd August - *To Lichborough. Too late for train at Shifnal. We drove in a fly from Coventry to Leamington. Had luncheon with the Storers to whom I had to be introduced.*[25] *Fete in the gardens at Lichborough and balloon going up. Mr Grant met us at the Station. Mr & Mrs Haddon staying in the house very pleasant people, she was a Miss Nesbitt, her family living in Wiltshire. He is Scotch and a barrister.*

Tuesday 3rd August - *We walked about as much as the rain would let us. Mr & Mrs Bevan, Miss Thornton and two brothers at dinner. Mrs Bevan was Miss Lorraine Smith. Mrs Haddon plays and sings very nicely.*

Wednesday 4th August - *Rainy - Drove to Tawsley. Henry and Mr Haddon riding. They called upon Sir CK. Mr & Mrs Smith came to dine.*

Thursday 5th August - *We left Lichborough and came to Malvern.*[6] *We have rooms with Mrs Whitmore. George and Sarah and their 2 children are here and Lucy's baby.*

Sunday 8th August - *The Abbey Church. Mr Rashdall preached from the difficult parable of the unjust steward - an excellent sermon.*

Monday 9th August - *The Isaacs came to dine and Mrs Rashdall and Capt Maude.*

Tuesday 10th August - *Walk on the North Hill, thunderstorm. Miss Saundersons - my birthday.*

Wednesday 11th August - *Emily not well. Luncheon at Mrs Stratton's, delightful Miss Lees. Engaged to dine at Lady Farnhams. Mr West could not go, fever and headache. Mrs Whitmore went, and George and Henry.*

Thursday 12th August - *George went to Kemberton. He gave me such a pretty purse as a birthday present and Henry the loveliest muslin.*

***Monday 16th August** - Apley Castle. Dearest Mama ill. Found the procession under the portice and Mr Charlton replying to the address. Met wagons loaded with raw beef covered with flowers. George went with us. 70 at luncheon, 40 at dinner. Sat in a wagon till I was tired watching the donkey races and climbing poles for hats. Came home about 12. Mama a little better.*

***Thursday 19th August - Luton Park** - Mr & Mrs R Jones, Kitty Garforth and Lucy Charlton joined us at the station at Wellington and we all went together. The Rockes there, the Egremonts, the Lysters, Hugh Wilson. Introduced Lord Wrottesley.*[26]

***Friday 29th August** - The ball at Apley Castle. It was in a tent lighted with small vauxhall lamps. Supper beautiful. Floor not very good had fall.*

***Sunday 2lst August** - Henry went to the Great dinner where he had to preside at the Charlton Arms.*[27]

***Monday 23rd August** - Mrs Garforth, Kitty and Maria*[4a] *and Miss Croft and Mr R Jones came for luncheon ("couleur de rose") They were hardly gone when Mrs Anstice and Mr & Mrs J Anstice*[24] *called. Henry was off for London in the evening.*

***Tuesday 24th August** - Mama and I drove to Willey in search of grapes for next Tuesday. Met Mr & Mrs John Pritchard*[37] *at Ironbridge. Arthur to be married on the 15th October.*

***Wednesday 25th August** - Henry came home in the evening.*

***Thursday 26th August** — Flower Show. All Bridgnorth came to it and everybody I think from our side. We stayed at Apley until Monday. Lord Lewisham*[38] *came with a large party. Mr Cheyney with 4 carriages, he asked us to dine.*

***Friday 27th August** - Dinner at Badger - Lady Louisa, Henry and I - 19. Dinner at half past 7. Mr Cheyney and his brother Edward, Archdeacon Sandford and Mrs and Miss Sandford. Mr Mrs and Miss Butler, Mr & Mrs Bentinck - she sings.*

***Saturday 28th August** - Visit from the Isaacsons. To Bridgnorth.*

***Sunday 29th August** - Went twice to church. Mama drove me in the pony carriage, the most of the party in the Brick. This has been a visitation, Henry had to come to Tom's place,*[9a] *he is in Ireland and nobody at the Flower Show to preside and give away the prizes.*

***Monday 30th August** - I went home early and Henry followed for dinner.*

***Tuesday 31st August** - Our first party here. Mr & Mrs Uvedale Corbett and a son and daughter, etc - We were 13 and Mrs Charlton was expected but she had a bad cold. Haunch of Venison.*

Wednesday 1st September - *Went to Dudmaston.*[39] *Henry rode and I went with Annie and the baggage. Found Miss Childe there and Mr Edward Childe, Admiral and Miss Bridgeman, Mrs Lowndes and Donald Carr joined the party at dinner - Music in the evening.*

Thursday 2nd September - *Mr Edward Childe and Henry went out shooting. We walked in the Dingle and then drove to Mr Whitmore's farm to see the Harvest Home dinner. Mr & Mrs Bellet at dinner and to stay the night. The Dean of Hereford (Dr Dave) and Mr Simmons - Walk by moonlight and Miss Agnes singing.*

Friday 3rd September - *Examination of Quat School by the Dean and Mr Bellet. Luncheon at Dudmaston*[39] *to more than 100 people, school children had tea - Blue Coat band. Row on the lake with Miss Moseley, Donald Carr and his sister and Miss Moseley's cousin. In the evening M Bellet stayed and made us play "This is to describe a noun of several meanings" any one of the party guessing it is not to name it, but to add to the description. The words we had were - Air, Train, Boa, Bore, Boar (which was hardly fair) - Flower and flour, Punch, Gate, gait - Perfect, vale, veil, bow, bough. Another game was to take the letters of the alphabet and make couplets the first person beginning "I am in Cat but not in Dog", the next "I am in Cat but not in Hog", and then to B, "I am in Bell but not in Church" etc. Sat up till half past 11.*

Saturday 4th September - *We left Dudmaston*[39] *- Battledore and Shuttlecock before breakfast. I joined Henry at Bridgnorth and we paid visits till the rain came. Mrs Smith James, a nice person wife of the Town Clerk, Mrs Wasey, Miss Davenport was staying there - she was a Miss Boncalton. Mrs Ellison, Mrs Purton, Mrs Bellet, Mrs Merryman, Mrs Phillips and Mrs Richards, Mrs Stringer (ill) Mrs Nock.*

Tuesday 7th September - *We went to Birmingham for the Music meeting, George with us - went to the Queens.*

Wednesday 8th September - *Christus - The Creation. Simms Reeves, Clara Novello, Viardot Garcia, Anna Terr, Mr Luckley, Formes. Luncheon at Mr George Wateley's. Concert in the evening, Loreley by Mendelsohn.*

Thursday 9th September - *The Messiah. Lady Louisa*[41] *and Nina and Mary came for it- George returned with them. Algernon not well. Concert in the evening. Beethoven's Symphony in D.*

Friday 10th September - *Samson - I held a plate. Dined at Mr Wateley's "The Laurels" a little way out of Birmingham. Lord Leigh, Mr Graham brother of Sir James, Mrs Milnes Gaskell and 2 plain daughters, Capt. Wynniat, Mr & Mrs Halsey.*

Saturday 11th September - *Returned home - called at Chesterton. A very ill, poor child. Henry had his pony and rode on to Bridgnorth. Found Mama not well.*

***Monday 13th September** - Henry went over to Kemberton[40] early and I was to ride his mare in the afternoon and return together. Just out of Madeley she galloped off with me and I could not stop her. Going down the hill into the Shifnal road met a man who flew at the mare screaming and struck her in the face with a thick stick - she jumped across the road and then went on around the dreadful sharp turns on to Kemberton.[40] I pulled her into a farmyard and she stopped. I rode Alice Gray home, Algernon not much better.*

***Tuesday 14th September** - We went to Kemberton[40] and stayed the night.*

***Friday 17th September** - We returned - Algernon better.*

***Saturday 18th September** - Too wet for Henry to go to Bridgnorth.*

***Monday 20th September** - Henry went to Bridgnorth. Mama not well. Went to Dudmaston.[39] Mrs and Miss Childe called.*

***Tuesday 21st September** - Mr Grant came. Mr Haughton dined and stayed the night.*

***Wednesday 22nd September** - Drove to Kemberton.[40] Mama still ill.*

***Thursday 23rd September** - We left Mr Grant at Coalbrookdale. Mama not well. Arrived at Bridgnorth in time for Mr Woodward's sermon. Then we went to Mrs Bellet's for luncheon and after called upon Mrs ? etc. Then when horses were to be had we went on to Kinlet, 9 miles of hilly road and through very pretty country. In the house, Mr Childe with 3 daughters and 3 sons. Mrs Arthur Childe not long married and not 18 and her Papa and Mama, Mr & Mrs Freeman, Hugh Owen Wilson - at dinner Mr & Mrs Essington.*

***Friday 24th September** - The gentlemen went out to shoot, we wrote and worked until luncheon. Miss Catty Childe and Mrs Fremantle and I drove out to see the views Hugh Wilson went away. The Flower Garden, the Owls. Sir Ed and Lady Blount and Miss Blount at dinner.*

***Sunday 26th September** - Sermon on the Duke of Wellington's death.*

***Wednesday 29th September** - 3 wet days, I not able to move. Today we drove in determined rain to Mrs Isaacson's to luncheon. Then we went on to Apley just in time for dinner at Leaton, Mr & Mrs Moseley and 2 daughters and one son, Mr & Mrs Charles Peel, Mr Bacon (Mrs Moseley's father) and a Mrs Cooper - charming music - Mrs Moseley's harp.*

***Thursday 30th September** - Went to Gatacre for luncheon after a very pleasant morning, we working and Mrs Moseley reading a novel to us (Miss Austen's Persuasion). Mr D Watts Russell and Donald Carr came to dinner.*

***Friday 1st October** - Left Leaton - paid visits. Mrs Taylor of Chicknell, Mr Kettle, Mrs Brazier (out). Davenport House with the Watts Russells. Home leaving Henry for his Club dinner at the Squirrell and to sleep at Apley. Mama and I went to call at Madeley Wood. Mrs WR Anstice,[24] the Pritchards[37] and two Miss P. Henry came home in the evening.*

Tuesday 5th October - *Lady Louisa*[41] *and Lady Elizabeth*[41] *and Miss Douglas and George and Sarah and 1 Miss Deacons came for luncheon and to see the Aloe.*

Thursday 7th October - *Ditto - Mrs Charlton and Dora. Henry had a Militia Meeting at Ironbridge and he brought back Lord Forester and Lord Newport. Afterwards we came over to Apley, Lady Elizabeth Douglas*[41] *and Miss Douglas here.*

Friday 8th October - *We all walked to the Terrace and sketched.*

Monday 11th October - *We had a very bad account of Mama. Louisa,*[41] *Lady Elizabeth,*[41] *Miss Douglas and I drove to Kemberton.*[40] *Lord Newport*[42] *came to luncheon.*

Tuesday 12th October - *We were to have gone to Gatacre, but Henry was so unhappy about Mama that he put it off and let me go over to her. I found her very ill but she would not let me stay. I came back really unhappy.*

Wednesday 13th October - *Henry went over with me to the Dale. Mama looked rather more like herself, gastric fever and dysentery. Dangerous for anyone and she now so weak and so thin. We saw Mr Rowland and he and she were positive to send us to Gatacre so we took another pair of horses before our Bridgnorth ones, arrived in time for dinner. Lucy and Col. Forbes*[9] *were arrived the day before - Miss Boycott and Mr G name forgotten, a clergyman at dinner. Finished "Uncle Tom's Cabin."*

Thursday 14th October - *Mr Gatacre drove us to Wolverhampton in his coach to see the Queen pass - saw a pink bonnet. Lord Anglesea there, Lord Wrottesley*[26] *took care of me through the crowd. Mrs Gatacre and I returned outside. The Carrs dined.*

Friday 15th October - *Henry went out shooting. Lucy and I for luncheon to Rudge - then to call upon Mrs Taylor at Chicknell and on the Actons. The Actons came to dinner.*

Saturday 16th October - *Took Mrs Clarke home with us. I went to Apley for luncheon. Henry rode home from Bridgnorth. My precious Mother is better.*

Sunday 17th October - *Henry's birthday - He had to go over to Apley about the Election petition. Tom*[9a] *says that Sir Robert's delinquence cannot affect him.*[28]

Monday 18th October - *Beautiful weather. Mrs Stevens called. To dinner at Willey,*[29] *Lady Louisa Whitmore*[41] *and Emily there. Rooms delightful looking on the lake. In the evening Mrs Anson, the General and daughter, Lady Newport,*[42] *Emiliers, old Major Forester, Orlando and Mrs Forester, Mr & Mrs Fane. Mr Fane went away after dinner and did not return during our visit.*

Tuesday 19th October - *Drove to Bridgnorth after luncheon. Mrs and Miss Anson, Lady Newport[42] and I. Mrs Forester and Orlando went away. Mr & Lady Charlotte Lyster came - also Major Powis. Henry went to Shrewsbury, glad he was not shooting.*

Wednesday 20th October - *Henry and I were obliged to return to receive the Actons at luncheon. After they were gone Lady Newport,[42] Mrs & Miss Anson, Mrs Fane, Mr & Lady Charlotte Lyster and Mrs Forester came over to see the Aloe - they took me back with them in the barouche. Miss Anson's playing and singing are fascinating. Today Lady Mary Bridgeman was married to Mr Robert Clive.*

Thursday 21st October - *Henry rode to Bridgnorth from Willey.[29] I went home and enjoyed the time with Mama immensely - she is much better. Very bad accounts from Brymbo they fear a heart complaint.[30] Found Mrs Cure and Capt Cheyne and Gatacres soon arrived. At dinner Mr & Mrs Twistleton, Mr Mrs and Miss Selwyn, Mrs and Miss Cure and Capt Cure the 3 Mr Cheyne. Music and Callotypes.*

Friday 22nd October - *Breakfast at 10. Walked in the Dingle (Dudmaston)[39] but rather wet. Dressed again for luncheon and when I came down found Lady Bradford[12] and Miss Moncrief there and Lady Powis[14] and Lady Harriet Clive and a Mr Herbert who stays here. We went to see Mr N Cheyne's rooms which are beautiful. We go to Weston next week.*

Saturday 23rd October - *The Gatacres and we left after breakfast, last evening a charming round game. Mrs Grant, Lily and Pauline came to luncheon and I returned just in time. They had been at Stanley.[43]*

Tuesday 26th October - *We went to Weston.[12] Lord and Lady (Riven pronounced) Ruthven spelt. Lord and Lady Newport,[42] Mr & Mrs George Bridgeman, the 2 Lady Bridgemans and Miss Moncriefs. Lady Ns 3 children have the whooping cough - the baby they hope will escape. Mr & Mrs Gatacre.*

Wednesday 27th October - *The same party in the house. We all were going out to drive but rain came on. Mrs and Miss Cludde[31] called after luncheon. In the evening we all worked and sometimes Lady Charlotte played. Annie had a sore throat and Lord Newport gave her some medicine from his box of Homeopathy - she got well but I think it was a gargle of brandy. Lady Ruthven draws rather well, and had a portfeuille of her own drawings and Lady Waterford's.*

Thursday 28th October - *We had to leave - They wished us to stay longer but Henry was going to Davenport to shoot and the Gatacres had also to return.*

Saturday 30th October - *Henry returned from Mr D Watts Russell's and brought Nina[11] with him to stay till Wednesday.*

Sunday 31st October - *We went to Buildwas Church in the afternoon and called on Mrs Nunn.*[21] *Tom*[9a] *drove over from Apley in his Dog Cart and returned, he came to meet Sir Robert Pigot but he did not arrive.*

Monday 1st November - *Henry, Nina and I went to Apley Castle for luncheon, most affectionate reception. Then we drove to call on the Cludde's at Wrockwardine.*[31] *Found them at home but just starting for Condover - called on the Bannings. Sir Robert Pigot did arrive about 9 o'clock. Mr & Mrs Stephens and Mr Hemphrey dined here to meet him.*

Tuesday 2nd November - *Sir Robert Pigot went to Bridgnorth for dinner. Nina and I walked out.*[32] *My Uncle Tothill called here and Gulson Reynolds. Mr & Mrs John Pritchard*[37] *came to dine and Mr George Pritchard.*

Wednesday 3rd November - *All except Mama went to Apley to luncheon and to take Nina home. Lord and Lady Bradford and Lady Ruthven drove over afterwards from Badger to Apley. On our return we found that Lady Newport, Mrs and Miss Anson, the George Bridgemans and Lady Lucy had paid Mama a visit and drank tea. Tom and George and Sarah came to dine. George and Sarah had been at Badger. It was a double birthday, Sir RP and Grandmama, we drank their healths and all the gentlemen went to see Grandmama and congratulated and kissed her.*

Thursday 4th November - *Sir Robert Pigot left very early. Miss Brocke called here.*

Friday 5th November - *Henry went to shoot at Apley and Louisa asked me to go too. The Isaacsons at luncheon.*

Saturday 6th November - *Henry went away for Malvern and London. Yesterday we had tea at Apley a great deal of thunder and lightning and some rain but we find that it was much more severe at the Dale, hailstones 2 and a half inches found and the glass broken at the Vinery and greenhouse and all the frames. Met Sorton Darby just come from Brymbo, very bad account of his father who is under the Homeopathic treatment!*[30] *I went to Kemberton for luncheon and then home.*

Sunday 7th November - *Such pouring rain, I could not go to church. Dearest Mama suffers so much from sore fingers.*

Tuesday 9th November - *At half past 4 in the morning all the household disturbed by an earthquake. The bed seemed lifted up and let down and then trembled with a seasickish motion. The china rattled and the stuffed bird cases danced on top of the wardrobe. Mama's bell rang and all the housemaids rushed downstairs. Toosie*[18] *never moved till he heard footsteps and then barked violently. I was dreadfully frightened. Henry took his seat.*

Thursday 11th November - *Mr & Mrs Nunn*[21] *came to spend a day or two.*

Saturday 13th November *- Mr & Mrs Nunn went home. The water being so out we had to drive to Lt Wenlock and they walked from there. Called on Mrs W Edmonds.*

Wednesday 17th November *- Henry took rooms for me at 20 South Audley Street and I came here today with Annie and Isaac and the Chattels. George came up with me. Dined at the Pigot's, Lord & Lady Keane, Mr Mrs and Miss Benmon.*

Thursday 18th November *- The Duke of Wellington's funeral. Everybody had to get up at 6 and nobody could sleep after. I went with the Charles Whitmores and a large party by water to our destination beyond the Temple. It was not affecting or solemn excepting perhaps the music. The troops moving to the Dead March in Saul, but it was a very grand military spectacle. There were detachments from every regiment in the service. The Lord Mayor and civic authorities joined in the procession in state carriages. Prince Albert and the Ministers. He and his suite in 3 carriages and 6. The Duke's horse was led by a groom. The funeral car was very ugly and heavy.*[33] *It was drawn by 12 immense black horses and the red velvet coffin at the top looked quite small and like a french pincushion. We went home by the way we came after a good luncheon. George dined with us. I so done up that I could hardly keep awake. Henry has a dreadful cold.*

Friday 19th November *- A good night has made me well again. Walked with Henry in the morning. George came for luncheon and they are gone to the House of Commons. It is my first evening alone but I have been too busy to be dull. I have very pretty rooms here.*

Saturday 20th November *- Lady Elizabeth Douglas*[41] *came to stay with me till Tuesday.*

Tuesday 23rd November *- Henry went to the Dale. Lady Eldon died therefore Lady Elizabeth*[41] *was not obliged to return home to Bute House therefore I asked her to stay with me. We paid visits to Mrs Henry Barnard, Mrs Brownrigg, Mrs Fitzroy and Mrs Cornwall and Mrs Charles Whitmore.*

Thursday 28th November *- Henry returned for a minute going to the House.*

Friday 26th November *- Lady Elizabeth returned home. Dreadful rain tonight. Alone reading the "Wide Wide World". Tommy*[9a] *called.*

Saturday 27th November *- Very late Division, Henry did not get away till 3 this morning too tired to say anything except "We have beaten them by 80." Lord Derby is safe now at present.*[34] *Long walk this morning fine and frosty and delicious. We chose for me a head-dress of red velvet and sequin pearls for tonight at Lady Derby's and a bonnet and black velvet gown. Miss Cornwall called and Mrs Fitzroy and Mrs George Holyoake.*

At Lady Derby's were all the foreign ministers and their wives and the foreign noblemen who have been sent by the different courts to attend the funeral of the Duke of Wellington. It was very splendid, the dresses were perfect, the supper most magnificent. Beautiful racing cups and the Coalport china made for Lord Derby and the Exhibition. Lady Derby not pretty but quiet looking and interesting. Lady Aylesbury and Lady Jersey were splendid. Mrs Milnes Gaskell, the Pigots, Lord Newport[42] and Lord Powis[14] there. Lord Derby said when Lord Palmerston entered, "I am sorry we have not a band, my lord, it should play 'Here comes the Conquering Hero"' which is esteemed very clever and polite.

Sunday 28th November - *We went twice to church, but it was very wet again.*

Monday 29th November - *Paid visits. Packingtons, William Russells, Downing St. Lady Elizabeth Tollemache.[11a] Nobody at home. Mrs Milnes Gaskell called while I was away. Invitation to dine with Lady Pigot but I was so happy on the way with the black cat that I refused. Henry at the House.*

Wednesday 1st December - *Mr Hamilton, Mr Bayley and Mr George Whitmore dine here. Called upon Mrs Gaskell who was at home, Lady Granville calling upon her at the same time.*

Thursday 2nd December - *Lord Drumlanrig came to breakfast and went with Henry to Salt Hill to see D and W.*

Friday 3rd December - *Walked with Henry to pay a visit to the Moltnes and to Sir Robert. Saturday, Sunday, Monday and Tuesday nothing but rain and wind.*

Wednesday 8th December - *Lord Bernard dined here. Very wet. I drove down Henry to the House of Commons and did some shopping. He gave me such a pretty gown with velvet.*

Monday 13th December - *I go tomorrow. Today we signed our settlements.*

Tuesday 14th December - *I came away from London by 10 o'clock train by the Trent Valley reaching Wellington at 4. Brought Isaac, Annie and the baggage. Hope Henry will be soon able to follow. Quite sorry to leave South Audley Street, Mrs Pitney and the black cat.*

Wednesday 15th December - *Found Mama was quite ill with spasms - we gave her brandy and water so hot that I was afraid to touch the glass and then she got upstairs. By the time Mr Rowland arrived she was eating a very good dinner!!!*

Thursday 16th November - *Mama and I drove to call on the Waynes and at Tickwood[35] - all at home these dark days are wet and cold.*

Friday 17th December - *Death of the short-lived Derby government.[34]*

Saturday 18th December - *Mama and I drove to Stanley*[43] *- Mrs Alfred looking very well and cheerful.*

Tuesday 21st December - *I came to Apley for Christmas. Henry arrived about an hour before me from London. Mr Douglas and Lady Jane here. Anything more flat is inconceivable. Wednesday and Thursday wet. Charlie Gage came.*

Friday 24th December - *The Douglas's left. I had a note from Mr Marshall with directions for the Altar Cloth. He says that the Stanley children were all baptised yesterday at Astley Abbots. We went to Bridgnorth after luncheon, saw Mr Wing, eldest boy has Alfred added to his names - Alfred Edmund William, Alice Mary and the Baby Alfreda Lucy.*

Saturday 25th December - Christmas Day - *Went to church in the morning of course. George and Sarah came, it will much improve matters. Henry and I stayed at the Isaacson's for luncheon. I enjoyed my walk back with him very much though it rained a little.*

Sunday 26th December - *It is like 2 Sundays together. We walked in the afternoon to Stockton church and back.*

Monday 27th December - *Last night the wind and rain was most tremendous. George and I walked to Stockton, the destruction was immense amongst the trees - they are broken very much in sight of the house.*

Tuesday 28th December - *Dearest Mama came over for luncheon only. Mrs Charlton arrived and Jane Jones. We walked in the flower garden and watched the hounds on the other side of the river. Mama says one of the cedars at home is blown down - not the finest but one of the two that Papa or his Aunt Rathbone planted, we cannot remember which it was. Singing in the evening. I played at chess with Charlie Gage and beat him in two games and should have done the same in the third so that will not do. We had oyster suppers and roasted oysters. Wednesday and Thursday were wet. Sarah and I sat in the morning room and worked, she making a Baby frock and I working my nine leaf bag which is for Louisa. Algernon and Cecy generally played there till 11. Then we had a very pleasant hour to ourselves, and Sarah gave a singing lesson to her nieces.*

Friday 31st December - New Year's Eve - *George and Sarah*[44] *and the children left, they go on Tuesday to Mrs Deacon at Mabledon, and a few weeks after Sarah's sister Fanny is to marry a Mr Ramsden. Henry and I went home to Mama for one day of which I was very glad. We sat up till 12 to see the New Year in - 1853. I was devising a Ball dress for Bridgnorth's on the 6th. It is to be my black lace flounces over white satin and bunches of red hollybocks with a wreath of same and silver grass. Henry gave them to me for St John Charlton's coming of age ball. We go back to Apley tomorrow. It is strongly advised that we should sell The Hay - for it is very much injured and pays very poor interest, £10,000 is offered for it.*[36]

NOTES

1. Mrs Whitmore would have been Catherine Whitmore, widow of Thomas Whitmore who had died in 1846. She was the mother of the three Whitmore sons, and was therefore the senior member of the family. Emily would have been Henry's cousin, the second daughter of Rev. Charles Whitmore, the former Rector of Stockton

1a. Stoke Court, Buckinghamshire was the home of Abraham Darby IV and Matilda, who was Adelaide's elder sister.

2. Lady Bandon was Catherine Whitmore (elder sister of Emily, see 1 above) who had married the Earl of Bandon.

3. The Giffard family came from Chillington, Staffordshire which they had occupied since the Norman Conquest. The Rev. Charles Whitmore, the former Rector of Stockton had been married to Anne Giffard.

4. Mrs Charles Whitmore was possibly the wife of Charles Whitmore Q.C., M.A., of Lower Slaughter in the Cotswolds. She was formerly Elizabeth Brownrigg. Lady Whitmore (née Lady Louisa Douglas) was the wife of Thomas Charlton Whitmore of Apley. Miss Brownrigg and Mr Brownrigg would have been related to Mrs Charles Whitmore (née Brownrigg). Mr Wolryche Whitmore was the owner of Dudmaston. This would have been a notable family gathering.

4a. The Garforth family came from Wigganthorpe Hall, 10 miles north of York.

5. Possibly a court/political usage.

6. The party from Malvern was possibly associated with Lt.-Col. Wilmot, DC, J.P. who 3 years later married Emily Whitmore (see note 1 above).

7. Wife of the Earl of Bradford of Weston Park, Shropshire.

8. See note 4 above.

9. Col. Forbes, Coldstream Guards, was married to Lucy Whitmore, daughter of Rev. Charles Whitmore, former Rector of Stockton. Lucy was the younger sister of Emily (see note 1 above) and they were both cousins of Henry Whitmore (see family tree).

9a. "Tommy" was Thomas Charlton Whitmore, eldest brother of Henry Whitmore.

10. Miss Sophia Whitmore of Connaught Place was probably Anna Sophia Whitmore, daughter of Thomas Whitmore of Apley (Henry's father) by his first marriage to Mary Whitmore (a cousin). Sophia was therefore a cousin of Henry Whitmore.

11. The entry for 10th June is confusing. Lady Louisa was the wife of Thomas Charlton Whitmore of Apley. Nina was the nickname of Caroline Whitmore (eldest daughter of Thomas Charlton Whitmore). Harry was probably Walter Henry Whitmore, sometimes nicknamed Harry (2nd son of Thomas Charlton Whitmore). Emily was the daughter of the former Rev. Charles Whitmore of Stockton. Lowndes Square where Adelaide went to stay was probably the London home of Rev. George Whitmore, the current Rector of Stockton. The reference to "George and another George Whitmore" was presumably to the Rev. George Whitmore (above) and the other George was probably one of the Lower Slaughter family.

11a. Lady Elizabeth Tollemache was a member of the Manners family.

12. Lord Bradford of Weston Park, Shropshire.

13. Miss Lucy Deacon was probably the sister of Mrs George Whitmore (née Sarah Deacon). She would therefore have been the sister-in-law of Rev. Whitmore, Rector of Stockton.
14. Lord Powys was a powerful figure in the Shropshire political scene. At the time of the Reform Act of 1832 he was the undisputed leader of "The Shropshire Whigs". He was still a person of great influence.
15. Lucy Gorgiana Whitmore, cousin of Henry Whitmore, had married Col. Forbes of the Coldstream Guards in 1849. Mr and Mrs William Whitmore and Mr John Whitmore were no doubt members of the London branch of the Whitmore family.
16. This was the first indication that there was to be a contest in the parliamentary election at Bridgnorth. It had been agreed that Thomas Charlton Whitmore, the existing Member for Bridgnorth would stand down. It was therefore necessary for Henry to seek nomination to stand in his stead.
17. Lady Louisa Whitmore, wife of Thomas Charlton Whitmore of Apley was the eldest daughter of the 5th Marquess of Queensbury, whose home was Bute House.
18. Toosie was a pet dog.
19. Mrs Frank Tothill, as Jane Digby, had married Francis Tothill, 3rd son of William and Hannah Tothill of Bristol (see family tree). Francis re-married in 1858 to Miss Galbraith.
20. Henry Whitmore was duly elected Member of Parliament for Bridgnorth. Second place went to Sir S. Pigot who had a majority of 77 over the representative of the Whigs.
21. Marnwood was the home of John Bartlett, the incumbent of Buildwas from 1822 until his death in 1861. Mrs Nunn was the wife of the curate.
22. Abraham Darby IV and Alfred Darby had bought five plots of land in Liverpool, totalling 272 acres of land at a cost of £138,921, as a speculative venture. Alfred had advised his sister to place her money in the project. His death in 1852 caused problems as the transfer of lands had not by then been completed. This necessitated an application to the Court of Chancery and the passing of a private Act of Parliament, the Darby Estate Act 1854. The whole project was therefore felt to be in jeopardy. Consequently Abraham IV and Matilda transferred to Mary their shares in the Coalbrookdale Company by way of compensation.
23. Presumably a miscarriage.
24. The Anstices were the proprietors of the Madeley Court Company and lived at Madeley Wood. Wroxeter was the home of Rev. and Mrs Egremont, where Rev. Egremont was the vicar. Capt Russell was married to Louisa their daughter.
25. The Whitmores were related by marriage to the Storers. An aunt of Henry, Elizabeth Whitmore had married Rev. John Storer, MA, Rector of Hawksworth, Notts, in 1818.
26. The 2nd Baron Wrottesley, of an ancient and important Staffordshire family. He was married to Sophia, 3rd daughter of Thomas Giffard of Chillington, Staffs. The 4th daughter (Anne) had been married to Rev. Charles Whitmore, the previous Rector of Stockton. Lord Wrottesley was one of the founders of the Royal Astronomical Society and was for some years President of the Royal Society.

27. The Charlton Arms in Wellington, Shropshire.
28. There must have been an alleged irregularity in the parliamentary election in July 1852, involving Sir Robert Pigot who came second in the count.
29. Home of Lord and Lady Forester.
30. This probably refers to Richard Darby of "Rosehill". Richard's two sons, William Henry and Charles Edward, after being trained in the Coalbrookdale Works, left the Dale to become joint Managers of the Brymbo Iron Works, near Wrexham, North Wales. Richard had purchased land nearby. Seemingly he may have suffered a heart attack.
31. The Cluddes were an old and distinguished family who owned land on the western and south-western outskirts of Wellington, Shropshire in Wrockwardine and Orleton. The origin of the family is commemorated in the name of the hamlet of Cluddley.
32. Possibly there had been a difference of view between the Whitmores and the Pigots over the election petition (see note 28 above).
33. The funeral carriage is now located at Stratfield Saye House, Berkshire, home of the Dukes of Wellington.
34. This was the occasion of Lord Derby's first administration, with Disraeli as Chancellor of the Exchequer. It only lasted a few weeks (see Journal 17th December) and was followed by a mixed government of Whigs and Peelites (i.e. Tories who followed Peel's later policy of Free Trade) under Lord Aberdeen. Despite its short life, it was a cause for celebration.
35. The Tickwood estate, west of Benthall and north of Much Wenlock was established by the Foresters in the 1820s. Tickwood House (later Hall) was built by 1828.
36. The Hay was acquired by Adelaide under the settlement following the death of her father, Francis Darby. It was sold to John Anstice of Madeley Wood in 1853.
37. Mr and Mrs John Pritchard were close friends of Adelaide. Mr Pritchard was a banker from Broseley.
38. Lord Lewisham was a member of the Dartmouth family from Pattingham, Staffordshire.
39. Dudmaston (now National Trust), situated 4 miles south east of Bridgnorth on the road to Kidderminster, was the home of William Wolryche Whitmore.
40. Kemberton, 4 miles east of Madeley, was the home of Rev. George Whitmore, Rector of Stockton, elder brother of Henry Whitmore and of Sarah his wife.
41. Lady Louisa Whitmore, wife of Thomas Charlton Whitmore, was the eldest daughter of the 5th Marquis of Queensbury of Bute House. Nina and Mary were two of her daughters. Lady Elizabeth Douglas was her sister.
42. Lord Newport was of the Bridgeman family (Lord and Lady Bradford of Weston Park, Shropshire).
43. Stanley Hall, near Bridgnorth, was the home of Rebecca Darby (née Christy) widow of Alfred Darby.
44. George was the Rev. George Whitmore, the Rector of Stockton and was the older brother of Henry Whitmore. Sarah was his wife. Before her marriage, she had been a Miss Deacon of Mabledon Court, Kent.

1852

CHARLES WHITMORE OF SOUTHAMPTON d. 1770 = MARY KELLY d. 1799

THOMAS WHITMORE d. 1773 (*inherited APLEY*) = MARY FOLEY

WILLIAM WHITMORE 1745-1815 (*inherited DUDMASTON*) = FRANCES BARBARA LISTER

THOMAS WHITMORE 1782-1846 =
1. MARY WHITMORE
a) MARY ANNE
b) ANNA SOPHIA
c) GEORGIANA

2. CATHERINE THOMASON = d. 1887

CHARLES WHITMORE = ANNE GIFFARD OF CHILLINGTON

CATHERINE = EARL OF BANDON

EMILY = LT. COL. WILMOT

LUCY = COL. FORBES

WILLIAM WOLRYCHE WHITMORE OF DUDMASTON 1787-1858 = LADY LUCY GEORGIAN BRIDGEMAN

THOMAS CHARLTON WHITMORE = LADY LOUISA DOUGLAS

1. THOMAS CHARLES DOUGLAS (*Sold APLEY 1867*)
2. WALTER HENRY
3. CAROLINE LOUISA (NINA)
4. MARY CATHERINE
5. EMILY HARRIET
6. LOUISA DOROTHEA
7. LUCY ALBINIA
8. EDITH GEORGINA
9. CECIL ELIZABETH
10. EVELYN OCTAVIA

REV. GEORGE WHITMORE = SARAH DEACON

1. ALGERNON 1849-1877
2. HENRY 1855-1909

HENRY WHITMORE 1813-1876 = **ADELAIDE ANNA DARBY 1817-1899**

1853

Comment

As already mentioned, the Journal by 1853 had become more of a diary, almost day by day, of visits made and of events in which Adelaide had become involved. They indicate an almost frenetic level of activity. On the domestic front the most notable event was the death of Adelaide's grandmother, Hannah Grant on 12th May 1853. She had been living at The White House for the past three years. At her funeral on 20th May at Leighton Buzzard they met Abraham and Matilda. Despite the embarrassment of the dispute over the family property, Adelaide was able to describe the meeting as "very amiable." This was followed by a visit to Stoke Court, (Abraham and Matilda's home) in July.

The affairs of the Company in Coalbrookdale are not mentioned, although, following the death of Alfred Darby in 1852 and the consequent appointment of Mr Crookes as Manager, Henry Whitmore had been appointed as one of a triumvirate to oversee the affairs of the Company on behalf of the partners. A great deal was happening as the Company was extending its ownership of property and mines in Lawley, Wellington and Dawley. Following the success of the Great Exhibition in Hyde Park in 1851, the Company took part in the International Exhibition in Dublin in August 1853. Henry Whitmore and Adelaide, attended on behalf of the company. The visit to Ireland was described quite fully and the Exhibition merited a brief mention but the Company's involvement in it was completely ignored in Adelaide's Journal. It was only the social scene in which she was interested. This included a visit to Bandon, the family seat of Lord Bandon to whom Henry's cousin, Catherine, was married.

On the political front there was the embarrassment of the Election Petition brought by Mr Cadogan the third placed candidate in the 1852 parliamentary election for Bridgnorth. As a result, Sir Robert Pigot (the second candidate) lost his seat, but Henry Whitmore was not affected. Sir Robert Pigot was replaced by Mr John Pritchard of Broseley. Parliamentary duties required prolonged stays in London and for that purpose, 29 Chesham Place was rented from February to July. The highlight of the London Season was the attendance at The Drawing Room in June 1853. This was a Royal Court Levée, although Adelaide did not disclose which, if any, of the Royal family were present.

Representing Bridgnorth as Member of Parliament, despite the prestige, must have been an expensive occupation. It is doubtful whether Henry Whitmore as a third son would have had sufficient resources to sustain that level of expenditure. His marriage to Adelaide probably made possible his ensuing political career and provided him with a family home.

The sale of Hay Farm in 1853 for £10,000 would have been a welcome addition to the family resources.

New Year's Day *- Apley Park - Rain, rain. I left Mama about.*[4] *Henry went to Bridgnorth in the morning. At Apley I found Captain Inge arrived - old, tall and ponderously polite, with a quantity of grey moustache and whiskers, clever and well informed.*

Sunday 2nd January *- So wet that we went in the family coach to church. Captain Inge with us. Lady Louisa*[1] *has a very bad cold. In the afternoon I walked to church with Mary and Douglas.*[1]

Monday 3rd January *- In time for Prayers. The Apley coppice and shrubbery were shot - 460 head of game killed. Mr Cotes, Mr Gatacre, Watts Russell, Captain Inge and Henry Foley - all stayed except Watts Russell. We were in the Drawing Room. I walked in the Park before luncheon reading "Bleak House." Captain Inge is long at breakfast and he talks a great deal - Knows Lord Bateman. When the ballad came out at Lord Bateman's, friends gave him the sobriquet of the "proud young Porter."*

Tuesday 4th January *- They shot the Patmarch. Only Mr Gatacre and Captain Inge came to dinner. Mr Gatacre left after.*

Wednesday 5th January *- Captain Inge went away after breakfast. Emily*[1a] *came. Henry and I went to pay visits at Bridgnorth. Mr & Mrs Harrison, the Mayor. To Stanley,*[36] *not at home. Mr & Mrs Bowen. Very cold but a fine day.*

Thursday 6th January *- Tom's birthday.*[8a] *Bridgnorth Ball, Sparkes, Kettles, Moseleys, Donald Carr and his sister, Mainwaring Owen, Mr Harnage, Lady Pigot in a brocaded silver poplin almost white - Red feathers in her hair, Lady Keane blue - Sir Robert and Mr Bennion. Danced once with Mr Harnage. Mr Midgeley came and spoke to me. I had quite forgotten him. I wore black lace flounces over white satin, hollyhocks and red and silver ribbons.*

Friday 7th January *- Emily*[1a] *and I walked to the Cave. Lady Pigot and Lady Keane and Mr Bennion came to luncheon. Saturday and Sunday in private life. Monday too wet to do anything but write letters.*

Tuesday 11th January *- Dined at the Mayor, Mr Harrison's with the Pigots. Drawing Room made into the Dining Room and the Nursery into a Drawing Room. Then we went to the Ball. Danced all the evening and did a great deal of duty. Lady Pigot beautifully dressed in a Spanish dress. My pretty embroidered tulle torn to bits! It was half past 3 when we got home. The Pigots were to leave at 6 in the morning.*

Wednesday 12th January *- Went over to the Dale. Henry and Emily*[1a] *and I to stay all night and Lady Louisa,*[1] *Nina, Mary, Walter, Douglas, Emmy and Lucy*[1] *for luncheon. Grandmama not very well in the evening.*

Thursday 13th January - *Drove over to the Infirmary Meeting.*[2] *Lovely morning but the river very high. In the Vestry - Bradfords, Powis's, Newports, Lysters, Bridgemans, Charltons, Corbets (Aston), Miss Jenkins, Wentworth Powis, Mr Slaney. Did not stay for the Ball. Called upon the Nunn's as we came home, left our horses at Ironbridge and were at Apley very sleepy in time for dinner. The Bishop of St. Asaph's sermon was very odd - Dogs, horses and fish and Angels. Lady Wynne held the plate - collection £286, Lord Powis Treasurer.*

Saturday 15th January - *Emily*[1a] *and Henry and I went out to pay visits at Bridgnorth, we went to Fir Grove, the Shepherd's.*

Sunday 16th January - *Went to luncheon to Capt. and Mrs Brazier's then to call upon Mrs Watts Russell and at Chesterton.*[3] *Emmy's birthday was kept (not the right day). Uncle Tom and Aunt Dinah, Emily, Such a good Uncle Tom. Tea in the Nursery.*

Tuesday 18th January - *Lucy's birthday kept. Gypsey and Boddingtons at luncheon. Very sad evening.*

Wednesday 19th January - *Mr Whitmore and Lucy went to take Douglas*[4] *to Eton for the first time. Emily went with them to return to Malvern. Henry and I stayed until after luncheon then came home for one week.*

Friday 21st January - *Miss F. Deacon*[5] *was married to Mr Ramsden. Henry had to go to London about his dreadful Election petition. I went with him to Apley Castle.*

Sunday 23rd January - *No rain, rather cold. Went to church very good sermon.*

Monday 24th January - *Mrs Alfred called and Mrs S Christie and Mr Alexander. Poor Sentinel too lame to go for Henry tomorrow. Wedding cake from Mr & Mrs Arthur Ramsden!!*[5]

Tuesday 25th January 1853 - *Dinner party. Mr & Mrs Sparkes and 2 daughters, Mr & Mrs Egremont,*[5a] *Lily and Mr Richards, Mr Fletcher. The Sparkes stayed the night.*

Wednesday 26th January - *Sparkes went away. Snow and rain. We went to Haughton*[6] *- Lord Wrottesley*[6a] *and Miss Wrottesley, Mr E. Bridgeman, Mr And Mrs Cuncliffe - she is very pretty and plays.*

Friday 28th January - *Shooting. Bad cold. Mr Newton Dickinson. Henry and I went to Davenport House to dine. Mr & Mrs Egerton Lee, Sir Francis Hopkins, Mr Robertson a traveller who has written books, Mrs Boddington, Mrs Broadbent, Miss Shepherd and Miss Wallington - charming evening. They acted Charades and we played games with the children - "The Post" and "Throwing Lights."*

Saturday 29th January - *The Storers came, Charlotte and Lois.*[7]

Friday 4th February - *We returned home bringing the Storers with*[7] *us for a few days. Went to Bridgnorth to attend a meeting of Irish missions. A most dull week, tho' I like the Storers immensely, a little cold.*

Sunday 6th February - *Drove to Buildwas Church in the afternoon. Mr Nunn.*

Wednesday 9th February - *Charlotte and Lois*[7] *went back to Apley and Henry went. Mama and I called at Severn House.*[8] *We go to London on Saturday.*

Saturday 12th February - *29 Chesham Place. We had 32 boxes and packages and only 1-16-0 to pay for overweight which we thought wonderful. A nice warm comfortable house. We dressed and went to dine with Mrs Garforth.*[7a] *Mr & Mrs Nepine, Mr Wooley, Admiral and Miss Bowles.*

Sunday 13th February - *We went to church in the morning but the cold was intense. I got a bad headache, dined with Mrs Garforth.*[7a] *A very agreeable Mr Lambert was there - he lives in Switzerland somewhere.*

Monday 14th February - *No letters until 11 o'clock on Valentine's day! My cook very* ***grand*** *"should I address you my Lady". Tom*[8a] *came in the evening about the Petition, he will have to stay some time, I think. We three went to dine with the Charles Whitmores.*[9] *Sir Robert and Miss Brownrigg, some nice music.*

Tuesday 15th February - *We walked out shopping. A visit from Augustus Tollemache*[9a] *and Mr Joseph Whitmore. Mr Sparkes dined. Our house is* ***very*** *pretty and comfortable.*

Wednesday 16th February - *The Committee*[11] *were called up to be sworn and Mr Dundas was missing and was in Paris. If he does not appear in 24 hours they must have another Committee. The delay does not matter much to us but Mr Cadogan has a multitude of witnesses.*

Thursday 17th February - *More snow. Dearest Mama not well. Sir Robert and Lady Pigot and Lady Keane coming to dinner and Augustus Tollemache.*[9a] *An Erard Pianoforte.*

Friday 18th February - *Henry and Tom*[8a] *went early to the House of Commons. Visit from Mrs R. Wrottesley.*[6a] *Went out and did a great deal of shopping. Called on Mrs Garforth*[7a] *and Mrs C. Whitmore.*[9] *Very cold and snowy.*

Saturday 19th February - *Mrs Garforth and Kitty and Maria*[7a] *called in the morning early after Henry and Tom*[8a] *were gone to their Committee*[11] *and they took me away with them to luncheon and we called upon Admiral and Miss Bowles and a nice Mrs Cleasby took me home in her carriage - cover a chair and wrote and practised.*

Sunday 20th February - *Went to Mr Liddell's St. Paul's, very cold, good sermon - all very popish. Lady Pigot and Lady Keane in the afternoon - no chance for Sir Robert I fear - he will lose his Election.*[11] *They say it is a bad Committee - Mr Bouverie the Chairman, Mr Dundas, Mr Locke King, Sir H. Willoughby. Augustus Tollemache*[9a] *came as I was writing in the twilight asked us to dine with Lady Elizabeth Tollemache on Wednesday. To me not well, nobody well.*

Monday 21st February - *Paying bills, and with Mrs Garforth*[7a] *to call on Mrs G W not at home. Then she went to call on Mrs Percival and came back talking of poor Sophie Beresford's death without an idea that I knew who she was talking about.*

Tuesday 22nd February - *Snow and rain, did not go out. Visit from Tommy.*[8a]

Wednesday 23rd February - *Tommy*[8a] *came to breakfast. Dined at Lady E. Tollemache's*[9a] *- Mr & Mrs Cowper, Mr Hubert de Burgh, Lord Drumlanrig. Augustus Tollemache was there but not his wife, she is ill. Went to see Lady Pigot this morning.*

Thursday 24th February - *I had a long hunt yesterday for nurses for Lucy.*[13] *The Petition is not yet ended.*[10] *Lady Wrottesley called.*[6a]

Friday 25th February - *Mrs Garforth and Maria*[7a] *before luncheon. Lady Elizabeth called and Augustus.*[9a] *I like them so much. Went to see Mrs Wrottesley*[6a] *who gave me some tea.*

Saturday 26th February - *The Garforths*[7a] *and Mr Hamilton dine here. The Petition ended and Henry safe and Sir Robert out for which I am sorry.*[11] *We hope Henry may get costs. Music and a pleasant evening.*

Sunday 27th February - *Went twice to Dr. Thorpe's chapel and called upon Mrs Charles Whitmore*[9] *to arrange about tomorrow for her to meet Mrs Garforth*[7a] *before the concert.*

Monday 28th February - *Mr Wilde Browne called and Mrs Wrottesley.*[6a] *Then I went out - visited Mrs Cornewall and Mrs Cutherbert's cards at the Deacons. Lady Henry Churchill and Mr Whatley, Mrs Graham Pigot. In the evening came the Charles Whitmores,*[9] *Mrs Garforth and Kitty and Maria*[7a] *- a great deal of music and very nice. Tommy*[8a] *went away during our absence. Mr Hope gone to Bridgnorth, And Uncle Wolryche*[12] *to London. Henry has got the chief of his costs given to the Petitioners and the Writ is postponed.*

Tuesday 1st March - *Henry has such a bad cold. Col Forbes*[13] *wrote to tell me to go to the servants Estate in Marlborough Street for Lucy's nurse tomorrow. Mr Wilde Browne came to dine.*

Wednesday 2nd March - *Mrs Garforth's concert. Ella*[13a] *managed it all. There were about 80 people. Sir James and Lady Campbell, Lady Herries,*

Miss Compton, the Nepines, Mrs Clearsby. Miss Duff sang very prettily Mendelsohn, Beethoven and Mozart, a grand piano forte - 4 violins.

Friday 4th March - *The Newports[14] dined with us and the Pigots, and Cecil and Lady Reaves - some of them went away to the House where Bridgnorth is being attacked [10] Mrs Garforth and Kitty came in after Ella's[13a] concert to hear Lady Pigot sing, which she did most amiably.*

Sunday 5th March - *I stayed at home all day expecting a Nurse to call for Lucy.[13] Came not. Dined at Mrs S's. Kitty's drawings beautiful. She is planning another concert - the Nepines, the Stevens.*

Sunday 6th March - *Walked to Berkeley Chapel - met Cecil Forester.[15] Tommy[8a] dined here.*

Monday 7th March - *Mrs Whitmore Jones[16] died very suddenly. We tried to fight off our mourning but it can't be.*

Tuesday 8th March - *Invited to the Garforth's[7a] but can't go. Henry went with me to the Heneages and Mrs Bristowe's and Lady Burgher's at Rutland St. Shopping since. Henry dined at Lord Salisbury's.*

Wednesday 9th March - *Lady Pigot wants our old lodgings. We walked to South Audley Street charming morning. Luncheon with Mrs Garforth[7a] who drove me home. Mr & Mrs A Tollemache,[9a] Sir Brownrigg, Mrs Wrottesley,[6a] Cecil Heneage and Kitty Garforth dine with us.*

Thursday 10th March - *Went with Mrs Garforth[7a] to her dancing academy, at Miss Birch's. Then called upon Mrs Edward Whitmore.[17] In the evening went with the Garforths to a concert at Lindsay Stoner's - singing good, Signor Ciabetti and Mr Benson.*

Friday 11th March - *Mama wrote that she wants a dressing case - we walked to Halstaffs for it.*

Saturday 12th March - *Pughs, - Lewis - Allenby - Howell and James, Miss Gladman for a bonnet, all failed! Went at last to Miss Clarke and they made me one that same evening.*

Sunday 13th March - *To Berkeley Chapel in the morning, such a good sermon. Went to Mrs Garforths[7a] for luncheon and to St. George's in the afternoon. It was a dreadful day. Kitty Garforth walked back with us after the 2nd service and she and George Whitmore[18] dined with us.*

Thursday 15th March - *I went out driving and shopping etc. In the evening we had a dinner party and the debate on Bridgnorth being late, Henry, Mr Halsey and Mr Hamilton arrived about 10, and dined at a side table! Mrs Garforth, Lord Annesley,[19] the Pigots, Lady Keane and George Whitmore came at 8 as they ought, and after waiting till half to 9, I ordered dinner and asked George Whitmore to be master of the house and take down Lady Keane. We* *did not get upstairs till half to 11 and then found Kitty and Maria Garforth had been there an hour!*

Wednesday 16th March - *Looked at a nurse for Lucy,[13] a lady whose husband is in Australia, she has 3 little girls but had never been out at service and is recommended by Lady Burton - so things turn up oddly enough. Mrs Garforth's[7a] second concert tonight. Henry is gone to dinner and go with Mr Wrottesley[6a] at 10. Charming evening, Lady Pigot sang. Music from le Prophete, Stradella, Beethovens Trio, Overture to Il Barbiere.*

Friday 18th March - *Tom[8a] came. I called on Mrs Mander. Everybody is going out of town for Easter - we go on Monday.*

Saturday 19th March - *We walked to Chesterfield Street. Mrs Garforth not well, fainted at Ella's[13a] - Lord Hotham there - Kitty and Maria dined here. Tom[8a] went home after breakfast.*

Sunday 20th March - *I went to Mr Liddell's church - In the evening, we walked to Mr Pelinne's church and then to Mrs Garforth's.[7a]*

Monday 21st March - *We left London by 5. Very cold and snowy. I reached home with Annie at half past 10. So snowy walked up the hill. Henry went to Shrewsbury with Lord Newport[14] for the Grand Jury.*

Wednesday 23rd March - *Henry came home, still very cold and snowy.*

Saturday 26th March - *Henry went to Apley to stay until Tuesday. Very busy making catalogue of books in the rosewood Bookcases in Library.*

Monday 28th March - *Went with Mama to call on the Pritchards.[23a] Ernestine de Satz was there.*

Tuesday 29th March - *I went to Apley to bring Henry home as George and Sarah[19a] were coming to stay day or two. Found Henry very ill but he got up and came.*

Wednesday 30th March - *George and Sarah,[19a] Miss Kate Deacon[20] and I went over the works at the Dale, Mama joined us and went to the new church - Henry still not well. In the afternoon we went to Buildwas Abbey and to see Mrs Nunn.*

Thursday 31st March - *They left us. Henry so ill! Mama and I went to call at Marnwood.[20a]*

Friday 1st April - *Came to Malvern. NB not to go again by Dudley Post.*

Saturday 2nd April - *Mr West ordered us a drive, Emily,[21] Henry and I.*

Sunday 3rd April - *Went twice to church. Henry not allowed to go out - Sermon for the Bible Society.*

Monday 4th April - *Drove to Mrs Stratton's to leave a note. Mr Scott and Col. Wilmot came to dine.*

Tuesday 5th April - Emily[21] and I went to Mrs Stratton's to alter an invitation, she was in great spirits and looking handsomer than ever and more like an old picture. She was in mourning with a quantity of grey hair in curls over her face and neck from under a Mrs Chapone cap. Miss Granville walked back with us to Malvern. Henry gets better very slowly.

Wednesday 6th April - *I might have gone up the hills but was not well enough.*

Thursday 7th April - *Mrs Stratton and Miss Granville - Mrs Candler and Mr Scott came to luncheon, a very merry luncheon it was. Called on Lady Church.*

Friday 8th April - *Henry gets better. Going to take Cod Liver Oil which did me so much good. We don't go back to London until Monday. I had a very bad headache all day and could not go out. Miss Cornwall called. Mr Rushdale and Mrs Brownlow, who recommended me to buy flowers at Callers in Ann's Place near Sloane Street. They gave me quantities of Brandy in the evening.*

Saturday 9th April - *Drove with Mrs Whitmore to Madresfield,[22] neither Lady Georgina nor Lord Beauchamp at home. Then some other visits and to the Candlers where Henry and Emily[21] had walked. Henry took my place in the carriage. Capt. Candler and his dog came with us almost to Malvern. Lucy and the Colonel had driven out in the pony carriage.*

Sunday 10th April - *Went to church twice. Henry did not go out all day. An east wind. Mr Rashdale preached a sermon I liked very much - as we came home met Col. Wilmot.[21] I have been very happy here and am sorry it is the last evening. I do not think I should ever be well long at Malvern and I am sure the drains are bad.*

Monday 11th April - *Returned to Chesham Street.*

Tuesday 12th April - *Paid visits. Lord Bernard[23] called.*

Wednesday 13th April - *Edward[17] came to ask me if I would see the Baroness Goldschmid. Called on the Pritchards[23a] and Mrs Gaskell. Mrs Ruskin at Paterson's very pretty in brown velvet and green bonnet.*

Thursday 14th April - *We dined at Lady Duncombes. Met Sir W. and Lady Herries and her sister. Major Tempest and the Garforths.[7a] Mr Hotham and a nameless young guardsman. Henry went back to the House. I went for him and waited long. At 12 we drove to Lady Bradfords where I had been afraid to go by myself. Found her party breaking up for a Ball at Lady Granville's. Mrs Deacon, Kate and Harry paid me a long visit.*

Friday 15th April - *Evening party and concert at Mrs Garforth's.[7a] Custs - Mitfords, etc. Lady Flower. Went by myself.*

Saturday 16th April - *Lord Bernard[23] and Henry were off early to Lord Derby's. I was to go with Mrs Garforth to the Houses of Lords and Commons,* *was 5 minutes too late and they were gone!! Drove by myself after them and caused a policeman to let me in after my party without a ticket. How magnificent it is. I found all the Garforth's and the Duncombes and Lady Herries and we went everywhere and saw everything. Even the committees sitting for New Ross and Cockermouth. Dine at Mrs Garforth's - the Durrants, Miss Willoughby, Mr Wooley, Mr Worsley, Miss Cust.*

Sunday 17th April - *Henry not well enough to go to church with me either time. We had a little walk together but he was very tired. Lord Bernard*[23] *dined here.*

Monday 18th April - *Henry went to consult Mr Stevenson - he cauterised his throat and made him faint with the stethoscope, said his mind worked too fast for his body - no more cod liver oil just yet.*

Tuesday 19th April - *George*[19a] *arrived.*

Wednesday 20th April - *Mr & Mrs Halsey, the J Pritchards,*[23a] *Sir Thomas Winnington, Mr & Mrs and Miss Holland dined here with us. Henry and I went to Mrs Disraeli's Reception*[23b] *afterwards, very pretty rooms they are, Henry introduced me to a great many people and some I liked. Lady Jersey, Lady Ely, Lady Georgiana Lygon (so pretty), Mr and Mrs Bateson, the great Hudson, Lord Hawarden and Hon. Miss Maude. Then in the Supper Room Lord John Manners, who said he had not forgotten me. Mrs Garforth was there, the Baldocks, Cecil Newport, everybody and the dresses splendid. There is a beautiful Madonna and very pretty modern pictures in the Dining Room.*

Thursday 21st April - *Tickets for the House of Commons. Stupid debate on the Budget but I was glad to be there malgre tout. Stayed till half past 11 then Henry got a pair. He came to me and introduced me to Mrs Cardwell and gave me some tea. George was just opposite in the Stranger's Gallery. In the Lady's Gallery we see and hear extremely well. Speech from Disraeli - good and very clear I am sure tho' I could not understand - consols at three per cent - very glad of supper.*

Saturday 23rd April - *George*[19a] *left us and then Henry and I came, with only Isaac to Windsor. Mr Stevenson said that he should have some country air and we thought we could come here and have Douglas*[4] *with us, and so also being arrived we find a letter from Douglas*[4] *and he is ill and in his bed.*

Sunday 24th April - *St George's Chapel - most beautiful it is with the banners of the Knights of the Garter, stained glass and dark oak. The music so perfect and the chanting. It was fine after luncheon and we walked to Eton, saw Douglas*[4] *and then went to church. Then we walked to the castle, and went to the top of the Round Tower - grand view! to the terrace and then home I thoroughly tired. Henry went again to Douglas and must I hope be better. Walter*[1] *with us all the time.*

Monday 25th April - *We left, and I drove about hunting for Lady Bernard's ribbon - failed. We were very comfortable at our Windsor Inn - the Castle.*

Tuesday 26th April - *Henry ordered to have leeches for his deafness - put them on at quarter to 7 - dinner being at half past - they sucked till 8, then we could not stop the bleeding. Augustus Tollemache[9a] and I dined together. At last it was stopped by pressing the lint very hard on the leeches.*

Wednesday 27th April - *Mrs Garforth[7a] was here by half past 10 to ask me to dine there and go this afternoon with them to the water colour exhibition. Mr Cook's pictures the best. I dined at Mrs Garforth's. Henry at Lord Hothams. We went together to Lady Eglinton's - great crush, beautiful rooms - everybody there - My amber gown with black lace. Lady Aylesbury's the only dress there at all like it.*

Friday 29th April - *A wet day. Henry had his throat most dreadfully cauterised yesterday. It cured the deafness for a time.*

Sunday 1st May 1853 - *Henry went with me to church in the morning. I to Mr Liddell's for the 2nd service. Then we walked across the Park to Mrs Garforth[7a] for the last time in Mrs Norton's pretty house in Chesterfield St. They move tomorrow into Curzon Street.*

Monday 2nd May - *Found Catleigh's pretty flower shop. The Garforths and Lord Bernard[23] came to dine. Visit from Mr Locke this morning and the Uvedale Corbetts.*

Tuesday 3rd May - *Very wet. Lady Bandon, Lady H Bernard and Mamey[23] came to pay me a visit. Henry dined at home very late, did not go back to the House.*

Wednesday 4th May - *Went out to pay visits, a long list - then to Hogarths for Mama. Dined at Lady Winningtons where we met Sir and Lady Domville and Miss Domville (her father, etc) Sir J Hopkins, Mr Packington, Mr Rushout, Sir John Hamer, Mr Adderley - 12. Then we went to Lady Newport's,[14] Lady Laura Gratton's. Found the Heneages at home.*

Friday 6th May - *Augustus Tollemache[9a] came whilst we were at breakfast. Then Mr & Mrs Charles Bernard before luncheon. Then Lord Bernard[23] and Mr Watts Russell, Mrs Charles Whitmore and Miss Whitmore of Charlton and Mrs Graham Pigot. I am going with the Pritchards[23a] to the French Play - Great was our surprise at finding Tom[8a] here on our return from the Theatre and Henry from the House of Commons.*

Saturday 7th May - *A wet day. I had a bad headache. We had 10 to dine. The Halseys, Mrs Garforth and Kitty, Mr Fitzroy, Sir J Hopkins, and Mr Price. The old trick of the Books and the key, and the new one of making a table turn.*

Sunday 8th May - *29 Chesham Street. Tom*[8a] *with us. Walked to church at Mr Nepeane's. Then to Mrs Garforth's and had luncheon. To the John Street Chapel in the evening - Mrs Creyke and Kitty dine with us.*

Monday 9th May - *Very wet and cold. I sat up reading Allison. Tom*[8a] *asleep. Henry at the House.*

Tuesday 10th May - *Henry and I went hunting for bargains - failed and found very impertinent people. Went about my Train and the flowers, wild roses and pink and white May and such beautiful white Moire.*

Wednesday 11th May - *Coalbrookdale - We know not what a day may bring. How happily we sat at breakfast with our letters unread. We had been very late. A summons from Mama and no hope either that I could see poor Grandmama alive. Mrs Garforth and Kitty and Maria*[7a] *came in - only one opinion, that I ought to go - We were to have dined with the Newports*[14] *- such a lovely silver and pink headress Henry had given me! Went by the Oxford line and Stour valley - NB not to go that way alone - was late. Took a fly from Wolverhampton and got here at half past 9. Grandmama still living and dearest Mama much comforted when I came. We watched by her till 3 and then went to bed.*

Thursday 12th May - *Our poor invalid lives - if only breathing can be called living. She has tasted nothing since Monday when she made a very good dinner of mutton chops. Tuesday she did not know anyone, but talked a great deal - repeating "going, going to be in heaven happy, happy to be with Jesus" - Then Mama wrote to me but after I came she could not speak - she tried but it was only a murmur - she never opened her eyes nor moved and today has uttered no sound. Sometimes a slight convulsion. Mr Edmonds passing by this evening came in and went up to see her. He offered up a beautiful prayer for the peace of the departing spirit. I could wish Matilda had come. We watched beside her till quarter to 1 o'clock in the morning - shortly before her countenance changed and she looked very happy and to our surprise we found that she was trying to speak and she presently said "Mother, Mother" in a low voice but quite distinctly and repeated it until almost the very last breath which was without a struggle of any kind. It was a very solemn death bed - midnight and the voice as it were of the departing spirit who seemed to see her Mother before waiting to conduct her throe' the dark valley of the shadow of death and that mother gone 70 years ago to that other blessed world. I can't be too thankful to have been with Mama.*

Saturday 14th May - *Henry came down in the evening.*

Thursday 19th May - *Such glorious weather. The funeral is to be tomorrow at Leighton (Buzzard). Matilda only meets us there alas. Mama goes on with us and then to Stoke Court.*[41]

Friday 20th May - *We were disappointed in getting the Express to stop for us at Leighton. Left Wellington at 1 and arrived there at a little before 6. It was a very fine day, and Mrs Anna Sturge and Barnard - Mr & Mrs Lawford - Miss Lawford and several others met us at the Station. Ridgway managed everything and it was well done. A hearse and six mourning coaches. Mr Grant had joined at Weedon - 3 women friends spoke and prayed beside the grave. The meeting was long and a great deal said, and quite full the Meeting House was. We drove to the Swan. Abraham and Matilda said they must go by the last train - they had some tea and went but were too late and came back to dine and sleep, very amiable all.*

Saturday 21st May - *We did not open the Will until Abraham and Matilda were gone this morning - Glad we did not. I wanted to give up half mine as Abraham refused the bank.*[24] *Mr Grant and Henry are agreed that Abraham would only esteem it an insult. Mama came with us to London.*

Sunday 22nd May - *We went to Dr Thorpe's church. Mrs Grant paid us a long sociable visit in the evening.*

Tuesday 24th May - *Mrs Whitmore and Emily arrived and suite. Tom*[8a] *lives here.*

Wednesday 25th May - *George and Sarah*[19a] *dined here.*

Thursday 26th May - *Mr Grant spent the morning on business here. He came also to dine. Pleasant evening.*

Friday 27th May - *Note from darling Mama. The Charles Bernards and Lady Herrick dined here and George,*[19a] *we are 5 - with Tom,*[8a] *Sarah*[19a] *and her sister*[20] *and Mamey and Miss Brodrick came in the evening.*

Sunday 29th May - *2 sermons by the Bishop of Oxford at Mr Nepeane's for the Cambridge Institution for soldiers and wives.*

Tuesday 31st May - *Mamey came to luncheon and we went to the Soho Bazaar and then shopping. Tom,*[8a] *George*[19a] *and Henry went to Greenwich.*

Wednesday 1st June - *Lord William Douglas*[25] *at luncheon - rather nice old man. Not well but had a pleasant dinner party - Lady Harriet and Mr Duncombe, Lord Hawarden and Miss Maude, Mr Forbes and Mr Knox - Mama sent us ducks. Henry gone to Lady Salisbury's, I thought on consideration it is too soon for me to go. Henry goes with the Garforths*[7a] *to the Drawing Room*[26] *tomorrow.*

Thursday 2nd June - *Went to see the Garforths dressed, very well they looked, White glace silk and green leaves to loop up the bouillones of tulle. In the evening the Pigots and Lady Keane and Lord Annesley*[19] *and Mrs Halsey dined here.*

Friday 3rd June - *We dined at Mrs Deacon's, Henry, E and I, we met a stupid Mr Scott who took me down to dine and a Mr & Mrs de Vass - she very* *pretty also 2 Mr Pyms and Miss Pym belonging to Mr Francis Pym of the Hazels. It was very pleasant.*

Saturday 4th June - *Paid visits and Mamey dined here and rang for us. Dearest Mama spent the morning with me from Stoke Court*[41] *she goes home Monday.*

Monday 6th June - *Hunted up Madame Zusy for my Court train - Edward Taylor called also Miss Levison who brought Mrs Whitmore such pretty flowers.*

Thursday 9th June - *The Garforths were to have dined with us but they went to Oxford instead to the Installation. Mr G came and Mrs Graham Pigot, Mrs Whitmore and Tom Storer.*[7] *The right Isidore dressed my hair beautifully and will do it for the Drawing Room*[26] *Tom*[8a] *came up on Tuesday and Brought the family diamonds for me to wear.*

Friday 10th June - *Went to the Exhibitions and Tom Storer*[7] *to dine.*

Saturday 11th June - *Mrs Whitmore*[27] *went to Brighton. We three and Tom Storer*[7] *to Chiswick in an open carriage and then to dine at Richmond after a party of 25, the Garforth's party, they began to dance and stayed late - we came away after dinner.*

Sunday 12th June - *Went to church in the Mayfair part of the world and then to say goodbye to the Garforths, who go on Tuesday.*

Tuesday 13th June - *Mr Whitmore*[27] *came back from Brighton to dress me - The Drawing Room*[26] *was not a full one. I was presented by Lady Calthorpe who found out at 12 o'clock that she was too ill to go. She did not let me know - so I went - It was very terrific but I hope I did nothing wrong. It was a great cram, I thought.*

Thursday 7th July - *Mr & Mrs Henry Bernard*[23] *came to dinner. - very sick and glad when it was over! Two Miss Brodricks came after. Went to Fulham to see Mrs Maude, whom we did not find at home.*

Friday 8th July - *Chobham - we left home at 9 in the open carriage. Posted all the way by Hounslow and Staines, such a beautiful sight I never saw before! Lovely weather but almost too hot. We found Mr Scott who introduced us to Capt. Neville and showed us Genl. Fane's tent. We had cold luncheon in the carriage and then went to see the Highlands Games and dancing by the 2nd. Lady Hardinge there. Then we drove to the camp of the Life Guards. Met Sir W Fraser and saw the stables and kitchen --mess room and hospital. About 3 hours going and returning. I was just in time to dress and drive to the Princess' Theatre where Ted and Pauline were with Mr & Miss Lamb and Miss Humphreys. Sardanapalus - the dresses and scenery are splendid and Mrs Charles Keane prettier than she used to be. Perhaps I knew the Tragedy too well and like it too much to be pleased with it put on the stage.*

Saturday 9th July - *George[19a] went away - Emily[1a] and I drove out in the open carriage. Found Mrs Egremont at home.*

Thursday 14th July 1853 *- A long melancholy week. Henry very ill - I had to leave him with Emily and go along to dine with the Pigots. Lord and Lady Keane, Colonel and Mrs de Voeux, Lord Hotham, Lord Annesley,[19] Mdme Montine, Capt. Vivian, Mr De Barry.*

Wednesday 18th July - *Henry and I went to Stoke Court[41] - the second invitation!! Mrs Egremont and her daughters and son were there - in the evening, 20 people at a most magnificent dinner and afterwards dancing. Bents, Rice Claytons, Hillersleys.*

Thursday 21st July - *Mrs Whitmore[27] and Emily left us for Scotland. We go on Saturday home.*

Friday 22nd July - *A day of days! Henry went with me to Mr Heath - shopping and packing. Went to dine at Mrs LeFroy's. met Lady Hayes in the evening and a Capt. Maxwell. All the rest strangers. Then to Lord Powis's Ball[28] where we found a great cram, everybody left in London, I should think. Mrs Gaskell and one daughter, Lady H Clive, Miss Bowles, Col. Wilmot, The Disraelis, Mr Leake.*

Saturday 23rd July - *I was quite low at leaving Chesham St! Matilda wrote to ask about my Mrs Olney who she wishes for as Cook, so I had a good deal to do at least. We went away in a patent safety and forgot poor Toozie![29] He came just in time. Found dearest Mama well and Miss Lawford with her.*

Monday 25th July - *Henry not very well - George[19a] came to dine and sleep. Henry and George went to Shrewsbury and then to Rhyl.*

Tuesday 28th July - *Dearest Mama's Birthday and she is 70, who could fancy it and she is so young and well. Not that she looks young.*

Thursday 28th July - *Henry came home, he looked better. Went to meet him at Wellington.*

Friday 29th July - *Henry and I went over to Apley for luncheon - I went to Bridgnorth with Louisa. The ponies behaved beautifully.*

Saturday 30th July - *Henry and Miss Lawford left us - he to go to London and she to Leighton. (Buzzard)*

Sunday 31st July - *Dearest Mama has not been well at all. I went to Mrs M's room in the morning, and Mama went with me to Buildwas church in the evening. Mr Nunn is going away to a good living in Suffolk.[30]*

Saturday 6th August - *A most melancholy week. My precious mother very ill from Tuesday when we went to Shrewsbury and she came back suffering intolerable pain. Thursday Mr Rowland's remedy appeared useless so I sent for Mr Webb who came and stayed the night. Next day the medicine had been so* *efficacious that the pain was gone. She has made some progress. Thank God, but she is very weak. Henry came home today.*

Monday 8th August - *Henry went to Kemberton*[31] *he goes to Apley tomorrow and has planned to keep my birthday. Mr Webb came again, his medicine has done great good, I am sure. She goes on well I hope and pray.*

Wednesday 10th August - *George and Sarah*[19a] *and Henry arrive for luncheon - a very happy birthday but much close gaspy weather. We drove as far as Leighton*[42] *and looked at the church. Canons and music at night for the passing of the Severn Valley Railway Bill.*

Thursday 11th August-*Mama and I went with George and Sarah*[19a] *to Kemberton.*[31] *Henry rode to Broseley. The A's take Cecil to school at Mr Chase's tomorrow.*

Friday 12th August - *The Storers 4. Lady Louisa, Nina, Mary, Emmy, Douglas and Walter,*[32] *came here for luncheon and stayed the afternoon. Oh, but I was tired. Mr & Mrs Nunn came to dine and stay the night. The living of Thorndon in Suffolk has been presented to him.*[30]

Saturday 13th August - *Henry went to Bridgnorth and Apley - Mama and I took the Nunn's home.*

Sunday 14th August - *Mama and I went to Little Wenlock to church, very good sermon. Then she walked till even I was tired. We go to Ireland*[33] *D/V on Tuesday.*

Tuesday 16th August - *We left Wellington about 12 and arrived at Holyhead somewhere about 7, later by an hour than it should have been. Landed at Kingstown and were at Rathbone's Hotel by one in the morning. After all the fine weather we had a wretched day, drizzling and foggy tho' the beautiful country about Chester and Ruabon and Penrhyn and pelting down right when we got past Bangor. Most awful was the passage yet not rough as all people said! - but almost everybody was sick and most miserable. Henry escaped wonderfully.*

Wednesday 17th August - *Still very uncomfortable and sick! Went by train to Dublin where Mr Hamilton's carriage met us, a most lovely perfect day and most enjoyable open carriage and such lovely country. The Phoenix Park with the beautiful Wicklow mountains in the distance. Abbotstown is a very pretty place - a good house and lovely park scenery and fine trees. At dinner Mrs Trant, Mr & Mrs Law, Miss Cane and 2 Miss Canes - 10.*

Thursday 18th August - *Not well yet, it is wretched to feel not up to anything when everybody is doing everything to please you - the Exhibition however did amuse me much.*[33] *It was delightful and the pictures very fine, Lord Ward's especially. At dinner Mr George Brooke and Lady Annabel their daughter, Col and Mrs Philip Hill and again Mrs Trant and Mrs Cayne (that is the name).*

Friday 19th August - *Mrs Trant and the Caynes went away. Henry and I went to the P Hill's for luncheon - on our return we walked about Abbotstown garden and shrubberies - fine trees, a Dingle like Dudmaston, the stables and farm buildings. Our party at night was Lady Annabel and Mr & Mrs Brooke, and Dr and Mrs Sadler, the clergyman of the Parish. Jon played some waltzes and polkas of his own. He is only 12 and so clever. Hans is very nice but he is older, 19, I think. I am very sorry this is our last day.*

Saturday 20th August - *Left at 9 with a jolly basket of provisions and sherry. Railway to Cork and then a little railway to Bandon*[34] *where Lord Bernard*[23] *and Mamey met us with the family coach. Such a lovely country and park with the Bandon river running thro'. Lady Bernard very handsome and all the children ditto. At dinner Lord Middleton, Miss Middleton, Miss Leveson and Mr John Scott, a nephew of Lady Bandon's.*[34]

Sunday 21st August - *Went to church at Bandon twice.*

Monday 22nd August - *Drive round the Park, thro' Bandon and to Lady Heriett's cottage.*

Tuesday 23rd August - *To Coolmaine, a large party - Lord Middleton, Miss Bodrid, Miss Leveson-Gower, Lady Bernard and I in the great family coach - Henry and Mr Scott outside. Lord Bandon*[34] *and Lady H. in the pony carriage. Coming back I went with "his lordship" and he drove me through the pretty grounds of Col. Alcock Stowell.*

Wednesday 24th August - *A wet day, we made nosegays for the Bazaar.*

Thursday 25th August - *The Bazaar in the Park - £80. Wet wretched day. Friday did not go out all day, wet and cold. Mr Scott left.*

Saturday 27th August - *Went to call on Col. & Mrs Alcock Stowel at Killerittan - walk after with Miss Leveson, a great deal of conversation.*

Sunday 28th August - *We went twice to church at Bandon - the organ fine and singing very good. Mr Blakeley and Mr Smith preached. Walk to the kitchen garden and "Echo Walk".*

Monday 29th August - *Miss Leveson Gower, Miss Brodrick, myself and Henry, Lord Bandon, Mamey and Lord Middleton went to Cone and Queenstown. Drove to Bandon thence by railway to Cork and by the steam packet to Cone - very pleasant. Called on the Admiral at Queenstown, and Henry, Miss Leveson and I remained in the garden and I made a sketch of Cone. Miss Leveson Gower was ill and could not appear at dinner. We had some charming music and singing. Mr & Mrs Blakeley, Mr Smith, Mr O'Sullivan, and Dr Ward dined here. Dr Ward has a fine bass voice. Mrs Blakeley plays very nicely.*

Tuesday 30th August - *Mrs H Bernard came over and we made bouquets for the Flower Show. Henry went to Cork - very wet.*

Thursday 1st September - *The Flower Show and Bazaar. As wet as it could be.*

Friday 2nd September - *A drive round the hill. Dined at Kilbregan - pretty house and beautiful pictures. Dr Ward, a handsome young Mr Freeman. Mr Spiller who acted as Auctioneer at the Bazaar. Mr & Mrs Gilmour, 2 odious children.*

Saturday 3rd September - *Most charming day at Castle Freke - We left Castle Bernard at 11 o'clock, Miss Brodrick, Lady Herriett, Miss Leveson, D Middleton and I in the great landau, Henry and Lord Bernard outside. It is 18 miles by Clonaketty - not very interesting country. Lord Shannon's property. Lord Carberry met us at the door - it is quite wonderful, how well he makes himself understood. After luncheon we drove to the gardens and then thro' shrubberies back close to the sea - this part between sandhills like Barmouth. I was in a pony carriage with Lady Carberry and Lord M. We reached Castle Bernard just in time to dress for dinner at 8.*

Monday 5th September - *Such beautiful weather - not a cloud nor a drop of rain since the Flower Show. We are thinking of Killarney - Charming drive, sketching. Walk to the Cabins with Miss Leveson Gower. In the evening Mr & Mrs and 2 Miss Gollocke, Mr Gilman and Mr & Mrs Charles Bernard.*

Tuesday 6th September - *To Cork by the Railway where we had to wait. I bought a little warm cloak - had luncheon and then we started for Killarney - Miss L Gower, Henry and I, Annie Isaac arrived about sunset.*

Wednesday 7th September - *Victoria Hotel. Drove to Mucross on an outside car. As we were sketching the beautiful ruins Mr Herbert rode by and gave Henry a note for his wife introducing us - most lovely place, a newly built house close to the Middle Lake. We had luncheon there and I liked Mrs Herbert. She had 2 little girls with a German governess, a boy is going to school. Sir John Warrender, her uncle, and 2 daughters, and Miss Herbert. Mrs Herbert showed us her portfolio of beautiful water colour drawings. We drove to the embarking place -* **Dinas**. *Went in the boat to Lady Kenmare's cottage Glenna. Home by a little moon.*

Thursday 8th September - *To the Gap of Dunlow, outside car first, then ponies - luncheon under the trees at a place called Brandon Cottage where we met Miss Leveson Gower Boat and servants. Upper Lake - Spelan with us and his bugle - Echoes. Innisfallen, Ross Castle. Quite dark as we got back to Killarney.*

Friday 9th September - *The first cloudy day - drove to Kenmare. The Dean of St Patrick and no horses for us! Rain as we approached. Before reaching the Tunnel when Bantry Bay opened upon us the country was like the Fete Noir over mountains magnificently wild with the most lovely views looking back upon the Killarney lakes and mountains.*

***Saturday 10th September** - Walked with a troop of little Irish boys to the lake, most lovely! Then on to Bantry. Bantry House, luncheon and then on with a great pair of very good horses to C.B. in time for dinner. Lord M and Miss B gone and only Mrs Frank Calthorpe here. The whooping cough.*

***Monday 12th September** - The Dean of St Patrick and Mrs Pakenham arrived - the daughters and son were sent to the Inn at Brandon to be out of the way of the whooping cough.*

***Tuesday 13th September** - A wet day, wrote letters and drew. The Dean and Mrs Pakenham went out to Lionise notwithstanding the rain. They leave tomorrow and we go to Coolmaine. Mr & Mrs Blakeley dine here.*

***Wednesday 14th September** - Coolmaine - Mr Bernard and Col. Alcock Stowell came to dine.*

***Thursday 15th September** - Fishing all day and sketching. Beautiful weather, caught crabs and Henry caught a wonderful stinging fish which came home. The Irish fishermen call it Delmy Down or Pin fish.*

***Friday 16th September** - Lady B and Lord Bernard came to take us home. Mrs Calthorpe and Miss Leveson still at CS.*

***Tuesday 20th September** - Went to see the Fleet leave at Cove. Yesterday, Mr & Mrs Blakeley and Dr Ward and Mr O'Sullivan dined here. I never was so sorry to leave any place. We go to Lady Cootes' - Ballyfinn on Thursday.*

***Thursday 22nd September** - Ballyfinn - It is a magnificent place - We found Mr & Mrs and Miss Stanley arrived and then came Lord & Lady Charleville, Lady Beaujolais, and Mr Dent and Mrs Marly.*

***Friday 23rd September** - We walked about the grounds and sketched and looked at the poultry yard and then came in to dress. Young Mr Marly came. Turning tables in the evening and Lady Beaujolais and Miss Coote played a great deal.*

***Saturday 24th September** - We left Ballyfin early only seeing Sir Charles - To Dublin by the railroad and then took our passage by the steam packet. Very ill again in the Race of Holyhead and again H. quite escaped.*

***Sunday 25th September** - Bangor - We came on here, I went to bed and was dosed and did not get up until luncheon time almost. Much better. Went to the Cathedral for the evening service which the old Bishop conducted but indifferently and kept losing his places in a pretty good sermon. We were going into Wales but the weather is so tempestuous that we think it will be better at home. Mama is still at Stoke Court.*[41]

***Monday 26th September** - We came home - a fine day and we went shopping at Chester.*

***Tuesday 27th September** - An invitation to Apley for 2 nights, we went. Tom[8a] gone into Cornwall. Lady Queensbury, (mother of Lady Louisa) and Bessie there and Charlie Gage.*

***Wednesday 28th September** - I drove over to call on Mrs Cure at Bridgnorth - found her in the Dingle - Had to take Nina, Mary and Emmy with me. George and Sarah,[19a] Miss Deacon and the new baby came over. Miss Sophie Whitmore came in the evening.*

***Thursday 29th September** - After luncheon came home. Mama had arrived 10 mins. From Leighton. (Buzzard)*

***Friday 30th September** - We lamed Alice Grey, at least rubbed her shoulder yesterday!*

***Sunday 2nd October 1853** - Henry and I drove over to Kemberton. (Home of George Whitmore) A sacrament day and 2 such excellent sermons from George.*

***Monday 3rd October** - George, Nina, Mary, Henry and I went to Shrewsbury for a concert at the Music Hall with Mario Ciabetti - Mdme. Doris, "Mistesori" and "Come gentil." A great many people there. The E's who Fielding Powys admitted. We slept at the Lion. The Stokes', Hugh Owen and H.O. Wilson.*

***Tuesday 4th October** - Called upon Lady Frances Wade. George left early with Nina and Mary. Henry and I dined at Broseley with the Pritchards,[23a] Mr and Mrs J Anstice[34a] - 2 Gordons' - Mr Smith (Emery) - Mdme. De Satze and 2 daughters.*

***Thursday 6th October** - Henry and I drove to Wenlock where was a Bazaar for an organ. Introduced to Mrs Dorall, Sir T. Boughey's sister - Pelhams' Bendons' H. Wilson.*

***Saturday 8th October** - Henry went to Malvern - I with him to the Station and to call on the Cunliffes. Then I went to Weston for luncheon. Happily found only Ld. Bathurst there besides the Newports[14] and George Bridgeman & themselves. Lady Mary Clive[35] has a daughter. Called at Aston and saw Mrs Watts Russell at Shifnal.*

***Sunday 9th October** - I went to the Schoolroom where Mr Marshall did not preach and in the afternoon Mama and I went to Little Wenlock. Aired Books and made catalogues till Thursday 13th when Henry met us at dinner at Stanley.[36] He had left Malvern on Wednesday for the Squirrel dinner. The Egremonts[37] were at Stanley and 2 Christys' and Mr Westcombe a man who is painting Mrs Alfred Darby's picture and one of Mary Darby in a hat and habit. Went with Henry to Bridgnorth and called on Mrs Clarke and at Apley.*

***Sunday 16th October** - Went to Little Wenlock at church. Henry not quite well.*

***Monday 17th October** - Henry's birthday - very wet but he went over to Apley. A dinner party - the Pritchards[23a] and 2 de Satzes, Mr and Mrs W.R. Anstice, Mr and Mrs J.D., Mr and Mrs H.D., George[19a] and Mr A. Christy.*

***Tuesday 18th October** - Algernon's birthday and Nina's. Henry went with George[19a] to Shrewsbury and then to Kemberton[31] to dine and sleep.*

***Wednesday 19th October** - Henry and I went to dine at Willey. (Foresters) Lady Pigot there without Sir Robert. He is not well at Newmarket. Lord and Lady Newport, Cecil, Emiline and old Major J, Mr George T, Capt Reeve, Mrs Fane, Lord Newport took me to the Dining room.*

***Thursday 20th October** - To Weston to stay until Saturday. Col. And Mrs Arthur Legge, Mr and Mrs Greaves, Mr and Mrs Bristowe, Mr Cecil Lane, Mr C. Wrottesley,[6a] John Bridgeman, George Bridgeman, Sir Thomas and Lady Boughey, and Miss Boughey at dinner.*

***Friday 21st October** - Wet but we walked and the gentlemen went out shooting. Henry rode to Kemberton[31] Lord Newport came from Willey, no other additions to our own very pleasant merry party at dinner. Music and work, very charming evening at Weston.*

***Saturday 22nd October** - I came home and Henry had to go to Malvern, - said good bye in our leavetaking room: At Shifnal - I called on Miss Brooke.*

***Monday 24th October** - Going to Bridgnorth to meet Henry. With Henry came Emily - 3 precious souls to stay at The Crown.*

***Tuesday 23rd October** - We three went to Apley for luncheon - great indignation that we were at Bridgnorth. Fortunate for all that Mrs Taylor called bringing Mrs Moseley and Miss Pulson - Met Lady C. Lyster - Mrs Anson - Mrs Fane - and Lily and Pauline came and George and we all dined at the Sparkes. Then the Concert which was good. Mrs and Mr Lockey, Mrs Endersohn, "When Sorrow Sleepeth Wake It Not." Then the supper! 100 people! All very jolly and happy and well fed and the thing said to be well done, and our healths were drunk and several others, and I fell in love with the Mayor and caught a cold.*

***Wednesday 26th October** - Emily went back to Malvern. The Pigots went home and we also for luncheon and then Henry and I went to Apley Castle for 2 nights. Found there 2 Miss Hills' - Capt. Bridgeman and his 2 pretty daughters - Mr M. Owen and Mr Cholmondley. Danced in the evening. The Sweetenhams were there and the Buchanans dined. I was so dead beat that I went to bed after one quadrille. Henry came much the worse for a young lady having rushed with her head into his mouth. He said his teeth were almost knocked out!*

***Tuesday 27th October** - The party dispersed. - the R. Jones' came.*

***Friday 28th October** - We came away after luncheon.*

***Saturday 29th October** - Left Mama early and came to Apley Park.*

***Thursday 3rd November** - Left Apley - Miss Sophia was there - but rather flat.*

***Tuesday 8th November** - Came to Malvern.*

***Friday 11th November** - Dinner party - Capt. And Mrs Caudler, Mr and Mrs R Astley, Miss Cornewall, Mrs Gordson, Mr Bootle, Mr Davis.*

***Monday 14th November** - Catty's 6th daughter was born, "Kathleen Frances."*

***Tuesday 15th November** - We left Malvern and came home.*

***Wednesday 16th November** - Henry went to Apley, I arranged my Ball dress.*

***Thursday 17th November** - Louisa, Tom and Nina[32] came here for the Ball! 13 miles! Louisa went with me in Mama's carriage, Henry with Tom and Nina in theirs. It was a very good ball and everybody there one wished to see. I had one quadrille with Lord Newport.[14] Black tulle gown, violets and silver. We got home about 5.*

***Friday 18th November** - How tired we were. Went with Tom, Louisa and Nina[32] thro' the Iron works! They left us after luncheon and Henry and I went to Wroxeter.[37] Mrs Moseley and her son and daughter dined there. The Russells in the house and Capt Lambrie.*

***Saturday 19th November 1853** - Wroxeter.[37] Went to Shrewsbury shopping. Mr and Mrs Henry Burton came to dine. Charade.*

***Sunday 20th November** - We went to Stanley[36] for luncheon, and saw Mrs Alfred Darby's picture and Mary Darby's. The Tothills were there, W. and S.H., called at the Albynes.*

***Thursday 24th November** - Henry went to Apley. So foggy we cannot get out!*

***Saturday 26th November** - Henry came home. The Company's Meeting.[38]*

***Sunday 27th November** - Went to church at Little Wenlock. Uncle Tothill and S.H. came to dine.*

***Monday 28th November** - Left home early and at Wolverhampton missed the train! Got to Wigganthorpe[39] in a fly and 4, very late. Mr Jones and Jane here and Col, and Mrs Hill.[39]*

***Tuesday 29th November** - Mrs and Miss Crumpton came.*

***Wednesday 30th November** - Tableaux vivants and charades. Henry hurt his foot in the Ballet dancing and Kitty fell on one knee.*

Thursday 1st December - *the first fine day since we came. Henry not able to move! But in the evening we had dressings in powder and of the age of George III Kitty and Maria looked well in powder and Jane was a Spanish lady, I. A. Jewess.*

Friday 2nd December - *I think yesterday was a quiet evening and this the dressing evening. Mrs and Miss Croft came to luncheon from Stillington.*

Saturday 3rd December - *Mrs and Miss Crompton went away. In the afternoon they dressed up a Mummy and at night sundry practical jokes. In bed about 2.*

Sunday 4th December - *Went to church at Terrington. I did not go to Scakleton in the evening, the fog was so thick.*

Monday 5th December - *Mr Jones and Jane went away to Stillington - very sorry! Mrs Clough and Maudie Clough came and Admiral and Mrs and Miss Mitford and Capt Taylor. Col. Hill and Henry went to York.*

Tuesday 5th December - *A fine day, we walked.*

Wednesday 7th December - *Henry and I went to Stillington to luncheon, very cold. Jane there, and Mr and Mrs and Miss Hawkins. Mrs and Miss Brigstock came in the evening - charming music.*

Thursday 8th December - *Arrived Miss Willoughy - Mrs Leggard and 2 Miss Beaumonts and Mr Hawk. Adml. Mrs and Miss Mitford went away, and Mr and Mrs Clough.*

Friday 9th December - *Mrs Garforth*[7a] *not well and in her room - Billiards. A walk and music in the evening.*

Saturday 10th December - *All the party dispersed this morning except Mrs and Miss Brigstock. Mrs Garforth still in her room.*

Sunday 11th December - *Went to church at Terrington and at Scakleton in the afternoon, very cold.*

Monday 12th December - *We left Wigganthorpe with great sorrow! Long, long cold journey to Birmingham. There we found George* [19a] *arrived and were all very comfortable at the Queens.*

Tuesday 13th December - *Poultry Show - Emily came with Major and Mrs Granville. I think we saw everybody there. The Duchess of Sutherland and Lady C.G., Corbets, Newports,*[14] *Foresters, Ansons, Wrottesleys,*[6a] *Lord Ward and his mother. Tom*[8a] *came and had a prize for his sheep. Saw Mary Colmore and Hugh and travelled home with Mr Bulkeley. Such a cram of people going by the train! All Shropshire. Got home in time for dinner, very tired indeed.*

Saturday 17th December - *Mr Grant came. We hear with sorrow of the death of Mrs George Bridgeman in her confinement. She was at Brighton with* *her mother and died of fever. The funeral is at Plymhill where she never lived but where everything was prepared for her. Richard Anstice has died at Wigginton of rheumatic fever, none knew of his illness at Madeley Wood in time to see him living.*

Sunday 18th December - *Went to church at Little Wenlock, very cold wind.*

Tuesday 20th December - *Mr Grant left us for Litchborough and Henry went to Apley and walked. Wednesday was a shooting day at Apley and J. Dick and Mr Sparkes were of the party.*

Thursday 22nd December - *Henry came home. Mama and I went to Kemberton.*[31]

Saturday 24th December - *Mrs Whitmore,*[27] *Emily,*[1a] *John and Lucy*[13] *are all settled at St. Leonards. George and Sarah*[19a] *were coming to us for Xmas week but Tom*[8a] *fixed the second shooting for that time so they kindly are willing to put it off until next week and come then.*

25th December Sunday and Christmas Day - *Henry and I drove to Stockton. Had luncheon at the Isaacsons*[40] *and went to both services but could not go to Apley, it is dark so soon! Lucy very low with a bad cold.*

Monday 26th December - *Henry went to shoot at Davenport House, and had a good day, but upset a man with a trombone and a great drum - part of the Broseley band - in returning. The bay pony kicked over the traces and came down, no harm done to pony or carriage, the new mare was as good as could be.*

Tuesday 27th December - *A deep snow. I forgot yesterday, George came over and he stayed for luncheon and walked with me to Marnwood.*[20a] *Mr Bartlett better. Henry is gone this afternoon. With Smith thro' all the snow to Apley. They expect Capt. Inge, Mr Cotes, Mr Lascelles, Mr Gatacre, and Henry to shoot but no womankind this year and quite right - right also if they had dispensed with the whole.*

Saturday 31st December - *The snow deeper and more terribly slippery. Smith went to bring Henry from Apley and Bridgnorth - how they got back safely I cannot tell but they did. We were all in bed before 12 - an event at any home but especially New Year's Eve.*

NOTES

1. Lady Louisa was the wife of Thomas Charlton of Apley. Nina, Mary, Walter, Douglas, Emmy and Lucy were their children.

1a. Emily was the second daughter of Charles Whitmore, the former Rector of Stockton. She lived with her father who was a widower at the Rectory at Stockton which was close to Apley. Her two sisters were married and had left home. She therefore spent a lot of time at Apley.

2. This was a regular fund raising occasion for the Shrewsbury Infirmary (hospital). The persons mentioned in the Vestry were the leading families in Shropshire.
3. Chesterton, a village south of Badger, Shropshire.
4. Douglas was Thomas Charles Douglas Whitmore, eldest child of Thomas Charlton Whitmore of Apley and Lady Louisa (née Douglas). He was born 1839.
5. Probably a sister of Mrs Sarah Whitmore (née Deacon) wife of Rev. George Whitmore, Rector of Stockton.
5a. Edward Egremont was the Vicar of Wroxeter.
6. Haughton is in Staffordshire, a few miles west of Stafford.
6a. The Wrottesley family were a leading Staffordshire family from Wolverhampton. John, 2nd Baron Wrottesley was noted for his scientific achievements and was one of the founders of The Royal Astronomical Society.
7. The Storers of Hawksworth, Notts were related by marriage to the Whitmore's and were regarded as "family".
7a. Mr and Mrs Garforth and their daughters Kitty and Maria, were a Yorkshire family from Wigganthorpe Hall, some 10 miles north of York. They had become close friends of Henry and Adelaide.
8. Home of Henry Dickson who was married to Deborah Darby, daughter of Lucy and Edmund Darby.
8a. Tom (Tommy) was Thomas Charlton Whitmore of Apley who was Henry Whitmore's eldest brother.
9. Probably Charles Whitmore of Lower Slaughter who was married to Elizabeth Brownrigg.
9a. Augustus Tollemache and Lady Elizabeth Tollemache were members of the Manners family. He became Vicar of Whitwick, Co. Leicester in 1874.
10. The Committee was a Committee of the House of Commons convened to consider the Election Petition of Mr Cadogan, the third-placed candidate in the Bridgenorth election.
11. Henry's attendance at a Committee of the House of Commons was for the hearing of an election petition submitted by Mr Cadogan, the third placed candidate at the 1852 parliamentary election for Bridgnorth. It appears to have concerned irregularities in the procedure on voting, by the second placed candidate Sir Robert Pigot. The petition succeeded and Sir Robert lost his seat, although Henry's position as the first-placed candidate was found to be safe. The vacant seat was filled by Mr John Pritchard, Adelaide's friend, from Broseley.
12. Uncle Wolryche was William Wolryche Whitmore of Dudmaston, Shropshire.
13. Col. Forbes, Coldstream Guards had married Lucy Whitmore (Henry's cousin) in 1849.
13a. John Ella (1802-88) was an English violinist, conductor and critic. From 1845-1880 he ran the Musical Union Subscription concerts, and from 1852 he started the Musical Winter evenings. These were exclusive gatherings. Henry and Adelaide Whitmore were subscribers as also were Abraham and Matilda Darby of Stoke Court, Bucks.

14. Lord and Lady Newport of Weston Park, Shropshire. The family name was Bridgeman and the principal title was held by Lord Bradford.
15. Cecil Forester of Willey, Shropshire.
16. The Whitmore Jones were another branch of the Whitmore family and lived at Chastleton (near Lower Slaughter) in the Cotswolds.
17. Edward Whitmore was probably a grandson of John Whitmore who was MP for Bridgnorth 1795-1812. Resident in London.
18. Possibly George Whitmore of Lower Slaughter, Cotswolds.
19. An Irish title (County Down). Probably the 4th Earl Annesley (1830-1874). The Annesley family had interests in Worcestershire. Adelaide had become acquainted with a branch of the Annesley family at the Arley fete.
19a. George was Rev. George Whitmore, who was the Rector of Stockton Church, near Apley. He was an elder brother of Henry Whitmore. Sarah was his wife and they lived at Kemberton, a few miles from Stockton. Before she married, Sarah was a Miss Deacon of Mabledon Park, Kent.
20. Sarah Whitmore's, sister.
20a. Marnwood Hall was on the road from Coalbrookdale to Buildwas. It had been built earlier in the century by Rev. Bartlett who was the incumbent of Buildwas Church.
21. Emily Whitmore who was to marry Col. (later Lt. Gen.) Wilmot of Malvern in 1855 (see note 1a above).
22. Madresfield is close to Malvern.
23. Lord Bernard of Castle Bernard, Bandon, Co. Cork was a relative of Lord Bandon who was married to Catherine (Whitmore) a cousin of Henry Whitmore (Lady Bandon). Bernard was the family name.
23a. The Pritchards were friends of Adelaide. John Pritchard was a banker in Broseley, Shropshire. After the election petition he replaced Sir Robert Pigot as Member of Parliament for Bridgnorth.
23b. Mrs Disraeli's reception was at Grosvenor Gate, a splendid house overlooking Hyde Park. She had inherited it from her first husband, Mr Wyndham Lewis, a wealthy Welsh coal owner.
24. This is a reference to the controversy which followed the death of John Grant, "grandmama's" husband. John Grant had, by his Will, left his holding in the Leighton Buzzard Bank to Abraham Darby IV in preference to Francis Darby who was married to his daughter, Adelaide's mother. There was a considerable dispute, and Abraham IV declined the share in the Bank.
25. Lord William Douglas was a relative of Lady Louisa Whitmore (née Douglas) wife of Thomas Charlton Whitmore, Henry's brother.
26. A Royal Court Levée.
27. Mrs Whitmore was the widow of Thomas Whitmore of Apley, who had died in 1846. She was the mother of Thomas Charlton, George and Henry. She was Adelaide's mother-in-law.
28. Lord Powys's Ball was an annual end-of-season event. Lord Powys was an important person in Shropshire's political and social life.
29. Toozie was a pet dog.
30. Rev. Bartlett was the incumbent of Buildwas Church until his death in 1861. Mr Nunn must have been employed as a curate.

31. Kemberton was the home of Rev. George Whitmore, and his wife Sarah. See note 19a above.
32. Lady Louisa was the wife of Thomas Charlton Whitmore (elder brother of Henry Whitmore) and Nina, Mary, Emmy (Emily) Douglas and Walter were their children.
33. Adelaide does not mention in her journal the reason for the visit to Ireland. This was because the Coalbrookedale Company had agreed to take part in the International Exhibition in Dublin in August 1853. Henry Whitmore and Adelaide attended the Exhibition on behalf of the Company. Not only was the Coalbrookdale Company not mentioned in her Journal, but the Company's exhibits did not even merit any comment, favourable or otherwise. The Exhibition did however "amuse (her) much and the pictures (were) very fine".
34. The visit to Ireland afforded an opportunity to visit Bandon near Cork, the county seat of the Earls of Bandon. A cousin of Henry Whitmore, Catherine, daughter of Charles Whitmore (George Whitmore's predecessor as Rector of Stockton) was married to the Earl of Bandon.
34a. Mr & Mrs John Anstice lived at Madeley Wood Hall on the north side of the River Severn, about 2 miles east of the Iron Bridge, near Coalport. They were distant relatives of the Darby family through the Reynolds family.
35. Lady Mary Clive was a Bridgeman.
36. Stanley Hall, home of the late Alfred Darby and Rebecca (Christy).
37. Wroxeter has the home of Rev. & Mrs Egremont.
38. Adelaide was probably not interested in the affairs of the Company but the meeting on the 26th November was an important one. After the death of Alfred Darby, Mr Crookes was appointed General Manager and the interests of the partners were vested in a triumvirate consisting of Henry Whitmore, Frank Tothill and Henry Dickinson. At the meeting on 26th November it was decided that all the various freehold interests held by individual partners should be vested in the members of the triumvirate in trust for the Coalbrookdale Company. The various deeds were executed in January 1854 by Abraham Darby, Richard Darby, William Tothill and Lucy Darby (S.R.R.C. 1681/178/10-15; 1681/179/9; 1681/181/55). They related, in the main to lands and collieries acquired by Sarah Darby and disposed of by her Will in 1821.
39. Wigganthorpe Hall is about a dozen miles north of York, situated between Terrington and Hovingham. It was the home of Mr and Mrs Garforth who had become close friends of Henry and Adelaide. Terrington and Sca[c]kleton are both nearby villages.
40. Rev. Isaacson was the Curate at Stockton where George Whitmore was the Rector.
41. Stoke Court, Bucks, was the home of Abraham Darby IV and Matilda.
42. Leighton (not to be confused with Leighton Buzzard) is a village a few miles west of Coalbrookdale.

1854

Comment

Life for Adelaide and Henry in 1854 continued at the same frantic pace that they had set in the previous two years. Adelaide had established herself as a political hostess of considerable merit and they appear to have lived life to the full. Henry had some difficulty in finding suitable accommodation for the London season and it was not until 6th March that they took up residence at 10 Lowndes Street which proved to be a very agreeable home, until they left in August. After a busy London season they returned to Shropshire where Henry's position as Member of Parliament for Bridgnorth meant that he and Adelaide mixed with the highest levels of society in the County and adjoining Staffordshire.

On the national level the beginning of the Crimea War was recorded and the Battles of the Alma, Balaclava and Inkerman were duly noted with the comments "Oh what times we have lived to see." This was before the arrival of the Russian winter and the suffering of the troops which caused such public outrage later.

An event within the family occurred in November 1854 of which Adelaide was unaware. This concerned Abraham IV and Matilda of Stoke Court, Bucks and their cousin Henry Dickinson and his wife Deborah (Abraham's sister) of Severn House, Coalbrookdale. It was early one morning in late November that Henry Dickinson arrived at Stoke Court with the devastating news that, two nights before, he had been sitting with his wife Deborah in his study at Severn House, when Mr Allen, the manager of the Shropshire Bank, Wellington, called to confess that he had speculated with the money placed in the Bank and had lost £200,000 and "that the Bank was cleaned out", and "£30,000 was given notice to be wanted by Mr Foster which there was no means to pay". £200,000 in 1854 was equivalent to £8 million in current money value,[1] and prior to the Limited Liability Act 1878, proprietors of banks were absolutely liable to the last penny of their means to repay their creditors. This was a truly dreadful blow, the more so as there was need for the utmost secrecy - only the two wives, Deborah and Matilda, were informed.

The effect on Abraham and Matilda was devastating. It is not known how they found the money to meet the demands on the Bank and to make up the loss, but within a few years, Abraham had sold the valuable collection of paintings and books which he had spent years amassing, and had moved to Ebbw Vale, South Wales where he became Manager and was able to concentrate on running and building up the Ironworks and Collieries, thus enabling him to sell Stoke Court in Buckinghamshire. The Bank survived and was taken over by Lloyds Bank in 1874.

The need for secrecy was so great that Adelaide was not informed, a situation which would have been unthinkable before the profound split which took place after the death of Francis Darby in 1850. The first indication that something was wrong came in 1857 (Adelaide's Journal, December 1857) when Adelaide recorded "Mama and I went to Stoke Court. We found Abraham and Matilda both ill from influenza and in trouble thinking they were coming to poverty!" It was ironic that whilst the circumstances of Matilda the elder sister were deteriorating, those of her younger sister Adelaide had escalated to the point at which she was moving in the highest circles in the land and enjoying a lifestyle of the highest quality.

New Year's Day - *So much snow we could not go to church, but read the afternoon service to the servants.*

Monday 2nd January - *George and Sarah*[2] *came to stay with us bringing the Baby (Gerald) - we despaired almost that they could come.*

Tuesday 3rd January - *George*[2] *and Henry went to Stockton to enquire after their uncle Charles*[3] *who is ill. They were obliged to take post horses - we did not stir out.*

Wednesday 4th January - *Nobody went out all day. No post in the evening.*

Thursday 5th January - *The snow went on all night! Drifted 6 ft deep between our house and the cottages. John digging slowly a path, looks lost in it! Waggons go tho' the field. George*[2] *and I walked for an hour in the snow. It was not cold to feel tho' the thermometer is 4 degrees below freezing.*

Saturday 7th January - *George and Sarah*[2] *went away - a thaw in the afternoon.*

Sunday 8th January - *We went to church at Madeley - Mr Gwyther preached an excellent sermon. Mama let us have the open carriage and horses and the roads were in such a condition that the wet snow and bits of ice splashed up into our faces.*

Monday 9th January - *Mrs Marshall called to take leave, she goes tomorrow and he preaches his farewell sermon next week.*[4]

Tuesday 10th January - *Joseph Dickinson*[5] *called to engage us to dine there next week from Bridgnorth. A cold thaw, still threatening snow. Catty*[21] *has written and Mamey*[21] *to ask me to work for a Bazaar Or Christmas Tree on the 19th so I am busy drawing. Also some music to copy for Sarah. Also my finery to prepare for Bridgnorth, a Ball on Thursday and concerts on Monday and Tuesday.*

Thursday 12th January - *Went to Bridgnorth for the Tradesmen's Ball. Black tulle gown embroidered with Straw, head dress of velvet and straw! Very tired.*

Friday 13th January - *Paid some visits thro' the ice and snow. Very bad headache.*

Saturday 14th January - *George[2] came to luncheon with us at The Crown. Went to Apley - probably the last visit we shall pay there - we staid over Sunday.*

Monday 16th January - *Went back to Bridgnorth for a concert and lecture on the Harp.*

Tuesday 17th January - *Paid visits all the morning, then drove to Oldbury[6] etc. Another concert.*

Wednesday 18th January - *To Faintree for luncheon - shopping. I hope the people have been pleased for all has been a great bore! We went to dine at the Albyne's[5] - Met Mr and Mrs Sparkes and 2 daughters, Mr and Mrs Anstice,[7] Mr and Mrs Thirsfield. Rather pleasant.*

Thursday 19th January - *Came home. Mr and Mrs Egremont[11] arrived for 2 days. The W R Anstices[7] came to dine.*

Friday 20th January - *George[2] came to luncheon. Mr and Mrs Egremont[11] and I walked to Marnwood. Henry's cold very bad indeed! Mr Marshall called to take leave.[4] Really going! It is too good to be true! The Edmonds came to dine.*

Saturday 21st January - *The Egremonts[11] left early. Mama and I and the dogs walked in the wind.*

Sunday 22nd January - *I went to church at the school room, Mr Gwyther preaching. Henry still very far from well.*

Monday 23rd January - *Mama and I called at Madeley Wood, Mrs Anstice[7] much altered.*

Tuesday 24th January - *Henry went to Kemberton.[2]*

Wednesday 25th January - *Henry went with me to call at the Rowleys in their new home. The Pritchards there and Mrs Forester.*

Thursday 26th January - *Went with Henry to Kemberton[2] for luncheon and he went on to Apley and stays over tomorrow for shooting.*

Saturday 28th January - *Henry came home - I busy about Scullery Maids!*

Sunday 29th January - *We went to church here, Mr Jettar preached.*

Monday 30th January - *Saw Henry off for London.*

Tuesday 31st January - *Mrs Clarke and her son went home after 3 days here. Mama and I went to Apley - Saw Louisa*[24] *for half an hour, she had gone over to Dudmaston.*[49]

Wednesday 1st February - *A pouring wet day.*

Thursday 2nd February - *Mama and I went to Kemberton for luncheon. Henry cannot find a house! We called on Mrs W R Anstice*[7] *and at Marnwood. Mr Bartlett*[8] *is better but altered.*

Saturday 4th February - *Mama and I went to Apley Castle and to Little Wenlock. Yesterday called upon Mr and Mrs Hayes at the Chesnuts*[9] *and like them.*

Sunday 5th February - *Went to the Schoolroom & Mama with me in the evening. 2 good sermons but the manner very dissenting.*

Monday 6th February - *Mr Knight to tune the piano. Matilda*[10] *came by the new 3 o'clock train!!! Looking very well and handsome.*

Tuesday 7th February - *Walked, we three, to the Church and School! I went to the top of the Tower - School left in utter ruin.*

Wednesday 8th February - *Went to Wroxeter.*[11] *They expected the Beresfords*[12] *in the evening!*

Thursday 9th February - *Henry came home. Matilda*[10] *and I walked to Severn House*[13] *and Dale House.*[13a] *Henry brought me a Daguerrotype of himself. He has taken No. 10, Lowndes Street.*

Friday 10th February - *Went to Stanley,*[14] *found nobody at home and to the Albynes.*[5]

Saturday 11th February - *Matilda*[10] *went away. Abraham said he would come and fetch her but she got a letter to say he had a cold and was gone home so she went and I spent 3 hours with her at Wellington waiting for a train.*

Sunday 12th February - *Laid up with quinzies - had to go out of church.*

Monday 13th February - *Henry went back to London with George.*[2] *We cannot have the house in Lowndes Street till March, so must be rather separated. Isaac left. Plate was packed. No end of notes and visits to enquire after Abraham.*[10] *Letter says Matilda*[10] *found him better. Mr Knight again tuned the piano.*

Monday 20th February - *A very happy week quite alone with Mama. Went on with the catalogue.*

Thursday 21st February - *Paid Mrs W R Anstice*[7] *a visit.*

Friday 24th February - *Henry came down from London and and Abraham and Matilda*[10] *came for one night. Smith's poor wife died last night after dreadful suffering from Dropsy. Mrs C D came to dine.*

Saturday 25th February - *Mr Hayes*[15] *came to breakfast. Abraham and Matilda*[10] *went away after luncheon.*

Sunday 26th February - *Henry and I walked to Little Wenlock in the afternoon.*

Monday 27th February - *I drove over to Apley - the Cattle Sale going on. George*[2] *there, Col and Mrs Arthur Legge at luncheon. Henry staid the night there and goes tomorrow to London.*

Tuesday 28th February - *Went to Shrewsbury. Mr Corbet, St Mary's Mrs DuGard.*

Friday 3rd March - *Mr Corbet and Edith came to spend the day. He brought some glass for the church and Mr Hayes*[15] *came to luncheon. Mrs Hayes and her sister came for the evening.*

Saturday 4th March - *Annie and Tappendon went with the carriage and three ponies to London and all the luggage.*

Sunday 6th March - *10 Lowndes Street, London. This is a very pretty house. I got here with Mrs Wooley and the scullery maid and Toozie*[16] *at 5. Henry came home to dinner.*

Thursday 7th March - *Mrs John Pritchard,*[17] *Mrs C Whitmore*[18] *and Mrs Calthorpe came to call upon us. Henry had unpacked all our pretty things and we look very nice.*

Saturday 11th March - *Henry went to the Speaker's Levée with Mr Foley, Mr Stanhope, who dined here - also Mr Forbes and George Whitmore.*[2]

Sunday 12th March - *Mr Bayley came to dine.*

Monday 13th March - *Emily*[37] *came from St Leonard's - All the week I was shut up with such a bad cold!*

Tuesday 14th March - *A fine day and we went to pay several visits.*

Wednesday 15th March - *We dined with George W in Park Street, beautiful pictures and china and excellent dinner.*

Saturday 18th March - *A dinner to give Mrs Wooley the benefit of a Man Cook, it was good! Mrs and Miss Brigstock, Mr and Mrs C Whitmore,*[18] *Mrs Forbes, Capt. Stuart Knox, Mr Whateley. Very pleasant evening.*

Tuesday 21st March - *Henry went to Shropshire for the Assizes. Lady E D came early with a dog for Mr Whateley. The cook from Woodcote came.*

Wednesday 22nd March - *Tappendon fell from Alice Gray and was taken to St George's Hospital, I am afraid it will be some time before he is well. The pony was not hurt at all. We had to dine with the Pritchards.*[17] *Miss Pritchard there and Mr Smith.*

Thursday 23rd March *- Mrs Wooley went home to Mama who wants her I am sure!*

Saturday 25th March *- Henry came back, bringing a good account of Mama.*

Thursday 30th March *- It has been a busy week preparing for the Drawing Room*[28] *today. My dress was approved of. Mdme Fusey, Isidore & Foster. The train Henry chose for me was a very beautiful brocade. It was a rather thin drawing room. Mrs Whitmore*[18a] *sent me her diamonds. The Royal party looked very serious and no wonder with war just declared.*[19]

Saturday 1st April *- Mrs and Miss Brigstock called and Mr Forbes and his daughter. Eliza's first dinner. Lady Laura and Mr Grattan, Miss Wrottesley,*[20] *Mr and Mrs John Pritchard, Lord Wm. Graham, Col Forester,*[38] *Mr Forbes and Mr Hamilton.*

Tuesday 4th April *- Mrs Whitmore*[18a] *came from St Leonards. She and Emily*[37] *went out together and Henry with me in the open carriage to the House and then my usual walk with Toozie*[16] *and lost my purse in Belgrave Square!!*

Wednesday 5th April *- Lord Bandon*[21] *and Catty*[21] *and all the children arrived in Lowndes Square. Henry could not get away to dine.*

Thursday 6th April *- Mamey*[21] *and Lord Bandon*[21] *and Col. Forbes*[22] *came to dine with us.*

Saturday 8th April *- Mrs Whitmore*[18a] *and Col Forbes*[22] *went back to St Leonards. Went to Sewell & Cross, Henry and I. He persuaded me to buy such a pretty forget-me-not gown!*

Tuesday 11th April *- Emily*[37] *went to St Leonards with the Castle Bernard*[26] *party, and we must go out of town tomorrow. It is deserted for Easter. Found the lost purse in my pocket.*

Wednesday 12th April *- Henry and I went to Leamington to the Regent. Found Mr Charles Whitmore*[18] *there and the Militia out and Major Granville in full regimentals.*

Thursday 13th April *- The review. We went to Mrs Storer*[23] *in the evening.*

14th April . Good Friday *- Twice at church. In the evening we went with Lois*[23] *to the Parish Church. Mr Craig not preaching yet - has just lost his wife! Staid an hour with poor Anne Fletcher. Mrs Hulton called and I was introduced to her, don't like her particularly. Saw Mrs Vaughton.*

Saturday 15th April *- We came away to Apley. Very hot! Very much like this day 2 years!*

16th April. Easter Sunday *- We staid for the Sacrament. Twice at Stockton Church.*

***Monday 17th April** - Louisa[24] took me to Cotsbrook. It is a very nice place just painted and papered. Will they go there!! Such lovely weather.*

***Tuesday 18th April** - A telegraphic summons for Louisa[24] from Bute House[25] - Tom[25] went with her.*

***Thursday 20th April** - Tom[21] returned in the evening, Lady Queensbury is better somewhat.*

***Friday 21st April 1854** - We came home to Mama, and I with a very bad cold.*

***Tuesday 25th April** - Henry had to return to London and George[2] is going too. I hope and think Elizabeth will make them comfortable for my cold is so bad they have decided I am to remain a few days.*

***Wednesday 26th April** - Fast Day - I could not go to church.*

***Friday 28th April** - Lady Queensbury's[24] death.*

***Monday 1st May** - I returned to London - George[2] here. Dreadful news of the loss of the Ercolane off Civitavecchia. The Halseys were on board and are lost with their beautiful little boy. Sir Robert Peel escaped by great activity and presence of mind. The poor Halseys have left one son of about 15 and at Eton.*

***Tuesday 2nd May** - Lord Bernard[26] dined with us and Douglas[27] is sent to us until the funeral.*

***Wednesday Mary 3rd** - Dined at Mrs Deacon's, Mr and Mrs Ramsden there.*

***Thursday 4th May** - The C Whitmores[18] dined with us. George Whitmore, Douglas[27] and George.*

***Friday 5th May** - Tom[24] arrived, dined and then went to Bute House.[25]*

***Saturday 6th May** - Lady Queensbury's funeral.[24] Douglas[27] went to it and returned at night with Tom[24] to dine. We dined with the Garforths.[51] George[2] returned home.*

***Tuesday 9th May** - Mrs Whitmore and Emily[37] came to take up their quarters at the "Family Hotel". Henry and I dined at The Annesleys.[52] Met the Ainsworths and in the evening a Bishop's visitation.*

***Wednesday 10th May** - Col Forbes[22] and Lucy[22] came to dine. Henry and I went to Mrs Gladstone's in the evening.*

***Saturday 13th May** - Lord Bernard[26] and Mamey[21] dined.*

***Tuesday 16th May** - I dined with the Garforths[51] and went with them to Drury Lane. Opera. Der Freischutz. The choruses very fine.*

***Wednesday 17th May** - Dinner party 12. Lady Wrottesley,[20] Mr and Mrs Baldock, Mr and Miss Garforth,[51] Mr Deacon, Sir J Hopkins, Mr Lefroy.*

Evening the Greatheds, Trants, Garforths and Miss Brigstock. Annie Cludde's marriage announced.[30]

Thursday 18th May *- Dinner 12. John and Lucy,*[22] *Mr Mrs and Miss L Forbes, Lord Bernard*[26] *and Henry Bernard.*[26]

Saturday 20th May *- The Birthday Drawing Room.*[28] *Dinner John and Lucy*[22] *and Mamey.*[21] *Lord Bernard*[26] *called for Mamey*[21] *and me to see the illuminations.*

Monday 22nd May *- Dined at Lady Laura Grattan's. Sir Robert and Lady Dallas, Mr and Mrs Lockhart, Sir J Guise and Miss Webb, Mr Bruce and a very agreeable Neapolitan, name unknown. He did not speak favourably of Lady Burghorsh's Carraxioli but it is decided. Mrs Lockhart is a foreigner, very handsome and entertaining.*

Wednesday 24th May *- Dinner 12. Lord and Lady Middleton,*[33] *Miss Brodrick, Lord Hawarden and Miss Maude, Mr Butler, John Pugh and Mr Price. Evening Albina Brodrick, Mamey,*[21] *Wrottesleys,*[20] *Trants and Garforths.*

Thursday 25th May *- Dinner 10. Mr and Lady Duncombe, John and Lucy,*[22] *Lord Bernard,*[26] *Mamey*[21] *and Tom Storer.*[23] *In the morning we all went to the United Services. Club, Jnr.*

Saturday 3rd June *- Dinner 12. Sir J and Lady Scott, Miss Hartopp, Capt Inge, Mr and Mrs Slaney, Col. Wilmot,*[37] *Mrs Cavendish Taylor. In the evening Garforths,*[51] *Charltons, John and Lucy.*[22]

Monday 5th June *- Henry went home. Emily*[37] *and I to Mrs Brigstock, in the evening. The new house cold.*

Wednesday 7th June *- Henry returned in the evening.*

Friday 9th June *- Dinner 12. Mrs Charlton, Lucy and Mr Jones, Willie Garforth and Maria,*[51] *G C Taylor and Mr E Taylor and George Whitmore.*[2] *Evening Trants, Cluddes, Mr Sweetenham, Jane and Dora, John and Lucy,*[22] *and Miss Forbes.*

Saturday 10th June *- Poor Mrs Baillie's funeral from the neat house. Very sad. Mrs Whitmore went with Lord Bernard*[26] *to Trowbridge, Sydenham. Henry, Emily*[37] *and I and George*[2] *went to the opening of The Crystal.*[29] *The Queen and her suite came. Clara Novello sang beautifully. G Whitmore dined with us.*

Wednesday 14th June *- Lady Powys' reception.*[30] *All London there to meet Miss Cludde.*[30] *Mrs Annesley*[52] *at home.*

Thursday 15th June *- Dined at Mrs Slaney's. Sir Offley Wakeman,*[31] *Mr H and Miss Richards, Mrs Campbell. Miss Sparling came in the evening. Mrs Garforth's concert.*

Friday 16th June - *Lady Harriet Duncombe to dine. Lord Charles Kerr, Garforths,*[51] *Lord and Lady Douglas. Miss Forbes came to go with us to Lady Bradford's Ball.*[32] *Did not go to Lady Spearman's.*[32]

Tuesday 20th June - *Went to Vauxhall with the Charltons - the fireworks very pretty.*

Wednesday 21st June - *Went with Miss Forbes and Emily*[37] *to the Flower Show in the Regent's Park. With Henry to Mrs Gaskell*[53] *in the evening.*

Thursday 22nd June - *Went to St George's to see Miss Cludde's*[30] *wedding. With Miss Forbes to see the pictures at Grosvenor House. John and Lucy*[22] *dined.*

Friday 23rd June - *The Storers*[23] *came at 12 to spend the day. Dinner and evening.*

Monday 26th June - *Richmond Dinner and Ball. I danced a good deal but stupid.*

Tuesday 27th June - *Matilda*[10] *came. We went to a Bazaar at Gore House. Dined at Mrs Ainsworths.*

Wednesday 28th June - *Henry and I dined with the Cotes. Met Lady H Herbert and Lord Powys,*[30] *Mr and Mrs Middleton,*[33] *Sir J and Lady Harmer and Mr Portman.*

Thursday 29th June - *Dined at Lord and Lady Middleton's.*[33] *The Bishop of Worcester and Mrs Pepys, Mr and Mrs Hutchins,*[34] *Lady Pakenham, Lord Waldegrave, and Lady Elizabeth W.*

Friday 30th June - *Dined at home. Lord Bernard*[26] *and Mamey, Mr and Miss Forbes, John and Lucy,*[22] *Sir Arthur Brooke, George*[2] *and Mr and Mrs Gatacre.*

Saturday 1st July - *We all dined at Lowndes Square.*

Monday 3rd July - *Rode May Queen to Clapham with John and Lucy Forbes.*[22] *Called on Mrs John Whitmore who could not see us and on F Levenson who was not at home.*

Wednesday 5th July - *Evening party at Lady Middleton's*[33] *where we met Mrs W Broderick for the first time.*

Thursday 6th July - *the Storers came for one day*[23] *and we went to Albert Smith's Ball.*

Friday 7th July - *The Ainsworths dined with us. Maria Garforth,*[51] *Major Powis, Sir John Hopkins.*

Tuesday 11th July - *Dined at home - 5 selves. Lord Adolphous Vane Tempest, Col Taylor, Mr Butler, Mr Knatchbull, Mr Stafford, Mr Stanhope - particularly pleasant.*

***Wednesday 12th July** - I dined at Mrs Garforth's[51] and went with them to the Fr. Plays. Les Diamants de la Couronne.*

***Friday 14th July** - Rode to Sydenham[29] with the Blackbournes, Col Knox, Mr Stanhope, etc. Visit to Sydenham for the day. With Mrs Whitmore and Emily and Henry to visit George and Sarah.[2]*

***Saturday 15th July** - Henry and I dined at the Blackbourne's, but Miss Blackbourne is so ill we met only Col Knox and Miss Vincent.*

***Monday 17th July** - I went to Beckenham with Mrs Whitmore and Emily.[37] It was to meet Mrs Robert Whitmore and Sophia and I liked it not.*

***Wednesday 19th July** - Henry went into Shropshire for the laying of a stone at Bridgnorth. About this time the church was consecrated at Coalbrookdale.[34] Rode to Sydenham[29] with the Blackbournes. Mr and Mrs Bromley, Mrs Greatheds' evening party. I went to it by myself. Mrs Taylor and Mrs Cavendish were there.*

***Thursday 20th July** - C and I went with the Garforth's[51] to the French Exhibition and the Water Colours.*

***Friday 21st July** - Mama came for one day only and Henry came back from Bridgnorth and settled with her for me to go to Stoke Court.[35]*

***Saturday 22nd July** - Mr and Miss Trant, and John and Lucy[22] dined here.*

***Monday 24th July** - I went to Stoke Court[35] taking with me May Anne Fuller, not yet my maid. At dinner Lady Sophia and Mr Towers, Lady Charlotte and Mr Blount, Mr Mrs and Miss Rice Clayton, Sir ------ Alexander, Mr and Mrs Hibbert, Sir T and Lady Willshire.*

***Tuesday 25th July** - Mrs Whitmore and Emily[37] left Lowndes Street.*

***Wednesday 26th July** - Dinner at Stoke Court.[35] Shaws, Wards, Bents, Waklins, Taylors, Gaskells.*

***Thursday 27th July** - I went back to Lowndes Square. Lucy[22] and Kitty dined.*

***Friday 28th July** - Mama came for one night. Lucy[22] dined.*

***Saturday 29th July** - Henry went into Shropshire for the Assizes. Mama and I to Stoke Court.[35]*

***Tuesday 1st August** - Mama went home from Stoke Court.[35] Abraham to Monmouth,[36] I stayed with Matilda.[10]*

***Wednesday 2nd August** - I returned to Lowndes Square and found Henry had arrived yesterday. Wrote to dismiss Fuller. Henry and I went to dine at Sydenham[29] with the Blackbourne's party. Mr Henry Turner went with us and we brought him and Mr Stanhope back to London in the rain and we finished at Astley's.*

Thursday 3rd August - *Lucy*[22] *dined with us.*

Friday 4th August - *Went to the Blackbourne's in the evening. Henry and I, Miss Vivian, Mr Stanhope & Mr and Mrs Blackbourne.*

Saturday 5th August - *Jane Abrams left and I have no maid. Dinner, Elinor Blackbourne, Lucy,*[22] *Col Taylor, Capt Storer and Mrs Stanhope.*

Sunday 6th August - *Went to the Blackbourne's for luncheon and with Emily*[37] *into Kensington Gardens.*

Tuesday 8th August - *Went with Mrs and 2 Miss Blackbournes to the Haymarket for the Spanish Dancers. Nena, the old Chateau, and as like as 2 peas. Mr Stanhope met us.*

Wednesday 9th August - *Matilda*[10] *came and spent the day.*

Saturday 12th August - *Jean Crawford came and I hope and trust she will do! Prorogation - the Queen reads beautifully. Lord Jocelyn's death of cholera.*

Tuesday 15th August - *We left Lowndes St. Indeed everybody fears to stay in London but John and Lucy*[22] *are in good spirits. Matilda*[10] *staying with Mama. We found Mama with a disfigured face, she had fallen down with a plate of fruit in the hall.*

Friday 18th August - *I went with Henry to Cotsbrook and Kemberton. Met George and Sarah Whitmore*[2] *with Mrs Charlton and Mrs Croft.*

Saturday 19th August - *Matilda*[10] *left us. Mama and I went with her to Wellington.*

Monday 21st August - *Mama and I went to Broseley.*

Tuesday 22nd August - *Henry went to Apley Castle and on our return we found Mr and Mrs Forester*[38] *& Cecil here. Mr Forester had had a letter from M desiring him to intercede with Henry about a footpath in the church to which Henry had never made an objection.*

Thursday 24th August - *Mrs Charlton and Lucy here. The Pritchards*[17] *called.*

Friday 25th August - *Mama, Henry and I to Kemberton for a School tea fete.*

Saturday 26th August - *Henry went to Bridgnorth.*

Tuesday 29th August - *Picnic at Apley. Miss Robertson, Emmy*[27] *and Lucy,*[27] *George and Sarah.*[2]

Thursday 31st August - *Flower Show at Davenport House. The Watts Russells were not at home. George and Sarah Whitmore*[2] *went with us, dined at Kemberton.*

Saturday 2nd September - *Tommy Charlton[24] came to go with Henry to Bridgnorth.*

Monday 4th September - *Music Meeting at Worcester. Lodgings at 45 High Street, Birbecks. Left home half past 3, arrived half past 8.*

Tuesday 5th September - *The Service in the Cathedral. The Dettingen Te Deum. Dined at Boughton. George and Sarah Whitmore[2] & Emily[37] are there. Concert, Mendelsohn's Midsummer Night's Dream.*

Wednesday 6th September - *Elijah & ------? Last Judgement. Dined at Boughton. Concert, Pastoral Symphony.*

Thursday 7th September - *The Creation. Dined at Boughton. The Miss Greathed's. Concert, Oberon and Mendelsohn's Symphony. Principal singers are Clara Novello, Viaroot Garcia, Mdme Weisse, Miss Dobby, whose place was taken twice by Mrs Lockey - Gardoni, Simms, Reeves, Lockey and Herr Founes.*

Friday 8th September - *Messiah. Luncheon at The Deanery. We did not go to the Ball but dined at Boughton for the last time. George and Sarah[2] gone to Malvern. 20 at dinner. Lady & Miss Holland, Mr Severne, Capt Arthur, Capt Arkwright, Mr Galton, Mr and Mrs Taylor Wynniats, Mrs Elwes.*

Saturday 9th September - *Emily[37] came over in the carriage ordered to take us to Malvern. Henry and I are at The Abbey Boarding House and they won't take in the servants.*

Wednesday 12th September - *The Poultry Show.*

Friday 15th September - *Review at Kensey. We went, Henry and I and Emily[37] with Miss Hewitt and Miss Granville in Lord Lifford's carriage.*

Saturday 16th September - *Went to Mrs Stratton's in the evening. Major, Mrs and Miss Granville, Mr Prideaux ------, Candlers, Berwicks ------.*

Monday 18th September - *Left Malvern for Dudmaston[49] for 2 nights. Admiral, Mrs and 2 Miss Bridgemans,[48] Mrs Taylor, Miss Shepherd, Mr W Moseley and Donald Carr.*

Wednesday 20th September - *Home.*

Thursday 21st September - *Col Forbes and Lucy came.[22]*

Friday 22nd September - *Went to Cotsbrook for luncheon.*

Saturday 23rd September - *Kemberton Do.*

Monday 25th September - *Mrs Clark came over for the day. The Rowleys and Tom and Louisa[24] came to dine.*

Tuesday 26th September - *Mr Bellet came to breakfast, they are gone to Bridgnorth.*

Wednesday 27th September - *John and Lucy*[22] *went to Scotland. Henry and I to Longford for the Weston Bow Meeting. Sir Baldwin and the Miss Leighton, Mrs W and Miss Pelham, Miss Childe, Capt Cotton, Mr Owen of Woodhouse.*

Thursday 28th September - *The Bow Meeting at Weston.*[48] *Dartmouths, Legges, Cheynes, Foresters, Newports, Miss Grey. We staid for the beginning of the Ball and then went back ourselves to Longford.*

Friday 29th September - *Henry went out shooting with Mr Pelham. Lady Hester Leake took the rest of the party a walk to Lilleshall Monument.*

Saturday 30th September - *Came home.*

Monday 2nd October - *Henry went to Apley Castle for shooting and then to Cotsbrook*[54] *until Thursday when we expect the Munros. Mama and I went to Wroxeter*[11] *after Luncheon Louisa Russell*[39] *there.*

Friday 6th October - *Col and Mrs Munro arrived having missed a train yesterday. In the afternoon drove to Marnwood,*[8] *Buildwas, and the Church. Mrs Edmund Darby and Mary Darby of Dale House,*[13a] *Mr and Mrs H Dickinson of Severn House,*[13] *Mrs Egremont of Wroxeter*[11]*, Miss Russell and Janet and Ted came to dinner.*

Saturday 7th October - *The Munro's left us. Henry and I went with them to the station and then on to Shrewsbury.*

Tuesday 10th October - *Henry and I went to Chicknell. Mrs Taylor has only her oldest son with her and Miss Cavendish. Miss Boycott dined.*

Wednesday 11th October - *Mrs Taylor took Henry and me to Enville, beautiful it is. Lady Stamford ill at Brighton.*

Friday 13th October - *Hale Hall*[40] *from Chicknell - a long day it was! We found only Elinor at home with Mr and Mrs Blackbourne, Mr and Mrs Edwin Corbett and Mrs John B.*

Saturday 14th October - *Liverpool - St George's Hall, Docks, Exchange.*

Tuesday 17th October - *Home. Elinor is really engaged to Mr Stanhope.*

Wednesday 18th October - *First Bridgnorth dinner. Mr and Mrs Richards, Mr Sparkes, Mr Thursfield, Mr Marshall, Mr Hayes,*[15] *2 Mr and Mrs Anstice.*[7]

Thursday 19th October - *Henry went to dinner at Willey.*[41] *I have brought home a bad cold from Hale*[40] *and cannot go there or to Bridgnorth.*

Friday 20th October - *Henry went to Bridgnorth for a "Prorogation Society" meeting, stayed one night and went to Cotsbrook till Monday.*

Tuesday 24th October - *We went to Millichope for two nights. Lady Diana, Mr Packington, Mr and Miss Smythe, Mr Cheyne and Col Rushwood. Very pretty country.*

Wednesday 25th October - *Battle of the Alma.*[42]

Thursday 26th October - *Came home, yesterday. We had a charming walk and most lovely country. Left snow on the Clee Hills.*

Monday 30th October - *Charlotte and Lois Storer came.*[23] *Tom*[24] *came on Saturday and staid to see them.*

Tuesday 1st November - *Dinner to the Bridgnorth Corporation. George and Sarah*[2] *and Miss Deacon came. Singing. It prospered very well but George and Sarah*[2] *had a mishap on their way - a fracture of wheels and springs and had to walk some part. It was 31st October but no matter.*

Friday 3rd November - *The T's, Henry and I went to Willey Rectory*[41] *to luncheon, called at Wenlock on Mrs Gaskell*[53] *and at Stanley.*[14] *Such lovely weather and all the leaves on the trees.*

Saturday 4th November - *The Hounds met at Apley and we drove over early in the Brake and then went on for luncheon to Bridgnorth. Mrs Sparkes asked us to C's wedding. It was a most pleasant day. Miss Ellen Deacon went with us, and as we turned up the Kemberton lane, I managed to tumble off and fainted and frightened everybody, but was not really hurt at all, which is a great blessing. It was just the place where the horse ran away.*

Sunday 5th November - *Balaklava.*[43] *I staid at home and was kept in bed most of the day, but Mr Webb says I am not one bit the worse. The Battle of Inkerman*[44] *- oh what times to have lived to see. Monday, Mary Darby*[13a] *with us.*

Tuesday 7th November - *Henry went to Bridgnorth and stayed all night and meets me tomorrow at Haughton.*[45] *The Storer's*[23] *left for Cotsbrook, and by the latest post I was so glad to see a letter from Lois*[23] *for Tom.*[24]

Wednesday 8th November - *Went to Haughton.*[45] *Called at Kemberton and upon the Spencers - the good people who took me in on Saturday. Took them some pears. At Haughton*[45] *Mr and Mrs Ince, Mr and Mrs Burroughs of Chetwynd, Mr William Congreave and Mr Mainwaring Owen.*

Thursday 9th November - *Henry went to Apley Castle. We called at Aston, saw the hounds. George and Sarah*[2] *and Miss Ellen Deacon came to dine.*

Friday 10th November - *Shooting at Sutton Wood. Mr Richard Brooke came.*

Saturday 11th November - *We came home. Dreadful stories in the Crimea*[44] *and poor Harry Croft was lost in the Rip Van Winkle, a horse transport which went down off Balaclava.*

Wednesday 15th November - *Henry and I went to Apley Castle. The Jones were there and Mrs C and Lucy*[27] *returned.*

Thursday 16th November - *Such a wet morning, only Henry went to the Infirmary Meeting.*[46] *Mrs Slaney and Miss Corbett held the plates and Mr Hill and Sir Henry Edwards. We went to the Ball - Jane, Robert and Dora - a very pleasant Ball.*

Friday 17th November - *We left Apley Castle after Henry had had a day's shooting. Got home to dine. Mr Grant here.*

Saturday 18th November - *Henry left early for Cotsbrook*[54] *to shoot and stay till Monday. Mr Grant went away too. The cold intense.*

Thursday 23rd November - *Henry went again to Cotsbrook*[54] *to shoot, he has a cold.*

Friday 24th November - *I went to Cotsbrook*[54] *to bring Henry home. Sophia there. Mr Bellet came to luncheon.*

Saturday 25th November - *Henry rode to Bridgnorth, he is not well. It is very cold.*

Thursday 28th November - *The Poultry Show at Shrewsbury. Everybody there! Wet day but warmer weather is a blessing.*

Wednesday 29th November - *Cut down the "fantastic larch".*

Friday 1st December - *Henry went to Malvern till Monday.*

Sunday 3rd December - *Mama went with me to church at night and Rebecca. The 39th ordered to the Crimea!*[44]

Monday 4th December - *Henry came home.*

Tuesday 5th December - *The Hawkstone Ball.*[47] *We went to dine at Shrewsbury where Tom,*[24] *Nina,*[27] *Mary*[27] *and Capt Cheyney met us, and we went together in the Aberystwyth coach for we could get no omnibus. 700 people. A tent for supper and a tent for dancing. Everything was perfectly arranged but in the tents rather cold. I was very happy, and met so many friends, Mama gave me a new gown after Henry's taste - green glace and my Brussels lace, a ruche of ribbons and pearls at the head of each flounce. Headdress a bouquet of mixed flowers, dark red poppies. Miss Deacon looked very nice.*

Wednesday 6th December - *Slept a few hours at Shrewsbury and came home. Henry off to shoot at Davenport for a few days. Gave up the Bridgnorth Concert, I am quite done up!*

Sunday 10th November - *Bernard D dined with us. Such a charming walk with Henry to Severn House*[13] *and Marnwood.*[8]

Monday 11th December - *Mama and I went to Shrewsbury for shopping, found the Militia assembling. Disagreeable. In the evening Mr Easton arrived from Downton.*

12th December - *Henry Whitmore went to London for a meeting of Parliament. Did not return until 23rd December. (Appendix to Journal for 1854 - not reproduced in this edition).*

Wednesday 13th December - *Pressing invitation to Mr Eaton to go to Mrs Moore Halsey's to paint some children. He went, he is very agreeable. Mama quite ill and overdone.*

Thursday 14th December - *I went to Weston*[48] *to luncheon. Lady Newport there and Alice, Anson and Mr G Bridgeman besides their own party. News of poor Harry Croft's death. He was lost in the ship Rip Van Winkle off Balaklava in the morning of 11th November. Another mourning.*

Friday 15th December - *News that Emily*[37] *is engaged to be married to Col Wilmot of Malvern.*

Tuesday 19th December - *Mama and I went to Cotsbrook.*[54] *Lady Louisa*[24] *of Malvern and Nina*[27] *and Mary*[27] *were gone to Woodcote.*

Thursday 21st December - *Caroline Sparkes was married to her cousin Frederick Isaac. I went myself, a pretty wedding and fineish day but some tears. Poor things going to Australia. 45 at the breakfast. Uncle Wolryche*[49] *filled Dudmaston for it, the presents very pretty and generally useless.*

Saturday 23rd December - *Henry came home. I went to Kemberton to meet him, train late.*

Sunday 24th December - *To Little Wenlock in the afternoon.*

Monday 25th December - Christmas Day - *Mama went with us to church here. George and Sarah*[2] *came in the evening to dine and spend the week.*

Wednesday 27th December - *George Whitmore, Sarah*[2] *and I went to Apley Castle to call.*

Thursday 28th December - *Henry went to shoot at Apley - said it was very sorrowful. The Edmonds*[50] *dined here.*

Friday 29th December - *Rebecca*[55] *came to dinner.*

Saturday 31st December - *New Year's Eve. I went to church myself for Henry has a cold. I am not happy about him at all and tomorrow if he can he goes to Malvern.*

NOTES

1. Equivalent contemporary values of the Pound; a Historical Series 1270 to 1900 - Bank of England.
2. George was Rev. George Whitmore, Rector of Stockton Church, near Apley. He was the elder brother of Henry Whitmore and was the middle one of the three Whitmore brothers (Thomas was the eldest). Sarah was his wife. Before her marriage she was Sarah Deacon of Mabledon Park, Kent. Their home was at Kemberton, a few miles away from Stockton. George's uncle, Charles Whitmore, the previous Rector of Stockton continued to occupy the Rectory at Stockton.
3. Rev Charles Whitmore who was Rector of Stockton before George Whitmore took over. He lived at the Rectory at Stockton.
4. Rev. Marshall was the first incumbent of the newly built Coalbrookdale Church.
5. Joseph Dickinson was the eldest child of Ann and Barnard Dickinson and was therefore Adelaide's cousin. He lived at the Albynes, between Bridgnorth and Broseley.
6. Oldbury is on the southern outskirts of Bridgnorth.
7. The Anstice family were based at Madeley Wood Hall, situated on the north side of the River Severn about 2 miles east of the Iron Bridge, near Coalport. They were distantly related to the Darby family through the Reynolds family. William Reynolds Anstice was a solicitor and was Steward of the Manor of Madeley.
8. Rev Bartlett lived at Marnwood Hall and was the incumbent of Buildwas Church.
9. The Chesnuts was given by Abraham IV to be the Vicarage for Coalbrookdale so Mr and Mrs Hayes were the successors to Mr and Mrs Marshall (see note 4 above).
10. Matilda Darby was Adelaide's elder sister. She was married to Abraham Darby IV. Until 1852 they lived at the Chesnuts, Coalbrookdale, while Abraham was manager of the Coalbrookdale company. In 1852, after "the painful family affair", they moved to Stoke Court, Buckinghamshire.
11. Mr & Mrs Egremont had been friends of Adelaide for many years. They lived at Wroxeter west of Coalbrookdale near to Atcham. Edward Egremont was Vicar of Wroxeter.
12. Archdeacon Beresford was at one time a suitor for Adelaide's hand in marriage.
13. Severn House (now the Valley Hotel, Ironbridge) was the home of Henry Dickinson and his wife, Deborah (neé Darby).

13a. Dale House, Coalbrookdale was the home of Mrs Edmund Darby (Lucy) and her daughter, Mary Darby.

14. Stanley Hall, Bridgnorth was the home of Mrs Alfred Darby (neé Christy), widow of Alfred Darby who died in 1852.
15. Mr Hayes was the Vicar of Holy Trinity, Coalbrookdale, in succession to Mr Marshall.
16. Toozie, the pet dog.
17. Mr and Mrs John Pritchard had been friends of Adelaide for some years. John Pritchard was a banker from Broseley. He was also the second Member of Parliament for Bridgnorth.

18. Mr and Mrs Charles Whitmore were possibly of the branch of the Whitmore family who had settled at Lower Slaughter in the Cotswolds.
18a. Mrs Whitmore was the mother of Henry Whitmore. No doubt the diamonds were family heirlooms.
19. This marked the beginning of the Crimean War. An ultimatum had been sent to the Czar of Russia at St. Petersburg by Britain and France on 27th February 1854 demanding the withdrawal of Russian troops from the Principalities of Moldavia and Wallachia which were subject to Turkish rule. No reply was received and war ensued.
20. The Wrottesley family were a leading Staffordshire family from Wolverhampton. Lord John Wrottesley, 2nd Baron Wrottesley was noted for his scientific achievements and was one of the founders of the Royal Astronomical Society. Lady Wrottesley was Sophia, daughter of Thomas Giffard of Chillington, Co. Stafford.
21. Lord and Lady Bandon (formerly Catherine Whitmore, cousin of Henry Whitmore) came from Castle Bernard, Bandon, Co. Cork. Catty and Mamey were members of their family.
22. Col. John Forbes, Coldstream Guards came from Callander, Scotland and was married to Lucy Whitmore, a cousin of Henry Whitmore. They had an address in Cadogan Place.
23. The Storers of Hawksworth, Nottinghamshire were related by marriage. Charlotte and Lois were members of the Storer family.
24. Louisa was Lady Louisa Whitmore (née Douglas). She was the daughter of the Marquis and Marchioness of Queensbury. She was married to Thomas Charlton Whitmore of Apley (called Tom or Tommy), eldest brother of Henry Whitmore.
25. Bute House was the home of Lord and Lady Queensbury.
26. Lord Bernard of Castle Bernard, Bandy, Co Cork was the same family as Lord and Lady Bandy. Bernard was the family name.
27. Douglas, the eldest child of Thomas Charlton Whitmore and Lady Louisa Whitmore (née Douglas). He was a pupil at Eton. There was another brother, Walter and seven sisters - Caroline (Nina), Mary, Emily (Emmy), Lucy, Edith, Cecil Elizabeth and Evelyn.
28. The Drawing Room was a Royal Court Levée. There were several during the London season.
29. After the Great Exhibition in Hyde Park in 1851, the Crystal Palace was taken down and re-erected at Sydenham, in south London.
30. Lord Powys was the leading political figure in Shropshire. The Cludde family, a very old Shropshire family of Orleton, Wellington were related to the Herbert family (Lord Powys). Miss Cludde was at the Reception prior to her wedding at St George's, Hanover Square on 22nd June.
31. Sir Offley Wakeman was a member of another leading Shropshire family.
32. June and July were regarded as the height of the London Season; Lady Bradford of Weston Park, Shropshire.
33. Possibly of Chirk Castle, Powys.
34. It was a condition of the settlement, following the death intestate of Francis Darby in 1850, that the land required for a new Anglican Church in Coalbrookdale which was to be provided and endowed by Abraham IV and

Matilda, would be conveyed, for a nominal consideration, to the Commission for New Churches, by Adelaide. The church was built between 1851 and 1854. It was consecrated as Holy Trinity Church Coalbrookdale in 1854. It seems strange that Adelaide did not attend the consecration. She provided the land for the church, even if she only did so in a nominal capacity.

35. Stoke Court in Buckinghamshire was the home of Abraham Darby IV and Matilda (Adelaide's sister). The House was built by a grandson of William Penn, the Quaker founder of Pennsylvania, U.S.A.
36. Abraham IV was one of the partners in the Ebbw Vale Company which they acquired in 1844. The company was in the middle of a process of expansion having acquired the Abersychan Ironworks in 1852 and was contemplating purchasing four blast furnaces and other works in Pontypool (acquired 1855).
37. Emily was a cousin of Henry Whitmore. She was destined to marry Col. (later Lt-Gen) Wilmot of Malvern in 1855.
38. The family seat of the Forester family was at Willey (between Broseley and Much Wenlock, Shropshire). Lord and Lady Forester (the former Lady Melbourne) lived there.
39. Louisa Russell, daughter of Rev and Mrs Egremont of Wroxeter was married to Capt Russell, a former suitor for Adelaide's hand in marriage.

39a. Weston Park, Shropshire, was the home of Lord and Lady Bradford and of Lord and Lady Newport. The family name was Bridgman.

40. Hale, Liverpool (south)
41. Willey Hall, home of the Forester family.
42. The first battle of the main part of the Crimean War, the Alma, took place in September 1864.
43. The second battle of the Crimean War, Balaclava, took place at the end of October 1864. It incorporated the "thin red line". (General Sir Colin Capbell and the 93rd Foot), the Charge of the Heavy Brigade (General Scarlett) and the more famous Charge of the Light Brigade (Lord Cardigan).
44. The third battle of the Crimean War, Inkerman took place in November 1854 and was an attempt by the Russian forces to relieve the Franco-British siege of Sevastopol. The attempt failed but there were heavy losses of horses and men and materials on both sides. This was followed by the Crimean winter which caused appalling misery and loss of life through sickness. Even as Adelaide was writing her entry for 5th November, Florence Nightingale was arriving at Scutari opposite Constantinople where the Army's health services were based. Her landmark actions combined with the activities of Sir William Russell, correspondent of The Times, kindled immense public indignation and led to the fall of the Aberdeen Government in February 1855.
45. Haughton is a village a few miles south-west of Stafford.
46. The Infirmary Meeting was the annual meeting held at St Chad's Church, Shrewsbury to raise funds for the Shrewsbury Infirmary (Hospital).
47. Hawkestone Park near Hodnet, Shropshire was the family seat of the Hill family. It is difficult to know why they travelled in the Aberystwith coach from Shrewsbury as Hawkstone is north-east of Shrewsbury, not west.
48. Weston Park, Shropshire, was the home of Lord and Lady Bradford and of Lord and Lady Newport. The family name was Bridgeman.

49. William Wolryche Whitmore was the owner of Dudmaston Hall near Bridgnorth, Shropshire.
50. George Edmonds was the Rector of Little Wenlock.
51. Mr and Mrs Garforth, and their daughters Kitty and Maria, were a Yorkshire family from Wigganthorpe Hall, some 10 miles north of York. They had become close friends of Henry and Adelaide.
52. The Annesley family had an Irish title. A branch of the family had interests in Worcestershire. Adelaide had become acquainted with them at the Arley fete.
53. The Gaskells were a well-known family from Much Wenlock, Shropshire.
54. Cotsbrook, about 2 miles northeast of Apley, had been purchased by Thomas Charlton Whitmore as a replacement home for Apley.
55. Rebecca was the daughter of Richard and Maria Darby of "Rosehill".

Edward Stanley (1799-1869), 14th Earl of Derby. Prime Minister three times: 1852, 1858-59 and 1866-68.

BY COURTESY OF THE NATIONAL PORTRAIT GALLERY, LONDON

Lord Henry Lennox (1821-86), son of the Duke of Richmond and a member of Disraeli's inner circle of friends.

BY COURTESY OF THE NATIONAL PORTRAIT GALLERY, LONDON

1855

Comment

Adelaide's last entry in her Journal for 1855 states "May God be thanked for such a happy year". She had been married to Henry Whitmore for three years and her marriage had proved successful. She experienced her third season in London and this proved to be a very busy time. She and her husband had rented 17 Eaton Terrace for six months. Life there seemed to consist of an endless round of dinners, receptions, assemblies, concerts and several appearances at Court, and she obviously felt that her life was very fulfilling.

After the London Season was over they went for a fortnight's holiday in Devonshire followed by another fortnight in Norfolk. From Norfolk they went to Malvern in Worcestershire. This was the home of Colonel (later Lt.-General) Wilmot who had married Emily Whitmore at St George's, Hanover Square on 15th February. Emily was a cousin of Henry Whitmore (see family tree, p.333) and had become a close associate of Adelaide.

The Journal does not disclose much information about Henry Whitmore's parliamentary career, except that in October he received a letter from Disraeli offering him a political appointment, which indicated that he was making progress within the new Conservative party which Disraeli was shaping. There also appeared on the scene a certain Mr Bluck, who thereafter became an almost constant presence in the Whitmore household. It is a matter of speculation as to the role he exercised, but he may have been an agent or secretary or some similar appointment.

On the national scene, the shadow overhanging life was the Crimean War. The death of the Czar in March was noted but this did not end the War. The turning point did not come until the capture of Sebastopol in September which was marked by a Thanksgiving Sunday on 30th September.

In Coalbrookdale the death took place on 29th September of Deborah (née Darby) wife of Henry Dickinson of Severn House. She was the younger daughter of Lucy Darby of Dale House and was the sister of Abraham Darby IV of Stoke Court. This was a dreadful blow to Lucy Darby coming after the loss of her younger son Alfred Darby in 1852. The death of a prominent member of the Darby family was always deeply felt in Coalbrookdale and the Works was closed on the day of the funeral.

Despite this sad loss, the year ended with visits to Longford and Weston Park in Shropshire, Haughton in Staffordshire and Hale in Liverpool.

Monday 1st January - New Year's Day - *Went with Henry to Wellington and saw him off. He is better I hope. Mama called on Mrs Graham and I went to fetch her home and we called on Mr and Mrs Hayes.*[1]

Wednesday 3rd January - *Henry returns today. He has a cold. So warm, it is quite Spring. Henry did not arrive until quite late, 11 - missing a train.*

Thursday 4th January - *The Tradesmen's Ball at Bridgnorth. I danced so much I was sick.*

Friday 5th January - *Not up before 2 - though tired all symptoms of having been tipsey. Paid a few visits, but it was a great waste of time.*

Saturday 6th January - *A great many visits - went to Aldenham (Bridgnorth) to call, did not find Lady Granville, came home to dine.*

Sunday 7th January - *Mr Hayes*[1] *gave us such a good sermon "Is it well with thee - is it well with thy husband" etc.*

Monday 8th January - *Henry went to Cotsbrook*[2] *for luncheon.*

Wednesday 10th January - *Piano forte tuned. Anxious letter from Matilda.*[3] *Henry and I go to Bridgnorth for the Aldenham Ball tonight. Drove over a gate and knocked off a lamp! The Avenue beautifully illuminated. Mr and Lady Margaret Leveson, Lady G. Fullerton, Major T, Lord Caernarvon, 2 Miss Pitts, Sir Robert and Miss Throckmorton in the house. The Waseys, Pritchards, Sparkes, Dorrells, Actons, Bensons and ourselves and Tennants and Tradesmen. Dancing, no supper.*

Thursday 11th January - *Took up Douglas and Walter*[4] *as we returned home - they staid to Saturday. Louisa*[4] *and Nina*[4] *came to fetch them.*

Tuesday 16th January - *Letter from Matilda*[3] *to say they were at Bangor and would call upon us. Spent an hour here. Dined at Dale House.*[45]

Thursday 18th January - *Dallicot to dine and sleep. Watts Russell, Pritchards,*[5] *Sparkes and little Bridie, Mr Gatacre, Mrs Leigh Smith and 2 sons and Miss Grazebrook, Mr Robertson.*

Friday 19th January - *Henry went to London, he left me at Norton.*

Sunday 21st January - *A deep snow and could not go out. Yesterday, took a walk thro' it and Sir J Acton called just as we returned - very agreeable.*

Sunday 28th January - *Henry returned yesterday - he has to go again to London tomorrow and we give up Woodcote.*[58] *The Government changing.*[6] *We have taken 17 Eaton Terrace, the Denman's house from 3rd February. £280. George*[23] *came yesterday to luncheon and Joseph Dickinson.*[57] *Snow all the week and Mama and I have hardly been out. Old Mrs Edwards*[7] *is dead and 2 weeks ago Mr Bache of Chesterton.*

Monday 29th January - *Note from Mr Cotes, he would not give up.*[58] *I went with Henry to Shifnal and he settled to come down tomorrow to Woodcote*[58] *with Sir J. Johnstone, and I should meet them there with his guns, etc.*

Tuesday 30th January - *Came to Woodcote*[58] *to dinner. Sir Johnstone brought me a note from Henry. He is laid up at Fentons with influenza!!*

Wednesday 31st January - *Henry writes that he is a little better, but I am not happy about him. Wrote to Mr Hamilton to ask him to go and see him.*

Thursday 1st February - *I came home from Woodcote.*[58]

Friday 2nd February - *Sent off William.*

Saturday 3rd February - *Packed up and Monday.*

Monday 5th February - *Came to 17 Eaton Terrace.*

Tuesday 6th February - *Spent the day in settling myself and the household in my pretty house, I am charmed with everything except the unfurnished kitchen.*

Wednesday 7th February - *Mrs Whitmore*[59] *and Emily*[8] *and their 2 maids and man arrived. Col Wilmot*[9] *dined here and Lucy.*[11]

Thursday 8th February - *A deep snow! Lucy*[11] *could not come out. The mail was delayed until evening. The old Col could not get out.*

Friday 9th February - *Out all day shopping. Col Wilmot*[9] *dined. Lucy*[11] *came to luncheon.*

Saturday 10th February - *Col Wilmot*[9] *and Lucy*[11] *at dinner. Mrs Garforth*[60] *called here. Kitty and Maria and Willie and his bride. Lady Miss Wrottesley*[13] *and Mrs Charles Whitmore.*

Sunday 11th February - *The cold is intense! We have a little church close to us where Mr Craig is preaching. What is to become of us all on Thursday! Gunter means to give the breakfast in the drawing room. Tom*[31] *is to have a lodging and the 3 daughters go to Lucy's*[11] *house. George Whitmore*[23] *came to dine and Col. Wilmot*[9] *- Emily's*[8] *presents are very pretty. Mrs W Whitmore is very ill at Westbourne Terrace.*

Monday 12th February - *George and Sarah*[23] *arrived in Portman Square. George dined here also the Colonel.*

Tuesday 13th February - *Lucy*[11] *received the news of the death of Mr Forbes at Callander. It is very sad. She cannot be here on Thursday. Tom*[31] *arrived with 3 bridesmaids. Dined here and George*[23] *and Col. Wilmot.*[9]

Wednesday 14th February - *Dinner of 20 - Mrs Whitmore employed Gunter. Col. Wilmot*[9] *and Emily,*[8] *George and Sarah,*[23] *Charltons, 4, Garforths,*[60] *5 Capt Storer,*[10] *Tom,*[31] *and the 3 daughters. After all were gone Tom*[31] *and Emily,*[8] *Henry and I turned all the drawing room furniture into the* *conservatory, arranged Emily's presents, and put away all my tables, ornaments, and finally sat down on the floor to have brandy and water. In bed about 2 and slept but little.*

Thursday 15th February - *A fine cold day. George[12] married them at St George's[12] 8 bridesmaids - 2 Garforths and 2 Charltons in white silk and pink, 3 Whitmores and Miss Douglas in white tarleton and blue. Beautiful breakfast from Gunter - 45. The Bride and Bridegroom, Tom[31] and the 3, George and Sarah,[23] Henry and I, Charltons 5, Garforths 5, Lord Drumlanrig, Douglas,[4] Capt and Mrs Maude, the C Whitmores, Fanny Leveson, Mrs John Whitmore, Col. Wilmot,[9] and 3 friends, Mr Rose, Mr Erskine and Mr Mitchell, Douglas[4] and Walter.[4] George and Sarah[23] dined with us and Tom[31] and 5, Tom Storer and Lucy[11]. I got the drawing room ready in time and was quite done up.*

Friday 16th February - *The Charltons came to dine and Tom,[31] and the Charles Whitmores. Mary[4] and Emmy[4] came in the evening. Nina[4] had been ill.*

Saturday 17th February - *Tom[31] and Nina[4] and Emmy[4] left. Mary was taken ill and remains behind putting off Mrs Whitmore's departure a little.*

Sunday 18th February - *Beautiful sermon from Mr Craig. In afternoon I went to Mr Liddell's church.*

Tuesday 20th February - *Mary Whitmore[4] was able to go yesterday with William Garforth.[60] Mrs Whitmore left today. I was out all the afternoon shopping and visiting. Toothache.*

Ash Wednesday, 21st February - *Went to Mr Craig's in the morning - "Father forgive them." George and Sarah[23] and Ellen Deacon (a relative of Sarah) came to dine. Toothache still.*

Tuesday 22nd February - *Laid up quite, Creosote and swelled face. Henry dined in*

Portman Square. Miss Greathed called and Mrs J Pritchard[5] and Lady Wrottesley.[13]

Friday 23rd February - *Better somewhat. Such wretched weather! Dark at half past one! Pipe burst.*

Sunday 25th February - *Wretched day but thaws. I did not go out at all. Mr Hamilton came to dine.*

Monday 26th February - *Quite dark! Lamps lighted at luncheon time.*

Thursday 1st March - *Went for luncheon to Cadogan Place. Col. Wilmot[9] and Emily[8] came up from Richmond for the day. Mrs Whitmore,[59] Emily[8] and I went shopping.*

Friday 2nd March - *Left Henry sitting to Mr Browning for his picture. Went to Stoke Court[14] and found Matilda alone - most kind - stayed until quite late. The Emperor of Russia dead.[15]*

Saturday 3rd March - *Went to see Henry's picture in the morning and sat finding faults. After luncheon a headache and went to call on Mrs Maude to take it off. Dinner, Mr Packington and Lady Diana, Kitty and Mr Garforth,[60] Colonel Vyse, Col. Taylor, Capt. Knox, Mr Grey, Mr Browning. Quite ill and bilious and sick.*

Sunday 4th March - *In bed till afternoon. Went to church then. Mr Bluck dined here.[16]*

Monday 5th March - *Paid a great many visits - found Lady Middleton and Mrs Brigstock at home, also Miss Greathed.*

Tuesday 6th March - *Bad cold which I nursed all day and at night went to Drury Lane with the Garforths[60] for the Etoile du Nord, Meyerbeer's music.*

Wednesday 7th March - *Went with Kitty to see Henry's picture at Montague Square - promising. Lucy[11] went to look at a house at Malvern. Saw Mrs Whitmore.[59] Henry dined at Mr Butler's.*

Thursday 8th March - *Nursed my cold in bed until luncheon time. Mrs Garforth and Maria called, Miss Greathed and Capt. Knox came to dine. Pleasant evening.*

Friday 9th March - *Snow again. Went to Mrs Garforth's[60] to tea. Mrs Parker there. Miss Beaumont, Miss Cleasby, Miss Wrangham, Miss Hill.*

Saturday 10th March - *Went to look over the remains of the Bernal collection. Cold much better. The Speaker's Levée. Dinner, Lord Wm. Graham, Sir Archibald Campbell, Mr Knatchbull, Mr Fitzwilliam Hune, Mr Bayley and Kitty Garforth. All in uniform, very charming.*

Sunday 11th March - *Went twice to Church. Mr Bluck[16] came to luncheon and dinner.*

Monday 12th March - *Wet all day. John and Lucy[11] quite laid up with influenza.*

Tuesday 13th March - *Mrs Garforth[60] and Maria early. Then the Middletons and Miss Brodrick, Mr and Mrs Halsey. Long walk and a lovely day.*

Wednesday 14th March - *Mrs Garforth,[60] Kitty and Maria, Mr Knatchbull, Capt. Knox, and Mr Pryce at dinner - charming.*

Thursday 15th March - *Dined at The Deacon's.[17] Mr and Mrs Gurney, Mr and Mrs and Miss Melville, Mr and Mrs C. Alexander, Mr and Mrs Briscoe - very stupid. First sitting for my picture, Kitty went with me.*

Saturday 17th March - *Second sitting for picture. The Garforths*[60] *dined with us.*

Sunday 18th March - *Twice went to church. Called in Cadogan Place. Mr Bluck came to dine.*

Monday 19th March - *I went for 3rd sitting. Dined with the Garforths*[60] *and went with them for the Olympic for "Tit for Tat" - The Lucky Friday and The Yellow Dwarf.*

Tuesday 20th March - *Henry last sitting. Mr Bluck*[16] *came to dine and go to the House.*

Wednesday 21st March - *The Fast Day. Salt fish and twice at Church - Henry went by the night train to Shrewsbury.*

Thursday 22nd March - *Went to Stoke Court,*[14] *Matilda*[3] *has been ill. Very glad to be with her.*

Friday 23rd March - *Very cold, Water colour drawings. Mrs Clayton called and Mrs Shaw.*

Saturday 24th March - *Came home with flowers and many kind gifts. Henry arrived last night.*

Sunday 25th March - *Mr Bluck here.*[16] *Planned to ask A.F.*

Monday 26th March - *Went to Dentist. Expect Tom.*[31]

Wednesday 28th March - *Dinner - Miss Wrottesley.*[13] *Miss Garforth.*[60] *Mr Foley, Capt. Knox, Mr Mullins, Mr Bluck.*[16]

Thursday 29th March - *Matilda*[3] *came to spend the day - Shopping, and C. Went in the evening to Ella's*[18] *last concert. Tom*[31] *and I dined in Chesterfield Street.*

Saturday 31st March - *Matilda*[3] *came to consult Mr Alexander about her eyes. Tom left.*[31] *Matilda spent the day.*

Sunday 1st April - *Bad cold and in bed. Mr Bluck here.*[16] *A.F. refused to come out in Passion week.*

Monday 2nd April - *At home nursing cold.*

Thursday 5th April - *We went home to Mama, fine and bright but cold. Mama not looking well.*

Saturday 7th April - *Henry and I went to Kemberton*[56] *and then to Cotsbrook*[2] *for luncheon. All at home except Tom.*[31] *Mr Bluck*[9] *arrived for dinner.*

Easter Sunday, 8th April - *We went to Church at The Dale. Henry and I stayed.*

***Monday 9th April** - Henry and Mr Bluck[16] walked to Apley.*

***Tuesday 10th April** - Henry and Mr Bluck[16] walked over to Kemberton.[56]*

***Wednesday 11th April** - Louisa[54] came to luncheon with the 6 eldest - George met them. Henry gave a school fete and we all went to it in the afternoon. Beautiful day.*

***Thursday 12th April** - Henry took Mr Bluck[16] to his brother's at Shrawardine[19] and left him there for a day.*

***Friday 13th April** - At Shrewsbury all of us, brought Mr Bluck home.*

***Saturday 14th April** - Henry and Mr Bluck[16] went to Bridgnorth. Mama and I walked to Marnwood[20] - I called on Mrs Hayes[21] and the Miss Edwards[21] who have lost their mother.*

***Sunday 15th April** - Our Wedding Day and such a happy day it has been, and such a happy visit to Mama.*

***Sunday 16th April** - Came back to Eaton Terrace.*

***Tuesday 17th April** - Ella's[18] first morning concert. Matilda[3] not able to come for it. Henry and Mr Bluck went to a Review at Windsor to see the French Emperor and Empress.*

***Wednesday 18th April** - I went to Stoke Court.[14] Found Matilda better than I had expected. She took me to Windsor to see the Royal party.*

***Thursday 19th April** - London quite mad! Running after the Emperor and Empress. We saw them several times as they came from a visit to the City. The Opera in the evening.*

***Friday 20th April** - Emily[8] and Col. Witmot[9] came to luncheon, also Mrs Whitmore[59] and John and Lucy.[6] I dined in Crystal Palace.*

***Saturday 21st April** - I went to call on Mrs E.W. at Montague Sq.*

***Sunday 22nd April** - Went to Westminster Abbey. Mr Bluck.*

***Tuesday 24th April** - The Wilmots[8] went to Malvern from Richmond and as we afterwards heard, had a very triumphal entry.*

***Wednesday 25th April** - Matilda and Abraham[3] came up for luncheon and to see maids. We dined with the Garforths,[60] Mr and Mrs and Miss Cleasby, Mr and Mrs Varden, John and Lucy,[11] Long table. Maria (Garforth) came in the evening.*

***Sunday 29th April** - Henry and I went to Mr Napean's. I am afraid the Garforths[60] are going. Mr Bluck.[16]*

***Tuesday 1st May** - Matilda and Abraham[3] came for Ella's[18] second concert. Very good, Halle played. I went with Abraham and Matilda[3] to Paddington Station. Dined with the Greigs. Col. Stephen took me down to dinner. The Arkrights, Capt. And Mrs Randolph. Mr Bluck[16] went with us.*

Wednesday 2nd May - *Frank, Mr Farnham, John and Lucy,[11] Miss Greathed and Mr Bluck[16] at dinner.*

Thursday 3rd May - *Went to see old Mrs Forbes and then with Lucy[11] to the Amateur Exhibition now at Burlington and wonderful pictures by the Princess Royal of the "Battlefields."*

Friday 4th May - *John and Lucy[11] came to luncheon, and Kitty. (Garforth)[60] Henry went with me to Clapham Common found both Miss Leveson and Mrs J. Whitmore.*

Saturday 5th May - *Dined at the Middleton's, and very pleasant evening. Mrs Deacon[17] and Ellen, Frank, Sir Walter Riddell, Col. Armitage and 3 daughters, the William Bowdricks, Mr and Mrs Hall, Mr Papillon.*

Monday 6th May - *Such a long day. Large party at the Crystal Palace.[22] Lady and 2 Miss Andersons, Lady Armitage, Miss Stirling, Mr Worsley, Mr Cooke, Maughams and Caleys. Went afterwards to Chesterfield Street to tea and round game. John and Lucy[11] there and my great hope. Mrs Durant in the evening.*

Tuesday 7th May - *Visiting all afternoon. Mr Bluck[16] at dinner.*

Wednesday 8th May - *Cold, very. Henry and I went to the flower show at the Regent's Park. Miss B. and Mr Bluck[16] dined with us.*

Thursday 9th May - *Dined at the Slaneys. Met Mr & Mrs Dod, Miss Printa, Miss Slaney, Miss Sparling, &c.*

Friday 11th May - *A thunder storm - but colder afterwards.*

Saturday 12th May - *Paid some visits. Lady Derby,[28] Slaney, Brooke Turners. Frank dined with us and John and Lucy[11] and Tom Storer.[10]*

Sunday 13th May - *Rains incessantly. Went to church in the morning. Mr Bluck here. George[23] is expected tomorrow.*

Monday 14th May - *George[23] came.*

Tuesday 15th May - *Mr Bluck dined here - Ecarté,[24] rather late. Henry went back to the House.*

Wednesday 16th May - *We dined at the Duncombe's, not a large party, pleasant. Mrs Garforth[60] and Lady Mary Gage, Mr Hall and Miss Elliot Yorke, Mr T. Croft, Mr Egerton.*

Thursday 17th May - *Dinner at home, 12. Mrs and Miss Trant, Mr and Mrs Bluck. John and Lucy[11] George Whitmore,[23] is expected tomorrow.*

Friday 18th May - *The Queen gave away the Crimea medals in front of the Horse Guards. We had excellent places in the Members Gallery, - Beautiful sight. Went to see Mrs Forbes and Louisa - Tea, George[23] with us. Took Henry back to the House to get a pair. Mr Bluck[16] for dinner and Ecarté.[24]*

Saturday 19th May - *George*[23] *left us. John and Lucy*[11] *are gone today to Malvern. Birthday Drawing Room*[25] *never was such a cram or so pretty a drawing room. Mr Bluck dined here.*

Sunday 20th May - *Bad stiff neck, did not go out. Augustus Tollemache*[26] *is come. Mr Bluck.*[16]

Tuesday 22nd May - *Evening at Lady Listowells. Bishop of Cashel, Lady Middleton and Miss B's and Mr Bes, Capt. and Mrs Maude, Lady Lurgan, Mr Rushall, Mrs Lilau.*

Wednesday 23rd May - *Henry and Mr Bluck went with me to the Exhibition and then to Eton. Henry dined here.*

Thursday 24th May - *Mr Bluck dined here and went with us to Mr Hassell's Assembly, a great crowd, very hot! Garforths,*[60] *Brigstocks, Adml. And Miss Bung, Percivals, &c.*

Friday 25th May - *Dined at the Leroys. Hon. Mr and Mrs King, Sir George Rich, Mr Crofton, &c.*

Saturday 26th May - *Dinner at home. Mr and Mrs. D. Packington, Mr and Mrs C. Corbet, Brigstocks, Frank and Kitty. Exhibition and Band at Burlington House.*

Whit Sunday, 27th May - *Mama not well. Henry goes tomorrow, perhaps me. At church twice, Mr Rashdale at St. Michaels.*

Monday 28th May - *The account of Mama was not good enough for me to stay behind so Henry took me with him. Miss Lawford*[27] *is with her but she is dreadfully weak and ill.*

Wednesday 30th May - *I stayed with Henry that one day Tuesday and Mama improved so far that we were able to leave her and go to Stoke Court*[14] *for one night - They are alone, but a grand dinner and the drawing room lighted up and fit for a Ball.*

Thursday 30th May - *Returned to Eaton Terrace and went to Lady Derby's*[28] *Reception, green gown and Brussels lace.*

Saturday 2nd June - *Dinner at home Lord and Lady H. Duncombe, Lord and Lady Middleton and Miss A. Brodrick, Mr and Mrs Herbert, Lady Elizabeth, Mr and Mrs Tollemache,*[26] *Mr Fitzroy, Mr Bluck. Matilda sent us strawberries and vegetables and 2 moulds of jelly and cream!*

Wednesday 6th June - *Dined at the Pritchards.*[5] *Mr and Mrs and Miss Gaskell,*[61] *Spearmans, Mr and Mrs Hoare, Sir T. Winngton.*

Thursday 7th June - *I went to Ascot with Mr Jones and Jane, his brother, Kitty Garforth, Tommy Charlton Whitmore*[31] *Tom Storer*[10] *- Beautiful day. Fandango the winner. Henry and Mr Bluck dined at Greenwich.*

Friday 8th June - *Shopping to buy muslins. Henry and Mr Bluck joined me and we went to the Surrey Gardens. In the evening Lady Knatchbull's party and Mrs Capel-Cure's concert from which I did not get home until 2 o'clock - Blue train made up and very handsome.*

Saturday 9th June - *Dinner at home. Mr and Mrs ------, Mrs Taylor, Miss Cavendish, Mrs Garforth,*[60] *Kitty and Maria, Capt. Storer,*[10] *Mr Hamilton and Mr Bluck.*

Monday 11th June - *Henry and Mr Bluck and I drove down to Richmond and dined. Most charming evening.*

Tuesday 12th June - *Henry not well and could not come to Ella's*[18] *concert which was very good. Hallé and Ernst. Henry had bad cold. Quiet evening.*

Wednesday 13th June - *Lady Bradford's*[29] *first Assembly. We had just a little dinner, George Whitmore,* [23] *Mr Jefferson and Mr Bluck.*[16]

Friday 15th June - *Hallé concert - Rain, rain! Mrs Garforth*[60] *called for me.*

Saturday 16th June - *Riding School Regent's Park Barracks. Band of The Blues*[26a] *played, all London there. Princess Mary of Cambridge came and the Grand Duchess of Mecklenburg Strelitz. Dancing. Dinner at home, Sir F. and Lady Scott, Heneages 3, Mr and Mrs Russell Stanhope, Capt. Knox, Mr Bluck and Mr Fitzroy who is going to be married.*

Monday 18th June - *George*[23] *came, went with us to Lady Donneraile's Assembly.*

Tuesday 19th June - *Ella's*[18] *5th Concert. Grand Matinée. Matilda did not come. Dined at the Garforths,*[60] *Henry and I, George*[23] *came in the evening. There was a grand party, - Hallé and Mrs Hallé there, Lady and Miss Stirling - Ella.*[18]

Wednesday 20th June - *Dinner at home - Lord Bandon,*[30] *Syanhopes, Mr Bluck and Capt. Storer.*[10] *First of all George and I went to Chiswick where we met the Garforths*[60] *&c. Lady Vernon's Assembly - Lady Bradford's*[29] *Assembly, a great Crush it was but very pleasant, - Everybody one had ever seen.*

Thursday 21st June - *I spent the day at Stoke Court.*[14] *Matilda alone. Henry and George dined with Sir T.H. at Greenwich.*

Friday 22nd June - *Cremorne Elephants - I caught cold.*

Saturday 23rd June - *George*[23] *went away.*

Sunday 24th June - *Staid in bed.*

Monday 25th June - *Staid at home - could not go to Mrs Rodham's Reception - Several visitors. Mrs and Miss Byng, Mrs and Miss Gratten, Mrs Cowper, Mrs Garforth,*[60] *Mr Edw. Wrottesley.*[13]

***Tuesday 26th June** - Could not go to Ella.*[18] *Matilda did not come. The Stanhopes had tickets.*

***Wednesday 27th June** - Dinner - Mr Whateley and Lady Henry Churchill, Mr and Lady Hester Leake, Mrs and Miss Jessell, Mr and Mrs Knight. After dinner came a "Reception" - the house very pretty and the supper - about 85 came and it was very successful. Col. Vyse and Mrs Baldock proposed dancing and it was pleasant.*

***Thursday 28th June** - Hallé's last Recital. I left the Garforths*[60] *and Lord H. there and came back to go with Miss Jessell and Henry and Mr Bluck to a fete at the Regent's Park Barracks. Col. Vyse presiding, it was very nice, Tea and claret cup. Lady Wrottesley*[13] *at home. - Dull.*

***Friday 29th June** - Dined at Mr and Lady Louisa Cote's. Lady Elizabeth and Mr Stanhope Lady Anne and Mr Mackenzie, Mrs Heron, Mr and Mrs Rodham, Dowage Lady and Miss Wrottesley.*[13]

***Saturday 30th June** - Dined at Mr and Mrs Baldock's. Sir George and Lady Westlake, Miss Gore, Mr and Mrs Stratton, &c.*

***Monday 2nd July** - Dined at Mrs Trant's - Sir Richard Levinge, Mrs Nugent, Miss Wrottesley,*[13] *Col. Coles, Mr Lennox Butler, &c.*

***Wednesday 4th July** - Dined - Col. and Mrs Creyke, Mr and Mrs Tollemache,*[26] *Mrs Garforth,*[60] *C. Whitmore, Mr Bluck.*[16] *Lady Diana Packington at home.*

***Wednesday 5th July** - C. Whitmore entrapped Henry's picture away to be photographed.*

***Friday 6th July** - Mama, came, alas: she looked very ill and so thin. After she was gone to bed Mr Bluck, Henry and I went to a Grand Concert at Mrs Jassell's, all the Opera people and really very nice.*

***Saturday 7th July** - Dinner at home - Mrs Garforth,*[60] *Henry and Matilda*[3] *and Miss Whitmore from Westbourne Terrace and Mr Bluck. Mama better.*

***Sunday 8th July** - Mob in the Park and Belgrave Square where they broke windows - Lord Robert Grosvenor having withdrawn his Sunday Bill one rather wonders what they can want. Persuaded Mama not to go to church. Went to sit in the Cadogan Gardens.*

***Monday 9th July** - Fete at Grosvenor House, Music - Theatricals in the Picture Gallery, Ice Tea and C. in the drawing room. Mrs and Miss Jassell and Mr Bluck at luncheon and Miss Jassel and he went with us. Mama I really think much better. Miss Roche came in at luncheon time, she is going to be married and go to India.*

***Tuesday 10th July** - Matilda*[3] *came for Ella's*[18] *last concert which was very nice. She took Mama with her to Stoke Court.*[14] *Henry and I dined at the*

Lennox Butlers - Very grand dinner - The Baldocks, Lord Pomfret, Sir F. Kelly and his daughter. Mrs Butler Johnstone and many more. Took Mr Bluck afterwards to Lady Knatchbull's Ball. Staid late, very pleasant, nice Mrs Dering and Miss Cunninghame. Henry danced a good deal, very hot.

Wednesday 11th July - *Rained all day, could not go out to Beckenham. Lady Vernon at home and Mrs Gaskell,[61] nice parties.*

Thursday 12th July - *Drove out, visits and shopping. Very warm. The Garforth's[60] went away on Monday.*

Friday 13th July - *Very hot - Paying Bills - Visits. Found Mrs Dering at home and Miss Cunninghame and Mrs Gaskell.[61] Mr Bluck[16] dined here - Ecarté.[24] Henry is gone to Lady Spearman's Ball.*

Saturday 14th July - Dinner - *Mrs H. Burton, Mr and Mrs Stanhope, Mr and Mrs Knight, Mrs Baldock, Capt. Knox, Mr Bluck. Matilda[3] sent us such good things - ducks, chickens, rabbits, flowers, grapes, strawberries and vegetables. Mrs Butler and Mrs Knight were great fun. Asked the Miss Percivals but they came not.*

Sunday 15th July - *To church at Mr Craig's and then to Westminster Abbey. Crowds of police in fear of another riot. Mr Bluck here.*

Monday 16th July - *Tom[31] came - wet all day.*

Tuesday 17th July - *Paying bills, &c. George Whitmore,[23] came to dinner - both went to sleep.*

Wednesday 18th July - *Tom[31] went away. Visit from Lady Pearson and Mr Craig. Dinner at Greenwich - Henry and I, Mr Bluck, Mr and Mrs Barton and Mr Stanley. Very pleasant, most lovely drive home.*

Thursday 19th July - *Went to Stoke Court[14] for the day - I think Mama is better.*

Friday 20th July - *Great Vexation! Mrs and Miss Jassell and a friend Miss Griffith dined here with Mr Bluck and Mr Jefferson to go to the Princess for Henry VIII we had stalls and were enjoying it immensely when I fainted.*

Saturday 21st July - *Did not feel quite right all day. Mr Bluck[16] dined here and Tom[31] returned from Beckenham.*

Sunday 22nd July - *Such a hot day. Tom[31] went with me to St. Barnabas' - Took Toozie[32] to Cadogan Gardens she was sent for to amuse a baby. Augustus Tollemache[26] and Mr Leake came to dine and Mr Bluck[16] and Tom[31] the denouement approaches.*

Monday 23rd July - *We went with Mr Bluck and the J's. to Mrs Laurence at Ealing Park, thunder storm and great destruction to clothes and tempers. Beautiful place.*

Tuesday 24th July **-** *So late last night that Tom*[31] *was very cross, no wonder - no dinner till half past 9.*

Wednesday 25th July **-** *Tom*[31] *asked Douglas*[4] *to come up from Eton for the day. Henry and I were engaged to dine at the Crystal Palace*[22] *- Mr Butler's party - 40 people and go to his house after for supper and dancing - Very pleasant. Miss Cunningham returned with us.*

Thursday 26th July **-** *Henry went to Kemberton*[56] *for the Assizes at Shrewsbury. Tom*[31] *returned with him to Shropshire. I went to Stoke Court.*[14] *Remarkable propositions.*

Friday 27th July **-** *Mr Grant came to stay at Stoke Court.*[14] *Mr and Mrs Shaw at dinner. Mama better.*

Saturday 28th July **-** *I came back to London (Hampers.) Dinner, Stanhopes Capt. Knox, Mrs and Miss Trant.*

Sunday 29th July **-** *Went to church here at Mr Liddell's. Mrs and Miss J called whilst away. I went into the garden at Lowndes Square with Toozie.*[32]

Monday 30th July **-** *Mama came to us from Stoke Court.*[14] *Beginning a toothache - Mama much better.*

Tuesday 31st July **-** *Last evening I got a note from Mrs F. - no, decidedly. Mr Bluck*[16] *dined here yesterday, and today. Mama and I shopping.*

Wednesday 1st August **-** *Drove out with Mama. Creosote in the evening! Henry went to dine with Mrs Farnham.*

Thursday 2nd August **-** *Laid up all day.*

Friday 3rd August **-** *Ditto - mama went with Henry to the Crystal Palace.*[22] *Beautiful day. They brought back Mr Bluck.*[16]

Saturday 4th August **-** *Little dinner for the last time. Mr and Mrs Knight and Mrs Butler Johnstone, Mr Bluck.*[16]

Sunday 5th August **-** *Mrs Garforth*[60] *called. I am getting well again but did not go out. I have been nearly starved.*

Monday 6th August **-** *Mama and I had a drive, very weak still. Henry at the House.*

Tuesday 7th August **-** *Shopping. Mr Bluck*[16] *to came to dine. Mama sitting to Mr Browning for such a pretty little picture.*

Wednesday 8th August **-** *Henry and I went to Four Oaks*[34] *'til Saturday. Staying in the house Mr and Mrs Pauncefoot Duncombe, Miss Howard, Mr Fraser, Capt. Cust, Mr Taylor, Major Shuckborough, Mr Boughey.*

Thursday 9th August - *We drove to Castle Bromwich[35] - found there a nice Col. and Mrs Slade, Captain Bridgeman, Howards, &c. Archery and The Maze.*

Friday 10th August - *Such a long day. The Meriden Archery Meeting.[36] Left Four Oaks in a Drag and Britiska, all the party at half past 10, and then the shooting then dancing and 15 miles to go and return - just in bed at 4 in the morning! Pleasant too. Mr Boughey, Lord and Lady Guernsey, Lord Dartmouth.[37]*

Saturday 11th August - *Dispersion of the party and we returned to London for 2 days.*

Sunday 12th August - *Went to church for the last time at Mr Craig's. Very few people! Very uncomfortable packing and taking leave.*

Monday 13th August - *Very busy all day packing and paying bills and ordering bonnet for Birmingham.*

Tuesday 14th August - *Interview with Mr Lennon at 11. Went at 12 to take things to Mr Bluck and to Lowndes Square. Clock, china, vases and lamps. At 12.50 we left Eaton Terrace. Met Mr Bluck at Paddington where Alice Gray galloped all the way. Came to Clevedon,[38] we 3 without servants, where we got into an omnibus and came to the Royal Hotel - dined there and we are to sleep at Buckingham House as they have no room. It is a very pretty place and sea rather muddy but there is a very pretty garden belonging to the Hotel.*

Wednesday 15th August - *Clevedon[38] to Highbridge where we stayed for luncheon - nothing pretty. Thence to Exeter and Barnstaple - Beautiful country between. Took an open carriage to Ilfracombe, 11 miles and most beautiful. Fine rocky coast and beautiful sunset. Britannia Hotel.*

Thursday 16th August - *Spent the morning walking about the beautiful rocks at Ilfracombe. Then drove in an open carriage to Lynton - Beautiful place walked down to the sea at Lynmouth and are very comfortable at the Castle Hotel overlooking the sea.*

Friday 17th August - *Lynton. Walked to the Valley of the Rocks. Had luncheon at Lynmouth at the Lyndale Hotel. Then sat by the sea and then rode on ponies by way of the East and West Lyne. Most beautiful the scenery is but the hills are steep beyond anything - we were very tired.*

Saturday 18th August - *Lynton. Spent all the day by the sea sketching and poking about the rocks and finding crabs and sea anemones and all sorts of shells. We carried our luncheon down to the beach - It was most charming.*

Sunday 19th August - *We went twice to church and a very nice church and most excellent clergyman. Walked in the afternoon to the Valley of the Rocks in wind and rain. I sat in a little cave above the sea watching the tide dashing in. It is quite magnificent.*

Monday 20th August - *Minehead. Left our beautiful Lynton by way of the grand road over mountains and downs with the sea below to Minehead. We had luncheon at Porlock a little wayside village - the hills were very long and steep almost as the sides of houses but our good horses never slipped. At Minehead Miss Bowditch who dined with us took us a long walk. It is very pretty but the sea runs far out over the sands - in 2 miles Dunster Castle.*

Tuesday 21st August - *Torquay. Left Minehead and Miss Bowdich and drove 24 miles to Taunton - then by the railroad to Exeter and past Dawlish and Teignmouth to Torquay. We are very comfortable at the Royal Hotel and it is a very pretty sea place and nice shops, a sort of Leamington by the sea.*

Wednesday 22nd August - *We have been to Babbacombe Bay in a sailing boat for the sake of fishing. They caught mackerel, 7 doz. and a half. We had luncheon at Babbacombe. Most charming day and so calm returning that I wrote letters in the boat.*

Thursday 23rd August - *Drove to Teignmouth. Had luncheon at the Hotel and sat on the sand sketching. Fine sea - great extent of grass and sandy beach with seaweed - rather dull. Walked afterwards to the Crescent and to "Daddy's Hole." Found curious small Hyacinth - Rifle practising.*

Friday 24th August - *Chepstow. Left Torquay by an 8 o'clock train to Bristol. Thence to Chepstow by the steam packet - to Wynd Cliff where we had rain then to Tintern which was most lovely - Quite done up.*

Saturday 25th August - *Home. We went to Chepstow Castle in the morning and most lovely ruin it is. To Gloucester where we parted with Mr Bluck.*[16] *Then on to Shifnal. Found Mama pretty well. Mr Grant and Arthur with her.*

Sunday 26th August - *Home. Henry quite tired and ill. Went to church with Mr Grant and Arthur.*

Monday 27th August - *Came to Lord Bradford's*[50] *for the Birmingham Festival. We have Mr E and Miss C. Childe, Mr Herbert, Mr Hanbury, George and Orlando Bridgeman, Lady Lucy and Lady Charlotte - Miss Moncrieffe is in Scotland.*

Tuesday 28th August - *Went to the first Oratorio - Elijah. Viardot, Miss Doby, Mdme. Rudersdorff, Simms, Reeves and Mr Weiss. Luncheon at Mr G. Whateley's. Drive with Lady Bradford to Pipe Hayes in the pony carriage. Held a plate with Sir J. Packington.*

Wednesday 29th August - *A page of the journal is missing between 29th August and Sunday 9th September.*

Monday 10th September - *Cromer. (Norfolk) Long walk on the beach to the Northward.*

Tuesday 11th September - *Wrote letters and took a long walk to the Southward on the beach and climbed up the cliffs to return. Most lovely weather - ever since we came. News today of the capture of Sebastopol! The Malakoff Tower was taken on the 9th and the Russians then began to sink their ships in the harbour and the place is now in the hands of the Allies!*[39] *Tonight as we had finished tea a great gun had begun to fire on the cliffs with cheering.*

Wednesday 12th September - *Still great rejoicing. Poked about on the beach and then walked north on the cliffs - caught shrimps and crabs.*

Thursday 13th September - *Brought home sea anemones.*

Friday 14th September - *Henry and Mr Bluck went out shooting with Capt. Ives. They say the country is beautiful.*

Saturday 15th September - *Rather ill and sick - plum tart. Dawdled out a little - cold.*

Sunday 16th September - *I did not go to church in the morning - rainy.*

Monday 17th September - *Very fine and warm - on the beach.*

Tuesday 18th September - *Henry and Mr Bluck went to shoot on Mr Eabell's property with Mr Keith and Captain Windham. Mr Bluck came back and went with me to the Lighthouse.*

Wednesday 19th September - *Henry out shooting again. Mr Bluck and I walked almost all day. Went to Felbrigg and made a sketch, Turnips, Pigstys. Found Henry returned - Beautiful country certainly and as warm as summer - saw quantities of game.*

Thursday 20th September - *Captain Windham insisted upon taking a last drive, he acting as chaperone. Took us to Felbrigg and over the house which is very handsome and comfortable. His brother who possessed it had not been dead six months. Then we went to Sheringham by way of the Lion's Mouth and Roman Camp. Most lovely wild country and hilly with the sea at a distance. Capt. Windham dined.*

Friday 21st September - *Very sorry to leave Cromer, a most charming morning drive to Holt and Dereham. Took the train to Lynn which is a curious and very dull looking old town. It has been fortified. Called upon Mrs Creswell but nobody at home, from Lynn we drove to Walsham to stay one night with Mr H.B.'s Pappa and Mamma. It is a very good house - fine old church.*

Saturday 22nd September - *Left Walsham early and came to London, ------. Such a pleasant walk for some shopping.*

Sunday 23rd September - *Sick and seedy all day - supposed to be the effect of Bitter Ale. Saw Mrs Denman.*

Monday 24th September - *We came to Malvern by the evening Express leaving Mr Bluck in London. John and Lucy*[11] *met us on the road. Mrs Whitmore*[59] *quite well.*

Tuesday 25th September - *Mt Pleasant. We went to Lyttleton House for luncheon and in the evening they came to dine. John and Lucy*[11] *and Col. David Forbes. Lucy's house is quite perfect. We only saw the children in the garden - they have had chicken pox. Visit from Lady Kenmore who is also staying in the house at Mt. Pleasant.*

Wednesday 26th September - *We all spent the day at Worcester. Louisa Forbes is lame and went to consult her Doctor. It was very pleasant and so fine. We went in Mrs Whitmore's*[59] *nice little open carriage and met John and Lucy*[11] *cousin David and 4 Miss Forbes and their Governesses.*

Thursday 27th September - *Went to see Mrs West in her new house. Visit from Mrs Stratton, Miss Granville Mr and Lady Charlotte Grenville. John, Lucy*[11] *and Col. David Forbes came to Mr P. to luncheon. Mrs Whitmore*[59] *not well and could not go with us to Lyttleton to dine. Miss Cornewall, 2 Miss Forbes Capt. Chandler, Mr Davies, Col. D. Forbes and Henry and I at dinner.*

Friday 28th September - *Coalbrookdale. We came home leaving Mrs Whitmore*[59] *much better and finding mama quite well. The first wet day for a long time.*

Saturday 29th September - *Henry went to Bridgnorth. Mr Bluck arrived in the afternoon.*

Sunday 30th September - *The Thanksgiving day for taking Sebastapol.*[39] *Good Sermon from Mr Hayes.*[1] *15th Psalm, verses 1 and 2.*

Monday 1st October - *Coalbrookdale. Letter from Matilda*[3] *from Paris I hope her sight is really better. Mama and I drove to Kemberton,*[56] *found George and Sarah*[23] *at home - then to Coalport.*[41]

Tuesday 2nd October - *Henry and Mr Bluck*[16] *went to see a pony to match Canvasser, Henry bought it. Mr and Mrs Hayes*[1] *called.*

Wednesday 3rd October - *A quite wet day! I finished shells and minerals in the Library.*

Thursday 4th October - *The Bridgnorth Poultry Show. Henry and Mr Bluck*[16] *went to it and the dinner. I staid with Mama and we drove to Broseley.*

Friday 5th October - *Rather wet day.*

Saturday 6th October - *Henry and Mr Bluck*[16] *at Bridgnorth.*

Sunday 7th October - *Walked to Little Wenlock in the afternoon. The Egremonts*[62] *have been to the Paris "Exposition". Also Abraham and Matilda*[3] *are just returned and her sight is quite restored.*

***Monday 8th October** - So busy preparing for the Bridgnorth dinner and for Mrs Whitmore.[59]*

***Tuesday 9th October** - Mrs Whitmore[59] came - Dinner to the Mayor and Corporation which appeared to prosper much. Some refusals left us 20. George and Sarah[23] came and she sang for us kindly. The desert was on the table and the wine coolers filled with flowers.*

***Wednesday 10th October** - Henry went to shoot at Apley. Mr Bluck and I went to Apley Castle for luncheon.*

***Thursday 11th October** - Dinner 14 - Dr and Mrs Rowley and Son, Mr and Mrs Barlett[20] and Mr Phillip Bartlett and Mr Reynolds, George and Sarah[23] 5 selves, very prosperous.*

***Friday 12th October** - Mrs Whitmore[59] left us to go to Cotsbrook,[2] very sorry to part with her. We all went to church and then went to try the new pony. He is so good and so handsome, Canvasser's own brother. Henry had yesterday a very gratifying letter from Disraeli offering him Lord Mandeville's appointment[40] which he could not help accepting and I hope it will not be too much for him. Mrs Whitmore[59] and Henry both at the same minute named the new pony "Whipper In."*

***Saturday 13th October** - Henry and Mr Bluck rode to Bridgnorth.*

***Sunday 14th October** - I have had a bad cold all the week and so today only went to church once.*

***Monday 15th October** - Henry and I went to Kinlet for 2 nights - only Col. Hill there. Mrs Charlton expected but not well.*

***Tuesday 16th October** - We all walked to Mr E. Childe's new Vicarage, very nice but not yet finished. Mr John Hunt a Clergyman arrived for the Kidderminster Musical Festival tomorrow.*

***Wednesday 17th October** - Henry's Birthday. All left Kinlet for the Kidderminster Festival except Miss C.C. and Col. Hill. We came home, Henry stopping for luncheon at the Cave.[63] Mr Bluck met him, my cold too bad to stay.*

***Thursday 18th October** - Henry and Mr Bluck went to the Mayor's dinner and stayed all night.*

***Friday 19th October** - Nursing my cold. A visit from Mr and Mrs Henry Dickinson.[44] Henry returned better.*

***Saturday 20th October** - Spent the day in Shrewsbury shopping - all 4 of us.*

***Sunday 21st October** - At church only once. Such a warm day.*

***Monday 22nd October** - Mama and I drove to Kemberton[56] to call on Mrs and Miss Deacon.[17] All at Shrewsbury.*

Tuesday 23rd October - *J. and Mr Bluck went to Kemberton. I very busy all day with Portfolios.*

Wednesday 24th October - *Mr Bluck[16] back to London. George, Sarah[23] and the 2 children and Mr and Miss Deacon[17] came to luncheon. Henry and I came to Willey.[42] Lady Newport here, Mr and Mrs Fane, Mr George Norman, Mrs Mytton, Mr George Forester, Major Forester.*

Thursday 25th October - *Mr Mytton gone. Mrs Joseph Dickinson[57] here and Dr Rowley here at dinner. Rain all day!*

Friday 26th October - *Drove to Coalport.[41] Colonel Forbes[11] came from London. At dinner Mr R. Thursfield and some people from Wenlock.*

Saturday 27th October - *Came home, called on Mrs Rowley.*

Sunday 28th October - *Henry not well. We went to church in the morning and he had to come away faint - sent for Mr Webb.[43]*

Monday 29th October - *Henry is better a little. This evening to our horror we hear that Mrs Henry Dickinson died this morning at Ness.[44] We knew that she was ill of inflammation of the bowels. They went last Wednesday with Mrs Edmund Darby and Mary to spent a day at Ness and the spasms she had had before came on that evening. R. Thursfield and 4 other doctors were in attendance.*

Tuesday 30th October - *Rain all day!*

Wednesday 31st October - *Incipient rain. Mr Webb[43] said he might leave Henry, I trust he has treated him well. Mama had a long letter from Henry Dickinson.*

Thursday 1st November - *Mama not at all well and Mr Browning coming to finish the picture, very unlucky. Such a fine day not a cloud but cold! The picture charming. Mrs Egremont[62] called and was sent away.*

Friday 5th November - *Mr Webb[43] saw Mama. Not at all well. Myself rheumatic.*

Saturday 3rd November - *The funeral. Mama well enough to go in the carriage. We walked afterwards and went to the Meeting. Henry went to a great luncheon at Severn House.[44] The Works closed! Abraham and Matilda are at Dale House.[45]*

Sunday 4th November - *I went to church and so did Abraham and Matilda.[3] Mama not well enough yet to go out. Seabrook asked to consult Mr Webb who gives no hope. I am very sorry. Called Tothills and many more. Abraham and Matilda[3] dined and spent the day here. More than couleur de rose.*

Monday 5th November - *Mama and I went to Severn House[44] and Dale House.[45] Very sad visits! Abraham came to dine, they go away tomorrow.*

Tuesday 6th November - *Fine warm day. Henry rode over to Apley.*

Wednesday 7th November - *Henry and I went to Longford.[49] We have Capt. And Mrs Kenyon, Mr and Mrs Edmund Bridgeman, Miss Childe, 2 Mr Clives (Styche) and Major Powys. Very pleasant. Visit from Mr Gaskell[61] before we left.*

Thursday 8th November - *We went to luncheon at Weston[50] and took Miss Childe, found all their own party and Lord and Lady Newport, Mr and Mrs Knight, Col. Hogg, Mr and Mrs Ralph Neville! As we returned a thunder-storm, and in it we called at Woodcote.[58] Saw Lady L.C. and Miss Brooke.*

Friday 9th November - *Kenyon and Clives left. Photography. Gentlemen out hunting. Lady H. Leake drove Mr Bridgeman and me to Chattle to see Mr Braltbees Pottery. At dinner Sir T, Lady and Miss Boughey and two Miss Hills Meertown.*

Saturday 10th November - *Came home. I went with Henry to the Newport Station whence he went to London. Mama better but has a cold.*

Sunday 11th November - *Went to church then a walk with Mama. Most lovely warm day.*

Monday 12th November - *Poor Seabrook goes to Malvern. Mrs Whitmore having offered to have him there to try Charcoal. George came for luncheon and we walked.*

Thursday 13th November - *A visit from Mrs W.E. Mama has a bad cold.*

Wednesday 14th November - *Henry returned from London. I went to meet him at Shifnal.*

Thursday 15th November - *Nora's Wedding Day. We went with four Greys and Henry bought me such a pretty new bonnet. All went off well. Excellent breakfast; Bridesmaids wore veils. We called at Kemberton,[56] Lady Newport has a daughter on the 13th. Having only left Weston and arrived at Wilton C. the day before. Nina,[4] Mary[4] and Emmy[4] have had Scarletina at Calwich, they are to go to Apley.*

Friday 16th November - *Henry gone to Apley for some possessions which may have risked Scarletina. But the expedition failed Mrs Bullock gone to Malvern and it appears that Lady Louisa[54] &c. go to Admaston[46] to perform quarantine. Mama and I went to call at Marnwood[20] and on Mrs W.R. Anstice.[64]*

Saturday 17th November - *Henry went to Bridgnorth. Mama's cold very bad still. Thick fog.*

***Sunday 18th November** - Henry and I went to Stockton[47] to church. The Bishop of Lichfield preached a Sermon for building a Parsonage at Oaken Gates.[48] Luncheon at the Isaacsons. The Bishop, Tom, Mr Cheyne, Mr Edward Cure, Mr and Mrs Austin and ourselves. We staid for the afternoon service. Very cold!*

***Monday 19th November** - To our great surprise a visit of 10 minutes from Abraham Darby. He brought me such a pretty collar and sleeves from Matilda[3] from Paris! Henry and I came to Weston[50] for 2 nights - we have here Lord Hatherton, Sir J. and Lady Packington, Miss Cure and her brother - now Col. Cure, Mr Edward Cheney, Mr George Bridgeman.*

***Tuesday 20th November** - Weston.[50] Drive before luncheon to Tong Castle[51] - Lord Bradford's new purchase. Tea and macaroons.*

***Wednesday 21st November** - Haughton.[52] We staid at Weston[50] till after luncheon. Lord Hatherton went away. We drove round by Neckton but saw no-one. At Haughton Mr and Mrs and 2 Miss Townshends, Mr Dugdale, Mr Buckanan, Mr M. Owen and Cavendish Taylor and Mr Leake and at dinner besides Mr and Mrs Cope and a Mr White.*

***Thursday 22nd November** - The gentlemen went out to shoot. Cold wet day, and I did not go out at all. At dinner Mr and Mrs Cunliffe, also Mr Legge in the house.*

***Friday 23rd November** - Home. Left Haughton[52] and came to Kemberton[56] for luncheon.*

***Saturday 24th November** - Home. Henry went to Bridgnorth. Mama and I drove to Apley Castle in the afternoon. Mr and Mrs Swetenham were there and Louisa and the 3 oldest girls performing quarantine at the Haygate. We went to enquire after them and take a basket.*

***Sunday 25th November** - Went to church in the morning and not out again, so piercingly cold.*

***Tuesday 27th November** - We went to call upon the Pritchards[5] - J.D. came to luncheon and told Mama we should soon hear some news which makes us very impatient. The W.R. Anstices[64] and J. Anstices[64] and Mr and Mrs Hayes[1] came to dinner and we had some nice singing.*

***Wednesday 28th November** - Hale. (Liverpool) We had to leave the Hayes with Mama this morning and make our expedition here. Fine day and not really cold. Staid at Warrington for Henry to have his ears syringed which was done most successfully. We find here Mr and Mrs Reginald Corbet (Alderley) Mr and Mrs Rigby, Mrs Brooke and Mr Brooke her brother-in-law, her husband being with his Regiment at the Cape (son of Sir Richd. Brooke), Col. and Mrs Wilbraham and Miss Kerr. Miss Blackburne and Jos (Fox?) are here.*

Thursday 29th November - *18 at dinner. Drive. Mr and Mrs Stapleton and Mr Ashton added to the party. Whist and round game and singing.*

Friday 30th November - *Hale. Mr and Mrs Rigby gone and Mr Brooke. Very pleasant walk with Jos. and Mrs Wilbraham - Singing.*

Saturday 1st December - *Hale. All the party dispersed except Mr Kerr and and ourselves. Wet cold day. Henry went to Liverpool, bought me a head-dress-pink roses and lace.*

Sunday 2nd December - *Went to church - cold - I am beginning a cold. "Illustration of the Industrial Arts of the XIX Century."*

Monday 3rd December - *Apley Castle. Left Hale this morning, Mr Kerr with us to Stafford. There we met Mr and Mrs Creyke who came with us here. We have Col. and Mrs Fred Hill and Miss Hill, Col. W. Hill and Tommy*[31] *and Mr Dodd and Dryden Corbet to dine.*

Tuesday 4th December - *Very bad cold. Mrs Creyke, Mrs Charlton, Dora and I went out walking, it was so mild. At dinner we had Mr and Mrs Banning and Mr and Mrs Buchanan.*

Wednesday 5th December - *Home. Left Apley Castle after breakfast. Cold very bad! Found Mama quite well. Every prospect of nursing the cold until the end of the week. Mrs Creyke gave me such a beautiful wreath and bouquet.*

Thursday 6th December - *Home. Poultry Show at Shrewsbury. Henry went not to that but to a "------ Reformatory Meeting" Myself all day in bed. Snow.*

Friday 7th December - *Home. Henry went to shoot at Apley and would stay at Bridgnorth till tomorrow.*

Saturday 8th December - *Henry came home to dine. Mama went out to Ironbridge. Very cold!*

Sunday 9th December - *Such a severe frost, but I am better.*

Monday 10th December - *Cold journey to Great Barr Hall.*[53] *Mr and Mrs J. Anstice*[64] *with us in the train. We have here Lord and Lady Hatherton, Lord and Lady Lifford, Mrs and Miss Herrick and Mr Mount.*

Tuesday 11th December - *Great Barr.*[53] *Lord Hatheron and Lord Lifford and Henry went again to Birmingham. We did not go out for the ground is covered with snow. Lady Hartopp brought over Sir J. and Lady Packington and Mr Newdegate.*

Thursday 13th December - *Came home. The party quite broken up. Poor Crawford after suffering dreadfully all the time we were at Barr was obliged to have a tooth out. We took her to Robertson who did it very well.*

Friday 14th December - *Henry went to London hoping to return tomorrow night. I had an early walk hoping the cold would be better.*

Saturday 15th December - *Mama not at all well - the old pain, Blue pill. Another early walk but certain they do no good.*

Sunday 16th December - *Late yesterday a telegraphic message from Henry that he could not come before Monday. Went to church - quite warm. Mama went out too.*

Monday 17th December - *I went to meet Henry at Shifnal. He has a very bad cold!*

Tuesday 18th December - *Crown Hotel. To Bridgnorth in the open carriage. Mr Bellet's Lecture on the Antiquities of Bridgnorth. George*[23] *here.*

Wednesday 19th December - *Very busy paying visits and very cold. Did a great deal! George* [23] *went away after breakfast.*

Thursday 20th December - *Met Louisa*[54] *for a few minutes and Walter.*[54] *Went to Stanley* [55] *to luncheon then home.*

Friday 21st December - *Mr Bluck*[16] *arrived - the cold is intense.*

Saturday 22nd December - *Colder then ever. I did not go out at all.*

Sunday 23rd December - *The Hill so slippery that I turned back and did not go to Church.*

Monday 24th December - *Mr and Mrs Augustus Tollemache*[26] *came to stay for a few days.*

Tuesday 25th December - Christmas Day - *Carol singing all the day and bands! The mud so deep we drove to church.*

Wednesday 26th December - *To Coalport.*[41] *Broke a spring in the Clarence and had to take a Fly. Went to Apley and had luncheon at the Cave.*[63] *It began to rain and we drove home but the morning was very fine.*

Thursday 27th December - *Henry and Mr Tollemache*[26] *went to shoot at Apley. Mrs Tollemache and I went to see the Works but there was not much to see it being Christmas. Dearest Mama all day ill in bed with a bilious attack. George and Sarah*[23] *came to dine and we had some music and singing - Telegraphic leave of absence for Mr Tollemache.*[26]

Friday 28th December - *Henry took Augustus Tollemaches*[26] *over to Kemberton.*[56] *Rather dull day and wet. Mama a little better.*

Saturday 29th December - *The Tollemaches*[26] *left us. Henry rode to Bridgnorth. The most lovely mild weather. Mama, Mr Bluck and I went to Coalport,*[41] *&c.*

Sunday 30th December - *Walked to Buildwas church in the afternoon. Mama brought the carriage to fetch us home. Bright mild evening, slightly frosty. Mr Reynolds and suite at Marnwood.*[20]

Monday 31st December - New Year's Eve *- H. and M. gone to Shrewsbury. Mama and I are to drive out it is so mild. Mr Bartlett and Mr Reynolds called. Mama and I went to see Mrs J. Anstice[64] who is not well. Went to Coalport,[41] Rose Du Barrie' set of Inkstands, &c. for Henry. He bought me such a pretty gown - embroidered black tulle. After 12 whilst the bells ring out the old year, we all exchanged our gifts. May God be thanked for such a happy year as 1855.*

NOTES

1. Rev. Hayes was the vicar of Coalbrookdale who lived at the Chesnuts.
2. Cotsbrook, 2 miles north-east of Apley, was the home of Thomas Charlton Whitmore (Henry's elder brother) and of Lady Louisa Whitmore (née Douglas) his wife. They used to live at Apley, but moved to Cotsbrook in 1854.
3. Matilda was Adelaide's older sister. She was married to Abraham Darby IV and lived at Stoke Court, Buckinghamshire.
4. Douglas (Thomas Charles Douglas Whitmore) and Walter were the sons of Thomas Charlton Whitmore and Lady Louisa Whitmore of Apley. There were also seven daughters - Caroline (Nina) Mary, Emily (Emmy), Lucy, Edith, Cecil Elizabeth and Evelyn.
5. Adelaide had known the Pritchards for some years. John Pritchard was a banker from Broseley. He was also, like Henry Whitmore, a member of Parliament for Bridgnorth.
6. This was a reference to the end of the administration of Lord Aberdeen who had been Prime Minister since 1852. This was caused by the public outrage at the appalling conditions suffered by the troops in the Crimea. In January 1855 Mr Roebuck, Member of Parliament for Sheffield brought forward a motion to appoint a Committee of Enquiry into the conduct of the War. This caused the resignation of Lord Aberdeen. Lord Derby tried to form a Conservative administration but found he had insufficient support. It was Lord Palmerston who became Prime Minister in February 1855 as the only man likely to finish the war satisfactorily.
7. "Old Mrs Edwards" who died in 1855 was the widow of William Edwards, the surgeon of Coalbrookdale who had died in 1828. The practice was continued by their two sons Edward and Benjamin Edwards.
8. Emily was a cousin of Henry Whitmore and was engaged to be married to Col. Wilmot.
9. Col. Wilmot came from Malvern and married Emily Whitmore on 15th February, 1855.
10. The Storers from Nottinghamshire and Leamington Spa (Warwickshire) were related by marriage to the Whitmore's and were treated as members of the family.
11. Lucy was a cousin of Henry Whitmore and was married to Col. John Forbes, Coldstream Guards.

12. George Whitmore, Rector of Stockton (and brother of Thomas and Henry Whitmore) married their cousin Emily to Col. Wilmot of Malvern at St. George's Hanover Square.
13. The Wrottesley's were a leading Staffordshire family; Sophia Lady Wrottesley was the wife of 2nd Baron Wrottesley of Wrottesley Hall, Wolverhampton. She was the daughter of Thomas Giffard of Chillington Co. Stafford who were near neighbours of the Whitmore family.
14. Stoke Court in Buckinghamshire was the home of Abraham Darby IV and his wife Matilda (sister of Adelaide). The property was built by a grandson of William Penn, the founder of Pennsylvania, U.S.A.
15. The death of the Czar was significant, although early hopes for an end to the war in the Crimea were dashed, his death did enable Russia to make concessions in due course which might not have been possible if he had lived.
16. Mr Bluck appears in Adelaide's Journal on 4th March. Thereafter he appears as a frequent visitor. He seemingly was introduced to Henry Whitmore just before 4th March, but it not clear what his status was. He may have been involved in the political scene, and it seems possible that he may have been an agent or had some secretarial appointment.
17. The Deacons were the family of Sarah Whitmore (George Whitmore's wife). Before she married George, she was a Miss Deacon of Mabledon Park, Kent.
18. John Ella (1802-1880) was an English violinist, conductor and critic. From 1845 to 1880 he ran the musical union subscription concerts, and from 1852 he started the Musical Winter evenings. These were exclusive gatherings. Henry and Adelaide were subscribers as also were Abraham and Matilda Darby of Stoke Court.
19. Shrawardine is near Montford Bridge west of Shrewsbury.
20. Marnwood Hall was situated off the road from Coalbrookdale to Buildwas. It was the home of Rev. Bartlett, the incumbent of Buildwas Church.
21. Mrs Hayes was the wife of the Vicar of Coalbrookdale and resident at The Chesnuts. The Miss Edwards' who had lost their mother were Elizabeth and Fanny Edwards sisters of Edward and Benjamin Edwards the surgeons of Coalbrookdale. They lived in Darby Road just below the Chesnuts.
22. After the Great Exhibition of 1851, the Crystal Palace was dismantled in Hyde Park and re-assembled at Sydenham, South London.
23. George Whitmore, Rector of Stockton,(near Apley) brother of Henry Whitmore. Sarah (née Deacon) was his wife.
24. Ecarté was a card game for two.
25. The Drawing Room was a Royal Court Levée.
26. Lady Elizabeth Tollemache and Augustus Tollemache, M.A. (1839-1923) were members of the Manners family. He became Vicar of Whitwick, Co. Leicester 1874-94.

26a. The Blues were The Royal Horse Guards.

27. Miss Lawford was a close friend from Leighton Buzzard.
28. Edward Stanley, 15th Earl of Derby was the leader of the Conservative (Tory) party.
29. Lady Bradford of Weston Park, Shropshire.
30. Lord Bandon of Castle Bernard, Bandon, Co. Cork was married to Henry Whitmore's cousin, Catherine, Lady Bandon.

31. Thomas Charlton Whitmore (Tom or Tommy) was Henry Whitmore's brother.
32. Toozie was the pet dog.
33. Douglas was the son of Thomas Charlton Whitmore and was a pupil at Eton College.
34. Four Oaks is west of Sutton Coldfield and north of Birmingham.
35. Castle Bromwich is south of Sutton Coldfield and east of Birmingham.
36. Meriden is between Birmingham and Coventry and is said to be the centre of England.
37. Lord Dartmouth of Patshull Co. Stafford near to Apley, Shropshire.
38. Clevedon, west of Bristol, on the Bristol Channel.
39. The capture of Sebastopol marked the practical end of the Crimean war. The French infantry took the Malakoff Redout, and although British forces failed to take the Redan, the Taking of the Malakoff rendered the Redan untenable and the Russians evacuated Sebastopol. Lord Palmerston set about ending the War and this was accomplished by the Treaty of Paris in May 1856.
40. This must have been a political appointment, (perhaps as a Party whip), Viscount Mandeville had been member of Parliament for Bewdley from 1848-1852 and for Huntington from 1852 to 1855. He succeeded as 7th Duke of Manchester in August 1855 at which time he gave up his seat.
41. Coalport was a settlement established by William Reynolds in the 1790s on the northern banks of the River Severn a few miles east of Ironbridge. It was the location of the Coalport China Works.
42. Willey Hall, Shropshire was the home of Lord and Lady Forester and was the seat of the Forester family.
43. Mr Webb was a surgeon from Shrewsbury.
44. Mrs Henry Dickinson of Severn House was Deborah (née Darby) (1810-1855) the younger of the two daughters born to Edmund and Lucy Darby. She was a sister of Abraham IV who had married Matilda, Adelaide's sister. Ness (Little Ness) was an estate of 1012 acres which Henry Dickinson had purchased in 1850 from the Earl of Powys. It is situated about six miles north west of Shrewsbury on the road (A5) to Oswestry.
45. Dale House in Coalbrookdale was built in 1717 by Abraham Darby I and became the accepted house of the Manager of the Coalbrookdale Company until Barnard Dickinson left to move to Eastfield, next to Severn House in 1838. Since that date it had been home to Lucy Darby, (Mrs Edmund Darby) mother of Deborah Dickinson who had just died.
46. Admaston Spa was built in the late 18th century and would have been used on this occasion for convalescence.
47. Stockton, near Apley was the church where Henry's brother, George Witmore was Rector.
48. Oakengates was an industrial town on the A5 east of Wellington and now like Wellington a part of Telford, Shropshire.
49. Longford is a village near Edgmond, west of Newport, Shropshire.
50. Weston Park, Shropshire, seat of the Earl of Bradford and the Bridgeman family, and Lord and Lady Newport.
51. Tong Castle a few miles south of Weston Park.

52. Haughton is a few miles west of Stafford.
53. Great Barr is north of Birmingham on the Walsall Road.
54. Louisa was Lady Louisa Whitmore wife of Thomas Charlton Whitmore and Walter was their second son.
55. Stanley Hall, near Bridgnorth, was the home of Rebecca Darby (née Christy) widow of the late Alfred Darby.
56. Kemberton was the home of George Whitmore, Rector of Stockton and of Sarah (née Deacon) his wife.
57. Joseph Dickinson was the eldest son of Barnard and Ann Dickinson. He lived at the Albynes between Broseley and Bridgnorth.
58. There is a Woodcote south of Newport, Shropshire. The references to Woodcote in Adelaide's Journal give no clues as to the location.
59. Mrs Whitmore was the widow of Thomas Whitmore who had died in 1846. She was the mother of Henry Whitmore and was Adelaide's mother-in-law. She seems to have lived at Malvern.
60. Mr and Mrs Garforth and their daughters, Kitty and Maria, and son William, were a Yorkshire family. They came from Wigganthorpe Hall, 10 miles north of York. They had become close friends of Henry and Adelaide.
61. The Gaskells were a well-known family from Much Wenlock, Shropshire.
62. Rev. and Mrs Egremont lived at Wroxeter, several miles west of Coalbrookdale. Edward Egremont was vicar of Wroxeter.
63. The Cave was just south of Apley Park, overlooking the River Severn.
64. The Anstice family were distantly related to the Darbys through the Reynolds family. They were the proprietors of the Madeley Wood Company. John Anstice was the managing partner. His brother William Reynolds Anstice, also a partner, was a solicitor and was Steward of the Manor of Madeley.

1856

Comment

The previous year Henry Whitmore had accepted from Benjamin Disraeli a political post within the Conservative Party. Although the party was headed by Edward Stanley, 14th Earl of Derby (1799-1869), the driving force and creative leader within the party was Benjamin Disraeli who was Chancellor of the Exchequer in Lord Derby's first abortive administration in 1852. Disraeli was ambitious and was not above manoeuvering to displace Lord Derby as head of the party and therefore potential Prime Minister (he did not succeed!) To this end he had a network of young MPs who assisted him in this political intrigue. There is no evidence that Henry Whitmore was actively involved in these manoeuvres. Unfortunately Adelaide's Journal contains very few comments on the political scene, but the few clues that she does give indicate that Henry's political career was in the ascendant. Apart from the usual round of receptions and balls he was invited to the Grand Banquet at the Mansion House (25th June) where he met Lord Derby. On a more personal level he had several meetings with Lord Henry Lennox, son of the Duke of Richmond, who was Disraeli's particular confidante at the time.

On the social side, the Journal noted the almost clandestine marriage of Lord Forester to Lady Melbourne. Unfortunately the year was punctuated by a number of deaths which caused some distress including the death of Lord Bandon and Kitty Garforth, Charles Whitmore, and the infant Gerald Whitmore. On a happier note, fences seemed to have been mended with Adelaide's sister Matilda of Stoke Court, Buckingham, and Abraham Darby IV.

In November, Sunniside, next to the White House was pulled down. This was a fine house built by Abraham Darby II in 1750/51. Although it had been inherited by Adelaide's father Francis Darby as part of the extended estate, Francis was reluctant to take possession of the property and it had remained empty for over 20 years. After Sunniside was demolished the name "Sunniside" was transferred to the White House.

Tuesday 1st January - New Year's Day - *We have only Mr Bluck with us, a very happy quiet day. The Bells came at dinner time.*

Wednesday 2nd January - *Mama and I went to Wellington to get Rose ribbons for my new gown - Henry's gift for the Bridgnorth Ball.*

Thursday 3rd January - *The Phillips Dinner and Bridgnorth Ball. Mr Bluck went with us. Tulle gown very pretty, Hollyhocks & veil growing out of them.*

Friday 4th January - *Very ill. Had to go home from the Crown but did not move till 3 o'clock. Went by Apley - Nina*[43] *& Mary*[43] *still there. Saw Douglas*[26] *riding.*

Saturday 5th January - *Very wet day! Henry was to have gone to shoot at Petmarsh but could not.*

Sunday 6th January - *I did not go out at all. The Munros arrived in England for a short leave.*

Monday 7th January - *Henry and Mr Bluck went to the Pritchards*[8] *for luncheon. George came here.*

Tuesday 8th January - *The warm weather is gone. Walk for ferns.*

Wednesday 9th January - *Henry went to Wroxeter*[1] *for 2 nights. Mr & Mrs Walcot there and Capt. Russell & Louisa*[1] *& 3 children. A charade. Mr & Mrs H. Burton & Mrs Heneage dined.*

Thursday 10th January - *The New Hunt Ball. Mrs Walcot came with us & we came away directly after supper. I enjoyed it very much, there was a large party from Pitchford*[2] *- Lord Hill*[3] *and his son, Lord & Lady Stafford, Lady Bradford & Bridgemans,*[4] *Herberts, Bougheys, Leightons, Capt. & Mrs ------, Lord Powis,*[5] *Charlton & Jones. We got home to Wroxeter and were asleep by 3.*

Friday 11th January - *Came home from Wroxeter. Henry went to Kemberton.*[66]

Saturday 12th January - *Henry at Bridgnorth. I went a long walk with Toozie.*[6] *Found Mrs Edmund Darby, Mary & Henry Dickinson here when I came back.*[7]

Sunday 13th January - *Joseph Dickinson*[32] *here, he is going to leave the Albynes & the T's are coming there again. Went to church in the morning. Mr Osborne Gordon preached.*

Monday 14th January - *Joseph Dickinson*[32] *left us early - very cold. Mama has a toothache.*

Tuesday 15th January - *Went to dine with the Pritchards.*[8] *Met Mr & Mrs Forester,*[9] *de Satze's & Miss Young, Mr Pritchard, Mr Osborne Gordon, Mr Smith. Blue Brocade & azaleas.*

Wednesday 16th January - *Henry and I went to Kemberton*[66] *where they were busy going away. Wet drive home & cold.*

Thursday & Friday 17th & 18th January - *Mama not well and we had very wet days. Mr Webb*[11] *came.*

Saturday 19th January - *Tom*[10] *came to stay till Tuesday. Rain, rain. Mama better.*

Sunday 20th January - *Mr Gwyther[12] preached. Our seat made smart with red.*

Monday 21st January - *We have had news this morning of Lucy,[13] she has another son. Poor John Storer[14] died at Nice on the 13th. George[15] came in the afternoon and we had a very merry evening.*

Tuesday 22nd January - *George[15] & Henry went to Leamington to see the poor Storers.[14] They came back to dinner. Tom[10] left us after breakfast.*

Wednesday 23rd January - *Mr & Mrs J. Pritchard,[8] Miss C. de Satze & Mr Pritchard came to dine & Mrs Alfred Darby[15a] to dine & sleep.*

Thursday 24th January - *Mrs Alfred Darby stayed till after luncheon. Then Mama & I took George[15] home to Kemberton & went to Shifnal about some Bills. Whilst we were away Mr Jones called on Henry and gave a poor account of Tommy.[10]*

Friday 25th January - *Henry and I went to Apley Castle for luncheon. Tommy[10] really ill, I am afraid. Mr & Mrs Forester[9] came over & had luncheon in our absence!!*

Saturday 26th January - *Henry went to Bridgnorth. Mama and I paid visits - at Dale House[64] Mrs Graham and Mrs Rose.*

Sunday 27th January - *Mr Richards of Dawley preached here - very good sermon. We went over to Kemberton for the afternoon service. Mama with us.*

Monday 28th January - *Henry went to Cotsbrook[67] to say goodbye.*

Tuesday 29th January - *Henry went to London - snow and very cold! Very dull.*

Wednesday 30th January - *Still very cold, went out a little.*

Thursday 31st January - *Mama and I went to Cotsbrook.[67] Saw Lady Louisa,[16] met the young ladies. Very cold. Settled for me to go to Stoke Court[17] with Henry on Monday. Hope of a house in Eaton Square.*

Friday 1st February - *Very busy packing for London.*

Saturday 2nd February - *Henry writes he has given up the house - Still, I must go to Stoke Court.[17] Called upon Mrs W.R. Anstice[68] at Severn House & Uncle Richard Darby.[18]*

Sunday 3rd February - *Went to church - Mr Hayes[19] returned.*

Monday 4th February - *I went with Crawford (her lady's maid) to Stoke Court[17] to meet Henry. We have taken 10 Lowndes St. I cannot help thinking of it as a Family Hotel. Miss Cust & Capt. Coleridge at Stoke Court.[17] Mrs Herbert's Bal Custome. We were very late & tired.*

Tuesday 5th February - *Went on to see the Royal Stag Hunt - Capt. Coleridge went away. Col. Taylor came for Col. Vyse's Ball. I enjoyed the Ball very much. I suppose the Belles were Lady Fitzmaurice & Miss Calvert! I admired a Mrs Cockayne & Miss Clarke.*

Wednesday 6th February - *Went to call on Mrs Hibbert at Chalfont Park. Miss Cust went away. We were alone in the evening.*

Thursday 7th February - *I came home to Mama. Henry went to London. Met Walter*[26] *at the station. Mrs Moseley in the train. Found Mama at Shifnal.*

Friday 8th February - *Such a warm day!*

Saturday 9th February - *We went to say goodbye to Mrs Edmonds. Then to Wellington to see about horse boxes, &c. Hot!*

Sunday 10th February - *At church in the morning. We had Mr Hayes.*[19]

Monday 11th February - *Cut down the old oak. The oldest thing I remember! It was quite decayed! Mama had a sore throat.*

Tuesday 12th February - *Mama better and we went out a little.*

Wednesday 13th February - *Rain all day. Oh, dear, we have no cook for Lowndes Street.*

Thursday 14th February - *The last day is always busy. Visit from Mr and Mrs Hayes!*[19]

Friday 15th February - *I came to Lowndes Street bringing Crawford & Seabrook.*[20] *Mary Anne & the Fenns, 3 ponies, 2 dogs and a cat. Found Henry had a tidy cook. Walked with him on his way to the House of Commons. He came home to dinner and stayed in the evening.*

Saturday 16th February - *So busy settling.*

Sunday 17th February - *We have the Greig's seats at St Michaels. Very good sermon in the morning against the opening of the Crystal Palace &c. on Sundays. Sir Joshua Walmesley's Motion. We begin to look very pretty. New carpets & chintz & everything very clean.*

Monday & Tuesday 18th & 19th February - *Cold days and I only walked out to pay visits & settle the hundred & one wants of our new home. Col. Taylor came to dine.*

Wednesday 20th February - *Walked again with Toozie.*[6] *Mr Bluck & his Mama dined here. Sunday Amusement Bill.*

Thursday 21st February - *Henry went with me to Portman Square but he has a very bad cold. Took him to the House of Commons & came home, it was so cold.*

Friday 22nd February - *I went out again in the carriage & came home for a long visit from Mrs Davison.*

Saturday 23rd February - *Mr Bluck dined here.*

Sunday 24th February - *Mr Bluck dined here and we went in the evening to John Street Chapel to hear Mr Broomfield.*

Monday 25th February - *Called upon Mrs Davison & saw her and Mr & Mrs Wolfe. Paid some more visits. Lord Henry Lennox[21] came home with Henry for dinner.*

Tuesday 26th February - *Called for Henry at the Carlton[22] & took him and Sir W. Jolliffe to the House of Commons.*

Wednesday 27th February - *Henry went to the Levée. Visit from Lady Elizabeth Tollemache.[25] Afterwards I went with Henry for shopping - Clarke & Black Tulle at Hardings. Miss Wrottesley[23] came in for an hour at dusk. Mr Bluck dines here.*

Thursday 28th February - *Went to leave our names at the Palace. Mr Charlton & Tommy[10] called.*

Friday 29th February - *Henry and I walked over to Paterson's to see the Charltons. Mrs Charlton came back with us to luncheon. Went with her to see Mrs Herbert. At Mrs Wrottesley's found Sir Robert Pigot.[24] Augustus[25] dined here.*

Saturday 1st March - *Bad headache because a dinner party! Mrs Davison, Mr & Mrs Wolfe, the Pritchards,[8] Miss Heneage, Sir Robert Pigot,[26] Mr Bluck.*

Sunday 2nd March - *Westminster Abbey in the afternoon such a good sermon and beautiful Anthems, & such perishing cold. Visit from Sir Wm. Davison. Mr Bluck here.*

Monday 3rd March - *Poor Toozie[6] not well - he twisted himself in his Master's lap and has been complaining since yesterday.*

Tuesday & Wednesday 4th & 5th March - *Cold days both. Toozie gradually better. Out driving both days in the open carriage. Henry & I called upon Miss Holland. Covent Garden Theatre.*

Thursday 6th March - *Douglas & Walter[26] arrived to spend the day. Abraham and Matilda[17] chose the same day. Henry had a bad account of George[15] which made us very unhappy - No telegraph to Shifnal! Henry took the Boys in the afternoon and I went out with Abraham & Matilda to call upon Mrs W. Brodrick & Mrs B. Harvey. They went back about 5. Mr Bluck dined here and the Boys went away. I went to Lady Wrottesley's[49] for an hour - came back for ecarté![27] Henry very tired and we both very anxious.*

Friday 7th March - *Called upon Mrs Calthorpe. Took Henry to the House. In the evening instead of Dinner went to Drury Lane Theatre for Charles Mathews in "The Bachelor of Arts" and the Pantomime.*

Saturday 8th March - *Such a sad day. Sarah's account of George*[15] *we thought not at all good. Henry telegraphed to Wellington & later in the afternoon the reply was "Better & down stairs!" Then we had an MP's Dinner which happily did well. Lord Henry Lennox,*[21] *Lord Wm. Graham, Lord Newport,*[28] *Lord Charles Clinton, Mr Newdegate,*[29] *Sir Wm. & Mr Jolliffe, Mr Hamilton, Colonel Vyse, and Col. Taylor. Mrs Dewison and ourselves made the unlucky number of 13. All were in uniform for the Speakers Levée and Lord Charles Clinton and Lord Henry Lennox came back with Henry.*

Sunday 9th March - *I did not go out in the morning. Mr Hamilton's in the afternoon. Mr Bluck here.*

Monday 10th March - *Very cold. Tom*[10] *came from Malvern.*

Tuesday 11th March - *I went to spend the day at Stoke Court.*[17] *The accounts of George*[15] *are still unfavourable.*

Wednesday 12th March - *We were alone tho' intending a dinner party. Tom*[10] *still here. Henry and I bought Mrs Clarke's gown & shawl.*

Thursday 13th March - *Mrs Davison dined here. In the morning I went with Tom*[10] *to Veitch's Gardens.*

Friday 14th March - *I go to dine and stay at Stoke Court.*[17] *Worse accounts of George.*[15] *Tom*[10] *and Henry go to Shropshire tomorrow. I joining them at Slough tomorrow morning. Caught cold in the hot houses. Dinner at Stoke Court. Rice Claytons. W. Brodricks, Bents, Penningtons & some clergymen.*

Saturday 15th March - *Matilda*[17] *took me to the station & we came home together stopping at Kemberton. George*[15] *up and down stairs but very far from well.*

Sunday & Monday 16th & 17th March - *I nursing my cold in bed. Henry at Kemberton, very cold. Home to dine. Mama so well.*

Wednesday 19th March - *Dr Evans came to Kemberton. Henry was much satisfied by his opinion of George.*[15] *Henry went on to the Assizes at Shrewsbury.*

Thursday 20th March - *I went to bring Henry from Kemberton. The Grand Jury not dismissed & Good Friday interval.*

Good Friday, 21st March - *I did not go to church for my cold is not gone. Henry at Kemberton.*

Saturday 22nd March - *Henry again had to go on the Grand Jury at Shrewsbury and Sarah made him return to Kemberton and stay over Easter Sunday whereat my mind was greatly tried.*

Easter Sunday, 23rd March - *I went to church by myself and stayed for the sacrament.*

Monday 24th March - *I went to Kemberton*[66] *to bring Henry home - doubtful if he would be allowed to leave, but there was no wish that he should remain. Sarah did thank me for letting him go on Easter Sunday and I said indeed he did not ask leave. Henry said "I am much too old to ask leave" & I laughed & said "I am much too old to expect it." I would not say I was glad he should stay but it was no time for being bad tempered for poor George*[15] *has been kept in bed ever since. Dr Evans saw him and they think him no better today. Henry very low & tired. It is a sad Easter Holiday & I fear can do him no good.*

Tuesday 25th March - *Mama and I to Bridgnorth. Henry was put down at the Cuckoo Oak*[30] *turnpike & we took him up again as we returned & Toozie.*[6] *Found Louisa and all the Cotsbrook*[67] *children & Mrs Alfred Darby*[15a] *& her family & a circus going on! George*[15] *a little better.*

Wednesday 26th March - *Henry still going to Kemberton*[66] *and returning to dinner.*

Thursday 27th March - *Mr and Mrs Bartlett*[31] *called, paid a long visit & Joseph Dickinson*[32] *who stayed luncheon. He left the Albyne's yesterday and the Stevens are returned.*

Friday 28th March - *Henry and I went to Cotsbrook*[67] *to luncheon - then to Kemberton.*[66]

Saturday 29th March - *Visit from Mrs Edmund Darby*[7] *& Mary. Certainly in very good spirits considering.*

Sunday 30th March - *Henry went with me to church, then he drove to Kemberton and I walked home with Mr and Mrs Hayes.*[19] *Very cold east wind. George*[15] *better but Henry still low at leaving him in bed and all.*

Monday 31st March - *Left dearest Mama. Peace is proclaimed.*[33] *We travelled with the Pritchards*[8] *to Lowndes St. very clean and comfortable but I do feel as if the world went the wrong way in that house! Henry came home to dinner and Mr Bluck.*

Tuesday 1st April - *Ella's*[34] *last concert. Matilda*[17] *came and Abraham. It was very good. Franchomme so very fine on the "violincello". Mr Bluck at dinner.*

Wednesday 2nd April - *I paid visits, only Lady Wrottesley*[23] *& Mrs John Pritchard*[8] *at home. In our vacation we had invitations to Wrottesley*[23] *for the Tong Sale and from the Farnhams to spend a week at Guondon. Mr Bluck at dinner.*

Thursday 3rd April - *Henry went back with me to Hardings & chose train & I bought & paid for a Persian shawl. Henry came home and we had a nice long evening.*

Friday 4th April - *To Brompton. Again to Hardings, brought away Train & Tulle & petticoat. Mr Baldock would be taken to the House. Mr Bluck & ecarté.*[27]

Saturday 5th April - *Henry and I and Mr Bluck went to Richmond. Henry called upon Lady Lyrwhitt and Mr Bluck and I walked on the Terrace. A lovely morning but turned out cold and rainy. Mr Bluck at dinner and ecarté.*[27] *A Headache. Dose and did not go out.*

Monday 7th April - *Matilda*[17] *came. We drove out & Mr Bluck came to dinner.*

Tuesday 8th April - *We drove out in the morning & went to hear Picco at St James Theatre. Mr Bluck and ecarté.*[27]

Wednesday 9th April - *Rain, but we went out in a shut up carriage. Dinner Party - Mr & Mrs Augustus Tollemache,*[25] *Mr & Mrs Charles Whitmore, Lady & Miss Wrottesley,*[23] *Mr Bayley, Mr Knatchbull, Mr Mullens and our 3 selves.*

Thursday 10th April - *Matilda*[17] *intended to have gone home but she was ill and could not get up with such a headache. Col. Taylor and Mr Farnham came to drive.*

Friday 11th April - *Abraham came for Matilda.*[17] *Bad account from Kemberton of little Gerald!*[35] *Catty*[37] *arrived yesterday & I drove in Lowndes Sq.*

Saturday 12th April - *Henry went down to Kemberton tho' we had a little better account from Sarah and I went to Stoke Court*[17] *both expecting to return Monday.*

Sunday 13th April - *Went to Stoke Court*[17] *and heard a very good sermon from Mr Shaw.*

Monday 14th April - *I expected to go back to London but Seabrook*[20] *arrived with letters. Poor little Gerald*[35] *died on Saturday night. Henry remains at Kemberton over the funeral. I stay on with Matilda.*

Tuesday, Wednesday, Thursday, Friday 15th, 16th, 17th & 18th April - *Mrs Whitmore*[69] *went to stay with Mama. Friday the child's funeral.*[35]

Saturday 19th April - *Met Henry at Paddington and we both came back to London. A very sad week for him! Mr Bluck at dinner.*

Sunday 20th April - *Twice at church, saw all Catty's*[37] *beautiful family.*

***Monday 21st April** - Paying visits and shopping with Henry. Mr Bluck at dinner. Henry gone again to the House of Commons.*

***Tuesday 22nd April** - Henry and I were out early about trimming for train. I had a great many visitors in the afternoon. Mrs Knight & Lady Dalrymple & Lady A. Duncombe & Lady Anne Drummond, Mrs & Miss Harrison, Mr Jefferson, Mr J. Taylor. Frank and Catty[37] dined with us & Mamey[37] & Lucy.[13]*

***Wednesday 23rd April** - I have been shocked this morning, to hear of the death of poor Louisa Burton! She had only left Paris a fortnight to visit her cousin in Gloucester Place and there she died from an attack of dysentery before her family were all aware of danger.*

***Thursday 24th April** - We dined with Frank and Catty.[37]*

***Friday 25th April** - Paid a great many visits and ended up with a headache.*

***Saturday 26th April** - Dearest Mama came. Mr Bluck dined.*

***Sunday 27th April** - Rain, rain all day. We could not go to church.*

***Monday 28th April** - We drove out but so cold. Mama had a Brougham.*

***Tuesday 29th April** - The Drawing Room.[36] Very full, Catty and Mamey[37] looked very well. Hair dressed at half past 9. Matilda and Abraham came. Took Mama to see the Queen go. Very cold. Mr Bluck here. Mrs Davison & Mrs Woulfe & George Whitmore came in afternoon. He was going to Lady Fremantle's concert.*

***Wednesday 30th April** - Mrs Harrison's Ball. We were late. If I remember so cold we never went out at all. Not 6 people we ever saw. Mr Bluck went with us.*

***Thursday 1st May** - Drove out but very cold.*

***Friday 2nd May** - Mama had a Brougham and we went to choose paper for Morning Room. Then to Westbourne Terrace and then to Leadenhall St. for spectacles and an opera glass for me.*

***Saturday 3rd May** - Mama went to Stoke Court[17] to spend Sunday. Dinner Party 12. Mr Mrs & Miss Fitzroy, Mrs Knight, Mr and Lady D. Pakington, Lord Bernard[37] & Mamey, Mr Boughey and Sir F. Hopkins.*

***Sunday 4th May** - Twice to church but cold. Long walk.*

***Monday 5th May** - I drove out. So glad to see Mama back. Mr Bluck at dinner.*

***Tuesday 6th May** - Drove out in open carriage.*

***Wednesday 7th May** - So cold & wet we never went out & saw nobody but Mr George Taylor. Mr Jefferson & Mr Bluck dined. The Duchess of*

Northumberland's reception in the evening. Magnificent house, many introductions. Mr & Mrs Disraeli, & Duke & Duchess of Manchester[37a] *very civil. Mr Warren.*

Thursday 8th May - *Out in a Brougham. Woodgates, Mamey*[37] *& Lucy*[13] *came to dine.*

Friday 9th May - *We went out with the ponies but still cold, shopping & then to the Academy to see the pictures. Not very good collection. Millais had a great many. Mr Bluck in the evening and ecarté.*[27] *Mama rather tired but very well. Matilda has a bad cold.*

Saturday 10th May - *Began the day early. Mama left us at 9. Visit to Catty*[37] *with Henry. Mr and 2 Miss Deacons*[38] *called. Dinner at home 12. Mr & Lady H. Duncombe, Lord & Lady & Miss Bernard.*[37] *Mr & Mrs Robert Herbert, Sir Adolphus & Lady Dalrymple, Edward Taylor. Lady Derby*[39] *at home. We got back before 12! The rooms were very full. Was introduced to Lord C. Russell & the Speaker. Lady Powis very kind.*

Sunday 11th May - *I was twice at church. Henry not at all well. But went to St Michael's in the afternoon & heard a very good sermon from Mr Fremantle. Mr Bluck here. Fine warm day.*

Monday 12th May - *Rain, rain. Henry not yet very well. Fanny Leveson came with Catty.*[37] *The Arcade. Mr Bluck in the evening.*

Tuesday 13th May - *Mamey*[37] *came to luncheon with me afterwards to Ella's.*[34] *We had Mme. Schumann & an excellent concert. I went off from the door to Paddington Station. Met Henry & servants & we went to Stoke Court*[17] *to dine & sleep. Mr Brodrick & Mr & Mrs Leicester Hibbert staying. At dinner Claytons Shaws.*

Wednesday 14th May - *Left Stoke Court for Malvern. Sent Crawford back to London. Lucy & Col. Forbes*[13] *at dinner & George & Sarah.*[15] *We had 3 hours at Oxford & Henry took me over Christ Church &c.*

Thursday 15th May - *Emily & I went to Lady Hilton's house. Then we dined at Lady Wilmots, Mrs Whitmore,*[69] *Col. Forbes & Lucy.*[13] *Mrs Isaac at luncheon.*

Friday 16th May - *News that Nina & Mary*[43] *want to come to us for the 29th. Drive with Mrs Whitmore,*[69] *Col. Wilmot & Emily*[13] *dined at Mt. Pleasant with us.*

Saturday 17th May - *Returned to Lowndes St. Sir J. Pakington in our carriage. Passed Leighton. Dined with the CW's. At dinner Gen'l & Mdme Cabrera. Mr & Mrs Wood. Miss Brownrigg, Mr Long, Lady Churchill & Mr Whateley, very pleasant.*

Sunday 18th May - *Henry's cold very bad. Did not go out at all. I went to Mr Liddell's in the morning. Mr Bluck, Catty*[37] *came. Great fear of a row because the Bands are stopped playing in Kensington Gardens.*

Monday 19th May - *Henry better. Drove out. Paid visits. Catty*[37] *got materials for camp stool. Housemaid ill again. Mr Teevan here. Mr Bluck & ecarté.*[27]

Tuesday 20th May - *John & Lucy Forbes*[13] *here at luncheon, and I took Lucy shopping. Eliza very ill & we have written to Mr Greig. Henry dined at the Carlton.*[22]

Wednesday 21st May - *Mr Greig came early. Eliza rather better. Sir F. Hopkins. Mr Hamilton at luncheon. Catty & Mamey.*[37] *Then we went out to Fosters about flowers. Then home & with Mr Bluck to nursery gardens for flowers (real). At dinner John & Lucy Forbes.*[13] *Mrs Brownlow!! and the 2 Miss Forbes. Henry and I to Northumberland House*[40] *in the evening.*

Thursday 22nd May - *Eliza is up & much better! Wet day. Lady Georgiana Douglas*[41] *and Mrs Ed. Wrottesley called.*[23] *Drove out. Mr Bluck. Mrs Capel-Cure at home & Mrs Annesley. At Mrs Capel-Cure are found so many Shropshire people we decided to ask them to an "at home". Sat up till 3 writing the cards.*

Friday 23rd May - *Mr Greig again. Drove out leaving our invitations & looking for lodgings for the Charltons - Alone this evening. Henry at dinner & coming to tea.*

Saturday 24th May - *Dined with the J. Pritchards,*[8] *Mrs & Miss Gurwards, Mr Pugh Spearmans - Lady Webster, Mons. Desanges, Miss Mosely. I had a busy morning writing to Mrs Whitmore*[69] *& Lady Louisa,*[16] *Nina & Mary*[43] *& Mrs Wall want to come here at the time of our party & I am sure we cannot do it.*

Sunday 25th May - *Mr Bluck. We tried to go to church again in the afternoon but were too late. Walked thro' the Park - very crowded.*

Monday 26th May - *I drove out to leave our cards for Wednesday.*

Tuesday 27th May - *Ella's 5th Concert.*[34] *Halle and a Septet of.......... such music! Matilda did not come she has Mrs Edmund Darby and Mary at Stoke Court.*[17] *Dined with Mr and Mrs Fitzroy. Mr & Mrs Hutchinson. Mrs Staples. Mrs Philip Crawley and the rooms filled in the evening. Rather pleasant.*

Wednesday 28th May - *Very early we began putting in the flowers - the furniture being moved away as much as it could and the rooms looking very nice I must say. We had Lord Burlington's cook. Cotes, Taylors, Hartopps, Sir Francis Scott, and John & Lucy Forbes came to dinner and about a hundred people in the evening. We asked 140, of those who came many were Shropshire friends. Lord & Lady Bradford, Mrs Wright, Miss Moncrieffe, Lady and 2*

Miss Bougheys, Mrs Mainwaring, Miss Sparling, Charltons, Leekes, Baldocks, Doneraile, Carberys, Brodricks, Leightons, Lloyds, Henages. We had music and one quadrille at last. It all prospered very much. Henry asked a great many political friends also.

Thursday 29th May - *A great bore it was to get up for the Drawing Room*[36] *this morning! And such a Drawing Room and such mobs in London. They were orderly mobs but I never saw such crowds. Catty and Mamey*[37] *both looked very well. I had wild roses put in my train &c. We got back to a 7 o'clock dinner. Then we walked across the Park to Mrs Disraeli's at Grosvenor Gate*[42] *and found the top of the house fitted up with lamps, carpets, chairs and grand people and there we saw the fireworks in great perfection - Very fine they were. 100 Rockets at a time, showers of gold, red, blue and green stars, feathers and wheat-sheaves. There was a grand "mine" and the fixed fireworks were very good but people complained it was too long and no variety. There was a grand supper and we watched the crowds disperse out of the park!! We walked towards Lord Ward's illuminations which was fit to be a matter of history and home by the French Embassy. Very tired.*

Friday 30th May - *We got letters & telegraphs this morning to say Nina & Mary*[43] *were coming to Paddington & would want to be taken to the London Bridge Station so I went and took them with the ponies. Lady H. Duncombe came in the afternoon & many other visitors and Lady H. Leeke. Mance...... won the Oaks.*

Saturday 31st May - *Wretched cold day. I did not go out but saw a great many visitors. Lady Carberry, Charltons, Mrs John Pritchard. This has been an eventful week - The Derby Week & in it Palmer's trial and the Peace Rejoicings on the Birth Day.*

Sunday 1st June - *Cold. Mr Bluck, once at church. Lowndes Square in the afternoon.*

Monday 2nd June - *We went to Lady Bradford's*[4] *in the evening & found a nice party, Packingtons, Leekes, Wrights, Lord and Lady Willoughby, &c. &c.*

Tuesday 3rd June - *We went to Lady Spearman's Ball for a small half hour.*

Wednesday 4th June - *Dined at Lord Wynford's. Met Lord and Lady Lanesborough, Lord Redesdale,*[45] *and Miss Mitford, &c. &c. &c. Then we went on to Lady Stracey's at home.*

Thursday 5th June - *Henry dined at the Carlton*[22] *& at 6 o'clock to go with the Charltons to the Princesses' for "The Winter's Tale" - Keanes.*

Friday 6th June - *Mrs Whitmore*[69] *arrived alone in the evening.*

Saturday 7th June - *Dinners 14. Lord & Lady Doncraile, Lord & Lady Carbery, Lord Bandon, Lord & Lady Bernard*[37] *& Mamey. Mr & Lady*

Hester Leake and Mrs Charlton. Great failure in the dinner, quite awful. Mrs Godfrey goes away on Monday.

Sunday 8th June - *Mr Bluck. The remains of a stiff neck but went twice to church. The Measles has appeared at Lowndes Square.*

Monday 9th June - *Sent away dreadful Mrs Godfrey. Our dinner from Gunter. Mr and Mrs Blackburne dined here, Miss Bluck and Fox. Col. Taylor & Mr Henry Turner. I engaged a little kitchen maid to help the Man cook for 1 week.*

Tuesday 10th June - *Matilda came up for the day and for Ella.*[34] *It was almost a Beethoven concert and so good! Ernst & Mdme Schumann. Mrs Whitmore had luncheon at Lady Kenmare's. We were at home in the evening. Henry at the House.*

Wednesday 11th June - *Dined with Lord & Lady Newport. Very pretty dinner. Mr and Lady Francis Lloyd, Admiral Bridgeman & Lady Lucy and Mr Forester came in the evening. Lord Forester was married very privately to Lady Melbourne*[46] *yesterday. Lord Palmerston gave her away.*

Thursday 12th June - *Dined with Mr & Mrs Farnham. She just came to London for her confinement & they have Sir Thos. Tronbridge's house in Eaton Place. We had Mr and Mrs Vaughan, Sir T. & Lady Scott, Linney Westerley, Sir ------ Tyrell & his daughter Mrs Palmer. Lady Carbery called in the morning with such a pretty little girl, & Mrs Slaney came in. She has Lucy & Dora with her for Ascot and wanted me to take them to the Opera tonight but one can't dine out and go to the Opera!*

Friday 13th June - *Wet all day! Dined at Mrs Deacon's.*[38] *20 people and I knew nobody, nor Henry hardly. An agreeable Mr Wilson took me to the dining room. Mr and Mrs Brabant and a Mr and Mrs Eardley Wilmott.*[47] *Took Henry to the House of Commons.*

Saturday 14th June - *Mrs Whitmore*[69] *left us. We drove to the Fosters and to Lord Derby's*[48] *and were caught in such rain! Then I went in the afternoon to Catty & drove with Henry and Mr Bluck to the Flower Show at Ashburnham House.*

Sunday 15th June - *Twice at Mrs Hamilton's. Mr Bluck here.*

Monday 16th June - *Miss Forbes went with us to Lady Hartopp's very good Ball! Henry did not arrive until late. It was very pleasant but I did not like my head dress of red feathers.*

Tuesday 17th June - *We had a quiet day. Henry late at the House and now the morning sittings begin, which is too much!*

Wednesday 18th June - *We drove out in the country to Wimbledon - so fresh & pleasant. In the evening Mrs and the Miss Lennox Butler's Ball. Very full* *and very nice. Not so much our set as Lady H's. Miss Forbes was going to a Crystal Palace Fete & too tired to come out.*

Thursday 19th June - *Dined with the Baldocks, a grand dinner. Mr & Lady Elizabeth Cust, Col. Forester - Mr & Lady Shafto - Mrs M. Biddulph - Capt. Martyn - Lord Kilmorey - Sir Henry & Lady Stracey.*

Friday 20th June - *A wet day and I could not go out after taking Henry to the House.*

Saturday 21st June - *Visit from Lady Carbery. Henry and I drove to the ship at Greenwich to dine with Sir Francis Hopkins. We were 13. 4 courses of fish & began with Turtle! Sir W. Clayton, Mr and Mrs S. Seymour, Col. Johnson, Mr Roberts, Mr and Miss Tottenham. Mr Jones Pautglas.*

Sunday 22nd June - *To St Michaels and in the afternoon to Mr Burgess's church where we heard such a good sermon. Mr Bluck here.*

Tuesday 24th June - *Matilda came for Ella's Grand Matinee.*[34] *We had Sivori & Viardot sang some songs. It was charming. We were too late for the train and I obliged to leave Matilda because we had coming to dine Miss Greathed, Mr G. Taylor, Sir Robert Pigot. Miss Forbes came to go with us to Lady Carbery's in the evening. She had a Band and the house beautifully decorated.*

Wednesday 25th June - *Grand Banquet at the Mansion House & Henry dined there to meet Lord Derby*[48] *&c.*

Thursday 26th June - *Henry dined at Lord Hotham's. Came for me to go to Lady Hartopp. It was a very pleasant party. Went to London Bridge to see George & Sarah*[15] *pass.*

Friday 27th June - *Henry had to go back to the House and very late we went to Mrs Harrison's Ball.*

Saturday 28th June - *We went to dine at Mrs Whateley's. Large party, Lord & Lady Allan, Sir & Lady & Miss Wightman, Lord Wynford & Miss Best Caberas. We spent the morning so charmingly at Kew.*

Monday 30th June - *George*[15] *came from Mabledon*[38] *to stay with us. He dined with Catty. We dined with Mr and Lady L. Cotes, met Mr and Lady Albreda Vernon, Sir J. and Lady Lyster Kaye, Mr and Mrs C. Herbert, Lady Wrottesley*[49] *and Linney, Lord J. Fitzroy, Mr Ford, Mr Dugdale.*

Tuesday 1st July - *Catty and Frank and all the Party except Lord Bandon*[37] *left London for Malvern. George*[15] *drove with me in the Park, &c.*

Wednesday 2nd July - *Little dinner at home. Lady Wrottesley*[49] *and Linney, Mrs and Miss Trant and Hans Hamilton, Major Stuart Knox, Mr G. Whitmore, Mr Browning.*

***Thursday 3rd July** - George[15] and I drove out. Did not go to Mrs Gratton's last night or Lady Spearman this night.*

***Friday 4th July** - G.H. and I drove down to Crystal Palace where we had luncheon & then a very good concert. Grisi & Gardoni in such a charming duet from Othello. Bosio, Drune's, Marai, Didier, Ranconi. The fountains beautiful. Henry could not get away from the House of Commons to dinner and I not well at all!*

***Saturday 5th July** - George[15] left us to go to Kent[38] for Sunday. We dined with the Gaskells. Met Lord and Lady Bradford,[4] Lord and Lady Newark, Mr and Mrs Hughes, Mr and Mrs Seymour, Mr Bruce, Mr Peacock, Mr Cheyney. Afterwards Lady Thesiger's Assembly. Grand House.*

***Sunday 6th July** - Went to church at St Michaels. We hear Kitty Garforth[52] is very ill.*

***Monday 7th July** - Henry not well yesterday. I had an early visit from Mrs Creswell, I think I like her. George returned here from Kent[38] in the evening.*

***Tuesday 8th July** - Matilda came for Ella's[34] last concert. Very full and very good. Halle and Sivoni. Lady Stracey's Ball, a great crowd it was.*

***Wednesday 9th July** - We were out early for the coming of the Guards! Went to the Oxford & Cambridge Club. Excellent view as they passed. Luncheon after. Then to the Park to see the Review after. Miss Forbes went with us. George left us for Mabledon.[38] Henry dined with Sir C. Burrell - Fetes at Apley Castle for Sir John's return.*

***Thursday 10th July** - I had a long and very pleasant day at Stoke Court.[17] Matilda alone.*

***Friday 11th July** - Mr and Mrs Trant went out driving with me. Mr Bluck came to dine. Henry went back to the House & a very late night they had.*

***Saturday 12th July** - Wet day. In the evening Henry and I and Mr Bluck went to the Italia Opera. Wagner in Lucretzia. Il Segreto.*

***Sunday 13th July** - St Michaels. Charity Sermon. Went to see Mrs Woulfe in the afternoon. Mr Bluck here.*

***Monday 14th July** - Mrs Butler and Lady Skipworth had a great party at the Crystal Palace, we did not go. A Ball afterwards.*

***Tuesday 15th July** - George came from Mabledon[38] for a day or two. John Forbes[13] here at luncheon and dinner. Went in the afternoon to Holland House. Lady H.[50] charming. The house beautiful. We went over the house & gardens. It is a lovely old place. The pictures by Sir Joshua Reynolds are very fine. Went to the House of Commons & Miss Trant met us. The Attorney General's defence of his conduct in the Sadleir affair. So warm after dinner we were all in the balcony. A thunder storm.*

Wednesday 16th July - *Day of the Review at Aldershot,*[51] *we did not go. Dinner Party. Lord Wynford & Miss Best, Mr Mrs and Miss Heneage. Col. Forester, Lord Hotham, Mr E. Talbot.*

Thursday 17th July - *George*[15] *left us. Went to Mrs Bett's Assembly. Sir Fenwick Williams and Baron Tricoupi.*

Friday 18th July - *Matilda and Abraham came to ask us to go to Stoke Court*[17] *in their absence in Scotland!! Matilda stayed luncheon & I came from the station, almost as Mama came! It is very nice. Henry came home to dine.*

Saturday 19th July - *Henry had to dine at the Carlton.*[22] *Mama and I drove about shopping &c.*

Sunday 20th July - *In the morning I went to church at Mr Liddell's. Mama and Henry stayed at home. Afterwards she and I went to St Michaels. It poured with rain, and Henry brought us a cab. Fine evening. Mr Bluck here.*

Monday 21st July - *Asked to a "Garden Party" at Mrs E. Wrottesley's.*[49] *Mrs Garforth*[52] *came with poor Kitty to Chesterfield St. She is very ill.*

Tuesday 22nd July - *Mama and I dressed to go to the "Garden Party" but Henry went with me to Chesterfield St. and we could not get away in time. Henry and I dined with the Capel Cures. Mr Bluck stayed with Mama. We met Mr and Mrs E. Wrottesley,*[49] *&c. &c.*

Wednesday 23rd July - *Mama and I to Stoke Court.*[17] *Henry to the Assizes at Shrewsbury. Heat terrific.*

Thursday 24th July - *Matilda took us to Burnham Beeches - Lovely weather, a little cooler.*

Friday 25th July - *I came back to Lowndes Street. Went to Mrs Garforth's.*[52] *Found poor Kitty very ill.*

Saturday 26th July - *We had a small dinner. Miss Greathed, Mr Stone, Mr Hawes, 2 Miss Leighs, twins - Mr Jefferson and Mr Bluck.*

Sunday 27th July - *Our last Sunday.*

Monday 28th July - *Mama and Matilda came up for the day. Matilda and Abraham go to Achnacarry - Lord Malmesbury's*[53] *moor. I recommended Isles for their absence for Stoke Court.*

Tuesday 29th July - *We dined with Mrs Trant and met Miss Percival &c. and heard a bad account of Jersey where we meant to have gone. Poor Kitty*[52] *a little better.*

Wednesday 30th July - *Henry, I and Mr Bluck left Lowndes St. Railway to Gloucester.*

Thursday 31st July - *Swansea - Park Wern.*

Friday 1st August *- Park Wern to Narberth Road & to Tenby by the coach.*

Saturday 2nd August *- Tenby, White Lion Hotel.*

Sunday, Monday, Tuesday 3th, 4th & 5th August *- Tenby, and very hot.*

Wednesday 6th August *- Tenby - Carew and Manorbier.*

Thursday 7th August *- Tenby - Pembroke & Baske.*

Friday 8th August *- Left Tenby, slept at Ivy Bush, Carmarthen.*

Saturday 9th August *- Carmarthen to Aberystwyth by Lampeter, the coach, pouring rain. Belle Vue.*

Sunday 10th August *- Aberystwyth.*

Monday 11th August *- Aberystwyth to Trefri by Borth Sands & the Ferry.*

Tuesday 12th August *- Trefri, Jane took us to Machynlleth. Tommy, Dora & Mrs Henry Corbett at Trefri.*

Wednesday 13th August *- Left Trefri. Came to Dolgelly, open carriage - showers.*

Thursday 14th August *- Left Dolgelly to Tan y Bwlch by Barmouth and Harlech.*

Friday 15th August *- Left Tan y Bwlch to Llanberis by Aberglaslyn & Beddgelert.*

Saturday 16th August *- Ascended Snowdon from Llanberis & came to Bangor. Drove to Carnarvon & thence the Railway.*

Sunday 17th August *- At Bangor.*

Monday 18th August *- We came home. Mama still at Lichborough.*

Tuesday 19th August *- Rain all day.*

Wednesday 20th August *- Rain - Drove to Kemberton.*

Thursday 21st August *- Dear Mama came home. I went to Apley Castle to luncheon. Mrs C. came to........ The worst possible accounts from Chesterfield Street of dear Kitty.*[52]

Friday 22nd August *- After luncheon Henry and Mr Bluck and I went to Shrewsbury. Called at Apley Castle afterwards. We had a very very bad account from Chesterfield Street.*[52]

Saturday 23rd August *- A letter to Henry from Mrs Daff. Poor Kitty died*[52] *on Thursday evening. It was to be expected but I cannot say how grieved we both are. It is like losing a sister. I went with Mama to Willey to the Gardens and Henry went to Kemberton.*

***Sunday 24th August** - What a sad day in Chesterfield St! We went to church in the morning. Henry and Mr Bluck in the afternoon to Little Wenlock. The funeral is to be on Tuesday the day Mrs Whitmore comes here for the Apley Bazaar.*

***Monday 25th August** - Henry went to London, I took him to Shifnal and then went to Kemberton, had luncheon there and took George & Sarah[15] to Apley where we found an immensity to do in arranging stalls &c. I never got back until past 7.*

***Tuesday 26th August** - Mrs Whitmore[69] came, she is very well indeed. Quite later Henry returned from London. Poor Kitty's[52] funeral was in the morning.*

***Wednesday 27th August** - Mrs Whitmore went to Apley Castle. Mr Bluck & Henry rode out and I prepared for the Bazaar & wrote to poor Mrs Garforth.[52]*

***Thursday 28th August** - The Bazaar and Flower Show at Apley. Great crowds and great heat & a great deal of money taken. I had about £10's worth of things in my stall and made £25 of it. Mr Bluck helping very much.*

***Friday 29th August** - A second day of the Bazaar. All things were sold. We were tired quite to death.*

***Saturday 30th August** - Mrs Whitmore, Mama and I went to call at the Rectory Broseley and on the Pritchards,[8] and only Mrs Pritchard at home. Such a perfect day.*

***Sunday 31st August** - We went to church in the morning and in the afternoon Mrs Whitmore, Mama, Mr Bluck and Henry went to Kemberton. I stayed and wrote letters.*

***Monday 1st September** - Louisa[16] came over from Cotsbrook[67] to luncheon bringing Lady Georgina and Lady Eliz., Nina, Mary, Emmy[43] & Walter & Douglas[54] rode, stayed the afternoon.*

***Tuesday 2nd September** - Mrs Whitmore[69] went with me to call at Willey - we saw the new Lady Forester[46] and were charmed with her. Went to see Dr and Mrs Rowley after. Henry and Mr Bluck went to Kemberton.*

***Wednesday 3rd September** - The Austins and Miss Lucina at luncheon. Mr and Mrs Hayes[19] & Mrs Edwards at dinner.*

***Thursday 4th September** - Henry and Mr Bluck went to Bridgnorth for the Annual Sermon. It was preached byy the Bishop of Hereford and a very good collection, £36. Lady Louisa and ourselves had luncheon at the Sparkes. George & Sarah[15] & Walter & Emily[54] were going to Dudmaston & we drove there also. The garden most beautiful. Uncle Wolryche[55] was at home and we saw the Gatacres & Miss Forbes and Adml. Bridgeman. Henry & Mr Bluck dined at Kemberton where I took them and came home very tired.*

Friday 5th September - *Mrs Whitmore*[69] *left us for Kemberton and the Wilmots*[47] *came to us from there.*

Saturday 6th September - *Col. Wilmot*[44] *spent the morning in devising a new flower garden & in the afternoon we went to Apley.*

Sunday 7th September - *Walked to church here in the morning and to Little Wenlock in the afternoon. Col. & Mrs Wilmot,*[44] *Henry, Mr Bluck and I.*

Monday 8th September - *Emily and Col. Wilmot,*[44] *Henry and I drove to Davenport to call upon Lord & Lady Newport. Met Mrs Whitmore and Sarah, Howards and Boddingtons! Called on Mrs Austin and Mrs Isaacson. Lady Louisa, Tom*[10] *& Nina*[43] *& Douglas*[26] *came to dine. Lovely weather. I wish we were at Achnacarry.*

Tuesday 9th September - *Mama, Mr Bluck and I went to Shrewsbury to see Mr Corbet's house before the sale. Emily & Col. Wilmot*[44] *and Henry went to Bridgnorth. Mr Edmonds*[56] *at dinner.*

Wednesday 10th September - *We were to have gone on a picnic to the Terrace but l'homme proposes et Dieu dispose! Uncle Charles*[57] *has been attacked with Paralysis. Henry & Emily*[47] *have been at Stockton all day! Col. Wilmot*[44] *has a bad cold.*

Thursday 11th September - *The same thing again. Henry & Emily*[44] *went to Stockton and Col. Wilmot*[44] *nursed his cold in the library. Mr Bluck fished in the Pond. Also it was arranged that the Wilmots*[44] *stayed until Monday.*

Friday 12th September - *Emily*[44] *did not go again today. Henry rode over.*

Saturday 13th September - *Emily and Henry went to Stockton, Col. Wilmot*[44] *made plans for a new Library Terrace. (at The White House)*

Sunday 14th September - *At church here in the morning. Drove to Stockton in the afternoon & went there to church & I saw Uncle Charles.*[57] *I think he will live yet some time by the way he spoke and looked.*

Monday 15th September - *Charlotte wrote from Stockton to ask Henry to go over before we go to Millichope. He went and found Uncle Charles*[57] *no worse. Col. Wilmot*[44] *& Emily & Mr Bluck started for London. Henry and I to Millichope. We found there Mrs Stockhouse Acton and Miss Boughton, Sir Offley Wakeman, Miss Shakespear & Mr Leighton.*

Tuesday 16th September - *Henry went out shooting. Miss Shakespear and I walked. Mr Hothman at dinner.*

Wednesday 17th September - *Henry shooting again. Miss Stoke, Miss Boughton and me a long walk - beautiful. Mrs C.P. had a bad cold. Edith Corbet is at Millichope, governess to the 3 pretty children.*

Thursday 18th September - *We came home. Henry rode to Kemberton & Stockton. Mrs Whitmore not well.*

Friday 19th September - *Henry and I went to Kemberton*[66] *for luncheon. We did not go to the Patshull Archery for the account was so bad of Uncle Charles*[57] *that we thought he might die and it rained torrents. Went to Stockton.*

Saturday 20th September - *Henry rode to Stockton. I went to Wellington to see Ellen Jones & wrote to Mrs Camae for her character.*

Sunday 21st September - *All day at Stockton. Luncheon with the Isaacsons.*

Monday 22nd September - *Henry rode to Stockton. I stayed at home very busy. Crawford*[20] *goes in a week.*

Tuesday 23rd September - *Mr Mrs and Miss Greig came to stay with us. Mama and I have colds.*

Wednesday 24th September - *We went all except Mama to Apley. Tea at The Cave. Hayes,*[19] *Mr Potter and Mr G. Edmonds*[56] *dined.*

Thursday 25th September - *Mr and Miss Gatacre, Henry and I went to Enville. Luncheon at Gatacre Park.*

Friday 26th September - *We walked. Henry rode to Stockton.*

Saturday 27th September - *Rain, rain, cold very bad. Mama better. We could not go out. Henry took Mrs & Miss Gatacre to Buildwas Abbey in the afternoon.*

Sunday 28th September - *Rain! drove to church.*

Monday 29th September - *Rain all day!*

Tuesday 30th September - *Crawford*[20] *left & Mrs Jones came. The Greigs left us. Mrs Charlton & Lucy at luncheon. Henry to Stockton.*

Wednesday 1st October - *Henry went to shoot at Hatton and I went with him & then on to Kemberton & after luncheon to Stockton. Poor Uncle Charles*[57] *has a nurse, Mrs Mincher, but very ill! George went with me. Mrs Whitmore*[69] *still at Kemberton.*[66]

Thursday 2nd October - *Henry and I to Dudmaston*[55] *till Saturday. Adml. and Mrs and 3 Miss Bridgemans,*[4] *Mr John Bridgeman & Mr Franks. Singing & Letters.*

Friday 3rd October - *Henry rode to Stockton, got very wet. Mr and Mrs & Miss Sparkes at dinner - Letters.*

Saturday 4th October - *Came home. Henry rode, pouring rain!*

Sunday 5th October - *Went to church here.*

Monday 6th October - *Henry and I to Kemberton*[66] *for luncheon. George*[15] *went with us to Stockton. Wet and cold.*

Tuesday 7th October - *Mama and I to Apley Castle for luncheon. Only Louisa and Douglas and Miss Wigginton at home. Henry to Stockton.*

Wednesday 8th October - *Henry to Stockton.*

Thursday 9th October - *Henry and I went to Bridgnorth Cattle Show and then to Stanley*[15a] *for 2 nights - Miss Egremont, Lily, Pauline & Ted. Mr & Mrs Ashworth, 2 Mr Leekes, 3 Mr Christies. At dinner Mr Bellet and his son, Mr Wing, Dr, Mrs and Miss Rowley.*

Friday 10th October - *Rain all day & we could not go out. Henry went out to shoot. Went over the house. Mr Mrs and Miss Sparkes at dinner & Miss Pritchard.*

Saturday 11th October - *Came home. We went to Bridgnorth and paid some visits and had luncheon and then to Stockton for an hour or two. Mr Bluck arrived.*

Sunday 12th October - *Went to church here.*

Monday 13th October - *We went to Stockton. Poor Uncle Charles*[57] *gets worse but goes thro' the form of dinner.*

Tuesday 14th October - *Our dinner to the Mayor and Corporation of Bridgnorth. George & Sarah*[15] *came and Mr and Mrs Webb!*

Wednesday 15th October - *We went to Willey until Friday. Mr and Mrs O. Forester, old Major Forester, Mr Fane & Lord Granby. The 2 Miss Anstices*[68] *dined and Rowleys.*

Thursday 16th October - *A long walk. Henry walked home. A very merry dinner considering Lady N. was not there.*

Friday 17th October - *We were asked to stay over today but could not. Photography. Came home. Henry rode to Stockton.*

Saturday 18th October - *Walked with Mama yesterday and got toothache. Laid up with it today.*

Sunday 19th October - *Better but did not go to church. Went to Stockton.*

Monday 20th October - *Not well but Mama and I went to Wenlock.*

Tuesday 21st October - *Better. Henry at Stockton.*

Wednesday 22nd October - *The Bazaar at Wenlock. Henry and I and Mr Bluck went to it. A great crowd. In the evening we went to dine with the Pritchards,*[8] *Capt. and Mrs Brazier, Mdme de Negro and Mrs Harrison, Mrs and Miss More, Mr and Mrs Anstice,*[68] *and Mr J.A. and Mrs Gildenmonds, Mr Wilde Browne.*

Thursday 23rd October - *Went to Stockton. Poor Uncle Charles*[57] *as ill as possible. We refused a visit at Chyknell as it is of no use to be able to expect to go.*

Friday & Saturday 24th & 25th October - *Both days Henry at Stockton, and I busy with the Book case. On Saturday Mama and I went to Madeley Wood to call on the W.R. Anstices*[68] *and to Dale House.*[64]

Sunday 26th October - *Went to Stockton in the afternoon, called for George & Sarah,*[15] *found Louisa*[16] *there and poor Uncle Charles*[57] *very ill. Charlotte said he had said Goodbye to her & thanked Mrs Mincher in the night. The dreadful wounds had to be dressed and he could hardly get any comfortable position whilst we stayed.*

Monday, Tuesday & Wednesday 27th, 28th & 29th October - *All 3 days Henry went to Stockton and I stayed and routed the Book case &c.*

Thursday 30th October - *Henry and I went after luncheon and found Uncle Charles*[57] *dying. A change came about half past 12 and he lay without much visible suffering except gasping for breath sometimes. He did not take any notice and did not appear to hear Mr Isaacson when he offered up the last Prayer. He died as peacefully as possible and George & Sarah*[15] *& Louisa*[16] *were all there in time to see the last at 4 o'clock. Poor Charlotte was very much distressed but she would not leave the house until the funeral is over. Mr Bellet came too late. Tom*[10] *in the evening. He only returned from his Irish tour on Monday. George & Sarah*[15] *stayed and we took them home. Quantities of letters. Henry and I felt very old and as if it had been a long day.*

Friday 31st October - *This day we should have been at Chyknell. Henry went over to Stockton. The funeral fixed for Monday.*

Saturday 1st November - *Very quiet day. All in the house. Mr and Mrs Hayes*[19] *called.*

Editors note:
The following entry for 1st November appears in an appendix at the end of the Journal for 1856. (See Comment 1856, p.407.)

1st November - *Began to pull down Sunniside House.*

Sunday 2nd November - *Henry and Mr Bluck went to Little Wenlock. I in bed with a stiff neck. We were shocked by a letter from Malvern, Lord Bandon*[37] *died suddenly on Friday.*

Monday 3rd November - *The day of the funeral. Henry returned announcing that George is to have Stockton.*[57] *Certainly bought for him by Mrs Whitmore*[69] *for £7000 owing to her.*

Tuesday 4th November - *Mama took me over to Stockton to say Goodbye to Charlotte. I found Louisa*[16] *there and George & Sarah*[15] *all inspecting the plate, &c. Henry not at all well.*

Wednesday 5th November - *Henry did not get up for breakfast but better. I busy with my Catalogues in the Library.*

Thursday 6th November - *Henry and Mr Bluck went to London. In the afternoon a long visit from Mr and Mrs H. Burton (or Barton). Lady Newport and Mrs Gaskell left cards.*

Friday 7th November - *Mama and I went to call at Haughton Aston and on Mrs Cunliffe. Found nobody at home! London so full Henry could not be taken in at Howchins, at 10 Arlington Street.*

Saturday 8th November - *Rain rain. I could not go out and I wanted to call at Willey.*

Sunday 9th November - *Rain and I did not go out. Mama in.*

Monday 10th November - *I went to Willey. Saw Lady Forester*[46] *and Mr Cotes - called at the Rectoryy and Mrs John Pritchard*[8] *but found nobody. It was cold and Lady Forester*[46] *had a bad cold.*

Tuesday 11th November - *Mama and I to Kemberton*[66] *in the open carriage from which I am afraid she suffered. George & Sarah*[15] *were at Stockton.*

Wednesday 12th November - *Henry came home & has brought such pretty things - a tulle gown and a shawl for me & Mama has given me a black moire antique & such a pretty violet & bead head dress from Foster's!*

Thursday 13th November - *The Infirmary Meeting.*[58] *I wore my shawl! Lady Forester*[46] *held the Plate with Mr John Pritchard.*[8] *Sir Vincent Corbet threw it over at the last. Miss Mary Childe & Col. Percy Herbert the others. Archdeacon Waring preached the Sermon & the collection was £280. We had 3 invitations to the Ball! Called at Apley Castle on our return.*

Friday 14th November - *Busy all day in the Library.*

Saturday 15th November - *Henry went to Bridgnorth. Mama and I to Marnwood*[31] *& Severn House.*

Sunday 16th November - *We went to church here and at Little Wenlock in the afternoon & paid such a long visit at the Rectory it was almost dark as we trotted home thro' the puddles. Mr and Mrs Edmonds are returned from Ireland.*

Monday 17th November - *I was busy with my Catalogue. Henry went to pay visits at home.*

Tuesday 18th November - *We came to Bridgnorth to stay at The Crown 'til Saturday. Henry walked from Stockton where the Sale is going on. George*[15] *is to have Stockton, Mr Wing*[60] *Astley Abbotts. After dinner & concert to which Louisa*[16] *came & brought 5 daughters - Mrs Sparkes & Mrs Alfred Darby.*[15a]

Wednesday 19th November - *We had a fine day and began our visits early and paid 19. We went out to the Woodlands and to Oldbury*[59] *- Dined at 6 and went to Church in the evening.*

Thursday 20th November - *We left early and called upon Mrs Smith and Mrs Bagott at Stanmore. Then luncheon at Gatacre & thence to Chyknell. So far everybody at home. Met the Kettles so could not do our duty at Dallicott and Lady Newport was not at Davenport so we did not call there. Mrs Brazier, Mrs Broadbent and then in the rain to see Mrs Clarke. We were very lucky in our day no rain to signify. We had our dinner at The Crown. Mr Mrs & Miss Bellet, Mr Merriman, Mr Marshall & Mr Wing*[60] *who goes to Hereford tomorrow to be inducted into his Living of Astley Abbotts.*

Friday 21st November - *To Jaintree - then visits to Bridgnorth until dark and Mr and Mrs Philips at dinner.*

Saturday 22nd November - *We shall have paid 60 visits altogether, have "done it very handsome" this time. Going home now. Stayed at Stockton saw George for a minute there. "Captain St John" came to dine and stayed over Sunday.*

Sunday 23rd November - *We went to church at the Ironbridge for a School Charity Sermon - not particularly edifying. Such lovely warm weather but I have a cold & not at all well!*

Monday 24th November - *St John left us this morning. Henry went for all day to a Propagation of the Gospel Meeting at Bridgnorth. Mama and I called upon Uncle Richard*[18] *who looks very ill! and Mrs Hayes*[19] *- And I lost Toozie*[6] *and such people rushing over the Park and found him myself sitting at the door of Dale House.*[64] *Henry has Mrs Whitmore's*[69] *letter about the Living. To be sure what wicked people there are!*

Tuesday 25th November - *The CBC M. Only Mr Roche came to it. Very cold day and snowing tonight. I busy amongst the Catalogues.*

Wednesday 26th November - *As I was very busy amongst the Books, St John came in to ask us to Apley Castle till Monday. We go.*

Thursday 27th November - *Henry and I went to Apley Castle. Mrs Garforth*[52] *and Maria there & Capt. Bridgeman and a Mr Coleman.*

Friday 28th November - *The Gentlemen went to shoot at Wytheford. We had a long walk and were caught in the snow.*

Saturday 29th November - *Mr and Mrs Browning at dinner. Mr Coleman went back to Ireland.*

Sunday 30th November - *Twice at church - Very cold. Tea with Lucy and Dora.*

Monday 1st December - *Henry left Apley Castle early to shoot at Apley - Deep snow. Mamey's dancing lessons. In the afternoon I went by the Railway* *to meet Henry at Aston. We had there Mrs and Miss Thursby Pelham - Capt. Kenyon and some other gentlemen. Mr Bottfield dined there. A charming round of game. Lottery Tickets.*

Tuesday 2nd December - *The Poultry Show at Birmingham. We went with the Uvedale Corbets, Pelhams &c., and Lord & Lady Newport got into the carriage. Walked to the Worcester Station and saw John & Lucy Forbes*[13] - *William Whitmore - Lady Louisa*[16] *& 3 daughters. At the show Hartopps, Scotts, & Foleys, Sir Thomas Winnington, Lord Dartmouth in great force, &c. Came home from Birmingham to receive Mrs Garforth*[52] *and Maria.*

Wednesday 3rd December - *Very cold. Mrs Garforth*[52] *went out by herself to the kitchen garden. St John came in the evening.*

Thursday 4th December - *A long walk with Mrs Garforth and Maria.*[52] *Henry in bed with a bad cold. Could not go to shoot with Tom and St John went by himself. Bitter cold. Mr and Mrs Anstice*[68] *and Mr J. Anstice*[68] *at dinner & some singing.*

Friday 5th December - *A thaw. In the house all day. Henry's cold very bad. Mr & Mrs Webb called.*

Saturday 6th November - *St John went away early - Mrs Garforth*[52] *and Maria after luncheon. I went to see Uncle Richard*[18] *& found him better. William Whitmore arrived.*

Sunday 7th December - *Went to church with Mr William Whitmore. Long walk also. Left Henry in bed.*

Monday 8th December - *Henry went to Shrewsbury for the Assizes - a Supernumerary Winter Assize on account of 2 murders. Mr William Whitmore went to see the "works" and in the afternoon Mama drove to Coalport.*[61] *Very warm. Mr William Whitmore left us then for Apley Castle. Henry not at all well - came home to dinner.*

Tuesday 9th December - *Henry and I came to Chetwynd*[62] *for three nights, 14 miles, ponies came in less than 2 hours. Mrs Uvedale Corbet here & Henry & Mildred. Miss Brooke & Mr John Bridgeman, Mr and Lester Leeke at dinner. Jones went with our things by the Railway & got taken to Longford.*[63]

Wednesday 10th December - *Rain - After luncheon it cleared up and Mrs Borough took Miss Brooke, Henry and I to call at Aquilate. We found Lady Baughey at home - Sir John Kynaston arrived - Mr Jellico at dinner.*

Thursday 11th December - *Walked in the Gardens. In the afternoon drove to Meretown where the Miss Hills live but are soon to leave it. The Gentlemen went out shooting, all but Sir John Kynaston who went with Miss Brooke, Miss Corbet and me in the "Sociable". Mr Borough drove Mrs Corbet in her pony carriage - afternoon & Mrs Eyton & Gen. Cumberland at dinner - she sings well.*

Friday 12th December - *Left Chetwynd.*[62] *The whole party breaking up. We went to Apley Castle for luncheon. Mrs G. and all still there. Tommy*[10] *arrived. Mrs Swetenham is there and her little boy - Came home.*

Saturday 13th December - *Henry went to Bridgnorth. Rain. Mama and I went to Shrewsbury shopping. Met St John who personated Henry and was told that he was "very like his Mother". Such an awful thing this morning. Dunbar tried to murder his wife and then cut his own throat, he still lives. We went to Mr Webb to ask about them and there is great doubt about both.*

Sunday 14th December - *Went to church here and Henry to Little Wenlock the afternoon.*

Monday 15th December - *Started directly after breakfast. Henry and I went to Kemberton*[66] *- to Weston for luncheon, Lord & Lady Bradford*[4] *there, Lady Lucy & Miss Moncrieffe to Patshull, to Badger and to Cotsbrook.*[67] *Afterwards Matilda & Abraham Darby were arrived when we got home.*

Tuesday 16th December - *Abraham Darby went away early. There was an examination at the school & Henry gave them tea and buns and there were Dissolving Views, we were there from 3 to 7 & I caught a cold.*

Wednesday 17th December - *Henry and I went to Longford*[63] *for two nights. Mr and Lady Augusta Mostyn were there and Mr Baughey.*

Thursday 18th December - *My cold beginning to be very tiresome. Did not go out. At dinner the Miss Hills and Mr Cavendish Taylor came to stay & shoot. Whist.*

Friday 19th December - *We did not leave until evening that Henry might shoot. We went out after luncheon to see a little cover shoot. Very cold as we drove home. Found Matilda and Mama all comfortable - and at dinner Mrs Edmund Darby & Mary.*[64] *Mr and Mrs & Miss G. Edmonds, Mr and Miss Hayes*[19] *- Rebecca. Cold very bad!*

Saturday 20th December - *Abraham Darby in the evening. Poor Dunbar died.*

Sunday 21st December - *I in bed. Abraham & Matilda & Henry went to church here & they went to luncheon at Dale House.*[64] *Henry to Little Wenlock.*

Monday 22nd December - *Abraham left us. Matilda and I painting all day. She and Mama went to pay some visits. Prince ill. Henry shooting at Apley. Douglas & Walter*[26] *came.*

Tuesday 23rd December - *Matilda went away. Douglas & Walter*[26] *here. Lord Queensbury's*[65] *death.*

Wednesday 24th December - *Douglas & Walter*[26] *went home and Henry with them to luncheon. Mr Bluck arrived. Hung up the mistletoe. Poor Prince getting better.*

Thursday 25th December - Christmas Day - *A deep snow & nobody could go out.*

Friday 26th December - *So cold and we all prisoners.*

Saturday 27th December - *The same sort of day but we went to Bridgnorth for me to try on my gown. Post horses & Mama's carriage.*

Sunday 28th December - *So slippery neither Mama nor I could go out. Henry and Mr Bluck did.*

Monday 29th December - *We put the Library to rights. Mr George Edmonds[56] called.*

Tuesday 30th December - *George & Sarah[15] came for two nights.*

Wednesday 31st December - New Year's Eve - *It was so warm that we sat with the windows open to hear the bells ringing at 12 o'clock. Games, &c. & Whist. It is always sad taking leave of an old year & beginning the New one. We don't know what the new one may bring us.*

NOTES

1. Wroxeter where Henry and Adelaide went for the New Hunt Ball, was the home of Rev. Edward Egremont, vicar of Wroxeter and his wife. Louisa was their daughter who had married Capt. Russell RN in 18??
2. Pitchford Hall is a fine timbered hall approximately six miles south of Shrewsbury.
3. Lord Hill was of the family based at Hawkestone Park and was related to Lord Berwick of Attingham Park.
4. Bridgeman was the family name of the Earl of Bradford of Weston Park, Shropshire. In 1856 Lord Bradford was George Augustus Frederick Henry (1789-1865) who was the 2nd Earl. Lady Bradford was his wife.
5. Lord Powys, a member of the Herbert family was probably still the leading political figure in Shropshire and mid-Wales. His home was at Powys Castle, Welshtown.
6. Toozie was the pet dog.
7. Mrs Edmund Darby was Lucy Darby, widow of Edmund Darby who had died in 1810. She lived at Dale House with her daughter Mary. Henry Dickinson lived at Severn House and had recently lost his wife Deborah Darby, younger daughter of Lucy and Edmund Darby.
8. John Pritchard was a banker at Broseley. He had become a second Member of Parliament for Bridgnorth after the Election Petition in 1852.
9. Mr and Mrs Forester were probably the brother (and his wife) of Lord and Lady Forester of Willey, Shropshire. Mr Forester succeeded to the title in 1874.
10. Tom or Tommy was Thomas Charlton Whitmore of Apley, the elder brother of Henry Whitmore and the previous Member of Parliament for Bridgnorth.
11. Mr Webb was the surgeon from Shrewsbury.
12. Mr Gwyther was the vicar of Madeley.

13. Lucy Forbes was a cousin of Henry Whitmore. She had married Col. John Forbes, Coldstream Guards in 1849.
14. John Storer MA, who died on 13th January 1856, was the Rector of Hawksworth, Notts. He had married Elizabeth Whitmore, an aunt of Henry Whitmore in 1818.
15. George Whitmore was the Rector of Stockton, near Apley. He was an elder brother of Henry Whitmore and lived with his wife Sarah (née Deacon) at Kemberton.
15a. Mrs Alfred Darby (née Christy) was the widow of Alfred Darby (brother of Abraham Darby IV) who died in 1852. She lived at Stanley Hall, Bridgnorth.
16. Lady Louisa Whitmore was the daughter of the Marquis of Queensbury and was married to Thomas Charlton Whitmore, eldest brother of Henry Whitmore.
17. Stoke Court in Buckinghamshire was the home of Abraham Darby IV formerly of The Chesnuts, Coalbrookdale who was married to Matilda, elder sister of Adelaide Whitmore.
18. Richard Darby of "Rosehill", Coalbrookdale was the younger brother of Francis Darby of The White House, Adelaide's father.
19. Mr Hayes was the vicar of Coalbrookdale.
20. Crawford and Seabrook were servants.
21. This was an important visit. Lord Henry Lennox (1821-86), son of the Duke of Richmond, was a close associate of Benjamin Disraeli and belonged to Disraeli's small circle of intimate young friends (mostly life-long batchelors) who sustained Disraeli and provided him with a network of social diplomacy and political information.
22. The Carlton Club in St James Street was the unofficial headquarters of the Conservative Party.
23. Possibly Miss Caroline Wrottesley, a relative of Lord Wrottesley, Co. Stafford.
24. Sir Robert Pigot, 4th Baronet, of Patshull. Related to the Dartmouth family. He had been elected as Member of Parliament for Bridgnorth in 1852 but lost his seat the following year on presentation of an election petition.
25. Lady Elizabeth Tollemache and Augustus Tollemache MA (1839-1923) were members of the Manners family. He became vicar of Whitwick, Leicester 1874-94.
26. Douglas and Walter were the sons of Thomas Charlton Whitmore (Henry's eldest brother) and Lady Louisa Whitmore of Apley. Douglas was a pupil at Eton.
27. Ecarté was a game of cards for two.
28. Lord Newport of Weston Park, Shropshire, was a member of the Bridgeman family (see note 4 above). He was a close associate and neighbour of the Whitmore family.
29. Possibly this was Charles Newdegate, a Whip in the House of Commons and a purchaser, in 1858 of Disraeli's newspaper *The Press*.
30. Cuckoo Oak is in Madeley on the A442.
31. Mr and Mrs Bartlett lived at Marnwood on the Coalbrookdale-Buildwas road. Mr Bartlett was the incumbent of Buildwas Church.
32. Joseph Dickinson was the eldest son of Barnard and Ann Dickinson of Eastfield, Coalbrookdale.

33. This marked the virtual end of the Crimean War. It was formalised by the Treaty of Paris of 30th May 1856.
34. John Ella (1802-88) was an English violinist, conductor and critic. From 1845 to 1880 he ran the Musical Union subscription concerts, and from 1852 he started the Musical Winter Evenings. These were exclusive gatherings. Henry and Adelaide Whitmore were subscribers as also were Abraham and Matilda Darby of Stoke Court.
35. Gerald was the infant son of George and Sarah Whitmore of Kemberton.
36. The Drawing Room was a Royal Court Levée.
37. Lord Bernard was a relative of Lord Bandon of Bandon and Castle Bernard Co. Cork (Lady Bandon was formerly Catherine Whitmore of Apley. "Mamey" and "Catty" were also members of the Bandon family.
37a. The Duke of Manchester was previously Lord Mandeville who succeeded to the Dukedom in August 1855. It was his political appointment within the Conservative Party that Henry Whitmore accepted in late 1855. This was the background to the civility which was shown to the Whitmores by Disraeli and the Duke of Manchester at the Duchess of Northumberland's Reception.
38. The Deacons came from Mabledon Park, Kent. George Whitmore's wife Sarah was formerly Miss Sarah Deacon (see note 15 above).
39. This was an "At Home" organised by Lady Derby. Her husband, Edward Stanley, 14th Earl of Derby was the leader of the Conservative Party, although Benjamin Disraeli was the intellectual driving force within the party.
40. The London house of the Duke and Duchess of Northumberland.
41. Douglas was the family name of the Marquis of Queensbury. Thomas Charlton Whitmore's wife was Lady Louisa Douglas, eldest daughter of the Marquis (see note 15a above).
42. Grosvenor Gate was a splendid house overlooking Hyde Park. Benjamin secured occupation of it through his marriage to Mary Anne, widow of Tommy Wyndham Lewis who had died in 1838. Mary Anne was left a life interest by Wyndham Lewis in Grosvenor Gate, which was far beyond Disraeli's means.
43. Nina, Mary and Emmy were daughters of Thomas Charlton Whitmore and Lady Louisa Whitmore. They were nieces of Henry Whitmore.
44. Col. Wilmot of Malvern, was married to Emily, who was Henry Whitmore's cousin.
45. Lord Redesdale of Kedleston Hall, Derbyshire.
46. This was the wedding of John George Weld Forester, 2nd Baron Forester PC, MP, and Countess Alexandria Julia Theresa Wilhelmina Sophia, widow of last Viscount Melbourne and daughter of Joachim Charles Louis Mortine Count von Maltzan.
47. Relatives of Col. Wilmot of Malvern who was married to Emily Whitmore.
48. Edward Stanley, 14th Earl of Derby was the acknowledged leader of the Conservative Party. His main interest was shooting and field sports. Intellectually he could not be compared with Benjamin Disraeli who really ran the party.
49. Lady Wrottesley was the wife of 2nd Baron Wrottesley (1798-1867) of Co. Stafford. She was the daughter of Thomas Giffard of Chillington, Staffordshire.

50. Possibly Lady "H" was Lady Elizabeth Holland who was a prominent member of the Whig Party.
51. The Review of the Army at Aldershot was organised to mark the successful outcome of the Crimean War and led to the establishment of Aldershot as the "Home of the British Army".
52. The Garforths of Wigganthorpe Hall, near York, had been close friends and associates of the Whitmores since their arrival in London and were involved in the political scene. Kitty was one of their daughters (Maria was the other) and was also a close friend. Sadly she died on 21st August 1856.
53. Lord Malmesbury was a prominent member of the Conservative Party and had been Foreign Secretary in Lord Derby's first Administration and later also in the second Administration. He became Lord Privy Seal in the third Administration.
54. Nina, Mary, Emmy (Emily), Walter and Douglas were all children of Thomas Charlton Whitmore and Lady Louisa.
55. William Wolryche Whitmore (1787-1858) was the owner of Dudmaston, south of Bridgnorth.
56. Mr George Edmonds was the Rector of Little Wenlock.
57. Rev. Charles Whitmore was the brother of Thomas Whitmore, Henry Whitmore's father. He was therefore Uncle Charles. He had also been the Rector of Stockton (near Apley) before Henry's brother, George became Rector. Charles continued to live at Stockton whilst George lived at Kemberton.
58. The Infirmary (Hospital) Meeting was the annual fundraising service at St Chads, Shrewsbury. It was supported by all the leading families in Shropshire. The privilege of holding the plate was an honour.
59. Oldbury is on the southern outskirts of Bridgnorth.
60. Mr Wing was the vicar nominated for the living at Astley Abbotts, north of Bridgnorth.
61. Coalport is at the eastern end of the Ironbridge Gorge. It was established in the 1790s by William Reynolds and was the home of the Coalport China Company.
62. Chetwynd is north west of Newport, Shropshire.
63. Longford is near Market Drayton, Shropshire.
64. Dale House, Coalbrookdale was the home of Lucy Darby (Mrs Edmund Darby) and Mary Darby, the mother and sister of Abraham Darby IV.
65. Lord Queensbury was the father of Lady Louisa Whitmore (née Douglas), wife of Thomas Charlton Whitmore.
66. Kemberton was the home of Rev. George Whitmore, elder brother of Henry Whitmore, and of Sarah Whitmore (née Deacon) his wife.
67. Cotsbrook was about 2 miles northeast of Apley. Thomas Charlton Whitmore and Lady Louisa his wife had moved there from Apley in 1854.
68. The Anstice family were distant relatives of the Darbys. They were the proprietors of the Madeley Wood Company. John Anstice, the principal partner, lived at Madeley Wood Hall. His brother William Reynolds Anstice, also a partner, was a solicitor and was Steward of the Manor of Madeley.
69. Mrs Whitmore was the mother of Henry Whitmore and was therefore Adelaide's mother-in-law.

1857

Comment

Henry Whitmore's uncle Rev. Charles Blaney Cavendish Whitmore MA (1787-1856), the former Rector of Stockton, near Apley, had died in October 1856. The Rectory in which he had lived seems to have been in the gift of the Whitmore family and it was therefore decided that the Rectory should become the home of Henry's brother Rev. George Whitmore MA (1812-1900) who had succeeded his uncle as Rector of Stockton. This removal to Stockton from Kemberton was duly recorded by Adelaide in her Journal.

Henry's parliamentary duties required his attendance in London and they rented No. 10 Lowndes Street for the season. Disraeli had been active on behalf of the Conservative Party during the recess and he immediately mounted an attack on Lord Palmerston's government about a secret treaty of December 1854 by which, in return for Austria's support in the Crimean War, England and France had guaranteed the security of Austrian possessions in Italy for the duration of the war. Much to Disraeli's discomfort, the House was singularly unimpressed by this revelation. The assault on the government was continued however by Disraeli and Gladstone over the Budget, but once again the attack failed. Success came with a third attack, over a Chinese vessel at Canton, manned by a Chinese crew but flying the British flag. A Mandarin arrested the Chinese crew and although they were released after protest, the Canton government refused to apologise. As a result British gunboats bombarded the port.

This incident was debated in the House and was noted in Adelaide's Journal for 27th February. Adelaide also recorded (3rd March) that the "Chinese question was decided against Government by 16, at 3 o'clock in the morning". Lord Palmerston immediately appealed to the country on the issue and was triumphantly returned with an increased majority. In Bridgnorth there was no contest and Henry was duly elected on 27th March with Adelaide recording that "the Bells rang there and at the Dale where we came home with 4 horses.

Apart from the Election the London political scene proceeded much as usual. Henry and Adelaide gave up No. 10 Lowndes Street but in October they took No. 1 Lowndes Street for the next two years.

1st January - New Year's Day - *George and Sarah left us.*[1] *Henry & Mr Bluck*[6] *rode over to Stockton, &c.*

Friday 2nd January - *Henry and I went to Weston*[2] *for 3 nights. Found there Uncle Wolryche,*[3] *Mr Cavendish Taylor, and all the rest Bridgemans.*[2]

Adml. and Mrs Bridgeman, 3 daughters and one son, the Edmund Bridgemans, Lady Lucy, Lady Charlotte & Miss Moncrieffe & Mr J. Hall & Capt. Orlando Bridgeman.

Saturday 3rd January - *Walk with Lady Bridgeman. Music & Whist in the evening.*

Sunday 4th January - *Twice at church. Mr George Bridgeman & a friend of his at dinner. New Year's Gift Books in the evening & Prayers in the Dining Room. 55 of us!*

Monday 5th January - *Came home.*

Tuesday 6th January - *In Bridgnorth for the Ball. Mrs Knock's gown for me very pretty - white silk & white crape petticoat. Above red ribbons & feather head dress. Pleasant rather.*

Wednesday 7th January - *Very ill, sick & sorry as usual. Came home about 3 o'clock. Had to walk down Lincoln Hill, post horses & so slippery. I went to bed directly.*

Thursday 8th January - *A thaw. Henry went to Cotsbrook*[4] *for luncheon.*

Friday 9th January - *John and Lucy*[5] *arrive.*

Saturday 10th January - *John and Lucy*[5] *& I went to call on the Rowleys & Mrs Forester. Such a fine day.*

Sunday 11th January - *Very wet, but twice at church, here and at Little Wenlock, post horses.*

Monday 12th January - *Henry took John and Lucy*[5] *to Apley for luncheon.*

Tuesday 13th January - *John and Lucy*[5] *left us to stay at Kemberton.*[1] *Henry and I & Mr Bluck went to dine at Apley Castle and then the Dispensary Ball at Wellington.*

Wednesday 14th January - *Mama took me to call upon the Isaacsons who are leaving. Met John and Lucy*[5] *and went to the Rectory where George & Sarah*[1] *were looking over the bare walls & floors, &c.*

Thursday 15th January - *The Hunt Ball. Mr & Mrs Anstice*[7] *& Miss Webb called here. Henry and I & Mr Bluck went from here to Shrewsbury and returned, about half past 4 in the morning, very good Ball. Tom*[4] *took his 3 daughters from Apley Castle.*

Friday 16th January - *Called at Severn House.*[8]

Saturday 17th January - *Mr and Mrs Dickinson & Bernard called here. Henry and Mr Bluck at Bridgnorth.*

Sunday 18th January - *At church. The bride .... in our seat.*

Monday 19th January - *Mr & Mrs Sparkes & Jeanette arrived to stay 2 nights.*

Tuesday 20th January - *Walked and paid visits. At dinner Mr & Mrs Dickinson, Henry Dickinson,*[8] *Mr and Mrs Hayes*[9] *& her sister, Mr Edmonds.*[10]

Wednesday 21st January - *Mr and Mrs Crookes*[11] *and a son & daughter came to dine and we persuaded the Sparkes to stay & help us. Went to call on Mrs W.R. Anstice*[7] *in the morning.*

Thursday 22nd January - *Mr and Mrs & Miss Sparkes left us. Yesterday Henry went to Stockton to help to give Mr Isaacson a testimonial. Today the Palmers.*

Friday 23rd January - *Henry not well, nor Mama either. Catalogue.*

Saturday 24th January - *Mama and I went to Wellington & there heard of the sad death of poor Edward Egremont*[12] *of typhus fever at Selaby. I am very very sorry.*

Sunday 25th January - *So wet and cold, could not go out.*

Monday 26th January - *.....an old woman and sat at dinner.*

Tuesday 27th January - *Mr Bluck*[6] *went away. Henry went to Kemberton*[1] *for luncheon. Mr and Mrs R.D. Jones came to stay till Thursday.*

Wednesday 28th January - *Henry, Mr and Mrs Jones, and I at Kemberton*[1] *for luncheon. Then to Stockton & to Cotsbrook,*[4] *Whist, and very late!*

Thursday 29th January - *Jane and Robert Jones left us after luncheon and Henry and I came to Woodcote to stay till Saturday. Sir Frederick and Lady Smythe, & Lord Newport*[2] *here.*

Friday 30th January - *Shooting. Snow & very cold. We walked out. Very pleasant in the evenings. Lady Smythe sings beautifully.*

Saturday 31st January - *Came home. Tom*[4] *arrived to stay until Monday.*

Sunday 1st February - *At church. Tom*[4] *and I walked.*

Monday 2nd February - *Henry went to London for the meeting of Parliament tomorrow. It began to snow very fast and Tom*[4] *stayed on.*

Tuesday 3rd February - *The snow deep but it was fine & Tom*[4] *went home.*

Wednesday 4th February - *Snow still and Mama not well.*

Thursday & Friday 5th & 6th February - *The same.*

Saturday 7th February - *Mama better, we went to Coalport*[13] *to order the plates.*

Sunday 8th February - *Mama better and we went out - rain.*

Monday 9th February - *Went to Stanley.[14] Mrs Alfred Darby not at home. Called on Mrs John Pritchard,[15] Rebecca[15a] came to dine.*

Tuesday 10th February - *Did not go out.*

Wednesday 11th February - *To Worcester, 2 Mrs Burtons there.*

Thursday 12th February - *To Kemberton,[1] most likely for the last time. They begin to move. Sarah and the children going to Portman Square.*

Friday 13th February - *To Marnwood[16] & Mrs Graham.*

Saturday 14th February - *Henry returned for Sunday.*

Sunday 15th February - *At church. Then came the end of packing. I called upon Uncle and Aunt Richard Darby.[17]*

Monday 16th February - *Came to 10 Lowndes Street. Dined with Mrs Garforth.[53] Isles has thrown us over and we have only the kitchen maid.*

Tuesday 17th February - *Inventories being taken. Chandeliers in bags - No muslim curtains & Mrs Bristowe called.*

Wednesday 18th February - *Begin to get settled. Afternoon Mrs Denman called.*

Thursday 19th February - *Walked to Mrs Garforth's.[53] Henry not home to dine!*

Friday 20th February - *Lord Henry Lennox[18] and Mr Hamilton came to dine - Our cook Mrs Brothwell won't do.*

Saturday 21st February - *I was out all day paying visits. Henry dined with the Speaker. Lord Henry Lennox came with him to have some tea.*

Sunday 22nd February - *Mr Bluck here.[6] Henry fagged rather. Mr Wm. Whitmore[19] called.*

Monday 23rd February - *Very late night at the House.[20]*

Tuesday 24th February - *George & Sarah[1] came to Portman Square. Went out for the first time with the ponies.*

Wednesday 25th February - *Henry went to the House early and George came afterwards to luncheon. I drove out to pay visits. Mrs Brothwell left and Mary Collins came and we had a good dinner. Mr Bluck here.*

Thursday 26th February - *To see Sarah and to Westbourne Terrace &c. Henry went with me. Late very.*

Friday 27th February - *We went out early, such lovely weather but Henry has a bad cold - Late, fight about the Chinese war.[21]*

Saturday 28th February - *Went out early. Henry went to Sir W.J. Letters to bring up the forces on Monday. Mrs Garforth & Marie[53] dined with us.*

Lord Graham, Col. Taylor and Mr Christy. Oh, the blessing of a decent cook, ours prospers at present.

Sunday 1st March - *Henry not well, did not go out. I went to church in the afternoon. Mr Bluck here.*

Monday 2nd March - *Lord Henry Lennox*[18] *at luncheon. Dined at Mrs Deacon's.*[23] *Henry got away to dine. George & Sarah*[1] *there, Mr and Mrs J. Deacon,*[23] *4 sisters & Mr Bosanquet, &c.*

Tuesday 3rd March - *Lord Henry Lennox*[18] *& George at dinner. The fight upon the Chinese question was decided against Government by 16 at 3 o'clock in the morning.*[21]

Wednesday 4th March - *I went to Stoke Court*[30] *for the day. Matilda has a cold. Flowers. Mr Bluck at dinner. Henry is tired.*

Thursday 5th March - *Called upon Lady Middleton. Henry had not to go back to the House in the evening. Instead of going out of office Lord Palmerston dissolves.*[21]

Friday 6th March - *Paid visits, found Lady Kinnare at home. Henry dined at the Carlton Club,*[22] *came home to tea so that we had a nice long evening.*

Saturday 7th March - *Luncheon with Mr Bluck.*[6] *Dinner before the Speaker's Levée. Lord Newport, Lord Ch. Clinton, Lord Bective, Lord Naas, Sir Wm. Jolliffe, Col. Taylor, Col. Cole, Mrs G. Hamilton, Mr Stafford, Mrs Garforth*[53] *came to help me.*

Sunday 8th March - *Not well, and deep snow, hail.*

Monday 9th March - *So cold, took Henry to the House, and soon home. Mr Bluck,*[6] *ecarté.*[25]

Tuesday 10th March - *Called on Mrs John Pritchard.*[15] *Mr Bluck at dinner. John and Lucy*[5] *came to Chesterfield Street.*

Wednesday 11th March - *An early visit from the Pritchards.*[15] *We were asked to dine with Major and Mrs Knox, could not go. Dinner at home. Mrs and 2 Miss Charltons, Lucy and Col. Forbes*[5] *and Miss Forbes, Mrs George Whitmore*[1] *and Miss Deacon and Mr W. Deacon,*[23] *Mr Farnham, Mr Bluck, Mr Fitzroy, Lord Derby's Reception.*[24] *Mrs Anson there.*

Thursday 12th March - *Henry all day busy with his Election committee. Reception at Lady Granvilles, but I could not go with Henry. Headache.*

Friday 13th March - *Not quite well. Mr Bluck*[6] *and ecarté.*[25]

Saturday 14th March - *Lucy*[5] *went out with me from Chesterfield Street. Lord Henry Lennox*[18] *at dinner, going to Speaker's Levée.*

Sunday 15th March - *Stormy. Lucy*[5] *came and went to church with us in the afternoon. George Whitmore*[1] *is here too.*

Monday 16th March - *Tom[4] arrived. I had a long day driving about.*

Tuesday 17th March - *Henry & I went to dine with the Pritchards.[15] Met the Spearmans, the Baldocks. Mr and Mrs Vane. Mr and Mrs Brett. Mrs and Miss Gaskell. Sir Graham Montgomery. Capt. E. Forester.[27]*

Wednesday 18th March - *Went to the Princesses to see King Richard II, Miss Forbes[5] joins Mr Bluck, Henry and I. Headache, &c.*

Thursday 19th March - *Not up early! Tom[4] & George[1] both here at luncheon. Henry at the Election Committee. Dined at Lord Middleton's. John & Lucy,[5] Mr and Mrs Brodrick & his brother, and 2 Miss Tolleys.*

Friday 20th March - *I went to church to hear Mr Fremantle. Henry and I to Lady Jersey's in the evening.*

Saturday 21st March - *Henry & I and Tom[4] left London. We got to Bridgnorth for the Election. No contest which is a great blessing. We are staying at the Crown. Dined at Mrs Sparkes. Jeanette staying at Dudmaston,[3] came over for the evening with Miss Whitmore Jones.[26] Mr Purton dined.*

Sunday 22nd March - *Three times at church. Beautiful Sermon from Mr Bellet in the evening.*

Monday 23rd March - *Henry began his canvass with Mr Bellet, Mr Marshall, Capt. Law &c. Mama came to fetch me home, looking so well.*

Tuesday 24th March - *The new tile floor in the hall is so pretty and nice! Col. Forester called.[27] His Election is quiet too (Borough of Wenlock).*

Wednesday 28th March - *Was wet all day.*

Thursday 26th March - *I went back to Bridgnorth, George arrived and he and I dined. Henry had no dinner for there was an oyster supper in the Crown.*

Friday 27th March - *The Election. Mr Gatacre proposed Henry, and Henry made a speech of which I was very proud. All was quiet. The Bells rang there and at the Dale where we came home with 4 horses.*

Saturday 28th March - *Henry went to Shrewsbury. Mr Huddleston defected & Major Phibbs, Mr Slaney & Mr Tomlins to be petitioned against.*

Sunday 29th March - *So wet could not go to church.*

Monday 30th March - *Packing and Mama and I went to call on Uncle Richard Darby,[17] the "Queen",[28] and Mrs Hayes.[9]*

Tuesday 31st March - *Henry and I came back to Lowndes Street. Lucy[5] dined with us, poor Mr Bluck[6] came in after. I forgot to say in the proper place that we were horrified to hear of his father's death from an accident in London.*

Wednesday 1st April - *We went to dine in Portman Square. 20 people. The Dean of Canterbury & Mrs Dean, Mr & Miss Melville, Sir Edwin and Lady*

Pearson, Mr and Mrs J. Deacon,[23] *Mr and Mrs Wollaston Blake, George & Sarah*[1] *& ourselves, Mr Waldegrave & Mr Hankey.*

Thursday 2nd April - *Pony has a cold in its eyes - Walk with Henry. Dinner at home 12. John and Lucy,*[5] *George & Sarah,*[1] *Miss Ellen D., Mrs Garforth & Marie*[53] *and Mr Bluck*[6] *came out. George & William Whitmore,*[19] *2 Miss Forbes in the evening.*

Friday 3rd April - *Walk with George and Henry, came on to rain. Went to Jessier's about a bracelet for Charlotte. Mr Bluck at dinner.*

Saturday 4th April - *Such a wet day could not go out & Toozie*[29] *had to go to the stable! Dined at Chesterfield Street, Mr Beaumont, Mrs Parker, Mrs Garforth,*[53] *Maria & Frank.*

Sunday 5th April - *Twice at church. Mr Bluck and George at dinner.*

Monday 6th April - *Rather fine day. Went out with the ponies and called upon poor Mrs Bluck. Henry dined at the Carlton.*[22]

Tuesday 7th April - *Drove out but it rained. Henry has a cold. Mr Bluck dined here.*

Wednesday 8th April - *Henry quite laid up. Went to Coutts for him. Mr Bluck.*

Thursday 9th April - *I went to Stoke Court,*[30] *only Matilda at home. Came away by early train and found Henry had not been out all day. Mr Bluck came.*

Good Friday 10th April - *I went to church in the morning at Mr Liddel's. Henry not out all day and I beginning a cold. Mr Bluck*[6] *with us.*

Saturday 11th April - *Henry better but did not go out. Myself laid up quite - cold and bilious. Rainy. Mr Bluck here.*

Easter Sunday 12th April - *Could not go out - very sorry. We are both better. Henry went out. Mr Bluck.*

Monday & Tuesday 13th & 14th April - *Packing and settling to go home.*

Wednesday 15th April - *Henry and I and Mr Bluck*[6] *came home to dearest Mama. Brought Jones with us & Edwin.*

Thursday 16th April - *Ball at Broseley. Henry and I went to dine with the Pritchards.*[15] *Good band and a clean room. Pritchards, Sparkes, Roses & some Bridgnorth people.*

Friday 17th April - *Rested ourselves. Cold.*

Saturday 18th April - *Henry and I went to Bridgnorth & paid visits - Douglas*[4] *at luncheon.*

Sunday 19th April - *A Mr Layton preached in Mr Hayes absence at Oxford. I have a sprained ankle & could not walk to Little Wenlock.*

Monday 20th April *- Henry went to luncheon at Cotsbrook.[4] Mama and I and Mr Bluck called at Dale House[31] and Mama and I at Uncle Richard Darbys.[17]*

Tuesday 21st April *- Henry and I called at the Chesnuts[32] on Mrs Layton. Lord Newport[2] came to luncheon. Capt. and Mrs Cotton called just as Henry and I were dressing to go to Bridgnorth to dine with the Sparkes & go to a concert.*

Wednesday 22nd April *- Henry went to Leamington & Malvern & took Walter.[4]*

Thursday 23rd April *- Went out walking - very cold.*

Friday 24th April *- Henry returned. I went to Shifnal to meet him.*

Saturday 25th April *- Henry rode to Bridgnorth, wretched cold day, all but snow.*

Sunday 26th April *- Mr Eardley preached such an excellent Sermon.*

Monday 27th April *- Settled my packing, &c.*

Tuesday 28th April *- I called at Dale House[31] & on Uncle Richard Darby[17] and Rebecca[15a] came back with me. Henry and Mr Bluck playing with gun powder.*

Wednesday 29th April *- Came back to Lowndes Street. We stopped at Leamington & had luncheon with the Storers[32a] - sent on servants and Mr Bluck took Toozie.[29]*

Thursday 30th April *- Tom[4] arrived as was thought for one day.*

Friday 1st May *- Paid visits, a very cold first of May.*

Saturday 2nd May *- Mama came. Henry went with me to meet her but she has a cold so did not come with us in the open carriage. We went to call on Mrs Forbes & Mrs Gatacre whose son is going to India. Mr Whitmore did not leave London as we expected but took a room in Pont Street and established himself for a period he does not mention.*

Sunday 3rd May *- Mama went to church with us to Mr Brookfield's, but she has a cold.*

Monday 4th May *- Dinner. Bristows, Charles Whitmore,[33] George Whitmore & a Miss Deacon,[23] Mr Huddleston, Mama, Tom[4] & ourselves.*

Tuesday 5th May *- To Week's Nursery, about Vines.*

Wednesday 6th May *- Mama, Henry and I went to Stoke Court[30] for the morning. Tom went at the same time to Eton to see his sons. Mr and Mrs John Pritchard[15] and Mr Bluck dined with us. George & Sarah[1] left Portman Square for Stockton.*

Thursday 7th May - *Visits & shopping. Parliament opened.*

Friday 8th May - *Rather cold but out all this afternoon.*

Saturday 9th May - *Mama, Henry and I went for the day to Leighton (Buzzard). Mr Lawford lent us his carriage & we went everywhere. Over Mr Bluck's new house & the old shrubbery. Luncheon at Mr Lawford's. Tom*[4] *left London.*

Sunday 10th May - *Mama went with me to church in the morning. Henry and I again afternoon. Mr Bluck.*

Monday 11th May - *Visits & shopping - Barry's - Mr Bluck - ecarté.*[25]

Tuesday 12th May - *Mr Blackburne. Mama left us to go to Stoke Court.*[30] *Henry and I & Mr Bluck*[6] *had a Box at the Opera. Alboni in Barbier & Prelini in the Ballet.*

Wednesday 13th May - *Henry and I to Lady Packingtons for Miss Thilluson's Recitations, a Miss Carleton sang. Ecarté.*[25]

Thursday 14th May - *Dinner at the Duncombe's. Lord & Lady Willoughby de Broke, Mr and Mrs Newton Lane, Mr Chiney, Sir G. and Lady Philips, Lady Janet Walrond & perhaps Mr Walrond, & a young lady. Mr Legard & another man name unknown. The dinner off the table.*

Friday 15th May - *Drove out, paid visits. Such a fine day. An evening by ourselves - but late planning invitations for a fortnight hence.*

Saturday 16th May - *Dine at Greenwich. Mr Bluck. Most lovely warm evening.*

Sunday 17th May - *Twice at church & walked a great deal.*

Monday 18th May - *Mrs Egremont*[12] *is in Baker Street & I went to take her out driving. Henry went with me to Bond Street for some muslins.*

Tuesday 19th May - *Ella's concert,*[34] *Sainton & Hallé. Mrs Charles Whitmore*[33] *went with me. Henry dined at the Carlton.*[22]

Wednesday 20th May - *Tilly (Matilda) sent me lovely flowers. A dinner party, 13. Lord Middleton & Miss Brodrick, Sir Edwin & Lady Pearson, Col. and Miss Taylor, the Robert Herbert's, Mr and Mrs Gathorne Hardy.*

Thursday 21st May - *I went again to take our Mrs Egremont.*[12] *Dearest Mama came from Stoke Court*[30] *with a cold. Mr Bluck*[6] *at dinner.*

Friday 22nd May - *So wet and so dark we never went out at all! Henry had to go back about the Princess Royal's fortune.*

Saturday 23rd May - *Mama and I drove out in the Park as well as a long list of visits.*

Sunday 24th May *- Such a bad stiff neck I have not been out. The Dean of Canterbury preached a Charity Sermon at St Michaels.*

Monday 25th May *- Drove out to shop & pay visits.*

Tuesday 26th May *- The same.*

Wednesday 27th May *- The Derby Day. Mama and I went to the French Exhibition and the Academy. Col. Forbes*[5] *and the Miss Forbes' and Mr Bluck and Mr Arthur Hankey dined here.*

Thursday 28th May *- Mama and I went out shopping and called upon Mrs Egremont.*[12] *After dinner Mr Bluck and a rather sad evening, Mama's last.*

Friday 29th May *- Mama went away to Stoke Court.*[30] *Henry did not come home to dinner. Then we had four parties. Mrs Bennet, Lady Verner, Mrs Capel-Cure & Mrs Harrison's Ball. Mrs Capel-Cure's was the pleasantest party to us. I was so tired before I came away from Mrs Harrison's Ball.*

Saturday 30th May *- Quite knocked up & sick occasionally. Better in the evening when we had a dinner party. Mr and Mrs Alfreda Vernon, Mr & Lady Louisa Cotes, Sir T. and Lady Scott, B. Boroughs, Capt. and Mrs George Wrottesley.*[35] *We prospered and it was pleasant. Matilda sent us lovely flowers & Henry put them all in water.*

Sunday 31st May *- In the afternoon we went to Westminster Abbey, where we could not hear the Sermon which was I believe, very good, by the Rev. Chevenix Trench. The Duchess of Sutherland opposite to us. Rather cold again. Mr Bluck here.*

Monday 1st June *- Bad dreams. Toozie*[29] *missing for half an hour. Henry and I went for one night to Stoke Court.*[30] *Abraham not at home. Mama there.*

Tuesday 2nd June *- Came back from Stoke Court.*[30] *Went to Ella's.*[34] *Then to Miss Clarke's about my train. Dined at Sir T. Scott's. Mrs Lloyd's in the evening.*

Wednesday 3rd June *- Tom*[4] *at luncheon, our evening party, 130 came, about 300 asked. Very prosperous.*

Thursday 4th June *- Tom*[4] *at luncheon. Miss Percival & Miss Taylor early. Mr Bluck at dinner. Lord Powys'*[36] *Ball. Very hot.*

Friday 5th June *- Tom*[4] *supposed to be at Beckenham,*[19] *spent the day here. I went to find Mrs Egremont*[12] *but missed her. The heat grows excessive.*

Saturday 6th June *- The Drawing Room.*[37] *There will be only 2 this year and no Birthday. Very full, very hot and no rain! Lady Pigot*[38] *great beauty. My train &c. from Miss Clarke - White moire with red pomegranites. Isidor could not come, but such a man did my hair very badly, and the wreath was* *not at all becoming, I think. Mr Bluck[6] at dinner. In the evening we went to Mrs Biddulph's & met the Bishop of Kilmore.*

Sunday 7th June - *So wet I did not go out in the morning. To Mr Liddel's in the afternoon. Sir Robert[38] and Lady Pigot and Miss Benyon called. Henry and I went into the Park. Mr Bluck here. Cooler.*

Monday 8th June - *Tom[4] spent the day here. I took Miss Perceval out driving. Rather showery. Called upon Mrs D. Griffiths "to enquire".*

Tuesday 9th June - *Matilda came for Ella's "extra matinee".[34] We had Rubenstein. Mdlle. Stubbe, Sivoti, &c. Tom[4] at luncheon. Mr Bluck & ecarté.[25]*

Wednesday 10th June - *I drove out a little and said goodbye to Mrs Forbes. Dined at Mr and Lady L. Cotes. Sir T. & Lady Smythe, Sir John & Lady Hammer. Mr and Lady Alfreda Vernon, Mr and Mrs Elliot, and Miss Ward. Evening Party at Lady Stracey's not many people we know except the Wrottesleys.[35]*

Thursday 11th June - *We dined at the Hardy's, such a family party, & Mr & Mrs Vance, Mrs Willoughby.*

Friday 12th June - *Drove to see Mrs Croft and nothing in the evening which was a comfort.*

Saturday 13th June - *Drive with Henry, saw the table set for dinner at the Carlton.[22] Henry dined at the Carlton - dinner to Sir Wm. Jolliffe.*

Sunday 14th June - *Mrs Croft came to breakfast & spent the day. We went in the afternoon to St Barnabas.*

Monday 15th June - *Visit from Miss Hartshorne & settled to take her to the Lennox Ball.[18]*

Tuesday 16th June - *Matilda came for Ella's concert.[34] Very good. Such a pleasant day. Evening party at Mrs Sparling's where we met all Shropshire & Mrs Butler's Ball where we met all London & took Miss Hartshorne. A great many pretty people.*

Wednesday 17th June - *Dinner at home. Lord, Lady & Miss Wrottesley.[35] C. Pemberton, Lady H. Leeke, Major and Mrs Stuart Knox. Disappointed of Mr Leeke, Sir James Jerynsson, and filled up their places with Mr Cane & John Hamilton. Dowager Lady and Miss Wrottesley,[35] Mrs and Miss Trent & Mrs Cane in the evening.*

Thursday 18th June - *Henry went to the Levée and very crowded. Afterwards I took him to the House & then called on Mrs Deacon.[23] At night an Assembly at Lady Londonderry's[39] - very brilliant indeed and beautiful.*

Friday 19th June - *Tickets for the House of Commons. Miss Wrottesley*[35] *went with me and we saw the witnesses in the matter of the Rochdale Election Petition brought to the Bar of the House. Henry had to go back at night.*

Saturday 20th June - *Henry and I and Mr Bluck went to spend the day at Brighton. Last night there was a thunder storm & deluges of rain so no dust & a most lovely day. We sat on the Pier and drove about. In the evening Tom*[4] *arrived.*

Sunday 21st June - *Archbishop of Canterbury preached at St Michael's for a Reformatory. Mrs Croft came to dine. Mr Bluck.*

Monday 22nd June - *We expected Mrs Croft to luncheon - Later she came & drove out with me to Kensington, &c. and in the Park. She is not well.*

Tuesday 23rd June - *Ella.*[34] *Matilda and Abraham & Mrs B. Harvey came to it but did not come here. We had Rubenstein. Changed Opera Glass.*

Wednesday 24th June - *Tom*[4] *went away with his servants about 1 o'clock for Paris, Strasbourg and Switzerland. Weather without a cloud & hot! hot ever since the thunder on Friday night last. Dinner Party. Pigots, Miss Benyon, Farnhams, Miss Hill, Sir R. Brownrigg,*[40] *Col. Taylor, C. Heneage, Mr John Bridgeman. Henry made ill, but good dinner.*

Thursday 25th June - *Jenn ill, and I could not go out. Very hot. Henry home for dinner, Mr Bluck & ecarté.*[25]

Friday 26th June - *The Queen distributed the Victoria Cross in Hyde Park.*[41] *We were there just before she arrived at 10. Very good places. The Queen rode and inspected the troops and then gave away the medals - The Prince of Prussia and Prince Albert, now Prince Consort on each side of her. There were Guards, Highlanders, Rifles, Sailors. The Regiments passed 3 times before the Queen the last in double quick time. It was interesting to see the Hospital Waggons & Mules for carrying the wounded. We got away about one. The heat was very great but the Queen must have had the worst of it. We dined at Adml. C. Duncombe's. Met Lord and Lady Muncastle, the Belgian Minister and Mdme. van der Weyn, Mr and Mrs and Miss Maxwell, &c. There is a very nice & pretty Miss Duncombe.*

Saturday 27th June - *We drove to Kensington Gardens. Henry and I and Mr Bluck and there sat in the shade. Henry dined at Sir Bulwer Lytton's, a man's dinner & very grand and good.*

Sunday 28th June - *Mrs Croft is gone to Norwood. At church once but such heat I could not go again! We called upon the Heneages & found Mrs Davison.*

Monday 29th June - *The Queen went to Manchester. I drove out very late - Very hot. Henry had to go back at 12. New work grounding of grapes.*

Tuesday 30th June - *Ella's Grand Matinee.*[34] *Matilda came up for it. She brought me some flowers and fruit. The Ballot, and Henry never got away to dine with the Sparlings, 18 people & an evening party.*

Wednesday 1st July - *Dined at Mrs John Biddulph's. Met Hussey Vivians, Mr Hamilton, Mrs Trant, Miss Perceval, &c. &c. Very wet day.*

Thursday & Friday 2nd & 3rd July - *Wet days. I worked at the sofa cushions for the Bazaar.*

Saturday 4th July - *Henry dined at Lord Eglington's, I went to fetch him and we went to Lady Derby's Reception.*[24] *Lord Belmore came with him & the Duchess of Cambridge & Princess Mary were there. Crowds of people, Mrs Anson, Mr & Mrs Butt, Duke of Manchester. Drove to see Mrs Croft at Norwood.*

Sunday 5th July - *I was not well. Did not go out & did not go to church. Mr Bluck.*

Monday 6th July - *We dined at Lady Laura Grattain's. Met Lord & Lady Devon, Lord & Lady Emelina Beauclerk, Mr Douglas, Mr Bruce, Mr Mackinnon, &c. &c. Concert at Mrs Biddulph's - Annulini, &c. Trants, Lennox's, Butlers, Capt. Cust, Bishop B. of Kilmore, Percivals, &c.*

Tuesday 7th July - *Dined at the Pritchards*[15] *- Hardys, Mrs and Miss King, Mrs Sandiland, Mr and Mrs Slaney. Lady Doneraile at home, beautiful home in Grosvenor Square. I am in a fuss about Collins leaving me. Mrs Walford came to tell me the Cook I had engaged was too ill at her house to go to service, Mrs Prescott refused to give up Collins even for a few days.*

Wednesday 8th July - *Dined at Mrs Farnham's. Mr and Mrs Adderley, Mrs & Miss Wycombe Martyn, Mr & Miss Lennox Battea, Lord Edwin Hill, Mr Hamilton, Mr Stanhope. In the evening, Mrs Mackinnon's Conversations - Hyde Park Place. Fine house, numbers of people.*

Thursday 9th July - *Henry went with me to Redmayne's to get 2 gowns, both are green. Collins went away this morning, and I took a Mrs Sims who we will keep if we can afford it. Mr Bluck & ecarté.*[25]

Friday 10th July - *The Jews' Bill was thrown out in the House of Lords by a very good majority, 34.*

Saturday 11th July - *Dinner at home. Mama and Tilly (Matilda) sent us a basket of fruit and flowers - Rather nervous but Mrs Sims did it very well indeed <u>very</u> well. Lady Louisa Gratten, Mr and Mrs W. Brodrick, Mr Mrs & Miss Capel Cure, Mrs B. Stanhope, Mr Bluck, Mr and Lady D. Pakington.*

Sunday 12th July - *Such a hot day. Mr Bluck here. Went once to church. The Park.*

Monday 13th July - *We had 3 evening parties. Lady Dalrymple's where we heard some wonderful singing from a Miss Treherne, Mrs Capel Cure's, and Mrs Trant's. This last a concert. Anichini &c. Mr Bluck*[6] *at dinner.*

Tuesday 14th July - *Henry had to go to the House later, rather a quiet day. Ella's last Matinee.*[34] *Matilda came.*

Wednesday 15th July - *Fete at Holland House where we saw the new beauty, the Countess Castiglione. Most lovely day & the whole thing quite beautiful. We got just in time for our dinner party. Mr & Lady Charlotte Lyster, Sir Wm., Lady and Miss Jolliffe, Lady J. and Mr Leake, Lady Beecher, Major Powys, Mr Henry Edwards - Mr and Mrs Knight came in the evening.*

Thursday 16th July - *Morning party at Mrs Edward Wrottesley's*[35] - *Wonderful performing dog played Whist and Dominoes. I took Miss Forbes with me. Henry dined at Lord Hotham's.*

Friday 17th July - *Such a late night at the House. There was an attempt by Lord John Russell to bring in a new Jews Bill - Henry did not get home till quarter to 5.*

Saturday 18th July - *Henry and I and Mr Bluck went to the Zoological Gardens where the Band played. Beautiful weather. We dined at the Gaskells, Lady and Miss Garnier, etc.*

Sunday 19th July - *Mr Bluck here. Called on the Fosters - saw Mr Forbes of Callander.*[5]

Monday 20th July - *My work, the grapes. I took Henry to the House. Dined at home but it was a late night.*

Tuesday 21st July - *Late again.*

Wednesday 22nd July - *George came from Rhyl. Dinner party - Baldocks, Pritchards, Biddulphs, Sparlings.*

Thursday 23rd July - *Drove out with Henry and George. Left Henry at the House and took George in the Park. Mr Bluck at dinner, late night.*

Friday 24th July - *Henry went with me to the Lowther Arcade for things for the Stanley Bazaar. In the Park. Mr Bluck at dinner.*

Saturday 25th July - *George went away. "Election Saty." at Eton but Henry did not go. We dined at Mr and Mrs Hollands. Mr Joley the only person we knew.*

Sunday 26th July - *Twice at church in the Park. Mr and Mrs Lloyd. Mr Bluck at dinner. London growing dull.*

Monday 27th July - *I went to Stoke Court*[30] *to stay one night. Hot, thunder. A toothache.*

***Tuesday 28th July** - I came back to London. Matilda and Abraham going tomorrow to Cornwall. Found Henry here and took him to the House of Commons. Mr Bluck at dinner.*

***Wednesday 29th July** - Henry and I and Mr Bluck went to the Opera. We had Ginglini, Alboni, Spezia in Il Travatore and a very pretty Ballet with Rosati afterwards - Marco Spada. It began so early, half past 7.*

***Thursday 30th July** - Not well this morning & in bed of course after the Opera.*

***Friday 31st July** - Mama came up for a few days. Very hot & stuffy. Went to Euston Square to meet Mama. Mr Bluck at dinner.*

***Saturday 1st August** - We walked out shopping. Dinner party in the evening. Mr Mrs and Miss Gaskell, Mrs and Miss Trent, Mr Coles, Mr Hamilton, Col. Taylor and Mr Bluck.*

***Sunday 2nd August** - Twice at church. Mama and I sat in the Cadogan Place gardens. Mr Bluck.*

***Monday 3rd August** - Tom[4] returned from the Continent.*

***Tuesday 4th August** - Tom[4] and I at luncheon and dinner.*

***Wednesday 5th August** - Mama busy chosing a carriage. Tom[4] went home.*

***Thursday 6th August** - South Kensington Museum,[42] Sheepshank's collection. Mr Bluck at dinner.*

***Friday 7th August** - Drove out - packing. Mr M. & ecarté.[25]*

***Saturday 8th August** - Mama came home and I with her & both our maids. The country is so nice. Henry could not come too. I am afraid he will only be able to come for the one day to the Stanley Bazaar.[14]*

***Sunday 9th August** - I went to church & stayed for the Sacrament.*

***Monday 10th August** - Mrs Whitmore[54] arrived. Very unlucky Mrs Wooley is ill - very ill, & Mrs Webb came quite late. Mama gave me a new muslin, very pretty - and Henry such a beautiful blue locket and chain! (Note: Adelaide's 40th birthday)*

***Tuesday 11th August** - I went over to Stanley[14] to help Mrs Alfred Darby to arrange the Bazaar and in the evening Henry arrived but can only stay till tomorrow after the Bazaar.*

***Wednesday 12th August** - Henry and I went to Stanley[14] in a Patent Safety and he went away to London that night! Mama and Mrs Whitmore[54] followed in the carriage later. The Bazaar was in a long tent. A fine day. We got £200 & the whole profit at last was more than £300. It was a fine day. I had a stall and did very well, about £30.*

Thursday 13th August *- Pouring rain with thunder. Mrs Whitmore,*[54] *Mama and I all day in the house.*

Friday 14th August *- I came back to Lowndes Street. Invitation to Westwood, we settled not to go as we must get to the sea and we give up No. 10 on the 22nd. Mrs Whitmore, the Forbes*[5] *and George*[1] *are all coming up for Marie's*[53] *wedding on the 1st of September. The Charltons also.*

Saturday 15th August *- Went to Merstham*[43] *until Monday. Met Sir Wm. Jolliffe at the station also Lady Adelaide and Mr Cadogan who were to be of the party at Merstham. Col. and Mrs Vyse were there. Grand game at a kind of Bagatelle with 9 pins & The Totums.*

Sunday 16th August *- Walked in the afternoon to Gatton Church. In the morning to Merstham.*

Monday 17th August *- Returned to Lowndes Street. Mr Bluck at dinner.*

Tuesday 18th August *- With Mrs Garforth*[53] *and Marie shopping. Called on Lady Middleton who is recovering slowly the broken leg and they hope soon to leave London. Went to No. 1 to see Mrs Law. Mr Bluck at dinner.*

Wednesday 19th August *- Henry went with me to buy Marie's present - an Inkstand, & candlesticks from Emily and Col. Wilmot.*[44]

Thursday 20th August *- Packing, packing. Mrs Garforth*[53] *& Marie called. Mr Bluck.*

Friday 21st August *- Packing & sending our things to No. 1.*[44a] *Left at 5 for Bognor which we did not like - therefore at 5 we left by the train and went to Portsmouth & slept at the George.*

Saturday 22nd August *- We crossed over to Ryde. It is Henry and I & Mr Bluck,*[6] *no servants. At Oldfield's York Hotel.*

Sunday 23rd August *- Twice at church - how the wasps did tease! In the afternoon such a good service, I don't know the clergyman's name - he was a sort of bishop? In the evening on the Pier and met Mr de Burgh.*

Monday 24th August *- Ryde too hot so we settled to go to Ventnor, where I expected to be hotter, but it is a mistake - We are at Bush's Marine Hotel and very clean and comfortable with a cat & kittens & garden & the sea before us.*

Tuesday 25th August *- Sat by the sea.*

Wednesday 26th August *- We dined at 4 and drove afterwards to Sandrock & Blackgang Chine - I thought I knew the Isle of Wight, but had forgotten this beautiful undercliffe. We got letters for the first time.*

Thursday 27th August *- Walked on the Cliffe beyond Steep Hill Castle. Mr Harmborough's - Such glorious weather - weeks now since we saw a cloud.*

Friday 28th August *- I resolved to brave the heat and so we walked after breakfast to Appuldurcombe Downs - The most lovely views. We took biscuits and sherry with us and it was too delightful.*

Saturday 29th August *- We left Ventnor, crossed from Ryde to Portsmouth & slept at Worthing where we had immense trouble to get taken in.*

Sunday 30th August *- We are very comfortable at the Steyne Hotel. Went to church and walked on the sands.*

Monday 31st August *- Our very happy little expedition was over. We came back to London. Henry and I to Howchin's. I was busy in Lowndes Street at 10 & 1.*

Tuesday 1st September *- Marie Garforth[53] was married to Mr Henry Beaumont. How strange it was to be in Chesterfield Street for such an event and only this August last year in the same sort of glorious heat the street with straw & poor Kitty! so dear & so pretty lying dying and so painfully. Well - Marie was married - & very <u>well</u> & she had 6 bridesmaids with wreaths of blue corn-flowers & George[1] performed the ceremony at St George's - So glad we were to get away, I to take off my finery - bonnet of gold beads & glace gown with lilac flounces & brussels shawl and we went to Leamington & slept at the Regent.*

Wednesday 2nd September *- Luncheon with the Storers[32a] who are to come and stay with us. Mr Bluck joined us at Birmingham with a sprained ankle & we came home.*

Thursday 3rd September *- At last, such a wet day!*

Friday 4th September *- The weather cleared up & we could go out.*

Saturday 5th September *- Henry and Mr Bluck to Stockton[1] and to Bridgnorth.*

Sunday 6th September *- We went to church at Little Wenlock and Henry and I twice. I not so very tired. We sat up to half past 12.*

Monday 7th September *- Henry and I to Cotsbrook[4] to luncheon & afterwards to Stockton.[1] It was a lovely day.*

Tuesday 8th September *- Wet. Henry and Mr Bluck were out riding and were caught in the rain. I busy with new work.*

Wednesday 9th September *- Mama and I to Marnwood.[16] Henry and Mr Bluck rode to Apley.*

Thursday 10th September *- Very gay....... meeting at Aston, Henry & I went. Mrs Sims went to No. 1.*

Friday 11th September *- Henry went to shoot at Sutton. I called on Uncle Richard Darby.[17]*

Saturday 12th September - *Alice came. Went to the Cave and had tea - Mama, Henry and Mr Bluck, Toozie*[29] *and I. It is like July and so lovely.*

Sunday 13th September - *Went to church, Mr Hayes.*[9] *Henry and Mr Bluck to Little Wenlock in the afternoon.*

Monday 14th September - *Henry went to Mr Bowen's. Mr Bluck fishing & I walked to see.*

Tuesday 15th September - *Alice well. Henry and Mr Bluck riding. Mama and I called at Madeley Wood.*[7]

Wednesday 16th September - *Henry shooting with Mr Brooke at Sutton. Lord & Lady Forester*[27] *called here.*

Thursday 17th September - *Henry and I and Mr Bluck came to Manchester. Could be taken in at no hotel! 12, Lever Street, and we dine at the Queen's, the table d'hote.*

Friday 18th September - *The Exhibition. Old Masters. Modern. Hertford Gallery. Dutch pictures and general works of art.*

Saturday 19th September - *Exhibition. The Water Colours. Photographs. Engravings. British Gallery of Portraits. Soulages Col. Indian Room, and works in precious metals. Came to Llangollen to sleep and spend Sunday.*

Sunday 20th September - *I was tired out and ill. However, in the evening recovered & walked up to Castell Dinas Bran.*

Monday 21st September - *Came home.*

Tuesday 22nd September - *Dudmaston*[3] *for 2 nights. The J. Pritchards*[15] *& Adml. Bridgeman*[2] *staying. At dinner the Sparkes & Mr Willey.*

Wednesday 23rd September - *Walked in the Dingle. Mrs C.B. went away to Lady Corbet who has a little girl. Mr & Mrs Postlethwaite dined. Played at letters.*

Thursday 24th September - *We were at home to luncheon. Mrs and Miss Storer*[32] *arrived in the afternoon till the 30th.*

Friday 25th September - *Indian meeting*[45] *at Bridgnorth. Henry and Lizzy and I went with the Post horses, called at Stockton.*

Saturday 26th September - *Mrs and Miss Storer,*[32a] *Henry and I went out with the ponies to Willey. Willey Rectory & Broseley. Mrs J. Pritchard left Dudmaston very ill but is better. I saw Mrs Forester.*

Sunday 27th September - *Went to church here. Wet afternoon.*

Monday 28th September - *Mr Marshall and Mrs Hudson came to luncheon. Mrs Storer, Mama and I drove to Buildwas, &c.*

Tuesday 29th September - *Mr and Mrs Hayes*[9] *came to dinner. Lizzy & Mrs M. had a long walk.*

Wednesday 30th September - *Mrs Storer*[32] *and Lizzy went to Stockton*[1] *and Charlotte and Lois*[32a] *came here the same day.*

Thursday 1st October - *Our dinner to the Mayor and Corporation of Bridgnorth. It was very successful. We had the "Dale Band" at dinner time and Charlotte and Lois*[32a] *sang for us after. Henry went off at 12 at night for the Leighton Cattle Show next day.*

Friday 2nd October - *I took Charlotte and Lois*[32a] *over to Stockton*[1] *after luncheon.*

Saturday 3rd October - *Henry returned having bought 3 fat black & very cross pigs.*

Sunday 4th October - *Rather wet in the afternoon.*

Monday 5th October - *We meant to go to Church Stretton but I spent the day at Shrewsbury for the trains did not fit as Bradshaw promised.*

Tuesday 6th October - *Charlotte and Lois*[32a] *left us to go to Stockton. Henry and Mr Bluck went with them.*

Wednesday 7th October - *The Fast Day. At church in the morning and Mr Bluck and Henry went in the evening.*

Thursday 8th October - *The Cattle Show at Bridgnorth. I did not go. The 3 pigs gained a prize.*

Friday 9th October - *Henry and I came to Hale.*[46] *Mama to meet Abraham and Matilda at Alderley. Mr Bluck to London. At Hale we found Mr and Mrs Barlowe at Sir Charles Douglas.*

Saturday 10th October - *To the Exhibition at Manchester. 2 Aunts, Miss Blackburnes arrived with a Marmozet. Mr Francis & Miss Fanny Blackbourne came to stay.*

Sunday 11th October - *Twice at church and a long walk besides. I forgot that Mr and Mrs Barlowe went away yesterday and everybody was sorry.*

Monday 12th October - *We went a large party to the exhibition at Old Trafford. Met Mama at last and Abraham and Matilda, Col. and Mrs Harvey Hopwood arrived at Hale. It is wonderful pleasure, the Exhibition.*

Tuesday 13th October - *Expedition to Speke Hall. Henry went to Manchester hearing G. would be there. Of course, they did not meet, and what was wonderful too he never saw Mama and Abraham and Matilda.*

Wednesday 14th October - *We left Hale, Mama joining us at Crewe to return home. We went to Longford.*[47]

Thursday 15th October - *At Longford. Lord and Lady Neville, the Bougheys at dinner. Called at Chetwynd.*[47]

Friday 16th October - *Left Longford*[47] *and had luncheon with Mama at home and then to Willey to dine & sleep. We could not make engagements fit to do more.*

Saturday 17th October - *At Willey there were staying Mr & Lady Clayton, Major Forester and Major Powys. The Ansons, Dr Rowley and Mr Potts at dinner. We came home today. Henry went to Bridgnorth & Mr Bluck came from London for Henry's birthday.*

Sunday 18th October - *Not at all well. Wet afternoon. Did not go out.*

Monday 19th October - *Mrs Anstice*[7] *called. Nice fine day. Henry and Mr Bluck out riding.*

Tuesday 20th October - *To Woodcote till Thursday. Mr J. Boughey. Mr and Mrs Robert Herbert, Mr and Mrs and Miss Hope Edwards, and 2 Miss Cotes.*

Wednesday 21st October - *Drove over to Longford.*[47]

Thursday 22nd October - *Home to luncheon. Miss Fowler came to luncheon. To Stanley*[14] *for 2 nights. 3 Christys, 1 Ashworth, 1 Hadwin. 23 at dinner. Ellisons, Partons, Mr and Miss Pritchard.*[15]

Friday 23rd October - *Mrs Edmund Darby, Mary*[28] *and Miss Fowler at luncheon - 25 at dinner. J. Pritchards,*[15] *Bingleys, J. Purtons, Sparkes.*

Saturday 24th October - *Came home. Henry to Bridgnorth.*

Sunday 25th October - *Walked to Little Wenlock. Henry and I and Mr Bluck and Toozie.*[29]

Monday 26th October - *Henry went to Shrewsbury & brought me such a lovely green gown, Mama's gift for Loton.*

Tuesday 27th October - *Taking fish out of the pool to mud it.*

Thursday 29th October - *Went to Aqualate till Saturday. Such a lovely moonlight drive.*

Friday 30th October - *Henry went to shoot with Sir Thomas Boughey. We had a long walk. In the evening, singing.*

Saturday 31st October - *We came home. They asked us to stay till Monday but we could not.*

Sunday 1st November - *At church in the morning. Mr Bluck went to Little Wenlock in the afternoon.*

Monday 2nd November - *Henry went to luncheon at Cotsbrook.*[4]

Tuesday 3rd November - *George & Sarah[1] came to luncheon. Wet day. At dinner 3 Anstices,[7] Henry Dickinson,[8] Rebecca,[15a] Mr Bluck and Mr Webb.*

Wednesday 4th November - *Ball at Loton. Henry and I went to the Lion at Shrewsbury to dine and sleep. Very good Ball and pleasant.*

Thursday 5th November - *Came home to luncheon. Pouring rain. Tired but not ill.*

Friday 6th November - *Catalogue. We 4 went to Admaston to see horses & Eliza and Mrs Alfred Darby called. She is going to Cannes for the winter!*

Saturday 7th November - *Henry and Mr Bluck went to Bridgnorth. Fog. Catalogue.*

Sunday 8th November - *At church here in the morning. Fog.*

Monday 9th November - *Mr Burton's Ball at Shrewsbury. Went to Wroxeter[12] for it.*

Tuesday 10th November - *Mr Bluck left Sunniside[48] for London. At Wroxeter.[12] Drove to Shrewsbury. At dinner, Mrs C. Jenkins, Mr Dodd and Mr Harnage. The Walcots.*

Wednesday 11th November - *To Berwick after luncheon from Wroxeter.[12] Lady Lane and Mr Levett Mainwaring of Oteley & Miss Duncombe. Mr and Mrs Reid and Mr Harding.*

Thursday 12th November - *Infirmary meeting[49] and the Hunt Ball. Went to both.*

Friday 13th November - *Came home from Berwick.*

Saturday 14th November - *Henry at Bridgnorth.*

Sunday 15th November - *Henry has a cold. At church this morning.*

Monday 16th November - *Mama and I went to Wellington.*

Tuesday 17th November - *Henry and I went to a concert at Bridgnorth.*

Wednesday 18th November - *Paid visits in the Upper Town at Bridgnorth. Home and dined with the Pritchards,[15] met Mr and Mrs Leighton Lowndes, Moseleys, Waynes.*

Thursday 19th November - *Catalogue. Henry went to shoot with Tom.[4]*

Friday 20th November - *Mr Mrs & Miss Moseley came to us from Broseley to dine and sleep and Tom[4] came to dine and brought ....*

Saturday 21st November - *Mr Mrs and Miss Moseley left us. Warmer again like summer.*

Sunday 22nd November - *At church.*

Monday 23rd November - *Henry went to London. I in the Library. Mama and I called at Marnwood*[16] *& found Mr Reynolds.*

Tuesday 24th November - *Snow on the ground. Uncle Tothill and Frank*[50] *called.*

Wednesday 25th November - *Company's meeting like last year. Uncle Tothill and Frank*[50] *dined here.*

Thursday 26th November - *I went to call upon Mrs Cunliffe at Aston and Haughton.*

Friday 27th November - *Finished the Catalogue. Mr and Mrs Bartlett*[16] *called.*

Saturday 28th November - *Lady Louisa and Nina*[4] *came to luncheon & brought the family diamonds to be mended.*

Advent Sunday 29th November - *Very cold. At church.*

Monday 30th November - *Packing for London.*

Tuesday 1st December - *Packing. A long visit from Mary Darby.*[28]

Wednesday 2nd December - *We came to London at No. 1 Lowndes Street. Mama and I bringing Jones, Sara, John & Betsy and Toozie.*

Thursday 3rd December - *Settled ourselves in the new house which still, Mrs Sims says, wants a great many things.*

Friday 4th December - *Mama and I went to Stoke Court*[30] *for the morning. We found Abraham and Matilda both ill from Influenza and in trouble thinking they are coming to poverty!*[51]

Saturday 5th December - *Henry and I went to Stoke Court*[30] *for luncheon with Tilly (Matilda). Met Abraham going to London. Mama came in afternoon to Stoke Court to stay over Monday. We came home to Lowndes Street. I rather happier! Mr Bluck and ecarté.*[25]

Sunday 6th December - *Raining and damp. At church in the afternoon. Mr Bluck.*

Monday 7th December - *Mama came back to us but desponds.*[51]

Tuesday & Wednesday 8th & 9th December - *Shopping. Cabinet hunting.*

Friday 11th December - *Lord Henry Lennox*[18] *expected at dinner & came, Col. Taylor & Mr Hamilton came without being expected. The Opposition sustained a defeat & Lord Palmerston appears stronger than ever!*[52]

Saturday 12th December - *Mr Jefferson came to dine and Mr Bluck.*

Sunday 13th December - *At church in the morning.*

Monday 14th December - *Cabinet hunting. Called on Lady Radstock to please Catty - she would not let us in.*

Tuesday 15th December - *Walked out shopping.*

Wednesday 16th December - *Mama went again to Stoke Court[30] for a day or two. Henry and I and Mr Bluck went to the St James's Theatre to see the famous conjuror Dr Wilgal, a Trickell, who did very wonderful things and with no table, nothing near to his operations.*

Thursday 17th December - *Henry was to convey Lois Storer[32a] across London - Her Dover train was too late, and they came back to luncheon.*

Friday 18th December - *Henry and I went to Stoke Court[30] to bring Mama back, but she stays till tomorrow.*

Saturday 19th December - *Out shopping. Miss Wrottesley[35] called. Told me Miss Coutts is to marry the Bishop of Oxford which I doubt! Mama came back to us. Mr Bluck at dinner.*

Sunday 20th December - *At church in the morning.*

Monday 21st December - *Shopping and then the Soho Bazaar.*

Tuesday 22nd December - *Came home. Mama, Henry and I, Jones, Sara, John & Betsy & Toozie try to follow.*

Wednesday 23rd December - *Busy day. Cabinet to be put up. In the afternoon suddenly dearest Mama not at all well and went to bed.*

Thursday 24th December - *Mama was worse, but would not send for Mr Webb. Mr Jefferson and Mr Bluck arrived.*

Friday 25th December - Christmas Day - *Mama better. Henry not well. I went to church and Mr Jefferson and Mr Bluck. Mr Bluck and I stayed for the Communion.*

Saturday 26th December - *Mama is really better and managed herself wonderfully with the blue pills. Henry took Mr Jefferson and Mr Bluck to Apley & Tom showed them the house and announced a Bazaar for Stockton Church. In the evening Whist.*

Sunday 27th December - *At church here. Walked to Little Wenlock in the afternoon. So dry & clean we took Toozie.[29]*

Monday 28th December - *Mr Jefferson left us. Henry went over to Stockton. Mr Bluck to Shrewsbury and Mama and I to Coalport.[13]*

Tuesday 29th December - *George & Sarah[1] came to stay for 2 nights. We are in the midst of levelling for our Terrace, in front of the house.*

Wednesday 30th December - *Douglas and Walter*[4] *came to luncheon and we then had a long walk. Abraham Darby came to dinner. He was at Dale House*[31] *and I was very glad to see him. Left next day.*

Thursday 31st December - *George and Sarah*[1] *left us. Rather cold. Henry and I and Mr Bluck went to buy a Cake for the servants' fete at Mrs Barclay's. So cold we came home. Made flags and a frill for the Cake. We sat up to hear the Bells & wish each other a Happy New Year and to give & receive our gifts. End of a very happy 1857.*

NOTES

1. George Whitmore was the Rector of Stockton, near Apley. He was an elder brother of Henry Whitmore, Adelaide's husband. Sarah Whitmore (née Deacon) was his wife and they lived until 1857 at Kemberton but they moved in 1857 to Stockton after the death of his uncle Charles Whitmore, the previous Rector of Stockton.
2. Weston Park, Shropshire, was the home of Lord and Lady Bradford and of Lord and Lady Newport. Their family name was Bridgeman.
3. William Wolryche Whitmore was the owner of Dudmaston Hall, Shropshire.
4. Cotsbrook was the home of Thomas Charlton Whitmore (Tom or Tommy), eldest brother of Henry Whitmore. He lived there with his wife Lady Louisa Whitmore (daughter of the late Marquis of Queensbury), their sons Douglas and Walter (both currently at Eton College), and their daughters Nina, Mary, Emily (Emmy), Louisa, Lucy, Edith and Elizabeth.
5. Lucy Forbes was a cousin of Henry Whitmore. She had married Col. John Forbes, Coldstream Guards of Callander in 1849.
6. Mr Bluck was a constant companion of Henry and Adelaide Whitmore. It has to be presumed that he was employed by Henry Whitmore in some capacity connected with his political career, possibly as an agent or secretary.
7. The Anstice family were based at Madeley Wood Hall on the north side of the River Severn a few miles east of Ironbridge. They were distantly related to the Darby family through the Reynolds family.
8. Severn House (now the Valley Hotel, Ironbridge) was the home of Henry Dickinson, a cousin of Adelaide Darby (see Family Tree). His wife Deborah (née Darby) had died in 1855. He married Susanna Hadwen in 1858.
9. Mr Hayes was the vicar of Coalbrookdale.
10. Mr Edmonds was the Rector of Little Wenlock.
11. Mr Charles Crookes was the manager of the Coalbrookdale Works and was also the prime mover in the construction of the Coalbrookdale Literary and Scientific Institution and School of Art.
12. Edward Egremont was the vicar of Wroxeter (5 or 6 miles west of Coalbrookdale). He and his wife had been very good friends of Adelaide since the 1840s.
13. Coalport was a settlement on the north side of the River Severn several miles east of Ironbridge. It was established by William Reynolds in the 1790's and included the Coalport China Works.
14. Stanley Hall, Bridgnorth, was the home of Mrs Alfred Darby, widow of Alfred Darby who died in 1852.

15. John Pritchard was a banker of Broseley. He was also the second Member of Parliament for Bridgnorth and was therefore a close political colleague of Henry Whitmore.
15a. Rebecca Darby was the daughter of Richard and Maria Darby and lived with them at "Rosehill" (see note 17).
16. Marnwood near Coalbrookdale was the home of Mr Bartlett, the incumbent of Buildwas Church.
17. Richard Darby was the brother of Adelaide's father, Francis Darby. He was then aged 69 and he lived with his wife Maria at the property now known as Rosehill, Coalbrookdale.
18. Lord Henry Lennox, son of the Duke of Richmond was a close confidante of Benjamin Disraeli who was the prime mover in the Conservative Party.
19. Probably Mr William Whitmore of Beckenham, Kent, a member of the London branch of the Whitmore family.
20. Adelaide does not elaborate much on her husband's activities in the House of Commons, although they were clearly of considerable significance. In February, proceedings in the House were electrified by Disraeli who accused the Government, under Lord Palmerston, of concealing a secret treaty made with France in December 1854 guaranteeing the security of Austrian possessions in Italy. Although Palmerston admitted the situation two days later, the House were not much interested in foreign affairs and Disraeli's manoeuvring fell rather flat. This may have been the background to Adelaide's reference to "very late night at the House", particularly in the light of the visits by Lord Henry Lennox on 20th and 21st February (see note 18 above).
21. Adelaide's reference to the "Chinese War" on 27th February was the issue which led to the dissolution of Parliament on 5th March. The background to the incident (a "War" as Adelaide described it) was that at Canton a Chinese Mandarin had arrested the Chinese crew of the "Arrow" which was flying the British flag. The crew were released after British protests, but the Canton government refused to apologise, whereupon British gunboats bombarded the port, several times. In Parliament, the Government lost by a narrow majority (see entry 3rd March) and Palmerston dissolved Parliament two days later (see 5th March). Palmerston won the resulting election and was returned with an increased majority.
22. The Carlton Club in St James' Street was (and still is) the unofficial headquarters of the Conservative Party.
23. The Deacon family were from Mapledon Park in Kent. Mrs George Whitmore of Kemberton/Stockton was a Miss Sarah Deacon before she married (see note 1 above).
24. Edward Stanley, 14th Earl of Derby was the acknowledged leader of the Conservative Party. His main interest was shooting and field sports. Intellectually he could not be compared with Benjamin Disraeli who really ran the party.
25. Ecarté was a game of cards for two.
26. The Whitmore Jones were a branch of the Whitmore family based at Chastleton, near Lower Slaughter in the Cotswolds.
27. The Forester family were from Willey, Shropshire. The title was held by John George Weld Forester 2nd Baron Forester who married Lady Melbourne in 1856.

28. The "Queen" probably refers (perhaps sarcastically) to Mary Darby, daughter of Lucy and Edmund Darby and sister of Abraham Darby IV. She lived at Dale House. Although Adelaide lived at the White House/Sunniside and regarded herself as the "Darby Heiress", she was by no means necessarily the most popular member of the Darby family. The residents of the Dale were far more discerning. Richard Darby and Lucy Darby as senior members of the family were highly esteemed but the top place in people's affections belonged to Mary Darby. She was very popular for manifold acts of kindness and generosity and her unfailing support for charities and every social and moral movement in the community. Her saintly behaviour led her to be known as the "Queen of the Valley". In 1858 she married Reverend Jones, vicar of Baschurch. This was the occasion of a week-long programme of celebrations in Coalbrookdale, Horsehay, Dawley and Lawley.
29. Toozie was the pet dog.
30. Stoke Court in Buckinghamshire was the home of Abraham Darby IV and Matilda who was Adelaide's elder sister.
31. Dale House, Coalbrookdale was built by Abraham Darby I in 1717. It was traditionally the home of the Manager of the Coalbrookdale Company. In 1857 it was occupied by Lucy Darby, mother of Abraham Darby IV and her daughter Mary Darby, the "Queen of the Dale" (see note 28 above).
32. The Chesnuts (sic), Coalbrookdale was built by Sarah Darby in the early 19th century out of the two cottages which she had purchased. It was subsequently occupied by Abraham Darby IV and Matilda his wife until they left Coalbrookdale to move to Stoke Court, Buckinghamshire after "the painful family affair" of 1851 (see Comment 1851). He then gave it to the Church Commissioners as a vicarage for the new Coalbrookdale parish church.
32a. The Storers were treated as "relatives" by the Whitmore family. In 1818 Elizabeth Whitmore, an aunt of Henry Whitmore married John Storer MA, Rector of Hawksworth, Notts. Charlotte and Lois were two daughters.
33. Charles Whitmore was probably of the branch of the Whitmore family of Lower Slaughter, Cotswolds.
34. John Ella (1802-88) was an English violinist, conductor and critic. From 1845 to 1880 he ran the Musical Union subscription concerts, and from 1852 he started the Musical Winter Evenings. These were exclusive gatherings. Henry and Adelaide Whitmore were subscribers as also were Abraham and Matilda Darby of Stoke Court.
35. The Wrottesley family were a leading Staffordshire family from Wolverhampton. Mrs George Wrottesley was possibly Margaret Anne, wife of Major-General George Wrottesley, son of the 2nd Baron Wrottesley.
36. Lord Powys, a member of the Herbert family, who was probably still the leading political figure in Shropshire and mid-Wales. His home was at Powys Castle, Welshtown.
37. The Drawing Room was a Royal Court Levée.
38. Sir Robert and Lady Pigot were related to the Dartmouth (Legge) family of Patshull, Co. Stafford. Sir Robert won second place in the 1852 Parliamentary election for Bridgnorth but lost his seat on an election petition soon after.
39. Frances Anne, Marchioness of Londonderry, was a confidante (and sponsor) of Disraeli. An invitation to one of her magnificent entertainments was

much sought after. These were normally held at Rosebank her summer villa at Fulham.

40. Sir Robert Brownrigg was probably a brother of Mrs Charles Whitmore (née Brownrigg) of Lower Slaughter, Cotswolds (see note 33 above).
41. The Victoria Cross was created after the Crimean War. The medal is fashioned from a piece of metal (which is still in existence) taken from a Russian gun captured during the campaign.
42. Now the Victoria and Albert Museum.
43. Merstham is near Redhill in Surrey.
44. Emily (née Whitmore) was a cousin of Henry Whitmore. She was married to Col. Wilmot of Malvern.

44a. Henry and Adelaide had taken a lease of No. 1 Lowndes Street for 2 years.

45. This may probably have been a meeting to discuss the repercussions of the Indian Mutiny which had started at Lucknow at the end of May 1857. The seige of Lucknow continued until 25th September, the day of the "Indian meeting" at Bridgnorth, but the Indian Mutiny continued until the summer of 1858. The political consequences (which perhaps the meeting discussed) was the passing of the Government of India Bill by Lord Derby's second Government in 1858 which transferred the government of India from the East India Company to the British Crown. Henry Whitmore was a member of that Government and it is tempting to speculate this may have been discussed at the meeting.
46. Hale is on the southern edge of Liverpool.
47. Longford is a mile or so west of Newport, Shropshire and Chetwynd is a mile or so north of Newport.
48. This was the White House, Coalbrookdale. It had been renamed "Sunniside" after the house of that name had been demolished in 1856.
49. The Infirmary meeting was the annual fundraising service at St Chad's Church, Shrewsbury for the hospital.
50. Uncle Tothill was William Tothill of Bristol, who was married to Hannah (née Darby), sister of Francis Darby, Adelaide's father. Frank was Francis Tothill, Williams' son. Frank was one of the triumvirate of partners who had been entrusted with the governance of the Coalbrookdale Company after the death of Alfred Darby in 1852. They had come to Coalbrookdale for the Company meeting which was held the following day.
51. The significant entries for 4th, 5th and 7th December are a reference to the fact that in 1854 the Manager of the Shropshire Bank in Wellington had confessed to losing £200,000, the whole of the Bank's assets (about £8 million in today's money) through speculation. The proprietors of the Bank, of whom Abraham Darby IV was one, were liable to the last penny of their means to repay creditors. This led to the disposal of Abraham's collection of valuable paintings and books and eventually, to the sale of Stoke Court. All this had to be done in great secrecy and it is not known how much (if anything) Adelaide knew of the situation.
52. This may have related to the situation in India.
53. Mr and Mrs Garforth, their daughter Maria and son William, of Wigganthorpe Hall, near York, had been close friends and associates of the Whitmores since 1852.
54. Mrs Whitmore was Henry Whitmore's mother. She seems to have lived in Malvern.

1858

Comment

The year 1858 marked the pinnacle of Henry Whitmore's political career. It came about in an unexpected manner. On 14th January 1858, while Henry and Adelaide were contemplating the good progress of the terrace in front of their home at Sunniside (formerly the White House), an Italian refugee named Orsini, based in England, made an unsuccessful assassination attempt on the life of the French Emperor Napoleon III. The bombs he used were made in England and this produced angry feelings in France. In February, Palmerston with his seemingly inpregnable position in Parliament, introduced a Conspiracy to Murder Bill which would have made it a felony to conspire to commit a murder whether in England or elsewhere. This seemed reasonable enough but public opinion took the view that the "bulldog" Palmerston was giving in to the French. An amendment to the Bill was moved and Palmerston lost the vote by 19 votes. Palmerston resigned and Lord Derby became Prime Minister on 21st February. Three days later, Henry Whitmore was appointed a Lord of the Treasury in Lord Derby's Administration with Benjamin Disraeli as Chancellor of the Exchequer. Henry Lennox who had been Henry's principal contact with Disraeli was appointed to the Admiralty.

With Henry in the Government, Adelaide's role as a political hostess became even more demanding. Their attendance at all the leading assemblies and receptions became almost more frenzied than before. This culminated in an invitation to the Lord Chancellor, Lord Chelmsford to visit Sunniside in the autumn. Although of course it was an informal visit it entailed visits to Willey, Patshull and Weston Park. The visit must have greatly enhanced the prestige of the family in Coalbrookdale and East Shropshire. On the other hand it was becoming clear that Adelaide, who regarded herself as "the Darby Heiress", had become detached from the daily life of the Dale. It was Mary Darby, sister of Abraham Darby IV and known locally as "the Queen of the Valley", who was probably the most popular and highly regarded member of the Darby family. On 27th October shortly after the visit of the Lord Chancellor, Mary Darby was married to Reverend Jones, vicar of Baschurch, Shropshire. This coincided with the completion of the Coalbrookdale Literary and Scientific Institution, which had been very much an initiative of Charles Crookes the Manager of the Works. It had been very much a community activity and all the materials were provided by the Company. The wedding of Mary Darby was the opportunity for week-long celebrations in Coalbrookdale, Horsehay, Dawley and Lawley. The centrepiece of the whole affair was a banquet in the newly completed Literary and Scientific

Institution, followed by an evening entertainment with a 15ft high bonfire and illuminations in the grounds of the Institution and of the Great Warehouse.

Adelaide was aware of these celebrations (see Journal for 27th October 1858) but Adelaide and Henry had no part in them. Their life had become increasingly London based.

Lord Derby's government in which Henry Whitmore was a Lord of the Treasury was short-lived and lasted little over a year. It commanded insufficient support in Parliament to be able to hold its own against the combined forces of the Whigs under Lord Palmerston, the Peelites under Lord John Russell and the Radicals under John Bright. They did however achieve one great success in 1858, which was the passing of the Government of India Bill under which the government of India was transfered from the East India Company to the Crown.

There was one pleasant by-product of Henry Whitmore's new status, and that was his appointment as Keeper of the Privy Seal to the Duchy of Cornwall. This was in the Queen's gift and it was in that capacity that he attended the Confirmation of the Prince of Wales, the future King Edward VII at Windsor Castle on 1st April. He could certainly claim to have reached the highest levels of society.

1st January - New Year's Day - *Fine bright day but cold. Henry rode over to Cotsbrooke[1] for luncheon.*

Saturday 2nd January - *Fog - Henry & I & Mr Bluck went to Bridgnorth.*

Sunday 3rd January *(2nd Sunday after Xmas) - At church in the morning. Henry and I stayed for the Communion.*

Monday 4th January - *We went to Bridgnorth for 2 nights, Henry and I and Mr Bluck, Jones & Fay. Stopped at Cotsbrooke[1] for the practice of the Lancers.*

Tuesday 5th January - *Finished our visit at Bridgnorth. Out all the day. The Break came over from Cotsbrooke filled. At night the Ball.*

Wednesday 6th January - *Came home as early as we could and I went to bed!*

Thursday 7th January - *Not at all well yet. Joseph Dickinson[2] here at luncheon.*

Friday 8th January - *Not at all well. Mrs Miss and Mr Ralph Wylde Browne here till tomorrow. Quite warm again like summer. Mr and Mrs Anstice[3] dined here and he sang several things and "Three fishers went sailing".*

Saturday 9th January - *The Wylde Brownes went away. Henry went to Bridgnorth and brought back with him Mrs Reynolds to stay here a few days.*

Sunday 10th January - *At church here in the morning. Mr Bluck*[5] *and Henry to Little Wenlock in the afternoon. I to meet them.*

Monday 11th January - *Such a lovely day. The Terrace makes progress. Ecarté*[4] *and Mrs Reynolds.*

Tuesday 12th January - *Henry and Mr Bluck*[5] *gone to Shrewsbury.*

Wednesday 13th January - *Dr and Mrs Rowley called. Dined at the John Pritchards.*[6] *Henry and I and Mr Bluck met Mr and Mrs Lowndes. Mdme de Satz, Mr and Mrs Macbarness & Miss Young, Dr Mrs and Miss Rowley and Mr & Mrs Bolton. Mr Osborne Gordon, Mr Pritchard. Singing which was good & music which was better.*

Thursday 14th January - *With Mama to call at Dale House*[7] *and on Mrs Hayes.*[11] *Henry and Mr Bluck gone to the New Hunt Ball.*

Friday 15th January - *Henry and Mr Bluck*[5] *came home last night, ie. at 5 this morning - were sleepy all day & then off to Apley Castle to dine & go to the Wellington Ball. Mr and Mrs Webb called.*

Saturday 16th January - *Henry went to Bridgnorth. Rather rainy and cold.*

Sunday 17th January - *Such a grand sermon from a stranger clergyman. The text from Judges, "I have a message for thee from God".*

Monday 18th January - *Henry and Mr Bluck went to London. Henry to return in a day or two.*

Tuesday 19th January - *Mama and I went to Willey to speak to the house-keeper about the maid for me. Called at the Pritchards*[6] *& on Mrs Forester whose house was totally deserted.*

Wednesday 20th January - *Such a high wind hardly went out except to Mrs Norris to get rid of the maid, Mary Whale.*

Thursday 21st January - *Henry came home. The Terrace makes rapid progress.*[8]

Friday 22nd January - *Very very sharp frost and cold. Contemplated the Terrace. Heard from Emily - Lucy*[9] *has another son, the 4th, on Wednesday evening. Lizzy Storer*[10] *there & John in Scotland and no nurse.*

Saturday 23rd January - *Tom*[1] *came for a day or two. Henry went to Bridgnorth.*

Sunday 24th January - *At church. Mr Hayes*[11] *- the text "The Sabbath was made for man not man for the Sabbath."*

Monday 25th January - *Tom*[1] *here. Mary Darby*[7] *called. Cloudy.*

Tuesday 26th January - *Tom[1] went home. Mrs Edmund Darby[7] came to stay with Mama whilst Mary goes to Henry Dickinsons[12] wedding. He is to marry Miss Hadwen tomorrow.*

Wednesday 27th January - *Came to London. Henry and I & Jones & a kitchen maid. We came by the North Western but Henry and I left the servants, ponies & carriage at Stafford and came on by an earlier train with Toozie.[13]*

Thursday 28th January - *Foggy & cold but it brightened up and Toozie[13] & I had a walk. Mr Bluck at dinner.*

Friday 29th January - *Still in the Library and still it smokes. Mr Bluck and Henry very busy hanging pictures, cold.*

Saturday 30th January - *The drawing room.[14] Our Princess Royal's last appearance. It was a wet day. My Court dress was a green moire train - Henry's Gift - and a white petticoat with Brussels lace flounces, Feathers, Green leaves, White frosted flowers, Gold berries & red geraniums, Mrs Whitmore's diamonds. The Queen looked grave and the little Princess took hardly any notice of any one. I believe the Prince Frederick William of Prussia is all that can be wished & that they really care for each other which is pleasant & rare in a Royal marriage.*

Sunday 31st January - *In bed with a bad cold & headache.*

Monday 1st February - *Still in bed - towards evening I had brandy and arrowroot & was cured. Mrs Brodrick called to see Henry's picture by Miss Day & promised to dine here.*

Tuesday 2nd February - *Snow - deep. The Prince & Princess in an open carriage. Poor child she is but 17 her eyes were streaming with tears and at the parting poor little Prince Albert cried bitterly - at Gravesend - I could not go out. They say the Princess wore a red velvet bonnet & white ostrich feathers (which must have been very ugly) & a black velvet Mantle. Our first dinner. The William Brodricks, John Pritchards,[6] 3 Greigs and Mr Bluck. We could not go to Lady D. Packington's, the Greigs stayed so late & the snow was so deep I was afraid.*

Wednesday 3rd February - *Snow going - sloppy and wet. Mr Bluck & ecarté.[4]*

Thursday 4th February - *Parliament meet. Rain.*

Friday 5th February - *Mr and Mrs Alfred Dick & Miss Burton called. Also Mr Greig. Paid visits & Foster's Bill. Lady Elizabeth Tollemache[24] at home & Lady Listowel & Mrs Denman, who says everybody about the Queen was devoted to the Princess Royal.*

Saturday 6th February - *Henry went to help to present the address to the Queen on the marriage of the Princess Royal. Paid visits. Lady Kenmare, Lady Wrottesley,*[15] *Miss Heneage - Henry dined with Mr Disraeli.*[16]

Sunday 7th February - *At church in the morning, Mr Hamilton alluded beautifully to the sudden death of Sir Henry Duckenfield only the other day. It was an illness of only 36 hours. He had preached the last day of the year from the text "In the midst of life we are in death".*

Monday 8th February - *Abraham*[17] *called here in the morning. Did Tyburnia. Quite late home! Henry came to dinner at half past 8 but to go back.*

Tuesday 9th February - *Shopping & visits. Lady Midleton & Miss Perceval. The Alien Bill*[18] *& Henry dined at the House of Commons.*

Wednesday 10th February - *This morning the sad news of Mr Creyke's death. He had not been well but nobody thought of any mischief going on when on Thursday morning poor Louisa found him unconscious and in high fever. I do not know if he ever became sensible again & on Sunday he died from congestion of the brain. We had a dinner party today. Sir Ralph and Lady Pigot, and Miss Benyon, Col. Vyse, Dowager Lady and Miss Wrottesley,*[15] *Mr Augustus Tollemache,*[24] *and Mr Bayley.*

Thursday 11th February - *A lost day for me, I was laid up with a headache.*

Friday 12th February - *Headache better in the afternoon. Visit from Mr Greig, and from Mr Garforth.*

Saturday 13th February - *Very wet & could not go out except late to give Toozie*[13] *a very dirty walk. Mr Rixon*[19] *in the morning with deeds of Trust for Matilda. Mr Bluck at dinner - ecarté.*[4]

Sunday 14th February - *Wet, wet! Henry had tickets for the Stalls at the Temple Church but we could not go out all day! Mr Bluck here.*

Monday 15th February - *Paid visits. Mrs Pritchard.*[6] *Mrs Brodrick whose little girl had fallen out of a brougham in Knightsbridge. She was hurt but not killed.*

Tuesday 16th February - *I went to Stoke Court*[17] *for the day. Col. Vyse gave me a "Times" & 2 eggs. Rather late night.*

Ash Wednesday 17th February - *Drive to pay Fuller's Bill.*

Thursday 18th February - *Long visit from Mrs Calthorpe. Henry went to the Levée. We dined with the Greigs. Mrs Arkwright & Mr Bluck.*

Friday 19th February - *Very very cold. Drive. Mrs Storer*[10] *has had a slight cold of paralysis but is better.*

Saturday 20th February - *Last night Henry could not come home to dine. The Government was beaten by 19 on Mr Milner Gibson's motion*[20] *concerning France.*

Sunday 21st February - *This has been a most exciting day. We did go to church and then with Sir J. and Lady Packington to their house but no tidings there of events! Lord Henry Lennox*[21] *here at luncheon, very low indeed. Mrs Disraeli had a written note saying Lord Derby had certainly refused to form a Government & the Queen had sent for Lord John Russell. Concluding "yours in dire dismay". Henry came home in the afternoon to tell me Lord Palmerston did indeed resign yesterday. Lord Derby kissed hands as Premier today at 3 o'clock.*

Monday & Tuesday 22nd & 23rd February - *Everybody in a fever of expectation and the change astonishing to all. All the world supports Lord Palmerston as firmly fixed in his seat as possible for years to come.*

Wednesday 24th February - *Visit from the old Miss Blackburnes. Dinner at home - 14. Miss Perceval. Mr Napier. Mr Blackburne. Col. Taylor. Mr Seymour Fitzgerald. Mr Whiteside. Mr Close. Mr Paull. Mr Vansitart. Mr Du Cane. Mr Robertson. Mr Bluck. This dinner was settled long before the change of Government, and curious it is that so many present had received appointments. Mr Seymour Fitzgerald to be Foreign Secretary. Mr Whiteside Attorney General for Ireland. Col. Taylor & Henry Lords of the Treasury.*

Thursday 25th February - *We called to congratulate Lady Thesiger. He is to be Lord Chancellor & Baron Chelmsford.*

Friday 26th February - *Henry was appointed Lord of the Treasury.*

Saturday 27th February - *Henry went off to Stockton for his election, and I to stay at Stoke Court.*[17]

Sunday 28th February - *Matilda is not at all strong, but shut up in the carriage we went to church in the morning.*

Monday, Tuesday & Wednesday 1st, 2nd & 3rd March - *Snow, snow, snow! I had a walk for the first time feeling headachy. Henry's Election today and no opposition.*

Thursday 4th March - *Henry went today to stay with Mama.*

Friday 5th March - *Left Stoke Court.*[17] *Met Henry at Paddington Station & came to Lowndes Street.*

Saturday 6th March - *Very cold & sloppy. Not out except walking. Mr Garforth called. Henry has the office of Keeper of the Privy Seal to the Duchy of Cornwall, the Queen's own gift. We dined today at Sir Edward Ryan's. Met C. Pembertin, C. Whitmores,*[22] *Slaneys, Mrs Wynne, Mr and Miss Mangles, Mr Blackwood, Mr Whitmore Jones.*[23]

Sunday 7th March - *Twice at St Michael's.*

Monday 8th March - *Cold but I went out driving, shopping & visiting. Mr Bluck & ecarté.*[4]

Tuesday 9th March - *Walked to Lady E. Tollemache*[24] *and Mrs Calthorpe. Mr Bluck & ecarté.*[4]

Wednesday 10th March - *Henry and I went in the snow paying visits. Dined with the Pritchards.*[6] *Met Sir C. and Lady Young, Butt, Bennets, &c.*

Thursday 11th March - *Sealing wax work. Snow. Mr Bluck & ecarté.*[4]

Friday 12th March - *Tom*[1] *arrived proposing a visit of a few days. Lady Bradford*[25] *and Miss M. called. Henry got home to dine.*

Saturday 13th March - *Headache. Dinner at home. Bennets, C. Whitmores,*[22] *C. Pembertons, Mrs Butt, Mr Ryes, Mr J. Whitmore and Tom.*[1]

Sunday 14th March - *I was laid up all day up to dinner.*

Monday 15th March - *I began Bradley's ether medicine. Eclipse, cloudy. Henry not home to dine.*

Tuesday 16th March - *Henry got home but had to go back after dinner.*

Wednesday 17th March - *Miss Fletcher came to luncheon. I took her home to Westbourne Terrace. Tom dined in Berkeley Square. Henry presented at the Levée. Dinner at Sir J. Packingtons. Lady Isabella Stuarts.*

Thursday 18th March - *Henry did not get home till late. Tom*[1] *sat up as well as me.*

Friday 19th March - *Called upon Miss Fletcher. Tom dined out. Henry came home to dine & stay. Mr Bluck & ecarté.*[4]

Saturday 20th March - *Dinner at home. The Speaker's Levée. Lord Henry Lennox,*[21] *Lord C. Hamilton, the O'Donnaghues, Mr Cole, Sir W. Jolliffe, Mr Hill, Col. Pakenham, Col. Forde, Mr Hamilton, Tom. Lady Derby's Assembly.*[35a]

Sunday 21st March - *Tom at church. Henry had a cold & stayed in bed. We went in the afternoon. Frank, Catty, Mamey, L. and J. came.*[26] *Mr Greig and Miss Perceval called.*

Monday 22nd March - *Early in the carriage with Henry. Tom*[1] *to Brighton for the day. Catty &c.*[26] *off to Brighton for a week or 2. Lady Salisbury's Reception.*

Tuesday 23rd March - *Lady Jersey's Reception where I went by myself and was greatly frightened. Duke of Cambridge & Princess Mary. Colonel Vyse found the carriage for me.*

Wednesday 24th March - *Dinner at home. Lord & Lady Donneraile, Lord & Lady Bandon & Mamey,*[26] *Mr Trefusis, Mr Lygon, Col. & Mrs Forbes,*[9] *Mr Noel, Mr Leslie. Reception at Northumberland House, the Hartshornes there. Mrs Darby Griffiths gave a party.*

Thursday 25th March - *Lady Hereford & Mrs Stanhope called. Lady Salisbury's 3rd Reception. Tom*[1] *went away.*

Friday 26th March - *Glad to rest!*

Saturday 27th March - *Went to dine at Lord Bradford's.*[25] *Lady Bradford was too ill to appear and Miss Moncrieffe took her place. Lady Colchester, 2 ladies Murray, Bishop of Rochester, Mr B. Stanhope, Lord & Lady Charles Clinton, Col. Taylor,*[27] *Sir John & Lady Packington.*

Sunday 28th March - *Passion Week. At church in the morning. In the afternoon Lord Henry Lennox*[21] *came & a chapter of grievances.*

Monday 29th March - *Drove & called on the Storers.*[10] *Mr Bluck.*

Tuesday 30th March - *The Storer's Charlotte & Lois*[10] *came to us before luncheon and I drove them home to Oxford Terrace. Mr Bluck.*

Wednesday 31st March - *Henry and I & Mr Bluck*[5] *went to stay at Stoke Court.*[17] *At dinner Mr and Mrs B. Harvey, Miss Creyke, Mr Ruthven, Mr Clayton.*

Thursday 1st April - *Henry went to Windsor Castle to attend the Confirmation of the Prince of Wales.*[27a] *Mrs B. Harvey & Miss Creyke came to luncheon.*

Friday 2nd April - Good Friday - *We went to church & heard a very good Sermon from Mr Shaw. Made Seals for the seal work.*

Saturday 3rd April - *Left Stoke Court.*[17] *Dinner at home. Lady Hereford & Col. Blackburne, Mr and Mrs Stanhope, Mr and Mrs Dick, Col. Forbes and Miss Forbes,*[9] *Mr Bluck, Mr W.W. Jones, 2 Storers.*[10]

Easter Sunday 4th April - *Went to a little church beyond Hans Place. Walk with Henry and Mr Bluck*[5] *in the afternoon.*

Monday 5th April - *Long visit from Mr W.W. Jones. Henry went to a dinner at the Mansion House.*

Tuesday 6th April - *Sunniside.*[28] *Came home to Mama. Henry and Mr Bluck. I did not take Jones, only Walters came. Rain.*

Wednesday 7th April - *Such rain. We could not go to Wroxeter*[29] *for the opening of the church.*

Thursday 8th April - *Wet and very cold. Mr Bluck*[5] *made models and I made seals for the service of the Bazaar for Stockton.*

Friday 9th April - *Mama and I went to call at Marnwood,*[30] *Severn House,*[31] *Dale House,*[7] *Madeley Wood.*[3]

Saturday 10th April - *Fine cold day. Henry went to Bridgnorth. Mr Bluck and I a walk. Mr and Mrs Henry Dickinson*[31] *& Mr and Mrs Anstice*[3] *came to dine.*

Sunday 11th April - *At church in the morning. Tom*[1] *came to luncheon and to see the alterations. The new Terrace is very promising but the wall cracks which is provoking.*

Monday 12th April - *We returned to Lowndes Street. Henry went at once to the House of Commons & kept there till 1 o'clock.*

Tuesday 13th April - *Ella's first concert at the new St James' Hall.*[33] *Abraham & Matilda and a Miss Evans came to luncheon. Lucy*[9] *is come to Chesterfield Square.*

Wednesday 14th April - *We dined with the Leveson-Gowers.*[34] *Met Frank & Mamey*[26] *& Mrs Long & her son. After, the Duchess of Northumberland's party.*

Thursday 15th April - *Dined at Mrs Saltmarche's. I went without Henry but he followed and was in time. John & Lucy,*[9] *Harrisons, G. & W. Whitmore, Charlotte & Lois (Storer),*[10] *Mrs Widdrington.*

Friday 16th April - *I went to see Catty*[26] *and Lucy.*[9]

Saturday 17th April - *Mrs Whitmore*[32] *came to stay with me.*

Sunday 18th April - *To Mr Hamilton's in the morning and Henry and I & Mr Bluck to Westminster Abbey in the afternoon. When we came home Catty*[26] *& all the family with Mrs Whitmore.*[32]

Monday 19th April - *Douglas*[35] *at breakfast. He is to join the Blues. Settled to go to the Drawing Room*[14] *on Thursday but my train is ready except flowers. Henry and I to Foster.*

Tuesday 20th April - *I went to the Opera with the Russell Stanhopes - Piccolomini in Don Pasquale. Lady Stracey at home but I could not go.*

Wednesday 21st April - *Marriage of Mr Hathaway to Miss Lennox Butler. We were at the Breakfast. Dinner at home. Frank & Catty & Mamey,*[26] *Lord & Lady Doneraile, John & Lucy,*[9] *Mr Lygon, Mr Noel, Mr Trefusis, Mr Leslie. Lady Derby's At Home.*[35a] *She was late from dining at the Palace & Lady Emma Stanley*[36] *received people beautifully.*

Thursday 22nd April - *My second Drawing Room.*[14] *Green train & white & lilac Rhododendrons, Brussels Lace. Dinner at Adml. Duncombe's, I went without Henry who could not get away from the House. Lady Grey Egerton &*

Miss Egerton, Lady H. Duncombe. Mr Abraham Darby[17] is just appointed to the Deanery of York.[37]

Friday 23rd April - *This is a season of great fuss respecting the affair of Lord Radstock and how it will end none can tell. I like it not!*

Saturday 24th April - *Dined with Lord C. & Lady Chelmsford,[38] Count Radetsky, Lord & Lady Donoughmore, Sir Wm. Jolliffe, Mr Mrs Hardy, Sir Hugh & Lady Cairns, Lord Hotham, Miss Earle, Col. Thesiger.[38] Could not go to Miss Blackburne's, it was so late. Came home & talked late in Mrs Whitmore's room.[32]*

Sunday 25th April - *Went to church.*

Monday & Tuesday 26th & 27th April - *Busy with Greenhouse.*

Wednesday 28th April - *Henry invited to Lord Salisbury's but went with me to dine at Mr J.H. Foley's. Very Whig dinner. Bishop of Worcester and Mrs Pepys, Mr and Mrs Richard Cavendish, Mrs Taylor, Sir Henry Cotrell, Lord W. Graham. Mr Rarey's secret of horse training begins to be known. He ties up one leg with a strap - but <u>how?</u> as in the case of Cruiser who was fed <u>thro' a hole</u> for some time before Mr Rarey operated upon him. Went to the Duchess of Northumberland's.*

Saturday 1st May - *Dinner at Mr & Mrs Malin's. Met the Lord Advocate, Mr and Mrs Mowbray, Mrs Dickinson.*

Monday 3rd May - *Mrs Whitmore[32] and I dined with Catty,[26] Lord & Lady Doneraile, Lord Bantry, 2 Storers,[10] Mr Brodrick, Mr Coloquhone, Bishop of Cashel.*

Tuesday 4th May - *Asked to dine at Mrs Slaney's & Mrs Butts - Went to Mrs Butts but Henry was ill in bed and I had to go alone. I met Lord and Lady Egmont, Mr and Mrs Cardwell, Mr and Mrs Reeve.*

Wednesday 5th May - *Catty[26] went to the Drawing Room. Henry rather better and Mr Bluck[5] came to dinner. I did not go to Northumberland House.*

Thursday 6th May - *Henry better and at the House. Went to take leave of Catty[26] & Lois (Storer).[10] Cold.*

Friday 7th May - *Did not go to Mrs Harrison's Ball.*

Saturday 8th May - *Dinner at home. Lord & Lady Bradford,[25] Sir W. & Lady & Miss Jolliffe, Mrs Taylor, Colonel Taylor,[39] Mr Cole, Mr & Mrs Hopwood, Lord Wm. Graham. Did not go to Mrs Bennet.*

Sunday 9th May - *Twice at church. Catty[26] and all the family here with Mrs Whitmore.[32] Mr Bluck.[5]*

Monday 10th May - *Went early with Mrs Whitmore*[32] *to the Exhibiton. Delayed by the Queen & the Queen of Portugal. Henry & I went to the Queen's Ball. White moire with double skirt and red & silver oleanders.*

Tuesday 11th May - *Ella's concert.*[33] *Matilda came but not to us. Did not go to Mrs Taylor's.*

Wednesday 12th May - *Dined at Sir Hugh and Lady Shipwith's. Met Lord and Lady Willoughy de Broke, Mr & Mrs Thornhill. We went to Mrs Derby Griffiths and to the Duchess of Northumberland.*

Thursday 13th May - *Went by myself to the Admiralty to Lady Pakington's At Home.*[40] *A great crush.*

Friday 14th May - *Wet. I went to Lady Keane's for some promised music but a poor lady Mrs Currie was dying at the next house and they had to give it up and did not play or sing a note until after the funeral. Henry got home to dine & Mr Bluck.*

Saturday 15th May - *The Birthday Drawing Room.*[14] *Henry dined with the Chancellor of the Exchequer.*[41] *I with Mrs Taylor & met Lord and Lady Waterpark, Mrs Musgrove, Mr C. Musgrove, Mrs Burton, Mr Carew. Full dress party at Lady Derby's in Downing Street.*[35a] *Oh dear me, but it was a squeeze on a narrow staircase! - Henry got the entree for me at the Drawing Room and it was very pleasant. Mauve train trimmings & lace.*

Sunday 16th May - *Twice at church. Mr Brockfield preached. It was a charity sermon but very excellent indeed.*

Monday 17th May - *Mrs Whitmore*[32] *went to Stoke Court*[17] *for the day. It was wet. George*[42] *arrived at Evetall's. Dined here & Henry came home.*

Tuesday 18th May - *I went with Mrs Stanhope to Harrington House for luncheon. Very wet so that we could not pay all the visits we intended.*

Wednesday 19th May - *Could not dine at Lord Midleton's. Went to Mrs Seymour Fitzgerald's,*[43] *met an immense party. Bishop of Exeter, & Mrs Phillpots, Sir Fitzroy Kelly, Hady, etc. Then went to Northumberland House. Lady Stracey's and Lady Spearman's. I was very seedy and glad when bed time came.*

Thursday 20th May - *Mrs Whitmore*[32] *went to dine with Catty.*[26] *Lady Pakington's*[40] *Assembly at the Admiralty but I did not go.*

Friday 21st May - *The Charltons at Paterson's & today they have news of the sudden death of Mrs Parr. Mr Cardwell's*[44] *note of censure on the Government was withdrawn.*

Saturday 22nd May - *Henry and I and Mr Bluck went to Veitch's about flowers for Wednesday. Mrs Bennet's dinner & evening party. A very mixed multitude.*

Sunday 23rd May - *Once at church. Rain. Lucy*[9] *& Dora called.*

Monday 24th May - *Henry at home and Mr Bluck at dinner.*

Tuesday 25th May - *Mrs Whitmore*[32] *left us. Dinner at home. Harrisons, Malins 2, Knights 2, Butler Johnsons 2, Sir J. Hopkins, Slaneys 2. 15.*

Wednesday 26th May - *"At Home." We dined with Catty*[26] *and met Lord and Lady Erne, Lord Blantyer and then I ran away for my evening party. Lord and Lady Harrington came early & stayed all the evening almost. Mrs Ashton Benyon came & sang a great deal for us & Lady Pigot & Lady Keane. It was a very successful evening but all spoilt to me by losing Toozie!*[13] *I took him into Cadogan Place and he ran into the garden and I lost him.*

Thursday 27th May - *The last day of Henry's little Whitsuntide holiday which has been quite spoilt by the loss of Toozie*[13] *- we are in bitter despair. Offered rewards, and went to consult Mr Bishop.*

Friday 28th May - *Henry again at the House. I went in the evening to Lady Laura Grattan's where she had a visiting young lady Miss Thompson whose powers are certainly remarkable. She is ten years old and recited from Hamlet with wonderful feeling. She is American.*

Saturday 29th May - *Darling Toozie*[13] *was brought home as we were dressing to dine with the Jolliffe's. Didn't we kiss him! He had not been stolen after all but having lost me he persuaded some servants to let him in. This morning the man saw our advertisement in the Times. Met at the Jolliffe's Mr and the Countess Bentinck, Count and Countess de Cetto, Lord and Lady Verulum.*

Sunday 30th May - *Once at church and then a walk. Mr Bluck.*

Monday 31st May - *Mamey*[26] *and I drove in the park. Lady Pigot at home. Large party, a great deal of singing. I had to go alone as usual, alas.*

Tuesday 1st June - *It is getting so very hot but our home is so nice. Henry got home today to dine. It was 3 o'clock in the morning & broad daylight before he could get home.*

Wednesday 2nd June - *Dinner at home - Mainwarings, Waterparks, Bandons.*[26] *In the morning, Harrington House & very hot. I went with Lady Laura Grattan & Miss Tollemache.*

Thursday 3rd June - *Ascot Cup Day.*

Friday 4th June - *Still very hot. Death of poor Mr R. Cavendish. I went to call on Mrs Moseley & Mrs G. Wrottesley.*[15]

Saturday 5th June - *Thunder and rain. Lady Blount At Home but we did not go - It was too pleasant to have Henry for once for an evening. Mr Bluck. Mrs Cavendish had a dreadful operation for cancer but was recovering, and it appears that no-one knew she had a heart complaint or probably they would* *not have given chloroform. From that and the heat she died quite unexpectedly 2 or 3 days after the operation.*

Tuesday 8th June - *Refused the Bennets & Richmonds - Sir J. Hopkins and Greenwich. Ella.*[33] *Lady Hereford At Home.*

Thursday 10th June - *Harrington House. Very large parties - the carpets up and people dancing in all the hottest afternoons! Dined at the Scotts. Henry could not come. Mrs Parry Nisbitt's evening party. I met Mrs Haddo. George arrived.*[42]

Friday 11th June - *Lady Scott at home & Lady Louisa Cotes' Concert. George*[42] *went to this last. It was Miss Cotes' Birthday.*

Saturday 12th June - *A dinner at home. Mr Mrs and Miss Blackburne, Sir Frederick and Lady Smythe, Admiral and Miss Byng, Mr A. Heneage, Lady Bandon,*[26] *Mamey,*[26] *George,*[42] *Mrs Egremont,*[29] *and a small party in the evening.*

Sunday 13th June - *To Dr Thorpe's and in the afternoon to St Michael's. I went to Catty*[26] *and then the Forbes.*[9] *Then in the Park with Henry and George.*[42]

Monday 14th June - *Miss Vansittart's At Home. Lady Bradford's*[25] *At Home, an immense party. George*[42] *went to it, I could not manage Miss Vansittart's & was vexed.*

Tuesday 15th June - *Mrs Cuthbert was to have gone to the House of Lords but she was taken ill. I went with Henry. George*[42] *& I dined with Catty.*[26] *I went to Mrs Annesley afterwards. Met Mrs and Miss Watts Russell.*

Wednesday 16th June - *Dined at Mr and Lady Mary Clive's. We met the Bishop of Worcester and Mrs Pepys &c.*

Thursday 17th June - *George*[42] *returned to Mableden.*

Friday 18th June - *The Queen's Concert, a great treat it was, and very splendid affair. Titiéns voice is beautiful. We had to give up dining with Lady Laura Grattan but went to Mrs Capel-Cure's Ball afterwards.*

Saturday 19th June - *Conversations at the Kensington Museum.*[45] *Mrs Gaskell at home but this we could not manage. Went to Mrs Bennet's for a few minutes. George*[42] *came back here.*

Sunday 20th June - *Henry laid up with a lame foot. I went once to church, St Michael's, with George.*[42]

Monday 21st June - *George*[42] *left us. A late night for Henry.*

Tuesday 22nd June - *Douglas*[35] *arrived. Took Mamey to Ella's*[33] *concert and then went to Dorset Place, Mrs Egremont*[29] *let me in. Henry home to dine.*

Wednesday 23rd June - *Mansion House dinner to meet Her Majesty's Ministers, oh it was a long affair, from half past 6 to 12 o'clock! Sir William Carden Mayor this year. I was glad to have seen the Loving Cup for once. The speeches very stupid. It was great fun to sit next to Henry. I had Mr Seymour Fitzgerald*[43] *on the other side. Afterwards we went to Mr Lennox Butler's Ball, which was very full and rather pleasant, but myself sleepy.*

Thursday 24th June - *Dined with Mr and Mrs Edwardes, met Lady Margaret Beaumont.*

Friday 25th June - *Douglas*[35] *left till Wednesday.*

Saturday 26th June - *Dinner at home. Hartopps, Vernons, Boroughs, Mr Boughey, Egremonts, Robert, Herbert, Mr Bluck. Henry and I afterwards to the Duchess of Manchester's Assembly.*[45a]

Sunday 27th June - *Lost pet blue locket (never found) advertised it.*

Monday 28th June - *Nice quiet day.*

Tuesday 29th June - *Did not go to Lady Pigot's Ball. I went to Mrs Taylor's in the evening and walked home.*

Wednesday 30th June - *Went with Henry to Sewell and Cross. Douglas*[35] *arrived. Dined at Lady Louisa Cotes. Met the Duke of Cleveland and Lady Augusta Paulet, Lord and Lady Delawarr, Mr and Mrs Mainwaring, Lord Redesdale, Miss Mitford. Afterwards Mrs Adderley's concert.*

Thursday 1st July - *Harrington House fete. Tom*[1] *here at luncheon. Douglas*[35] *went out to dine.*

Friday 2nd July - *Tom*[1] *here from Beckenham.*[46] *Douglas*[34] *and I an evening alone.*

Saturday 3rd July - *Tom*[1] *here and took Douglas*[35] *with him to Beckenham*[46] *till Monday. Henry and I went to the Exhibition. Henry dined at the Trinity House to meet Prince Albert.*

Sunday 4th July - *To church and in the afternoon to Westminster Abbey.*

Monday 5th July - *Tom*[1] *here on his way home. I shopping. Waited dinner for Douglas*[35] *but he went to the theatre.*

Tuesday 6th July - *Dinner at Mr and Mrs Christy's.*[47] *Sir J. Elphinstone, Mr Dundee, Mr and Mrs Bentley, Sir Archibald Hope, &c.*

Wednesday 7th July - *Ball at the Mansion House, a tremendous thunder storm, could not go to Mrs Waldo Sibthorpe's Concert.*

Thursday 8th July - *I went to Stoke Court*[17] *for fete. Lady Jersey at home and Lady Hartopp's Ball.*

Friday 9th July - *Rain, rain, for the Cremoine Fete. Douglas*[35] *dined out quite accidentally.*

Saturday 10th July - *Rain. Dinner at home. Lady Scott, Sir Francis was too ill. Mrs Taylor, Mr and Mrs J. Pritchard,*[6] *Mr and Mrs Boville, Mr Mrs and Miss Edwardes, Mr G.A. Hamilton, Douglas,*[35] *Major Powys, Mr Leeke, Mr Baldock.*

Sunday 11th July - *Bad cold which began with the Stoke Park fete on a cold day. Not out. Colonel Forbes*[9] *called. Douglas,*[35] *Mr Wingfield and Mr Bluck at dinner. Douglas*[35] *left us for the Barracks.*

Monday 12th July - *Warmer. Out driving. Henry came home to dine.*

Tuesday 13th July - *No morning sitting. Called on Lady Hartopp and Lady Jolliffe.*

Wednesday 14th July - *Drove out with Henry in the afternoon. Dined with the Gaskells. 16. Sir Watkin and Lady Wynne, Sir J. and Lady Doyle, Capel-Cures, Capt. Cheney, Mr Gaugh and Mr Phillimore.*

Thursday 15th July - *Colonel Forbes*[9] *at breakfast time. Douglas*[35] *came to luncheon.*

Saturday 17th July - *Dearest Mama came to us for a day or two. We had the Queen's Box at the Princesses for Shylock and Charles Keen. Dined at the Capel Cures who came with us and brought their party. Lady Ashbrook & Lord Ashbrook, &c. Mr and Miss Bluck and Mr Jefferson & Douglas*[35] *came in.*

Sunday 18th July - *Went to church in the afternoon. Cold bad. Mr and Miss Bluck and Douglas*[35] *at dinner.*

Monday 19th July - *Mama and I shopping and to call on Lady Wrottesley*[15] *and Mrs Taylor.*

Tuesday 20th July - *Shopping & the Exhibition. Henry home to dine.*

Wednesday 21st July - *Mama left us for Stoke Court.*[17] *Dined with Sir Wm. and Lady Hartopp, Lord and Lady Newark, Lady Clifford Constable, Lord Earlsworth, Sir H. Vane, Mr Adderley.*

Thursday 22nd July - *Wet day. Took Henry to the House. At work for Bazaar and miss Mama very much.*

Friday 23rd July - *Settling wages and at work for the Bazaar.*

Saturday 24th July - *Ministerial White Bait dinner at Greenwich. I went for the day to Stoke Court*[17] *- Mama there.*

Sunday 25th July - *At church at St Michael's.*

Monday 26th July - *Shopping and paying bills.*

Tuesday 27th July - *Douglas*[35] *came for luncheon.*

Wednesday 28th July - *Henry and I went to Stoke Court*[17] *to dine & sleep.*

Thursday 29th July - *Came back early from Stoke Court.*[17]

Friday 30th July - *Not at all well, laid up.*

Saturday 31st July - *Better. Packing. Drove out with Henry for some last shopping.*

Sunday 1st August - *Not at church. A visit from Mr and Mrs Beaumont. She looking so well and happy.*

Monday 2nd August - *Parliament prorogued. Marie came to see me again. Everything put away and me miserable.*

Tuesday 3rd August - *Servants, carriage and horses early to Coalbrookdale. Henry and I and Mr Bluck to the Burlington Hotel, Eastbourne.*

Wednesday 4th August - *We like Eastbourne and they have given us better rooms than at first.*

Thursday 5th August - *Lovely weather but rather cold! I feel so well.*

Friday 6th August - *Walked in the evening to the wind mills & found such a dear cat.*

Saturday7th August - *The country is very pretty for walking through, at first we thought it flat & ugly - the sea beautiful and the weather & everything so fresh. We went to Hastings & St Leonards & Fairlight Downs. Walked 7 miles.*

Sunday 8th August - *I was tired and rather stiff but twice at church. Charity sermons for the schools but very good.*

Monday 9th August - *Dreadful news. Last Friday Lord Queensbury*[48] *(Archie Drumlanrig) was found shot through the heart on his own moor at Kenmount.*

Tuesday 10th August - *We drove after dinner to Beachy Head. Such magnificent cliffs.*

Wednesday 11th August - *Rather hot - Walked to the wind mills to feed our cat.*

Thursday 12th August - *Walked on the beach but very misty towards Beachy Head.*

Friday 13th August - *More bad news. We must leave this on Monday. Poor Uncle Wolryche*[49] *is dead. He was not well but no-one had thought of danger altho' he had been altered of late. He was found dead about 10 o'clock in the day. Dr Wall having left him to sleep some hours before. This was last Wednesday.*

Saturday 14th August - *Mr Bluck went to Brighton for the day. Douglas*[35] *came to spend Sunday. I not over well.*

Sunday 15th August - *I still rather seedy and did not go to church.*

Monday 16th August - *Henry & I & Mr Bluck & Douglas*[35] *left Eastbourne for Lowndes Street. Douglas spent the day with us. Shopping.*

Tuesday 17th August - *Shopping, shopping, for I have to get mourning for the Birmingham Festival as well as for that Bazaar. At half past 5 left for Stoke Court.*[17]

Wednesday 18th August - *Left Stoke Court.*[17] *Abraham is much recovering from the lameness & walked with a stick. He strained or broke the tendon Achilles dancing some Highland dance. Met Mr Bluck at Slough and came home.*

Thursday 19th August - *Mama very well.*

Friday 20th August - *Henry to Dudmaston for the sad funeral.*[49] *The place never can be the same again! It is left to Mr F. Laing when the debt of £50,000 is paid off.*

Saturday 21st August - *Sting with wasp! Mr and Mrs Henry Dickinson*[12] *and Mr and Mrs W.E. called.*

Sunday 22nd August - *Went to church and a Mr Brook. Mr Forester's Curate preached. Rain.*

Monday 23rd August - *Henry and I and Mr Bluck drove to Apley to see the Bazaar preparations. Walked over the Park to Stockton. The Pritchards called.*

Tuesday 24th August - *Mr Henry Dickinson*[12] *to see stall. Mrs Alfred Darby*[50] *& Miss Christy & 2 Mr Christys to luncheon & to contribute.*

Wednesday 25th August - *Mrs Anstice*[3] *came to see stall.*

Thursday 26th August - *The first day of the Bazaar and Flower Show. Henry and I and Mr Bluck to dine at Stockton. Mrs Whitmore*[32] *there and John and Lucy*[9] *- Home with Post Horses, Mama's brake broken.*

Friday 27th August - *Second day of the Bazaar and not much done.*

Saturday 28th August - *Henry to Cotsbrooke.*[1] *Charlotte & Lois (Storer)*[10] *are there. Mr Bluck fishing.*

Sunday 29th August - *I did not go to church, the old wasp's sting beginning to be so tiresome.*

Monday 30th August - *Henry and I and the servants go to Great Barr for the week for the Birmingham Festival. Mrs Washington Hibbert, Mr Fane, Sir J. Harrison and Sir Henry Edwardes.*

Tuesday 31st August - *To Birmingham for the first day of the Festival. Elijah. C. Novello, Castellan, Miss Dolby, Sims, Reeves.*

Wednesday 1st September - *Elijah - George & Miss Deacon came to Birmingham. All had luncheon both days at the G. Whateleys.*

Thursday 2nd September - *The Messiah. The Hall filled. Mrs Egremont*[29] *& 3 daughters there. A younger Miss Hartopp arrived at Barr and Captain Hanbury.*

Friday 3rd September - *Judith. Beethoven's Mass in C. Mendelssohn's Hymn.*

Saturday 4th September - *We came home and the party broke up. Nobody can tell what I suffered all through the week with the wasp's sting on my ankle, and it was all but erysipelas!*

Sunday 5th September - *Did not go out in the morning. In the afternoon all went to church at Little Wenlock, Mama in the carriage.*

Monday 6th September - *Mr Webb*[51] *came to see the sting, and a second wasp gave me a second sting as he was preparing to look at it!*

Tuesday 7th September - *Henry and Mr Bluck fishing. Walter*[1] *came for a few days. Mr Webb*[51] *& Coulard water.*

Wednesday 8th September - *All three went to fish. Whist.*

Thursday 9th September - *All of us at Shrewsbury. Nice pleasant day.*

Friday 10th September - *Henry went to shoot at Apley. Walter*[1] *& Mr Bluck to fish. Mama and I called on Uncle Richard Darby.*[52]

Saturday 11th September - *Walter*[1] *left us. Henry and Mr Bluck to Bridgnorth. Mrs Whitmore*[32] *came to stay with us from Apley Castle. Mrs Edmund Darby*[7] *& Mary called.*

Sunday 12th September - *Henry and Mr Bluck to Little Wenlock in the morning. Sermon for schools. In the afternoon to Sutton. Mrs Whitmore,*[32] *Mama, Mr Bluck, Henry and I. Mr Aston, "It is high time to awake out of sleep."*

Monday 13th September - *Mrs Whitmore,*[32] *Mama and I to Stanley.*[50] *Very hot. Saw Comet last night in the north. Henry shooting with Mr Sparkes. George*[42] *came for 2 nights.*

Tuesday 14th September - *Colder. The Corporation Dinner (Bridgnorth). The Queen's Haunch of Venison. Mr and Mrs Webb*[51] *came.*

Wednesday 15th September - *Mrs Whitmore and I to Bridgnorth to luncheon. Left George*[42] *at Stockton. Called on Mrs Sparkes - Bellets - Mr Marshall. Miss Whitmore's Vesi.*

Thursday 16th September - *Mrs Whitmore,*[32] *Mama and I went to call at Uncle Richard Darby's,*[52] *Dale House,*[7] *Severn House,*[12] *Marnwood*[30] *and Buildwas Park.*[53]

Friday 17th September - *Miss Croft came to luncheon and Miss Haughton and Mrs Whitmore left us going back with them to Apley Castle. Ponies turned out.*

Saturday 18th September - *Henry and Mr Bluck to Bridgnorth.*

Sunday 19th September - *Went to church here, Mr Hayes.*[11] *In afternoon, Henry & I & Mr Bluck went to Little Wenlock.*

Monday 20th September - *Not at all well in the evening.*

Tuesday 21st September - *Comet beautiful.*

Wednesday 22nd September - *Wet and cold. Sat and worked. Fussed about myself.*

Thursday 23rd September - *Henry went to Apley Castle for luncheon and to bring Mrs Whitmore*[32] *here again for a week.*

Friday 24th September - *A walk. Rebecca's fall from her horse. Mrs & 2 Miss Egremonts. Mr Mrs and Miss Rowley at dinner. Colonel Forester & Miss Anson called & had luncheon.*

Saturday 25th September - *Mrs Whitmore went with me to luncheon at Willey. Called on the Rowleys, O. Foresters and J. Pritchards.*[6] *Ballon. Mr and Mrs W.D. called.*

Sunday 26th September - *To Broseley church. Mrs Whitmore,*[32] *Henry and I and Mr Bluck to hear Mr Aston preach.*

Monday 27th September - *We all left home. Mr Bluck for London, Mrs Whitmore, Henry & Mama and I to the Regent at Leamington. This was for the benefit of Mr Middleton's advice for me but he says nothing can be known yet & we must wait. The Storers*[10] *came too.*

Tuesday 28th September - *Mama and I and Henry left the Regent and came home.*

Wednesday 29th September - *Henry and I came to Kinlet*[54] *- 4 horses from Bridgnorth and pretty the country was about Bewdley & such lovely weather. All this time I did not think I should live & very sweet the pleasures of life seemed. Yet I do not know that there was a clinging to life that might be imagined. Often it was a thought like "The sooner it is over, the sooner to sleep and pray that when the last days of life may really be supposed drawing near that it may please God to give me the same resignation & the same blessed sense of Forgiveness through His grace who alone can save."*

Thursday 30th September - *At Kinlet, we have Mr and Mrs Stevens and Emily Bridgeman. I went with the 2 Miss Childes to call at Morley on Lady Blount. Henry found a kitten.*

Friday 1st October *- Drive around the Park at Kinlet. It is beautiful and the day was beautiful. In the evening Mrs Stevens played and we had Whist and the Comet.*

Saturday 2nd October *- We left Kinlet leaving the kitten in Miss Bridgeman's care. Posted thro' Bewdley Forest to Bewdley & Worcester to Malvern. Shall I ever forget that drive! I was Very Happy and yet thought perhaps I am not to see another summer in this world. We dined at Lyttleton Hall.*

Sunday 3rd October *- We are at the Abbey Hotel. Twice at church. Emily*[55] *came to dine with us.*

Monday 4th October *- Luncheon at Rose Bank. The Conjuror. Bad toothache but it got better and we went to dine at Madresfield.*[56] *Lord and Lady Raglan, Canon and Mrs Wood, Mr Dyson, Miss Brownlow, Miss Cornewall.*

Tuesday 5th October *- Luncheon at Rose Bank. Lady Church, John & Lucy, Mrs Whitmore.*[32] *To Madresfield & Mr Packington's with E. & E. Dined at Lyttleton Hall. Met Capt. & Mrs Chandler, Mrs Davis, E. & E. The Comet within centre of ?*

Wednesday 6th October *- Called on Miss Cornewall and went to Lyttleton Hall for luncheon. Ballons. To Westwood, a fine old house. Lord Chancellor & Lady Chelmsford,*[38] *Miss Thesiger, Lord Redesdale & Miss Mitford, Mrs Murray.*

Thursday 7th October *- A wet day. At dinner the Mayor of Worcester and Mr & Mrs Pidcock, the Dean of Worcester & Mrs Pepys. Singing.*

Friday 8th October *- Drove to Witley*[57] *after luncheon. Beautiful day - the Comet at night. At dinner the Bishop of Worcester & Mrs Pepys.*

Saturday 9th October *- Left Westwood to return home by Bridgnorth where we met George*[42] *& had luncheon. Tom*[1] *gave us a Haunch of Venison & no end of game for the Chancellor's visit.*

Sunday 10th October *- So wet nobody could go out, so we settled Henry's dressing room for Lord Chancellor.*

Monday 11th October *- The Lord Chancellor & Lady Chelmsford & Miss Thesiger arrived for luncheon. We drove to Willey*[58] *and saw the old Major & Mrs Anson as she was getting off her horse. Mr Bluck arrived. At dinner Mr and Mrs Anstice,*[3] *Mr Edmonds,*[59] *George & Sarah.*[42]

Tuesday 12th October *- The Fishing at Patshull.*[60] *Went all in our carriage with 4 post horses. At dinner Mr and Mrs John Pritchard*[6] *& Mr and Mrs Hayes.*[11]

Wednesday 13th October *- Went to Bridgnorth for luncheon. Apley. At dinner Tom & Lady Louisa - Nina & Mary,*[1] *Wally Garforth, Col. Forester,*[58] *St John.*

Thursday 14th October - *The Lord Chancellor & Lady Chelmsford, Miss Thesiger, Henry and I to Weston Park*[25] *for 2 nights.*

Friday 15th October - *The Lady Bridgemans very busy with the photographs. Expedition to Lilleshall. We have at Weston Mr and Mrs Noireys, Mr Robert Eyton and Mr Richard Brooke.*

Saturday 16th October - *The party broke up. Saw the Chelmsfords off at Shifnal. Discomfort in the Establishment - John Speke of Rowton must be sent away.*

Sunday 17th October - *Such glorious weather. Twice at church here and at Little Wenlock. Henry & I and Mr Bluck.*

Monday 18th October - *Pouring rain! what a pity! Miss C. and Mr E. Childe arrived in the evening.*

Tuesday 19th October - *Windy & wet but we all went to Apley & called at Stockton. Miss C.C. being very brave.*

Wednesday 20th October - *Catty and Mr E. Childe left us. Rather wet still.*

Thursday 21st October - *Henry and I went to Willey*[58] *for 3 nights. Today Isabel Leighton is to marry Mr Botfield.*

Friday 22nd October - *At Willey.*[58] *Lady Ailsbury, Mrs and 2 Miss Ansons, Colonel and Mrs Curzon, Col. Forester, Major Forester, Mr & Mrs Doyrell, Mr Mytton of Shipton.*

Saturday 23rd October - *Henry and I and Geraldine Anson walked to call on Mrs Layton Lowndes - this was yesterday. Henry to Bridgnorth.*

Sunday 24th October - *Mr Bluck not well & Mama has a cold. Henry & I at church.*

Monday 25th October - *Great rummage in my affairs!*

Tuesday 26th October - *Sermon at Bridgnorth by the Bishop of Cape Town. Luncheon at Mrs Sparkes.*

Wednesday 27th October - *Mary Darby*[7] *was married at Stoke Court to Mr Jones of Baschurch.*[61] *Noisy days here. Very fine.*

Thursday 28th October - *Very wet day. Mama not at all well.*

Friday 29th October - *Henry and Mr Bluck gone to Fair at Bridgnorth. Mr Hayes*[11] *called. Mrs Henry Dickinson*[12] *and Rebecca, Mama saw them but she is very ill!*

Saturday 30th October - *Accounts of the Stoke Court wedding not pleasant. Mama so far from well that Mr Webb*[51] *came twice & we sat up.*

Sunday 31st October - *I did not leave Mama at all. It is like rheumatic fever. Henry once at church & Mr Bluck.*

Monday 1st November - *Fine bright day. Mama in the Drawing Room in the evening.*

Tuesday 2nd November - *Beautiful warm day. In the afternoon Henry and I and Mr Bluck drove to Marnwood*[30] *to call on Mrs Anstice.*

Wednesday 3rd November - *Dearest Mama makes some progress now the effect of the opium is gone off.*

Thursday 4th November - *Henry and I and Mr Bluck drove to Willey.*[58] *Everybody gone to the opening of Linley Church. Left some Pears. Mama a little better.*

Friday 5th November - *Henry and I and Mr Bluck went in cold rain to call on Mrs H. Wayne at Tickwood. Called on Uncle Richard Darby*[52] *in the morning.*

Saturday 6th November - *Mrs Egremont met Lillie here at luncheon, returning from Stoke Court*[17] *and Stanley. Very bad account from Stoke Court*[17] *of Mrs Edmund Darby.*[7] *Mama very tired.*

Sunday 7th November - *At church - Sacrament. Henry and Mr Bluck to Buildwas. Douglas*[35] *came over. Mama tired but came down to dine.*

Monday 8th November - *Henry and Mr Bluck left for London. Mr Graham ill - I went to see poor Mrs S.G. The Joseph Dickinsons called.*[2]

Tuesday 9th November - *Mama better and we had a little drive. Poor Mr Graham died last night. Mr Edmonds*[59] *called. Henry would dine at the Guildhall.*

Wednesday 10th November - *Fog, fog, or we should have gone out. Sad accounts from Stoke Court.*[62]

Thursday 11th November - *Inventories of Plate. Mama is much better & stronger. Mr & Mrs Hayes called.*[11]

Friday 12th November - *Mrs Henry Dickinson*[12] *& Miss Sturge called. Mama and I went out to call on Mrs Graham.*

Saturday 13th November - *Settling to go to Lowndes Street next week. Stoke Court news gets worse and worse.*[62]

Sunday 14th November - *At church. Mr Graham's funeral. Mr & Mrs Sturge called.*

Monday 15th November - *Visit from Mr Layton Lowndes - This night was the dreadful night at Weston*[25] *and Lady Lucy and Lady Charlotte Bridgeman burnt in a terrible manner.*

Tuesday 16th November - *Mama and I went to London by the North Western in a* through *carriage. The 2 maids & Walter.*

Wednesday 17th November - *Lady Forester*[63] *has a still-born son. Our before luncheon shopping. Mrs Garforth*[65] *called.*

Thursday 18th November - *Shopping Clarkes. Dr Bence Jones who gives me no hope of being better but I am to take a medicine.*

Friday 19th November - *Mr Greig called. Douglas*[35] *dined here. Whist.*

Saturday 20th November - *Drive with Mrs G. to Brompton. Mr & Mrs Taylor. Asbestos stove. Mr Bluck and whist.*

Sunday 21st November - *Thick fog. I went to church in the afternoon. Cold. Mr & Mrs Fitzroy called and Mrs Garforth.*[65] *Douglas*[35] *and Mr Bluck at dinner.*

Monday 22nd November - *Called on Mrs Garforth*[65] *with Mama. Mrs C. Wand, Mrs Brisbowe. Mr Bluck and Whist.*

Tuesday 23rd November - *Walked out shopping. Bought a hat. Douglas*[35] *at dinner.*

Wednesday 24th November - *Mama and I out shopping. Met Lady Radstocke & Missy. Douglas*[35] *at luncheon. Mr Jefferson and Mr Bluck.*

Thursday 25th November - *A very long shopping Mama & me. At dinner Mr Bluck & Whist. Soho Bazaar. Henry and I to call upon Lady Chelmsford.*[38] *Lady Elizabeth Tollemache.*[24] *I to Lady Wrottesley.*[15] *Mama and I to Mrs Greig. Douglas*[35] *& Mr Bluck dined here. Whist. Poor Lady Charlotte Bridgeman*[25] *died today of locked jaw from the burns.*

Saturday 27th November - *Mama and her maid to Stoke Court.*[17] *Henry & I & servants to Guys Cliffe to stay with the Percys. Lord & Lady Villiers, Sir George and Lady Phillips, Mr Knightley.*

Sunday 28th November - *To church at Warwick. In the afternoon Henry & I & Mr Percy to Leamington over the fields. Came back here in the dark in a fly & Henry jumping out in the dark hurt his leg, horribly, jumping out!*

Monday 29th November - *The Poultry show at Birmingham. Henry could not go nor did I, oh dear, but it is unfortunate. Mr Doherty at dinner.*

Tuesday 30th November - *We left Guys Cliffe. Had some luncheon at Leamington at Mrs Storer's*[10] *and Henry saw a doctor. Went to Longford. Capt. & Mrs Clement Hill, Sir J. Kynaston, Mrs Cavendish Taylor, Sir John Charlton, Mr Palmer, Bougheys at dinner.*

Wednesday 1st December - *Lady Hester drove over to Weston*[25] *with Mrs Clement Hill and me to enquire after poor Lady Lucy Bridgeman - as ill as possible.*

Thursday 2nd December - *We returned to Lowndes Street - Sir J. Kynaston ordered a through carriage for us by the North Western. Lord Vane as far as Stafford. Toozie so glad to see us.*

Friday 3rd December - *Lady Lucy Bridgeman died today, the day of Lady Charlotte's funeral.*

Saturday 4th December - *Yesterday we went off to pay a visit to Stoke Court[17] but were stopped by a note from Tilly (Matilda) when we got to Slough. One of Mrs Alfred's[50] children then at Stoke Court had been taken ill. We telegraphed back for some dinner and returned by the next train. It was a glorious sunset. Today Henry's Duchy meeting. Gave up going to Stanley[50] next week for he is still lame and under Mr Cumberbach. Lady Clementina Villiers dead of ague today.*

Sunday 5th December - *At church in the morning, Mrs Danson & Mrs Woulfe, Douglas[35] and Mr Bluck at luncheon and dinner.*

Monday 6th December - *Henry so lame. Mr Cumberbach says we must stay on. Dark & foggy. Mr Bluck & dancing.*

Tuesday 7th December - *Dark & foggy. Did not go out. Mr Percy called. Mr Bluck & dancing.*

Wednesday 8th December - *Abraham Darby[17] brought Mama for the day to see us. Mr Bluck and dancing. Whist.*

Thursday 9th December - *I went to Stoke Court[17] for the day, Mama, Mrs Edmund Darby and Miss Nicoll. In the evening Mr Bluck, Douglas[35] and Whist.*

Friday 10th December - *Long day of shopping & visiting. Forbes, Mrs Brisbowe &c. &c. Today Lady Lucy Bridgeman's[25] funeral. We dined at Lady Elizabeth Tollemache's.[24] Met the Augustus Tollemache's[24] and Mrs Leycester.*

Saturday 11th December - *We came home picking up Mama at Slough. Mr Palmer as far as Reading. Then Dora and Tom Megriete who had been staying with Lord & Lady Ferrers.*

Sunday 12th December - *At church in the morning. Henry still a little lame. We 3 are alone and it is very nice. Foy is gone to live with the Bishop of Hereford. We have a new man out of livery, Felix Court by name, & Walter is still here.*

Monday 13th December - *Henry shooting at Apley. Busy in the Library. Mr & Mrs Hayes[11] called.*

Tuesday 14th December - *Cold. Mama to consult Mr Anstice about a Leighton lease. Called at Marnwood.[30]*

***Wednesday 15th December** - The Bells rang all day, as we guess for Mrs Jones[64] coming to Severn House. Cold and wet.*

***Thursday 16th December** - Cold & wet. Library all day. Mr & Mrs Jones at Severn House.[64] We went out.*

***Friday 17th December** - Henry shooting at Apley. Visit from Rebecca. Library.*

***Saturday 18th December** - Henry at Bridgnorth. Walter[1] came here with him in returning to spend Sunday. Thunder storm after such a wet morning.*

***Sunday 19th December** - Mr Hayes[11] Sermon on the Church at Philadelphia.*

***Monday 20th December** - Abraham Darby[17] came to stay with Mama. Henry and I to call at Decker Hill - Aston Haughton - and on Mrs Cunliffe.*

***Tuesday 21st December** - Company's Meeting. Nothing good. Henry and I to Oteley Park. Left Abraham Darby[17] with Mama. At Oteley, Mr & Lady Leeke, Mrs Taylor and Capt. Taylor, Mr Mrs and Miss Bullen, Capt. Cotton, Mr Salisbury Mainwaring who is 15, and at Eton. Shooting. Mrs Mainwaring and I walked in the grounds. Whist. This on Wednesday. Sir John Kynaston came to dine.*

***Thursday 23rd December** - I woke up so ill! The Hounds met at Oteley - I came home. Henry going on to Shifnal, to sleep at Stockton[42] and shoot tomorrow at Apley. Sick & seedy all day.*

***Friday 24th December** - Much better! Busy in Library. Mr Bluck[5] arrived just a little before Henry.*

***Saturday 25th December - Christmas Day** - We went to church and stayed the Sacrament, but so wet we drove there and back. Carols all day long. Mr Bluck has given me such a lovely pair of Whist Markers, Henry an ivory pair of glove openers and Mama a Bag, her own pretty work. Carols, Carols!*

***Sunday 26th December** - At church. Douglas[35] came over to call. Mr Bluck[5] to church at Buildwas.*

***Monday 27th December** - Henry shooting at Apley. Library. Dora rode over. I called on Uncle Richard Darby.[52]*

***Tuesday 28th December** - The Library. Photography.*

***Wednesday 29th December** - We were to have gone over to Stockton[42] for a Christmas Tree at the school but heavy rain gave us a great escape.*

***Thursday 30th December** - Henry and I to Apley Castle. Mr Beaumont & Marie, the Robert Jones and their 2 boys, Miss Corbet Aston, Mr Brooke, St John, Mr Merrick from Admaston. Music in the evening. William Whitmore was of the party.*

Friday 31st December - New Year's Eve *- The old year ended very foggy and dark. Nobody went out walking. Henry went to Shrewsbury in the service of the Charades. At night they acted some very good ones - Butterfly, Madrigal, Ballot, and they ended with a Tableau of the Old Year. Henry managed all. Yesterday poor Mrs Anson drank laudanum by mistake and died, notwithstanding every effort to save her. She was at Mrs Isted's at Eckton.*

Infirmary Meeting
November 1858

Treasurer - Lod Wenlock.

Plates held by: Lady Mary Clure,
Sir Charles Boughton,
Miss Cotes,
Mr Boughey.

Sermon preached by the Hon. & Rev. Lawley.

NOTES

1. Cotsbrooke was the home of Thomas Charlton Whitmore (Tom or Tommy), the eldest of the three Whitmore brothers (George and Henry being the others) and of Lady Louisa Whitmore (née Douglas) his wife who was the daughter of the Marquis of Queensbury. It was also home to their children Douglas, Walter, Nina, Mary, Emily (Emmy), Louisa, Lucy, Edith and Elizabeth.
2. Joseph Dickinson was a cousin of Adelaide. He was the eldest son of Barnard and Ann Dickinson and had for a few years been manager of the Horsehay works. In 1842 he married Lucy Midgley who died in 1854. He then married in 1856 Eliza Ormiston of Ruabon.
3. The Anstice family were based at Madeley Wood Hall on the north side of the River Severn, a few miles east of Ironbridge. They were distantly related to the Darby family through the Reynolds family.
4. Ecarté was a game of cards for two.
5. Mr Bluck was a constant companion of Henry and Adelaide Whitmore. He must have been employed by Henry Whitmore in some political capacity, perhaps as an agent or secretary or as a steward.
6. John Pritchard was a banker of Broseley. He was also the second Member of Parliament for Bridgnorth and was therefore a close political colleague of Henry Whitmore.
7. Dale House, Coalbrookdale, was built by Abraham Darby I in 1717. In 1858 it was occupied by Lucy Darby (Mrs Edmund Darby), mother of Abraham Darby IV, and by her daughter Mary Darby, known locally as the "Queen of the Dale" (see note 28, 1857).

8. The terrace was on the south eastern side of the White House/Sunniside.
9. Lucy was a cousin of the Whitmores. She had married Col. John Forbes, Coldstream Guards of Callander, Scotland in 1849. Her husband was clearly away in Scotland when their fourth child was born.
10. The Storers, including Charlotte and Lois were distant relatives of the Whitmores. They were treated as members of the family.
11. Mr Hayes was the vicar of Holy Trinity Church, Coalbrookdale.
12. Henry Dickinson was a cousin of Adelaide. He was the sixth child of Ann (née Darby) and Barnard Dickinson and lived at Severn House, Coalbrookdale (now the Valley Hotel, Ironbridge). He had been married to Deborah Darby, sister of Abraham Darby IV, but she had died in 1855. On 27th January 1858 he married for the second time Susanna Hadwen, daughter of Isaac Hadwen, a banker of Liverpool at Mosley, Lancashire.
13. Toozie was the pet dog.
14. The Drawing Room was a Royal Court Levée.
15. The Wrottesley family were a leading Staffordshire family from Wolverhampton. Lady Wrottesley would have been Sophia, daughter of Thomas Giffard of Chillington, Staffs, who was married to John, 2nd Baron Wrottesley who was noted for his scientific achievements and was one of the founders of the Royal Astronomical Society.
16. This must have been a significant lunch. Henry Whitmore had become part of Disraeli's circle of friends. The following month Henry was appointed a Lord of the Treasury in Lord Derby's second Administration with Disraeli as Chancellor of the Exchequer.
17. Abraham Darby IV was married to Matilda, Adelaide's elder sister. They used to live at The Chesnuts, Coalbrookdale, but after the "painful family affair" in 1552, they moved to Stoke Court, Buckinghamshire.
18. Adelaide's reference to "The Alien Bill" was almost certainly the Conspiracy to Murder Bill introduced to Parliament by Lord Palmerston, which was to lead to the downfall of his government. The background was that on 14th January 1858, an Italian called Orsini tried to assassinate Napoleon III outside the Opera House in Paris. Orsini was a member of a gang of refugees who had been granted asylum in England. The French were outraged and for a time there was war fever in France. The Conspiracy to Murder Bill sought to make it a felony to conspire to commit a murder whether inside or outside the United Kingdom. Although the Bill was reasonable enough, the public and Parliament took the view that they were being dictated to by a foreign power (France) and the Bill was thrown out.
19. Mr Rixon was a solicitor. The background to this entry was that Mrs Edmund Darby, mother of Abraham IV had decided to give to Abraham her shares in the Coalbrookdale Company. Mr Rixon had advised her that because of Abraham's potential liabilities following the embezzlement of money from the Shropshire Bank by its manager, it would be better if the shares were transferred to Matilda, Abraham's wife, on trust for Abraham. Adelaide and Henry Whitmore were the trustees of the transaction.
20. This was a motion of amendment to the Conspiracy to Murder Bill (see note 18 above) which amounted to a vote of censure. It was moved by the Radicals

Milner Gibson and John Bright, and was passed by the House by 19 votes whereupon Lord Palmerston resigned.

21. Lord Henry Lennox, son of the Duke of Richmond, was a close confidante of Benjamin Disraeli, and was the channel of communication between Disraeli and members of the Conservative Club.
22. Charles Whitmore, probably of the branch of the Whitmore family of Lower Slaughter, Cotswolds.
23. The Whitmore Jones were a branch of the Whitmore family based at Chastleton, near Lower Slaughter, Cotswolds.
24. Lady Tollemache was a member of the Manners family as also was Augustus Tollemache MA, a friend of the Whitmores, who became vicar of Whitwick, Co. Leicester in 1874.
25. Lord and Lady Bradford and Lord and Lady Newport were from Weston Park, Shropshire and were therefore near neighbours of the Whitmore family. Their family name was Bridgeman.
26. Frank, Catty, Mamey &c were all members of Lady Bandon's family from Castle Bernard, Bandon, Co. Cork. Lady Bandon (née Catherine Whitmore) was a cousin of Henry Whitmore.
27. Col. Taylor was a Lord of the Treasury with Henry Whitmore.
27a. Henry Whitmore attended as Keeper of the Privy Seal to the Duchy of Cornwall.
28. Formerly known as the White House, Coalbrookdale.
29. Wroxeter was the home of Mrs Egremont. Her husband, Rev Edward Egremont, vicar of Wroxeter had died in 1857.
30. Marnwood, situated on the road from Coalbrookdale to Buildwas was the home of Rev and Mrs Bartlett, of Buildwas Church.
31. Severn House was the home of Henry Dickinson and his new wife.
32. Mrs Whitmore was the mother of Thomas, George and Henry Whitmore. She was Adelaide's mother-in-law.
33. John Ella (1802-88) was an English violinist, conductor and critic. From 1845 to 1880 he ran the Musical Union subscription concerts, and from 1852 he started the Musical Winter Evenings. These were exclusive gatherings. Henry and Adelaide Whitmore were subscribers as also were Abraham and Matilda Darby of Stoke Court.
34. Leveson Gower was the name of the family originally from Wolverhampton which owned Lilleshall Hall, Shropshire, and the Lilleshall Company. The head of the family in the mid 19th century was Granville Leveson Gower who was created Viscount Granville in 1865 and Earl Granville in 1833.
35. Douglas was Thomas Charles Douglas Whitmore, the eldest child of Thomas Charlton Whitmore of Apley (see note 1 above). He had been at Eton and was now in the process of purchasing a commission in the Royal Horse Guards, one of the top Cavalry regiments in the Army (the Blues).
35a. As Henry Whitmore was a Lord of the Treasury in Lord Derby's government, Lady Derby's Assembly At Home (and later at Downing Street) must have been a priority engagement for Henry and Adelaide.
36. Lady Emma Stanley was Emily, daughter of Lord and Lady Derby.
37. Perhaps this ecclesiastical appointment was a recognition of Abraham's part in endowing the building of Holy Trinity Church, Coalbrookdale.

38. Lord Chelmsford was Lord Chancellor in Lord Derby's government in which Henry Whitmore was a Lord of the Treasury. Lord Chelmsford's family name was Thesiger so Col. Thesiger (and Miss Thesiger) were presumably relatives. Col. Thesiger was probably the son of Lord and Lady Chelmsford. He succeeded to the title and became Commander-in-Chief of the British Army in the Zulu War in Natal in 1879.
39. Col. Taylor was a Lord of the Treasury with Henry Whitmore.
40. Sir John Pakington was at the Admiralty in Lord Derby's government having previously been Colonial Secretary.
41. The Chancellor of the Exchequer was Benjamin Disraeli.
42. George Whitmore was the elder brother of Henry Whitmore. He was the Rector of Stockton, near Apley, Shropshire. He was married to Sarah (née Deacon) who came from Mabledon Park, Kent. George and Sarah had recently moved from Kemberton, their previous home, to the Rectory at Stockton, previously occupied by his uncle, the late Rev Charles Whitmore.
43. Mr Seymour Fitzgerald was Foreign Secretary in Lord Derby's government.
44. Edward Cardwell, who later became Secretary of State for War in Gladstone's government and was responsible for the military reforms of the 1870s.
45. Now the Victoria and Albert Museum.
45a. The Duke of Manchester was formerly Lord Mandeville. It was his elevation to the peerage which facilitated Henry's political advancement.
46. The home of William Whitmore, a member of the London branch of the Whitmore family.
47. This was probably the home of Mr and Mrs Christy at the Woodbines, Kingston, the parents of Rebecca Darby, widow of the late Alfred Darby.
48. Lord Queensbury was the father of Lady Louisa Whitmore, wife of Thomas Charlton Whitmore (Tom), Henry's eldest brother (see note 1).
49. Uncle Wolryche was William Wolryche Whitmore. He owned Dudmaston Hall, Shropshire.
50. Mrs Alfred Darby was the widow of Alfred Darby. Before she married she was Rebecca Christy of the Woodbines, Kingston (see note 47). She lived at Stanley Hall, Bridgnorth.
51. Mr Webb was a surgeon from Shrewsbury.
52. Uncle Richard Darby was the brother of Adelaide's father and lived in Darby Road, Coalbrookdale in the property now known as "Rosehill".
53. Buildwas Park was situated south of the River Severn, about a mile west of Buildwas Abbey and to the east of Sheinton.
54. Kinlet is a village about 8 miles south of Bridgnorth.
55. Emily Wilmot (née Whitmore) was a cousin of Henry Whitmore. She was married to Col. Wilmot of Malvern.
56. Madresfield is a village on the outskirts of Malvern.
57. Witley is about 10 miles north west of Worcester.
58. Willey was the home of Lord and Lady Forester.
59. George Edmonds was the Rector of Little Wenlock.
60. Patshull (Staffs) was the home of Lord Dartmouth.
61. Mary Darby was the daughter of Lucy and Edmund Darby. She was the sister of Abraham IV of Stoke Court and she was a cousin of Matilda, Abraham's wife. (She was also a cousin of Adelaide.) She was very popular

in Coalbrookdale (see note 7 above). She owned property in Baschurch and this presumably was how she came to know Reverend Jones, vicar of Baschurch. She was married to Rev Jones at Stoke Court, Buckinghamshire, her brother's home. The wedding prompted a week-long programme of celebrations in Coalbrookdale, Horsehay, Dawley and Lawley. The centre-piece of the whole affair was a banquet in the newly constructed Literary and Scientific Institution followed by an evening entertainment with a 15ft high bonfire with illumination of the grounds of the Institution and of the Great Warehouse. The unanswered question is why Adelaide was not involved in these important events.

62. The entries for 10th and 13th November need to be read in conjunction with the entries for 4th, 5th and 7th December 1857 (see note 51 for 1857). Adelaide does not elaborate on the "sad accounts" and a certain amount of speculation is therefore involved, but it seems almost certain that the bad news was occasioned by the fact that in 1854 the Manager of the Shropshire Bank in Wellington (Shropshire) had confessed to losing £200,000, the whole of the Bank's assets (about £8 million in today's money) through speculation. The proprietors of the Bank, of whom Abraham Darby IV was one, were liable to the last penny of their means to repay creditors. This led to the disposal of Abraham's collection of valuable paintings and books, and eventually to the sale of Stoke Court.
63. Lady Forester was the former Lady Melbourne. She was married to the 2nd Baron Forester in 1857.
64. Mrs Jones must have been the former Mary Darby who was married at Stoke Court on 27th October 1858 (see note 61 above). Their residence at Severn House must have been temporary as Severn House was the home of Mr and Mrs Henry Dickinson.
65. The Garforths were a Yorkshire family. Their home was Wigganthorpe Hall, about 10 miles north of York. They had become close friends of the Whitmores.

1860 and 1861

Comment

Adelaide's Journal came to an end in 1858. There is no explanation for the ending of the Journal. Two possible causes may be surmised . First, the Journal for 1858 (27th and 29th September and 2nd October) indicates that Adelaide experienced a health scare, sufficiently serious to make her contemplate the possibility of death. Secondly, it is evident that life in London had become very demanding. Henry's position as a member of the government required his presence, with Adelaide, at a number of functions, which otherwise they might not have attended. This pressure, combined with possible ill-health may have compelled the cessation of the Journal at the end of 1858. There is therefore no information about the end of the Derby Government in 1859, nor of Disraeli's abortive attempt to extend the franchise (the "Fancy Franchises" Bill which was thrown out by the Commons in June 1859).

Adelaide added two brief appendices for the years 1860 and 1861. The following information is extracted from those appendices.

1860 – BRIEF SUMMARY

3rd February - *The death of Maria Darby, aged 68 after a long illness. She was the wife of Richard Darby of "Rosehill", who was Adelaide's uncle.*

11th April - *Lois Storer married Major Hardwick. Lois Storer and her sister Charlotte had been popular members of the Whitmore "family".*

18th May - *The death of Joseph Dickinson, aged 54. He was the eldest of the children of Barnard and Ann Dickinson. He was a cousin of Adelaide.*

7th August - *The death of Richard Darby, aged 72, Adelaide's uncle. He died in Brussels where he had been with his daughter Rebecca.*

December - *On 18th December, Abraham Darby IV and Matilda arrived to visit Hannah Darby, mother of Matilda and Adelaide. She had been ill. On 20th December, Adelaide recorded "Our most precious mother was taken from us... it was a dark, dark time".*

1861 – BRIEF SUMMARY

9th January - *"There never dawned a year so sad." Henry Whitmore made a plan for adding to the old house, work which was nearly completed by the end of the year.*

16th March - *The Duchess of Kent (the Queen's mother) died. The Queen was heartbroken.*

1st June - *Toozie (the pet dog) died, aged 12-13 years old.*

27th July - *Matilda visited Stoke Court for the last time as Abraham and Matilda were moving to Monmouthshire to take charge of the Ebbw Vale Ironworks.*

2nd December - *Henry and Adelaide moved to Eaton Place and stayed there until the New Year. "It was a great comfort to be away at Christmas - - - - London was under the darkest cloud from the death of the Prince Consort.*

1862-1902
CONCLUSION – THE REST OF THE STORY "THE TWILIGHT OF THE GODS"

Adelaide's Journal ended in 1861 except for a few months between March and June 1873 in which she describes a visit to the European Continent with Henry, and an unidentified aunt. They seem to have retraced the same route that they had followed in July 1871, shortly after the Franco-Prussian War of 1870 when parts of Paris had been devastated. They proceeded via Paris and Lyons to the south of France and the Italian Riviera. From Milan they explored the Italian Lakes and thence over the Simplon Pass to Switzerland, and then to Munich, and Austria, where the account ends abruptly with the words "We have to dine..." This sudden ending suggests that some event intervened while she was writing her Journal and that it was of sufficient moment to prevent her from resuming her writing. However, there is not the slightest clue as to what that event was!

In 1873 Henry Whitmore had enjoyed three years of retirement after a distinguished political career (he was still only 59 years of age). He had accepted the Chiltern Hundreds (ie. retired from politics) in February 1870. He had been Member of Parliament for Bridgnorth for 18 years. His family had represented the seat almost continuously since 1621, but he was the last to do so.

As a member of the Conservative Party he had experienced some years of frustration in opposition, but between March 1858 and June 1859 he was a Lord of the Treasury and Keeper of the Privy Seal to the Prince of Wales in Lord Derby's second administration with Benjamin Disraeli as Chancellor of the Exchequer. Adelaide's Journal records that experience in 1858 but, sadly, not for 1859 when her Journal falls silent. Henry returned to the opposition back benches for the next seven years.

During that period, Henry was able to devote some of his energies to the building of a substantial enlargement of Sunniside (formerly The White House). The original White House (the central portion) was occupied by Rebecca Darby after the death of her husband (Abraham Darby III, builder of the Iron Bridge) in 1789. The east wing, a very substantial structure was built by her son Francis Darby (Adelaide's father) in about 1808. A considerable terrace was added to this east wing by Adelaide and Henry. Between 1862 and 1865 Henry built a very substantial west wing which reflected Francis Darby's east wing. This greatly increased the living space and the facilities of the house, and perhaps made it more of a country house appropriate to a past and potential future member of the government.

There was little point in opposing the Whig government during the life of Lord Palmerston but he died in October 1865. There had been an election the previous July when the Liberals (as they had then come to be known) were returned to power. Henry Whitmore was unsuccessful in that election but he submitted an Election Petition which was successful, and he resumed his seat in March 1866. He was in time to see Gladstone as Chancellor of the Exchequer (under the premiership of Lord John Russell who had taken over on the death of Palmerston) introduce a Reform Bill to extend the parliamentary franchise. This proved contentious and it was wrecked by a breakaway movement of the Liberal Party, who thereafter became known as the Adullamites (after the biblical rebels who gathered round King David in the Cave of Adullam). The Bill was rejected and the government resigned.

Henry Whitmore found himself once more as a Lord of the Treasury and Keeper of the Privy Seal to the Prince of Wales in Lord Derby's third administration with Benjamin Disraeli again as Chancellor of the Exchequer. His period in this high office lasted from July 1866 to December 1868. The outstanding achievement of that government was the passing of the Reform Act of 1867 (the "Fancy Franchises" Bill) which was memorably described by Lord Derby as "a leap in the dark".

Lord Derby's government was succeeded in December 1868 by William Gladstone's first (of four) governments. He stated, on entering the premiership, that "My mission is to pacify Ireland". This mission started in 1869 with an Act to disestablish the church in Ireland. Henry Whitmore was strongly opposed to this measure which he considered to be "strenuously supported by those who openly desire the separation of Church and State". In parliamentary terms he is most remembered for his views on this subject. After the Act became law, he decided to retire from politics. He was only 56 years of age, so whether he was disillusioned with politics or was suffering ill health, or some other reason, we do not know, nor unfortunately do we have the benefit of Adelaide's Journal to enlighten us. The following year, 1871 we know from Adelaide's final Journal that they went on a journey to the Continent and two years later in 1873 they went on the same journey as described in the final Journal.

That same year, 1873, Abraham Darby IV retired as Managing Director of the Ebbw Vale Steel Iron and Coal Company Ltd. Abraham and Matilda had been living at the Company's official residence Ebbw Vale Park since they had moved from Stoke Court, Buckinghamshire in 1861. Abraham's mother, Lucy Darby also lived there with them until her death in 1870.

By contrast with Adelaide's opulent and possibly extravagent lifestyle, her older sister Matilda had fared rather badly. As young ladies, it was

Matilda who seemed to be the more fortunate. She had married her childhood sweetheart, her cousin Abraham Darby IV, who was the Manager of the Coalbrookdale Company. Adelaide, who had confidently expected to marry early, found herself "on the shelf" as she passed the critical age of 30 years. The situation changed with the death of their father, Francis Darby in 1850. He had refused to sign a Will which had been forcefully advocated by his wife, which would have transferred most of his assets to his wife and to Adelaide. Francis expected that by not signing the Will, there would be an intestacy under which his estate would be split as equally as possible between Matilda and Adelaide as his co-heiresses. This was not acceptable to his widow who campaigned somewhat ruthlessly for the terms of the unsigned Will to be followed. The result of this "rather painful family affair" (as it was described by Matilda) was that Matilda was deprived of her inheritance and she and Abraham left Coalbrookdale (in disgust) to live at Stoke Court, Buckinghamshire. The other result was that Adelaide, as the "Darby Heiress" was sufficiently wealthy to make a good marriage to Henry Whitmore of Apley Park, a third son of one of the leading Shropshire families.

Apart from the inevitable ill-feeling between the two sisters (which was gradually overcome) the situation was still acceptable because Abraham IV was sufficiently wealthy to maintain his and Matilda's status. Unfortunately, this was not to last due to the disastrous embezzlement by the Manager of the funds of the Shropshire Bank in which Abraham IV was a partner. The amount of the loss in modern day terms was £8 million, and this cast a blight over Abraham's finances for the rest of his life, leading first to the sale of his valuable collection of paintings and books, and eventually to the sale of Stoke Court, their home in Buckinghamshire. Writing many years later, in 1887 (SRRC 1987/51/2/3), Matilda wrote "We were a good deal straitened.... But we did our best, my husband to earn, and I to learn details and to make the best of smaller means." Abraham took over full-time management of the extensive Ebbw Vale Ironworks and collieries in 1862. The partners at that time comprised Abraham IV, Henry Dickinson, William Tothill, Joseph Robinson (of Liverpool) and Thomas Brown (the previous manager). The enterprise had expanded very considerably since 1844 when it was first acquired by the partnership. By 1862 it comprised 19 blast furnaces, 142 puddling furnaces, 99 heating furnaces and 1200 workmen's houses. The colliery leases comprised 75,000 acres of land. All in all, it was a much bigger operation than the Coalbrookdale Company.

In the same year that Abraham took over the management, Parliament passed the Companies Act 1862, which introduced the concept of limited liability into Company Law. Two years later in 1864, Abraham took the lead in converting the company from a partnership into a limited liability company with a capital of £4 million. Abraham became the Managing Director.

Until then the company had been operating under their own patents, some of which pre-dated the Bessemer process for making mild steel. In 1866 Bessemer purchased their patents for £80,000 and thereafter the Company operated the Bessemer process. This also involved a further reconstruction of the Company as the Ebbw Vale Steel Iron and Coal Company Ltd. The Company prospered under Abraham's inspired leadership and continued to expand. In 1873, Abraham retired as Managing Director. He was then 69 years of age and his wife Matilda was 64 years of age. That same year (1873) his younger sister Mary who was married to Rev. Jones, Vicar of Baschurch died aged 65 years, so Abraham was left as the last member of his family, except for his nephew Alfred II, son of his brother Alfred I who had died in 1852.

Abraham and Matilda had the option of returning to Coalbrookdale, their birthplace, but they rejected this, and instead they retired to Llangorse Lake, a beauty spot near Brecon.

Back in Coalbrookdale, the Company was under the wise and able management of William Gregory Norris, a Quaker whose family had been with the company since 1714 when Thomas Luccock, a relative of Abraham I's stepmother (and ancestor of Norris), had been taken into apprenticeship with the Company. In 1873, when Abraham and Matilda retired, the Company was making great progress. In that year the Company won the Medal of Progress at the International Exhibition in Vienna, the highest award available. Ironically however, it was the work which Abraham IV and Bessemer and others like them, had been doing which was spelling the end of the older ironworks, particularly those away from the coast without access to ores from overseas. The Industrial Revolution which had been built on the development of the Iron, Coal and Steam industries was now being overtaken by the development of Steel, Engineering, and soon, Electricity. By 1876, William Gregory Norris was reporting that the Company's activities had been affected with a great difficulty and anxiety and that work had been reduced.

It was in that same year that Henry Whitmore, Adelaide's husband died, aged 62 years. Much had happened in the Whitmore family in the meantime. Henry's eldest brother Thomas Charlton Whitmore (referred to as Tom or Tommy in Adelaide's Journal) had died in 1865. His son Thomas Charles Douglas Whitmore (referred to as Douglas in Adelaide's Journal) had succeeded to the Apley estate but had sold it two years later in 1867 when he married. That left Henry's other older brother George, married to Sarah (née Deacon) who remained at Stockton where he was Rector. Other members of the extended family had passed away. Henry's cousin, Lady Bandon died in 1873 and another cousin Lucy who was married to Col. Forbes of the Coldstream Guards had died the previous year. Adelaide was therefore left with a diminishing circle of relatives and friends. No doubt also the frenetic round of dinners, assemblies, receptions in which Adelaide catalogued in her Journal in the 1850s and which presumably continued into the 1860s was considerably curtailed after 1870 when Henry had retired from politics. After Henry's death her level of activity may well have been even more reduced. Perhaps she may have been content to spend more time at Sunniside. If she did, she would have found that the atmosphere in Coalbrookdale had become even more desperate.

In 1877 the whole area was devastated by the closure of the Old Park Furnaces in Dawley, and the pressure on the Coalbrookdale Company to survive became more intense. Matters were not helped by the death in 1878 of Abraham Darby IV aged 75 years. He was symbolic of the great days leading up to the Great Exhibition of 1851 and he was regarded with the greatest respect and affection by the people of the Dale. Although he died in Breconshire, his body was brought by train to Coalbrookdale railway station and thence in procession through "an immense concourse of people" to Holy Trinity Church, which he had built and endowed. Every house in Coalbrookdale and Ironbridge had drawn blinds or closed shutters.

By 1880 it had become evident that if it was to survive, the Company faced a massive retrenchment of its operations involving the closure of works and the disposal of premises and warehouses. It was therefore decided to convert the partnership (which had been in existence in various forms since 1714) into a limited liability Joint Stock company. This was done in July 1881. Matilda and Adelaide remained as shareholders in the new company.

In 1883 the Lightmoor and Dawley Castle furnaces were closed down and for the first time since 1709 the Company ceased altogether to smelt iron ore. Despite this depressing environment, Adelaide expanded the Sunniside estate to its final ultimate size by the acquisition of Green Bank Farm to the east of the Sunniside estate. In 1886, Alfred Edmund William Darby (Alfred II) the son of Alfred Darby (Abraham IV's brother), who had died in 1852, became Chairman of the new Company. Slowly the Company weathered the economic storm and was restored to profitability. The effects on the locality had however been appalling. The population of Dawley which had been over 11,000 in 1861 was reduced to 7,000 in 1891, a reduction of 40%. The dereliction of the former workings and their spoil mounds became a dreadful memorial to the depression of the 1870s and 1880s.

Henry Dickinson, of Severn House, died in 1886, and then the only members of the Darby family left in Coalbrookdale were Rebecca, daughter of Richard and Maria Darby who was living at "Rosehill" and Adelaide who was living at Sunniside (The White House). Adelaide seems also to have retained her London address at 68 Eaton Place, and it is probable that towards the end of her life she spent an increasing amount of time at her London address.

Adelaide died on 10th July 1899 aged 82 years. The previous year she had made a Will leaving the Sunniside estate and Green Bank Farm to her older sister Matilda, who was living in Breconshire. Perhaps in some way this was a final reconciliation of the "painful family affair" of 1851. Despite her age, Matilda moved back to her birthplace at Sunniside and lived there for two years until her death aged 93, on 16th December 1902. This brought to an end the saga of the two sisters, Adelaide and her sister "dearest Tilly".

Editor's footnote

Adelaide's Journal was transcribed by Lady Rachel Labouchere before she died on 22nd March 1996. Rachel was descended through her maternal line from Abraham Darby I. Through her paternal line she was born Rachel Hamilton-Russell, a granddaughter of the 8th Viscount Boyne. During the Second World War she met and married George Labouchere, later Sir George Labouchere, who from 1960-1966 was British Ambassador to Madrid.

It was through her aunt on the maternal side, Muriel Cope-Darby, that Rachel inherited large quantities of family papers, as well as furniture, furnishings, silver and porcelain belonging to the Darby family. While she was President of the Ironbridge Gorge Museum Trust (from 1973-1987) she purchased for the Trust the premises known as "Rosehill", Darby Road, Coalbrookdale. In 1985 after the house had been restored it was opened as a Darby family home. Rachel donated the family furniture which she had inherited from Muriel Cope-Darby together with family silver, porcelain, pictures and other artefacts to be displayed in period and interpretation rooms at Rosehill.

Amongst the family papers which she inherited, were manuscripts of Journals written by Abiah Darby (1716-1793), Rebecca Darby (1754-1810) and Adelaide Darby (1817-1899). The first two were published in 1988 and 1993. The third of the Trilogy is now published as a memorial to her work. Rachel Labouchere was deeply sympathetic to her Quaker background and was very proud of her Darby pedigree. She would have been delighted to see her Trilogy completed. It is offered in memory of a lovely English lady.

There is one final, but vital, tribute to be paid, and that is to William K. Sessions, President, The Ebor Press, York. During the preparation and publication of Rachel Labouchere's previous books on Abiah Darby and Rebecca Darby she received immense support and encouragement from Bill Sessions and especially from his late wife Margot Sessions, with their deep understanding of Quaker affairs. When Rachel Labouchere died with her third book incomplete, Bill Sessions felt a profound commitment for the completion of Rachel's work. He thus gave repeated encouragement which helped this editor to persevere in editing Adelaide's year-upon-year Journal.

EMYR THOMAS